CONTRACT THEORY

CONTRACT THEORY

Patrick Bolton and Mathias Dewatripont

The MIT Press
Cambridge, Massachusetts
London, England

This book was set in Times Ten by SNP Best-set Typesetter Ltd., Hong Kong, and was printed and bound in the United States of America.

Library of Congress Cataloging-in-Publication Data

Bolton, Patrick, 1957–
   Contract theory / Patrick Bolton and Mathias Dewatripont.
     p. cm.
   Includes bibliographical references and index.
   ISBN-13: 978-0-262-02576-8
   ISBN-10: 0-262-02576-0
   1. Contracts—Methodology.   I. Dewatripont, M. (Mathias)   II. Title.

K840.B65   2004
346.02′01—dc22

2004055902

10 9 8 7 6 5 4

Contents

To Our Families

Preface

Contract theory, information economics, incentive theory, and organization theory have been highly successful and active research areas in economics, finance, management, and corporate law for more than three decades. A number of founding contributors have been rewarded with the Nobel prize in economics for their contributions in this general area, including Ronald Coase, Herbert Simon, William Vickrey, James Mirrlees, George Akerlof, Joseph Stiglitz, and Michael Spence. There is now a vast literature relating to contract theory in leading economics, finance, and law journals, and yet a relatively small number of core notions and findings have found their way into textbooks. The most recent graduate textbooks in microeconomics[1] devote a few chapters to basic notions in incentive and information economics like *adverse selection, moral hazard,* and *mechanism design,* but this material serves only as an introduction to these enormous topics.

The goal of this book is to provide a synthesis of this huge area by highlighting the common themes and methodologies that unite this field. The book can serve both as a complementary text for a graduate or advanced undergraduate course in microeconomics and for a graduate course in contract theory. Although we aim to provide very broad coverage of the research literature, it is impossible to do justice to all the interesting articles and all subfields that have emerged over the past 30 years. As a remedy against the most obvious gaps and omissions, we make a limited attempt to provide a short guide to the literature at the end of each chapter. Even if this book leaves out large portions of the literature, it still contains far too much material for even a full-semester course in contract theory. Our intention was to give instructors some discretion over which chapters to emphasize and to leave it to the students to do the background reading.

The book also presents methodological results in the key application areas where they have been developed, be they in labor economics, organization theory, corporate finance, or industrial organization, for example. In this way, the book can also serve as a reference source for researchers interested in the very many applications of contract theory in economics. The philosophy of the book is to stress applications rather than general theorems, while providing a simplified yet self-contained treatment of the key models and methodologies in the literature.

We owe an immeasurable intellectual debt to our advisers, Oliver Hart, Andreu Mas-Colell, Eric Maskin, John Moore, and Jean Tirole. Their

---

1. See, for example, the books by Kreps (1990) and Mas-Colell, Whinston, and Green (1995).

influence is visible on almost every page of this book. And although we have not had the good fortune to have them as our advisers, the intellectual influence of Bengt Holmström, Jean-Jacques Laffont, Paul Milgrom, James Mirrlees, and Roger Myerson has been just as important. The inspiration and support of our coauthors, Philippe Aghion, Christopher Harris, Ian Jewitt, Bruno Jullien, Patrick Legros, Steve Matthews, Patrick Rey, Alisa Röell, Gérard Roland, Howard Rosenthal, David Scharfstein, Ernst-Ludwig von Thadden, Michael Whinston, and Chenggang Xu, has been invaluable. In particular, Philippe Aghion and Patrick Rey have played a major role throughout the long gestation period of this book.

Over the years, every chapter of the book has been tested in the classroom. We thank our students at ECARES (Université Libre de Bruxelles), Tilburg, Princeton, MIT, Helsinki, and the summer schools in Oberwesel and Gerzensee for their comments. We also thank Philippe Aghion and Oliver Hart for using our manuscript in their contract theory courses at Harvard and for their feedback. We are grateful to Kenneth Ayotte, Estelle Cantillon, Antonio Estache, Antoine Faure-Grimaud, Denis Gromb, Christopher Hennessy, Andrei Hagiu, Jacques Lawarrée, Joel Shapiro, Jean Tirole, and three anonymous MIT Press readers for comments and advice. We are particularly grateful to Kathleen Hurley, Diana Prout, and Ellen Sklar for all their help in preparing the manuscript. We are also enormously grateful to our editors, Terry Vaughn and John Covell, for their continuing support and for making sure that we bring this project to completion.

1 Introduction

Economics is often defined as a field that aims to understand the process by which scarce resources are allocated to their most efficient uses, and markets are generally seen as playing a central role in this process. But, more fundamentally, the simple activity of exchange of goods and services, whether on organized exchanges or outside a market setting, is the basic first step in any production or allocation of resources. For a long time economic theory has been able to analyze formally only very basic exchange activities like the barter of two different commodities between two individuals at a given place and point in time. Most microeconomics textbooks[1] begin with an analysis of this basic situation, representing it in the classic "Edgeworth box." A slightly more involved exchange situation that can also be represented in an Edgeworth box is between two individuals trading at different points in time. Simple lending, investment, or futures contracts can be characterized in this way. However, such a simple reinterpretation already raises new issues, like the possibility of default or nondelivery by the other party in the future.

Until the 1940s or 1950s only situations of simple exchange of goods and services were amenable to formal analysis. More complex exchange activities like the allocation and sharing of risk began to be analyzed formally only with the introduction of the idea of "state-contingent" commodities by Arrow (1964) and Debreu (1959) and the formulation of a theory of "choice under uncertainty" by von Neumann and Morgenstern (1944) and others. The notion of exchange of state-contingent commodities gave a precise meaning to the exchange and allocation of risk. Preference orderings over lotteries provided a formal representation of attitudes toward risk and preferences for risk taking. These conceptual innovations are the foundations of modern theories of investment under risk and portfolio choice.

In the late 1960s and 1970s yet another conceptual breakthrough took place with the introduction of "private information" and "hidden actions" in contractual settings. The notions of "incentive compatibility" and incentives for "truth telling" provided the basic underpinnings for the theory of incentives and the economics of information. They also provided the first formal tools for a theory of the firm, corporate finance, and, more generally, a theory of economic institutions.

---

1. See, for example, Part 4 of the celebrated book by Mas-Colell, Whinston, and Green (1995).

Finally, much of the existing theory of long-term or dynamic contracting was developed in the 1980s and 1990s. Contract renegotiation, relational contracts, and incomplete contracts provided the first tools for an analysis of "ownership" and "control rights." These notions, in turn, complete the foundations for a full-fledged theory of the firm and organizations.

There are by now many excellent finance and economics textbooks covering the theory of investment under risk, insurance, and risk diversification. As this is already well-explored territory, we shall not provide any systematic coverage of these ideas. In contrast, to date there are only a few books covering the theory of incentives, information, and economic institutions, which is generally referred to in short as *contract theory*.[2] There has been such a large research output on these topics in the last 30 years that it is an impossible task to give a comprehensive synthesis of all the ideas and methods of contract theory in a single book. Nevertheless, our aim is to be as wide ranging as possible to give a sense of the richness of the theory—its core ideas and methodology—as well as its numerous possible applications in virtually all fields of economics.

Thus, in this book we attempt to cover all the major topics in contract theory that are taught in most graduate courses. Part I starts with basic ideas in incentive and information theory like screening, signaling, and moral hazard. Part II covers the less well trodden material of multilateral contracting with private information or hidden actions. In this part we provide an introduction to auction theory, bilateral trade under private information, and the theory of internal organization of firms. Part III deals with long-term contracts with private information or hidden actions. Finally, Part IV covers incomplete contracts, the theory of ownership and control, and contracting with externalities. Exercises are collected in a specific chapter at the end of the book.

There is obviously too much material in this book for any one-semester course in contract theory. Rather than impose our own preferences and our own pet topics, we thought that it would be better to cover all the main themes of contract theory and let instructors pick and choose which parts to cover in depth and which ones to leave to the students to read.

Consistent with our goal of providing broad coverage of the field, we have aimed for a style of exposition that favors simplicity over generality or rigor.

---

2. See in particular the textbooks by Salanié (1997) and Laffont and Martimort (2002).

Our primary goal is to illustrate the core ideas, the main methods in their simplest self-contained form, and the wide applicability of the central notions of contract theory. More often than not, research articles in contract theory are hard to penetrate even for a well-trained reader. We have gone to considerable lengths to make the central ideas and methods in these articles accessible. Inevitably, we have been led to sacrifice generality to achieve greater ease of understanding. Our hope is that once the main ideas have been assimilated the interested reader will find it easier to read the original articles.

In the remainder of this chapter we provide a brief overview of the main ideas and topics that are covered in the book by considering a single concrete situation involving an *employer* and an *employee*. Depending on the topic we are interested in we shall take the employer to be a *manager* hiring a *worker*, or a *farmer* hiring a *sharecropper*, or even a company *owner* hiring a *manager*. Throughout the book we discuss many other applications, and this brief overview should not be taken to be the leading application of contract theory. Before we proceed with a brief description of the multiple facets of this contracting problem, it is useful to begin by delineating the boundaries of the framework and stating the main assumptions that apply throughout this book.

The benchmark contracting situation that we shall consider in this book is one between two parties who operate in a market economy with a well-functioning legal system. Under such a system, any contract the parties decide to write will be enforced perfectly by a court, provided, of course, that it does not contravene any existing laws. We shall assume throughout most of the book that the contracting parties do not need to worry about whether the courts are able or willing to enforce the terms of the contract precisely. Judges are perfectly rational individuals, whose only concern is to stick as closely as possible to the agreed terms of the contract. The penalties for breaching the contract will be assumed to be sufficiently severe that no contracting party will ever consider the possibility of not honoring the contract. We shall step outside this framework only occasionally to consider, for example, the case of self-enforcing contracts.

Thus, throughout this book we shall assume away most of the problems legal scholars, lawyers, and judges are concerned with in practice and concentrate only on the economic aspects of the contract. We shall be primarily interested in determining what contractual clauses rational economic individuals are willing to sign and what types of transactions they are willing to undertake.

If the transaction is a simple exchange of goods or services for money, we shall be interested in the terms of the transaction. What is the price per unit the parties shall agree on? Does the contract specify rebates? Are there penalty clauses for late delivery? If so, what form do they take? And so on. Alternatively, if the transaction is an insurance contract, we shall be interested in determining how the terms vary with the underlying risk, with the risk aversion of the parties, or with the private information the insuree or the insurer might have about the exact nature of the risk. We begin by briefly reviewing the simplest possible contractual situation an employer and employee might face: a situation involving only two parties, transacting only once, and facing no uncertainty and no private information or hidden actions.

1.1 Optimal Employment Contracts without Uncertainty, Hidden Information, or Hidden Actions

Consider the following standard bilateral contracting problem between an employer and employee: the employee has an initial endowment of time, which she can keep for herself of sell to the employer as labor services, because the employer can make productive use of the employee's time. Specifically, we can assume therefore that the parties' utility functions depend both on the allocation of employee time and on their purchasing power. Let us denote the employer's utility function as $U(l, t)$ where l is the quantity of employee time the employer has acquired and t denotes the quantity of "money"—or equivalently the "output" that this money can buy[3]—that he has at his disposal. Similarly, employee utility is $u(l, t)$, where l is the quantity of time the employee has kept for herself and t is the quantity of money that she has at her disposal.

Suppose that the initial endowment of the individuals is $(\hat{l}_1, \hat{t}_1) = (0, 1)$ for the employer (hereafter *individual 1*) and $(\hat{l}_2, \hat{t}_2) = (1, 0)$ for the employee (hereafter *individual 2*). That is, without any trade, the employer gets no employee time but is assumed to have all the money, while the employee has all of her time for herself but has no money.

---

3. Indeed, the utility of money here reflects the utility derived from the consumption of a composite good that can be purchased with money.

Both individuals could decide not to trade, in which case they would each achieve a utility level of $\overline{U} = U(0, 1)$ and $\bar{u} = u(1, 0)$, respectively. If, however, both utility functions are strictly increasing in both arguments and strictly concave, then both individuals may be able to increase their joint payoff by exchanging labor services l for money/output. What will be the outcome of their contractual negotiations? That is, how many hours of work will the employee be willing to offer and what (hourly) wage will she be paid?

As in most economics texts, we shall assume throughout this book that contracting parties are rational individuals who aim to achieve the highest possible payoff. The joint surplus maximization problem for both individuals can be represented as follows. If we denote by l_i the amount of employee time actually consumed and by t_i the amount of output consumed by each party $i = 1, 2$ after trade, then the parties will solve the following optimization problem:

$$\max_{l_i, t_i} U(l_1, t_1) + \mu u(l_2, t_2) \tag{1.1}$$

subject to aggregate resource constraints:

$$l_1 + l_2 = \hat{l}_1 + \hat{l}_2 = 1 \quad \text{and} \quad t_1 + t_2 = \hat{t}_1 + \hat{t}_2 = 1$$

Here μ can reflect both the individuals' respective reservation utility levels, $\overline{U}$ and $\bar{u}$, and their relative bargaining strengths.

When both utility functions are strictly increasing and concave, the maximum is completely characterized by the first-order conditions

$$U_l + \mu u_l = 0 = U_t + \mu u_t \tag{1.2}$$

which imply

$$\frac{U_l}{U_t} = \frac{u_l}{u_t}$$

See Figure 1.1, where indifference curves are drawn.

In other words, joint surplus maximization is achieved when the marginal rates of substitution between money and leisure for both individuals are equalized.

There are gains from trade initially if

$$\frac{U_l}{U_t} > \frac{u_l}{u_t}$$

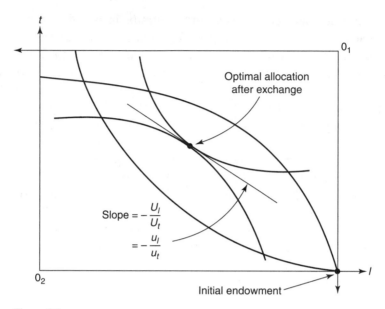

Figure 1.1
Classical Edgeworth Box

How these gains are shared between the two individuals is determined by μ. The employee gets a higher share of the surplus the higher μ is. The highest possible utility that the employee can get is given by the solution to the following optimization problem:

$$\max_{l_2, t_2} u(l_2, t_2) \quad \text{subject to} \quad U(1 - l_2, 1 - t_2) \geq \overline{U}$$

Similarly, the highest payoff the employer can get is given by the solution to

$$\max_{l_1, t_1} U(l_1, t_1) \quad \text{subject to} \quad u(1 - l_1, 1 - t_1) \geq \overline{u}$$

These extreme problems can be interpreted as simple bargaining games where one party has all the bargaining power and makes a take-it-or-leave-it offer to the other party. Note, however, that by increasing $\overline{u}$ in the employer's constrained maximization problem or $\overline{U}$ in the employee's problem one can reduce the surplus that either individual gets. Thus a given division of the surplus can be parameterized by either μ, $\overline{U}$, or $\overline{u}$, depending on how the joint surplus maximization problem is formulated.

Throughout this book we shall represent optimal contracting outcomes as solutions to constrained optimization problems like the two preceding problems. We thus take as starting point the Coase theorem (1960), that is, the efficient contracting perspective, as long as informational problems are not present.[4] Although this representation seems quite natural, it is important to highlight that behind it lie two implicit simplifying assumptions. First, the final contract the parties end up signing is independent of the bargaining process leading up to the signature of the contract. In reality it is likely that most contracts that we see partly reflect prior negotiations and each party's negotiating skills. But, if the main determinants of contracts are the parties' objectives, technological constraints, and outside options, then it is not unreasonable to abstract from the potentially complex bargaining games they might be playing. At least as a first approach, this simplifying assumption appears to be reasonable.

Second, as we have already mentioned, the other relevant dimension of the contracting problem that is generally suppressed in the preceding formal characterization is the enforcement of the contract. Without legal institutions to enforce contracts many gains from trade are left unexploited by rational individuals because one or both fear that the other will fail to carry out the agreed transaction. In the absence of courts or other modes of enforcement, a transaction between two or more parties can take place only if the exchange of goods or services is simultaneous. Otherwise, the party who is supposed to execute her trade last will simply walk away. In practice, achieving perfect simultaneity is almost impossible, so that important gains from trade may remain unexploited in the absence of an efficient enforcement mechanism.

1.2 Optimal Contracts under Uncertainty

There is more to employment contracts than the simple characterization in the previous section. One important dimension in reality is the extent to which employees are insured against economic downturns. In most developed economies employees are at least partially protected against the risk of unemployment. Most existing unemployment insurance schemes are

---

4. As we shall detail throughout this book, informational problems will act as constraints on the set of allocations that contracts can achieve.

nationwide insurance arrangements, funded by employer and employee contributions, and guaranteeing a minimum fraction of a laid-off employee's pay over a minimum time horizon (ranging from one year to several years with a sliding scale). A fundamental economic question concerning these insurance schemes is how much "business-cycle" and other "firm-specific" risk should be absorbed by employers and how much by employees. Should employers take on all the risk, and if so, why? One theory, dating back to Knight (1921) and formalized more recently by Kihlstrom and Laffont (1979) and Kanbur (1979), holds that employers (or "entrepreneurs") should take on all the risk and fully insure employees. The reason is that entrepreneurs are natural "risk lovers" and are best able to absorb the risk that "risk-averse" employees do not want to take.

To be able to analyze this question of optimal risk allocation formally one must enrich the framework of section 1.1 by introducing uncertainty. At one level this extension is extremely simple. All it takes is the introduction of the notions of a state of nature, a state space, and a state-contingent commodity. Arrow (1964) and Debreu (1959) were the first to explore this extension. They define a state of nature as any possible future event that might affect an individual's utility. The state space is then simply the set of all possible future events, and a state-contingent commodity is a good that is redefined to be a new commodity in every different state of nature. For example, a given number of hours of work is a different commodity in the middle of an economic boom than in a recession.

The difficulty is not in defining all these notions. The important conceptual leap is rather to suppose that rational individuals are able to form a complete description of all possible future events and, moreover, that all have the same description of the state space. Once this common description is determined, the basic contracting problem can be represented like the preceding one, although the interpretation of the contract will be different. More precisely, it is possible to represent a simple insurance contract, which specifies trades between the employer and employee in different states of nature, in an Edgeworth box. Before doing so, let us consider a pure insurance problem without production.

1.2.1 Pure Insurance

Consider the simplest possible setting with uncertainty. Assume that there are only two possible future states of nature, θ_L and θ_H. To be concrete, let θ_L represent an adverse output shock, or a "recession," and θ_H a good output realization, or a "boom." For simplicity, we disregard time endowments. Then the state of nature influences only the value of output each individual has as endowment. Specifically, assume the following respective endowments for each individual in each state:

$$(\hat{t}_{1H}, \hat{t}_{1L}) = (2, 1), \quad \text{for individual 1}$$

$$(\hat{t}_{2H}, \hat{t}_{2L}) = (2, 1), \quad \text{for individual 2}$$

The variable $\hat{t}_{ij}$ therefore denotes the endowment of individual i in state of nature θ_j. Note that in a "recession" aggregate output—2—is lower than in a boom—4.

Before the state of nature is realized each individual has preferences over consumption bundles (t_L, t_H) represented by the utility functions $V(t_L, t_H)$ for the employer and $v(t_L, t_H)$ for the employee.

If the two individuals do not exchange any contingent commodities, their ex ante utility (before the state of nature is realized) is $\overline{V} = V(2, 1)$ and $\overline{v} = v(2, 1)$. But they can also increase their ex ante utility by coinsuring against the economic risk. Note, however, that some aggregate risk is uninsurable: the two individuals can do nothing to smooth the difference in aggregate endowments between the two states. Nevertheless, they can increase their ex ante utility by pooling their risks.

As before, the efficient amount of coinsurance is obtained when the final allocations of each contingent commodity $\{(t_{1L}, t_{2L}), (t_{1H}, t_{2H})\}$ are such that

$$V_{t_L} + \mu v_{t_L} = 0 = V_{t_H} + \mu v_{t_H} \tag{1.3}$$

which implies

$$\frac{V_{t_L}}{V_{t_H}} = \frac{v_{t_L}}{v_{t_H}}$$

See Figure 1.2, where indifference curves are drawn.

It should be clear by now that the analysis of pure exchange under certainty can be transposed entirely to the case with uncertainty once one enlarges the commodity space to include contingent commodities.

However, to obtain a full characterization of the optimal contracting problem under uncertainty one needs to put more structure on this framework. Indeed, two important elements are hidden in the preceding characterization of the optimal insurance contract: one is a description of

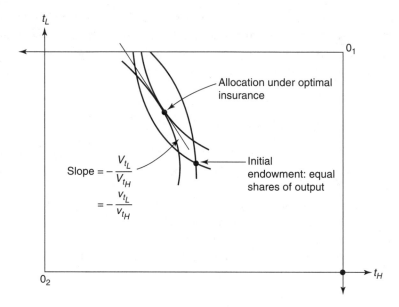

Figure 1.2
Optimal Coinsurance

ex post utility once the state of nature has been realized, and the other is the probability of each state occurring.

The first complete framework of decision making under uncertainty, which explicitly specifies the probability distribution over states and the ex post utility in each state, is due to von Neumann and Morgenstern (1944). It is this framework that is used in most contracting applications. Interestingly, even though there is by now a large literature exploring a wide range of alternative models of individual choice and behavior under uncertainty, there have been relatively few explorations of the implications for optimal contracting of alternative models of behavior under uncertainty.

In the setup considered by von Neumann and Morgenstern, individual ex post utility functions are respectively $U(t)$ and $u(t)$ for the employer and employee, where both functions are increasing in t. If we call $p_j \in (0, 1)$ the probability of occurrence of any particular state of nature θ_j, the ex ante utility function is simply defined as the expectation over ex post utility outcomes:

$$V(t_{1L}, t_{1H}) = p_L U(t_{1L}) + p_H U(t_{1H})$$

and

$$v(t_{2L}, t_{2H}) = p_L u(t_{2L}) + p_H u(t_{2H})$$

The easiest way of thinking about the probability distribution $\{p_j\}$ is simply as an objective distribution that is known by both individuals. But it is also possible to think of $\{p_j\}$ as a subjective belief that is common to both individuals. In most contracting applications it is assumed that all parties share a common prior belief and that differences in (posterior) probability beliefs among the parties only reflect differences in information. Although this basic assumption is rarely motivated, it generally reflects the somewhat vague idea that all individuals are born with the same "view of the world" and that their beliefs differ only if they have had different life experiences. Recently, however, there have been some attempts to explore the implications for optimal contracting of fundamental differences in beliefs among contracting parties.

It is instructive to consider the optimal insurance conditions (1.3) when the individuals' ex ante utility function is assumed to be the Von Neumann–Morgenstern utility function that we have specified. In that case the marginal rate of substitution between commodities 1 and 2 is given by

$$\frac{V_{tL}}{V_{tH}} = \frac{p_L}{p_H} \frac{U'(t_{1L})}{U'(t_{1H})}$$

As this expression makes clear, the marginal rate of substitution between the two contingent commodities varies with the probability distribution. Moreover, the marginal rate of substitution is constant along the 45° line, where $t_{1L} = t_{1H}$.

1.2.2 Optimal Employment Contracts under Uncertainty

Using the framework of von Neumann and Morgenstern, let us come back to the contracting problem of section 1.1 with two goods, leisure l and a consumption good t, which can be readily extended to include uncertainty as follows:

Let (l_{1L}, t_{1L}) and (l_{1H}, t_{1H}) represent the two different state-contingent time/output bundles of the employer, and (l_{2L}, t_{2L}) and (l_{2H}, t_{2H}) the two different state-contingent time/output bundles of the employee. Also let $(\hat{l}_{ij}, \hat{t}_{ij})$ denote their respective initial endowments, $(i = 1, 2; j = L, H)$. Then the optimal insurance contract signed by the two individuals can be represented as the solution to the optimal contracting problem:

$$\max_{l_{ij},\, t_{ij}} [p_L U(l_{1L}, t_{1L}) + p_H U(l_{1H}, t_{1H})]$$

subject to

$$p_L u(l_{2L}, t_{2L}) + p_H u(l_{2H}, t_{2H}) \geq \bar{u} \tag{1.4}$$

and

$$l_{1j} + l_{2j} \leq \hat{l}_{1j} + \hat{l}_{2j} \quad \text{for } j = L, H$$

$$t_{1j} + t_{2j} \leq \hat{t}_{1j} + \hat{t}_{2j} \quad \text{for } j = L, H$$

where

$$\bar{u} = p_L u\big(\hat{l}_{2L}, \hat{t}_{2L}\big) + p_H u\big(\hat{l}_{2H}, \hat{t}_{2H}\big)$$

One important advantage of the von Neumann and Morgenstern formulation is that an individual's attitude toward risk can be easily characterized by the curvature of the ex post utility function. Thus, if both $U(\cdot)$ and $u(\cdot)$ are strictly concave, then both individuals are risk averse and want to share risk, whereas if both $U(\cdot)$ and $u(\cdot)$ are strictly convex, then both individuals are risk loving and want to trade gambles with each other.

For now, suppose that both individuals are risk averse, so that their ex post utility functions are strictly concave. Then the contract-maximizing joint surplus is fully characterized by the first-order conditions:

$$\frac{U_l(l_{1j}, t_{1j})}{U_t(l_{1j}, t_{1j})} = \frac{u_l(l_{2j}, t_{2j})}{u_t(l_{2j}, t_{2j})} \tag{1.5}$$

$$\frac{U_l(l_{1j}, t_{1j})}{u_l(l_{2j}, t_{2j})} \quad \text{constant across } \theta_j\text{'s} \tag{1.6}$$

$$\frac{U_t(l_{1j}, t_{1j})}{u_t(l_{2j}, t_{2j})} \quad \text{constant across } \theta_j\text{'s} \tag{1.7}$$

Condition (1.5) is the familiar condition for efficient trade ex post. This means that ex ante efficiency is achieved if and only if the contract is also ex post efficient. We shall see that when incentive considerations enter into the contracting problem there is usually a conflict between ex ante and ex post efficiency.

Conditions (1.6) and (1.7) are conditions of optimal coinsurance. Condition (1.7) is sometimes referred to as the *Borch rule* (1962): optimal coinsurance requires the equalization of the ratio of marginal utilities of money across states of nature.

A risk-neutral individual has a constant marginal utility of money. Thus, if one of the two individuals is risk neutral and the other individual is risk averse, the Borch rule says that optimal insurance requires that the risk-averse individual must also have a constant marginal utility of money across states of nature. In other words, the risk-averse individual must get perfect insurance. This is exactly the solution that intuition would suggest.

To summarize, optimal contracting under uncertainty would result in perfect insurance of the employee against economic risk only if the employer is risk neutral. In general, however, when both employer and employee are risk averse, they will optimally share business risk. Thus the simple Knightian idea that entrepreneurs perfectly insure employees is likely to hold only under special assumptions about risk preferences of entrepreneurs. An individual's attitude toward risk is driven in part by initial wealth holdings. Thus it is generally accepted that individuals' absolute risk aversion tends to decrease with wealth. If extremely wealthy individuals are approximately risk neutral and poor individuals are risk averse, then one special case where the Knightian theory would be a good approximation is when wealth inequalities are extreme and a few very wealthy entrepreneurs provide nearly perfect job security to a mass of poor employees.

It should be clear from this brief overview of optimal contracting under uncertainty that the presumption of rational behavior and perfect enforceability of contracts is less plausible in environments with uncertainty than in situations without uncertainty. In many contracting situations in practice it is possible that the contracting parties will be unable to agree on a complete description of the state space and that, as a consequence, insurance contracts will be incomplete. The rationality requirements imposed on the contracting parties and the enforcement abilities assumed of the courts should be kept in mind as caveats for the theory of contracting when faced with very complex actual contractual situations where the parties may have limited abilities to describe possible future events and the courts have limited knowledge to be able to effectively stick to the original intentions of the contracting parties.

Another important simplifying assumption to bear in mind is that it is presumed that each party knows exactly the intentions of the other contracting parties. However, in practice the motives behind an individual's willingness to contract are not always known perfectly. As a consequence, suspicion about ulterior motives often may lead to breakdown of contracting. These considerations are the subject of much of this book and are briefly reviewed in the next sections of this chapter.

1.3   Information and Incentives

The preceding discussion highlights that even in the best possible contracting environments, where comprehensive insurance contracts can be written, it is unlikely that employees will be perfectly insured against business risks. The reason is simply that the equilibrium price of such insurance would be too high if employers were also averse to risk.

Another important reason employees are likely to get only limited insurance is that they need to have adequate incentives to work. If the output produced by employees tends to be higher when employees exert themselves more, or if the likelihood of a negative output shock is lower if employees are more dedicated or focused on their work, then economic efficiency requires that they receive a higher compensation when their (output) performance is better. Indeed, if their pay is independent of performance and if their job security is not affected by their performance, why should they put any effort into their work? This is a well-understood idea. Even in the egalitarian economic system of the former Soviet Union the provision of incentives was a generally recognized economic issue, and over the years many ingenious schemes were proposed and implemented to address the problem of worker incentives and also factory managers' incentives. What was less well understood, however, was the trade-off between incentives and insurance. How far should employee insurance be scaled back to make way for adequate work incentives? How could adequate work incentives be structured while preserving job security as much as possible? These remained open and hotly debated questions over the successive five-year plans.

Much of Part I of this book will be devoted to a formal analysis of this question. Two general types of incentive problems have been distinguished. One is the *hidden-information* problem and the other the *hidden-action* problem. The first problem refers to a situation where the employee may have private information about her inability or unwillingness to take on certain tasks. That is, the information about some relevant characteristics of the employee (her distaste for certain tasks, her level of competence) are hidden from her employer. The second problem refers to situations where the employer cannot see what the employee does—whether she works or not, how hard she works, how careful she is, and so on. In these situations it is the employee's actions that are hidden from the employer.

Problems of hidden information are often referred to as *adverse selection,* and problems of hidden actions as *moral hazard.* In practice, of course, most incentive problems combine elements of both moral hazard and adverse selection. Also, the theoretical distinction between a hidden-action and a hidden-information problem can sometimes be artificial. Nevertheless, it is useful to distinguish between these two types of incentive problems, in part because the methodology that has been developed to analyze these problems is quite different in each case.

1.3.1 Adverse Selection

Chapters 2 and 3 provide a first introduction to optimal contracts with hidden information. These chapters examine optimal bilateral contracts when one of the contracting parties has private information. Chapter 2 explores contracting situations where the party making the contract offers is the *uninformed* party. These situations are often referred to as *screening* problems, since the uninformed party must attempt to screen the different pieces of information the informed party has. Chapter 3 considers the opposite situation where the *informed* party makes the contract offers. These situations fall under the general descriptive heading of *signaling* problems, as the party making the offer may attempt to signal to the other party what it knows through the type of contract it offers or other actions.

The introduction of hidden information is a substantial break from the contracting problems we have already considered. Now the underlying contracting situation requires specification of the private information one of the parties might have and the beliefs of the other party concerning that information *in addition to* preferences, outside options, initial endowments, a state space, and a probability distribution over states of nature.

In the context of employment contracts the type of information that may often be private to the employee at the time of contracting is her basic skill, productivity, or training. In practice, employers try to overcome this informational asymmetry by hiring only employees with some training or only high school and college graduates.

In a pathbreaking analysis Spence (1973, 1974) has shown how education can be a signal of intrinsic skill or productivity. The basic idea behind his analysis is that more-able employees have a lower disutility of education and therefore are more willing to educate themselves than less-able employees. Prospective employers understand this and therefore are willing to pay educated workers more even if education per se does not add any value. We review Spence's model and other contracting settings with signaling in Chapter 3.

Another way for employers to improve their pool of applicants is to commit to pay greater than market-clearing wages. This tends to attract better applicants, who generally have better job opportunities and are more likely to do well in interviews. Such a policy naturally gives rise to equilibrium unemployment, as Weiss (1980) has shown. Thus, as Akerlof, in his 1970 article, and Stiglitz, in many subsequent writings, had anticipated, the presence of private information about employee characteristics can potentially explain at a microeconomic level why equilibrium unemployment and other forms of market inefficiencies can arise. With the introduction of asymmetric information in contracting problems economists have at last found plausible explanations for observed market inefficiencies that had long eluded them in simpler settings of contracting under complete information.

Or at least they thought so. Understandably, given the importance of the basic economic issue, much of the subsequent research on contracting under asymmetric information has tested the *robustness* of the basic predictions of market inefficiencies and somewhat deflated early expectations about a general theory of market inefficiencies.

A first fundamental question to be tackled was, Just how efficient can contracting under asymmetric information be? The answer to this question turns out to be surprisingly elegant and powerful. It is generally referred to as the *revelation principle* and is one of the main notions in contract economics. The basic insight behind the revelation principle is that to determine optimal contracts under asymmetric information it suffices to consider only one contract for each type of information that the informed party might have, but to make sure that each type has an incentive to select only the contract that is destined to him/her.

More concretely, consider an employer who contracts with two possible types of employees—a "skilled" employee and an "unskilled" one—and who does not know which is which. The revelation principle says that it is optimal for the employer to consider offering only two employment contracts—one destined to the skilled employee and the other to the unskilled one—but to make sure that each contract is *incentive compatible*. That is, that each type of employee wants to pick only the contract that is destined to her. Thus, according to the revelation principle, the employer's optimal contracting problem reduces to a standard contracting problem, but with additional incentive compatibility constraints.

As a way of illustrating a typical contracting problem with hidden information, let us simplify the previous problem with uncertainty with a simple form of private information added. Suppose first that employee time and output enter additively in both utility functions: define them as $U[\alpha\theta(1-l) - t]$ for the employer and $u(\theta l + t)$ for the employee, where

- $(1 - l)$ is the employee time sold to the employer, and l is the time the employee keeps for herself;
- t is the monetary/output transfer from the employer to the employee;
- α is a positive constant; and
- θ measures the "unit value of time," or the skill level of the employee.

The variable θ is thus the state of nature, and we assume it is learned *privately* by the employee before signing any contract. Specifically, the employee knows whether she is skilled, with a value of time θ_H, or unskilled, with a value of time $\theta_L < \theta_H$. The employer, however, knows only that the probability of facing a skilled employee is p_H.

When the employer faces a skilled employee, the relevant reservation utility is $\bar{u}_H = u(\theta_H)$, and when he faces an unskilled employee, it is $\bar{u}_L = u(\theta_L)$.[5] Assume that the employee's time is more efficient when sold to the employer; that is, assume $\alpha > 1$. Then, if the employer could also learn the employee's type, he would simply offer in state θ_j a contract with a transfer $t_j = \theta_j$ in exchange for all her work time (that is, $1 - l_j = 1$). Such a contract would maximize production efficiency, and since the employee's *individual rationality constraint*, $u(t_j) \geq u(\theta_j)$, would be binding under this contract, it would maximize the employer's payoff.

When employee productivity is private information, however, the employer would not be able to achieve the same payoff, for if the employer offers a wage contract $t_j = \theta_j$ in exchange for 1 unit of work time, all

---

5. Indeed, in state θ_j, the employee's endowment $\hat{l}_{2j} = \theta_j$.

employee types would respond by "pretending to be skilled" to get the higher wage θ_H.

Note that for the employee type to be truly private information it must also be the case that the employee's output is not observable. If it were, the employer could easily get around the informational asymmetry by including a "money-back guarantee" into the contract should the employee's output fall short of the promised amount. Assumptions similar to the nonobservability of output are required in these contracting problems with hidden information. A slightly more realistic assumption serving the same purpose is that the employee's output may be random and that a "no-slavery" constraint prevents the employer from punishing the employee ex post for failing to reach a given output target. If that is the case, then an inefficient employee can always pretend that she was "unlucky." Even if this latter assumption is more appealing, we shall simply assume here for expositional convenience (as is often done) that output is unobservable.

Under that assumption, the only contracts that the employer can offer the employee are contracts offering a total payment of $t(l)$ in exchange for $(1 - l)$ units of work. Although this class of contracts is much simpler than most real-world employment contracts, finding the optimal contracts in the set of all (nonlinear) functions $\{t(l)\}$ could be a daunting problem. Fortunately, the revelation principle offers a key simplification. It says that all the employer needs to determine is a menu of two "point contracts": (t_L, l_L) and (t_H, l_H), where, by convention, (t_j, l_j) is the contract chosen by type j. The reason why the employer does not need to specify a full (nonlinear) contract $t(l)$ is that each type of employee would pick only one point on the full schedule $t(l)$ anyway. So the employer might as well pick that point directly. However, each point has to be incentive compatible. That is, type θ_H must prefer contract (t_H, l_H) over (t_L, l_L), and type θ_L contract (t_L, l_L) over (t_H, l_H).

Thus the optimal *menu* of employment contracts under hidden information can be represented as the solution to the optimal contracting problem under complete information:

$$\max_{(l_j, t_j)} \{ p_L U[\alpha\theta_L(1 - l_L) - t_L] + p_H U[\alpha\theta_H(1 - l_H) - t_H] \}$$

subject to

$$u(l_L\theta_L + t_L) \geq u(\theta_L)$$

and

$$u(l_H\theta_H + t_H) \ge u(\theta_H)$$

but with two additional *incentive constraints:*

$$u(l_H\theta_H + t_H) \ge u(l_L\theta_H + t_L)$$

and

$$u(l_L\theta_L + t_L) \ge u(l_H\theta_L + t_H)$$

The solution to this constrained optimization problem will produce the most efficient contracts under hidden information. As this problem immediately reveals, the addition of incentive constraints will in general result in less efficient allocations than under complete information. In general, optimal contracts under hidden information will be second-best contracts, which do not achieve simultaneously optimal allocative and distributive efficiency. Much of Chapter 2 will be devoted to the analysis of the structure of incentive constraints and the type of distortions that result from the presence of hidden information. The general economic principle that this chapter highlights is that hidden information results in a form of *informational monopoly power* and allocative inefficiencies similar to those produced by monopolies. In the preceding example, the employer might choose to suboptimally employ skilled employees (by setting $1 - l_H$ < 1) to be able to pay unskilled employees slightly less.[6] In a nutshell, the main trade-off that is emphasized in contracting problems with hidden information is one between informational rent extraction and allocative efficiency.

---

6. One option is to have a contract with allocative efficiency, that is, $l_H = l_L = 0$ and $t_H = t_L = \theta_H$. This leaves informational rents for the unskilled employee relative to her outside opportunity. It may therefore be attractive to lower skilled employment (that is, set $l_H > 0$)— at an allocative cost of $(\alpha - 1)l_H$—in order to lower t_L without violating the incentive constraint:

$$u(l_L\theta_L + t_L) \ge u(l_H\theta_L + t_H)$$

Intuitively, lowering skilled employment allows the employer to lower t_H by a significant amount, since the skilled employee has a high opportunity cost of time. Therefore, "pretending to be skilled" becomes less attractive for the unskilled employee (who has a lower opportunity cost of time), with the result that a lower transfer t_L becomes compatible with the incentive constraint. The trade-off between allocative efficiency and rent extraction will be detailed in the next chapter.

If the presence of hidden information may give rise to allocative inefficiencies such as unemployment, it does not follow that public intervention
is warranted to improve market outcomes. Indeed, the incentive constraints
faced by employers are also likely to be faced by planners or public authorities. It is worth recalling here that the centrally planned economy of the
Soviet Union was notorious for its overmanning problems. It may not have
had any official unemployment, but it certainly had huge problems of
underemployment. Chapters 7 and 13 will discuss at length the extent to
which market outcomes under hidden information may be first- or second-
best efficient and when the "market mechanism" may be dominated by
some better institutional arrangement.

Our discussion has focused on a situation where the employee has an
informational advantage over the employer. But, in practice, it is often the
employer that has more information about the value of the employee's
work. Chapter 2 also explores several settings where employers have
private information about demand and the value of output. As we highlight,
these settings are perhaps more likely to give rise to unemployment.
Indeed, layoffs can be seen as a way for employers to credibly convey to
their employees that the economic environment of their firm has worsened
to the extent that pay cuts may be needed for the firm to survive.

1.3.2   Moral Hazard

Chapter 4 introduces and discusses the other major class of contracting
problems under asymmetric information: *hidden actions.* In contrast to
most hidden information problems, contracting situations with hidden
actions involve informational asymmetries arising after the signing of a
contract. In these problems the agent (employee) is not asked to choose
from a menu of contracts, but rather from a menu of action-reward
pairs.

Contracting problems with hidden actions involve a fundamental incentive problem that has long been referred to in the insurance industry as
moral hazard: when an insuree gets financial or other coverage against a
bad event from an insurer she is likely to be less careful in trying to avoid
the bad outcome against which she is insured. This behavioral response to
better insurance arises in almost all insurance situations, whether in life,
health, fire, flood, theft, or automobile insurance. When a person gets better
protection against a bad outcome, she will rationally invest fewer resources
in trying to avoid it. One of the first and most striking empirical studies of

moral hazard is that of Peltzman (1975), who has documented how the introduction of laws compelling drivers to wear seat belts has resulted in higher average driving speeds and a greater incidence of accidents (involving, in particular, pedestrians).

How do insurers deal with moral hazard? By charging proportionally more for greater coverage, thus inducing the insuree to trade off the benefits of better insurance against the incentive cost of a greater incidence of bad outcomes.

Incentive problems like moral hazard are also prevalent in employment relations. As is now widely understood, if an employee's pay and job tenure are shielded against the risk of bad earnings, then she will work less in trying to avoid these outcomes. Moral hazard on the job was one of the first important new economic issues that Soviet planners had to contend with. If they were to abolish unemployment and implement equal treatment of workers, how could they also ensure that workers would work diligently? As they reluctantly found out, there was unfortunately no miracle solution. For a time ideological fervor and emulation of model workers seemed to work, but soon major and widespread motivation problems arose in an economic system founded on the separation of pay from performance.

Employers typically respond to moral hazard on the job by rewarding good performance (through bonus payments, piece rates, efficiency wages, stock options, and the like) and/or punishing bad performance (through layoffs). As with insurance companies, employers must trade off the benefits of better insurance (in terms of lower average pay) against the costs in lower effort provision by employees. The most spectacular form of incentive pay seen nowadays is the compensation of CEOs in the United States. Arguably, the basic theory of contracting with hidden actions discussed in Chapter 4 provides the main theoretical underpinnings for the types of executive compensation packages seen today. According to the theory, even risk-averse CEOs should receive significant profit- and stock-performance based compensation if their (hidden) actions have a major impact on the firm's performance.[7]

While it is easy to grasp at an intuitive level that there is a basic trade-off between insurance and incentives in most employment relations, it is

---

7. Actual CEO compensation packages have also shown some serious limitations, which the theory has addressed too; more on this topic will follow.

less easy to see how the contract should be structured to best trade off effort provision and insurance.

Formally, to introduce hidden actions into the preceding employment problem with uncertainty, suppose that the amount of time $(1 - l)$ worked by the employee is private information (a *hidden action*). Suppose, in addition, that the employee chooses the action $(1 - l)$ *before* the state of nature θ_j is realized and that this action influences the *probability* of the state of nature: when the employee chooses action $(1 - l)$, output for the employer is simply θ_H with a probability function $p_H[1 - l]$, increasing in $1 - l$ (and θ_L with a probability function $p_L[1 - l] = 1 - p_H[1 - l]$).[8] The usual interpretation here is that $(1 - l)$ stands for "effort," and more effort produces higher expected output, at cost $1 - l$ for the employee, say.[9] However, it is not *guaranteed* to bring about higher output, since the bad state of nature θ_L may still occur. Note that if output were to increase deterministically with effort then the unobservability of effort would not matter because the agent's hidden effort supply could be perfectly inferred from the observation of output.

Since effort $(1 - l)$ is not observable, the agent can be compensated only on the basis of realized output θ_j. The employer is thus restricted to offering a compensation contract $t(\theta_j)$ to the employee. Also the employer must now take into account the fact that $(1 - l)$ will be chosen by the employee to maximize her own expected payoff under the output-contingent compensation scheme $t(\theta_j)$. In other words, the employer can now make only a best guess that the effort level chosen by the employee is the outcome of the employee's own optimization problem:

$$(1-l) \in \operatorname*{argmax}_{\tilde{l}} \{p_L[1-l]u[t(\theta_L)+l]+p_H[1-l]u[t(\theta_H)+l]\}$$

Therefore, when the employer chooses the optimal compensation contract $\{t(\theta_j)\}$ to maximize his expected utility, he must make sure that it is in the employee's best interest to supply the right level of effort $(1 - l)$. In other words, the employer now solves the following maximization problem:

$$\max_{t(\theta_j)} \{p_L[1-l]U[\theta_L-t(\theta_L)]+p_H[1-l]U[\theta_H-t(\theta_H)]\}$$

8. Where $p_H[\cdot]$ (respectively $p_L[\cdot]$) is an increasing (respectively, decreasing) *function* of $(1 - l)$.

9. For simplicity, we assume here that the opportunity cost of time for the employee is independent of the state of nature.

subject to

$$p_L[1-l]u[t(\theta_L)+l]+p_H[1-l]u[t(\theta_H)+l] \geq \bar{u} = u(1) \tag{IR}$$

and

$$(1-l) \in \underset{l}{\operatorname{argmax}}\{p_L[1-l]u[t(\theta_L)+l]+p_H[1-l]u[t(\theta_H)+l]\} \tag{IC}$$

As in contracting problems with hidden information, when the action supplied by the employee is not observable the employer must take into consideration not only the employee's individual rationality constraint but also her incentive constraint.

Determining the solution to the employer problem with both constraints is not a trivial matter in general. Chapter 4 provides an extensive discussion of the two main approaches toward characterizing the solution to this problem. For now we shall simply point to the main underlying idea that an efficient *trade-off* between insurance and incentives involves rewarding the employee most for output outcomes that are most likely to arise when she puts in the required level of effort and punishing her the most for outcomes that are most likely to occur when she shirks. The application of this principle can give rise to quite complex compensation contracts in general, often more complex than what we see in reality. There is one situation, however, where the solution to this problem is extremely simple: when the employee is risk neutral. In that case it is efficient to have the employee take on all the output risk so as to maximize her incentives for effort provision. That is, when the employee is risk neutral, she should fully insure the employer.

One reason why this simple theory may predict unrealistically complex incentive schemes is that in most situations with hidden actions the incentive problem may be multifaceted. CEOs, for example, can take actions that increase profits, but they can also manipulate earnings, or "run down" assets in an effort to boost current earnings at the expense of future profits. They can also undertake high-expected-return but high-risk investments. It has been suggested that when shareholders or any other employer thus face a multidimensional incentive problem, then it may be appropriate to respond with both less "high powered" and simpler incentive schemes. We explore these ideas both in Chapter 6, which discusses hidden action problems with multiple tasks, and in Chapter 10, which considers long-term incentive contracting problems where the employee takes repeated hidden actions.

Chapter 6 also considers multidimensional hidden information problems as well as problems combining both hidden information and hidden actions. All these problems raise new analytical issues of their own and produce interesting new insights. We provide an extensive treatment of some of the most important contracting problems under multidimensional asymmetric information in the research literature.

Part I of our book also discusses contracting situations with an intermediate form of asymmetric information, situations where the informed party can *credibly disclose* her information if she wishes to do so. These situations, which are considered in Chapter 5, are mostly relevant for accounting regulation and for the design of mandatory disclosure rules, which are quite pervasive in the financial industry. Besides their obvious practical relevance, these contractual situations are also of interest because they deal with a very simple incentive problem, whether to *disclose or hide* relevant information (while *forging* information is not an available option). Because of this simplicity, the contractual problems considered in Chapter 5 offer an easy introduction to the general topic of contracting under asymmetric information. One of the main ideas emerging from the analysis of contracting problems with private but verifiable information is that incentives for voluntary disclosure can be very powerful. The basic logic, which is sometimes referred to as the "unraveling result," is that any seller of a good or service (e.g., an employee) has every incentive to reveal good information about herself, such as high test scores or a strong curriculum vitae. Employers understand this fact and expect employees to be forthcoming. If an employee is not, the employer assumes the worst. It is for this reason that employees have incentives to voluntarily disclose all but the worst piece of private verifiable information. This logic is so powerful that it is difficult to see why there should be mandatory disclosure laws. Chapter 5 discusses the main limits of the unraveling result and explains when mandatory disclosure laws might be warranted.

Finally, it is worth stressing that although our leading example in this introduction is the employment relation, each chapter contains several other classic applications, whether in corporate finance, industrial organization, regulation, public finance, or the theory of the firm. Besides helping the readers to acquaint themselves with the core concepts of the theory, these applications are also meant to highlight the richness and broad relevance of the basic theory of contracting under private information.

1.4   Optimal Contracting with Multilateral Asymmetric Information

The contracting situations we have discussed so far involve only one-sided private information or one-sided hidden actions. In practice, however, there are many situations where several contracting parties may possess relevant private information or be called to take hidden actions. A first basic question of interest then is whether and how the theory of contracting with one-sided private information extends to multilateral settings. Part II of this book is devoted to this question. It comprises two chapters. Chapter 7 deals with *multilateral private information* and Chapter 8 with *multilateral hidden actions*. Besides the obvious technical and methodological interest in analyzing these more general contractual settings, fundamental economic issues relating to the constrained efficiency of contractual outcomes, the role of competition, and the theory of the firm are also dealt with in these chapters.

While the general methodology and most of the core ideas discussed in Part I extend to the general case of multilateral asymmetric information, there is one fundamental difference. In the one-sided private information case the contract design problem reduces to a problem of controlling the informed party's response, while in the multilateral situation the contracting problem becomes one of controlling the strategic behavior of several parties interacting with each other. That is, the contract design problem becomes one of *designing a game with incomplete information*.

One of the main new difficulties then is predicting how the game will be played. The best way of dealing with this issue is in fact to design the contract in such a way that each player has a unique *dominant strategy*. Then the outcome of the game is easy to predict, since in essence all strategic interactions have then been removed. Unfortunately, however, contracts where each party has a unique dominant strategy are generally not efficient. Indeed, in a major result which builds on Arrow's (1963) impossibility theorem, Gibbard (1973) and Satterthwaite (1975) have shown that it is impossible in general to attain the full-information efficient outcome when there are more than two possible allocations to choose from and when the contracting parties' domain of preferences is unrestricted (that is, when the set of possible types of each contracting party is very diverse). Rather than stick to predictable but inefficient contracts, it may then generally be desirable to agree on contracts where the outcome is less predictable but on average more efficient (that is, contracts where each party's response depends on what the other contracting parties are expected to do). From a theorist's perspective this is a mixed blessing because the proposed efficient contracts (or "mechanisms," as they are often referred to in multilateral settings) may be somewhat fragile and may not always work in practice as the theory predicts.

1.4.1   Auctions and Trade under Multilateral Private Information

Perhaps the most important and widely studied problem of contracting with multilateral hidden information is the design of *auctions* with multiple bidders, each with his or her own private information about the value of the objects that are put up for auction.[10] Accordingly, Chapter 7 devotes considerable space to a discussion of the main ideas and derivation of key results in auction theory, such as the *revenue equivalence theorem* or *the winner's curse*. The first result establishes that a number of standard auctions yield the same expected revenue to the seller when bidders are risk neutral and their valuations for the object are independently and identically distributed. The second idea refers to the inevitable disappointment of the winner in an auction where bidders value the object in a similar way but have different prior information about its worth: when she learns that she won she also finds out that her information led her to be overoptimistic about the value of the object.

In recent years there has been an explosion of research in auction theory partly because of its relevance to auction design in a number of important practical cases. Covering this research would require a separate book, and Chapter 7 can serve only as an introduction to the subject.

Auction design with multiple informed bidders is by no means the only example of contracting with multilateral hidden information. Another leading example, which is extensively discussed in Chapter 7, is trade in situations where each party has private information about how much it values the good or the exchange.

A major economic principle emerging from the analysis of contracting with one-sided hidden information is the trade-off between allocative efficiency and extraction of informational rents. If the bargaining power lies

---

10. Despite its relative fragility, the theory of contracting with multilateral hidden information has proved to be of considerable practical relevance, as for example in the design of spectrum and wireless telephone license auctions (see for example Klemperer, 2002).

with the uninformed party, as we have assumed, then that party attempts to appropriate some of the informational rents of the informed party at the expense of allocative efficiency. But note that if the informed party (e.g., the employee in our example) has all the bargaining power and makes the contract offer, then the contracting outcome is always efficient. So, if the overriding objective is to achieve a Pareto efficient outcome (with, say, no unemployment), then there appears to be a simple solution when there is only one-sided hidden information: simply give all the bargaining power to the informed party.

In practice, however, besides the difficulty in identifying who the informed party is, there is also the obvious problem that generally all parties to the contract will have some relevant private information. Therefore, the natural contracting setting in which to pose the question of the efficiency of trade under asymmetric information and how it varies with the bargaining power of the different parties is one of multilateral asymmetric information. A fundamental insight highlighted in Chapter 7 is that the main constraint on efficient trade is not so much eliciting the parties' private information as ensuring their participation. Efficient trade can (almost) always be achieved if the parties' participation is obtained before they learn their information, while it cannot be achieved if participation is decided when they already know their type.

Applying this insight to our labor contracting example, the analysis in Chapter 7 indicates that labor market inefficiencies like unemployment are to be expected in an otherwise frictionless labor market when employers have market power and employees private information about their productivity, or when there is two-sided asymmetric information. It must be stressed, however, that policy intervention that is not based on any information superior to that available to the contracting parties will not be able to reduce or eliminate these inefficiencies. But labor market policies that try to intensify competitive bidding for jobs or for employees should lower inefficiencies caused by hidden information.

1.4.2 Moral Hazard in Teams, Tournaments, and Organizations

Contracting situations where several parties take hidden actions are often encountered in firms and other organizations. It is for this reason that the leading application of contracting problems involving multisided moral hazard is often seen to be the internal organization of firms and other economic institutions. Some prominent economic theorists of the firm like

Alchian and Demsetz (1972) or Jensen and Meckling (1976) go as far as arguing that the resolution of *moral-hazard-in-teams* problems (where several agents take complementary hidden actions) is the raison d'être of a firm. They contend that the role of a firm's owner or manager is to monitor employees and make sure that they take efficient actions that are hidden to others. Hence, the analysis of contracting problems with multisided moral hazard is important if only as an indirect vehicle for understanding economic organizations and firms.

Accordingly, Chapter 8 covers multiagent moral hazard situations with a particular focus on firms and their internal organization. To illustrate some of the key insights and findings covered in this chapter, consider the situation where our employer now contracts with two employees, A and B, each supplying a (hidden) "effort" $(1 - l_A)$ and $(1 - l_B)$. A key distinction in contracting problems with multisided moral hazard concerns the measure of performance: Is each employee's performance measured separately, or is there a single aggregate measure of both employees' contributions?

In the former case, when the output of each employee is observable and is given by, say, θ_{Aj} with probability p_{Aj} and θ_{Bj} with probability p_{Bj}, for $j = L, H$, the employer's problem is similar to the single-agent moral hazard problem described earlier, with the new feature that now the employer can also base compensation on each employee's *relative performance:*

$$\theta_{A_j} - \theta_{B_j}$$

An important class of incentive contracting situations in which agents are rewarded on the basis of how well they did relative to others is *rank-order tournaments.* Many sports contests are of this form, and promotions of employees up the corporate ladder can also be seen as a particular form of tournament.

Thus, in our employment problem with two employees and observable individual outputs, the employer may be able to provide better incentives with less risk exposure to the two employees by basing compensation on how well they perform relative to each other. This possibility can be seen as one reason why firms like to provide incentives to their employees through promotion schemes, appointing only the better employees to higher paying and more rewarding jobs. The reason why relative performance evaluation improves incentives is that when employees are exposed to the same exogenous shocks affecting their performance (changes in demand for their output or quality of input supplies, say), it is possible to shield them against these risks by *filtering out the common shock* from their performance measure. To see how this works, think that the probability p_{Aj} (resp., p_{Bj}) depends not only on individual effort $(1 - l_A)$ [resp., $(1 - l_B)$] but also on a random variable *that affects both agents*. In this case, it makes sense to link an employee's compensation positively to her own performance but *negatively* to the other employee's performance. Chapter 8 discusses extensively how to make the best use of relative performance measures in general problems with multisided moral hazard.

It is worth noting here that as compelling and plausible as the case for relative performance may be, many critical commentators on CEO compensation in the United States have pointed to the absence of such relative performance evaluation for CEOs. For example, Bebchuk, Fried, and Walker (2002) have criticized CEO compensation contracts in the United States for not optimally correcting compensation by filtering out common stock market shocks through indexing. They argue that this is a major deviation from optimal incentive contracting and is evidence of a failure in corporate governance in most large U.S. companies. Others, however, have rationalized the absence of explicit indexing as an optimal way of getting managers to do their own hedging when this is cheaper, or as an optimal response to competitive pressures in the market for CEOs (see Garvey and Milbourn, 2003; Jin, 2002).

Let us now turn to the second case, where observable output is a *single aggregate measure* given by

$$\theta_{Aj} + \theta_{Bj}$$

with the probability of higher realizations that depends positively on each employee's effort. Then the employer faces a moral-hazard-in-teams problem. Indeed, the amount of time worked by either of the two employees is a public good because, by raising joint output, it benefits both employees. As is easy to understand, in such situations a major difficulty for the employer is to prevent *free riding* by one employee on the other employee's work.

Alchian and Demsetz (1972) proposed that free riding of employees can be prevented through monitoring by the employer. That is, the employer's main role in their view is one of supervising employees and making sure that they all work. They also argue that the employer should be the residual claimant on the firm's revenues and that employees should be paid fixed wages to make sure that the employer has the right incentives to monitor.

When monitoring is too costly or imperfect, however, then employees also need to be motivated through compensation based on aggregate performance. An important insight of Holmström (1982), which we discuss in Chapter 8, is that optimal provision of incentives by giving shares of aggregate output to employees requires *budget breaking* in general. That is, the sum of the shares of the team members should not always add up to one. The residual should then be sold to a third party, which can be thought of as outside shareholders.

When the number of employees to be monitored is large, it is not reasonable to think that a single employer is able to effectively monitor all employees. Multiple supervisors are then required, and someone will have to monitor the monitors. If the number of supervisors is itself large, then multiple monitors of supervisors will be needed. And so on. Thus, by specifying the *span of control* of any supervisor (the number of employees that can reasonably be monitored by a single supervisor) and the *loss of control* as more tiers of supervisors are added (intuitively, there will be an overall reduction in efficiency of supervision of bottom-layer employees as more layers are added between the top and the bottom of the *hierarchy*), one can develop simultaneously a simple theory of the optimal firm size and the optimal hierarchical internal organization of the firm. Again, Chapter 8 gives an extensive treatment of this theory of organizations.

One of the reasons why there may be a loss of control as more supervisory tiers are added is that midlevel supervisors may attempt to *collude* with their employees against top management or the firm's owners. Recent corporate scandals in the United States have painfully reminded investors of the risk of collusion between auditors and the agents they are meant to monitor. These examples vividly draw attention to the importance of considering the possibility of collusion in multiagent contracting situations. Chapter 8 provides an extensive discussion of some of the main models of optimal contracting with collusion. It emphasizes in particular the idea that beyond incentive and participation constraints, optimal multilateral contracts are also constrained by "no-collusion constraints."

1.5   The Dynamics of Incentive Contracting

In practice, many if not most contracting relations are repeated or long term. Yet the theory we develop in the first two parts of the book deals only with static or one-shot contracting situations. In Part III we provide systematic coverage of long-term incentive contracting, mostly in a bilateral contracting framework. In Chapter 9 we discuss dynamic adverse selection and in Chapter 10 dynamic moral hazard.

Methodologically, there is no significant change in analyzing optimal multiperiod contracts as long as the contracting parties can *commit* to a single comprehensive long-term contract at the initial negotiation stage. As we have already noted in the context of intertemporal coinsurance contracting problems, when full commitment is feasible the long-term contract can essentially be reduced to a slightly more complex static contract involving trade of a slightly richer basket of state-contingent commodities, services, and transfers. What this conclusion implies in particular for contracting under hidden information is that the revelation principle still applies under full commitment.

However, if the contracting parties are allowed to *renegotiate* the initial contract as time unfolds and new information arrives, then new conceptual issues need to be addressed and the basic methodology of optimal static contracting must be adapted. Mainly, incentive constraints must then be replaced by tighter *renegotiation-proofness* constraints.

A number of new fundamental economic issues arise when the parties are involved in a long-term contractual relation. How is private information revealed over time? How is the constrained efficiency of contractual outcomes affected by repeated interactions? How does the possibility of renegotiation limit the efficiency of the overall long-term contract? To what extent can *reputation* serve as a more informal enforcement vehicle that is an alternative to courts? We discuss these and other issues extensively in this third part of the book.

1.5.1   Dynamic Adverse Selection

There are two canonical long-term contracting problems with hidden information: one where the informed party's type does not change over time and the other where a new type is drawn every period. In the first problem the main new conceptual issue to be addressed relates to *learning* and the gradual reduction of the informed party's informational advantage over time. The second class of problems is conceptually much closer to a static contracting problem, as the information asymmetry between the two contracting parties remains stationary. The main novel economic question in this class of problems concerns the trade-off between within-period and intertemporal insurance or allocative efficiency.

To see one important implication of learning of the informed party's type over time, consider again our employment-contracting problem with private information of the employee's productivity. That is, suppose that the employee can supply labor $(1 - l)$ to produce output $\alpha\theta_H(1 - l)$ when she is skilled and output $\alpha\theta_L(1 - l)$ when she is unskilled at opportunity cost $(1 - l)\theta_j$ $(j = H,L)$, where her productivity and opportunity cost of labor are hidden information. And suppose, as before, that the employer knows only the probability of facing a skilled employee, p_H. As we have seen, in a static contracting situation the employer would pursue an optimal trade-off between rent extraction and allocative inefficiency with a menu of employment contracts. The contract for the skilled employee would specify an inefficiently low level of employment, and the contract for the unskilled employee would leave her an informational rent relative to her outside opportunity.

Now, consider a twice-repeated relation with spot contracting in each period. In this situation the menu of contracts that we have described would no longer be feasible in the first period: indeed, if in the first period the type-j employee chooses option (l_j, t_j), she will have identified herself to the employer. In the second period the employer would then know her outside opportunity, and would in particular not leave any informational rent anymore to the unskilled employee. Therefore, unless the employer commits not to respond in this way, the unskilled employee will be reluctant to reveal her type by separating. Consequently more pooling of types is to be expected in early stages of the contracting relation.

Note that this commitment issue is a very general one that arises in many different contexts. It was known for example to analysts of the Soviet system as the *ratchet effect* (see Weitzman, 1976), which denotes the behavior of central planners that dynamically increase firm performance targets when they realize that they are facing very productive firms.

Under full commitment to a comprehensive long-term contract the preceding problems disappear. But full commitment will not be feasible if the contracting parties are allowed to sign long-term contracts but cannot commit not to renegotiate them in the future if they identify Pareto-improving opportunities. Indeed, in our employment example, the contracting parties will always want to renegotiate the optimal long-term contract, as this contract specifies an inefficiently low labor supply for the skilled employee. Once the high skill of the employee is revealed, there are gains from trade to renegotiating the contract to a higher level of labor supply. But if this renegotiation is anticipated, then the unskilled employee will again want to pretend to be skilled. In general, then, the optimal *renegotiation-proof* contract will differentiate the types less in the early stages of the relation, and the hidden information about the employee's type will only gradually be revealed to the employer. Chapter 9 provides an extensive discussion of the dynamics of contracting under adverse selection. It also illustrates the relevance of these ideas with several applications.

One general lesson emerging from our analysis in this chapter is that there are no gains from enduring relationships when the type of the informed party is fixed. Indeed, the best the contracting parties can hope to achieve is to repeat the optimal static contract. In contrast, when the informed party's type changes over time, there are substantial gains from repeating the relationship. While it is stretching our imagination to think that an employee's intrinsic productivity may change randomly over time, it is much more plausible to think of the hidden type as an unobservable income shock and to think of the contracting problem as an insurance problem with unobservable income shocks. Indeed, the first formal model of this problem by Townsend (1982) considers exactly this application.

The starting point of this analysis is that there can be no gains from contracting at all in a one-shot contracting relation because the informed party will always claim to have had a low income realization in order to receive an insurance compensation. But even in a twice-repeated contracting relation there can be substantial gains from insurance contracting. The reason is that in a relation that is repeated twice or more, greater insurance against income shocks within the first period can be traded off against better intertemporal allocation of consumption. In very concrete terms an individual who gets a low-income shock in the first period can borrow against her future income to smooth consumption. Vice versa, an individual who gets a high income in the first period can save some of this income toward future consumption. The key insight of Townsend and the subsequent literature on this problem is that borrowing and lending in a competitive debt market provides inefficiently low insurance. The optimal long-term incentive-compatible contract would provide more within-period insurance against low-income shocks. As we highlight in Chapter 9, this insight is particularly relevant for understanding the role of banks and their greater ability in providing liquidity (that is, within-period insurance) than financial markets.

1.5.2   Dynamic Moral Hazard

Dynamic contracting problems with moral hazard have a similar structure to dynamic adverse selection problems where the type of the informed party is drawn randomly every period. As with these contracting problems, there are gains from enduring relations, and the optimal long-term contract induces a similar distortion in intertemporal consumption allocations relative to what would obtain under repeated-spot-incentive contracting and simple borrowing and lending. That is, an optimal long-term employment contract with hidden actions by the employee will induce her to consume relatively more in earlier periods. If the employee were free to save any amount of her first-period income at competitive market rates, then she would choose to save more than is optimal under a long-term incentive contract, which would directly control her savings. The broad intuition for this general result is that by inducing the employee to consume more in early periods the employer can keep her "hungry" in subsequent periods and thus does not need to raise her level of compensation to maintain the same incentives.

Chapter 10 begins with a thorough analysis of a general twice-repeated contracting problem with moral hazard and of the general result we just mentioned. It then proceeds with a detailed discussion of the different effects in play in a repeated relation with moral hazard and identifies two important sources of gains and one important source of losses from an enduring relation. A first positive effect is that repetition of the relation makes the employee less averse to risk, since she can engage in "self-insurance" and offset a bad output shock in one period by borrowing against future income. A second potential positive effect comes from better information about the employee's choice of action obtained from repeated output observations. Offsetting these two positive effects, however, is a negative effect, which comes from the greater flexibility afforded the employee to act in response to dynamic incentives. In an enduring relation she can slack off following a good performance run or make up for poor performance in one period by working extra hard the next period.

It is this ability to modulate her effort supply in response to good or bad output changes that drives a striking insight due to Holmström and Milgrom (1987) concerning the shape of the optimal long-term incentive contract. One would think that when the relation between an employer and employee is enduring, the complexity of the employment contract would grow with the length of the relation, so much so that the optimal contract predicted by incentive theory in any realistic setup would become hopelessly complex. One might then fear that this extreme complexity could easily defeat the practical use of the theory. Holmström and Milgrom, however, argue that as the employee's set of possible actions grows with the length of the relation, the set of incentive constraints that constrict the shape of the optimal contract becomes so large that the incentive-compatible long-term contract ends up taking a simple linear form in final accumulated output. In short, under an enduring relation the optimal long-term contract gains in simplicity. This observation, which tends to accord well with the relative simplicity of actual employment contracts, is, however, theoretically valid only under some specific conditions on preferences and technology.

Another important simplification that is available under fairly general conditions is that the incentive effects under an optimal long-term incentive contract may be replicable with a sequence of spot contracts. This observation may be of particular relevance for evaluating long-term CEO compensation contracts. A common practice is to let CEOs exercise their stock options and sell their equity stake early but to "reload" their stock options to provide continuing incentives to CEOs. This has been viewed as an inefficient practice by some commentators (e.g., Bebchuk, Fried, and Walker, 2002), but it may also be seen as consistent with the idea of replication of the efficient long-term contract through a sequence of short-term contracts.

Explicit long-term employment contracts may also take a simple form in practice because in an ongoing employment relation efficiency may be attained by providing a combination of *explicit and implicit incentives*. The explicitly written part of the contract may then appear to be simple because it is supplemented by sophisticated implicit incentives. Loosely speaking, the term "implicit incentives" refers to notions like reputation building, career concerns, informal rewards, and *quid pro quos*. In reality many long-term employment relations do not provide a complete specification of employer obligations and employee duties. Instead they are sustained by implicit rules and incentives. Reliance on such incomplete explicit contracts may often be a way of economizing on contract-drafting costs. Accordingly, Chapter 10 provides an extensive treatment of so-called *relational contracts*, which combine both explicit and implicit incentives, and of the implicit incentives derived from "market" perceptions about employee "talent" and their implications, for example, in terms of outside offers.

The chapter also deals with renegotiation. As with dynamic adverse selection, the possibility of renegotiation undermines efficient incentive provision. Once a risk-averse employee has taken her action, there is no point in further exposing her to unnecessary output risk, and gains from renegotiation open up by letting the employer provide better insurance to the employee. But if such renegotiation is anticipated, then the employee will have lower incentives to put in effort. This issue is particularly relevant for CEO compensation where the "action" to be taken by the CEO may be the implementation of a new investment project or a new business plan. Once the project has been undertaken, there is no point in exposing the CEO to further risk, and it may be efficient to let her sell at least part of her equity stake. This is indeed the prediction of optimal incentive contracting with renegotiation, as we explain in Chapter 10.

1.6   Incomplete Contracts

Our discussion of explicit and implicit incentives already alludes to the fact that most long-term contracts in practice are *incomplete*, in that they do not deal explicitly with all possible contingencies and leave many decisions and transactions to be determined later. It is easy to understand intuitively why this is the case. Most people find it hard to think through even relatively simple dynamic decision problems and prefer to leave many decisions to be settled at a later stage when they become more pressing. If this is true for dynamic decision problems, then this must be the case a fortiori for dynamic contracting problems, where the parties must *jointly* think through and agree on future transactions or leave them to be determined at a later stage.

Our formulation of optimal contracting problems in the first three parts of the book abstracts from all these issues. There are no contract-drafting costs, there are no limits on contract enforcement, and parties are able to instantly determine complex optimal long-term contracts. This is clearly a drastic albeit convenient simplification. In the fourth and final part of the book we depart from this simple framework and explore the implications of contractual incompleteness.

As in Part III, Part IV is concerned with long-term contracts. But the focus is different. When contracts are incomplete, some transactions and decisions must be determined by the contracting parties at some later stage. The question then arises, Who makes these decisions? The principal focus of this part of the book will be to address this question. The form of the (incomplete) long-term contract will be prespecified exogenously in at least some dimensions, and the optimizing variables will be mainly the allocation among contracting parties of ownership titles, control rights, discretion, authority, decision-making rules, and so on.

Hence, the formulation of the basic incomplete contracting problem involves a major methodological change. Indeed, to emphasize this change we consider mostly problems involving little or no asymmetric information at the contracting stage. This part of the book also involves a fundamental substantive change: In the first three parts the focus was exclusively on monetary rewards for the provision of incentives. In contrast, in Part IV the focus will be on the incentive effects of *control* and *ownership protections*. In other words, this part emphasizes other institutional factors besides monetary remuneration in the provision of incentives. In a nutshell, the incomplete contracting approach offers a vehicle to explore the analysis of economic institutions and organizations systematically.

1.6.1   Ownership and Employment

In Chapter 11 we begin our treatment of incomplete contracts by assuming that an inability to describe certain events accurately before the fact is the principal reason why contracts are incomplete. We shall, however, assume that after the fact these events are easily described and their implications fully understood. It has been a matter of debate how much limitations on language are a constraint for drafting fully comprehensive contracts both in theory and in practice. We provide an extensive discussion of this debate in Chapter 12.

In Chapter 11 we specify exogenously which events the contract cannot be based on and focus on the implications of contractual incompleteness for institution design. We shall be interested primarily in the role of two ubiquitous institutions of market economies, ownership rights and employment relations.

The first formal model of an incomplete contracting problem by Simon (1951) deals with a fundamental aspect of the employment relation we have not hitherto considered: the *authority relation* between the employer and employee. So far we have described an employment contract like any other contract for the provision of an explicit service or "output." But in reality most employment contracts define only in very broad terms the duties of the employee and leave to the discretion of the employer the future determination of the specific tasks of the employee. In short, employment contracts are highly incomplete contracts where the employee agrees to put herself under the (limited) authority of the employer. Employment contracts thus specify a different mode of transaction from the negotiation mode prevalent in spot markets. It is for this reason that Simon, Coase, Williamson, and others have singled out the employment relation as the archetypal form of an economic institution that is different from market exchange.

Simon views the choice between the two modes of transaction as a comparison between two long-term contracts: a "sales contract," in which the service to be provided is precisely specified in a contract, and an "employment contract," in which the service is left to the discretion of the buyer (employer) within some contractually specified limits. The employment contract is preferred when the buyer is highly uncertain at the time of contracting about which service he prefers and when the seller (employee) is close to indifferent between the different tasks the employer can choose from. Chapter 11 discusses the strengths and limitations of Simon's theory and provides an extensive treatment of a "modernized" version of his theory that allows for *ex ante relation-specific investments* and ex post renegotiation. Chapter 12 further builds on Simon's theory by explicitly modeling "orders" or "commands" given by the employer, to which the employee responds by either "quitting" or "executing" the order.

The notion that the presence of relation-specific investments creates the need for modes of exchange other than trade in spot markets has been articulated and emphasized forcibly in Williamson's writings (1975, 1979, 1985). In a pathbreaking article that builds on his insights, Grossman and Hart (1986) developed a simple theory and model of *ownership rights* based on the notion of *residual rights of control*. They define a firm as a collection of assets owned by a common owner, who has residual rights of control over the use of the assets. A key new notion in their article is that ownership serves as a protection against future *holdups* by other trading partners and thus may give stronger incentives for ex ante relation-specific investments. That is, the owner of an asset has a bargaining chip in future negotiations over trades not specified in the initial incomplete contracts. He can sell access to the productive asset to future trading partners who need the asset for production. The owner can thus protect the returns from ex ante relation-specific investments.

Building on these notions, Grossman and Hart are able to provide a simple formal theory of the costs and benefits of integration and the boundaries of the firm. Chapter 11 provides an extensive treatment of this theory. The advantage of integration is that the bargaining position of the owner of the newly integrated firm is strengthened. This stronger position may induce him to invest more. The drawback, however, is that the previous owner's bargaining position is weakened. This agent may therefore invest less. Depending on the relative size of these costs and benefits of integration, Grossman and Hart are able to determine when it is optimal to integrate or not. They are thus able to articulate for the first time a simple and rigorous theory of the boundaries of the firm, which has been further elaborated by Hart and Moore (1990) and synthesized by Hart (1995).

1.6.2   Incomplete Contracts and Implementation Theory

While this theory of the firm has improved our understanding of the special role of ownership, a major theoretical issue remains only partially resolved, at least in its initial versions. As Maskin and Tirole (1999a) have pointed out, there is a basic logical tension in the theory. On the one hand, contracting parties are assumed to be able to fully anticipate the consequences of their current actions for the future, like the potential for holdups or the protections given by ownership. And yet, on the other hand, they are also assumed to be unable to limit expected future abuse by trading partners with explicit contractual clauses. All they can do to improve their future negotiating position is to trade a very standardized contract: ownership titles.

We discuss the delicate theoretical issues relating to this basic logical tension in Chapter 12. This chapter begins by covering the theory of *Nash implementation* (Maskin, 1977) and its subsequent developments. This theory deals with issues of contract design in situations where an event is difficult to describe ex ante (or identify by a third party) but easily recognized by all contracting parties ex post. It exploits the idea that contracts can be made contingent on such events by relying on reports by the parties on which event occurred. A striking general result of implementation theory is that by designing suitable *revelation games* for the contracting parties it is often possible to achieve the same outcomes as with fully contingent contracts.

Thus the challenge for the theory of incomplete contracts, which relies on the distinction between observability and nonverifiability (or non-describability) of an event, is to explain why the contracting parties do not attempt to contract around this constraint by designing sophisticated revelation games (or *Maskin schemes* as they are commonly called). This is not necessarily an abstruse theoretical issue, as Chapter 12 illustrates with examples of plausible optionlike contracts that achieve efficiency in contracting problems involving relation-specific investments and holdup problems. As is readily seen, these contracts can be interpreted as simple revelation games.

One way the challenge has been taken up is to argue that Maskin schemes have limited power in improving efficiency over simple incomplete contracts in *complex* contracting environments where there may be many different states of nature or potentially many different services or goods to be traded (see Segal, 1999a). Chapter 12 provides an extensive discussion of these arguments. It also explores another foundation for the theory of authority, based on actions that are *both ex ante and ex post non-contractable*. If one assumes that one can contract on who *controls* these actions, one can derive predictions about the optimal allocation of authority within organizations, either in a one-shot or in a repeated context.

1.6.3   Bilateral Contracts and Multilateral Exchange

Finally, Chapter 13 deals with another common form of contractual incompleteness: the limited participation of all concerned parties in a single comprehensive multilateral contract. Employment contracts, for example, are generally bilateral contracts between an employer and an employee even in situations where the employee works together in a team with other employees, or in situations where the employer is involved in a whole *nexus of contracts* with suppliers, clients, lenders, and other providers of capital. When (incomplete) bilateral contracts are written in such multilateral contract settings, any bilateral contract may impose an externality on the other parties. The equilibrium outcome of the contracting game may then be inefficient. Thus a central focus of this chapter is the characterization of situations where bilateral contracting results in efficient outcomes.

An important distinction that is drawn in the literature is whether the bilateral contract is *exclusive* or *nonexclusive*—that is, whether the employee can sign only an exclusive contract with one employer or whether she can sign up with several employers for several part-time jobs. Interestingly, most employment contracts are exclusive. But this is not always the case for other contracts. For example, for health insurance it is generally possible for the insuree to acquire supplementary insurance. Similarly, with credit card debt or other loans, a borrower can build up debt on several different cards or take out loans from several different lenders. Exactly why exclusivity is required for some types of contracts but not others involving externalities has not been fully explored. Intuitively, one should expect to see exclusive contracts when the externality is potentially large and when exclusivity is easy to enforce. Whether exclusivity is enforced or not, however, one should expect inefficient equilibrium outcomes to obtain in general in bilateral contracting games, since bilateral contracts alone are insufficient to fully internalize all externalities across all affected parties. This is a central theme in the *common agency* literature, which studies multiple bilateral incentive contracting between a single agent and several principals (see, for example, Bernheim and Whinston, 1985, 1986a, 1986b). Chapter 13 provides an extensive treatment of this important contracting problem.

Because of the presence of a potential externality, an obvious concern is whether the bilateral contracting game has a well-defined equilibrium outcome. An early focus of the contracting literature has indeed been the potential nonexistence of equilibrium in such contracting games. In a landmark article Rothschild and Stiglitz (1976) have thus shown that if two insurers compete for exclusive bilateral contracts with one or several insurees who have private information about their likelihood of facing an adverse shock (or accident), then a well-defined equilibrium outcome of the contracting game may not exist. The reason is that each insurer has an incentive to respond to the contract offers of the other insurer by only *cream skimming* the good risks and leaving the high-risk insurees to contract with their rival. Chapter 13 discusses this striking result and the vast literature it has spawned.

Other important topics are touched on besides these two broad themes, such as the strategic value of contracting in duopoly or barrier-to-entry settings, or the impact of product-market competition on the size of agency problems. But it is fair to say that Chapter 13 does not attempt to provide a systematic treatment of the existing literature on bilateral contracting with competition (whether static or dynamic, with adverse selection, moral hazard, or both) simply because the existing literature that touches on this topic is at this point both too vast and too disconnected to be able to provide a systematic and comprehensive treatment in only one chapter.[11]

1.7   Summing Up

The analysis of optimal contracting in this book highlights the fact that common contract forms and institutions that we take for granted, like employment contracts and ownership rights, are sophisticated and multi-faceted "institutions." For a long time economists have been able to give only an oversimplified analysis of these contract forms, which ignored uncertainty, asymmetric information, incentives, and control issues. As this introductory chapter makes clear, however, a basic economic relation like the employment relation has to deal with these various facets.

The goal of this book is therefore to explain how existing contract theory allows one to incorporate these features, not just in employment relations but also in many other applications. In fact, we have chosen to illustrate contract-theoretic analyses in many different contexts, typically choosing the application that has been the most influential in economics for the particular general problem under consideration.

The book gives an overview of the main conceptual breakthroughs of contract theory, while also pointing out its current limitations. As contract theory has grown to become a large field, we have been forced to limit our coverage by making difficult choices on what to leave out. While we have given careful consideration to what material to cover, our choices inevitably also reflect our limited knowledge of the field and our own personal preferences. As the reader may already have noted, our biases have likely been in the direction of overemphasizing economic ideas, insights, and simplicity over generality.

11. For example, we do not cover here the growing literature on contracting in a "general equilibrium" setting, for example, the impact of credit rationing on macroeconomic fluctuations (see Bernanke and Gertler, 1989, and Kiyotaki and Moore, 1997) or income distribution (see Banerjee and Newman, 1991, 1993, and Aghion and Bolton, 1997). Nor do we cover more traditional general equilibrium analysis with moral hazard or adverse selection (see Prescott and Townsend, 1984, and Guesnerie, 1992). Indeed, providing a self-contained treatment of these various topics would require dealing with many technical issues that go beyond contract theory.

The final chapter of the book contains a set of exercises, which serve two purposes. First and foremost, these exercises help the reader to master some of the basic analytical techniques to solve optimal contracting problems and to develop a deeper understanding of the most important arguments. The second purpose of this chapter is to cover some classic articles that we have not had the space to cover in the main chapters. For this reason it may be worth leafing through this chapter even if the reader does not intend to try to solve any of the problems.

I STATIC BILATERAL CONTRACTING

The first part of this book deals with the classical *theory of incentives and information* in a static bilateral contracting framework. The fundamental conceptual innovation in the contracting problems considered here relative to the classical decision problems in microeconomics textbooks is that one of the contracting parties, the *principal,* is now controlling the decision problem of another party, the *agent.* That is, the principal's optimization problem has another optimization problem embedded in its constraints: the agent's optimization problem. The first part of this book provides a systematic exposition of the general methods that have been developed to analyze this type of nested optimization problem.

The first two chapters are concerned with the general problem of contracting under *hidden information.* Chapter 2 considers optimal contracts designed by the *uninformed party.* This is generally referred to as the *screening problem.* Chapter 3 turns the table and considers optimal contracts offered by the *informed party.* This involves a *signaling problem* and is generally referred to as the *informed principal problem.* Chapter 4 deals with the contracting problem involving *hidden actions.* This is generally known as the *moral hazard* problem. Much of the material in these three chapters can also be found in advanced microeconomics textbooks, such as Mas-Colell, Whinston, and Green (1995) and in the contract theory textbooks of Salanié (1997) and Laffont and Martimort (2002). Chapter 5, on the other hand, covers the general problem of *disclosure* of verifiable private information and introduces material that is not found in other texts. This chapter deals with a subclass of contracting problems under hidden information, which is relevant in particular to auditing and securities regulations. The next chapter (Chapter 6) covers richer contracting problems that involve multidimensional private information or hidden actions, and also a combination of hidden information and hidden actions. Again, most of the material in this chapter is not covered in depth in other textbooks.

2   Hidden Information, Screening

In this chapter we focus on the basic static adverse selection problem, with one principal facing one agent who has private information on her "type," that is, her preferences or her intrinsic productivity. This problem was first formally analyzed by Mirrlees (1971). We first explain how to solve such problems when the agent can be of only two types, a case that already allows us to obtain most of the key insights from adverse selection models. We do so by looking at the problem of nonlinear pricing by a monopolistic seller who faces a buyer with unknown valuation for his product.

We then move on to other applications, still in the case where the informed party can be of only two types: credit rationing, optimal income taxation, implicit labor contracts, and regulation. This is only a partial list of economic issues where adverse selection matters. Nevertheless, these are all important economic applications that have made a lasting impression on the economics profession. For each of them we underline both the economic insights and the specificities from the point of view of contract theory.

In the last part of the chapter we extend the analysis to more than two types, returning to monopoly pricing. We especially emphasize the continuum case, which is easier to handle. This extension allows us to stress which results from the two-type case are general and which ones are not. The methods we present will also be helpful in tackling multiagent contexts, in particular in Chapter 7.

2.1   The Simple Economics of Adverse Selection

Adverse selection naturally arises in the following context, analyzed first by Mussa and Rosen (1978), and subsequently by Maskin and Riley (1984a): Consider a transaction between a buyer and a seller, where the seller does not know perfectly how much the buyer is willing to pay for a good. Suppose, in addition, that the seller sets the terms of the contract. The buyer's preferences are represented by the utility function

$$u(q, T, \theta) = \int_0^q P(x, \theta)dx - T$$

where q is the number of units purchased, T is the total amount paid to the seller, and $P(x, \theta)$ is the inverse demand curve of a buyer with preference characteristics θ. Throughout this section we shall consider the following special and convenient functional form for the buyer's preferences:

$$u(q, T, \theta) = \theta v(q) - T$$

where $v(0) = 0$, $v'(q) > 0$, and $v''(q) < 0$ for all q. The characteristics θ are private information to the buyer. The seller knows only the distribution of θ, $F(\theta)$.

Assuming that the seller's unit production costs are given by $c > 0$, his profit from selling q units against a sum of money T is given by

$$\pi = T - cq$$

The question of interest here is, What is the best, that is, the profit-maximizing, pair (T, q) that the seller will be able to induce the buyer to choose? The answer to this question will depend on the information the seller has on the buyer's preferences. We treat in this section the case where there are only two types of buyers: $\theta \in \{\theta_L, \theta_H\}$, with $\theta_H > \theta_L$. The consumer is of type θ_L with probability $\beta \in [0, 1]$ and of type θ_H with probability $(1 - \beta)$. The probability β can also be interpreted as the proportion of consumers of type θ_L.

2.1.1   First-Best Outcome: Perfect Price Discrimination

To begin with, suppose that the seller is perfectly informed about the buyer's characteristics. The seller can then treat each type of buyer separately and offer her a type-specific contract, that is, (T_i, q_i) for type θ_i ($i = H, L$). The seller will try to maximize his profits subject to inducing the buyer to accept the proposed contract. Assume the buyer obtains a payoff of $\bar{u}$ if she does not take the seller's offer. In this case, the seller will solve

$$\max_{T_i, q_i} T_i - cq_i$$

subject to

$$\theta_i v(q_i) - T_i \geq \bar{u}$$

We can call this constraint the participation, or individual-rationality, constraint of the buyer. The solution to this problem will be the contract $(\tilde{q}_i, \tilde{T}_i)$ such that

$$\theta_i v'(\tilde{q}_i) = c$$

and

$$\theta_i v(\tilde{q}_i) = \tilde{T}_i + \bar{u}$$

Intuitively, without adverse selection, the seller finds it optimal to maximize total surplus by having the buyer select a quantity such that marginal utility equals marginal cost, and then setting the payment so as to appropriate the full surplus and leave no rent to the buyer above $\bar{u}$. Note that in a market context, $\bar{u}$ could be endogenized, but here we shall treat it as exogenous and normalize it to 0.

Without adverse selection, the total profit of the seller is thus

$$\beta(T_L - cq_L) + (1 - \beta)(T_H - cq_H)$$

and the optimal contract maximizes this profit subject to the participation constraints for the two types of buyer. Note that it can be implemented by *type-specific two-part tariffs,* where the buyer is allowed to buy as much as she wants of the good at unit price c provided she pays a type-specific fixed fee equal to $\theta_i v(\tilde{q}_i) - c\tilde{q}_i$.

The idea that, without adverse selection, the optimal contract will maximize total surplus while participation constraints will determine the way in which it is shared is a very general one.[1] This ceases to be true in the presence of adverse selection.

2.1.2 Adverse Selection, Linear Pricing, and Simple Two-Part Tariffs

If the seller cannot observe the type of the buyer anymore, he has to offer the same contract to everybody. The contract set is potentially large, since it consists of the set of functions $T(q)$. We first look at two simple contracts of this kind.

2.1.2.1 Linear Pricing

The simplest contract consists in *traditional linear pricing,* which is a situation where the seller's contract specifies only a price P. Given this contract the buyer chooses q to maximize

$$\theta_i v(q) - Pq, \quad \text{where } i = L, H$$

From the first-order conditions

$$\theta_i v'(q) = P$$

we can derive the demand functions of each type:[2]

---

1. This idea also requires that surplus be freely transferable across individuals, which will not be the case if some individuals face financial resource constraints.
2. The assumed concavity of $v(.)$ ensures that there is a unique solution to the first-order conditions.

$$q_i = D_i(P)$$

The buyer's net surplus can now be written as follows:

$$S_i(P) = \theta_i v[D_i(P)] - PD_i(P)$$

Let

$$D(P) \equiv \beta D_L(P) + (1 - \beta)D_H(P)$$

$$S(P) \equiv \beta S_L(P) + (1 - \beta)S_H(P)$$

With linear pricing the seller's problem is the familiar monopoly pricing problem, where the seller chooses P to solve

$$\max_{P}(P - c)D(P)$$

and the monopoly price is given by

$$P_m = c - \frac{D(P)}{D'(P)}$$

In this solution we have both positive rents for the buyers $[S(P) > 0]$ and inefficiently low consumption, that is, $\theta_i v'(q) = P > c$, since the seller can make profits only by setting a price in excess of marginal cost and $D'(\cdot) < 0$. Note that, depending on the values of β, θ_L, and θ_H, it may be optimal for the seller to serve only the θ_H buyers. We shall, however, proceed under the assumption that it is in the interest of the seller to serve both markets.

Can the seller do better by moving away from linear pricing? He will be able to do so only if buyers cannot make arbitrage profits by trading in a secondary market: if arbitrage is costless, only linear pricing is possible, because buyers would buy at the minimum average price and then resell in the secondary market if they do not want to consume everything they bought.

2.1.2.2 Single Two-Part Tariff

In this subsection we shall work with the interpretation that there is only one buyer and that β is a probability measure. Under this interpretation there are no arbitrage opportunities open to the buyer. Therefore, a single two-part tariff (Z, P), where P is the unit price and Z the fixed fee, will improve upon linear pricing for the seller. Note first that for any given price P, the minimum fixed fee the seller will set is given by $Z = S_L(P)$. (This is the maximum fee a buyer of type θ_L is willing to pay.) A type-θ_H buyer will always decide to purchase a positive quantity of q when charged a two-part tariff $T(q) = S_L(P) + Pq$, since $\theta_H > \theta_L$. If the seller decides to serve both types of customers and therefore sets $Z = S_L(P)$, he also chooses P to maximize

$$\max_P S_L(P) + (P - c)D(P)$$

The solution for P under this arrangement is given by

$$S_L'(P) + D(P) + (P - c)D'(P) = 0$$

which implies

$$P = c - \frac{D(P) + S_L'(P)}{D'(P)}$$

Now, by the envelope theorem, $S_L'(P) = -D_L(P)$, so that $D(P) + S_L'(P)$ is strictly positive; in addition, $D'(P) < 0$, so that $P > c$. Thus, if the seller decides to serve both types of customers [and therefore sets $Z = S_L(P)$], the first-best outcome cannot be achieved and underconsumption remains relative to the first-best outcome.[3] Another conclusion to be drawn from this simple analysis is that an optimal single two-part tariff contract is always preferred by the seller to an optimal linear pricing contract [since the seller can always raise his profits by setting $Z = S_L(P_m)$]. We can also observe the following: If P_m, P_d, and P_c, respectively, denote the monopoly price, the marginal price in an optimal single two-part tariff, and the (first-best efficient) competitive price, then $P_m > P_d > P_c = c$. To see this point, note that a small reduction in price from P_m has a second-order (negative) effect on monopoly profits $(P_m - c)D(P_m)$, by definition of P_m. But it has a first-order (positive) effect on consumer surplus, which increases by an amount proportional to the reduction in price. The first-order (positive) effect dominates, and, therefore, the seller is better off lowering the price from P_m when he can extract the buyer's surplus with the fixed fee $Z = S_L(P_m)$. Similarly, a small increase in price from P_c has a first-order (positive) effect on $(P_c - c)D(P_c)$, but a second-order (negative) effect on $S(P_c)$, by definition of P_c.

---

3. If he decides to set an even higher fixed fee and to price the type-θ_L buyer out of the market, he does not achieve the first-best outcome either; either way, the first-best solution cannot be attained under a single two-part tariff contract.

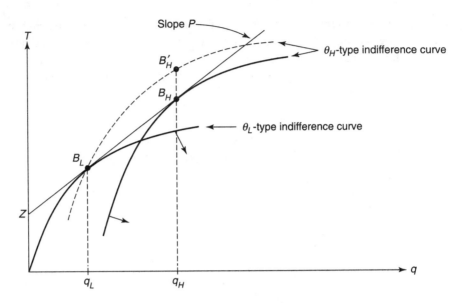

Figure 2.1
Two-Part Tariff Solution

An important feature of the optimal single two-part tariff solution is that the θ_H-type buyer strictly prefers the allocation B_H to B_L, as illustrated in Figure 2.1. As the figure also shows, by setting up more general contracts $C = [q, T(q)]$, the seller can do strictly better by offering the same allocation to the θ_L-type buyer, but offering, for example, some other allocation $B_H' \neq B_H$ to the θ_H-type buyer. Notice that at B_H' the seller gets a higher transfer $T(q)$ for the same consumption (this is particular to the example). Also, the θ_H buyer is indifferent between B_L and B_H'. These observations naturally raise the question of the form of optimal nonlinear pricing contract.

2.1.3   Second-Best Outcome: Optimal Nonlinear Pricing

In this subsection we show that the seller can generally do better by offering more general nonlinear prices than a single two-part tariff. In the process we outline the basic methodology of solving for optimal contracts when the buyer's type is unknown. Since the seller does not observe the type of the buyer, he is forced to offer her a set of choices independent of her type. Without loss of generality, this set can be described as

$[q, T(q)]$; that is, the buyer faces a schedule from which she will pick the outcome that maximizes her payoff. The problem of the seller is therefore to solve

$$\max_{T(q)} \beta[T(q_L) - cq_L] + (1-\beta)[T(q_H) - cq_H]$$

subject to

$$q_i = \arg\max_q \theta_i v(q) - T(q) \quad \text{for } i = L, H$$

and

$$\theta_i v(q_i) - T(q_i) \geq 0 \quad \text{for } i = L, H$$

The first two constraints are the incentive-compatibility (IC) constraints, while the last two are participation or individual-rationality constraints (IR). This problem looks nontrivial to solve, since it involves optimization over a schedule $T(q)$ under constraints that themselves involve optimization problems. Such adverse selection problems can, however, be easily solved step-by-step as follows:

Step 1: Apply the revelation principle.

From Chapter 1 we can recall that without loss of generality we can restrict each schedule $T(q)$ to the pair of optimal choices made by the two types of buyers $\{[T(q_L), q_L] \text{ and } [T(q_H), q_H]\}$; this restriction also simplifies greatly the incentive constraints. Specifically, if we define $T(q_i) = T_i$ for $i = L, H$, then the problem can be rewritten as

$$\max_{T_i, q_i} \beta(T_L - cq_L) + (1-\beta)(T_H - cq_H)$$

subject to

$$\theta_H v(q_H) - T_H \geq \theta_H v(q_L) - T_L \qquad (ICH)$$

$$\theta_L v(q_L) - T_L \geq \theta_L v(q_H) - T_H \qquad (ICL)$$

$$\theta_H v(q_H) - T_H \geq 0 \qquad (IRH)$$

$$\theta_L v(q_L) - T_L \geq 0 \qquad (IRL)$$

The seller thus faces four constraints, two incentive constraints $[(IC_i)$ means that the type-θ_i buyer should prefer her own allocation to the allocation of the other type of buyer] and two participation constraints

[(IR_i) means that the allocation that buyer of type θ_i chooses gives her a nonnegative payoff]. Step 1 has thus already greatly simplified the problem. We can now try to eliminate some of these constraints.

Step 2: Observe that the participation constraint of the "high" type will not bind at the optimum.

Indeed (IRH) will be satisfied automatically because of (IRL) and (ICH):

$$\theta_H v(q_H) - T_H \geq \theta_H v(q_L) - T_L \geq \theta_L v(q_L) - T_L \geq 0$$

where the inequality in the middle comes from the fact that $\theta_H > \theta_L$.

Step 3: Solve the relaxed problem without the incentive constraint that is satisfied at the first-best optimum.

The strategy now is to relax the problem by deleting one incentive constraint, solve the relaxed problem, and then check that it does satisfy this omitted incentive constraint. In order to choose which constraint to omit, consider the first-best problem. It involves efficient consumption and zero rents for both types of buyers, that is, $\theta_i v'(\tilde{q}_i) = c$ and $\theta_i v(\tilde{q}_i) = \tilde{T}_i$. This outcome is not incentive compatible, because the θ_H buyer will prefer to choose $(\tilde{q}_L, \tilde{T}_L)$ rather than her own first-best allocation: while this inefficiently restricts her consumption, it allows her to enjoy a strictly positive surplus equal to $(\theta_H - \theta_L)\tilde{q}_L$, rather than zero rents. Instead, type θ_L will not find it attractive to raise her consumption to the level $\tilde{q}_H$: doing so would involve paying an amount $\tilde{T}_H$ that exhausts the surplus of type θ_H and would therefore imply a negative payoff for type θ_L, who has a lower valuation for this consumption. In step 3, we thus choose to omit constraint (ICL). Note that the fact that only one incentive constraint will bind at the optimum is driven by the *Spence-Mirrlees single-crossing condition*, which can be written as

$$\frac{\partial}{\partial \theta}\left[-\frac{\partial u/\partial q}{\partial u/\partial T}\right] > 0$$

This condition means that the marginal utility of consumption (relative to that of money, which is here constant) rises with θ. Consequently, optimal consumption will have to rise with θ.

Step 4: Observe that the two remaining constraints of the relaxed problem will bind at the optimum.

Remember that we now look at the problem

$$\max_{T_i, q_i} \beta(T_L - cq_L) + (1-\beta)(T_H - cq_H)$$

subject to

$$\theta_H v(q_H) - T_H \geq \theta_H v(q_L) - T_L \qquad\qquad\qquad (ICH)$$

$$\theta_L v(q_L) - T_L \geq 0 \qquad\qquad\qquad\qquad\qquad\qquad (IRL)$$

In this problem, constraint (ICH) will bind at the optimum; otherwise, the seller can raise T_H until it does bind: this step leaves constraint (IRL) unaffected while improving the maximand. And constraint (IRL) will also bind; otherwise, the seller can raise T_L until it does bind: this step in fact relaxes constraint (ICH) while improving the maximand [it is here that having omitted (ICL) matters, since a rise in T_L could be problematic for this constraint].

Step 5: Eliminate T_L and T_H from the maximand using the two binding constraints, perform the unconstrained optimization, and then check that (ICL) is indeed satisfied.

Substituting for the values of T_L and T_H in the seller's objective function, we obtain the following unconstrained optimization problem:

$$\max_{q_L, q_H} \beta[\theta_L v(q_L) - cq_L] + (1-\beta)[\theta_H v(q_H) - cq_H - (\theta_H - \theta_L)v(q_L)]$$

The first term in brackets is the full surplus generated by the purchases of type θ_L, which the seller appropriates entirely because that type is left with zero rents. Instead, the second term in brackets is the full surplus generated by the purchases of type θ_H *minus her informational rent* $(\theta_H - \theta_L)v(q_L)$, which comes from the fact that she can "mimic" the behavior of the other type. This informational rent increases with q_L.

The following first-order conditions characterize the unique interior solution (q_L^*, q_H^*) to the relaxed program, if this solution exists:[4]

$$\theta_H v'(q_H^*) = c$$

$$\theta_L v'(q_L^*) = \frac{c}{1 - \left(\dfrac{1-\beta}{\beta} \dfrac{\theta_H - \theta_L}{\theta_L}\right)} > c$$

---

4. If the denominator of the second expression is not positive, then the optimal solution involves $q_L^* = 0$, while the other consumption remains determined by the first-order condition.

This interior solution implies $q_L^* < q_H^*$. One can then immediately verify that the omitted constraints are satisfied at the optimum ($q_i^*, T_i^*, i = L, H$) given that (ICH) binds. Indeed,

$$\theta_H v(q_H^*) - T_H^* = \theta_H v(q_L^*) - T_L^* \qquad\qquad (ICH)$$

together with $\theta_L < \theta_H$ and $q_L^* < q_H^*$, implies

$$\theta_L v(q_H^*) - T_H^* \leq \theta_L v(q_L^*) - T_L^* \qquad\qquad (ICL)$$

We have therefore characterized the actual optimum. Two basic economic conclusions emerge from this analysis:

1. The second-best optimal consumption for type θ_H is the same as the first-best optimal consumption ($\tilde{q}_H$), but that of type θ_L is lower. Thus only the consumption of one of the two types is distorted in the second-best solution.

2. The type-θ_L buyer obtains a surplus of zero, while the other type obtains a strictly positive "informational" rent.

These two conclusions are closely related to each other: the consumption distortion for type θ_L is the result of the seller's attempt to reduce the informational rent of type θ_H. Since a buyer of type θ_H is more eager to consume, the seller can reduce that type's incentive to mimic type θ_L by cutting down on the consumption offered to type θ_L. By reducing type θ_H's incentives to mimic type θ_L, the seller can reduce the informational rent of (or, equivalently, charge a higher price to) type θ_H. Looking at the first-order conditions for q_i^* indicates that the size of the distortion, $\tilde{q}_L - q_L^*$, is increasing in the potential size of the informational rent of type θ_H—as measured by the difference $(\theta_H - \theta_L)$—and decreasing in β. For β and $(\theta_H - \theta_L)$ large enough the denominator becomes negative. In that case the seller hits the constraint $q_L \geq 0$.

As the latter part of the chapter will show, what will remain true with more than two types is the inefficiently low consumption relative to the first best (except for the highest type: we will keep "efficiency at the top") and the fact that the buyer will enjoy positive informational rents (except for the lowest type). Before doing this extension, let us turn to other applications.

2.2 Applications

2.2.1 Credit Rationing

Adverse selection arises naturally in financial markets. Indeed, a lender usually knows less about the risk-return characteristics of a project than the borrower. In other words, a lender is in the same position as a buyer of a secondhand car:[5] it does not know perfectly the "quality" of the project it invests in. Because of this informational asymmetry, inefficiencies in the allocation of investment funds to projects may arise. As in the case of secondhand cars, these inefficiencies may take the form that "good quality" projects remain "unsold" or are denied credit. This type of inefficiency is generally referred to as "credit rationing." There is now an extensive literature on credit rationing. The main early contributions are Jaffee and Modigliani (1969), Jaffee and Russell (1976), Stiglitz and Weiss (1981), Bester (1985), and De Meza and Webb (1987). We shall illustrate the main ideas with a simple example where borrowers can be of two different types.

Consider a population of risk-neutral borrowers who each own a project that requires an initial outlay of $I = 1$ and yields a random return X, where $X \in \{R, 0\}$. Let $p \in [0, 1]$ denote the probability that $X = R$. Borrowers have no wealth and must obtain investment funds from an outside source. A borrower can be of two different types $i = s, r$, where s stands for "safe" and r for "risky." The borrower of type i has a project with return characteristics (p_i, R_i). We shall make the following assumptions:

A1: $p_i R_i = m$,   with $m > 1$

A2: $p_s > p_r$ and $R_s < R_r$

Thus both types of borrowers have projects with the same expected return, but the risk characteristics of the projects differ. In general, project types may differ both in risk and return characteristics. It turns out that the early literature mainly emphasizes differences in risk characteristics.

A bank can offer to finance the initial outlay in exchange for a future repayment. Assume for simplicity that there is a single bank and excess

---

5. Akerlof (1970), in a pioneering contribution, has analyzed the role of adverse selection in markets by focusing in particular on used cars. See Chapter 13 on the role of adverse selection in markets more generally.

demand for funds: the bank has a total amount $\alpha < 1$ of funds, and it faces a unit mass of borrowers. The proportion of "safe" borrowers is β (and that of "risky" borrowers is $1 - \beta$). Assume, moreover, that $\alpha > \max \{\beta, 1 - \beta\}$, so that available funds are sufficient to avoid crowding out either type of borrower completely.

What type of lending contract should the bank offer a borrower in this situation? Under symmetric information and no contractual restrictions, the bank would lend all of α and would be indifferent about financing either type of borrower: it would specify a repayment D_i for borrower of type i, with $D_i = R_i$, which it would obtain with probability p_i.

What about adverse selection? The early literature on credit rationing does not allow for much contractual flexibility: it considers only contracts where the bank specifies a fixed repayment, D, in exchange for the initial outlay $I = 1$. Assume that type-i borrowers apply for funds if and only if $D \leq R_i$. If $D > R_s$, only "risky" borrowers will consider applying. In this case, setting $D = R_r$ is optimal and gives the bank a profit of

$$(1 - \beta)(m - 1) \tag{2.1}$$

Instead, if $D \leq R_s$, both types of borrowers will apply. Assuming each applicant has an equal chance of being financed, the bank then finds it optimal to set $D = R_s$ and obtains

$$\alpha[\beta(m - 1) + (1 - \beta)(p_r R_s - 1)] \tag{2.2}$$

This second outcome allows the bank to use its funds fully. However, it is now earning less than m on "risky" borrowers, since they repay only R_s, with the relatively low probability p_r. Whether expression (2.1) or (2.2) is higher will depend on parameter values. Ceteris paribus, expression (2.2) will be higher than expression (2.1) when $1 - \beta$ is small enough, or when p_r is close enough to p_s. When this is the case, one can say that credit rationing arises: some "risky" borrowers cannot get credit; they would be ready to accept a higher D, since they obtain strictly positive surplus when financed; however, the bank finds it optimal not to raise D, because it would then lose the "safe" borrowers.

This story begs the following question, however: Can't the bank do better by offering more sophisticated contracts? Let us keep the restriction to debt contracts, or fixed-repayment contracts (more on this topic will follow), but assume that the bank can offer contracts that differ both in terms of repayment and in terms of probability of obtaining the scarce funds. Specifically, call (x_i, D_i) a contract that offers financing with probability x_i and repayment D_i. The bank then sets its contracts to solve the following problem:

$$\max_{x_i, D_i}[\beta x_s (p_s D_s - 1) + (1 - \beta)x_r (p_r D_r - 1)]$$

subject to

$$0 \le x_i \le 1 \quad \text{for all} \quad i = s, r \tag{2.3}$$

$$D_i \le R_i \quad \text{for all} \quad i = s, r \tag{2.4}$$

$$x_i p_i (R_i - D_i) \ge x_j p_i (R_i - D_j) \quad \text{for all} \quad i, j = s, r \tag{2.5}$$

$$\beta x_s + (1 - \beta)x_r \le \alpha \tag{2.6}$$

where expression (2.3) is a set of feasibility constraints; expressions (2.4) and (2.5) are the individual rationality and incentive compatibility constraints; and expression (2.6) is the resource constraint given by the bank's availability of funds.

Since $D_i \le R_i$, one can easily see that the binding individual rationality constraint is

$$D_s \le R_s$$

while the binding incentive constraint is

$$x_r (R_r - D_r) \ge x_s (R_r - R_s) \tag{2.7}$$

The binding incentive constraint implies that extracting all the rents on risky borrowers $(D_r = R_r)$ requires excluding safe ones from borrowing $(x_s = 0)$. Instead, giving both types equal access to credit $(x_r = x_s)$ implies equal repayments when successful $(D_r = R_s)$. These two outcomes are the ones discussed earlier. Can the bank do better? To answer this question, note that the binding incentive constraint (2.7) can be rewritten as

$$D_r = R_r - \frac{x_s}{x_r}(R_r - R_s)$$

so that the preceding problem becomes

$$\max_{x_s, x_r}\{\beta x_s (p_s R_s - 1) + (1 - \beta)[x_r (p_r R_r - 1) - x_s p_r (R_r - R_s)]\}$$

subject to

$$0 \leq x_s \leq x_r \leq 1$$

$$\beta x_s + (1 - \beta)x_r \leq \alpha$$

Since $p_s R_s = p_r R_r = m$, this problem leads to $x_r = 1$: there is no distortion at the top, that is, no rationing of risky borrowers. As for safe ones, we have $x_s = 0$ whenever

$$\beta(p_s R_s - 1) - (1 - \beta)p_r(R_r - R_s) < 0$$

while $x_s = [\alpha - (1 - \beta)x_r]/\beta$ otherwise.

Intuitively, in this solution, the bank trades off the rents extracted from "risky" borrowers with the ability to lend all its funds. When "safe" borrowers are numerous enough, it does not make sense to exclude them by setting $x_s = 0$. As a result, risky borrowers earn rents. However, it is possible to do better than financing everybody with a repayment R_s: one induces "risky" borrowers to choose a higher repayment by giving them preferential access to funds. The bank ends up going "all the way" when setting $x_r = 1$.

Note that *credit rationing has disappeared here*: whether or not "risky" borrowers earn rents (that is, whether $x_s > 0$ or $x_s = 0$), they are not rationed. The only ones who are not fully funded are "safe" borrowers, who are in fact indifferent about being funded, since they never earn rents when financed. Credit rationing reappears, however, when assumption Al is replaced by

A3: $p_s R_s > 1$,   but $p_r R_r < 1$

while assumption A2 is maintained. In this case, the bank would like to turn away "risky" borrowers but is unable to do so. Consequently, either both types of projects are funded and there is cross-subsidization between types—this outcome occurs whenever $[\beta p_s + (1 - \beta)p_r]R_s \geq 1$—or neither project is funded and there is "financial collapse," a severe form of credit rationing. This happens when $[\beta p_s + (1 - \beta)p_r]R_s < 1$.[6]

The preceding example leads to several remarks:

1. The example illustrates that even though asymmetric information is likely to be a pervasive phenomenon in financial markets, it does not in

---

6. Note that the lender would never set a contract with $D \geq R_s$, since then only "risky" projects (with a negative net present value) would be funded.

itself inevitably give rise to credit rationing. It may be possible to achieve allocative efficiency despite asymmetric information. Moreover, even if there are inefficiencies resulting from asymmetric information, they may not take the form of credit rationing. Negative-net-present-value projects may be funded.

2. When assumptions A1 and A2 hold, credit market inefficiencies arise only as a result of exogenous restrictions imposed on the allowable set of contracts. To see this point, suppose that the lender can set an arbitrary repayment schedule contingent on realized returns: D_s if $X = R_s$ and D_r if $X = R_r$. Then it suffices to set $D_i = R_i$, and there is no longer a need to try to discriminate between borrower types, since ex post each borrower type ends up paying the relevant contingent repayment. Thus in this example the potential inefficiencies arising from asymmetric information can be overcome if the lender can freely decide how to structure the investment contract. This approach works very straightforwardly here because the ex post returns are different for the two types. It should be stressed, however, that even in more general examples it is more efficient to discriminate between borrower types by offering general-return-contingent repayments. When such contracts are allowed, the incidence of credit rationing is much lower. The reader may wonder at this point why loan contracts in practice do not specify general-return-contingent repayments if they are so much more efficient. We shall return to this important question in Chapter 11.

3. When assumptions A3 and A2 hold instead, then inefficiencies may arise even if a general-return-contingent repayment schedule can be specified. In this case the lender does not want to finance projects of type r. It can attempt to discourage type-r applicants by setting $D_r = R_r$. However, even with such a high repayment, type-r applicants may still want to apply. Suppose, for example, that the borrowers get positive utility just by undertaking the project; then type-r borrowers would want to apply for funding even if their expected monetary return (net of repayments) from undertaking the project is zero. The maximum expected return for the lender in that case is given by

$$\beta p_s R_s + (1 - \beta) p_r R_r - 1$$

When β is sufficiently large, this return is positive and there is cross-subsidization. However, when β is small the expected return is negative and there is financial collapse.

We close this subsection with a brief discussion of the economic significance and implications of credit rationing. The presence of asymmetric information between borrowers and lenders is undeniable. However, it does not follow that inefficiencies in financial markets arise as a result of adverse selection between borrowers, as our example illustrates. Also, even if some inefficiencies arise, they may not fundamentally change the functioning of financial markets, or they may not take the form of credit rationing. A heated debate (both theoretical and empirical) has been raging in the macroeconomics community about the relevance of credit rationing.

One implication of credit rationing for monetary intervention aimed at smoothing out business fluctuations is that a policy that mainly varies the supply of investment funds may not have the desired impact on investment. For example, it may not help much to increase the supply of funds in a recession if a large fraction of firms is credit rationed. A policy aimed at subsidizing investment more directly may be more effective. Another implication of credit rationing is that credit markets may amplify rather than dampen business fluctuations. An unexpectedly large drop in aggregate consumption may be only partially offset by an increase in investment, for example, if credit rationing is prevalent. Finally, credit rationing may have important implications for economic and financial development. Informational asymmetries are if anything worse in less developed economies. These economies may therefore have a handicap in catching up with the more developed and informationally transparent economies.[7]

2.2.2   Optimal Income Taxation

A central theme of this chapter is the trade-off between allocative efficiency and distribution in the presence of adverse selection. This trade-off has first been highlighted by Mirrlees (1971) in the context of redistributive taxation, where distributional concerns are weighed against incentive efficiency when lump-sum taxation is not feasible. One central reason why lump-sum taxation may not be feasible is that the size of the lump-sum tax is limited by the lowest income. To be able to raise higher tax revenues, the tax must inevitably be based on unobservable variables like an individual's earnings potential or productivity.

7. See Banerjee (2003) for a survey of these issues.

More formally, consider the following setup where "income" q is produced with "effort" e according to the production function: $q = \theta e$. Here, θ is an individual productivity parameter that can take two values, θ_L and θ_H, with $\theta_L < \theta_H$. Suppose that a proportion β of individuals has low productivity θ_L and a proportion $(1 - \beta)$ high productivity θ_H. All individuals have the same utility function given by

$$u[q - t - \psi(e)]$$

where t is the net tax (subsidy) the individual has to pay (receive) from the government and $\psi(e)$ is an increasing and convex cost function. The government's budget constraint is given by

$$0 \le \beta t_L + (1 - \beta)t_H \tag{2.8}$$

where t_L is the (possibly negative) tax levied on low-productivity individuals and t_H the tax on high-productivity individuals. In the absence of adverse selection, a utilitarian government, maximizing the sum of individual utilities, solves the following problem:[8]

$$\underset{\substack{t_H, t_L \\ e_H, e_L}}{\text{Max}} \{\beta u[\theta_L e_L - t_L - \psi(e_L)] + (1 - \beta)u[\theta_H e_H - t_H - \psi(e_H)]\} \tag{2.9}$$

subject to condition (2.8). Note that we assume here that the government can impose its tax scheme on individuals, so that it does not face any individual rationality constraints. At the optimum, condition (2.8) must be binding, and the first-order conditions yield

$$u'_L \equiv u'[\theta_L e_L - t_L - \psi(e_L)] = u'[\theta_H e_H - t_H - \psi(e_H)] \equiv u'_H$$

$$\psi'(e_L) = \theta_L$$

$$\psi'(e_H) = \theta_H$$

In words, the utilitarian optimum is attained when marginal utilities are equalized across individuals (that is, $u'_L = u'_H$). When all individuals have the same utility function, then they all reach identical utility levels if $u(\cdot)$ is concave. The other condition for an optimum is that the marginal cost of effort is equal to its marginal productivity for each type.

---

8. Note that when the government can observe θ_i it can also tell how much effort an individual has supplied when observing the individual output $q = \theta_i e$. Hence, by setting type-contingent output targets $q_i = \theta_i e_i$, the government can effectively control individual effort.

Under adverse selection, the following set of incentive constraints must be imposed on the government's optimization problem:

$$\theta_L e_L - t_L - \psi(e_L) \geq \theta_H e_H - t_H - \psi\left(\frac{\theta_H e_H}{\theta_L}\right) \tag{2.10}$$

$$\theta_H e_H - t_H - \psi(e_H) \geq \theta_L e_L - t_L - \psi\left(\frac{\theta_L e_L}{\theta_H}\right) \tag{2.11}$$

Indeed, when the government cannot identify each productivity type, it can only offer everybody an income-contingent tax, where t_i has to be paid if income $q_i = \theta_i e_i$ is produced. This would allow an individual with productivity θ_j to pay t_i by producing q_i at the cost of an effort level $\theta_i e_i/e_j$. As always, the incentive constraints ensure that this behavior is not attractive for either type of individual.

When $u(\cdot)$ is concave, the complete information optimum is such that

$$q_L - t_L - \psi(e_L) = q_H - t_H - \psi(e_H)$$

This allocation, however, violates incentive constraint (2.11): high-productivity individuals would then prefer to choose (q_L, t_L) instead of (q_H, t_H).[9] Therefore, condition (2.11) must be binding in a second-best optimum, and the same is of course true of the budget constraint (2.8). Using these two constraints to eliminate the tax levels from the maximand and taking the first-order conditions with respect to e_H and e_L then yields

$$\psi'(e_H) = \theta_H \tag{2.12}$$

and

$$\psi'(e_L) = \theta_L - (1-\beta)\gamma\left[\psi'(e_L) - \frac{\theta_L}{\theta_H}\psi'\left(\frac{\theta_L e_L}{\theta_H}\right)\right] \tag{2.13}$$

where $\gamma = (u_L' - u_H')/[\beta u_L' + (1-\beta)u_H']$.

That is, γ represents the difference between the marginal utilities of low- and high-ability individuals as a percentage of average marginal utilities.

Condition (2.12) tells us, as is by now familiar, that the second-best allocation for type θ_H is efficient (efficiency at the top). Condition (2.13) tells

---

9. Note that this conclusion is robust to changes in the utility function: it would remain true, for example, if effort appeared additively outside the utility function {e.g., if we assume a payoff $u[q - t] - \psi(e)$, with $\psi(\cdot)$ being linear or convex in effort}.

us that type θ_L underprovides effort. Indeed, first-best efficiency requires that $\psi'(e_L) = \theta_L$. But since $\theta_L < \theta_H$, we have $0 < \psi'(e_L)(1 - \theta_L/\theta_H) < \psi'(e_L) - \theta_L/\theta_H \, \psi'(\theta_L e_L/\theta_H)$. Moreover, for any strictly increasing, concave utility function $u(\cdot)$, γ is strictly positive, since then $u'_L > u'_H > 0$. Therefore, the second term of the right-hand side (RHS) of condition (2.13) is strictly positive, resulting in underprovision of effort. The reason why it is second-best efficient to underprovide effort here is that a lower e_L limits the welfare difference between high- and low-productivity individuals, which is given by

$$[\theta_H e_H - t_H - \psi(e_H)] - [\theta_L e_L - t_L - \psi(e_L)] = \psi(e_L) - \psi\left(\frac{\theta_L e_L}{\theta_H}\right) \tag{2.14}$$

when the incentive constraint (2.11) is binding. This brings about a first-order gain in the utilitarian welfare function that exceeds the second-order loss from a reduction in productivity of the low type. A reduction in e_L brings about a reduction in inequality of welfare because high-productivity individuals have the option to produce output q_L while saving a proportion $(\theta_H - \theta_L)/\theta_H$ of the effort e_L that low-productivity individuals have to exert.

How can we reinterpret conditions (2.12), (2.13), and (2.14) in terms of existing features of the income tax code? One can think of governments first setting *marginal tax rates* as well as *uniform tax rebates*, while individuals respond by choosing effort. In this perspective,

- Equation (2.12) implies that the marginal tax rate at output $q_H = \theta_H e_H$ should be *zero*, in order to induce efficient effort.

- By contrast, the marginal tax rate at output $q_L = \theta_L e_L$ should be *positive, and equal to*

$$\left\{(1 - \beta)\gamma\left[\psi'(e_L) - \frac{\theta_L}{\theta_H} \psi'\left(\frac{\theta_L e_L}{\theta_H}\right)\right]\right\}\bigg/\theta_L \tag{2.15}$$

where γ and e_L are the second-best values; indeed, this marginal tax rate is needed to induce the (inefficiently low) choice of e_L given by equation (2.13).

- In between these two output levels, the marginal tax rate should be positive and such that the additional tax payment coming from high-productivity individuals will be sufficient to reduce the ex post utility difference between the two types to that given by condition (2.11) [recall that, from budget constraint (2.8), all marginal tax revenues are returned to individuals, in the form of uniform tax rebates].

This framework thus seems to plead for positive marginal tax rates at low income levels, and for zero marginal tax rates at high income levels. This result appears paradoxical, since we started from a government objective that was tilted toward redistribution. In fact, there is of course positive redistribution here, through the uniform tax rebate. And the positive marginal tax rate at low incomes is there to achieve higher redistribution, as explained earlier. The theory in fact offers a rationalization for the widespread practice of making various welfare benefits conditional on having low incomes: this results in very high effective marginal tax rates at low income levels. As for the zero-marginal-tax-rate-at-the-top result, it should not be overemphasized: If we allowed for a continuum of types (as in section 2.3), this zero marginal tax rate would appear only at the very maximum of the income distribution.

We close this subsection by analyzing the effect of changes in the government's information structure in this setup. Following Maskin and Riley (1985), we could indeed ask the following question: how would tax levels be affected if, instead of observing "income" $q = \theta \cdot e$, the government observed individual "input," that is, effort (or, equivalently, hours of work)? Would this new information structure result in more or less inequality, and more or less allocative distortion?

In comparison with the preceding analysis, only the incentive constraints (2.10) and (2.11) would be affected. They would become

$$\theta_L e_L - t_L - \psi(e_L) \geq \theta_L e_H - t_H - \psi(e_H) \tag{2.16}$$

$$\theta_H e_H - t_H - \psi(e_H) \geq \theta_H e_L - t_L - \psi(e_L) \tag{2.17}$$

since individuals now face effort-contingent taxes, instead of output-contingent taxes. As before, the problem is to prevent high-ability individuals from mimicking the choice of low-ability individuals. Consequently, condition (2.17) must be binding at the optimum, and the inequality in welfare between the two types is given by

$$[\theta_H e_H - t_H - \psi(e_H)] - [\theta_L e_L - t_L - \psi(e_L)] = (\theta_H - \theta_L)e_L \tag{2.18}$$

Thus, for a given e_L, welfare inequality is higher in equation (2.18) than in equation (2.14) whenever $\theta_H > \psi'(e_L)$. This is always the case at the optimum, since $\theta_H > \theta_L > \psi'(e_L^*)$. Intuitively, an effort-contingent tax makes it more attractive for the high type to mimic the behavior of the low type, since a given effort level allows the high type to enjoy comparatively more output than the low type, thanks to his higher productivity. Instead, in an income-contingent scheme, mimicking the low type really means sticking to a low income. It is true that this allows the high type to save on effort cost, but with a convex effort cost, the benefit of this lower effort is limited.

Solving the optimum tax problem with equation (2.17) instead of equation (2.11), one can show that efficient effort results again for the high type. Instead, the effort of the low type is further distorted downward, in comparison with the income tax case: when welfare inequality is higher, the marginal benefit from reducing inequality at a given allocative cost is also higher. In this setting, effort monitoring is thus inferior to income monitoring, since it leads both to more inequality and to more allocative inefficiency.

This last discussion is especially relevant when the principal is able to make decisions about which information structure to put in place. It would apply naturally, for example, in the context of the internal organization of a firm, where decisions have to be made about which information systems to set up for monitoring purposes. On this subject, see the general analysis of Maskin and Riley (1985) on the superiority of output- over input-monitoring schemes.

2.2.3   Implicit Labor Contracts

The optimal labor contracting approach has been used since the 1970s to try to understand labor-market fluctuations, particularly perceived wage rigidities and employment variability over the business cycle. It is not our purpose here to discuss the debates among macroeconomists surrounding the stylized facts, but simply to illustrate how the contracting paradigm may or may not be consistent with perceived facts.

2.2.3.1   Contracting without Adverse Selection

The first wave of labor contract models (see Azariadis, 1975; Baily, 1974; Gordon, 1974) abstract from adverse selection to focus solely on risk sharing. They are based on the idea that employment relationships typically involve set-up costs (e.g., specific training) so that firms and workers have an interest in organizing their future relations through a long-term contract that has to be contingent on random future events. Because of imperfect insurance markets, moreover, parties to the contract are risk averse. This observation is especially true of workers, whose human capital is much less easily diversifiable than financial capital. Consequently, labor contracts serve both to set production decisions and to allocate risk efficiently.

Formally, consider a firm that can produce output q using a technology $q = \theta Q(L)$, where θ is a random productivity parameter, L is the level of employment, and $Q(\cdot)$ is an increasing concave function. The firm can hire from a pool of identical workers whose utility is $u[w + G(\bar{\ell} - \ell)]$, where w is the wage level, $\bar{\ell}$ is the individual's potential working time, ℓ is effective individual labor time, and G is a positive constant. We thus assume here perfect substitutability between money and leisure (more on this topic to follow). Let us normalize $\bar{\ell}$ to 1 and assume indivisibilities to be such that ℓ can only take the values 0 or 1.

In contrast to the analysis of this chapter so far, contracting now takes place at the *ex ante* stage, that is, before the realization of θ is known. Assume symmetric information at this stage: all parties expect $\theta \in \{\theta_L, \theta_H\}$ and expect $\text{Prob}[\theta = \theta_i] = \beta_i$, with $\beta_L + \beta_H = 1$. Moreover, these beliefs are common knowledge. The problem has two stages:

Stage 1 (ex ante stage): Hiring and contracting decisions.

Stage 2 (ex post stage): θ_i is learned by all parties, and the contract is executed.

Call L the stock of workers hired in stage 1 and $\alpha_i L$ the employment level given θ_i in stage 2, so that $(1 - \alpha_i)L$ corresponds to the workers that are laid off. A contract determines, for each θ_i, the values of α_i, and of w_i, and w_{si}, the wage and severance pay levels. Assume that workers have market opportunities that amount to $\bar{u}$ in utility terms, and that the firm has an increasing and concave utility function $V(\cdot)$ of profits. The firm then solves

$$\underset{w_i, \alpha_i, L}{\text{Max}} \sum_i \beta_i V[\theta_i Q(\alpha_i L) - w_i \alpha_i L - w_{si}(1 - \alpha_i)L]$$

subject to

$$\sum_i \beta_i [\alpha_i u(w_i) + (1 - \alpha_i)u(w_{si} + G)] \geq \bar{u}$$

and the feasibility constraints

$$\alpha_i \leq 1 \quad \text{for} \quad i = L, H$$

Denoting firm profits in each state θ_i by

$$\Pi_i = \theta_i Q(\alpha_i L) - w_i \alpha_i L - w_{si}(1 - \alpha_i)L$$

the first-order conditions with respect to w_i and w_{si}, respectively, yield, for $i = L, H$,

$$-\beta_i V'(\Pi_i)\alpha_i L + \lambda \beta_i \alpha_i u'(w_i) = 0 \tag{2.19}$$

$$-\beta_i V'(\Pi_i)(1 - \alpha_i)L + \lambda \beta_i (1 - \alpha_i)u'(w_{si} + G) = 0 \tag{2.20}$$

Whenever workers are risk averse ($u'' < 0$), equations (2.19) and (2.20) imply $w_i = w_{si} + G$: for a given total monetary payment to workers it makes no sense for the firm to have individual workers bear risk over who is retained and who is dismissed. In fact, given that they have identical productivity and outside opportunities, it is optimal to give them each exactly u in expected terms ex ante.

In this model, therefore, there is no involuntary unemployment, since workers are indifferent between being laid off and staying on the job. What about wage rigidity across the business cycle? Stretching interpretation, state θ_H could be described as a "boom" and state θ_L ($<\theta_H$) as a "recession." The extent of wage rigidity is determined by the following condition:

$$\frac{u'(w_L)}{u'(w_H)} = \frac{V'(\Pi_L)}{V'(\Pi_H)}$$

This is simply the Borch rule, which requires that $w_L = w_H$ if the firm is risk neutral ($V'' = 0$). This model thus predicts complete wage "rigidity," in the special case where firms are risk neutral. But is risk neutrality a good assumption? Diversifiability of financial capital does suggest that V is less concave than u, and that wages should be more stable than profits. However, macroeconomic shocks are by definition hard to diversify, so that risk neutrality of the firm is too extreme an assumption in this case.

Still, what are the consequences of the predicted wage "rigidity" across states of nature? Does it lead to excessive employment fluctuations, as in the usual spot-market view of macroeconomic textbooks? To assess this issue, consider the first-order condition with respect to α_i, for $i = L, H$. If α_i is strictly between 0 and 1, we have

$$\beta_i V'(\Pi_i)[\theta_i Q'(\alpha_i L) - (w_i - w_{si})]L + \lambda \beta_i [u'(w_i) - u'(w_{si} + G)] = 0$$

But since $w_i = w_{si} + G$, this is equivalent to $\theta_i Q'(\alpha_i L) = G$. In other words, inefficient underemployment never occurs (note also that we always have $\alpha_L \leq \alpha_H = 1$: indeed, it only makes sense to hire workers that will at least be retained in the good state of nature). Thus, as in other applications, allocative efficiency obtains under symmetric information.

What is somewhat paradoxical about the preceding formulation is that employment is not only ex ante efficient, but also *profit maximizing ex post*, given that $w_i = w_{si} + G$. It is thus not even necessary to set α_i ex ante, because it would be self-enforcing given w_i and w_{si}.

Finally, what can we say about hiring decisions? The first-order condition with respect to L is not particularly illuminating. It simply says that hiring decisions are such that expected marginal cost of labor (given the outside opportunity $\bar{u}$) is set to be equal to expected marginal productivity.

To sum up, the model predicts wages that are stable relative to profits (at least when the firm is risk neutral), but this stability does not come at the expense of allocative efficiency, nor does it induce job rationing (since workers are indifferent ex post between being retained or being laid off). That is, this theory cannot offer a rationale for either inefficient under-employment or involuntary unemployment.

How robust are these insights? It turns out that changing workers' utility functions matters for their comparative ex post treatment. For example, one could drop the perfect substitutability between money and leisure, and take a utility function $u(w, \bar{\ell} - \ell)$, where leisure is a normal good. Take, for example, the following Cobb-Douglas formulation:

$$u(w, \bar{\ell} - \ell) = \log w + \log(K + \bar{\ell} - \ell)$$

where K is a positive constant. The individual rationality constraint now becomes

$$\sum_i \beta_i [\alpha_i (\log w_i + \log K) + (1 - \alpha_i)(\log w_{si} + \log(K + 1))] \geq \bar{u}$$

and the first-order conditions with respect to w_i and w_{si} yield

$$w_i = w_{si}$$

Although allocative efficiency obtains, the relation between employed and laid-off workers has now changed: one can now speak of *involuntary employment!* Ex ante, it is Pareto optimal to equate the marginal utility of money across workers, and here this means setting $w_i = w_{si}$. This feature of involuntary employment is in fact present for any utility function where leisure is a normal good (see Azariadis and Stiglitz, 1983). Note also that the contract cannot leave the firm the freedom to set employment ex post anymore: with the severance pay equal to the wage, the firm has an incentive to choose α_i as high as possible, whatever θ_i.

2.2.3.2   Contracting with Adverse Selection

A second wave of labor contract models (see Azariadis, 1983; Chari, 1983; Green and Kahn, 1983; and Grossman and Hart, 1983) have added adverse selection to the previous framework. In earlier sections, adverse selection introduced a trade-off between rent extraction and allocative efficiency. In this subsection, this will translate into a trade-off between insurance and allocative efficiency, because contracting takes place at the ex ante stage and not at the interim stage. In the previous subsection, the optimal contract was efficient and reproduced the spot-market allocation [that is, we had $\theta_i Q'(\alpha_i L) = G$ whenever layoffs occurred, that is, whenever $\alpha_i < 1$]. Assume now instead that contract execution takes place at a time when *only the firm* knows the value of θ. As a result of this information asymmetry, incentive constraints must be imposed on the optimal contracting problem. To keep things simple, assume perfect substitution between money and leisure and set $\bar{l} = 1$. Moreover, assume $L = 1$, and interpret α_i now as the number of *hours* worked by each individual worker, while w_i is individual compensation.[10] We thus have the utility function $u[w_i + (1 - \alpha_i)G]$.

Under these assumptions, the firm's optimization problem becomes

$$\underset{w_i, \alpha_i}{\text{Max}} \sum_i \beta_i V[\theta_i Q(\alpha_i) - w_i]$$

subject to

$$\alpha_i \leq 1 \quad i = L, H$$

$$\sum_i \beta_i u[w_i + (1 - \alpha_i)G] \geq \bar{u} \quad i = L, H$$

$$\theta_i Q(\alpha_i) - w_i \geq \theta_i Q(\alpha_j) - w_j \quad i, j = L, H$$

As before, this problem can be solved by first looking at the incentive constraint that is violated in the first-best outcome. An interesting special

---

10. We thus abstract away here from the issue of potential unequal treatment among workers.

case occurs when the firm is risk neutral, for then it is optimal to fully insure workers and set

$$w_L + (1 - \alpha_L)G = w_H + (1 - \alpha_H)G$$

so that the incentive constraints reduce to

$$\theta_i Q(\alpha_i) - w_i \geq \theta_i Q(\alpha_j) - (\alpha_j - \alpha_i)G - w_i$$

But these conditions are automatically satisfied when α_i is ex post efficient: intuitively, by setting a wage level that rises by G times the employment level α_i, the optimal contract induces firms to internalize the value of leisure that workers lose when they have to work, and to choose ex post efficient employment levels.

On the one hand, under firm risk neutrality, adverse selection does not change the optimal contract here. On the other hand, when the firm is risk averse, it is efficient to reduce w_L relative to w_H, in order to share risk with workers. This action, however, creates an incentive problem in that the firm may want to claim falsely to be in state θ_L in order to reduce its wage cost. This problem arises whenever $V(\cdot)$ *is sufficiently concave relative to* $u(\cdot)$.

To make the point, consider the extreme case where the firm is risk averse ($V'' < 0$) but the worker is risk neutral [$u'' = 0$, or $u(x) = x$]. In this case, the relevant incentive constraint is

$$\theta_H Q(\alpha_H) - w_H = \theta_H Q(\alpha_L) - w_L$$

Since the individual rationality constraint is also binding at the optimum, we have a maximization problem with two equality constraints. The first-order conditions with respect to w_i and α_i are then given by

$$-\beta_L V'(\Pi_L) + \lambda_a \beta_L + \lambda_b = 0 \tag{2.21}$$

$$-\beta_H V'(\Pi_H) + \lambda_a \beta_H - \lambda_b = 0 \tag{2.22}$$

$$\beta_L V'(\Pi_L)\theta_L Q'(\alpha_L) - \lambda_a \beta_L G - \lambda_b \theta_H Q'(\alpha_L) \geq 0 \tag{2.23}$$

$$\beta_H V'(\Pi_H)\theta_H Q'(\alpha_H) - \lambda_a \beta_H G + \lambda_b \theta_H Q'(\alpha_H) \geq 0 \tag{2.24}$$

where λ_a and λ_b are the Lagrange multipliers for the individual-rationality and incentive constraints, respectively.[11]

11. Remember that, by the feasibility constraints, $\alpha_i \leq 1$.

Conditions (2.22) and (2.24) yield

$$\theta_H Q'(\alpha_H) \geq G \tag{2.25}$$

while conditions (2.21) and (2.23) yield

$$\theta_L Q'(\alpha_L) \geq G + \frac{\lambda_b}{\lambda_a} \frac{\theta_H - \theta_L}{\beta_L} Q'(\alpha_L) \tag{2.26}$$

Moreover, these two conditions are binding whenever workers are fully employed, that is, whenever $\alpha_i = 1$. Finally, conditions (2.21) and (2.22) imply

$$\Pi_H > \Pi_L \tag{2.27}$$

since $\lambda_b > 0$.

The intuition for these results is as follows: Because the incentive constraint binds, risk sharing is imperfect, and underemployment occurs, but only in the bad state of nature θ_L [see equations (2.25) and (2.26)]. We thus obtain again the result of no distortion at the top. Note that while these results have been obtained under worker risk neutrality, allowing for a little concavity for $u(\cdot)$ would keep these results unchanged, provided the firm is (sufficiently) risk averse.

This model thus generates underemployment in bad states of nature, but not wage stability relative to profits: underemployment relies on the sufficient concavity of $V(\cdot)$ relative to $u(\cdot)$. Moreover, interpreting $\theta = \theta_L$ as a recession is difficult, since θ has to be private information to the firm (see, however, Grossman, Hart, and Maskin (1983), for a macroeconomic extension of this framework that is immune to this criticism). Finally, the underemployment result is itself dependent on the particular choice of utility functions: assume instead firm risk neutrality ($V'' = 0$) and a Cobb-Douglas utility function for workers [$u(\cdot) = \log w + \log(K + 1 - \alpha)$]. In this case, the first-best allocation ($\alpha_L < \alpha_H$ and $w_L = w_H$) violates the incentive constraint of the firm when it is in the bad state of nature θ_L: since total payments to workers do not depend on the realization of θ but employment is higher in the good state θ_H, announcing $\theta = \theta_L$ is never incentive compatible. Solving the model with the incentive constraint

$$\theta_L Q(\alpha_L) - w_L = \theta_L Q(\alpha_H) - w_H$$

then yields ex post efficient employment when $\theta = \theta_L$ and possible *overemployment* when $\theta = \theta_H$, thus overturning the previous prediction of underemployment.

In conclusion, the optimal contracting approach, by stressing the insurance role of labor contracts, has offered an interesting motive for wage stability. However, it has failed to deliver robust predictions on involuntary unemployment or underemployment. From this perspective, moral hazard models based on "efficiency wages" have been more successful (see Chapter 4).

2.2.4   Regulation

Regulation of natural monopolies is another area where adverse selection ideas have been emphasized, because public regulators are often at an informational disadvantage with respect to the regulated utility or natural monopoly. Baron and Myerson (1982) have written a pioneering contribution in the field, deriving the optimal output-contingent subsidy scheme for a regulator facing a firm with a privately known productivity parameter that belongs to a continuous interval.[12] Later, Laffont and Tirole (1986) pointed out that in reality subsidy schemes are also cost contingent and built a model where accounting costs are observable, but reflect both "intrinsic productivity" and an "effort to cut costs." Interestingly, this framework combines both an adverse selection and a moral hazard (hidden action) element. In this subsection, we study the simplest possible version of the Laffont-Tirole model, which is the cornerstone of the "new economics of regulation" (see their 1993 book).

The basic economic problem involves a regulator concerned with protecting consumer welfare and attempting to force a natural monopoly to charge competitive prices. The main difficulty for the regulator is that he does not have full or adequate knowledge of the firm's intrinsic cost structure. More formally, consider a natural monopoly with an exogenous cost parameter $\theta \in \{\theta_L, \theta_H\}$. Define $\Delta\theta = \theta_H - \theta_L$. The firm's cost of producing the good is $c = \theta - e$, where e stands for "effort." Expending effort has cost $\psi(e) = [\max\{0, e\}]^2/2$, which is increasing and convex in e. Assume that the regulator wants the good to be produced against the lowest possible payment $P = s + c$ (where s is a "subsidy," or payment to the firm in excess of accounting cost c). Minimizing the total payment to the firm can be justified on the grounds that it has to be financed out of distortionary taxa-

---

12. This paper has been very influential in terms of dealing with adverse selection with more than two types (see section 2.3).

tion, which a benevolent regulator should be anxious to minimize. The payoff of the firm is $P - c - \psi(e) = s - \psi(e)$. If the regulator observes the value of the cost parameter θ, it tries to achieve

$$\min s + c = s + \theta - e$$

subject to the individual-rationality constraint

$$s - [\max\{0, e\}]^2 / 2 \geq 0$$

This approach yields an effort level $e^* = 1$ and a subsidy $s^* = 0.5$. One can interpret this outcome as the regulator offering the firm a fixed total payment P, which induces the firm to minimize $c + \psi(e)$, and thus to choose $e^* = 1$. This is what the regulation literature calls a "price-cap scheme"; the opposite of price caps is a "cost-plus" scheme, where the firm receives a constant subsidy s irrespective of its actual cost (such a scheme would result in zero effort, as is easy to see). Between these two extreme regulatory regimes, we have cost-sharing agreements, where the incentive scheme induces more effort the closer it is to the price cap. With adverse selection, price caps may be suboptimal because they fail to optimally extract the regulated firm's informational rent (see Laffont and Tirole, 1993, for discussions of regulation issues).

Indeed, assume that the regulator cannot observe the cost parameter of the firm but has prior belief as follows: $\Pr(\theta = \theta_L) = \beta$. Call (s_L, c_L) the contract that will be chosen by type θ_L (who then expends effort $e_L = \theta_L - c_L$), and call (s_H, c_H) the contract that will be chosen by type θ_H (who then expends effort $e_H = \theta_H - c_H$). The regulator chooses these contracts so as to minimize $\beta(s_L + c_L) + (1 - \beta)(s_H + c_H)$, or, equivalently (since the θ's are exogenous), to solve

$$\min\{\beta(s_L - e_L) + (1 - \beta)(s_H - e_H)\}$$

subject to participation and incentive constraints

$$s_L - [\max\{0, e_L\}]^2 / 2 > 0$$

$$s_H - [\max\{0, e_H\}]^2 / 2 \geq 0$$

$$s_L - [\max\{0, e_L\}]^2 / 2 \geq s_H - [\max\{0, e_H - \Delta\theta\}]^2 / 2$$

$$s_H - [\max\{0, e_H\}]^2 / 2 \geq s_L - [\max\{0, e_L + \Delta\theta\}]^2 / 2$$

The first two inequalities are participation constraints, and the next two are incentive constraints. Achieving c_H implies effort level e_H for type θ_H but effort level $e_H - \Delta\theta$ for type θ_L, and similarly for cost c_L.

We shall be interested in avoiding corner solutions. Accordingly, we assume that $e_H = \theta_H - c_H > \Delta\theta$, so that $\theta_L - c_H > 0$. This is a condition involving equilibrium effort, and we shall express it directly in terms of exogenous parameters of the model.

The first-best outcome has the same effort level for both types (since both effort cost functions and marginal productivities of effort are identical) and therefore the same level of subsidy, but a higher actual cost for the inefficient type. The incentive problem in this first-best outcome arises from the fact that the efficient type wants to mimic the inefficient type, to collect the same subsidy while expending only effort $e^* - \Delta\theta$, and achieving actual cost c_H. As a result, the relevant incentive constraint is that of the efficient type, while the relevant participation constraint is that of the inefficient type, or

$$s_L - e_L^2/2 = s_H - (e_H - \Delta\theta)^2/2$$

$$s_H - e_H^2/2 = 0$$

Rewriting the optimization problem using these two equalities yields

$$\min\left\{\beta\left(e_L^2/2 - e_L + \left[e_H^2/2 - (e_H - \Delta\theta)^2/2\right]\right) + (1-\beta)(e_H^2/2 - e_H)\right\}$$

which implies as first-order conditions

$$e_L = 1$$

and

$$e_H = 1 - \frac{\beta}{1-\beta}\Delta\theta$$

We thus have again the by-now-familiar "ex post allocative efficiency at the top" and underprovision of effort for the inefficient type, since this underprovision reduces the rent of the efficient type [which equals $e_H^2/2 - (e_H - \Delta\theta)^2/2$]. Because of the increasing marginal cost of effort, a lower actual cost c_H benefits the efficient type less than the inefficient type in terms of effort cost savings. The incentive to lower e_H increases in the cost parameter differential and in the probability of facing the efficient type, whose rents the regulator is trying to extract.

In terms of actual implementation, the optimal regulation therefore involves offering a menu that induces the regulated firm with cost parameter θ_L to choose a price-cap scheme (with a constant price $P_L = s_L + c_L = s_L + \theta_L - e_L$, where θ_L and e_L are the solutions computed previously) and the regulated firm with cost parameter θ_H to choose a cost-sharing arrangement (with a lower price plus a share of ex post costs that would make effort e_H optimal and leave it zero rents). As appealing as this solution appears to be, it is unfortunately still far from being applied systematically in practice (see Armstrong, Cowan, and Vickers, 1994).

2.3   More Than Two Types

We now return to the general one-buyer/one-seller specification of section 2.1 and, following Maskin and Riley (1984a), discuss the extensions of the basic framework to situations where buyers can be of more than two types. We shall consider in turn the general formulation of the problem for $n \geq 3$ types and for a continuum of types. This latter formulation, first analyzed in the context of regulation by Baron and Myerson (1982), is by far the more tractable one.

2.3.1   Finite Number of Types

Recall that the buyer has a utility function

$$u(q, T, \theta_i) = \theta_i v(q) - T$$

But suppose now that there are at least three different preference types:

$$\theta_n > \theta_{n-1} > \ldots > \theta_1$$

with $n \geq 3$. Call β_i the proportion of buyers of type θ_i in the population. Let $\{(q_i, T_i); i = 1, \ldots, n\}$ be a menu of contracts offered by the seller. Then, by the revelation principle, the seller's problem is to choose $\{(q_i, T_i); i = 1, \ldots, n\}$ from among all feasible menus of contracts to solve the program

$$\begin{cases} \max_{\{(q_i, T_i)\}} \sum_{i=1}^{n} (T_i - cq_i)\beta_i \\ \text{subject to} \\ \text{for all } i \quad \theta_i v(q_i) - T_i \geq 0 \\ \text{for all } i, j \quad \theta_i v(q_i) - T_i \geq \theta_i v(q_j) - T_j \end{cases}$$

Just as in the two-type case, among all participation constraints only the one concerning type θ_1 will bind; the other ones will automatically hold given that

$$\theta_i v(q_i) - T_i \geq \theta_i v(q_1) - T_1 \geq \theta_1 v(q_1) - T_1 \geq 0$$

The main difficulty in solving this program is to reduce the number of incentive constraints to a more tractable set of constraints [in this program, there are $n(n-1)$ incentive constraints]. This reduction can be achieved if the buyer's utility function satisfies the Spence-Mirrlees single-crossing condition:

$$\frac{\partial}{\partial \theta}\left[-\frac{\partial u/\partial q}{\partial u/\partial T}\right] > 0$$

With our chosen functional form for the buyer's utility function, $\theta_i v(q) - T$, this condition is satisfied, as can be readily checked. This observation leads us to our first step in solving the problem:

Step 1: The single-crossing condition implies monotonicity and the sufficiency of "local" incentive constraints.

Summing the incentive constraints for types $\theta_i \neq \theta_j$, that is

$$\theta_i v(q_i) - T_i \geq \theta_i v(q_j) - T_j$$

and

$$\theta_j v(q_j) - T_j \geq \theta_j v(q_i) - T_i$$

we have

$$(\theta_i - \theta_j)[v(q_i) - v(q_j)] \geq 0$$

Since $v'(q) \geq 0$, this equation implies that an incentive-compatible contract must be such that $q_i \geq q_j$ whenever $\theta_i > \theta_j$. That is, consumption must be monotonically increasing in θ when the single-crossing condition holds.

It is this important implication of the single-crossing property that enables us to considerably reduce the set of incentive constraints. To see why monotonicity of consumption reduces the set of relevant incentive constraints, consider the three types $\theta_{i-1} < \theta_i < \theta_{i+1}$, and consider the following incentive constraints, which we can call the *local downward incentive constraints*, or LDICs:

$$\theta_{i+1}v(q_{i+1}) - T_{i+1} \geq \theta_{i+1}v(q_i) - T_i$$

and

$$\theta_i v(q_i) - T_i \geq \theta_i v(q_{i-1}) - T_{i-1}$$

This second constraint, together with $q_i \geq q_{i-1}$, implies that

$$\theta_{i+1}v(q_i) - T_i \geq \theta_{i+1}v(q_{i-1}) - T_{i-1}$$

which in turn implies that the downward incentive constraint for type θ_{i+1} and allocation (q_{i-1}, T_{i-1}) also holds:

$$\theta_{i+1}v(q_{i+1}) - T_{i+1} \geq \theta_{i+1}v(q_{i-1}) - T_{i-1}$$

Therefore, if for each type θ_i, the incentive constraint with respect to type θ_{i-1} holds—in other words, the LDIC is satisfied—then all other downward incentive constraints (for θ_i relative to lower θ's) are also satisfied if the monotonicity condition $q_i \geq q_{i-1}$ holds. We are thus able to reduce the set of downward incentive constraints to the set of LDICs and the monotonicity condition $q_i \geq q_{i-1}$. One can easily show that the same is true for the set of upward incentive constraints (that is, for θ_i relative to upper θ's).

We can thus replace the set of incentive constraints by the set of local incentive constraints and the monotonicity condition on consumption. The next question is whether the set of incentive constraints can be reduced still further.

Step 2: Together with the monotonicity of consumption, the relevant set of incentive constraints is the set of LDICs, which will bind at the optimum.

Just as in the two-type analysis of section 2.1, we can start by omitting the set of local upward incentive constraints (LUICs) and focus solely on monotonicity of consumption together with the set of LDICs. Then it is easy to show that the optimum will imply that all LDICs are binding. Indeed, suppose that an LDIC is not binding for some type θ_i, that is,

$$\theta_i v(q_i) - T_i > \theta_i v(q_{i-1}) - T_{i-1}$$

In this case, the seller can adapt his schedule by raising all T_j's for $j \geq i$ by the same positive amount so as to make the preceding constraint binding. This method will leave unaffected all other LDICs while improving the maximand.

In turn, the fact that all LDICs are binding, together with the monotonicity of consumption, leads all LUICs to be satisfied. Indeed,

$$\theta_i v(q_i) - T_i = \theta_i v(q_{i-1}) - T_{i-1}$$

implies

$$\theta_{i-1} v(q_i) - T_i \le \theta_{i-1} v(q_{i-1}) - T_{i-1}$$

since $q_{i-1} \le q_i$. Therefore, if the single-crossing condition is verified, only the LDIC constraints are binding when the monotonicity condition $q_{i-1} \le q_i$ holds, so that the seller's problem reduces to

$$\begin{cases} \max_{\{(q_i, T_i)\}} & \sum_{i=1}^{n} (T_i - cq_i)\beta_i \\ \text{subject to} & \\ & \theta_1 v(q_1) - T_1 = 0 \\ \text{for all } i & \theta_i v(q_i) - T_i = \theta_i v(q_{i-1}) - T_{i-1} \\ \text{and} & q_i \ge q_j \quad \text{where } \theta_i \ge \theta_j \end{cases}$$

Step 3: Solving the reduced program.

The standard procedure for solving this program is first to solve the relaxed problem without the monotonicity condition and then to check whether the solution to this relaxed problem satisfies the monotonicity condition.

Proceeding as outlined, consider the Lagrangian

$$\mathcal{L} = \sum_{i=1}^{n} \{[T_i - cq_i]\beta_i + \lambda_i[\theta_i v(q_i) - \theta_i v(q_{i-1}) - T_i + T_{i-1}]\} + \mu[\theta_1 v(q_1) - T_1]$$

The Lagrange multiplier associated with the LDIC for type θ_i is thus λ_i, while μ is the multiplier associated with the participation constraint for type θ_1. The first-order conditions are, for $1 < i < n$,

$$\frac{\partial \mathcal{L}}{\partial q_i} = \lambda_i \theta_i v'(q_i) - \lambda_{i+1}\theta_{i+1} v'(q_i) = c\beta_i$$

$$\frac{\partial \mathcal{L}}{\partial T_i} = \beta_i - \lambda_i + \lambda_{i+1} = 0$$

and, for $i = n$,

$$\frac{\partial \mathcal{L}}{\partial q_n} = \lambda_n \theta_n v'(q_n) = c\beta_n$$

$$\frac{\partial \mathcal{L}}{\partial T_n} = 0 \Leftrightarrow \beta_n = \lambda_n$$

Thus, for $i = n$, we have $\theta_n v'(q_n) = c$. In other words, consumption is efficient for $i = n$. However, for $i < n$, we have $\theta_i v'(q_i) > c$. In other words, all types other than n underconsume in equilibrium.

These are the generalizations to n types of the results established for two types. If one wants to further characterize the optimal menu of contracts, it is more convenient to move to a specification where there is a continuum of types. Before doing so, we briefly take up an important issue that our simple setting has enabled us to sidestep so far.

2.3.2   Random Contracts

So far, we have restricted attention to deterministic contracts. This restriction involves no loss of generality if the seller's optimization program is concave. In general, however, the incentive constraints are such that the constraint set faced by the seller is nonconvex. In these situations the seller may be able to do strictly better by offering random contracts to the buyer. A random contract is such that the buyer faces a lottery instead of buying a fixed allocation:

$$L(\theta_i) = \{[q(\theta_i, \alpha), T(\theta_i, \alpha)]; A(\theta_i, \alpha) = \text{Probability of } \alpha \text{ given } \theta_i\}$$

We shall consider a simple example where stochastic contracts strictly dominate deterministic contracts: Let $[q(\theta_i), T(\theta_i)]$, $i = 1, 2$, be an optimal deterministic contract. Assume a utility function $u(q, T, \theta)$ that is concave in q and such that the buyer of type θ_2 is more risk averse than the buyer of type θ_1 (where $\theta_2 > \theta_1$). Since both types of buyers are risk averse, they are willing to pay more for q_i than for any random $\tilde{q}_i$ with mean q_i. In particular, if type θ_1 is indifferent between $(\hat{T}_1, \tilde{q}_1)$, where $\hat{T}_1$ is fixed, and (T_1, q_1), we must have $\hat{T}_1 < T_1$. In other words, by introducing a random scheme, the seller is certain to lose money on type θ_1, so the only way this can be beneficial is if he can charge type θ_2 more. By assumption, type θ_2 is more risk averse, so that she strictly prefers (T_1, q_1) to $(\hat{T}_1, \tilde{q}_1)$. The seller can therefore find $\delta > 0$ such that type θ_2 (weakly) prefers $(T_2 + \delta, q_2)$ to $(\hat{T}_1, \tilde{q}_1)$. If type θ_2 is sufficiently more risk averse than type θ_1, the seller's gain of δ outweighs the loss of $T_1 - \hat{T}_1$. Instead, if type θ_2 is less risk averse than type θ_1, then the random contract does not dominate the optimal deterministic contract.[13] This intuition is indeed correct, as Maskin and Riley (1984a) have shown. It stems from the fact that the relevant incentive constraints are the downward constraints; there is therefore no point in offering type θ_2 a random allocation, since it involves an efficiency loss for this type without any gain in terms of rent extraction on the other type, who is already at her reservation utility level.

An example of a random contract in the real world is an economy-class airline ticket, which comes with so many restrictions relative to a business-class ticket that it effectively imposes significant additional risk on the traveler. It is in part because of such restrictions that business travelers, who often feel they cannot afford to take such risks, are prepared to pay substantially more for a business-class ticket.

2.3.3   A Continuum of Types

Suppose now that θ does not take a finite number of values anymore but is distributed according to the density $f(\theta)$ [with c.d.f. $F(\theta)$] on an interval $[\underline{\theta}, \overline{\theta}]$. Thanks to the revelation principle, the seller's problem with a continuum of types can be written as follows:

$$
\begin{cases}
\max_{q(\theta),T(\theta)} \quad \int_{\underline{\theta}}^{\overline{\theta}} [T(\theta) - cq(\theta)]f(\theta)d\theta \\
\text{subject to} \\
\text{(IR)} \quad \theta v[q(\theta)] - T(\theta) \geq 0 \qquad\qquad\quad \text{for all } \theta \in [\underline{\theta}, \overline{\theta}] \\
\text{(IC)} \quad \theta v[q(\theta)] - T(\theta) \geq \theta v[q(\hat{\theta})] - T(\hat{\theta}) \quad \text{for all } \theta, \hat{\theta} \in [\underline{\theta}, \overline{\theta}]
\end{cases}
$$

Note first that we can replace the participation constraints (IR) by

(IR′) $\underline{\theta} v[q(\underline{\theta})] - T(\underline{\theta}) \geq 0$

given that all (IC)'s hold. Note also that the seller may want to exclude some types from consumption; this can be formally represented by setting $q(\theta) = T(\theta) = 0$ for the relevant types.

It is convenient to decompose the seller's problem into an *implementation problem* [which functions $q(\theta)$ are incentive compatible?] and an

---

13. In fact, one can show that the optimal contract is deterministic in our simple case where $u(q,T,\theta) = \theta v(q) - T$.

optimization problem [among all implementable $q(\theta)$ functions, which one is the best for the seller?].

2.3.3.1   The Implementation Problem

With a continuum of types it is even more urgent to get a tractable set of contraints than in the problem with a finite set of types n. As we shall show, however, the basic logic that led us to conclude that all incentive constraints would hold if (1) consumption $q(\theta)$ is monotonically increasing in θ and (2) all *local downward incentive constraints* are binding also applies in the case where there is a continuum of types.

More formally, we shall show that if the buyer's utility function satisfies the single-crossing condition

$$\frac{\partial}{\partial \theta}\left[-\frac{\partial u/\partial q}{\partial u/\partial T}\right] > 0$$

as it does under our assumed functional form

$$u(q, T, \theta) = \theta v(q) - T$$

then the set of incentive constraints in the seller's optimization problem is equivalent to the following two sets of contraints:

Monotonicity:

$$\frac{dq(\theta)}{d\theta} \geq 0$$

Local incentive compatibility:

$$\theta v'[q(\theta)]\frac{dq(\theta)}{d\theta} = T'(\theta) \quad \text{for all } \theta \in [\underline{\theta}, \overline{\theta}]$$

To see this point, suppose, first, that all incentive constraints are satisfied. Then, assuming for now that the consumption $q(\theta)$ and transfer $T(\theta)$ schedules are differentiable, it must be the case that the following first- and second-order conditions for the buyer's optimization problem are satisfied at $\hat{\theta} = \theta$:

$$\theta v'[q(\hat{\theta})]\frac{dq(\hat{\theta})}{d\hat{\theta}} - T'(\hat{\theta}) = 0 \qquad\qquad \text{FOC}$$

and

$$\theta v''[q(\hat{\theta})]\left(\frac{dq(\hat{\theta})}{d\hat{\theta}}\right)^2 + \theta v'[q(\hat{\theta})]\frac{d^2q(\hat{\theta})}{d\hat{\theta}^2} - T''(\hat{\theta}) \le 0 \qquad\qquad \text{SOC}$$

Thus the first-order conditions of the buyer's optimization problem are the same as the local incentive compatibility constraints earlier. If we further differentiate the local incentive compatibility condition with respect to θ we obtain

$$\theta v''[q(\theta)]\left(\frac{dq(\theta)}{d\theta}\right)^2 + v'[q(\theta)]\frac{dq(\theta)}{d\theta} + \theta v'[q(\theta)]\frac{d^2q(\theta)}{d\theta^2} - T''(\theta) = 0$$

but from the buyer's SOC, this equation implies that

$$v'[q(\theta)]\frac{dq(\theta)}{d\theta} \ge 0$$

or, since $v'[q(\theta)] > 0$, that

$$\frac{dq(\theta)}{d\theta} \ge 0$$

Suppose, next, that both the monotonicity and the local incentive compatibility conditions hold. Then it must be the case that all the buyer's incentive compatibility conditions hold. To see this result, suppose by contradiction that for at least one type θ the buyer's incentive constraint is violated:

$$\theta v[q(\theta)] - T(\theta) < \theta v[q(\hat{\theta})] - T(\hat{\theta})$$

for at least one $\hat{\theta} \ne \theta$. Or, integrating,

$$\int_\theta^{\hat{\theta}}\left[\theta v'[q(x)]\frac{dq(x)}{dx} - T'(x)\right]dx > 0$$

By assumption we have $dq(x)/dx \ge 0$, and if $\hat{\theta} > \theta$, we have

$$\theta v'[q(x)] < x v'[q(x)]$$

Therefore, the local incentive constraint implies that

$$\int_\theta^{\hat{\theta}}\left[\theta v'[q(x)]\frac{dq(x)}{dx} - T'(x)\right]dx < 0$$

a contradiction. Finally, if $\hat{\theta} < \theta$, the same logic leads us to a similar contradiction. This result establishes the equivalence between the monotonicity condition together with the local incentive constraint and the full set of the buyer's incentive constraints.

2.3.3.2   The Optimization Problem

The seller's problem can therefore be written as

$$\max_{q(\theta);T(\theta)} \int_{\underline{\theta}}^{\overline{\theta}} [T(\theta) - cq(\theta)] f(\theta) d\theta$$

subject to

$$\underline{\theta} v[q(\underline{\theta})] - T(\underline{\theta}) \geq 0 \tag{2.28}$$

$$\frac{dq(\theta)}{d\theta} \geq 0 \tag{2.29}$$

$$T'(\theta) = \theta v'[q(\theta)] \frac{dq(\theta)}{d\theta} \tag{2.30}$$

The standard procedure for solving this program is first to ignore the monotonicity constraint and solve the relaxed problem with only equations (2.28) and (2.30). This relaxed problem is reasonably straightforward to solve given our simplified utility function for the buyer.

To derive the optimal quantity function, we shall follow a procedure first introduced by Mirrlees (1971), which has become standard. Define

$$W(\theta) \equiv \theta v[q(\theta)] - T(\theta) = \max_{\hat{\theta}} \{\theta v[q(\hat{\theta})] - T(\hat{\theta})\}$$

By the envelope theorem, we obtain

$$\frac{dW(\theta)}{d\theta} = \frac{\partial W(\theta)}{\partial \theta} = v[q(\theta)]$$

or, integrating,

$$W(\theta) = \int_{\underline{\theta}}^{\theta} v[q(x)] dx + W(\underline{\theta})$$

At the optimum the participation constraint of the lowest type is binding, so that $W(\underline{\theta}) = 0$ and

$$W(\theta) = \int_{\underline{\theta}}^{\theta} v[q(x)] dx$$

Since

$$T(\theta) = \theta v[q(\theta)] - W(\theta)$$

we can rewrite the seller's profits as

$$\pi = \int_{\underline{\theta}}^{\bar{\theta}} \left[\theta v[q(\theta)] - \left[\int_{\underline{\theta}}^{\theta} v[q(x)]dx \right] - cq(\theta) \right] f(\theta) d\theta$$

or, after integration by parts,[14]

$$\pi = \int_{\underline{\theta}}^{\bar{\theta}} (\{\theta v[q(\theta)] - cq(\theta)\} f(\theta) - v[q(\theta)][1 - F(\theta)]) d\theta$$

The maximization of π with respect to the schedule $q(\cdot)$ requires that the term under the integral be maximized with respect to $q(\theta)$ for all θ. Thus we have

$$\theta v'[q(\theta)] = c + \frac{1 - F(\theta)}{f(\theta)} v'[q(\theta)] \tag{2.31}$$

or

$$\left[\theta - \frac{1 - F(\theta)}{f(\theta)} \right] v'[q(\theta)] = c$$

From this equation, we can immediately make two useful observations:

1. Since first-best efficiency requires $\theta v'[q(\theta)] = c$, there is under-consumption for all types $\theta < \bar{\theta}$.

---

14. Remember that

$$\int_{\underline{\theta}}^{\bar{\theta}} uv' = [uv]_{\underline{\theta}}^{\bar{\theta}} - \int_{\underline{\theta}}^{\bar{\theta}} u'v$$

Here, let $v' = f(\theta)$ and $u = \int V[q(x)]dx$ so that

$$\int_{\underline{\theta}}^{\bar{\theta}} \left(\int_{\underline{\theta}}^{\theta} V[q(x)]dx \right) f(\theta) d\theta = \left[\int_{\underline{\theta}}^{\theta} V[q(x)]dx \, F(\theta) \right]_{\underline{\theta}}^{\bar{\theta}} - \int_{\underline{\theta}}^{\bar{\theta}} V[q(\theta)]F(\theta) d\theta$$

which is equal to

$$\int_{\underline{\theta}}^{\bar{\theta}} V[q(\theta)][1 - F(\theta)] d\theta$$

2. We can obtain a simple expression for the *price-cost margin:* Let $T'(\theta)$ $\equiv P[q(\theta)]$. Then from equation (2.30) in the seller's optimization problem we have $P[q(\theta)] = \theta v'[q(\theta)]$. Substituting in equation (2.31), we get

$$\frac{P-c}{P} = \frac{1-F(\theta)}{\theta f(\theta)}$$

It finally remains to check that the optimal solution defined by equations (2.31) and (2.30) satisfies the monotonicity constraint (2.29). In general whether condition (2.29) is satisfied or not depends on the form of buyer's utility function and/or on the form of the density function $f(\theta)$. A sufficient condition for the monotonicity constraint to be satisfied that is commonly encountered in the literature is that the *hazard rate,*

$$h(\theta) \equiv \frac{f(\theta)}{1-F(\theta)}$$

is increasing in θ.[15]

It is straightforward to verify that if the hazard rate is increasing in θ, then condition (2.29) is verified for the solution given by equations (2.31) and (2.30). Indeed, letting

$$g(\theta) = \left[\theta - \frac{1-F(\theta)}{f(\theta)}\right]$$

the first-order conditions can be rewritten as

$$g(\theta)v'[q(\theta)] = c$$

Differentiating this equation with respect to θ then yields

$$\frac{dq}{d\theta} = -\frac{g'(\theta)v'[q(\theta)]}{v''[q(\theta)]g(\theta)}$$

Since $v(\cdot)$ is concave and $g(\theta) > 0$ for all θ, we note that $dq/d\theta > 0$ if $g'(\theta) > 0$. A sufficient condition for $g'(\theta) > 0$ is then that $1/h(\theta)$ is decreasing in θ.

---

15. In words, the hazard rate is the conditional probability that the consumer's type belongs to the interval $[\theta, \theta + d\theta]$, given that her type is known to belong to the interval $[\theta, \bar{\theta}]$.

The hazard rate $h(\theta)$ is nondecreasing in θ for the uniform, normal, exponential, and other frequently used distributions; therefore, the preceding results derived without imposing the monotonicity constraint (2.29) are quite general. The hazard rate, however, decreases with θ if the density $f(\theta)$ decreases too rapidly with θ, in other words, if higher θ's become relatively much less likely. In this case, the solution given by equations (2.31) and (2.30) may violate condition (2.29). When the monotonicity constraint is violated, the solution that we obtained must be modified so as to "iron out" the nonmonotonicity in $q(\theta)$. For the sake of completeness, we now turn to this case.

2.3.3.3   Bunching and Ironing

Call the solution to the problem without the monotonicity constraint (2.29) $q^*(\theta)$. So we have

$$\left[\theta - \frac{1-F(\theta)}{f(\theta)}\right]v'[q^*(\theta)] = c$$

Assume that $dq^*(\theta)/d\theta < 0$ for some $\theta \in [\underline{\theta}, \bar{\theta}]$, as in Figure 2.2.

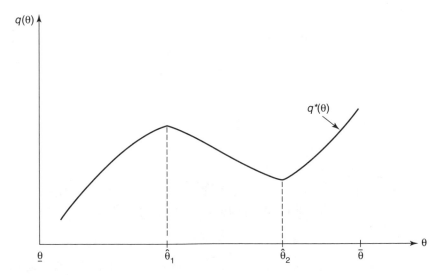

Figure 2.2
Violation of the Monotonicity Constraint

This could be the case when the hazard rate $h(\theta)$ is not everywhere increasing in θ. Then the seller must choose the optimal $q(\theta)$ [which we will call $\bar{q}(\theta)$] to maximize the constrained problem

$$\max_{q(\theta)} \pi = \int_{\underline{\theta}}^{\bar{\theta}} \left[\theta v[q(\theta)] - cq(\theta) - \frac{v[q(\theta)]}{h(\theta)} \right] f(\theta) d\theta$$

subject to

$$\frac{dq(\theta)}{d\theta} \geq 0$$

Assume that the objective function is strictly concave in $q(\theta)$ and that the unconstrained problem is such that $dq^*(\theta)/d\theta$ changes sign only a finite number of times. Then the following "ironing" procedure can be applied to solve for the optimal nonlinear contract: Rewrite the seller's problem as

$$\max_{q(\theta)} \pi = \int_{\underline{\theta}}^{\bar{\theta}} \left[\theta v[q(\theta)] - cq(\theta) - \frac{v[q(\theta)]}{h(\theta)} \right] f(\theta) d\theta$$

subject to

$$\frac{dq(\theta)}{d\theta} = \mu(\theta)$$

$$\mu(\theta) \geq 0$$

The Hamiltonian for this program is then

$$H(\theta, q, \mu, \lambda) = \left[\theta v[q(\theta)] - cq(\theta) - \frac{v[q(\theta)]}{h(\theta)} \right] f(\theta) + \lambda(\theta)\mu(\theta)$$

And by Pontryagin's maximum principle, the necessary conditions for an optimum $[\bar{q}(\theta), \bar{\mu}(\theta)]$ are given by

1. $H[\theta, \bar{q}(\theta), \bar{\mu}(\theta), \lambda(\theta)] \geq H[\theta, q(\theta), \mu(\theta), \lambda(\theta)]$
2. Except at points of discontinuity of $\bar{q}(\theta)$, we have

$$\frac{d\lambda(\theta)}{d\theta} = -\left[\left(\theta - \frac{1}{h(\theta)} \right) v'[\bar{q}(\theta)] - c \right] f(\theta) \tag{2.32}$$

3. The transversality conditions $\lambda(\underline{\theta}) = \lambda(\bar{\theta}) = 0$ are satisfied.

These conditions are also sufficient if $H[\theta, q(\theta), \mu(\theta), \lambda(\theta)]$ is a concave function of q.[16]

Integrating equation (2.32), we can write

$$\lambda(\theta) = -\int_{\underline{\theta}}^{\theta}\left[\left(\theta - \frac{1}{h(\theta)}\right)v'[\bar{q}(\theta)] - c\right]f(\theta)d\theta$$

Using the transversality conditions, we then have

$$0 = \lambda(\bar{\theta}) = \lambda(\underline{\theta}) = -\int_{\underline{\theta}}^{\bar{\theta}}\left[\left(\theta - \frac{1}{h(\theta)}\right)v'[\bar{q}(\theta)] - c\right]f(\theta)d\theta$$

Next, the first condition requires that $\mu(\theta)$ maximize $H(\theta, q, \mu, \lambda)$ subject to $\mu(\theta) \geq 0$. This requirement implies that $\lambda(\theta) \leq 0$ or

$$\int_{\underline{\theta}}^{\theta}\left[\left(\theta - \frac{1}{h(\theta)}\right)v'[\bar{q}(\theta)] - c\right]f(\theta)d\theta \geq 0$$

Whenever $\lambda(\theta) < 0$ we must then have

$$\bar{\mu}(\theta) = \frac{d\bar{q}(\theta)}{d\theta} = 0$$

Thus we get the following complementary slackness condition:

$$\frac{d\bar{q}(\theta)}{d\theta} \cdot \int_{\underline{\theta}}^{\theta}\left[\left(\theta - \frac{1}{h(\theta)}\right)v'[\bar{q}(\theta)] - c\right]f(\theta)d\theta = 0$$

for all $\theta \in [\underline{\theta}, \bar{\theta}]$.

It follows from this condition that if $\bar{q}(\theta)$ is strictly increasing over some interval, then it must coincide with $q^*(\theta)$. To see this conclusion, note that

$$\bar{\mu}(\theta) = \frac{d\bar{q}(\theta)}{d(\theta)} > 0 \Rightarrow \lambda(\theta) = 0 \Rightarrow \frac{d\lambda(\theta)}{d\theta} = 0 \Rightarrow \left(\theta - \frac{1}{h(\theta)}\right)v'[\bar{q}(\theta)] - c = 0$$

But this is precisely the condition that defines $q^*(\theta)$. It therefore only remains to determine the intervals over which $\bar{q}(\theta)$ is constant. Consider Figure 2.3. To the left of θ_1 and to the right of θ_2, we have

---

16. See Kamien and Schwartz (1991), pp. 202, 205.

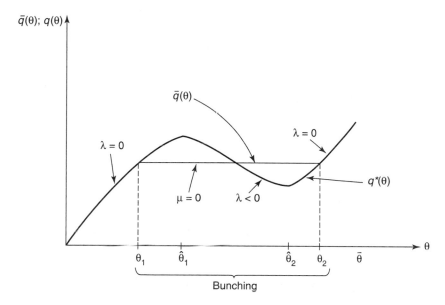

Figure 2.3
Bunching and Ironing Solution

$$\lambda(\theta) = 0 \quad \text{and} \quad \mu(\theta) = \frac{d\bar{q}(\theta)}{d\theta} = \frac{dq^*(\theta)}{d\theta} > 0$$

And for any θ between θ_1 and θ_2, we have

$$\lambda(\theta) < 0 \quad \text{and} \quad \mu(\theta) = 0$$

By continuity of $\lambda(\theta)$, we must have $\lambda(\theta_1) = \lambda(\theta_2) = 0$, so that

$$\int_{\theta_1}^{\theta_2} \left[\left(\theta - \frac{1}{h(\theta)} \right) v'[\bar{q}(\theta)] - c \right] = 0$$

In addition, at θ_1 and θ_2 we must have $q^*(\theta_1) = q^*(\theta_2)$. This follows from the continuity of $\bar{q}(\theta)$. Thus we have two equations with two unknowns, allowing us to determine the values of θ_1 and θ_2. An interval $[\theta_1, \theta_2]$ over which $\bar{q}(\theta)$ is constant is known as a *bunching* interval.

To gain some intuition for the procedure, consider the density function depicted in Figure 2.4. This density does not have a monotonically increasing hazard rate. In this example, there is little likelihood that the buyer's type lies between θ_1 and θ_2. Now suppose that the seller offers some strictly

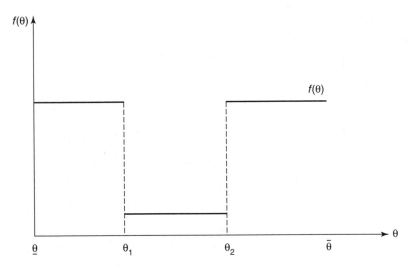

Figure 2.4
Violation of the Monotone Hazard Rate Condition

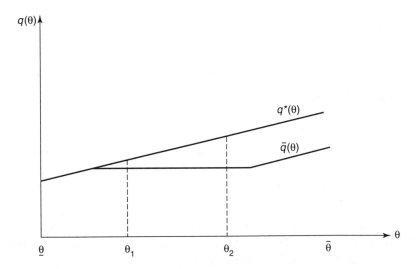

Figure 2.5
Improvement over Strictly Monotonic Consumption

increasing schedule $q*(\theta)$. Remember that consumer surplus $W(\theta) = \theta v[q(\theta)] - T[q(\theta)]$ can be rewritten as

$$W(\theta) = \int_{\underline{\theta}}^{\theta} v[q(x)]dx$$

so that the utility of a buyer of type θ increases at a rate that increases with $q(\theta)$. Now the seller can reduce the rent to all types $\theta \geq \theta_1$ by specifying a schedule $\bar{q}(\theta)$ that is not strictly increasing, as in Figure 2.5.

This rent reduction involves a cost, namely, that all types $\theta \in [\theta_1, \theta_2]$ will pay a lower transfer than the total transfer that could be extracted from them without violating the incentive constraints. But there is also a benefit, since the incentive constraints for the types $\theta \geq \theta_2$ are relaxed, so that a higher transfer can be extracted from them. The benefit will outweigh the cost if the likelihood that the buyer's type falls between θ_1 and θ_2 is sufficiently low.

2.4   Summary

The basic screening model described in this chapter has been hugely influential in economics. We have detailed the way in which it can be solved and its main contract-theoretic insights, as well as a number of key applications. We can summarize the main results in terms of pure contract theory as follows:

• The two-type case provides a useful paradigm for the screening problem, since many of its insights carry over to the case with more than two types.

• When it comes to solving the screening problem, it is useful to start from the benchmark problem without adverse selection, which involves maximizing the expected payoff of the principal subject to an individual rationality constraint for each type of agent. At the optimum, allocative efficiency is then achieved, because the principal can treat each type of agent separately and offer a type-specific "package."

• In the presence of adverse selection, however, the principal has to offer all types of agents the same menu of options. He has to anticipate that each type of agent will choose her favorite option. Without loss of generality, he can restrict the menu to the set of options actually chosen by at least one type of agent. This latter observation, known as the revelation principle, reduces the program of the principal to the maximization of his expected payoff subject to an individual-rationality constraint and a set of incentive constraints for each type of agent.

• In the nonlinear pricing problem with two types, one can moreover (1) disregard the individual rationality constraint of the high-valuation type, as well as the incentive constraint of the low-valuation type; (2) observe that a reduction of the consumption of the low-valuation type lowers the informational rent of the high-valuation type. The optimal contract then trades off optimally the allocative inefficiency of the low-valuation type with the informational rent conceded to the high-valuation type. In contrast, there is no allocative inefficiency for the high-valuation type and no rent for the low-valuation type, since no buyer wants to pretend that an object is worth more to her than it really is.

• In other applications, the technical resolution method is broadly the same as in the nonlinear pricing problem. While the structure of incentive constraints is similar across applications, the same is not always true for individual rationality constraints: (1) for example, in the labor-contract application, contracting takes place ex ante, before the firm learns its type, so that there is a single individual-rationality constraint for the firm; (2) in the optimal-income-tax application, the government is able to force participation of the agent; its utilitarian objective function, together with its budget constraint, induces a specific trade-off between allocative efficiency and the distribution of rents across individuals; (3) finally, in the credit-rationing and regulation problems, we have the same trade-off between rent extraction and allocative efficiency—and the same type of individual-rationality constraints—as in the nonlinear pricing problem of section 2.1.

• For generalizations to more than two types, the continuous-type case is often easiest to analyze, because the set of incentive constraints can often be replaced by a simple differential equation plus a monotonicity condition for the allocations of each type of agent (itself implied by the "Spence-Mirrlees" monotonicity condition on the agent utility with respect to her type). The problem with a continuum of types reveals that what is robust in the two-type case is the existence of positive informational rents and of allocative inefficiency (indeed, these two features happen for all types in the interior of the interval of types, so that they are "probability-one events").

• Under natural restrictions on the distribution of types (e.g., a monotone hazard rate), we have "full separation"; that is, any two different types end up choosing different points in the menu of options offered by the principal, implying that the monotonicity condition is strictly satisfied. The point-wise choice of options in the contract is the outcome of the same type of trade-off as in the two-type case between allocative efficiency and rent extraction.

• In some cases, the distribution of types does not lead to full separation—for example, when there are intermediate types that the principal considers to be of low prior probability, as in the case of a multimodal type distribution. There would then be an incentive for the principal to have severe allocative inefficiency for these types, in order to reduce the rents of adjacent types. But this incentive conflicts with the monotonicity condition mentioned earlier. In this case, a procedure of "bunching and ironing" has been outlined to solve for the optimal contract, relying on Pontryagin's maximum principle. The monotonicity condition then binds for some intervals of types where bunching occurs. These intervals are derived by trading off allocative efficiency and rent extraction *with respect to the bunching interval as a whole*.

Beyond these contract-theoretic insights, there are important economic lessons to be obtained from the screening paradigm:

• The analysis of nonlinear pricing has rationalized quantity discounts, which increase allocative efficiency relative to linear pricing.

• Adverse selection in financial markets can rationalize the phenomenon of equilibrium credit rationing, even though this result is sensitive to the set of financial contracts that is allowed (see Chapter 11 in particular on optimal financial contract design).

• Redistributive concerns by a government that has imperfect information about individual types can rationalize distortionary income taxation, that is, positive marginal income tax rates and therefore inefficiently low labor supply, especially by low-productivity individuals, in order to reduce the income gap between less and more productive individuals.

• A desire by the government not to abandon too many rents to regulated firms can rationalize deviations from "price cap regulation" in favor of partial coverage of costs, at the expense of efficient cost cutting by regulated firms.

• Finally, the screening paradigm has been used to investigate the effect of optimal labor contracting on equilibrium levels of employment. Although labor contracts clearly have a (partial) insurance role, the theory reveals that the introduction of adverse selection does not produce robust predictions on deviations from efficient employment.

2.5   Literature Notes

The material covered in this chapter is "classical" and has by now generated a huge literature. In this section, we stress only pathbreaking contributions that have been at the origin of this literature, surveys of its various branches, and selected key recent advances that go beyond the scope of our book.

The pioneering article developing the formal approach to the basic adverse selection problem is Mirrlees (1971). The revelation principle, which also applies in a multi-agent context, has appeared in various contributions, e.g., Gibbard (1973), Green and Laffont (1977), Myerson (1979), and Dasgupta, Hammond, and Maskin (1979). The solution to the problem with a continuum of types owes much to Baron and Myerson (1982). See also (1) Guesnerie and Laffont (1984) for a general characterization of "necessary and sufficient" conditions for the existence of a second-best optimum in the one-dimensional case and (2) Jullien (2000) and Rochet and Stole (2002) for explorations of type-dependent and random individual rationality constraints.

Some key applications involving adverse selection and screening are the following:

• Mussa and Rosen (1978) on nonlinear pricing, and Maskin and Riley (1984a), on which section 2.1 is based. For an in-depth exploration of nonlinear pricing, the book by Wilson (1993) is also an excellent source.

• A central reference on credit rationing is Stiglitz and Weiss (1981). See also the surveys by Bester and Hellwig (1987), Bester (1992), and Harris and Raviv (1992), which covers financial contracting more generally.

• On optimal taxation, beyond the classic contribution by Mirrlees (1971), see also the surveys by Mirrlees (1986) and Tuomala (1990). Recent contributions not covered here that further operationalize the Mirrlees framework are Roberts (2000) and Saez (2001), for example.

• On implicit labor contracts under adverse selection, our discussion is based on the papers by Azariadis (1983), Chari (1983), Green and Kahn

(1983), and Grossman and Hart (1983). See also the summaries provided by Azariadis and Stiglitz (1983) and Hart (1983a).

• Finally, for regulation under adverse selection, beyond the initial contribution by Baron and Myerson (1982), we should mention the paper by Laffont and Tirole (1986) which allows for the observability of costs and which has led to a vast research output culminating in their 1993 book. See also the survey by Caillaud, Guesnerie, Rey, and Tirole (1988).

3 Hidden Information, Signaling

In Chapter 2 we considered a contracting problem where the party making the contract offer (the principal) is attempting to reduce the informational rent of the other party (the agent). In this chapter we consider the opposite case where the principal has private information and may convey some of that information to the agent either through the form of the contract offer or through observable actions prior to the contracting phase. This type of contracting problem under asymmetric information is commonly referred to as a *signaling* or *informed principal* problem.

The classic example of a signaling problem is the model of education as a signal by Spence (1973, 1974). We shall base our exposition of the general principles of contracting by an informed principal on that model.

The basic setup considered by Spence is a competitive labor market where firms do not know perfectly the productivity of the workers they hire. In the absence of any information about worker productivity, the competitive wage reflects only expected productivity, so that low-productivity workers are overpaid and high-productivity workers underpaid. In this situation the high productivity workers have an incentive to try to reveal (or signal) their productivity to the firms.

Spence considered the idea that education prior to entering the labor market may act as a signal of future productivity. In a nutshell, his idea was that education might be less difficult or costly for high-productivity workers. They could therefore distinguish themselves by acquiring more education. It is important to emphasize that Spence did not argue that education per se would raise productivity, nor did he argue that education would reveal ability through test scores. His point was rather that high education would signal high productivity because it would be too costly for low-productivity types to acquire high education.

Spence's idea is the first example of a precontractual signaling activity. For later reference it is useful to point out that the form of signaling considered by Spence is one where the informed principal (the worker) takes an action to convey information prior to contracting. As we shall see, this is a form of signaling that is different from signaling in the contracting phase through the form of the proposed contract. An example of the latter type of signaling would be the sale of shares in a company by the original owner: by selling a larger or smaller fraction of the firm's shares the owner may signal what he knows about the value of the company (see Leland and Pyle, 1977).

The informed-principal problem raises new conceptual difficulties. The reason is that an informed principal's action, by conveying new information to the agent, changes the agent's beliefs about the type of principal he is facing. Therefore, to determine equilibrium actions, one needs to understand the process by which the agent's beliefs are affected by these actions.

The approach initiated by Spence, subsequently refined by Kreps and Wilson (1982) and others, has been to begin by specifying the agent's prior beliefs about the principal's type, as well as the agent's beliefs about what action each type of principal will take, then to determine each principal type's action given the agent's beliefs, and finally to define an equilibrium outcome as a situation where the agent's beliefs about what action each type of principal takes are correct (that is, the action believed to be chosen by a given type is indeed the action chosen by that type) and where, given the agent's updated beliefs (following the action), each type of principal is acting optimally.

Unfortunately, the additional conceptual difficulty is not just to understand this complex process of revision of beliefs following an action by the principal. Indeed, one of the unresolved problems with this approach is that the equilibrium outcome cannot be perfectly predicted, since there are too many degrees of freedom in choosing the agent's prior beliefs about each principal type's action. This issue is addressed in subsequent work by Cho and Kreps (1987) and Maskin and Tirole (1992) in particular.

In this chapter, we detail the original Spence model as well as its subsequent theoretical developments. We then turn to several finance applications that illustrate the general relevance of signaling models.

3.1   Spence's Model of Education as a Signal

We shall consider only the simplest version of Spence's model with two productivity levels: a worker's productivity can be either r_H or r_L, with $r_H > r_L > 0$. Let $\beta_i \in [0,1]$ be the firm's prior belief that $r = r_i$. Workers are willing to work at any wage $w > 0$, and firms are willing to hire any worker at a wage less than the worker's expected productivity.

A worker of type $i = L, H$ can get e years of education at cost $c(e) = \theta_i e$ before entering the labor market.[1] The key assumption here is that $\theta_H < \theta_L$, or, in words, that the marginal cost of education is lower for high-

---

1. This is a model of voluntary education acquisition; $e = 0$ thus means that the worker does not acquire any education beyond the minimum legal requirement.

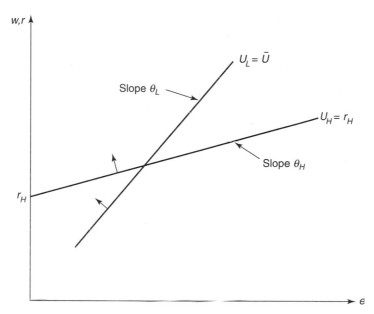

Figure 3.1
Single-Crossing Condition

productivity workers. Under this assumption the indifference curves of a high-productivity and low-productivity worker can cross only once, as indicated in Figure 3.1.

Note that it is assumed here that education does not affect future productivity and is therefore purely "wasteful": its only purpose is to allow highly productive workers to distinguish themselves. This extreme, and unrealistic, assumption can easily be relaxed. Its advantage here is to allow us to identify very clearly the signaling role of education.

In his original article, Spence considers a competitive labor market, where workers determine their level of education anticipating that when they enter the labor market the equilibrium wage is set equal to the expected productivity of the worker conditional on observed education. We shall postpone any discussion of equilibrium determination in a competitive market until Part IV, as the analysis of competition in the presence of asymmetric information raises subtle new issues. For now, we shall consider only the problem of education as a signal in a bilateral contracting setting with one firm and one worker.

In a first stage the worker chooses education, and in a second stage the wage is determined through bargaining. To stick as closely to Spence's original analysis, we assume that in the bargaining phase the worker has all the bargaining power.[2]

Suppose, to begin with, that the worker's productivity is perfectly observable. Then it should be obvious that each worker type chooses a level of education $e_i = 0$. Indeed, since the worker's productivity is known, the highest offer the firm is willing to accept is $w_i = r_i$ regardless of the level of education of the worker.

Now suppose that productivity is not observable. Then the first-best solution $e_L = e_H = 0$ and $w_i = r_i$ can no longer be an equilibrium outcome. To proceed further with our analysis of contracting under asymmetric information we need to specify precisely the game played by the worker and firm, as well as the notion of equilibrium.

In the first stage of the game the worker chooses a level of education, possibly randomly, to maximize his expected return. Let $p_i(e)$ denote the probability that the worker/principal of type i chooses education level e. In the second stage of the game the outcome is entirely driven by how the agent's beliefs have been affected by the observation of the principal's education level. Let $\beta(\theta_i|e)$ denote the agent's revised beliefs about productivity upon observing e. Then the equilibrium wage in the second stage is given by

$$w(e) = \beta(\theta_H|e)r_H + \beta(\theta_L|e)r_L$$

where $\beta(\theta_L|e) = 1 - \beta(\theta_H|e)$. This is the maximum wage the firm is willing to pay given its updated beliefs.

As we hinted at earlier, the key difficulty in this game is determining the evolution of the agent's beliefs. Imposing the minimum consistency requirements on the agent's conditional beliefs in equilibrium leads to the definition of a so-called perfect Bayesian equilibrium:

DEFINITION   A perfect Bayesian equilibrium (PBE) is a set of (possibly mixed) strategies $\{p_i(e)\}$ for the principal's types and conditional beliefs $\beta(\theta_i|e)$ for the agent such that

---

2. Note that in the opposite case, where the employer has all the bargaining power, the equilibrium wage is $w = 0$ no matter what the worker's productivity is. In this case, it is not in the worker's interest to acquire costly education so as to signal his productivity.

1. All education levels observed with positive probability in equilibrium must maximize workers' expected payoff: that is, for all e^* such that $p_i(e^*) > 0$, we have

$$e^* \in \arg\max_e \{\beta(\theta_H|e)r_H + \beta(\theta_L|e)r_L - \theta_i e\}$$

2. Firms' posterior beliefs conditional on equilibrium education levels must satisfy Bayes' rule:

$$\beta(\theta_i|e) = \frac{p_i(e)\beta_i}{\sum_{i=1}^{2}\beta_i p_i(e)}$$

whenever $p_i(e) > 0$ for at least one type.

3. Posterior beliefs are otherwise not restricted: if $p_i(e) = 0$ for $i = L, H$ (so that $\sum_{i=1}^{2}\beta_i p_i(e) = 0$, and Bayes' rule gives no prediction for posterior beliefs), then $\beta(\theta_i|e)$ can take any value in $[0, 1]$.

4. Firms pay workers their expected productivity:

$$w(e) = \beta(\theta_H|e)r_H + \beta(\theta_L|e)r_L$$

When a PBE is taken to be the outcome of this signaling game, essentially the only restriction that is imposed is that in equilibrium the agent's beliefs are consistent with the agent's knowledge of the optimizing behavior of the principal.

To solve for a PBE one typically proceeds as follows. Using one's basic understanding of how the game works, one guesses conditional beliefs $\beta(\theta_i|e)$ for the agent. Then one determines the principal's best response $p_i(e)$ given these beliefs. Finally one checks whether the beliefs $\beta(\theta_i|e)$ are consistent with the principal's optimizing behavior. In signaling games the difficulty is usually not to find a PBE. Rather, the problem is that there exist too many PBEs.

Using our intuitive understanding of Spence's model, we can easily guess the following PBE. If the observed education level is high, it is likely that the worker has high productivity. Indeed, even if a low-productivity worker could obtain a wage $w = r_H$ by acquiring education, he would not be willing to choose a level of education above $\hat{e}$, where $\hat{e}$ is given by $r_H - \theta_L\hat{e} = r_L$. Thus a candidate for a PBE is to set $\beta(\theta_H|e) = 1$ for all $e \geq \hat{e}$ and $\beta(\theta_H|e) = 0$ for all $e < \hat{e}$. If the principal optimizes against these beliefs, then he chooses no education when he has low productivity [$p_L(e) = 0$ for all $e > 0$] and he chooses the level of education $\hat{e}$ when he has high productivity. It is easy to see that with this best response by the principal, the agent's beliefs are consistent in equilibrium.

The PBE we have identified captures in a simple and stark way Spence's idea that the level of education can act as a signal of productivity. The high-productivity worker distinguishes himself by acquiring a level of education $e \geq \hat{e}$ and obtains a high wage, r_H, while the low-productivity worker does not acquire any education and gets a low wage, r_L.

However, the intuitively plausible PBE we have identified is by no means the only one, so that the effectiveness of education as a signal is by no means guaranteed. There are many PBEs, which can be classified into three different categories:

1. Separating PBEs such as the one we have identified, where the signal chosen by the principal identifies the principal's type exactly.

2. Pooling PBEs, where the observed signal reveals no additional information about the principal's type.

3. Semiseparating PBEs, where some but not all information about the principal's type is obtained from the observation of the signal.

We focus here on giving a precise definition and characterization of the set of separating and pooling equilibria, while commenting briefly on semiseparating PBEs whenever appropriate (indeed, this last type of equilibrium is not very important in this economic context, as will be explained later).[3]

DEFINITION   A separating equilibrium is a PBE where each type of principal chooses a different signal in equilibrium: $e_H \neq e_L$ so that $\beta(\theta_H|e_H) = 1$, $\beta(\theta_L|e_L) = 1$, and $w_i = r_i$.

It is straightforward to check that the set of separating equilibrium levels of education is given by

$$S_s = \left\{ (e_H, e_L) \,|\, e_L = 0 \text{ and } e_H \in \left[\frac{r_H - r_L}{\theta_L}, \frac{r_H - r_L}{\theta_H} \right] \right\}$$

We illustrate one separating equilibrium in Figure 3.2. Intuitively, since the low-productivity type is getting the worst possible wage, he has

---

3. For more on signaling models, see game theory texts, such as Fudenberg and Tirole (1991).

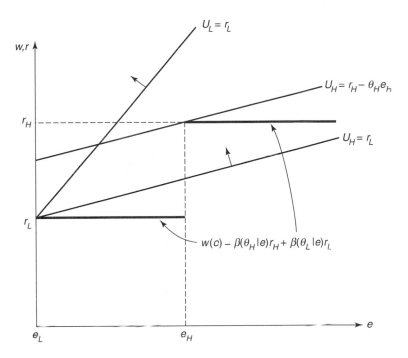

Figure 3.2
Separating Equilibrium

no incentive to acquire education: he can obtain this wage with no education at all. Instead, the high-productivity type is getting the highest possible wage r_H. Incentive compatibility requires $r_H - \theta_L e_H \leq r_L$; otherwise, the low-productivity type would prefer to acquire education level e_H in order to get wage r_H. Similarly, we need $r_H - \theta_H e_H \geq r_L$; otherwise, the high-productivity type would prefer no education and a wage of r_L. Beyond these restrictions, it is easy to find out-of-equilibrium beliefs that support any e_H in S_s. For example, as in Figure 3.2, $\beta(\theta_H|e) = 1$ whenever $e \geq e_H$, and $\beta(\theta_H|e) = 0$ otherwise; under these beliefs, only 0 and e_H can ever be optimal worker choices.

DEFINITION   A pooling equilibrium is a PBE where each type of principal chooses the same signal in equilibrium: $e_H = e_L$ so that $\beta(\theta_H|e_H) = \beta_H$, $\beta(\theta_L|e_L) = \beta_L$, and $w(e_H) = w(e_L) = \beta_L r_L + \beta_H r_H \equiv \bar{r}$.

Again, it is straightforward to verify that the set of pooling equilibrium levels of education is

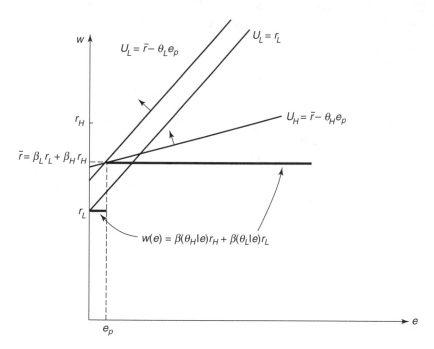

Figure 3.3
Pooling Equilibrium

$$S_p = \left\{ (e_H, e_L) \,|\, e_L = e_H = e_p \text{ and } e_p \in \left[0, \frac{\beta_L r_L + \beta_H r_H - r_L}{\theta_L} \right] \right\}$$

A pooling equilibrium is illustrated in Figure 3.3. Intuitively, S_p is determined by the fact that the worker could obtain a wage of at least r_L without any education. This option is particularly attractive for the low-productivity type. Incentive compatibility thus requires $\bar{r} - \theta_L e_p \geq r_L$. It is then easy to find out-of-equilibrium beliefs that support any e_p in S_p. For example, as in Figure 3.3, $\beta(\theta_H|e) = \beta_H$ and $\beta(\theta_L|e) = \beta_L$ whenever $e \geq e_p$, and $\beta(\theta_H|e) = 0$ otherwise. Under these beliefs, only 0 and e_p can ever be optimal worker choices.

Finally, note that there also exists a set of semiseparating equilibria, where at least one type of principal is mixing between two signals, one of which is also chosen with positive probability by the other type of principal. The key requirement here (as stressed in part 1 of the definition of a PBE) is that, for mixing to be optimal, the type of principal who is mixing has to be indifferent between the two signals that are played with positive probability.

3.1.1 Refinements

The fact that there may be so many different equilibria suggests at the very least that the theory of contracting with an informed principal is incomplete. Indeed, in his original work Spence suggested that additional considerations, such as social custom or conventions, are relevant in determining how a particular equilibrium situation may come about. Spence did not venture into the difficult terrain of social customs and was rather agnostic as to what type of signaling equilibrium might be supported by social custom.

Subsequently, a large body of research in game theory has attempted to develop criteria based on theoretical considerations alone for selecting a particular subset of equilibria.[4] The basic idea behind this research program is to enrich the specification of the game by introducing restrictions on the set of allowable out-of-equilibrium beliefs using the observation that some types of players are more likely to choose some deviations than others.

3.1.1.1 Cho and Kreps' Intuitive Criterion

The most popular refinement used in signaling games is the so-called *Cho-Kreps intuitive criterion* (see Cho and Kreps, 1987). The basic observation this selection criterion builds on is that most deviations from equilibrium play can never be in the interest of some principal types. Beliefs conditional on out-of-equilibrium actions, therefore, ought to reflect the fact that these actions are more likely to be chosen by some types than others. In other words, beliefs conditional on out-of-equilibrium actions must be restricted to reflect the fact that only some types are ever likely to choose these actions.

Formally, the restriction imposed by Cho and Kreps on beliefs conditional on out-of-equilibrium actions in our simple example is the following:

DEFINITION   Cho-Kreps intuitive criterion: Let $u_i^* = w_i^*(e_i) - \theta_i e_i$ denote the equilibrium payoff of type i. Then, $\beta(\theta_j|e) = 0$, for $e \neq (e_i; e_j)$, whenever $r_H - \theta_j e < u_j^*$ and $r_H - \theta_i e \geq u_i^*$ ($i = L, H; i \neq j$).

The Cho-Kreps intuitive criterion is essentially a stability requirement about out-of-equilibrium beliefs: it says that when a deviation is *dominated*

---

4. See, for example, Fudenberg and Tirole (1991).

for one type of player but not the other one, this deviation should not be attributed to the player for which it is dominated. By dominated, one means that the player is getting a *worse* payoff than his equilibrium payoff for *any* belief of the uninformed party following the deviation. Here, the most favorable belief following a deviation is $\beta(\theta_H|e) = 1$, leading to a wage of r_H, so that a deviation is dominated for type θ_j but not θ_i if and only if $r_H - \theta_i e \geq u_i^*$ and $r_H - \theta_j e < u_j^*$. In this case, the Cho-Kreps criterion says that the out-of-equilibrium belief should be $\beta(\theta_j|e) = 0$. Any equilibrium that does not satisfy this criterion should be discarded.

Applying this test to pooling equilibria, one is led to discard all of them. Indeed, at any pooling equilibrium, the indifference curves of the two types must cross as shown in Figure 3.4. But then the θ_H type can always find a profitable deviation, by, say, increasing his education level to e_d (see Figure 3.4). At e_d the firm is ready to accept a wage of $w(e_d) = r_H$, since at that wage the deviation can be profitable only for a θ_H type, while it is dominated for the other type. Using an argument similar to the one for pooling equilibria, it can easily be shown that all semiseparating equilibria can be discarded.

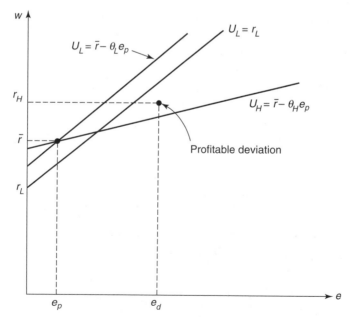

Figure 3.4
Cho-Kreps Unstable Pooling Equilibrium

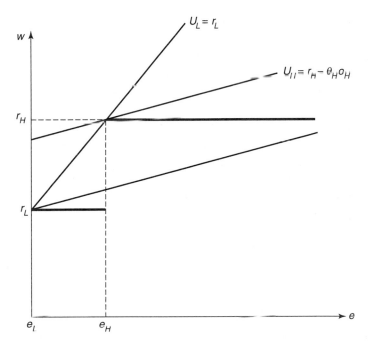

Figure 3.5
Least-Cost Separating Equilibrium

Next, applying the Cho-Kreps intuitive criterion to all separating equilibria, one eliminates all but one equilibrium, the so-called "least-cost" separating equilibrium in which $e_L = 0$ and $e_H = (r_H - r_L)/\theta_L$. Figure 3.5 details this equilibrium. The Cho-Kreps intuitive criterion thus selects a unique pure-strategy equilibrium, which is given by the "least-cost" separating equilibrium.

This extension of the original theory, which places greater demands of rationality on the formation of beliefs than does Spence's theory, makes a strong and unambiguous prediction: when signals such as education are available to allow higher ability workers to distinguish themselves from average workers, these signals will be correctly understood by employers and, consequently, will be used by the higher ability workers to separate themselves out.

As plausible as the Cho-Kreps intuitive criterion may be, it does seem to predict implausible equilibrium outcomes in some situations. Note in particular that the "least-cost" separating equilibrium is the same for all values of $\beta_i > 0$; $i = L, H$. Suppose now that β_L, the prior probablity that a worker of type θ_L is present, is arbitrarily small ($\beta_L = \delta \to 0$). In that case, it seems an excessive cost to pay to incur an education cost of $c(e_H; \theta_H) = \theta_H(r_H - r_L)/\theta_L$ just to be able to raise the wage by a commensurately small amount [$\Delta w = r_H - (1 - \delta)r_H - \delta r_L = \delta(r_H - r_L) \to 0$]. Indeed, in that case the pooling equilibrium where no education costs are incurred seems a more plausible outcome, since it Pareto-dominates the Cho-Kreps equilibrium.[5] Moreover, note that without adverse selection at all, that is, $\beta_L = 0$, no education is chosen in equilibrium, with the result that it is the pooling equilibrium without education that is the limit of this complete-information case, and not the Cho-Kreps equilibrium.

This particular argument should serve as a useful warning not to rely too blindly on selection criteria such as Cho and Kreps' intuitive criterion to single out particular PBEs.[6] It is fair to say nevertheless that the Cho-Kreps criterion has acquired preeminence in the many applications of the signaling approach.

3.1.1.2   Maskin and Tirole's Informed-Principal Problem

Interestingly, the problem of multiplicity of PBEs is reduced when the timing of the game is changed so as to let the principal offer the agent a contingent contract before the choice of the signal. This is one important lesson to be drawn from Maskin and Tirole (1992). To see this, consider the linear model of education specified previously, and invert the stages of contracting and education choice. That is, now the worker offers his employer

5. In all equilibria, firms earn zero profits and are therefore indifferent. As for the low-productivity worker, his preferred equilibrium is the pooling one without education, where he is subsidized by the high-productivity worker without having to incur education costs. Finally, for β_L low enough, the education level required to separate from the low-productivity worker is too expensive for the high-productivity worker in comparison with the pooling wage (but not in comparison with the low-productivity wage, of course).

6. Some game theorists cast further doubt on such selection criteria that do not "endogenize" out-of-equilibrium strategies: while it makes sense not to attribute a deviation to a type for whom the deviation is dominated, why attribute it to the other type, since by construction of the PBE the deviation gives the player a lower payoff than his equilibrium payoff, given the original beliefs about out-of-equilibrium strategies? It would therefore be better to build a theory of equilibrium selection that would embody a theory of out-of-equilibrium strategies. For more on these issues, see, for example, Fudenberg and Tirole (1991).

a contract before undertaking education. This contract then specifies a wage schedule contingent on the level of education chosen by the worker after signing the contract.

Let $\{w(e)\}$ denote the contingent wage schedule specified by the contract. There are two different cases to consider:

1. $\bar{r} - \beta_H r_H + \beta_L r_L \leq r_H - \theta_H (r_H - r_L)/\theta_L$. In this case a high-productivity worker is better off in the "least-cost" separating equilibrium than in the efficient pooling equilibrium.

2. $\bar{r} > r_H - \theta_H (r_H - r_L)/\theta_L$. Here, on the contrary, the high-productivity worker is better off in the efficient pooling equilibrium.

In the first case, the least-cost separating equilibrium is "interim efficient," in that there is no other incentive-compatible contract that manages to strictly improve the equilibrium payoff of the firm or of at least one type of worker without causing another payoff to deteriorate. In this case, the unique equilibrium contract to be signed is the one that specifies the same wage schedule as in the "least-cost" separating equilibrium:

$$w(e) = \begin{cases} r_H & \text{for } e \geq \dfrac{r_H - r_L}{\theta_L} \\ r_L & \text{otherwise} \end{cases}$$

Indeed, note first that the firm is willing to accept this contract. If it does, the high-productivity worker then chooses an education level $e_H = (r_H - r_L)/\theta_L$ and the low-productivity worker, being indifferent between e_H and $e_L = 0$, chooses $e_L = 0$. In either case the firm breaks even, so that it is willing to accept this contract irrespective of whether it originates from a low- or a high-productivity worker. Second, it is easy to verify that in the case where $\bar{r} \leq r_H - \theta_H (r_H - r_L)/\theta_L$ the high-productivity worker cannot do better than offering this contract, nor can the low-productivity worker. More precisely, the high-productivity worker strictly prefers this contract over any contract resulting in pooling or any contract with more costly separation. As for the low-productivity worker, he cannot offer a better incentive-compatible contract that would be acceptable to the firm. In this case, therefore, changing the timing of the game leads to a unique PBE.

In the alternative case however, that is, when $\bar{r} > r_H - \theta_H (r_H - r_L)/\theta_L$, the least-cost separating equilibrium can be improved upon in a Pareto sense. In that case, Maskin and Tirole show that the equilibrium set of this game consists in the incentive-compatible allocations that weakly Pareto-dominate the least-cost separating equilibrium. This multiplicity of equilibria brings us back to the lack of restrictions imposed on out-of-equilibrium beliefs by the PBE concept.

Changing the timing of the game so that a contracting stage precedes the stage when workers choose their education levels is thus particularly significant in situations where the least-cost separating equilibrium is interim efficient, since it is then selected as a unique PBE, and this without having to appeal to restrictions on out-of-equilibrium beliefs.

3.2   Applications

3.2.1   Corporate Financing and Investment Decisions under Asymmetric Information

One of the founding blocks of modern corporate finance is the Modigliani-Miller theorem (1958), which states that capital structure (in other words, the form and source of financing) is irrelevant for firms' investment decisions when there are no tax distortions, transactions costs, agency problems, or asymmetries of information. In a frictionless capital market firms maximize profits when they decide to undertake investment projects if and only if the net present value (NPV) of the project is positive. Considerations other than cash-flow and investment costs, such as dividend policy and debt-equity ratios, are irrelevant for investment decisions. The basic reasoning behind this theorem is the following: since shareholders can buy and sell financial assets at will, they can design the payout stream from the firm that best suits their needs. The firm has no advantage over investors in designing a particular payout stream.

In Chapter 2 we showed how in the presence of adverse selection some firms may be unable to fund their positive NPV projects with debt. Here, we apply the signaling paradigm to show how the choice of firm financing—equity or debt—may affect a firm's investment policy when the firm has better information about investment returns than outside investors, thus leading to a departure from Modigliani-Miller irrelevance.

Much of the following discussion is based on the article by Myers and Majluf (1984). These authors attempt to explain the following stylized fact: new equity issues on average result in a drop in the stock price of the issuer. This is somewhat paradoxical, since a new issue reveals to the market that the firm has new investment opportunities available. If these are positive-NPV projects, the stock price should go up rather than down.

Myers and Majluf show, however, that if the firm has private information about the value of its assets and new investment opportunities, then the negative-stock-price reaction following the announcement of a new equity issue can be explained as a rational response by less well informed investors.

When the firm has private information, the stock issue may act as a signal of firm value and thus convey information to the market. In other words, the firm faces a signaling situation, where the signal is the firm's decision to raise new capital.

We shall consider a generalization of the simple example introduced by Myers and Majluf that incorporates uncertainty. In this example a firm run by a risk-neutral manager has assets in place whose value can be 0 or 1 in the future, and a new investment project whose gross value can also be 0 or 1; the start-up cost of the new project is 0.5.

Denote by γ_i and η_i the respective success probabilities for the assets in place and the new project in state of nature i (with outcomes uncorrelated conditional on these probabilities). Suppose that there are only two states of nature, $i = G, B$, each occurring with probability 0.5. In state G, the good state, we have $\gamma_G \geq \gamma_B$ and $\eta_G \geq \eta_B$. We introduce private information by assuming that the manager observes the true state of nature before making the investment decision, but that outside investors do not observe the underlying state the firm is in.

Assume that the firm is initially fully owned by its manager. Then, if she had 0.5 in cash, she would start the investment project in state i if and only if $\eta_i \geq 0.5$. Suppose, however, that the new investment project has to be fully funded externally by a risk-neutral investor.

3.2.1.1   Case 1: $\eta_G \geq \eta_B \geq 0.5$

In Case 1 it is always efficient to undertake the new project. But we shall see that the manager may be led to make inefficient investment decisions because of her informational advantage over the market. Let us begin by specifying the financial contract used to raise new funds. To this end, denote by r_j the ex post repayment when the gross value of the firm V is respectively $j = 1, 2$. Since the ex post value of the asset in place and the new project can be either 0 or 1, the total ex post value of the firm can be either 2 (when both asset in place and new project are worth 1), 1 (when only one of the two assets has ex post value of 1), or 0 (when neither asset has a value of 1). Note also that when the ex post value is 0 the firm cannot make any repayment. Therefore, we need to specify only r_1 and r_2 to describe a general investment contract.

Equity Financing

We begin by considering the signaling game the firm plays when it is constrained to raising capital in the form of a new standard equity issue. This amounts to

$$r_2 = 2r_1$$

Under this constraint the firm faces a very simple signaling problem with only two actions: "issue new equity and invest in the new project" and "do not issue."

In state B the firm always wants to issue and invest, since, at worst, investors correctly believe that the state of nature is bad and are willing to invest 0.5 in the firm in exchange for an equity stake of at least

$$\frac{0.5}{\gamma_B + \eta_B}$$

of the shares of the firm. Indeed, with such a stake new investors obtain an expected return of $(\gamma_B + \eta_B)[0.5/(\gamma_B + \eta_B)] = 0.5$, equal to their initial investment. In a competitive capital market with a discount rate of zero they are willing to accept such an offer from the firm. This offer leaves the firm with a payoff equal to

$$(\gamma_B + \eta_B)\left(1 - \frac{0.5}{\gamma_B + \eta_B}\right) = \gamma_B + \eta_B - 0.5$$

which is, by assumption, higher than γ_B, the payoff the firm obtains when not undertaking the project.

If, in equilibrium, the firm were to issue shares in both states of nature, investors would not be able to infer the state of nature from the firm's action. Unable to observe the state, they would then value the firm's assets at $0.5(\gamma_G + \eta_G) + 0.5(\gamma_B + \eta_B)$ and ask for an equity stake of

$$\frac{0.5}{0.5\sum_i (\gamma_i + \eta_i)}$$

in return for an initial investment of 0.5. Under such an offer the firm is overvalued by investors in state B and undervalued in state G.

In state G the firm then obtains the following expected payoff if it goes ahead with the investment:

$$(\gamma_G + \eta_G)\left(1 - \frac{1}{\sum_i (\gamma_i + \eta_i)}\right) = \gamma_G + \eta_G - 0.5 - 0.5\frac{(\gamma_G + \eta_G) - (\gamma_B + \eta_B)}{\sum_i (\gamma_i + \eta_i)} \qquad (3.1)$$

The last term represents the subsidy from the firm to investors in state G, resulting from the undervaluation of the firm in that state. This subsidy is sometimes referred to as a "dilution cost" associated with a new equity issue. It should be clear from this expression that if this subsidy is too high, the manager's payoff from issuing equity will be lower than γ_G, the payoff when she does not undertake the investment project. Thus, whenever

$$\eta_G - 0.5 < 0.5\frac{(\gamma_G + \eta_G) - (\gamma_B + \eta_B)}{\sum_i (\gamma_i + \eta_i)}$$

the firm issues equity only in the bad state. In that case, the firm's action perfectly reveals the firm's information, and we have a separating equilibrium.

There are two important observations to be drawn from this equilibrium outcome:

1. The value of the firm is lower than it would have been, had it had the necessary cash to fund the investment project beforehand, since it fails to undertake a positive-NPV project in the good state of nature.

2. When the firm announces a new equity issue, investors learn not only that it has a new investment project available but also that the firm is in state B; as a result, firm value drops from $0.5\gamma_G + 0.5(\gamma_B + \eta_B - 0.5)$ to $\gamma_B + \eta_B - 0.5$. Thus in this separating equilibrium there is a negative stock-price reaction to the announcement of a new equity issue. It is worth emphasizing that despite the expected drop in stock price it is in the firm's interest to go ahead with the issue.

When instead

$$\eta_G - 0.5 \geq 0.5 \frac{(\gamma_G + \eta_G) - (\gamma_B + \eta_B)}{\sum_i (\gamma_i + \eta_i)}$$

then a pooling equilibrium exists where the firm issues equity in both states. However, it is not the only equilibrium if the following condition also holds:

$$(\gamma_G + \eta_G)\left(1 - \frac{0.5}{\gamma_B + \eta_B}\right) < \gamma_G \tag{3.2}$$

When these two conditions hold simultaneously, then both the pooling and the separating equilibria exist. Here investors' beliefs can be self-fulfilling: the firm in state G issues equity if and only if the market thinks that it does. If the market believes that the firm in state G issues equity, it is ready to give the firm more favorable terms, which in turn makes it more attractive for the firm to issue equity.

Finally, if

$$(\gamma_G + \eta_G)\left(1 - \frac{0.5}{\gamma_B + \eta_B}\right) \geq \gamma_G \tag{3.3}$$

then only the pooling equilibrium exists. Note that this condition always holds when $\gamma_G = \gamma_B$ (no asymmetric information on the value of existing assets) or, equivalently, when the new project is funded entirely externally, as an independent firm. In such cases, all positive-NPV projects are undertaken.

Note finally that all the equilibria we have described satisfy the Cho-Kreps intuitive criterion. This is trivially the case for the separating equilibrium, where both signals are used with positive probability in equilibrium and no out-of-equilibrium beliefs need be specified. But it is also trivially satisfied for the pooling equilibrium, for which deviating means not issuing equity, so that out-of-equilibrium beliefs are irrelevant.

Debt Financing

We have seen that whenever

$$\eta_G - 0.5 < 0.5 \frac{(\gamma_G + \eta_G) - (\gamma_B + \eta_B)}{\sum_i (\gamma_i + \eta_i)}$$

there is such a high dilution cost involved in issuing new equity in state G that the firm prefers to forgo a profitable investment opportunity. This result raises the question of whether under these conditions alternative modes of financing, such as debt, are available that would allow the firm to reduce the cost of outside financing enough to go ahead with the new investment.

To this end, we can express the difference between equity and debt in terms of r_j, the ex post repayment when the gross value of the firm is, respectively, $j = 1, 2$. We defined a standard equity contract as one where $r_2 = 2r_1$. In contrast, a standard (risky) debt contract with face value D is such that

$$r_1 = \min\{D, 1\} \quad \text{and} \quad r_2 = \min\{D, 2\}$$

so that $r_2 < 2r_1$ whenever $D < 2$. Thus, under debt financing, the firm repays relatively more when the ex post firm value is 1 than under equity financing. Indeed, it is a feature of debt repayment to be concave in firm value, while equity repayment here is linear in firm value (and becomes convex in firm value when debt has also been issued, since debt has priority over equity).

Because of these differences in repayment functions it is likely that the dilution costs associated with these two instruments will be different. In particular, it seems plausible that debt financing would reduce the subsidy from the firm to the market in state G if the mispricing problem is less severe when the value of the firm is 1 rather than 2, that is, whenever

$$\frac{\text{Prob}(V = 1|B)}{\text{Prob}(V = 1|G)} > \frac{\text{Prob}(V = 2|B)}{\text{Prob}(V = 2|G)}$$

or

$$\frac{\gamma_B(1 - \eta_B) + (1 - \gamma_B)\eta_B}{\gamma_G(1 - \eta_G) + (1 - \gamma_G)\eta_G} > \frac{\gamma_B \eta_B}{\gamma_G \eta_G} \tag{3.4}$$

an inequality that is always satisfied under our assumption that $\gamma_G \geq \gamma_B$ and $\eta_G \geq \eta_B$.

We now show that debt financing reduces the subsidy to the market in state G if and only if condition (3.4) holds. To see this, consider the local deviation from equity contract, where instead of repaying $(r_1, r_2) = (r_1, 2r_1)$ the firm agrees to repay $[r_1 + \delta, 2r_1 - \varepsilon(\delta)]$, where $\delta \geq 0$ and $\varepsilon(\delta)$ is chosen so as to keep the expected repayment constant:

$$\left[0.5\sum_i \gamma_i(1-\eta_i)+(1-\gamma_i)\eta_i\right](r_1+\delta)+\left[0.5\sum_i \gamma_i\eta_i\right](2r_1-\varepsilon)=k$$

where k is a constant. If the subsidy under the deviation is lower than under the equity contract, then clearly debt financing involves lower dilution costs.

The subsidy, S, in state G under a contract $[r_1 + \delta, 2r_1 - \varepsilon(\delta)]$ is given by the difference between the true value of the repayment stream $[r_1 + \delta, 2r_1 - \varepsilon(\delta)]$ and the investor's valuation of this stream:

$$S = (r_1+\delta)[\gamma_G(1-\eta_G)+(1-\gamma_G)\eta_G]+[2r_1-\varepsilon(\delta)]\gamma_G\eta_G - \left[0.5\sum_i \gamma_i(1-\eta_i)+(1-\gamma_i)\eta_i\right](r_1+\delta)+\left[0.5\sum_i \gamma_i\eta_i\right](2r_1-\varepsilon)$$

Now consider the change in the subsidy, S, when δ is increased but the expected repayment is kept constant:

$$\frac{dS}{d\delta} = \gamma_G(1-\eta_G)+(1-\gamma_G)\eta_G-\gamma_G\eta_G\frac{d\delta}{d\varepsilon}$$

$$= \gamma_G(1-\eta_G)+(1-\gamma_G)\eta_G-\gamma_G\eta_G\frac{[0.5\sum_i \gamma_i(1-\eta_i)+(1-\gamma_i)\eta_i]}{[0.5\sum_i \gamma_i\eta_i]}$$

Rearranging and simplifying, it is easy to check that $dS/d\delta < 0$ if and only if condition (3.4) holds. Thus, under our assumptions, debt finance would be better than equity finance. But, debt finance, in turn, is dominated by internal finance, since, as we pointed out, internal finance does not involve any "dilution" cost. These observations are consistent with the "pecking-order theory of finance" put forward by Myers (1977), which suggests that retained earnings are the best source of finance, followed by debt, and finally, equity, which is the least efficient form of finance. Strictly speaking, equity would never be used by the firm in the narrow context of our model. This finding has led some critics to argue that the theory proposed by Myers and Majluf is not empirically plausible because it leads to the conclusion that firms never issue equity. However, it is not difficult to extend the model to introduce bankruptcy costs and thus to obtain some equity financing in equilibrium in order to reduce the firm's exposure to these costs. Perhaps a more important criticism is that this pecking order suggested by Myers does not hold for all relevant parameter values. If, for example, condition

(3.4) does not hold, then equity is the preferred instrument over debt, and the pecking order is changed. Furthermore, the theory considered here predicts that in general neither equity nor debt is the most suitable instrument, as we shall illustrate.

Optimal External Financing

While debt is a better way of financing the firm externally than equity, it is not necessarily optimal. The optimal form of external finance is the one that minimizes the difference in value of repayment across states of nature. This finding may mean that the repayment should not be monotonic in the revenue of the firm. Consider, for example, the case where $1 = \eta_G > \eta_B = 0.5$ and $\gamma_G = 0.5 > \gamma_B = 0$. In this case, $\text{Prob}(V = 1)$ is 0.5 in both states of nature. Consequently, a repayment stream such that $r_1 = 1$ and $r_2 = 0$ satisfies the investor's participation constraint and eliminates the subsidy to new investors in state G.

While the example is extreme in terms of allowing for a repayment burden that is identical across states of nature, it illustrates in a stark way the criterion that dictates the attractiveness of financing modes in this setup. Note, however, that one unattractive feature of this contract is that the firm could make money here by borrowing secretly to artifically boost its revenue and thereby reduce its total repayment. As will be discussed in Chapter 4 (in a moral hazard context), Innes (1990) has analyzed optimal financial contracting under "monotonicity constraints," which require repayments to be weakly increasing in the revenue of the firm, and has derived conditions under which debt then becomes an optimal contract.

3.2.1.2   Case 2: $\eta_G > 0.5 > \eta_B$

We close our discussion of this model with a few remarks about the case where the efficient outcome is separating and has the firm undertake the new investment project only in the good state of nature. If this were an equilibrium, investment would take place if and only if the new project had positive NPV, since the market would correctly perceive the state of nature the firm is in. However, in this situation, the market would subsidize the firm if it were in state B and decided to invest. For example, under equity finance, the firm would then obtain a payoff of

$$(\gamma_B + \eta_B)\left(1 - \frac{0.5}{\gamma_G + \eta_G}\right) = \gamma_B + \eta_B - 0.5 + 0.5\frac{\gamma_G + \eta_G - (\gamma_B + \eta_B)}{\gamma_G + \eta_G}$$

The last term of this expression is the subsidy from the market to the firm. If it is large enough, the manager's payoff will be higher than γ_B, and an efficient separating equilibrium will not exist under equity financing. A separating equilibrium may, however, exist under alternative financing modes—for sure under self-financing, but possibly also under debt financing. Indeed, as in Case 1, debt finance is preferable to equity finance here, for an identical reason: financing instruments are better the more stable is the repayment burden across states of nature.

3.2.2 Signaling Changes in Cash Flow through Dividend Payments

The Modigliani-Miller theorem states not only that corporate capital structure is irrelevant for firms' investment decisions, but also that changes in dividend policy do not have any effect on firm value (when capital markets are competitive, there are no tax distortions, and the firm has no informational advantage over outside investors). To see the basic logic behind the Modigliani-Miller theorem (1958) more clearly, consider the following highly simplified formal argument that underlies their result. Take two firms that are identical in every respect, except for their dividend policy. To keep things as simple as possible, we shall reduce a firm to a cash flow and a dividend policy. Suppose that the two firms have the same cash flow, $C_1^t = C_2^t = C^t$, but a different dividend policy, $d_1^t \neq d_2^t$ for $t = 0, 1, 2 \ldots, \infty$. Let $\rho \geq 0$ denote the constant market interest rate, m_i^t the number of new shares issued (or bought) by firm $i = 1, 2$ at date t, and P_i^t the market price of a share in firm $i = 1, 2$ at date t. Then the net present value of each firm at date $t = 0$ can be written as

$$V_i = \sum_{t=0}^{\infty} \left[\frac{d_i^t + m_i^t P_i^t}{(1+\rho)^t} \right]$$

In words, the current net value of firm $i = 1, 2$ is simply the discounted value of dividend payments and share repurchases (or new issues). In other words, it is the discounted value of all net payments from the firm to the shareholders. It would seem from this formula that the current value of both firms must differ because they have different dividend policies. As Modigliani and Miller have pointed out, however, this assumption is not correct, since we have failed to take into account the basic accounting identity:

$$C_i^t = d_i^t + m_i^t P_i^t$$

which states that in any period, revenue (C_i^t) must be equal to expenditure ($d_i^t + m_i^t P_i^t$), as an accounting construction. Once we take this identity into account, it is obvious that the two firms' current values cannot be different if they have the same cash flows.

As compelling as the Modigliani-Miller logic is, in reality dividend policy does matter, and firm value is significantly affected by changes in dividend policy. For example, it has been widely documented that a firm's share price drops substantially following the announcement of a dividend cut. Similarly, firms that have never paid any dividends see their stock price increase significantly (on average) following the announcement of a change in policy to positive dividend payouts (see Asquith and Mullins, 1983).

The reason why dividend policy matters is still not well understood. Perhaps the best available explanation is that, in a world where managers have better information than investors about cash flow, dividend policy serves as a signal of cash flow, and changes in dividend policy as a signal of changes in cash flow. The first model of signaling through dividends is due to Bhattacharya (1979). We shall consider an extremely simple example adapted from his model. This example highlights the common structure between the signaling problems considered by Bhattacharya and by Myers and Majluf. It also introduces a more satisfactory objective function for the manager.

Consider a firm run by a manager who owns an equity stake $\alpha > 0$ in the firm. This firm generates a cash flow in periods $t = 1$ and $t = 2$ that can take two possible expected values, $\gamma \in \{\gamma_G, \gamma_B\}$, where $\gamma_G > \gamma_B$. As in the model of Myers and Majluf considered earlier, we shall suppose that in each period there is a random (i.i.d.) draw of cash flows and that realized cash flows can take only the value zero or one. The variable $\gamma_i (i = G, B)$ thus denotes the probability that realized cash flow in any period is equal to one. At date $t = 0$ the manager learns the true value of γ, but other shareholders remain uninformed. Shareholders' prior beliefs are given by $\beta = \Pr(\gamma = \gamma_G)$.

The manager of the firm is risk neutral but has *uncertain liquidity preferences*; that is, she does not know in advance when she will need to consume. We model this problem as in the celebrated paper by Diamond and Dybvig (1983) (see Chapter 9 for further discussion of this issue). Specifically, we assume that the manager's state-contingent utility function takes the following simple form:

$$u(c_1, c_2) = \begin{cases} c_1 & \text{with probability } p \\ c_2 & \text{with probability } 1-p \end{cases}$$

where, $c_t (t = 1, 2)$ denotes consumption in period t, and p is the ex ante probability that the manager wants to consume in period $t = 1$. The idea is the following: at date $t = 0$ the manager does not yet know when she wants to consume; she learns her preferred consumption date only at the beginning of period $t = 1$. If it turns out that she wants to consume in period $t = 1$, then she needs to sell her stake α in the firm. Thus at date $t = 0$ the manager cares both about the final value of her stake at date $t = 2$ and the market value of her stake at date $t = 1$.

The precise timing of events in period $t = 1$ is as follows: (1) the firm's cash flow for that period is realized and observed by both manager and shareholders; (2) the firm borrows whatever is needed to meet its dividend payments; (3) the manager learns her consumption preferences; (4) the manager decides whether or not to liquidate her stake in the firm.

We shall consider the decision faced by a manager of a firm with expected cash flow per period of γ_G. In a world of symmetric information the value of the firm at date $t = 0$ would be $2\gamma_G$ (assuming a discount rate of zero), but in the absence of any information identifying the type of the firm, the market would value this firm only at $2[\beta\gamma_G + (1 - \beta)\gamma_B]$.

We shall now show that the manager could raise the market value of the firm by announcing a dividend payout d such that $1 \geq d > 0$ at date $t = 1$. In other words, the announced dividend payout can act as a signal of the firm's cash flow. As usual, the promised dividend payout works as a signal if and only if it is too costly for a firm with low cash flow, γ_B, to commit to such a payout stream. The costs from commiting to a dividend payout d arise here from the cost of borrowing that must be incurred when realized cash flow in period 1 falls short of the promised dividend payment.

Let $\delta > 0$ denote the unit deadweight cost of borrowing,[7] and suppose that the market's posterior belief about the firm's cash-flow type conditional on an announced dividend payment $\hat{d}$ is given by

---

7. Note that the presence of a strictly positive deadweight cost of borrowing is essential for the theory. This cost might be a debt-mispricing cost or a debt-collection cost, or simply a monitoring cost. Whatever interpretation one takes of this cost, it is worth emphasizing that the signaling theory works only if there is also an imperfection in credit markets.

$$\beta(\hat{d}) = \Pr(\gamma = \gamma_G \,|\, \hat{d}) = \begin{cases} 1 & \text{for } \hat{d} \geq d \\ 0 & \text{for } \hat{d} < d \end{cases}$$

It is then too costly for a manager of a low-cash-flow firm to commit to a dividend payout d if and only if

$$\alpha 2\gamma_B \geq \alpha[2\gamma_G - d(1-\gamma_B)\delta] \tag{3.5}$$

The left-hand side (LHS) of this inequality is the manager's payoff if she commits to no dividend payout. In that case, the market identifies her firm as a low-cash-flow firm and correctly values her stake at $\alpha 2\gamma_B$. The RHS is the manager's payoff if she commits to a payout of d. In that case, the market is fooled to identify her firm as a high-cash-flow firm at date $t = 1$. Given that the market is then led to overvalue the firm, it is in the manager's interest to liquidate her stake at date $t = 1$, whether she wants to consume in that period or not. Also, given that the manager sells her stake after the realization of cash flow (and, therefore, after the firm's outstanding debt has been determined), her expected ex ante payoff from that strategy is

$$\gamma_B(\alpha 2\gamma_G) + (1-\gamma_B)\alpha(2\gamma_G - d\delta) = \alpha[2\gamma_G - d(1-\gamma_B)\delta]$$

Similarly, it is worth commiting to a dividend of d for a manager of a high-cash-flow firm if and only if

$$\alpha[2\gamma_G - d(1-\gamma_G)\delta] \geq \alpha[p2\gamma_B + (1-p)2\gamma_G]$$

The LHS of this inequality is the manager's expected payoff if she commits to a dividend of d and thus induces the market to correctly value the firm at $2\gamma_G$ minus the expected deadweight cost of borrowing $d(1 - \gamma_G)\delta$. The payoff on the RHS can be understood as follows: on the one hand, if the manager makes no dividend payment, the firm is identified as a low-cash-flow firm at date $t = 1$, and the manager is forced to sell her stake below the true value whenever she has a liquidity need (with probability p); on the other hand, if she does not have any liquidity need, she can hold on to her stake until date $t = 2$ and realize the full value of her stake without incurring any deadweight cost of borrowing.

Rearranging and simplifying these two inequalities, we obtain

$$\frac{2p(\gamma_G - \gamma_B)}{(1-\gamma_G)\delta} \geq d \geq \frac{2(\gamma_G - \gamma_B)}{(1-\gamma_B)\delta}$$

Thus, as long as δ is large enough (so that $d \le 1$),[8] and

$$p \ge \frac{(1-\gamma_G)}{(1-\gamma_B)}$$

then it is possible to find a separating equilibrium, where a high-cash-flow firm commits to a dividend payment of $d > 0$, incurring an expected deadweight cost of borrowing of $(1 - \gamma_G)\delta d$, and a low-cash-flow firm would not commit to any dividend payment. Intuitively, a high p helps the existence of a separating equilibrium, since it raises the cost of not committing to a dividend payment for the high-cash-flow firm; and the same is true for an increase in γ_G or a decrease in γ_B, which amplify the difference between the two types and therefore the difference between their expected deadweight cost of borrowing.

Even though the signaling theory of dividends, as outlined in this simple example, is rather plausible and is also consistent with U.S. data (see Bernheim and Wantz, 1995), it is not entirely satisfactory. One major difficulty with the theory is that its results are sensitive to small, seemingly innocuous changes in specific timing assumptions. For instance, if the manager could liquidate her stake any time after the announcement of d but before the realization of cash flows at date $t = 1$, then it would be easy to see that dividends could no longer act as credible signals of cash flow. Indeed, in that case condition (3.5) becomes

$$\alpha 2\gamma_B \ge \alpha[2\gamma_G - d(1-\gamma_G)\delta]$$

However, we also have

$$\alpha[2\gamma_G - d(1-\gamma_G)\delta] \ge \alpha[p2\gamma_B + (1-p)2\gamma_G]$$

so that it is impossible to find a dividend payment that would be chosen only by a high-cash-flow firm. More generally, a central difficulty with the theory outlined here is that a dividend policy is in essence a "promise to pay" and not an "obligation to pay." The signaling theory outlined here assumes that when a firm has announced a future dividend of d, then it always sticks to its commitment ex post. But it is not obvious that it is in

---

8. The condition that $d \le 1$ is stronger than necessary. It is possible to allow for higher values of d, but then our expressions for the manager's payoff would be changed. Also, if d is too large, the policy is not credible because the firm would not be able to borrow the full amount needed in case of cash-flow shortfall.

the firm's interest not to renege on its promise. To establish that it is in the firm's interest to stick to its word, the theory needs to be enriched by bringing in reputation considerations.

3.3   Summary and Literature Notes

As the analysis in this chapter highlights, signaling models involve more sophisticated game-theoretic arguments than screening models. In the latter class of models the principal simply solves an optimization problem constrained by a set of incentive constraints. That is, the revelation principle and the fact that the uninformed party moves first allow for a simple transformation of the bilateral contracting problem into a decision problem.

In contrast, in signaling models it is the informed party who moves first. This fact enriches the set of equilibrium outcomes because many conditional beliefs of the uninformed party can be self-fulfilling. The multiplicity of equilibria is due to the fact that Bayes' rule provides no restrictions on beliefs for zero-probability contract offers "off the equilirium path."

In an attempt to provide sharper predictions on likely equilibrium outcomes in signaling games, a large literature on equilibrium refinements has emerged following Spence's contribution. The basic approach of this literature is to introduce some noise into the contracting game, which guarantees that all "off the equilibrium" paths are reached with positive probability, so that beliefs can be tied down everywhere using Bayes' rule (see van Damme, 1983, for an extensive treatment of equilibrium refinements). The most popular refinement is the one by Cho and Kreps (1987). It is based on the following heuristic argument: when a deviation from equilibrium behavior is observed that is dominated for some types of the informed party but not others, then this deviation should not be attributed to the types for which it is dominated. Application of this refinement cuts down the equilibrium set, often to a unique refined equilibrium. For example, in the original model by Spence it uniquely selects the "least-cost separating equilibrium." As we have shown, although this refinement has considerable intuitive appeal, it may select a Pareto-inefficient equilibrium. In contrast, when one allows the uninformed party to restrict the set of contracts from which the informed party can choose prior to the signaling action, as in Maskin and Tirole (1992), then the least-cost separating equilibrium is the unique perfect Bayesian equilibrium only when it is also

Pareto efficient. When it is not, all incentive-compatible payoffs that Pareto-dominate the least-cost separating payoffs may be supported as perfect Bayesian equilibria.

The influence of signaling models in economics is considerable and on par with the screening models considered in Chapter 2. Remarkably, signaling ideas have also influenced subjects as far afield as evolutionary biology. An extremely successful application of signaling theory, for example, has been to explain the striking yet unwieldy shape of male peacock tails! A widely accepted explanation nowadays is that peacock tails signal strength, for only the fittest peacocks would be able to survive with such a handicap (see Grafen, 1990; Zahavi, 1975).

In economics, signaling ideas have found prominent applications, for example, in labor and education, corporate finance, and industrial organization:

• **Labor:** Following the pioneering work of Spence (1973, 1974), education has been seen as not only a human-capital-enhancing activity but also as a selection device (see, e.g., Weiss, 1983, for a model combining both elements). Some of the subsequent theoretical literature on education as a signal has been concerned with robustness issues of the basic theory proposed by Spence. For example, Noldeke and van Damme (1990) have explored the issue of the value of education as a signal when prospective job applicants cannot commit to a particular duration of education. Other aspects of labor markets involving elements of signaling have also been explored. It has been argued, for instance, that a spell of unemployment may be a way of signaling worker productivity, for only productive workers can afford to stay without a job for long (see Ma and Weiss, 1993).

• **Corporate Finance:** Besides the classic contributions of Bhattacharya (1979) and Myers and Majluf (1984) discussed in this chapter, other important examples of signaling behavior by corporations in financial markets have been explored. To just name the first application of signaling in finance, Leland and Pyle (1977) show how a risk-averse owner-manager can signal the underlying quality of the firm it is floating in an initial public offering (IPO) by retaining a substantial undiversified stake in the firm. This is an effective signal because owner-managers of low-quality firms face greater costs of retaining large stakes in their firm. Each of these classic contributions has spawned its own literature testing the robustness of the proposed theory. For example, Brennan and Kraus (1987), Constantinides and

Grundy (1989), and Goswami, Noe, and Rebello (1995), among several other studies, explore the robustness of the "pecking-order theory" of corporate finance implied by the analysis of Myers and Majluf. Similarly, John and Williams (1985) and Bernheim (1991), among other studies, extend Bhattacharya's signaling theory of dividends to include, among other things, dividend taxation. Finally, Welch (1989) and Allen and Faulhaber (1989), among others, have extended Leland and Pyle's theory of signaling in IPOs.

• **Industrial Organization:** Limit (or predatory) pricing, introductory pricing, and advertising are three prominent examples of signaling in industrial organization. The classic contribution by Milgrom and Roberts (1982) has put new life in an old discredited theory of entry prevention through low pricing by an incumbent monopolist. The authors show how low prices may be a signal of low cost or low demand. Their article has spawned a large literature exploring various extensions and robustness of the theory (see Tirole, 1988, for a discussion of this literature). As for advertising, Milgrom and Roberts (1986a) show how a firm selling a high-quality good can signal the quality of its product through wasteful advertising expenditures. Like the peacock's tail, only a firm selling high-quality goods can bear the burden of such expenditures. In an important later contribution Bagwell and Riordan (1991) show how introductory pricing can act as a signal in a way similar to advertising (see Bagwell, 2001, for a survey of the substantial literature on pricing and advertising as signals of quality that has been spawned by these early contributions).

Other examples of signaling in industrial organization that are more directly linked to contracting include Aghion and Bolton (1987), Aghion and Hermalin (1990), and Spier (1992), among others. These contributions take the form of the contract to be the signal. Aghion and Bolton, for example, show how short-term or incomplete contracts offered by an informed seller to buyers can signal a low probability of future entry by rival sellers. Similarly, Spier shows how complex complete contract offers, like prenuptial agreements, may never be made in equilibrium, for they may signal a tough-minded streak in the party making the proposal and thus scare off the other contracting party. Aghion and Hermalin explore how mandatory legal rules, such as bankruptcy laws, can improve on incomplete contractual outcomes that result from a signaling game at the contract negotiation stage.

4 Hidden Action, Moral Hazard

In this chapter we analyze the following contracting problem between a principal and an agent: the principal hires the agent to perform a task; the agent chooses her "effort intensity" a, which affects "performance" q. The principal cares only about performance. But effort is costly to the agent, and the principal has to compensate the agent for incurring these costs. If effort is unobservable, the best the principal can do is to relate compensation to performance. This compensation scheme will typically entail a loss, since performance is only a noisy signal of effort.

This class of principal-agent problems with moral hazard has been widely used as a representation of various standard economic relations. Among the most well-known applications are the theory of insurance under "moral hazard" (Arrow, 1970, and Spence and Zeckhauser, 1971, provide early analyses of this problem); the theory of the managerial firm (Alchian and Demsetz, 1972; Jensen and Meckling, 1976; Grossman and Hart, 1982); optimal sharecropping contracts between landlords and tenants (Stiglitz, 1974; Newbery and Stiglitz, 1979); efficiency wage theories (Shapiro and Stiglitz, 1984); and theories of accounting (see Demski and Kreps, 1982, for a survey). There are of course many other applications, and for each of them specific principal-agent models have been considered.

The basic moral hazard problem has a fairly simple structure, yet general conclusions have been difficult to obtain. As yet, the characterization of optimal contracts in the context of moral hazard is still somewhat limited. Very few general results can be obtained about the form of optimal contracts. However, this limitation has not prevented applications that use this paradigm from flourishing, as the short list in the preceding paragraph already indicates. Typically, applications have put more structure on the moral hazard problem under consideration, thus enabling a sharper characterization of the optimal incentive contract. This chapter begins by outlining the simplest possible model of a principal-agent relation, with only two possible performance outcomes. This model has been very popular in applications. Another simple model, which we consider next, is that of a normally distributed performance measure together with constant absolute risk-averse preferences for the agent and linear incentive contracts. Following the analysis of these two special models, we turn to a more general analysis, which highlights the central difficulty in deriving robust predictions on the form of optimal incentive contracts with moral hazard. To do so, we build in particular on the classical contributions by Mirrlees (1974, 1975, 1976), Holmström (1979), and Grossman and Hart (1983a). We then turn to two applications, relating to managerial incentive schemes and the optimality of debt as a financial instrument, respectively.

4.1   Two Performance Outcomes

Suppose for now that performance, or output q, can take only two values: $q \in \{0, 1\}$. When $q = 1$ the agent's performance is a "success," and when $q = 0$ it is a "failure." The probability of success is given by $\Pr(q = 1 | a) = p(a)$, which is strictly increasing and concave in a. Assume that $p(0) = 0$, $p(\infty) = 1$, and $p'(0) > 1$. The principal's utility function is given by

$$V(q - w)$$

where $V'(\cdot) > 0$ and $V''(\cdot) \leq 0$. The agent's utility function is[1]

$$u(w) - \psi(a)$$

where $u'(\cdot) > 0$, $u''(\cdot) \leq 0$, $\psi'(\cdot) > 0$, and $\psi''(\cdot) \geq 0$. We can make the convenient simplifying assumption that $\psi(a) = a$, which does not involve much loss of generality in this special model.

4.1.1   First-Best versus Second-Best Contracts

When the agent's choice of action is observable and verifiable, the agent's compensation can be made contingent on action choice. The optimal compensation contract is then the solution to the following maximization problem:[2]

$$\max_{a, w_i} p(a)V(1 - w_1) + [1 - p(a)]V(-w_0)$$

subject to

$$p(a)u(w_1) + [1 - p(a)]u(w_0) - a \geq \bar{u}$$

where $\bar{u}$ is the agent's outside option. Without loss of generality we can set $\bar{u} = 0$. Denoting by λ the Lagrange multiplier for the agent's individual-

---

1. It is standard in the literature to assume that the agent's utility is separable in income and effort. This assumption conveniently eliminates any considerations of income effects on the marginal cost of effort. In the general model without wealth constraints it guarantees that the agent's individual rationality constraint is always binding at the optimum.

rationality constraint, the first-order conditions with respect to w_1 and w_0 yield the following optimal coinsurance, or so-called Borch rule, between the principal and agent (see Borch, 1962):

$$\frac{V'(1-w_1)}{u'(w_1)} = \lambda = \frac{V'(-w_0)}{u'(w_0)}$$

The first-order condition with respect to effort is

$$p'(a)[V(1-w_1)-V(-w_0)]+\lambda p'(a)[u(w_1)-u(w_0)]-\lambda = 0$$

which, together with the Borch rule, determines the optimal action a.

Example 1: Risk-Neutral Principal $[V(x) = x]$ The optimum entails full insurance of the agent, with a constant wage w^* and an effort level a^* such that

$$u(w^*) = a^* \quad \text{and} \quad p'(a^*) = \frac{1}{u'(w^*)}$$

That is, marginal productivity of effort is equated with its marginal cost (from the perspective of the principal, who has to compensate the agent for her cost a^*).

Example 2: Risk-Neutral Agent $[u(x) = x]$ The optimum entails full insurance of the principal, with

$$w_1^* - w_0^* = 1 \quad \text{and} \quad p'(a^*) = 1$$

Once again, marginal productivity of effort is equated with its marginal cost for the principal.

When the agent's choice of action is unobservable, the compensation contract cannot be made contingent on action choice. Then the agent's output-

---

2. Alternatively, the maximization problem can be formulated as

$$\max_{a,w_i}\{p(a)u(w_1)+[1-p(a)]u(w_0)-a\}$$

subject to

$$p(a)V(1-w_1)+[1-p(a)]V(-w_0) \geq \overline{V}$$

By varying $\overline{V}$ or $\overline{u}$ it is possible to allow for any division of surplus between the principal and agent. This is a useful shortcut that allows us to separate the analysis of the form of the optimal contract from the bargaining game between principal and agent.

contingent compensation induces her to choose an action to maximize her payoff:

$$\max_a p(a)u(w_1)+[1-p(a)]u(w_0)-a$$

The second-best contract is then obtained as a solution to the following problem:

$$\max_{a,w_i} p(a)V(1-w_1)+[1-p(a)]V(-w_0)$$

subject to

$$p(a)u(w_1)+[1-p(a)]u(w_0)-a\geq 0$$

and

$$a\in\arg\max_{\hat{a}} p(\hat{a})u(w_1)+[1-p(\hat{a})]u(w_0)-\hat{a} \tag{IC}$$

The first-order condition of the agent's optimization problem is given by

$$p'(a)[u(w_1)-u(w_0)]=1 \tag{4.1}$$

Given our assumptions on $p(\cdot)$ and $u(\cdot)$, there is a unique solution to this equation for any compensation contract $(w_0;w_1)$. We can therefore replace the agent's incentive constraint (IC) by the solution to equation (4.1). In general, replacing the agent's incentive constraint by the first-order conditions of the agent's optimization problem will involve a strict relaxation of the principal's problem, as we shall see. However, in this special two-outcome case the principal's constrained optimization problem remains unchanged following this substitution. This substitution simplifies the analysis enormously, as will become clear subsequently. We begin by analyzing the second-best problem in two classical cases: in the first case, principal and agent are risk neutral, but the agent faces a resource constraint; in the second case, at least one of the contracting parties is risk averse.

4.1.2 The Second Best with Bilateral Risk Neutrality and Resource Constraints for the Agent

When the agent is risk neutral, so that $u(x)=x$, first-best optimality requires that $p'(a^*)=1$. The first-order condition of the agent's optimization problem then also becomes $p'(a)(w_1-w_0)=1$, so that the first-best action could be implemented with $w_1^* - w_0^* = 1$. This solution can be interpreted as an upfront "sale" of the output to the agent for a price $-w_0^* > 0$.

If $w_0 = 0$ and $w_1 - w_0 = 1$, the agent would obtain an expected payoff equal to

$$p(a^*) - a^*$$

which is strictly positive, since $p''(a)$ is strictly negative and $p'(a^*) = 1$. By contrast, the principal would obtain a zero payoff, since he is selling the output upfront at a zero price. A risk-neutral principal faced with the constraint $w_0 \geq 0$ would therefore choose $w_0 = 0$ and, faced with $w_1 = 1/p'(a)$ in the second-best problem, would choose a to solve the following problem:

$$\max_a p(a)(1 - w_1)$$

subject to

$$p'(a)w_1 = 1$$

Solving this problem yields

$$p'(a) = 1 - \frac{p(a)p''(a)}{[p'(a)]^2}$$

As can be readily checked, the solution to this equation is smaller than a^*. This result is intuitive, since inducing more effort provision by the agent here requires giving her more surplus.

4.1.3   Simple Applications

The results just presented can be interpreted in several ways. For example, one can think of the agent as a manager of a firm and the principal an investor in this firm. Then w_1 is interpreted as "inside" equity and $(1 - w_1)$ as "outside" equity (Jensen and Meckling, 1976); or, still thinking of the agent as a manager and w_1 as inside equity, $(1 - w_1)$ can be thought of as the outstanding debt of the firm (Myers, 1977); an alternative interpretation is that the agent is an agricultural laborer under a sharecropping contract (Stiglitz, 1974). Under all these interpretations a lower w_1 reduces incentives to work, and it can even become perverse for the principal, generating a form of "Laffer curve" effect. This can mean, for example, that reducing the face value of debt can increase its real value by reducing the debt burden "overhanging" the agent (Myers, 1977).

The standard agency problem assumes that actions are unobservable but output is observable. But for some contracting problems in practice even performance may be difficult to observe or describe. To capture these types of situations some applications involving moral hazard assume that contracting on q is too costly but actions can be observed at a cost through monitoring. One important example of such applications is the efficiency wage model (Shapiro and Stiglitz, 1984). In this model the focus is on trying to induce effort through monitoring. Assume, for example, that effort can be verified perfectly at a monitoring expense M. The full monitoring optimum then solves

$$\max_{a,w} p(a) - w - M$$

subject to

$$w - a \geq 0$$

and

$$w \geq 0$$

which yields $w^* = a^*$ and $p'(a^*) = 1$.

But suppose now that the principal is able to verify the agent's action with probability 0.5 without spending M. If the agent is found shirking, it is optimal to give her the lowest possible compensation. In this case, with a limited wealth constraint, $w \geq 0$, the variable w is set equal to 0. If the principal decides not to spend M, his problem is

$$\max_{a,w} p(a) - w$$

subject to

$$w - a \geq 0.5w$$

The LHS of the incentive constraint is the agent's payoff if she chooses the prescribed action a. The RHS is the agent's maximum payoff if she decides to shirk. In that case it is best not to exert any effort and gamble on the possibility that the agent will not be caught. Now the principal has to give the agent a compensation that is twice her effort level. In other words, the principal gives the agent rents that she would lose when caught shirking.

Having to concede rents once again lowers the principal's desire to induce effort, so that optimal effort is lower than a^*. Finally, the choice of whether or not to monitor depends on the size of M.

4.1.4 Bilateral Risk Aversion

Let us now return to our simple theoretical example. In the absence of risk aversion on the part of the agent and no wealth constraints, the first best can be achieved by letting the agent "buy" the output from the principal. In contrast, if only the agent is risk averse, the first-best solution requires a constant wage, independent of performance. Of course, this completely eliminates effort incentives if effort is not observable. Optimal risk sharing under bilateral risk aversion does not provide for full insurance of the agent, but risk aversion on the part of the agent still prevents first-best outcomes under moral hazard in this case. Indeed, the principal then solves

$$\max_{a,w_i} p(a)V(1-w_1)+[1-p(a)]V(-w_0)$$

subject to

$$p(a)u(w_1)+[1-p(a)]u(w_0)-a\geq 0 \tag{IR}$$

and

$$p'(a)[u(w_1)-u(w_0)]=1 \tag{IC}$$

Letting λ and μ denote the respective Lagrange multipliers of the (IR) and (IC) constraints and taking derivatives with respect to w_0 and w_1 yields

$$\frac{V'(1-w_1)}{u'(w_1)}=\lambda+\mu\frac{p'(a)}{p(a)}$$

and

$$\frac{V'(-w_0)}{u'(w_0)}=\lambda-\mu\frac{p'(a)}{1-p(a)}$$

When $\mu=0$, we obtain the Borch rule. However, at the optimum $\mu>0$ under quite general conditions, as we shall show, so that optimal insurance is distorted: the agent gets a larger (smaller) share of the surplus relative to the Borch rule in case of high (low) performance. Specifically, in order to induce effort, the agent is rewarded (punished) for outcomes whose frequency rises (falls) with effort. In our two-outcome setting, this result is particularly simple: $q = 1$ is rewarded, and $q = 0$ is punished.

Paradoxically, the principal perfectly predicts the effort level associated with any incentive contract and realizes that the reward or punishment corresponds only to good or bad luck. Nevertheless, the incentive scheme is needed to induce effort provision.

4.1.5   The Value of Information

Assume now that the contract can be made contingent not only on q but also on another variable $s \in \{0, 1\}$. This variable may be independent of effort (think of the state of the business cycle) or may depend on it (think of consumer satisfaction indices, if the agent is a salesperson). However, the variable s does not enter directly into the agent's or the principal's objective functions. Specifically, assume $\Pr(q = i, s = j \mid a) = p_{ij}(a)$. The principal can now offer the agent a compensation level w_{ij}, to solve

$$\max_{a, w_{ij}} \sum_{i=0}^{1} \sum_{j=0}^{1} p_{ij}(a) V(i - w_{ij})$$

subject to

$$\sum_{i=0}^{1} \sum_{j=0}^{1} p_{ij}(a) u(w_{ij}) \geq a \qquad \text{(IR)}$$

$$\sum_{i=0}^{1} \sum_{j=0}^{1} p_{ij}'(a) u(w_{ij}) = 1 \qquad \text{(IC)}$$

Again, letting λ and μ denote the respective Lagrange multipliers of the (IR) and (IC) constraints, and taking derivatives with respect to w_{ij}, one obtains the following first-order conditions with respect to w_{ij}:

$$\frac{V'(i - w_{ij})}{u'(w_{ij})} = \lambda + \mu \frac{p_{ij}'(a)}{p_{ij}(a)}$$

Hence the variable s drops out of the incentive scheme (i.e., $w_{ij} = w_i$ for $i = 0, 1$) if for all a

$$\frac{p_{i0}'(a)}{p_{i0}(a)} = \frac{p_{i1}'(a)}{p_{i1}(a)} \quad \text{for } i = 0, 1$$

where a denotes the second-best action choice.

Integrating these conditions yields

$$p_{i0}(a) = k_i p_{i1}(a) \quad \text{for } i = 0, 1$$

where the k_i's are positive constants. The condition for s to be absent from the agent's incentive scheme is thus that, for each q, changing effort yields the same change in relative density whatever s may be. When this is satisfied, one says that q is a "sufficient statistic" for (q, s) with respect to a, or that s is not "informative" about a given q.

When q is not a sufficient statistic for a, taking s into account improves the principal's payoff by allowing for a more precise signal about effort, and thus a more favorable trade-off between effort provision and insurance.

The sufficient statistic result is due to Holmström (1979) (see also Shavell, 1979a, 1979b; and Harris and Raviv, 1979). It extends to general settings, as will be shown later on in this chapter and in Chapters 6 and 8.

4.2   Linear Contracts, Normally Distributed Performance, and Exponential Utility

Next to the two-performance-outcome case, another widely used special case involves linear contracts, normally distributed performance, and exponential utility. Performance is assumed to be equal to effort plus noise: $q = a + \varepsilon$, where ε is normally distributed with zero mean and variance σ^2. The principal is assumed to be risk neutral. The agent has constant absolute risk-averse (CARA) risk preferences represented by the following negative exponential utility function:

$$u(w, a) = -e^{-\eta[w - \psi(a)]}$$

where w is the amount of monetary compensation and $\eta > 0$ is the agent's coefficient of absolute risk aversion ($\eta = -u''/u'$). Note that in contrast with the earlier formulation, effort cost here is measured in monetary units. For simplicity the cost-of-effort function is assumed to be quadratic: $\psi(a) = \frac{1}{2} c a^2$.

Suppose that the principal and agent can write only linear contracts of the form

$$w = t + sq$$

where t is the fixed compensation level and s is the variable, performance-related component of compensation. The principal's problem is then to solve

$$\max_{a,t,s} E(q-w)$$

subject to

$$E(-e^{-\eta[w-\psi(a)]}) \geq u(\overline{w}) \tag{IR}$$

and

$$a \in \arg\max_a E(-e^{-\eta[w-\psi(a)]}) \tag{IC}$$

where $u(\overline{w})$ is the reservation utility level of the agent and $\overline{w}$ denotes the minimum acceptable certain monetary equivalent of the agent's compensation contract.

Maximizing expected utility is equivalent to maximizing

$$E\left(-e^{-\eta\left(t+s(a+\varepsilon)-\frac{ca^2}{2}\right)}\right)$$

$$= \left(-e^{-\eta\left(t+sa-\frac{1}{2}ca^2\right)}\right)E(e^{-\eta s\varepsilon})$$

Moreover, when a random variable ε is normally distributed with zero mean and variance σ^2, we have,[3] for any γ

$$E(e^{\gamma\varepsilon}) = e^{\gamma^2\sigma^2/2}$$

Therefore, maximizing expected utility is equivalent to maximizing

$$-e^{-\eta\left(t+sa-\frac{1}{2}ca^2-\frac{\eta}{2}s^2\sigma^2\right)} \equiv -e^{-\eta\hat{w}(a)}$$

---

3. Indeed, $E(e^{\gamma\varepsilon})$ is then equal to

$$\frac{1}{\sqrt{2\pi}\sigma}\int_{-\infty}^{+\infty} e^{\gamma\varepsilon}e^{-\frac{\varepsilon^2}{2\sigma^2}}\,d\varepsilon = \frac{1}{\sqrt{2\pi}\sigma}\int_{-\infty}^{+\infty} e^{-\frac{\left(\varepsilon^2-\gamma\varepsilon 2\sigma^2\right)}{2\sigma^2}}\,d\varepsilon$$

$$= \frac{1}{\sqrt{2\pi}\sigma}\int_{-\infty}^{+\infty} e^{-\frac{\left(\left(\varepsilon-\gamma\sigma^2\right)^2-\gamma^2\sigma^4\right)}{2\sigma^2}}\,d\varepsilon = e^{\gamma^2\sigma^2/2}\frac{1}{\sqrt{2\pi}\sigma}\int_{-\infty}^{+\infty} e^{-\frac{\left(\varepsilon-\gamma\sigma^2\right)^2}{2\sigma^2}}\,d\varepsilon$$

This last expression is equal to $e^{\gamma^2\sigma^2/2}$ since

$$\frac{1}{\sqrt{2\pi}\sigma}\int_{-\infty}^{+\infty} e^{-\frac{\left(\varepsilon-\gamma\sigma^2\right)^2}{2\sigma^2}}\,d\varepsilon$$

is the area under a normal distribution with mean $\gamma\sigma^2$ and variance σ^2, that is, 1.

where $\hat{w}(a)$ is the *certainty equivalent compensation* of the agent, which is thus equal to her expected compensation net of her effort cost and of a risk premium, which, for a given s, is increasing in the coefficient of risk aversion η and in the variance of output σ^2. It is also increasing in s, since the higher the s, the more the agent bears the risk associated to q.

Thus the exponential form of the expected utility function makes it possible to obtain a closed-form solution for the certainty equivalent wealth $\hat{w}(a)$ here. An explicit solution is generally not obtainable for other functional forms.

The optimization problem of the agent is therefore:

$$a \in \arg \max \hat{w}(a) = \left[t + sa - \frac{1}{2}ca^2 - \frac{\eta}{2}s^2\sigma^2 \right]$$

which yields the simple result $a = s/c$. This equation gives us the agent's effort for any performance incentive s. Knowing that $a = s/c$, the principal solves

$$\max_{t,s} \frac{s}{c} - \left(t + \frac{s^2}{c} \right)$$

subject to

$$t + \frac{s^2}{c} - \frac{c}{2}\frac{s^2}{c^2} - \frac{\eta}{2}s^2\sigma^2 = \overline{w}$$

This derivation yields

$$s = \frac{1}{1 + \eta c\sigma^2}$$

Effort and the variable compensation component thus go down when c (cost of effort), η (degree of risk aversion), and σ^2 (randomness of performance) go up, a result that is intuitive.

4.3   The Suboptimality of Linear Contracts in the Classical Model

The previous case is attractive in that it leads to a simple and intuitive closed-form solution under standard assumptions: normally distributed performance and a CARA utility function for the agent. Unfortunately, however, linear contracts are far from optimal in this setting.

To see this point, consider first a simple case where performance is such that $q = a + \varepsilon$ and where the support of ε is given by $[-k, +k]$, where $\infty > k > 0$. Suppose for simplicity that ε is uniformly distributed on this interval. Through her choice of action, the agent can then move the support of q. This seems, at first glance, to be a reasonable description of the agent's technology. Unfortunately, under this specification, the agency problem disappears altogether: the first best can always be achieved. Call a^* the first-best action, and w^* the first-best transfer. With bounded support, the principal can rule out certain performance realizations, provided the agent chooses a^*. Thus by punishing the agent very severely for performance outcomes outside of $[a^* - k, a^* + k]$ the principal can give the right incentives to the agent. At the same time, the principal can perfectly insure the agent, since when the latter chooses a^*, she has a constant transfer w^* irrespective of the performance realizations in $[a^* - k, a^* + k]$.

One response to this observation is to assume that ε has a fixed or unbounded support and thus avoid having perfectly informative signals about the agent's action choice. As Mirrlees (1975) has shown, however, performance signals may be arbitrarily informative even when ε has unbounded support. This is the case, for example, when ε is normally distributed.

Mirrlees considers the same setting as before:

$$q = a + \varepsilon, \quad \text{where } \varepsilon \sim N(0, \sigma^2)$$

Now, with a normal density we have

$$\frac{f_a(q|a)}{f(q|a)} = \frac{d}{da}[\log f(q|a)] = \frac{(q-a)}{\sigma^2}$$

In other words, the likelihood ratio f_a/f can take any value between plus and minus infinity. That is, the principal can get an almost exact estimate of *a at the tails of the distribution*. Mirrlees shows that this information can be used to approximate the first best arbitrarily closely. That is, the principal can choose $\underline{q}$ such that, for all $q < \underline{q}$, the transfer to the agent $w(q)$ is very low (a form of extreme punishment), but for $q \geq \underline{q}$ the transfer is fixed at $w(q) = w^* + \delta$, slightly higher than the first-best wage level. Under such a compensation scheme the agent faces a negligible risk of getting punished when she chooses a^*, so that her (IR) constraint is satisfied if she is offered a fixed wage $w^* + \delta$, with δ positive but arbitrarily small.

To see this point, let K be the (very low) transfer the agent receives when failing to achieve output of at least $\underline{q}$. For any arbitrary $\underline{q}$ the value of K can be set so as to induce the agent to choose the first-best level of effort a^*, that is,

$$\int_{-\infty}^{\underline{q}} u(K) f_a(q,a^*)dq + \int_{\underline{q}}^{\infty} u(w^*) f_a(q,a^*)dq = \psi'(a^*)$$

where $\psi(a)$ is the (convex) cost-of-effort function. This incentive scheme violates the agent's (IR) constraint only by the positive amount

$$\int_{-\infty}^{\underline{q}} [u(w^*) - u(K)] f(q,a^*)dq$$

However, we know that for any arbitrarily large M, there exists a $\underline{q}$ low enough such that

$$\frac{f_a(q|a)}{f(q|a)} < -M$$

for all $q < \underline{q}$.

Therefore, the shortfall to meet the (IR) constraint is less than

$$\frac{-1}{M} \int_{-\infty}^{\underline{q}} [u(w^*) - u(K)] f_a(q|a^*)dq$$

which, using the incentive constraint, is equal to

$$\frac{-1}{M} \int_{-\infty}^{\infty} u(w^*) f_a(q|a^*)dq - \psi'(a^*)$$

Finally, as

$$f_a(q|a^*) = \frac{(q - a^*)}{\sigma^2} f(q|a^*)$$

this expression is given (and finite) for a given M and tends to zero for M large enough. As a result, the first best can be approximated by setting extreme punishments that are almost surely avoidable provided that the agent chooses the optimal action a^*. Unbounded punishments are of course crucial for the argument here. It is paradoxical that they are used against a risk-averse agent—and they are: the first best can be approximated but not achieved; a constant w^* generates no effort whatsoever! But the key insight is that, as the size of the punishment grows, its relative occurrence falls very fast.

While the result of this subsection casts a shadow over the linear— CARA—normal model, Holmström and Milgrom (1987) have identified conditions under which linear contracts are optimal. Beyond assuming CARA preferences, they consider a dynamic model where effort is chosen in continuous time by the agent. The Holmström–Milgrom result, discussed in Chapter 10, provides foundations, under admittedly specific assumptions, to this user-friendly model discussed in the previous subsection, and has partly contributed to its popularity.

4.4   General Case: The First-Order Approach

4.4.1   Characterizing the Second Best

As the previous subsection has highlighted, linear incentive schemes, while easy to analyze, are, however, not optimal in general. Following Mirrlees (1974, 1975, 1976) and Holmström (1979) in particular, we now turn to the characterization of general nonlinear incentive schemes in a framework where performance measures are described in broad terms as $q = Q(\theta, a)$, where $\theta \in \Theta$ is some random variable representing the state of nature, and $a \in A \subseteq \mathcal{R}$ denotes the agent's effort or action. The principal may be risk averse and has a utility function given by

$$V(q - w)$$

where $V'(\cdot) > 0$ and $V''(\cdot) \leq 0$. The agent is risk averse and also incurs private effort costs. Her utility function takes the general separable form

$$u(w) - \psi(a)$$

where $u'(\cdot) > 0$, $u''(\cdot) \leq 0$, $\psi'(\cdot) > 0$, and $\psi''(\cdot) \geq 0$.[4] As in the two-outcome case, it is convenient to formulate the optimal contracting problem by specifying a probability distribution function over output that is conditional on the agent's action choice. One advantage of this formulation is that it gives very intuitive necessary conditions for an optimal contract. Suppose that performance is a random variable $q \in [\underline{q}, \overline{q}]$ with cumulative distribution

---

4. It is standard in the literature to assume that the agent's utility is separable into income and effort.

function $F(q \mid a)$, where a denotes the agent's action choice. Let the conditional density of q be $f(q \mid a)$. Then the principal's problem can be written as

$$\max_{\{w(q),a\}} \int_{\underline{q}}^{\bar{q}} V[q - w(q)] f(q \mid a) dq$$

subject to

$$\int_{\underline{q}}^{\bar{q}} u[w(q)] f(q \mid a) dq - \psi(a) \geq \bar{u} \tag{IR}$$

and

$$a \in \arg\max_{\hat{a} \in A} \left\{ \int_{\underline{q}}^{\bar{q}} u[w(q)] f(q \mid \hat{a}) dq - \psi(\hat{a}) \right\} \tag{IC}$$

As in the case with only two output outcomes, it is tempting to replace the (IC) constraint by the first- and second-order conditions of the agent's problem:

$$\int_{\underline{q}}^{\bar{q}} u[w(q)] f_a(q \mid a) dq = \psi'(a) \tag{ICa}$$

$$\int_{\underline{q}}^{\bar{q}} u[w(q)] f_{aa}(q \mid a) dq - \psi''(a) < 0 \tag{ICb}$$

In fact, what many authors do is to leave aside the second-order condition (ICb) and replace (IC) by condition (ICa) only. Proceeding in this way and replacing the (IC) constraint by the agent's first-order condition, we obtain the Lagrangean

$$\mathcal{L} = \int_{\underline{q}}^{\bar{q}} \{ V[q - w(q)] f(q \mid a) + \lambda[u(w(q)) f(q \mid a) - \psi(a) - \bar{u}]$$
$$+ \mu[u(w(q)) f_a(q \mid a) - \psi'(a)] \} dq$$

Differentiating with respect to $w(q)$ inside the integral sign, we obtain the by-now-familiar first-order conditions for the principal's problem. An optimal incentive compensation scheme $w(q)$ is such that for all q

$$\frac{V'[q - w(q)]}{u'[w(q)]} = \lambda + \mu \frac{f_a(q \mid a)}{f(q \mid a)} \tag{4.2}$$

These conditions reduce to Borch's rule for optimal risk sharing if $\mu = 0$. However, intuition suggests that generally $\mu = 0$ cannot be an optimum when a is not observed by the principal. Indeed, as a way of inducing the agent to put in higher effort, one would expect the principal to pay the agent more for higher q's than would be optimal for pure risk-sharing reasons. Implicit in this intuition, however, is the idea that higher effort tends to raise output. This assumption is true, however, only if one assumes at least that the conditional distribution function over output satisfies first-order stochastic dominance: $F_a(q \mid a) \leq 0$ with a strict inequality for some value of q. This condition means that, for all $\tilde{q} \in [\underline{q}, \overline{q}]$, there is always a weakly (and at times strictly) lower probability that $q \leq \tilde{q}$ when effort is higher (see Figure 4.1 for an illustration). Note that in the two-outcome case, first-order stochastic dominance is implied by the assumption that effort raises the probability of success.

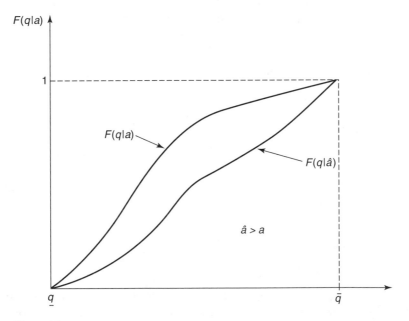

Figure 4.1
First-Order Stochastic Dominance

With this additional assumption on $F(\cdot)$ and our other assumptions on $\psi(a)$ we can show that $\mu > 0$ if the agent is risk averse (if the agent is risk neutral, she can be made residual claimant and moral hazard is not an issue, since we do not have resource constraints here). To do so, proceed by contradiction and assume instead that $\mu \leq 0$. Take the derivative of the Lagrangian with respect to u:

$$\int_{\underline{q}}^{\overline{q}} \{V[q - w(q)]f_a(q\,|\,a) + \lambda[u(w(q))f_a(q\,|\,a) - \psi'(a)])$$

$$+ \mu[u(w(q))f_{aa}(q\,|\,a) - \psi''(a)]\}dq = 0$$

Using the first- and second-order conditions of the agent's optimization problem (ICa) and (ICb), we note that $\mu \leq 0$ is equivalent to

$$\int_{\underline{q}}^{\overline{q}} V[q - w(q)]f_a(q\,|\,a)dq \leq 0 \tag{4.3}$$

Call the first-best wage schedule $w_{FB}(q)$. By Borch rule, $w_{FB}(q)$ and $q - w_{FB}(q)$ are (weakly) monotonically increasing in q. When $\mu \leq 0$, by (4.2), the second-best wage will be weakly below $w_{FB}(q)$ for output levels q such that $f_a(q\,|\,a) > 0$, and it will be above $w_{FB}(q)$ for output levels q such that $f_a(q\,|\,a) < 0$. Consequently, we have

$$\int_{\underline{q}}^{\overline{q}} V[q - w(q)]f_a(q\,|\,a)dq \geq \int_{\underline{q}}^{\overline{q}} V[q - w_{FB}(q)]f_a(q\,|\,a)dq \tag{4.4}$$

However, since $F_a(\underline{q}, a) = F_a(\overline{q}, a) = 0$ for all a, integration by parts implies

$$\int_{\underline{q}}^{\overline{q}} V[q - w_{FB}(q)]f_a(q\,|\,a)dq = -\int_{\underline{q}}^{\overline{q}} V'[q - w_{FB}(q)][1 - w'_{FB}(q)]F_a(q\,|\,a)dq \tag{4.5}$$

Moreover, differentiating the optimality condition (4.2) with $\mu = 0$ yields

$$w'_{FB}(q) = \frac{V''[q - w_{FB}(q)]}{\lambda u''[w_{FB}(q)] + V''[q - w_{FB}(q)]}$$

When the agent is risk averse (that is, $u'' < 0$), this implies $1 > w'(q) \geq 0$ (which simply means that a risk averse agent should not be fully residual claimant in an optimal risk-sharing contract). Since $V'[q - w(q)] > 0$, first-order stochastic dominance implies that (4.5) is strictly positive and, in turn, that conditions (4.3) to (4.5) are incompatible. This contradiction proves that μ must be positive at the second-best outcome. This also means that the principal would like to raise the effort of the agent in the second-best contract.

When $\mu > 0$, the first-order conditions of the principal's problem with respect to $w(q)$ summarize the trade-off between risk sharing and incentives. To better interpret these conditions it is helpful to consider the special case where the agent can choose only among two levels of effort, a_H and a_L ($a_H > a_L$). Then, assuming that it is optimal to elicit a_H, the first-order conditions are rewritten as

$$\frac{V'[q - w(q)]}{u'[w(q)]} = \lambda + \mu\left[1 - \frac{f(q \mid a_L)}{f(q \mid a_H)}\right]$$

If the principal is risk neutral, this equation simplifies to

$$\frac{1}{u'[w(q)]} = \lambda + \mu\left[1 - \frac{f(q \mid a_L)}{f(q \mid a_H)}\right]$$

This equation tells us that $w(q)$ is higher if $f(q \mid a_L)/f(q \mid a_H) < 1$: the agent gets a higher transfer for an output performance that is more likely under a_H. Vice versa, if $f(q \mid a_L)/f(q \mid a_H) > 1$, she gets a lower transfer than under optimal risk sharing. The agent is thus punished for outcomes that *revise beliefs* about a_H down, while she is rewarded for outcomes that revise beliefs up. As Hart and Holmström (1987, page 80) have put it:

The agency problem is not an inference problem in a strict statistical sense; conceptually, the principal is not inferring anything about the agent's action from q

because he already knows what action is being implemented. Yet, the optimal sharing rule reflects precisely the pricing of inference.

Because the transfer function $w(q)$ is directly related to the likelihood ratio, it will be difficult to derive strong properties about this function without making strong assumptions about $F(q \mid a)$. Thus, $w(q)$ is not monotone in general even under first-order stochastic dominance, $F_a(q \mid a) \leq 0$. To see this fact consider the following example.

Example: Nonmonotone Transfer Function   Suppose that there are only three possible performance realizations ($q_L < q_M < q_H$), and that the agent has two possible effort levels ($a_L < a_H$). The conditional densities $f(q \mid a_H)$ and $f(q \mid a_L)$ are given in the following table:

	$f(q_L \mid a)$	$f(q_M \mid a)$	$f(q_H \mid a)$
a_L	0.5	0.5	0.0
a_H	0.4	0.1	0.5

Here, the second-best transfer function is such that

$$w(q_H) > w(q_L) > w(q_M)$$

The point is that when $q = q_L$ it is almost as likely that the agent chose a_H as a_L. Therefore, the principal does not want to punish the agent too much for low performance realizations.

One should expect to have a monotone transfer function only if lower performance observations indicate a lower effort choice by the agent. This intuitive requirement corresponds to the statistical assumption of a *monotone likelihood ratio property* (MLRP). When $f(q \mid a)$ satisfies MLRP, a high-performance realization is good news about the agent's choice of effort (see Milgrom, 1981a). To see this point, consider the necessary conditions for an optimal compensation in the two-action case, when the principal is risk neutral:

$$\frac{1}{u'[w(q)]} = \lambda + \mu\left[1 - \frac{f(q\mid a_L)}{f(q\mid a_H)}\right]$$

We know that $u'(\cdot) > 0$, so that

$$\frac{dw}{dq} > 0 \Leftrightarrow \frac{d}{dq}\left[\frac{f(q\mid a_L)}{f(q\mid a_H)}\right] \leq 0$$

This last inequality is precisely the MLRP condition. In the continuous-action case, the MLRP condition takes the following form:

$$\frac{d}{dq}\left[\frac{f_a(q\mid a)}{f(q\mid a)}\right] \geq 0$$

To get a monotonic transfer function, we must therefore make strong assumptions about $f(q\mid a)$. To obtain optimal *linear* incentive schemes, even stronger assumptions are required. This is unfortunate, as optimal linear incentive schemes are relatively straightforward to characterize. Also, in practice such schemes are commonly observed (as in sharecropping, for example). However, one also observes nonlinear incentive schemes like stock options for CEOs or incentive contracts for fund managers.

A final comment on the monotonicity of the transfer function: Perhaps a good reason why the function $w(q)$ must be monotonic is that the agent may be able to costlessly reduce performance, that is, "burn output". In the preceding example, he would then lower output from q_M to q_L whenever the outcome is q_M.

4.4.2   When Is the First-Order Approach Valid?

4.4.2.1   An Example where the First-Order Approach Is not Valid

We pointed out earlier that in general one cannot substitute the (IC) constraint with the agent's first-order condition (ICa). The following example due to Mirrlees (1975) provides an illustration of what can go wrong.[5] Mirrlees considers the following principal-agent example:

---

5. This example is admittedly abstract, but this is the only one to our knowledge that addresses this technical issue.

The principal's objective is to maximize

$$-(x-1)^2 - (z-2)^2$$

with respect to z.

The agent, however, chooses x to maximize her objective:

$$u(x, z) = ze^{-(x+1)^2} + e^{-(x-1)^2}$$

For any z, the first-order condition of the agent's maximization problem is

$$z(x+1)e^{-(x+1)^2} + (x-1)e^{-(x-1)^2} = 0$$

or

$$z = \frac{1-x}{1+x} e^{4x}$$

Now the reader can check that for z between 0.344 and 2.903 there are three values of x that solve this equation, one of which is the optimal value for the agent. To see which is the optimal value, observe that

$$u(z, x) - u(z, -x) = -(z-1)(e^{4x} - 1)e^{-(x+1)^2}$$

Thus, for $z > 1$ the maximum of u occurs for negative x. When $z < 1$, the maximum of u occurs for positive x. In either case, this observation identifies the optimal value of x. When $z = 1$, u is maximized by setting $x = 0.957$ or $x = -0.957$.

By sketching indifference curves for the principal

$$(x-1)^2 + (z-2)^2 = K$$

in a diagram, one finds that the solution of the maximization problem of the principal is $x = 0.957$ and $z = 1$.

This solution is not obtained if one treats the problem as a conventional maximization problem with the agent's first-order condition as a constraint. One then obtains instead the following first-order conditions to the principal's problem:

$$(2-z) + (1-x)\frac{dx}{dz} = 0$$

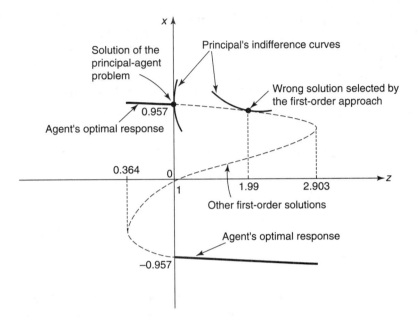

Figure 4.2
Solution of "Relaxed Problem" under the First-Order Approach

where

$$\frac{dz}{dx} = e^{4x}\left(\frac{4(1-x^2)-2}{(1+x)^2}\right)$$

$$= 2z\left(\frac{2(1-x^2)-1}{(1+x)(1-x)}\right)$$

So that

$$2z(2-z) = \frac{(1-x^2)^2}{(1+x)(2x^2-1)}$$

There are three solutions x to this equation. One of those, defined by $z = 1.99$ and $x = 0.895$, achieves the highest value for the maximand

$$-(x-1)^2 - (z-2)^2$$

but this solution does not maximize $u(x, z)$. This solution is only a local maximum.[6]

---

6. The second solution is ineligible on all possible grounds: it is a local minimum of $u(x, z)$. The third solution is a global maximum of $u(x, z)$ but does not maximize the principal's payoff.

Graphically the problem pointed out by Mirrlees can be represented as seen in Figure 4.2. The points on the bold curve represent the solutions to the agent's maximization problem. These points are global optima of the agent's problem. The point ($x = 0.957$; $z = 1$) is the optimum of the principal-agent problem. As the figure illustrates, by replacing the agent's (IC) constraint by only the first-order conditions of the agent's problem (ICa), we are in fact relaxing some constraints in the principal's optimization problem. As a result, we may identify outcomes that are actually not attainable by the principal (in this case, the point $x = 0.895$; $z = 1.99$).

4.4.2.2   A Sufficient Condition for the First-Order Approach to Be Valid

If the solution to the agent's first-order condition is unique and the agent's optimization problem is concave, then it is legitimate to substitute the agent's first-order condition for the agent's (IC).

Rogerson (1985a) gives sufficient conditions that validate this substitution: if MLRP, together with a convexity of the distribution function condition (CDFC) holds, then the first-order approach is valid. The CDFC requires that the distribution function $F(q|a)$ be convex in a:

$$F[q|\zeta a+(1-\zeta)a']\leq\zeta F(q|a)+(1-\zeta)F(q,a')$$

for all $a, a' \in A$, and $\zeta \in [0,1]$.

The two conditions essentially guarantee that the agent's optimization problem is concave so that the first-order conditions fully identify global optima for the agent. The following heuristic argument shows why, under MLRP and CDFC, the agent's first-order conditions are necessary and sufficient. Suppose that the optimal transfer function $w(q)$ is differentiable almost everywhere.[7] The agent's problem is to maximize

$$\int_{\underline{q}}^{\bar{q}} u[w(q)]f(q|a)dq - \psi(a)$$

with respect to $a \in A$.

---

7. Note that since $w(q)$ is endogenously determined, there is no reason, a priori, for $w(q)$ to be differentiable.

Integrating by parts, we can rewrite the agent's objective function as follows:

$$u[w(\overline{q})] - \int_{\underline{q}}^{\overline{q}} u'[w(q)]w'(q)F(q\,|\,a)dq - \psi(a)$$

Differentiating this expression twice with respect to a, we obtain

$$-\int_{\underline{q}}^{\overline{q}} u'[w(q)]w'(q)F_{aa}(q\,|\,a)dq - \psi''(a)$$

Then, by MLRP [$w'(q) \geq 0$] and CDFC [$F_{aa}(q\,|\,a) \geq 0$], the second derivative with respect to a is always negative.

Unfortunately, CDFC and MLRP together are very restrictive conditions. For instance, none of the well-known distribution functions satisfy both conditions simultaneously. Jewitt (1988) has identified conditions somewhat weaker than CDFC and MLRP by making stronger assumptions about the form of the agent's utility function.

Notice, however, that the requirement that the agent's first-order conditions be necessary and sufficient is too strong. All we need is that the substitution of (IC) by its first-order condition yields necessary conditions for the principal's problem. These considerations suggest that an alternative approach to the problem that does not put stringent restrictions on the conditional distribution function $F(q|a)$ is useful. Such an approach has been developed by Grossman and Hart (1983a).

4.5   Grossman and Hart's Approach to the Principal-Agent Problem

This approach relies on the basic assumption that there are only a finite number of possible output outcomes. Thus, suppose that there are only N possible q_i: $0 \leq q_1 < q_2 < \ldots < q_N$, and let $p_i(a)$ denote the probability of outcome q_i given action choice a. The agent's action set A is taken to be a compact subset of $\mathcal{R}^n$. To keep the analysis simple we take the principal to be risk neutral: $V(\cdot) = q - w$. The agent's objective function, however, now takes the more general form

$$\tilde{u}(w, a) = \phi(a)u[w(q)] - \psi(a)$$

Under this specification, the agent's preferences over income lotteries are independent of her choice of action.[8] This utility function contains as special cases the multiplicatively separable utility function [$\psi(a) \equiv 0$ for all a] and the additively separable utility function [$\phi(a) \equiv 1$ for all a]. Moreover, $u[w(q)]$ is such that $u(\cdot)$ is continuous, strictly increasing, and concave on the open interval $(\underline{w}, +\infty)$ and

$$\lim_{w \to \underline{w}} u(w) = -\infty$$

The principal's problem is to choose $a \in A$ and $w_i \equiv w(q_i) \in (\underline{w}, +\infty)$ to maximize

$$V = \sum_{i=1}^{N} p_i(u)(q_i - w_i)$$

subject to the agent's (IR) constraint

$$\sum_{i=1}^{N} \{\phi(a)u(w_i) - \psi(a)\} p_i(a) \geq \bar{u}$$

In addition, if a is unobservable the principal also faces the (IC) constraint

$$\sum_{i=1}^{N} \{\phi(a)u(w_i) - \psi(a)\} p_i(a) \geq \sum_{i=1}^{N} \{\phi(\hat{a})u(w_i) - \psi(\hat{a})\} p_i(\hat{a})$$

for all $\hat{a} \in A$.

Suppose, to begin with, that a is observable to the principal. Since the agent is risk averse and the principal risk neutral, the (first-best) optimal contract insures the agent perfectly. The optimal transfer is determined by maintaining the agent on her individual rationality constraint. Then the principal can implement the first best by setting

---

8. This is the most general representation of the agent's preferences such that the agent's participation (or IR) constraint is binding under an optimal contract. Under a more general representation, such that the agent's cost of effort depends on the agent's income or exposure to risk, it may be optimal for the principal to leave a monetary rent to the agent so as to lower the cost of effort and induce a higher effort choice. In that case the IR constraint would not be binding. As a consequence the optimal incentive contract would be substantially more difficult to characterize.

$$w = u^{-1} \left[\frac{\bar{u} + \psi(a)}{\phi(a)} \right]$$

and choosing a to maximize

$$V = \sum_{i=1}^{N} p_i(a)q_i - u^{-1} \left[\frac{\bar{u} + \psi(a)}{\phi(a)} \right]$$

Now suppose that a is not observable to the principal. The innovation in this approach is to divide the principal's problem into two stages: first determine the minimum transfers to the agent that implement any given action a, then maximize over actions:

Stage 1: Implementation   This stage involves solving the following problem

$$\min_{(w_1, \cdots, w_N)} \sum_{i=1}^{N} p_i(a)w_i$$

subject to

$$\sum_{i=1}^{N} p_i(a)\{\phi(a)u(w_i) - \psi(a)\} \geq \bar{u} \tag{IR}$$

$$\sum_{i=1}^{N} p_i(a)\{\phi(a)u(w_i) - \psi(a)\} \geq \sum_{i=1}^{N} p_i(\hat{a})\{\phi(\hat{a})u(w_i) - \psi(\hat{a})\} \quad \text{for all } \hat{a} \in A \tag{IC}$$

This program is solved for any action $a \in A$. Notice that we have a finite number of constraints so that the Kuhn-Tucker theorem can be applied here. But the program as we have written it is not necessarily concave. The trick is then to make a simple transformation and take $u_i \equiv u(w_i)$ rather than w_i as the principal's control variables. Define also $h \equiv u^{-1}$ and $u_i \equiv u(w_i)$ so that $w_i = h(u_i)$.

This approach requires an additional technical assumption. Let

$$\mathbb{U} = \{u \,|\, u(w) = u \text{ for some } w \in (\underline{w}, +\infty)\}$$

Then assume that

$$\frac{[\bar{u} + \psi(a)]}{\phi(a)} \in \mathbb{U} \quad \text{for all } a \in A$$

In words, for every effort a, there exists a wage that meets the participation constraint of the agent for that effort.

Then the transformed program is

$$\min_{(u_1,\cdots,u_N)} \sum_{i=1}^{N} p_i(a)h(u_i)$$

subject to

$$\begin{cases} \displaystyle\sum_{i=1}^{N} p_i(a)\{\phi(a)u_i - \psi(a)\} \geq \overline{u} & \text{(IR)} \\ \displaystyle\sum_{i=1}^{N} p_i(a)\{\phi(a)u_i - \psi(a)\} \geq \sum_{i=1}^{N} p_i(\hat{a})\{\phi(\hat{a})u_i - \psi(\hat{a})\} & \text{for all } \hat{a} \in A \quad \text{(IC)} \end{cases}$$

We now have linear constraints and a convex objective, so that the Kuhn-Tucker conditions are necessary and sufficient.

Let $\mathbf{u} = (u_1, \ldots, u_N)$ and define

$$C(a) = \inf\left\{ \sum_{i=1}^{N} p_i(a)h(u_i) \,\middle|\, \mathbf{u} \text{ implements } a \right\}$$

Note that for some $a \in A$ there may exist no $\mathbf{u}$ that implements a. For such actions, let $C(a) = +\infty$.

Grossman and Hart show that when $p_i(a) > 0$ for $i = 1, \ldots, N$, there exists a solution $(u_1^*, \ldots, u_N^*)$ to the preceding minimization problem, so that the cost function $C(a)$ is well defined. As the Mirrlees example highlights, a potential difficulty here is that some components of $\mathbf{u}$ may be such that $h(u_i)$ is unbounded even if $C(a)$ remains bounded. If this is the case, a solution to the maximization problem may not exist. One can rule this problem out by assuming that $p_i(a) > 0$, so that $C(a)$ also becomes infinitely large when $h(u_i)$ is unbounded for some u_i's. An infinitely large $C(a)$ cannot be optimal, so that one can then safely assume that all relevant $h(u_i)$ are bounded and that the constraint set is compact. The existence of a solution in the set

$$\left\{ \sum_{i=1}^{N} p_i(a)h(u_i) \,\middle|\, \mathbf{u} \text{ implements } a \right\}$$

then follows by Weierstrass's theorem.

Stage 2: Optimization   The second step is to choose $a \in A$ to solve

$$\max_{a \in A} \left\{ \sum_{i=1}^{N} p_i(a) q_i - C(a) \right\}$$

Once the cost function $C(a)$ has been determined, this is a straight-forward step.

We have now completed our outline of the approach proposed by Grossman and Hart to solve the principal-agent problem. Notice that the only assumption on the distribution function over output they make to obtain an optimal contract is that $p_i(a) > 0$. The remainder of their article establishes results obtained in previous formulations (in this more general setting) and also some new results. Particulary noteworthy are the following new results:

First, as already discussed, the (IR) constraint is binding if the agent's utility function is additively or multiplicatively separable and

$$\lim_{w \to \underline{w}} u(w) = -\infty$$

Second, even if MLRP holds, the incentive scheme may not be mono-tonic. This result is due to the possible indifference of the agent between several actions at an optimum (see example 1 in Grossman and Hart). To obtain monotonicity, one needs an even stronger *spanning condition* (see Grossman and Hart).

Beyond these results, the most that can be said about optimal incentive schemes, when no restrictions are put on $p_i(a)$, except for $p_i(a) > 0$, is that the transfers $w_1, \ldots, w_N$ cannot be decreasing everywhere in performance, nor increasing everywhere faster than performance. That is, while the Borch rule requires that

$$0 \le \frac{w_i - w_{i-1}}{q_i - q_{i-1}} \le 1$$

in this general case the most that can be said is that we do not have

$$\frac{w_i - w_{i-1}}{q_i - q_{i-1}} < 0$$

everywhere, nor

$$\frac{w_i - w_{i-1}}{q_i - q_{i-1}} > 1$$

everywhere!

These are rather weak predictions. Just as sharp characterizations of the optimal incentive scheme are not obtainable in general, simple comparative statics results are unavailable. For instance, a reduction in the agent's cost of effort can make the principal worse off, as this may make it easier for the agent to take some undesirable actions (see Grossman and Hart for an example). Finally, it should come as no surprise that sharp characterizations of the agent's second-best action are also not obtainable. The second-best action can be higher or lower than the first-best action. There is no general reason that hidden actions necessarily result in underprovision of effort.

4.6 Applications

As the introductory and concluding sections of this chapter stress, there is a paradox in moral hazard theory: While the model is very relevant for many real-world contexts, the above discussion indicates that it delivers very few general predictions. Only when significant simplifying assumptions are introduced can we obtain clean and intuitive results. This explains why applications in the area take these simplifying assumptions on board. This section details two such applications.

4.6.1 Managerial Incentive Schemes

The conflict of interest between shareholders and managers of a firm is a classic example of a principal-agent problem. Indeed, management compensation packages are perhaps the best-known examples of incentive contracts. The design of executive compensation schemes has become a sophisticated art, so much so that most companies nowadays hire the services of consultants specialized in managerial compensation issues to design the remuneration packages of their executives. It is therefore natural to ask what lessons can be drawn from principal-agent theory for the design of managerial compensation contracts and whether current practice is consistent with the predictions of the theory.

In most cases a manager's compensation package in a listed company comprises a salary, a bonus related to the firm's profits in the current year, and stock options (or other related forms of compensation based on the firm's share price). The overall package also includes various other benefits, such as pension rights and severance pay (often described as "golden parachutes").[9] In other words, a manager's remuneration can broadly be divided into a "safe" transfer (the wage), a short-term incentive component (the bonus), and a long-term incentive component (the stock option).

At first sight, the overall structure of this package is difficult to relate to the optimal contracts considered in this chapter. This difficulty should not come as a surprise given that the problem of providing adequate incentives to managers is much richer than the stylized principal-agent problems we have considered in this chapter. First, the relationship between a manager and shareholders is long-term. Second, the manager can often manipulate performance measures such as profits. Third, and perhaps most importantly, the managerial incentive problem does not just boil down to eliciting more effort from the manager. It also involves issues of risk taking, efficient cost cutting, adequate payout provisions, empire building, hubris, and so on. If anything, what is surprising is the relative simplicity of observed managerial compensation packages given the complexity of the incentive problem.

Another important difference between practice and theory is the contracting protocol. In the abstract problem we have considered in this chapter, a single principal makes a take-it-or-leave-it offer to the agent. In practice, however, it is the manager (or a compensation committee, often appointed by the manager) who draws the compensation package and gets it approved by the directors (who are, for all practical purposes, on the manager's payroll). It comes as no surprise then that managers are often generously rewarded even when their company is doing poorly. A key focus of corporate governance regulation is precisely on this contractual protocol. A number of SEC or other securities regulations are aimed at reducing the risk of capture of the remuneration committee and the board by management. Despite these regulations, many commentators have argued that managerial compensation has more to do with rent extraction than with providing incentives to CEOs (see, for example, Bebchuk, Fried, and Walker, 2002).

---

9. In some cases the problem is not so much to insure the manager against job loss as to tie the manager to the firm. Then the compensation package might include a "golden handcuff" (which is essentially a payment from the manager to the firm if the manager leaves the firm before the expiration of his contract) instead of a "golden parachute." Another, more exotic, type of clause that is sometimes observed is a "golden coffin" (which is essentially an exceptionaly generous life insurance for executives).

With all these differences between theory and practice it would seem that the simple principal-agent theory developed in this chapter has little to say about the problem of managerial compensation. We shall show, however, that a slightly reformulated version of the general model considered in this chapter can yield the general structure of the managerial compensation package we have described and provide insights as to how the package should vary with the environment the manager operates in.

Consider a single manager who contracts with a single representative shareholder (say, the head of the remuneration committee). The manager takes hidden actions $a \in A$, which affect both current profits q and the stock price P. Take profits q to be normally distributed with mean a and variance σ_q^2:

$$q = a + \varepsilon_q$$

where $\varepsilon_q \sim N(0, \sigma_q^2)$. Similarly, take the stock price to be normally distributed with mean a and variance σ_P^2:

$$P = a + \varepsilon_p$$

where ε_p is a normally distributed random variable: $\varepsilon_p \sim N(0, \sigma_P^2)$.

In general, the stock price variable behaves differently from the profit variable because stock prices incorporate information other than that contained in profit reports. For example, the stock price may reflect information stock analysts have acquired directly about the manager's actions (see Holmström and Tirole, 1993, for a more detailed model of managerial compensation that illustrates how analyst's information gets reflected in stock prices). Even if they behave differently, however, they are likely to be correlated random variables. Thus, let σ_{qP} denote the covariance of q and P.

Take the manager to have constant absolute risk-averse (CARA) preferences, and represent her preferences with the negative exponential utility function

$$u(w, a) = -e^{-\eta[w-\psi(a)]}$$

where, as before, $\psi(a) = 1/2ca^2$. The principal, however, is assumed to be risk neutral.[10]

---

10. This assumption is justified as an approximation if we think of the principal as a representative shareholder with a well-diversified portfolio.

As in section 4.2, restrict attention to linear incentive packages. This is a common (though not innocuous) simplification in the economics or accounting literature on managerial compensation contracts. Suppose that the manager gets a compensation package w of the form

$$w = t + sq + fP$$

where t denotes the salary (independent of performance), s the fraction of profits the manager obtains as a bonus, and f the manager's share of equity capital.[11]

We shall think of the owner as a "buy and hold" investor, who cares only about the firm's profit performance. That is, the owner is not concerned about selling his shares in the secondary market at a good price and therefore is not directly concerned about stock price. Thus the owner's problem is

$$\begin{cases} \max_{a,t,s,f} E[q-w] \\ \text{subject to} \\ a \in \arg\max_a E\left[-e^{-\eta\left(w - c\frac{a^2}{2}\right)} \right] \\ \text{and} \\ E\left[-e^{-\eta\left(w - c\frac{a^2}{2}\right)} \right] \geq -e^{-\eta\bar{w}} \end{cases}$$

where, as before, $\bar{w}$ denotes the manager's reservation wage.

As we have shown in section 4.2, we can rewrite the principal's and agent's objectives in terms of their certainty-equivalent wealth and thus obtain the following simple reformulation of the principal's problem:

$$\begin{cases} \max_{a,t,s,f}(1-s-f)a-t \\ \text{subject to} \\ a \in \arg\max_a\left\{ (s+f)a+t-\frac{1}{2}ca^2 - \frac{1}{2}\eta[s^2\sigma_q^2 + 2sf\sigma_{qP} + f^2\sigma_P^2] \right\} \\ \text{and} \\ (s+f)a+t-\frac{1}{2}ca^2 - \frac{1}{2}\eta[s^2\sigma_q^2 + 2sf\sigma_{qP} + f^2\sigma_P^2] \geq \bar{w} \end{cases}$$

11. Note that by restricting attention to linear incentive schemes we rule out (nonlinear) stock option plans.

As in section 4.2, we can solve this problem using the first-order approach. Accordingly, we substitute the incentive constraint with the first-order conditions for the agent's problem:

$$a = \frac{s+f}{c}$$

The owner's problem is then simplified to

$$
\begin{cases}
\max_{t,s,f} (1-s-f)\dfrac{s+f}{c} - t \\[2mm]
\text{subject to} \\[2mm]
\left\{ (s+f)\dfrac{s+f}{c} + t - \dfrac{1}{2}c\left(\dfrac{s+f}{c}\right)^2 - \dfrac{1}{2}\eta[s^2\sigma_q^2 + 2sf\sigma_{qP} + f^2\sigma_P^2] \right\} = \overline{w}
\end{cases}
$$

Substituting for the value of t in the individual-rationality constraint and maximizing with respect to s and f, one then obtains the following solution for the optimal linear compensation package:

$$s^* = \frac{\sigma_P^2 - \sigma_{qP}}{\sigma_q^2 + 2\sigma_{qP} + \sigma_P^2} \frac{1}{1+\eta c\Omega}$$

$$f^* = \frac{\sigma_q^2 - \sigma_{qP}}{\sigma_q^2 + 2\sigma_{qP} + \sigma_P^2} \frac{1}{1+\eta c\Omega}$$

where

$$\Omega = \frac{\sigma_q^2\sigma_P^2 - \sigma_{qP}^2}{\sigma_q^2 + 2\sigma_{qP} + \sigma_P^2}.$$

These expressions determine how the manager's compensation package varies as a function of the underlying environment the firm operates in. Specifically, the compensation package can be directly tied to the stochastic structure of the firm's cash flow and stock price. To see how the compensation package varies with the volatility of cash flow or stock price, consider first the special case where ε_q and ε_P are independently distributed. In that case, $\sigma_{qP} = 0$, and the expressions for s^* and f^* reduce to

$$s^* = \frac{\sigma_P^2}{\sigma_q^2 + \sigma_P^2 + \eta c\sigma_P^2\sigma_q^2}$$

$$f* = \frac{\sigma_q^2}{\sigma_q^2 + \sigma_P^2 + \eta c \sigma_P^2 \sigma_q^2}$$

It is easy to see from these expressions that as the firm's stock price becomes more volatile (σ_P^2 increases), the manager's shareholding decreases ($f*$ is smaller), but the share of profit increases ($s*$ increases). Similarly, if profit becomes more volatile, the manager's stock participation goes up, but the profit participation is reduced. Another interesting observation is that the manager does not become a 100% equity holder of the firm even when she is almost risk neutral (as $\eta \to 0$). However, she does become the sole residual claimant since $s* + f* \to 1$ as $\eta \to 0$.

Consider next the special case where $\varepsilon_P = \varepsilon_q + \zeta$, where ζ is an independently normally distributed random variable: $\zeta \sim N(0, \sigma_\zeta^2)$. In that case the stock price is a more noisy signal of the manager's effort than profits. In other words, profits are then a sufficient statistic, and the result due to Holmström (1979) suggests that there should be no stock participation in the manager's compensation package. Under this stochastic structure, $\sigma_P^2 = \sigma_q^2 + \sigma_\zeta^2$ and $\sigma_{qP} = \sigma_q^2$, so that $f* = 0$ and $s* = 1/(1 + \eta c \sigma_q^2)$, as the general theory would predict.

An important assumption in the agency theory of executive compensation that we have outlined is that the stock market is informationally efficient, so that the stock price is an unbiased estimate of the firm's fundamental value and the CEO's action choice a. When one allows for the possibility of speculative bubbles in stock markets, then the optimal compensation contract may put more weight on short-term stock price performance than on long-term fundamental value, as Bolton, Scheinkman, and Xiong (2003) have shown.

4.6.2 The Optimality of Debt Financing under Moral Hazard and Limited Liability

In Chapter 3 we discussed why debt financing can be a cheaper source of funding for firms than equity or any other form of financing when the firm has private information about the expected value of its assets and investments. Since under a debt contract the repayment to investors varies less with performance than under any other financial contract, this repayment stream is likely to be less underpriced by uninformed investors than the payment stream under any other form of financing.

We now illustrate that when (costly and hidden) managerial/entrepreneurial effort raises the return on investment, then the most incentive-efficient form of outside financing of the entrepreneur's project under limited liability may be some form of debt financing. A special case of this result has first been established by Jensen and Meckling (1976), who have pointed out that when the investment project can be financed entirely with "safe debt"—that is, debt that is repaid in full for sure—then a risk-neutral entrepreneur will have first-best incentives to provide effort. The reason is simply that in this case the entrepreneur gets to appropriate the entire marginal return from her effort. Innes (1990) has shown that the incentive efficiency of debt financing extends to situations where debt is "risky"—that is, debt is not always repaid in full—if the set of feasible investment contracts is such that the repayment to investors is always (weakly) increasing in the return on investment.

Innes's theory, along with Myers and Majluf's and several others we discuss in later chapters, provide several compelling explanations for why most small firms and most households raise outside funds primarily in the form of debt. Until recently debt financing was the only form of outside financing available to firms and households. And even though it is possible nowadays to get funding in the form of venture capital financing or equity participation by an investment fund, debt financing is still the most prevalent form of outside financing.

Innes's basic idea is that, in the presence of limited liability, when the downside of an investment is limited both for the entrepreneur and the investor, the closest one can get to a situation where the entrepreneur is a "residual claimant" is a (risky) debt contract. In other words, a debt contract provides the best incentives for effort provision by extracting as much as possible from the entrepreneur under low performance and by giving her the full marginal return from effort provision in high-performance states where revenues are above the face value of the debt.

The basic setup is as follows. Suppose that a risk-neutral entrepreneur can raise revenues from investment q by increasing effort a. Specifically, suppose that revenues are distributed according to the conditional density $f(q|a)$ and the conditional cumulative distribution $F(q|a)$. The entrepreneur's utility function is separable in income and effort (as usual) and is given by $v(w, a) = w - \psi(a)$, with ψ', $\psi'' > 0$.

Suppose also that the risk-neutral entrepreneur has no funds and that the firm's setup cost I must be funded by a risk-neutral investor in exchange for a revenue-contingent repayment $r(q)$. We now show that if the firm is a limited liability corporation and if feasible investment contracts must specify repayments that are monotonically increasing in q, then the uniquely optimal investment contract is a risky debt contract taking the form $r(q) = D$ for $q \geq D$ and $r(q) = q$ for $q < D$, where $D > 0$ is set so that (discounted) expected repayments are equal to the initial investment I.

More formally, the key restrictions imposed on the set of feasible contracts $r(q)$ are

1. A two-sided limited liability constraint $0 \leq r(q) \leq q$

2. A monotonicity constraint $0 \leq r'(q)$

The first restriction means that the entrepreneur cannot be asked to pay back more than she earns $[r(q) \leq q]$, and also that the investor cannot be asked to pay more than I in total (this latter part of the constraint is not important for the result in the end). The second restriction seems less natural at first. It can, however, be justified as follows: Suppose that $0 > r'(q)$ for a subset of revenue outcomes q. In that case the entrepreneur would strictly gain by borrowing money at par from another source and thus marginally boost her profit performance,

$$\frac{d\{[q - r(q)] - q\}}{dq} = -r'(q) > 0$$

If this kind of borrowing can go on undetected, then any contract such that $0 > r'(q)$ would simply encourage the entrepreneur to engage in this type of arbitrage activity. Note that the second restriction would also be required if the principal were able to costlessly reduce profits ex post.

Under these restrictions, a striking conclusion emerges: If the density function $f(q\,|\,a)$ satisfies the monotone likelihood ratio property (MLRP), an optimal investment contract is a debt contract. Moreover, Innes shows that under the optimal investment contract there is always underprovision of effort relative to the first best, where the entrepreneur does not need to raise any outside funding. Let us provide the intuition for this result.

We begin by showing that in the absence of any monotonicity constraint $0 \leq r'(q)$, MLRP implies that it is optimal to "punish" the entrepreneur for "bad" performance ($q \leq Z$) by taking away all the revenues from her $[r(q)$

= q], and to "reward" her for "good" performance ($q > Z$) by leaving her all the revenues of the investment [$r(q) = 0$].

Formally, the entrepreneur's optimal contracting problem is to maximize her expected net return from the investment, subject to meeting (1) an incentive compatibility constraint, (2) the investor's break-even condition, and (3) the two-sided limited liability constraint. If we substitute the incentive compatibility constraint by the first-order condition of the entrepreneur's optimization problem with respect to a, then we can write the constrained optimization problem as follows:

$$\max_{\{r(q),a\}} \int_0^{\bar{q}} [q - r(q)] f(q|a) dq - \psi(a) - I$$

subject to

$$\int_0^{\bar{q}} [q - r(q)] f_a(q|a) dq = \psi'(a) \tag{IC}$$

$$\int_0^{\bar{q}} r(q) f(q|a) dq = I \tag{IR}$$

$$0 \le r(q) \le q \tag{LL}$$

As we have explained, in general, substitution of the incentive constraints with the first-order conditions of the agent's problem results in a "relaxed" problem for the principal. However, here the restrictions on the set of feasible contracts as well as the MLRP ensure that the substitution of the incentive constraints with the first-order conditions does not result in a strictly relaxed problem. We leave it to the reader to verify this finding as an exercise.

Letting μ and λ denote the Lagrange multipliers associated with the constraints (IC) and (IR), respectively, we can write the Lagrangean of this problem as

$$\mathcal{L} = \int_0^{\bar{q}} [q - r(q)] f(q|a) dq - \psi(a) + \mu \left[\int_0^{\bar{q}} [q - r(q)] f_a(q|a) dq - \psi'(a) \right]$$
$$+ \lambda \left[\int_0^{\bar{q}} r(q) f(q|a) dq - I \right]$$

Rearranging, the Lagrangean can be rewritten as

$$\mathcal{L} = \int_0^{\bar{q}} r(q) \left[\lambda - \mu \frac{f_a(q|a)}{f(q|a)} - 1 \right] f(q|a) dq$$

$$+ \int_0^{\bar{q}} q \left[1 + \mu \frac{f_a(q|a)}{f(q|a)} \right] f(q|a) dq - \psi(a) - \mu \psi'(a) - \lambda I$$

This formulation of the problem makes it clear that the objective is linear in $r(q)$ for all q. Therefore, provided that the constraint (IC) is binding and therefore that $\mu > 0$,[12] the optimal repayment schedule $r^*(q)$ is such that

$$r^*(q) = \begin{cases} q & if \ \lambda > 1 + \mu \dfrac{f_a(q|a)}{f(q|a)} \\ 0 & if \ \lambda < 1 + \mu \dfrac{f_a(q|a)}{f(q|a)} \end{cases}$$

We can then conclude from this analysis that it is optimal to "reward" the entrepreneur for revenue outcomes such that the likelihood ratio $f_a(q|a)/f(q|a)$ is higher than the threshold $(\lambda - 1)/\mu$. Under MLRP the likelihood ratio $f_a(q|a)/f(q|a)$ is increasing in q. Therefore, there exists a revenue level Z such that it is optimal to set

$$r^*(q) = \begin{cases} 0 & if \ q > Z \\ q & if \ q < Z \end{cases}$$

See Figure 4.3 for an illustration of this contract. Note that this contract is highly nonmonotonic and does not resemble the description of a standard debt contract $\{r_D(q)\}$ such that

$$r_D(q) = \begin{cases} D & if \ q > D \\ q & if \ q \leq D \end{cases}$$

However, if one imposes the additional constraint that $r'(q) \geq 0$, it is clear from the preceding argument that the constrained optimal contract takes the form a standard debt contract $r_D(q)$ where D is the lowest value that solves the (IR) constraint:

---

12. Otherwise, the first-best can be reached.

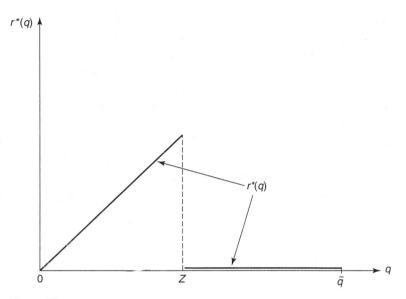

Figure 4.3
Optimal Nonmonotonic Contract

$$\int_0^D qf(q\,|\,a^*)dq + [1 - F(D\,|\,a^*)]D = I$$

and a^* is given by the (IC) constraint

$$\int_D^q (q - D)f_a(q\,|\,a^*)dq = \psi'(a^*)$$

The intuition of Innes's result is straightforward. The incentive problem is to try to induce the entrepreneur to supply high effort. Given that high revenue outcomes are most likely when the entrepreneur works hard, it makes sense to reward her as much as possible for high-revenue performance.

One important implication of this result is that when external financing is constrained by limited liability, it will generally not be possible to mitigate the debt-overhang problem, which was highlighted by Myers (1977) and discussed at the beginning of this chapter, by looking for other forms of financing besides debt. Indeed, Innes's result indicates that under quite general conditions it is not possible to get around this problem by structuring financing differently. Debt is already the financial instrument that minimizes this problem when there is limited liability.

One key feature Innes abstracts from is risk aversion. While debt provides maximum effort incentives, it is not good from the point of view of insuring the entrepreneur against risk. In Chapter 10, we discuss, however, the contribution of Dewatripont, Legros, and Matthews (2003), who show that Innes's insight survives in a dynamic setting where the initial financial contract can be renegotiated after the investor has observed the effort choice of the entrepreneur. The renegotiated contract can then be relied upon to provide optimal insurance, while the role of the initial contract is to maximize effort incentives. For this purpose, starting with debt financing is optimal.

4.7 Summary

The notion of moral hazard has for a long time been confined to the insurance industry and mainly been discussed by actuaries. Nowadays, however, this is a widely understood notion, which is seen as highly relevant in many different subdisciplines ranging from international finance to economic development. Although the trade-off between risk sharing and incentives is widely recognized, there is unfortunately no tractable general model that is as widely used. In this chapter, we have highlighted some of the conceptual and mathematical difficulties inherent in a general contracting problem with hidden actions. Despite these difficulties, several general lessons emerge from our analysis.

• When the agent is risk neutral and wealthy, a simple solution to any contracting problem with moral hazard is to let the agent be a "residual claimant" on the output she produces.

• When the agent is risk neutral but has limited wealth, then the incentive problem is worse the poorer is the agent. Sometimes the poverty of the agent may be so extreme that it pays the principal to hand over wealth to the agent in the form of aid or an efficiency wage. Much of development policy to very poor countries can be rationalized on these grounds.

• When the agent is risk averse, then more incentives come at the cost of a risk premium that the principal must pay the agent. Whether the principal should expose the agent to less risk when the agent is more risk averse, however, is generally not clear. Similarly, whether the principal should optimally elicit higher effort from the agent when the agent's effort cost decreases is not generally clear.

• Among the main general predictions of the model is the informativeness principle, which says that the incentive contract should be based on all variables that provide information about the agent's actions. Also, in general the agent must be exposed to some risk to provide adequate incentives.

• When the distribution of output conditional on the agent's action choice satisfies the monotone likelihood ratio property (MLRP), then the agent's remuneration is increasing in her performance (provided that the agent is not also subject to a limited liability or wealth constraint). But in general there is no reason to expect the optimal reward function of the agent to be linear.

• Some of the main areas of application of the principal-agent framework with hidden actions have been to executive compensation, corporate finance, and the theory of the firm. But this framework has also been applied widely in international finance, agricultural economics, and macroeconomics. A leading application in macroeconomics has been to the incentive problem of central bankers (see Walsh, 1995).

4.8   Literature Notes

The topics covered in this chapter are standard material. Since references for key applications were mentioned in the introduction, we concentrate here on theoretical references. Arrow's (1970) essays on risk bearing have played an important role in exposing the economics profession to the ideas of moral hazard and the widespread problems of incentives when actions are hidden. The first article to characterize the first-best optimal risk-sharing rule is due to Borch (1962). Wilson (1968) considers a more general problem than Borch, and his article is the first to formally touch on the problem of optimal risk sharing with hidden actions. Much of the discussion in Wilson (1968) and later in Spence and Zeckhauser (1971) and Ross (1973) is confined to the question of identifying situations where the first best can be achieved with hidden actions. The pioneering articles that first attempt to formulate the second-best problem are due to Mirrlees (1974, 1975, 1976). Later, Holmström (1979) (see also Shavell, 1979a, 1979b and Harris and Raviv, 1979) built on Mirrlees' work to provide the first articulation of the informativeness principle (see also Kim, 1995 and Jewitt, 1997) on the value of information systems in moral hazard settings). Sappington (1983) and Kahn and Scheinkman (1985) have provided solutions to the bilateral risk neutrality problem with resource constraints for the agent. Finally, the research effort of formulating a general framework for the second-best problem culminates with the model and approach proposed by Grossman and Hart (1983a) and the characterization of sufficient conditions under which the first-order approach is valid by Rogerson (1985a) and the later generalizations proposed by Jewitt (1988).

The static bilateral contracting problem with hidden actions has of course been subsequently extended in many different directions, most of which we explore in detail in subsequent chapters. Thus we consider multitask extensions as well as hybrid models involving both hidden information and action in Chapter 6. Multiagent and dynamic extensions are pursued further in Chapters 8 and 10. One important extension, however, that we have not been able to cover is the framework considered by Baker (1992, 2000), where the contract is signed before the agent learns her true cost of effort. This assumption not only is realistic, but also provides a contracting structure that is fairly tractable and gives rise to sharper characterizations.

5 Disclosure of Private Certifiable Information

Up to now we have considered situations where private information is neither observable nor verifiable. That is to say, we have considered private information about such things as individual preferences, tastes, ideas, intentions, quality of projects, and effort costs, which cannot be measured objectively by a third party. But there are other forms of private information, such as an individual's health, the servicing and accident history of a car, potential and actual liabilities of a firm, and earned income, that can be certified or authenticated once disclosed. For these types of information the main problem is to get the party who has the information to disclose it. This is a simpler problem than the one we have considered so far, since the informed party cannot report false information. It can only choose not to report some piece of information it has available.

There is a small but nonetheless significant literature dealing with the problem of disclosure of verifiable information. Our review of the main results and ideas of this literature is based on Townsend (1979), Milgrom (1981a), Grossman and Hart (1980), Grossman (1981), Gale and Hellwig (1985), Okuno-Fujiwara, Postlewaite, and Suzumura (1990), Shavell (1994), and Fishman and Hagerty (1995).

In many situations where one contracting party may have private verifiable information, a standard regulatory response is to introduce mandatory disclosure laws. This practice is particularly prevalent in financial markets, where firms that issue equity or bonds are required to regularly disclose information about their performance and activities. Also, financial intermediaries are required to disclose information about their trading activities and pricing decisions. Although at first sight mandatory disclosure laws may seem like a rather sensible regulatory response to overcome some forms of informational asymmetry, we shall see that some of these laws are controversial, at least in financial markets. The reason is simply that according to the theory outlined in this chapter there are sufficient incentives for contracting parties to voluntarily disclose information. Therefore, it is often argued, mandatory disclosure laws are at best redundant and may impose unnecessary costs on the contracting parties. We begin this chapter by considering the incentives for voluntary disclosure. We then identify situations where there may be inefficient voluntary disclosure and investigate the merits of mandatory disclosure regulations. We close the chapter with a discussion of costly information production and disclosure. We show that when there are positive disclosure or verification costs it is optimal to minimize overall disclosure costs and to commit to produce and disclose only the most relevant or essential information. We illustrate how this basic logic can be applied to the design of financial contracts and financial reporting. In particular, we cover the arguments by Townsend (1979) and Gale and Hellwig (1985) that debt contracts have the desirable property that they minimize the extent of costly financial reporting.

5.1 Voluntary Disclosure of Verifiable Information

Since mandatory disclosure laws are particularly prevalent in financial markets, we shall address the problem of disclosure of verifiable information in the context of a finance application. Specifically, we shall consider the problem of a firm issuing equity on a stock market. In practice, securities laws and stock markets impose a number of rather stringent disclosure requirements on any member firm. These requirements are often invoked as an important reason why some firms may prefer not to go public.

Consider again the model of Myers and Majluf (1984) introduced in Chapter 3. Recall the basic elements of their model:

• A risk-neutral owner-manager of a firm with assets in place is considering issuing equity to finance a new project.

• The final value of the assets in place is uncertain and may be either 1 with probability γ or 0 with probability $1 - \gamma$.

• The setup cost of the new project is 0.5, and its expected discounted gross value is also uncertain; it may be either 1 with probability η or 0 with probability $1 - \eta$, where $\eta > 0.5$.

• The owner-manager has private information about the expected value of assets in place. She knows whether $\gamma = \gamma_G$ or $\gamma = \gamma_B$, where $\gamma_G > \gamma_B$.

• Outside investors, however, know only that $\gamma = \gamma_G$ with probability 0.5. Since they are all risk neutral, they value the assets in place at $0.5(\gamma_G + \gamma_B)$.

As a benchmark, we begin by briefly reviewing the equilibrium outcomes in this model when the private information of the owner-manager is not certifiable. We then show how the equilibrium outcome is drastically changed when information is certifiable.

5.1.1 Private Uncertifiable Information

If the owner-manager's private information about γ_i is not certifiable, then we are dealing with a signaling problem similar to that analyzed in Chapter

3. Recall that in this signaling problem the owner-manager always wants to issue shares and invest in the new project if $\gamma = \gamma_B$. Indeed, even if outside investors have the most pessimistic valuation of the firm's assets in place and demand a share of equity of $0.5/(\gamma_B + \eta)$ in return for an investment of 0.5 (to cover the setup costs of the new project) the owner-manager gets a payoff equal to

$$(\gamma_B + \eta)\left(1 - \frac{0.5}{\gamma_B + \eta}\right) = \gamma_B + \eta - 0.5$$

which is, by assumption, higher than γ_B, the payoff the owner-manager would obtain if she did not undertake the new investment project.

If $\gamma = \gamma_G$, however, then the owner-manager may or may not issue new equity, depending on how much outside investors undervalue the firm's assets in place. In a pooling equilibrium the owner-manager issues shares whether assets in place have a high or low expected value. In that case the owner-manager's action reveals no information, and outside investors value the firm at $0.5(\gamma_G + \gamma_B) + (\eta - 0.5)$. In a separating equilibrium the owner-manager issues shares only when the expected value of assets in place is low $(\gamma = \gamma_B)$.[1]

Since $\gamma > 0.5$, only the pooling equilibrium is efficient. But for some parameter constellations only the separating equilibrium exists. Moreover, for a wide range of parameter values both types of equilibrium may exist, and there is no guarantee that the pooling equilibrium is the natural outcome of the signaling game.

5.1.2 Private, Certifiable Information

If the firm is able to disclose its information about the value of assets in place by certifying the true value of γ_i, then the equilibrium outcome in this model is radically different. To see this, suppose that the firm can get an underwriter, a rating agency, or an accounting firm to certify the true value

---

1. Recall that a separating equilibrium exists if and only if

$$(\gamma_G + \eta)\left(1 - \frac{1}{\sum_i(\gamma_i + \eta)}\right) = \gamma_G + \eta - 0.5 - 0.5\frac{\gamma_G - \gamma_B}{\sum_i(\gamma_i + \eta)} < \gamma_G$$

or if

$$\eta - 0.5 < 0.5\frac{\gamma_G - \gamma_B}{\sum_i(\gamma_i + \eta)}$$

of γ_i at a cost $K > 0$. Then, whenever $\gamma = \gamma_G$, the owner-manager would want to disclose her certified information if outside investors believe that the value of assets in place is strictly less than $(\gamma_G + \eta)/(1 + 2K) - \eta$. Indeed, following disclosure the owner-manager can then get financing of 0.5 in return for a stake of $0.5/(\gamma_G + \eta)$ and obtain a payoff of $\gamma_G + \eta - 0.5 - K$, while if she does not disclose her information she gets no more than γ_G (under an inefficient separating equilibrium) or $(\gamma_G + \eta)[1 - (0.5 + K)/(\gamma_G + \eta)] = \gamma_G + \eta - 0.5 - K$ (under an efficient pooling equilibrium). In other words, by disclosing the value of assets in place, the owner-manager can overcome the undervaluation problem in the Myers and Majluf model.

When $\gamma = \gamma_B$, however, it is not in the interest of the firm to disclose that outside investors may be overvaluing assets in place, so that no voluntary disclosure of information takes place in that event. But rational investors can infer as much information from the firm's equity issue decisions as from the firm's disclosure actions, and here the firm's decision not to disclose its information when $\gamma = \gamma_B$ inevitably reveals its type.

To summarize, when the firm is able to certify its private information about assets in place at sufficiently low cost, then the unique equilibrium outcome is for the firm to disclose good information, to always invest in the new project, and to raise new funding by issuing equity at fair terms.

5.1.3   Too Much Disclosure

It is tempting to conclude from the preceding discussion that efficiency is always improved by making disclosure possible (say, by introducing a new information-certification technology). However, since certification is costly, it would be more efficient to have a pooling equilibrium. Yet if the technology were available, the firm might want to use it to prevent a pooling equilibrium. Indeed, a firm with assets in place worth γ_G might want to disclose its private information about the value of these assets so as to obtain better terms for the equity issue. More precisely, as long as certification costs are lower than the subsidy to investors [which is equal to $0.5 \, (\gamma_G - \gamma_B)/(\sum_i (\gamma_i + \eta))$], in a pooling equilibrium, the firm would want to certify the value of its asset γ_G.

It is only against a separating-equilibrium situation that disclosure is welfare enhancing. In such a situation, certification by type G has no impact on the payoff of type B, so that it occurs if and only if it is efficient. All in all, then, there is too much disclosure in this model, even if disclosure is voluntary. A mandatory disclosure law would only make things worse here.

5.1.4   Unraveling and the Full Disclosure Theorem

One striking conclusion emerging from the analysis of this simple model is that (when certification costs are not too high) the firm ends up revealing all private information in equilibrium. In other words, the firm is unable to exploit its informational advantage when it can credibly disclose this information. An obvious question is whether this result extends to more general settings.

A central result in the literature on disclosure of information (due to Grossman and Hart (1980), Grossman (1981), and Milgrom (1981a)) is that when certification is costless ($K = 0$), there is full disclosure of information in equilibrium under very general conditions. In particular, the full-disclosure theorem holds not just with two types, but with any number of types. The basic logic behind this full-disclosure theorem is as follows.

Suppose that assets in place can now take N different values, $\gamma_i \in \Gamma = \{\gamma_1, \gamma_2, \ldots, \gamma_N\}$, where $\gamma_1 < \gamma_2 < \ldots < \gamma_N$. Since outside investors have only a probability distribution over all possible values γ_i, the expected market value $\bar{\gamma}$ is strictly less than γ_N (unless the probability distribution is degenerate). As a result, type γ_N has a strict incentive to disclose so as to eliminate the market's undervaluation of assets in place.

Hence, if the firm does not disclose any information, outside investors are able to infer that assets in place are worth at most γ_{N-1} and probably less than that. This downward revision in market expectations in turn prompts type γ_{N-1} to disclose also, so that no disclosure of information leads outside investors to believe that assets in place are worth only γ_{N-2}. This logic can be repeated for types γ_{N-2}, γ_{N-3}, and so on.

To complete the induction argument, suppose that some type $i > 1$ does not disclose. Consider the highest such type, say, type $j \geq i$. By disclosing, type j could obtain funding at actuarially fair terms. By not disclosing, type j is pooled with at least type 1, for whom disclosing is a weakly dominated strategy. But then type j gets financing at worse than actuarially fair terms, so that type j is strictly better off disclosing its type.

Note that we have heavily relied on the assumption that disclosure involves no costs ($K = 0$) to obtain this rather striking result. Of course, if K is very high, then disclosure may not pay even for type N. In that case, the firm's problem reduces to a signaling game akin to that analyzed in Chapter 3. With intermediate values of K, however, partial disclosure can obtain. To see this possibility, take, for example, $\gamma_i \in \{\gamma_1, \gamma_2, \gamma_3\}$ with $\gamma_1 < \gamma_2 < \gamma_3$, but $\gamma_2 - \gamma_1$ small relative to $\gamma_3 - \gamma_2$. Then the incentive for type 3 to disclose is much higher than for type 2. We then obtain disclosure for all types above a given level γ_i and no disclosure for lower types. This simple dichotomy obtains because the net incentive to disclose increases with γ_i.

As hinted at earlier, the full-disclosure theorem has implications for mandatory-disclosure laws. If all private information is already disclosed voluntarily, then mandatory-disclosure laws are at best superfluous. More-over, they may be harmful to the extent that they may force firms to dis-close totally irrelevant information. Perhaps a more important implication of this result and its underlying logic is that it suggests that "privacy" laws, such as the right to keep one's health history private, may be ineffective if they do not also punish voluntary disclosure of this information. In other words, if any healthy employee is allowed to volunteer the information of her good health to her employer by providing an updated medical exami-nation, then employees with health problems get no protection at all from any privacy laws. The only way to enforce privacy in that case would be to allow individuals to forge health certificates and to prevent courts from punishing such forgery, even if private contracts explicitly were to allow for such punishments!

5.1.5   Generalizing the Full-Disclosure Theorem

How general is the full-disclosure theorem? We have shown so far that it holds for an arbitrary number of types when disclosure is costless and when it is common knowledge that the firm knows its type γ_i. Would the result still hold if, for example, the firm did not know its type perfectly but knew only that it belongs to a subset of all possible types? Okuno-Fujiwara, Postlewaite, and Suzumura (1990) have investigated this issue. They provide two sufficient conditions under which full disclosure obtains, as well as examples where it fails when any of these conditions are not satisfied. Their full-disclosure theorem essentially generalizes as much as is possible the underlying unraveling logic outlined previously. The main interest of their result lies in the identification of two conditions, which in fact are almost necessary in the sense that examples where either of the conditions does not hold give rise to partial or no disclosure in equilibrium.

Let $\pi(\gamma_i, b)$ be the manager's equilibrium payoff when the true value of the firm's assets is γ_i but outside investors have belief b about this value.

Beliefs are (possibly degenerate) probability distributions over Γ [so that, for each b, calling $b(\gamma_i)$ the probability that the value of the firm's assets is γ_i under belief b, we have $b(\gamma_1) + b(\gamma_2) + \ldots + b(\gamma_N) = 1$]. Beliefs may be influenced (through Bayesian updating) by certified statements that the manager sends. These certified statements are assumed to be subsets of Γ, and for each γ_i, the manager has access to a set of certified statements that all include γ_i. In other words, the manager can certify with more or less accuracy that the value of her assets is at least as high as γ_i or no greater than γ_i, but she cannot lie and announce that her true type is in a given subset when it is not. Okuno-Fujiwara, Postlewaite, and Suzumura (1990) define the following two conditions:

1. For any γ_i, the manager can certify to the market that her type is at least γ_i. More formally, the manager can send a certified statement whose minimum element is γ_i.

2. For any belief b, consider belief b' that first-order stochastically dominates b: that is, for all γ_i,

$$\sum_{\gamma_j \leq \gamma_i} b'(\gamma_j) \leq \sum_{\gamma_j \leq \gamma_i} b(\gamma_j)$$

where a strict inequality holds for at least one γ_i. Then $\pi(\gamma_i, b') > \pi(\gamma_i, b)$.

Condition 1 says that the set of certifiable statements is rich enough to allow the manager to prove that the assets in place are worth at least their true value. Condition 2 is a monotonicity condition on beliefs, which says that the manager's payoff is higher when market beliefs are more optimistic about the value of the assets of the firm.

We have argued that, following a statement $c \subseteq \Gamma$, outside investors use Bayes' rule in order to revise their beliefs from b to $b(c)$. Okuno-Fujiwara, Postlewaite, and Suzumura (1990) also define beliefs to be *skeptical* if, following a statement c, updated beliefs $b(c)$ put full probability weight on the lowest element of c.

In this setup, they establish the following full-disclosure theorem: *Under conditions 1 and 2, the equilibrium involves full revelation of information and skeptical market beliefs.*

This theorem can be proved in three steps:

• First, one can rule out incomplete disclosure in equilibrium (which is itself incompatible with skeptical beliefs). Indeed, incomplete disclosure means that there exist several types of manager sending the same certified statement c. Consider the highest type of manager who is to be pooled with some other type(s). By condition 1, she could separate from such type(s) by sending a certified statement with her true type as lowest element of the statement. She would then be either fully separated or pooled with higher types than hers. In any case, by condition 2, she would have strictly raised her payoff. Thus there does not exist a partial-disclosure equilibrium.

• Consider next a full-disclosure equilibrium where there exists a report c (which might or might not be sent with positive probability in equilibrium) for which the associated equilibrium belief is not skeptical. In this case, it would be in the interest of the lowest type included in c to deviate and send this report: she would thereby strictly raise her equilibrium, full-revelation payoff, because she would have generated beliefs that first-order stochastically dominate the (correct) equilibrium belief. Thus there does not exist an equilibrium without skeptical beliefs.

• Finally, it is clear that it is an equilibrium for each type to send a report with one's true type as lowest element, and for investors to anticipate this behavior, that is, to have skeptical beliefs.

5.2   Voluntary Nondisclosure and Mandatory-Disclosure Laws

If the conditions of the above full-disclosure theorem always held in practice, then mandatory-disclosure laws would be redundant. We begin this section by showing that when either or both of the conditions of their full-disclosure theorem do not hold, then there may be only partial disclosure in equilibrium. We then proceed by analyzing the manager's incentives to acquire costly information in the first place when this information may be wasted ex post through voluntary disclosure. Finally, we close this section by showing that an implicit assumption behind the full-disclosure theorem is that the informed party is always on one side of the transaction. That is, the informed party is always a buyer or always a seller. If, however, the informed party is sometimes a buyer and sometimes a seller, then full disclosure breaks down even when both conditions of the theorem hold.

5.2.1 Two Examples of No Disclosure or Partial Voluntary Disclosure

Although conditions 1 and 2 are only sufficient conditions, they appear to be the right conditions, since the full-disclosure result easily breaks down in examples where either one of them does not hold. To see this point, consider the following two examples, where in turn conditions 1 and 2 are not satisfied.

Example 1   In this example the manager may not know her true type. In other words, with positive probability the manager may be as uninformed as outside investors. If there are only two possible values for assets in place—γ is either γ_G or γ_B—then there are three types of managers in this example: those who know that $\gamma = \gamma_B$, those who know that $\gamma = \gamma_G$, and those who do not know anything. We denote that last manager type by $\gamma = \gamma_{GB}$. Thus, let the set of types be $\Gamma = \{\gamma_B, \gamma_{BG}, \gamma_G\}$, where $\gamma_B < \gamma_{BG} < \gamma_G$. This example satisfies condition 2, since the manager's payoff is monotonic in γ_i. But it violates condition 1. The reason is simply that it is not possible to prove one's ignorance, so that type γ_{BG} cannot certify that her type is at least γ_{BG}. As a result, the equilibrium is such that type γ_G discloses, but type γ_B is able to pool with type γ_{BG} (only, of course, as long as issuing equity is optimal for type γ_{BG}).

Example 2   This example is rather contrived within our simplified setting; based on an example from Okuno-Fujiwara, Postlewaite, and Suzumura (1990) it conveys its general idea, but does not do full justice to it. In this example, disclosure of information exogenously reduces the manager's payoff so that condition 2 is violated. In Okuno-Fujiwara, Postlewaite, and Suzumura (1990), disclosure reduces the manager's payoff because of the increased competition generated by the news that the firm has a high value of assets in place.[2] Here, keeping this story in reduced form, let $\Gamma = \{\gamma_B, \gamma_G\}$, with $\gamma_B < \gamma_G$, and assume that if type γ_G discloses her type, then her payoff

---

2. Concretely, consider a pharmaceutical company for which certifying that it has assets in place that are worth a lot means disclosing results on preliminary testing of a new wonder drug. In such a case, it is conceivable that, as a result of the disclosure, its future profits are reduced because of the increased future competition by other pharmaceutical companies that are working in parallel with this company. If competition is expected to be sufficiently fierce, the firm may well decide not to disclose its information (see, for example, Green and Scotchmer, 1995, on the issue of disclosure and patenting with sequential innovations).

drops from γ_G to $\gamma_G - \Delta$. Disclosure of type γ_G would, of course, improve the firm's financing terms and make the new investment profitable to undertake. But if disclosure leads to an excessive reduction in the value of assets in place (that is, if Δ is too large), a type-γ_G firm may well decide not to disclose. In a pooling equilibrium situation, disclosing leads to more favorable financing terms for the type-γ_G firm if $\gamma_G - \Delta > 0.5(\gamma_G + \gamma_B)$. This condition does not imply that disclosure will happen, however: if $\Delta > \eta - 0.5$, the loss of value on assets in place exceeds the net present value of the investment, so that a type-γ_G manager prefers not to disclose her type and not to invest in the new project even though this decision means passing up a valuable investment opportunity.

Example 1 identifies an important reason why full disclosure may not occur in equilibrium. If there is any doubt about whether the manager is at all informed, then full voluntary disclosure may not occur because managers who receive bad information can always claim that they are uninformed. Given that voluntary disclosure results in only partial disclosure, it appears that there may be a role for mandatory-disclosure laws in this case. Indeed, if mandatory-disclosure laws are effective, they may bring about full disclosure. There are, however, potentially two objections against this line of argument. First, it is not clear that full disclosure is desirable. Suppose that there are strictly positive disclosure costs ($K > 0$); then, as long as type γ_{BG} is willing to invest in the new positive-net-present-value project (in a situation where it might be pooled with type γ_B), there is nothing to be gained from full disclosure. Second, even if mandatory disclosure is desirable, it may not be effective. Indeed, if the manager is unable to prove that she is ignorant, how can a judge do so?

5.2.2   Incentives for Information Acquisition and the Role of Mandatory-Disclosure Laws

So far we have not found very compelling reasons for introducing mandatory-disclosure laws. The only possible justification we have found is that voluntary disclosure may only be partial when there is some uncertainty about whether the manager is informed or not. We shall pursue this line further here by asking what the source of this uncertainty might be. Specifically, we shall consider a stage prior to the information-disclosure stage where the manager can endogenously determine how much information she acquires.

Formally, this approach involves considering a model combining both moral hazard elements (how much information to acquire) and adverse selection elements (how to act on the basis of the information acquired). The model we shall analyze is a simplified version of Shavell (1994). In the information-acquisition stage we allow the manager to randomize over becoming informed about her type or not. If she randomizes, then her choice of probability p of acquiring information is private information. We also assume that information acquisition is costly and involves a cost $\psi > 0$.[3] To allow for the possibility that the information acquired by the manager is socially valuable, we let the manager's type affect the value of both the assets in place and a new investment opportunity. Thus we assume that $\gamma_G \geq \gamma_B$, and also that $\eta \in \{\eta_G, \eta_B\}$ with $\eta_G \geq \eta_B$. The information acquired by the manager then has positive (gross) social value whenever $\eta_G \geq 0.5$ and $\eta_B < 0.5$. We shall consider in turn two cases—the first, when the information has no social value, and the second, when the information has strictly positive social value.

5.2.2.1   When Information Acquisition Has Zero Gross Social Value

We first consider the manager's incentive for information acquisition under voluntary disclosure when $\eta_G \geq \eta_B \geq 0.5$. To see the effects of endogenous information acquisition in the first stage, it is important to bear in mind that in the information-disclosure stage the problem is essentially identical to Example 1. The manager has a positive incentive to discover her type here if outside investors believe that she is likely to be uninformed in the information-disclosure stage, for she can then hide behind type γ_{BG} whenever she learns that her true type is γ_B. Moreover, if she learns that her type is γ_G, she can surprise outside investors by disclosing this information and obtain better financing terms. These benefits must, of course, be balanced against the information-acquisition cost ψ. Also, these benefits are likely to be smaller the more outside investors believe that she is in fact informed. It thus appears that there may be some subtle feedback effects between outside investors' beliefs and the manager's incentive to acquire information.

As before, we suppose that outside investors form their beliefs rationally, and consequently we define the outcome of this game to be a perfect Bayesian equilibrium (PBE) where the manager's actions are a best

---

3. In practice, the certification process plays the role both of improving the manager's information and of credibly disclosing to the market information the manager may already possess, so that the acquisition and disclosure of information can also be thought of as a joint action.

response to investors' beliefs and investors form their beliefs using Bayes' rule given the manager's best response function. We begin by determining the manager's best response function. Suppose investors believe that the manager acquires information with probability p. Then, conditional on getting the information, the manager is of type γ_G with probability 0.5. In this case, she voluntarily discloses her type, obtains financing at actuarially fair terms, and invests in the new project. With equal probability, her type is γ_B, in which case she does not disclose her type, obtains funding at actuarially favorable terms, and invests in the new project.

How favorable the terms are depends on whether the manager has an incentive to invest in the new project when she remains uninformed. On the one hand, if she decides to invest even when she is uninformed, then type γ_B can hide behind type γ_{BG} and obtain better than actuarially fair terms. If, on the other hand, the manager prefers not to invest when uninformed, then type γ_B can obtain only actuarially fair terms. Indeed, by seeking investment funds and not disclosing her type she actually reveals her type, since type γ_{BG} does not want to raise funds.

Consider first the situation where the manager invests in the new project even when uninformed. Then outside investors' expectation of firm value conditional on no disclosure is

$$V_p = \frac{0.5(1-p)(\gamma_G + \eta_G) + 0.5(\gamma_B + \eta_B)}{1 - 0.5p}$$

Notice that $dV_p/dp = 0.25(\gamma_B + \eta_B - \gamma_G - \eta_G)/(1 - 0.5p)^2 < 0$. In words, the market value of the firm conditional on no disclosure is decreasing in the probability that the manager is informed. This result is quite intuitive: the less likely type γ_{BG} is, the more weight outside investors put on type γ_B when there is no disclosure. Given the market's conditional expectation V_p, the firm's cost of capital when the manager remains uninformed is given by

$$\frac{0.5}{V_p}\{0.5(\gamma_G + \eta_G + \gamma_B + \eta_B)\}$$

However, when the manager informs herself, the expected cost of capital is

$$0.5\left\{0.5 + \frac{0.5}{V_p}(\gamma_B + \eta_B)\right\} + \psi$$

Therefore, the manager decides to become informed (with positive probability) if and only if

$$0.5 + \frac{0.5}{V_p}(\gamma_B + \eta_B) + 2\psi \le \frac{0.5(\gamma_G + \eta_G + \gamma_B + \eta_B)}{V_p}$$

There, is therefore,

1. A (pure-strategy) PBE without information acquisition if and only if

$$\psi \ge \frac{\gamma_G + \eta_G - \gamma_B - \eta_B}{4(\gamma_G + \eta_G + \gamma_B + \eta_B)}$$

2. A (pure-strategy) PBE with information acquisition if and only if

$$\psi \le \frac{\gamma_G + \eta_G - \gamma_B - \eta_B}{4(\gamma_B + \eta_B)}$$

3. A mixed-strategy PBE if and only if

$$V_p = \frac{\gamma_G + \eta_G}{1 + 4\psi}$$

or if and only if

$$1 > p = \frac{(1 + 4\psi)(\gamma_G + \eta_G + \gamma_B + \eta_B) - 2(\gamma_G + \eta_G)}{(\gamma_G + \eta_G)4\psi} > 0$$

that is, if and only if

$$\frac{\gamma_G + \eta_G - \gamma_B - \eta_B}{4(\gamma_G + \eta_G + \gamma_B + \eta_B)} < \psi < \frac{\gamma_G + \eta_G - \gamma_B - \eta_B}{4(\gamma_B + \eta_B)}$$

We first conclude that when the cost of information acquisition ψ is high, there is a unique pure-strategy equilibrium with no information acquisition. When instead the cost of information acquisition falls below $(\gamma_G + \eta_G - \gamma_B - \eta_B)/[4(\gamma_B + \eta_B)]$, the manager may acquire information with positive probability. There is a unique full-information equilibrium when the cost of information acquisition falls below $(\gamma_G + \eta_G - \gamma_B - \eta_B)/[4(\gamma_G + \eta_G + \gamma_B + \eta_B)]$. In other words, as soon as the cost of information acquisition is sufficiently low, the manager has a strict incentive to acquire information, and there is then too much information acquisition in equilibrium. Interestingly, when ψ falls below $(\gamma_G + \eta_G - \gamma_B - \eta_B)/$ $[4(\gamma_G + \eta_G + \gamma_B + \eta_B)]$, the manager's attempt to take advantage of her private information fails, and the cost of information acquisition is completely wasted. The reason is that with full information acquisition ex ante there is also unraveling and full disclosure ex post.

To summarize, when $\eta_G \geq \eta_B \geq 0.5$, equilibria with voluntary disclosure tend to induce excessive information acquisition. Only when the information acquisition cost is high is the social optimum attained. There is, however, a simple way of restoring efficiency here. It suffices to adopt a mandatory-disclosure law, that is, to threaten to punish the manager *for failing to disclose any information she might have acquired.* Then the manager obtains no return from information acquisition. But, as noted before, mandatory-disclosure laws may be ineffective here if it is difficult to prove that the manager is informed.

5.2.2.2   When Information Acquisition Has Positive Gross Social Value

Consider now the manager's incentive for information acquisition under voluntary disclosure when $\eta_G \geq 0.5 \geq \eta_B$. Two cases have to be distinguished: one where it is efficient to invest when uninformed about the value of η, that is, when $0.5(\eta_G + \eta_B) > 0.5$; the other when it is not worth investing, that is, when $0.5(\eta_G + \eta_B) < 0.5$.

In the second case, the equilibrium outcome is easy to see: when the manager is uninformed, she does not invest in the new project; therefore, once information has been acquired, type γ_B cannot "hide" behind type γ_{BG}. The net value of information acquisition for the manager, computed ex ante, is then $0.5(\eta_G - 0.5) - \psi$. This also happens to be the net social value of information. Therefore, in the subcase where $0.5(\eta_G + \eta_B) < 0.5$, the manager has the correct incentives for information acquisition under voluntary disclosure. Note that in this subcase a mandatory disclosure law would not make any difference.

In the former subcase, where $0.5(\eta_G + \eta_B) > 0.5$, the manager's net value of information is at most $0.5(0.5 - \eta_B) - \psi$: the value of finding out that it is not worth investing if the manager's type is γ_B. In this case, the manager also has the correct incentives for information acquisition under voluntary disclosure. A mandatory disclosure law here would again make no difference. But, if the manager prefers to invest when her type is γ_B, then there may be too much or too little information acquisition relative to the social optimum. A type-γ_B manager here invests if and only if

$$(\gamma_B + \eta_B)\left(1 - \frac{0.5}{V_p}\right) \geq \gamma_B$$

Given that $\eta_B \leq 0.5$, the manager would not have an incentive to invest if $p = 1$, since then

$$(\gamma_B + \eta_B)\left(1 - \frac{0.5}{V_1}\right) = \gamma_B + \eta_B - 0.5 \leq \gamma_B$$

But the manager may have a strict incentive to invest if, at $p = 0$,

$$(\gamma_B + \eta_B)\left(1 - \frac{0.5}{V_0}\right) = \gamma_B + \eta_B - \frac{\gamma_B + \eta_B}{\gamma_G + \eta_G + \gamma_B + \eta_B} \geq \gamma_B$$

There is then a mixed-strategy equilibrium given by

$$V_p = 0.5 \frac{\gamma_B + \eta_B}{\eta_B}$$

or

$$p = \frac{\eta_B(\gamma_G + \eta_G + \gamma_B + \eta_B) - (\gamma_B + \eta_B)}{\eta_B(\gamma_G + \eta_G) - 0.5(\gamma_B + \eta_B)}$$

In this mixed-strategy equilibrium the manager acquires too little information relative to the social optimum when $0.5(0.5 - \eta_B) > \psi$, and too much when $0.5(0.5 - \eta_B) < \psi$. These distortions can again be corrected by imposing a mandatory-disclosure law, since under such a law the mixed-strategy equilibrium breaks down, and the type-γ_B manager strictly prefers not to invest, so that the manager's incentives for information acquisition are aligned with social incentives.

5.2.2.3   Conclusion

We have found that, when the manager can acquire information at a cost, there often tends to be too much (but at times too little) information acquisition under voluntary disclosure. In this setup, mandatory-disclosure laws, which threaten to punish managers for failing to disclose any information they might have acquired, have been shown to correct these distortions and to lead to socially optimal information acquisition. This finding assumes, however, that such laws are effective, that is, that managers cannot succeed in falsely claiming to be uninformed.

5.2.3 No Voluntary Disclosure When the Informed Party Can Be Either a Buyer or a Seller

As we show in this section, limited voluntary disclosure of information can easily result when the informed party is not always on the same side of a transaction, as we have assumed so far by letting the informed party always be a seller of equity. We shall explore this insight by considering information disclosure by traders in financial markets. Financial market regulations sometimes require some investors to disclose their trades. For example, corporate managers and insiders in the United States (investors who own more than 5 percent of a firm's stock) must disclose their trades in the firm's stock.

We provide a simple example adapted from Fishman and Hagerty (1995) illustrating how informed traders who may decide to buy or sell a stock have little or no incentive to voluntarily disclose their information or their trades. Therefore, mandatory-disclosure rules may be required to make that information public. We show, however, that these rules may not necessarily benefit uninformed traders.

Consider the secondary market for shares of the firm discussed earlier, and suppose for simplicity that there are no new investment opportunities available to the firm. Recall that the final value per share of the firm is uncertain and may be either 1, with probability γ, or 0, with probability $1 - \gamma$. Therefore, the current expected value of a share in the secondary market, assuming away discounting, is γ. The manager of the firm may have private information about the expected final value of shares. With probability β she learns whether the shares are worth $\gamma_G > \gamma$ or $\gamma_B < \gamma$. Uninformed shareholders, however, know only that $\gamma = \gamma_G$ with probability 0.5. Since they are all assumed to be risk neutral, they value each share at $0.5(\gamma_G + \gamma_B) = \gamma$ ex ante.

Suppose that there are two trading dates, $t = 1$ and $t = 2$, and that each shareholder can buy or sell only one share per trading date. The example can be adapted to allow for trading of a finite number of shares at each trading date. What is important for the example is that trades are spread over the two trading dates. Although we do not model them explicitly here, there are good reasons why this would be the case in practice: most importantly, concentration of trades in a single trading period would result in both higher price risk and more adverse terms of trade.

Suppose, in addition, that trading in the secondary market is anonymous and that the size of the manager's trades is small relative to the market, so that she cannot move the price. With probability $(1 - \beta)$, the manager is uninformed. She is then assumed to be equally likely to buy or sell one share for liquidity or portfolio-rebalancing reasons. When she is informed, however, she sells one share at date 1 when she learns that the final expected value is γ_B and buys one share when she learns that the final expected value is γ_G. Her net payoff from trading at date 1 (her "informational rent") when she is informed is then

$$0.5(\gamma_G - \gamma) + 0.5(\gamma - \gamma_B) = 0.5(\gamma_G - \gamma_B) \equiv 0.5\Delta\gamma$$

Therefore, if she does not disclose her information or her trade at date 1, the manager can expect to get a total payoff of $2\beta 0.5\Delta\gamma$. If she discloses her trade at date 1, however, the price at which she can trade at date 2 will move against her. If she discloses a "buy," the price of shares in the secondary market will rise from γ to

$$\beta\gamma_G + (1 - \beta)\gamma$$

The price moves to this level because uninformed traders update their beliefs that the underlying expected value of shares is γ_G following a "buy" by the informed party. They reason that the manager could have bought a share because she was informed (with prior probability β) or because she was uninformed but repositioned her portfolio [with prior probability $(1 - \beta)$]. The informed manager's payoff from trading at date 2 is then only

$$(1 - \beta)(\gamma_G - \gamma)$$

Similarly, if she discloses a "sell," the price will fall from γ to

$$\beta\gamma_B + (1 - \beta)\gamma$$

and her payoff from trading at date 2 is only

$$(1 - \beta)(\gamma - \gamma_B)$$

Clearly, an informed manager would prefer not to disclose her date-1 trade. When her trade was a "buy," she would lose $\beta(\gamma_G - \gamma)$, and when it was a "sell," she would lose $\beta(\gamma - \gamma_B)$. If her private information were verifiable, she would also not want to disclose her information. Often, however, private information is not verifiable, and only trades are. It is for this reason that regulation concentrates on disclosure requirements of trades.

What about the disclosure incentives of an uninformed manager? Ironically, uninformed managers have a weak incentive to disclose their trades here. Indeed, if their disclosure is taken as news by the market, they stand to gain from the resulting price manipulation. Suppose, for example, that an uninformed manager discloses a date-1 "buy." This could result in a price increase, which the manager knows to be unjustified. She could then gain from this price move by selling one share at date 2. She knows the share's expected value is γ, but she would be able to sell it for a higher price. Of course, in a perfect Bayesian equilibrium this could not be the case: since only uninformed managers would disclose, disclosure would simply be ignored by the market.

There are two reasons why informed managers cannot be induced to voluntarily disclose their trades here. First, and foremost, the market here cannot punish nondisclosure, since it does not know the nature of the information. If the market interprets nondisclosure as the manager withholding bad news, then the manager can profit by buying shares in the secondary market, and vice versa by selling shares. The second reason why the manager does not disclose information voluntarily is that her first trade does not move the market. Suppose that trading in the secondary market was not anonymous; then any party trading with the manager at date 1 would only accept to sell a share at price $\beta\gamma_G + (1 - \beta)\gamma$ and to buy a share from the manager at price $\beta\gamma_B + (1 - \beta)\gamma$. If the manager had no choice but to trade at those prices, she would be indifferent between disclosing or not disclosing her first trade.

If there is no voluntary disclosure of trades by the informed manager, can a case be made for mandatory disclosure? Note first that mandatory disclosure can be justified here only as a way of protecting uninformed traders. Indeed, in this simple example, trading under asymmetric information does not induce any distortions. It affects only the distribution of value across shareholders. In a richer setup, however, one can imagine that some traders' informational advantage might adversely affect liquidity and investment. Disclosure policy might then be directed at minimizing such investment or liquidity distortions. It is conceivable that this might require protecting uninformed investors.

Interestingly, even if the objective of protecting uninformed investors is taken for granted, there is not always a case for introducing mandatory-disclosure rules in this simple example. That is, there may be situations where a mandatory-disclosure rule actually benefits the manager at the expense of other shareholders. How can such situations arise? We have shown that an informed manager is always worse off as a result of the disclosure of her date-1 trade. Therefore, if there is a gain to be obtained from a mandatory-disclosure rule, it would have to be for uninformed managers. As we have hinted, uninformed managers actually gain under mandatory disclosure. They obtain an informational advantage because they know that the price move following the disclosure of their trade was not warranted. Following disclosure of a "buy," uninformed managers obtain a net expected gain from a date-2 "sell" of

$$\beta(\gamma_G - \gamma)$$

and following disclosure of a "sell," they obtain a net expected gain by buying a share at date 2 of

$$\beta(\gamma - \gamma_B)$$

Thus, on average, an uninformed manager gains $(\beta/2)(\gamma_G - \gamma_B)$ under mandatory disclosure, but an informed manager can expect to lose $(\beta/2)(\gamma_G - \gamma_B)$. The net gain from mandatory disclosure is therefore

$$-\beta\left[\frac{\beta}{2}(\gamma_G - \gamma_B)\right] + (1-\beta)\left[\frac{\beta}{2}(\gamma_G - \gamma_B)\right]$$

In other words, if the manager is less likely to be informed than uninformed (that is, $\beta < \frac{1}{2}$), it is she, and not uninformed investors, who gains from a mandatory-disclosure rule.

This example brings out the close connection between disclosure and market manipulation. Here mandatory disclosure may facilitate market manipulation by increasing the credibility of the disclosed information. If disclosure was voluntary, rational uninformed participants would simply ignore the information, since they understand that only an uninformed manager would have an incentive to disclose.[4]

Let us end this subsection by stressing that Fishman and Hagerty's example is yet another illustration of the subtle effects of mandatory-disclosure rules. Their analysis and Shavell's actually do not make a strong case for mandatory-disclosure rules. A more recent article by Admati and

---

4. Interestingly, for some parameter values, one can check that mandatory disclosure could actually lead to an extreme form of market manipulation here, where the *informed* manager would begin by selling when observing γ_G so as to be able to buy shares back on the cheap.

Pfleiderer (2000) makes a stronger case. They assume that disclosure of information involves transaction costs and that there is an informational externality on other firms. In other words, disclosure is partly a public good. Since individual firms do not capture the full social informational value of disclosure and since they must pay the full cost, there will generally be underprovision of information in equilibrium. To improve the production of socially valuable information, Admati and Pfleiderer argue that mandatory-disclosure rules may be required.

5.3   Costly Disclosure and Debt Financing

We close this chapter with a treatment of an influential research line on financial engineering, the *costly state verification* (CSV) approach. The CSV perspective starts from the premise that when disclosure (or verification) of a firm's performance (profits or earnings) is costly, the design of financial contracts may be driven to a large extent by the objective of minimizing disclosure (or audit) costs. A striking and central result of the CSV approach to financial engineering is that it is generally optimal to commit to a partial, state-contingent disclosure rule. What is more, under some admittedly strong conditions, the optimal rule is implemented by a standard debt contract for which there is no disclosure of the debtor's performance as long as debts are honored, but there is full disclosure or verification in the event of default. Viewed from the CSV perspective, the main function of bankruptcy institutions is to establish a clear inventory of all assets and liabilities and to assess the net value of the firm.

The CSV approach to financial contracting considers a slightly different disclosure problem than we have seen so far in this chapter. The informed party now has to make a decision whether to certify its information to be able to disclose it credibly.

The financial contracting problem considered by Townsend (1979) and Gale and Hellwig (1985) involves two risk-neutral agents, an entrepreneur with an investment project but no investment funds, and a financier with unlimited funds. In its simplest form the contracting problem is as follows: The fixed investment requires a setup cost of $I > 0$ at $t = 0$ and generates random cash flows at $t = 1$ of $\pi \in [0, +\infty)$, with density function $f(\pi)$. The entrepreneur observes realized cash flows and can credibly disclose π to the investor only by incurring a certification cost $K > 0$. The contract-design problem is to specify in advance which cash-flow realizations should be certified and which not.

It is easy to see that absent any certification the entrepreneur will never be able to raise funding for the project. Indeed, the rational investor then anticipates that at $t = 1$ the entrepreneur will always pretend that $\pi = 0$ to avoid making any repayments to the investor.

One way, of course, of guaranteeing financing is to always verify or audit the realized return of the project. Securities regulations mandating the periodic disclosure of firm performance can be seen as instances of such systematic verification of performance. Interestingly, the CSV perspective highlights the potential inefficiency of such regulations. Indeed, we shall explain that such systematic disclosure rules tend to impose excessive disclosure costs.

The set of contracts from which the contracting parties can choose is described as follows: In general terms, the contract will specify whether an audit should take place following the realization of cash flows and what fraction of realized cash flows the entrepreneur should pay back to the investor. More formally, we can reduce the set of relevant contracts by appealing to the *revelation principle* (see Chapter 2).

Thus, following the realization of π, the entrepreneur (truthfully) reveals π, and the contract can specify the probability $p(\pi) \in [0, 1]$ of certifying (or auditing) cash flows. When there is no certification, the contract can only specify a repayment $r(\pi)$. But, when there is certification of cash flows the contract can specify a repayment contingent on both the announced cash flow $\hat{\pi}$ and the (true) cash flow certified by the audit π, $r(\hat{\pi}, \pi)$. Application of the revelation principle will, of course, ensure that in equilibrium the entrepreneur always truthfully reports cash flows: $\hat{\pi} = \pi$, for all π. Nevertheless, the contract will specify a different repayment when $\hat{\pi} \neq \pi$ as a threat (which will never be exercised in equilibrium) to provide incentives to the entrepreneur to tell the truth. It is easy to see that, since this threat is not exercised in equilibrium, it is efficient to provide maximum incentives to tell the truth by maximizing the punishment for lying and setting $r(\hat{\pi}, \pi) = \pi$ whenever $\hat{\pi} \neq \pi$.[5] Under such a threat there is no benefit from falsely reporting a cash flow that triggers an audit for sure. Consequently, such

---

5. Since the entrepreneur has no resources to start with, it is impossible to induce a repayment in excess of π.

cash-flow realizations are always truthful, and we can denote the repayment for audited cash flows simply as $r_a(\pi)$.

As we already alluded to, a central result of the CSV approach to financial contracting is that standard debt contracts may be optimal financial contracts. This result only obtains, however, under fairly strong assumptions. One critical assumption, in particular, is that financial contracts can specify only deterministic certification policies:

ASSUMPTION: For all π, $p(\pi) \in \{0, 1\}$.

In other words, commitment to random audits is not feasible. We now show how under this assumption a standard debt contract is an optimal financial contract.

Assuming that the project has a positive net present value, the optimal contracting problem reduces to a problem of minimizing expected audit costs, subject to meeting the entrepreneur's incentive constraints for truth telling, and the financier's participation constraint:

$$\min_{p(\pi),r(\pi),r_a(\pi)} \quad K\int_0^{+\infty} p(\pi)f(\pi)\,d\pi$$

subject to:

(1) the investor's individual-rationality constraint:

$$\int_0^{+\infty} p(\pi)[r_a(\pi) - K]f(\pi)d\pi + \int_0^{+\infty}[1 - p(\pi)]r(\pi)f(\pi)d\pi \geq I$$

(2) a set of incentive constraints:

$r_a(\pi_1) \leq r(\pi_2)$ for all $\pi_1 \neq \pi_2$ such that $p(\pi_1) = 1$ and $p(\pi_2) = 0$

$r(\pi_1) = r(\pi_2) = r$ for all $\pi_1 \neq \pi_2$ such that $p(\pi_1) = 0 = p(\pi_2)$

and

(3) a set of limited wealth constraints:

$r_a(\pi) \leq \pi$ for all π such that $p(\pi) = 1$

$r(\pi) \leq \pi$ for all π such that $p(\pi) = 0$

The incentive constraints have a particularly simple structure. For any two cash-flow realizations that do not require certification, the repayment to the financier has to be the same. Obviously, if this were not the case, the

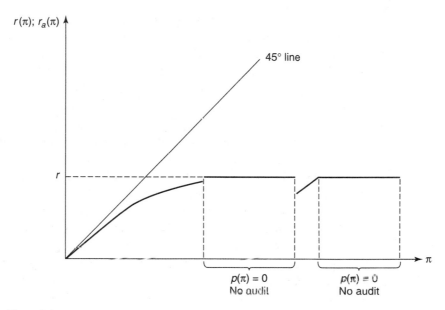

Figure 5.1
An Incentive-Compatible Repayment Schedule

entrepreneur would want to lie about realized cash flows and announce the
one with the lower repayment. Similarly, a cash-flow realization π_1 that
requires certification should not entail a higher repayment $r_a(\pi_1)$ than the
repayment for a cash-flow realization π_2 that does not involve certification
$r(\pi_2)$. If that were the case, then the entrepreneur would want to lie about
the realization of π_1 and thus make a smaller repayment. The set of incentive and limited wealth constraints thus imposes sweeping limits on the set
of feasible contracts. As Figure 5.1 illustrates, all feasible contracts have the
two features that repayments outside the certification subset must be independent of realized cash flows, and that repayments in the certification
subset must be less than those outside the set.

Basically, the only dimensions along which the financial contract can be
varied are (1) the certification subset and (2) the size of the repayment in
the certification subset. Characterizing the optimal contract can be achieved
thanks to the following observations. First, it is easy to see that any feasible contract must include the cash-flow realization $\pi = 0$ in the audit subset.
If this were not the case, then the entrepreneur could always claim to have
a cash flow of zero, thus avoiding an audit as well as any repayments to
the financier. Second, it is also straightforward to see that any contract that

minimizes expected audit costs must be such that for any cash-flow realization π in the audit subset, $r_a(\pi) = \min\{\pi, r\}$. This result can be seen as follows. Suppose first that $r < \pi$. Then incentive compatibility precludes any $r_a(\pi) > r$, as we have already noted. But a contract with $r_a(\pi) < r$ would involve inefficiently high audit costs. Indeed, it would be possible to raise $r_a(\pi)$ to r without violating any incentive or wealth constraints. Doing so would relax the financier's participation constraint by generating higher expected repayments and thus would make it possible to slightly reduce the audit subset (and therefore expected audit costs) without violating the participation constraint. Suppose now that $\pi < r$. Then any contract such that $r_a(\pi) < \pi$ would be inefficient for the same reason. Figure 5.2 modifies the repayment schedule of Figure 5.1 to take advantage of these observations.

The third and final observation is that any contract with a disconnected audit subset $[0, \hat{\pi}] \cup [\underline{\pi}, \overline{\pi}]$ (with $\hat{\pi} < \underline{\pi}$) as depicted in Figure 5.3 would be inefficient, since then an obvious improvement is available by shifting to a connected subset with the same probability mass (see Figure 5.4). Such a shift would make it possible to raise r, and therefore also to raise expected audit repayments $r_a(\pi)$. Once again, the higher expected repayments thus generated would relax the participation constraint and enable a small saving of expected audit costs.

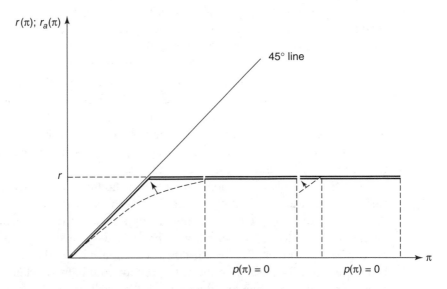

Figure 5.2
Incentive-Compatible Repayment Schedule with $r_a(\pi) = \min\{\pi, r\}$

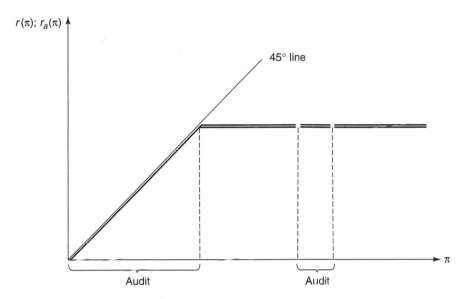

Figure 5.3
Inefficient Audit Region

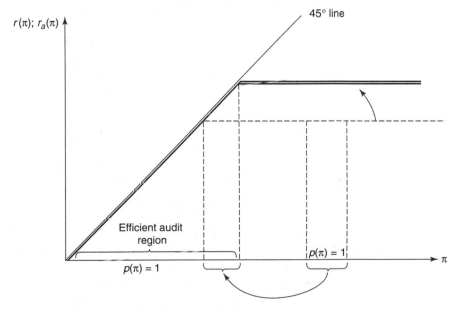

Figure 5.4
Efficient Audits

Piecing all these observations together, we are able to conclude that the uniquely optimal financial contract, which minimizes expected audit costs, is such that (1) there is a single connected audit region $\Pi_a = [0, \bar{\pi}]$, with $\bar{\pi} < \infty$; (2) over this region audit repayments are $r_a(\pi) = \pi$; and (3) for cash flows $\pi > \bar{\pi}$, which are not audited, the repayment is $r = \bar{\pi}$. The unique cutoff $\bar{\pi}$ is given by the solution to the participation constraint

$$\int_0^{\bar{\pi}} (\pi - K)f(\pi)d\pi + [1 - F(\bar{\pi})]r = I$$

and expected audit costs are $F(\bar{\pi})K$.

In other words, the optimal financial contract is equivalent to a *standard debt contract* with face value $\bar{\pi}$, which also gives the creditor the right to all "liquidation proceeds" π in the event of default. Under this interpretation K is a fixed bankruptcy cost that must be borne to be able to obtain any liquidation proceeds.

That standard debt contracts have the property that they minimize expected certification or disclosure costs is an insightful and important observation. It sheds light on another desirable property of debt contracts, and it highlights the potential costs of mandatory-disclosure regulations that require equal disclosure of performance whether good or bad. Interestingly, the CSV approach highlights the benefits of more fine-tuned disclosure regulations, which would call for more disclosure when performance is bad.

It is important to bear in mind, however, that the optimality of standard debt contracts in a CSV framework only obtains under strong assumptions. As Gale and Hellwig (1985) have shown, standard debt contracts are no longer optimal when the entrepreneur is risk averse (see Question 19 in Chapter 14). Similarly, when random audit policies are introduced, standard debt is no longer optimal (see Mookherjee and Png, 1989).

Another important weakness of the CSV approach is that standard debt contracts are optimal only if the parties can commit to the audit policy specified in the contract at $t = 0$. If they cannot commit to the audit policy, they would not want to carry out the audit called for by the contract ex post, since to do so would be wasteful. Indeed, if the entrepreneur expects the audit to take place as specified in the contract, then she will always report cash-flow realizations truthfully. But if truthful reporting is anticipated, there is no point in carrying out the audit. Interestingly, the need for a commitment device could provide a justification for mandatory-disclosure rules, since such rules typically cannot be renegotiated by individual contracting parties.

Finally, the result that standard debt contracts are optimal financial contracts does not extend to slightly richer settings, where the firm may invest in more than one project, where the investment extends over more than one period, or in the presence of multiple financiers (see Gale and Hellwig, 1989; Chang, 1990; Webb, 1992; Winton, 1995).

5.4 Summary and Literature Notes

The private-but-certifiable-information paradigm is very useful and relevant for a wide range of applications, including health, innovation, auditing, and financial market trading. Under this variation of the adverse selection paradigm detailed in Chapter 2, the informed party is not allowed to claim to be of a type different from her true type: her only choice is between full disclosure, partial disclosure, and no disclosure of the truth. Such a paradigm has generated a key result, known as the "full-disclosure theorem," first established by Grossman and Hart (1980), Milgrom (1981a), and Grossman (1981), and subsequently generalized by Okuno-Fujiwara, Postlewaite, and Suzumura (1990). This result highlights that full disclosure obtains in equilibrium when the following four conditions are satisfied: (1) it is common knowledge that the informed party is indeed informed about her type: (2) the type space is one-dimensional, and types can be ranked monotonically in terms of payoffs of the informed party; (3) the informed party is able to send a certified message proving that her type is not below (resp. above) her true type; and (4) disclosure is costless. An important implication of this result is that when the conditions for full disclosure are met, one should not expect "privacy laws" to be very effective. Even if individuals have the right not to disclose parts of their personal history or to refuse undergoing a test, if they are likely to be drawn into disclosing this information voluntarily, then these privacy protections do not have much bite. To strengthen these laws one might also have to let individuals get away with *forging* certificates. Otherwise "good types" will want to voluntarily certify their types, thus inducing "worse types" to do so as well.

When all conditions for full disclosure are not met, voluntary disclosure is not going to be sufficient in general to generate all relevant public information. Mandatory-disclosure rules may then be desirable. Only a few formal analyses of the role of mandatory-disclosure rules as a supplement to deficient voluntary disclosure exist. Shavell (1994) and Fishman and Hagerty (1995) identify conditions when mandatory-disclosure rules may be desirable given that voluntary disclosure is incomplete. Interestingly, both analyses point out that when mandatory-disclosure laws are desirable they also tend to be difficult to enforce. One reason is that mandatory disclosure is generally desirable in situations where the informed party can pretend to be ignorant. But then it is much more difficult to prove that one is uninformed (or, for example, that one does not possess a weapon).

The last section of the chapter has detailed the *costly state verification* approach to optimal financial contracting. This approach focuses on a one-shot financing problem of an entrepreneur who privately observes the return of the project while the financier observes it only at a positive cost. Townsend (1979) and Gale and Hellwig (1985) have shown that the optimal financing mechanism, that is, the mechanism that minimizes expected verification costs, is a *standard debt contract,* under the following assumptions: (1) only deterministic contracts are possible; (2) both parties are risk neutral; and (3) the parties can commit in advance to undertaking the costly verification policy. These papers therefore provide an alternative justification to the optimality of debt contracts to the moral-hazard-based one due to Innes (1990), discussed in Chapter 4.

6 Multidimensional Incentive Problems

Most economic contracting problems cannot be easily reduced to pure one-dimensional adverse-selection or pure one-dimensional moral-hazard problems. Either they involve multidimensional characteristics or multiple tasks, or they combine both adverse-selection and moral-hazard features. This chapter illustrates how the pure cases of adverse selection and moral hazard can be extended to incorporate multidimensional aspects and how hidden-action and hidden-information considerations can be combined within a single framework. These extensions do not involve any fundamental reformulation of the general theory of contracting under asymmetric information. As will become clear, most extentions can be analyzed by adapting the methods outlined in previous chapters.

There are, obviously, many different ways of introducing multidimensional incentives into the standard frameworks. Indeed, many different extensions have already been explored in the literature—far too numerous to be all covered in this chapter. We shall explore only three of the most important extensions. The first introduces multidimensional aspects into the standard screening problem and the second into the standard moral-hazard problem. The third combines adverse selection and moral hazard in a simple way.

6.1 Adverse Selection with Multidimensional Types

The classic situation of adverse selection with multidimensional types is the multiproduct monopoly problem. This is the problem of any seller with some market power who sells at least two different goods. An extreme example of a multiproduct monopoly problem is that faced by a large supermarket or department store. A supermarket sells several thousand different items. It can offer quantity discounts on any one of these items and special deals on any bundle of them. So the optimal nonlinear pricing problem of a large supermarket is potentially very complex.

One approach to this problem might be to simply consider each good in isolation and determine a nonlinear price for that good separately. This would involve only a minor conceptual extension of the basic single-product monopoly problem. But the multiproduct monopolist may fail to maximize profits by taking this approach. Indeed, it is easy to construct examples where he would gain by bundling different goods together (and sell the bundle at a different price from the sum of the component parts). We shall provide one example later. This bundling option cannot be analyzed naturally as a one-dimensional screening problem; a full analysis requires a multidimensional extension of the basic theory considered in Chapter 2. Because such an extension can be technically rather involved, we begin by considering the simplest bundling problem, with two goods, and with one unit of each good only. We then proceed to analyze the multiunit case.

The bundling problem of a multiproduct monopoly was first analyzed by Adams and Yellen (1976). They consider a monopolist selling two different items, good 1 and good 2. The buyer's reservation values for each of the two goods are given by $(v_1, v_2) \geq 0$, and the costs of production of each good are $c_1 \geq 0$ and $c_2 \geq 0$. The seller does not know the true reservation values and has prior beliefs represented by the cumulative distribution function $F(v_1, v_2)$.

Note that this formulation excludes any complementarities in consumption. If such complementarities were present, there would be a natural reason for bundling the two products together. What is more interesting and surprising is that even in the absence of any complementarities the seller may gain by bundling the two products.

The seller has three different pricing strategies: (1) sell each good separately; (2) offer the two goods only as a bundle; and (3) sell either separately or bundled. We begin our discussion with an example, due to Adams and Yellen (1976), illustrating how the seller can benefit by selling the two goods either bundled or separately.

6.1.1 An Example Where Bundling Is Profitable

In this example $c_i = 0$, and the buyer may have four different characteristics, each with equal probability; that is, the reservation prices (v_1, v_2) may take four different values given in the following table:

State of Nature	v_1	v_2	Prob
A	90	10	$\frac{1}{4}$
B	80	40	$\frac{1}{4}$
C	40	80	$\frac{1}{4}$
D	10	90	$\frac{1}{4}$

It is easy to verify that, when selling each good separately, the seller maximizes expected profits by setting individual prices, $P_1 = P_2 = 80$. In this case, each good is sold with probability $\frac{1}{2}$, and expected profits are 80.

When offering the bundle only ("pure bundling"), the seller maximizes profits by setting the price of the bundle, P_b, at 100, at which it is sold with probability 1, thereby improving upon "no bundling." Finally, selling both separately and bundled, a strategy Adams and Yellen refer to as "mixed bundling," the optimal prices are $P_1 = P_2 = 90$, $P_b = 120$. This is the optimal strategy, since expected profits are then 105: the bundle is sold with probability $\frac{1}{2}$, and each good is sold individually with probability $\frac{1}{4}$.

Having established that bundling may be profitable, the next question is, How broad is the range of cases where bundling dominates? On the basis of this example, as well as others, Adams and Yellen conclude that mixed bundling tends to dominate selling each good separately whenever "the correlation coefficient linking an individual's valuation of one good to his valuation of the other good is not strongly positive." A more general characterization is given by McAfee, McMillan, and Whinston (1989), hereafter MMW.

6.1.2   When Is Bundling Optimal? A Local Analysis

Following MMW, we consider general environments where the cumulative distribution $F(v_1,v_2)$ representing the prior beliefs of the seller is continuously differentiable with support $[\underline{v}_1, \overline{v}_1] \times [\underline{v}_2, \overline{v}_2]$. Also, we define $G_i(v_i|v_j)$ [and $g_i(v_i|v_j)$] as the associated conditional cumulative distribution (and density) functions, and $H_i(v_i)$ [and $h_i(v_i)$] as the associated marginal distribution (and density) functions for $i = 1, 2$. Following MMW, we can distinguish between the "home bundling" case, where the buyer can "construct her own bundle" by buying each good separately, and the case where the seller can prevent the buyer from purchasing more than one good separately. In the first case the seller faces the constraint that $P_b \leq P_1 + P_2$. We assume here that home bundling is possible and let (P_1^*, P_2^*) be the monopoly prices under separate sales. When would the introduction of bundling raise profits above those obtained with separate monopoly pricing? A sufficient condition for bundling to dominate is easily obtained by asking whether a policy of introducing a bundle at price $P_b = P_1^* + P_2^*$ and selling good 2 at the slightly higher price $P_2 = P_2^* + \varepsilon$ ($\varepsilon > 0$) raises the seller's expected profits. Under such a bundling policy,

• All consumer types with $v_1 \geq P_1^*$ and $v_2 \leq P_2^*$ would consume good 1 only.

• All consumer types with $v_2 \geq P_2^* + \varepsilon$ and $v_1 \leq P_1^* - \varepsilon$ would consume good 2 only.

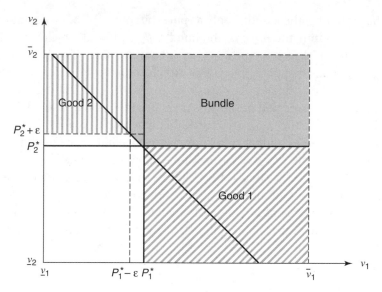

Figure 6.1
Mixed Bundling

• All consumer types with $v_1 + v_2 \geq P_1^* + P_2^*$, $v_2 \geq P_2^*$, and $v_1 \geq P_1^* - \varepsilon$ purchase the bundle (see Figure 6.1).

Notice that the introduction of a bundle at price $P_b = P_1^* + P_2^*$ and the increase in price for good 2 to $P_2 = P_2^* + \varepsilon$ affect neither the purchasing decisions of consumer types with $v_1 > P_1^*$ nor the price they end up paying. Any gain from introducing bundling must therefore be obtained from the consumer types with $v_1 < P_1^*$. The seller's profit from these consumer types as a function of ε is

$$\pi(\varepsilon) = \left(P_2^* + \varepsilon - c_2\right)\int_{\underline{v}_1}^{P_1^* - \varepsilon}\left[\int_{P_2^* + \varepsilon}^{\bar{v}_2} f(v_1, v_2)dv_2\right]dv_1$$

$$+ \left(P_1^* + P_2^* - c_1 - c_2\right)\int_{P_1^* - \varepsilon}^{P_1^*}\left[\int_{P_2^* + P_1^* - v_1}^{\bar{v}_2} f(v_1, v_2)dv_2\right]dv_1 \tag{6.1}$$

For ε small, this equation can be rewritten as

$$\pi(\varepsilon) = \left(P_2^* + \varepsilon - c_2\right)\int_{P_2^* + \varepsilon}^{\bar{v}_2}\left[\int_{\underline{v}_1}^{P_1^*} f(v_1, v_2)dv_1\right]dv_2$$

$$+ \left(P_1^* - c_1\right)\int_{P_1^* - \varepsilon}^{P_1^*}\left[\int_{P_2^*}^{\bar{v}_2} f(v_1, v_2)dv_2\right]dv_1$$

Intuitively, raising ε above 0 has two effects: (1) the usual monopoly trade-off between price and quantity, but limited to those buyers who consider buying good 2 or no good at all, because $v_1 < P_1^*$; and (2) an increase in the sale of good 1, bundled with good 2, for those buyers for whom v_1 is "just below" P_1^* while $v_2 > P_2^*$. The second effect is positive, so that bundling is attractive for the seller, provided the first effect is not too negative.

It is thus a sufficient condition for bundling to be profitable that the derivative of $\pi(\varepsilon)$ with respect to ε be positive at $\varepsilon = 0$, that is, that

$$\int_{P_2^*}^{\bar{v}_2}\left[\int_{\underline{v}_1}^{P_1^*} f(v_1, v_2)dv_1\right]dv_2 - \left(P_2^* - c_2\right)\int_{\underline{v}_1}^{P_1^*} f\left(v_1, P_2^*\right)dv_1$$
$$+ \left(P_1^* - c_1\right)\int_{P_2^*}^{\bar{v}_2} f\left(P_1^*, v_2\right)dv_2 > 0$$

which can be rewritten as

$$\int_{\underline{v}_1}^{P_1^*}\left\{\left[1 - G_2\left(P_2^*|v_1\right)\right] - \left(P_2^* - c_2\right)g_2\left(P_2^*|v_1\right)\right\}h_1(v_1)dv_1$$
$$+ \left(P_1^* - c_1\right)\left[1 - G_2\left(P_2^*|P_1^*\right)\right]h_1\left(P_1^*\right) > 0P_1^*$$

The second term in this inequality corresponds to the area *abcd* in Figure 6.2. It represents the additional profit the monopolist can generate through bundling from those consumers who without bundling would buy only good 2 but with bundling are encouraged to buy both goods (effect 2). This term is always positive. The sign of the first term, which represents the monopoly trade-off for buyers for whom $v_1 < P_1^*$ (effect 1), is ambiguous. It turns out, however, that, if the reservation values are independently distributed, this first term is of second order, because P_2^* is also the monopoly price for buyers for whom $v_1 < P_1^*$. It therefore vanishes, and bundling strictly dominates. To see this result, note that, in this case, the preceding inequality simplifies to

$$H_1\left(P_1^*\right)\left\{\left[1 - H_2\left(P_2^*\right)\right] - \left(P_2^* - c_2\right)h_2\left(P_2^*\right)\right\}$$
$$+ \left(P_1^* - c_1\right)\left[1 - H_2\left(P_2^*\right)\right]h_1\left(P_1^*\right) > 0$$

Since P_2^* is the monopoly price under separate sales, we must have $[1 - H_2(P_2^*)] - (P_2^* - c_2)h_2(P_2^*) = 0$, so that the inequality reduces to

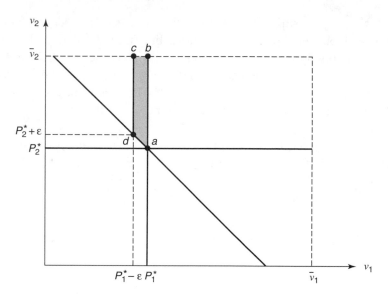

Figure 6.2
Additonal Sales through Bundling

$$\left(P_1^* - c_1\right)\left[1 - H_2\left(P_2^*\right)\right]h_1\left(P_1^*\right) > 0 \tag{6.2}$$

This condition always holds provided that there is a positive measure of reservation values above cost.

In sum, bundling is optimal for the multiproduct monopoly for a large range of cases. In particular, it is optimal in the case where the demands for the two goods by the consumer are unrelated (or independent).

6.1.3   Optimal Bundling: A Global Analysis in the 2 × 2 Model

From MMW's analysis we were able to identify sufficient conditions under which bundling dominates no bundling locally. Following Armstrong and Rochet (1999), we now provide a global analysis of the optimal bundling problem in the special case where there are only two possible valuations for each good: $v_1 \in \{v_1^L, v_1^H\}$ with $\Delta_1 = v_1^H - v_1^L > 0$, and $v_2 \in \{v_2^L, v_2^H\}$ with $\Delta_2 = v_2^H - v_2^L > 0$. There are then only four possible types of consumers, (v_L, v_L), (v_L, v_H), (v_H, v_L), and (v_H, v_H). The seller's prior probability distribution over the buyers' types is $\Pr(v_i, v_j) = \beta_{ij}$; $i = L, H$; $j = L, H$. We shall make the innocuous simplifying assumption that $\beta_{LH} = \beta_{HL} = \beta$.

The seller's problem here is to offer a menu of contracts $\{T_{ij}, x_1^{ij}, x_2^{ij}\}$ to maximize his net expected profit, where T_{ij} denotes the payment and x_1^{ij} (resp. x_2^{ij}) the probability of getting good 1 (resp. good 2) for buyer type (v_i, v_j). The seller's expected profit is then

$$\pi = \sum_{ij} \beta_{ij} \left(T_{ij} - x_1^{ij} c_1 - x_2^{ij} c_2 \right)$$

and the buyer's net surplus (or informational rent) is

$$R_{ij} = x_1^{ij} v_1^i + x_2^{ij} v_2^j - T_{ij}$$

A more convenient expression for the seller's expected profit is

$$\pi = S(x) - \sum_{ij} \beta_{ij} R_{ij}$$

where

$$S(x) = \sum_{ij} \beta_{ij} \left[x_1^{ij} (v_1^i - c_1) + x_2^{ij} (v_2^j - c_2) \right]$$

denotes the expected social surplus.

The constraints faced by the seller are, as usual, incentive-compatibility (IC) and individual-rationality (IR) constraints. As in the one-dimensional problem, the individual-rationality constraint $R_{LL} \geq 0$ and the incentive compatibility constraints imply that the other individual-rationality constraints are satisfied. As for the set of incentive constraints, it can be written as

$$R_{ij} \geq R_{kl} + x_1^{kl}(v_1^i - v_1^k) + x_2^{kl}(v_2^j - v_2^l) \quad \text{for all } ij \text{ and } kl$$

As in the one-dimensional problem, incentive compatibility implies monotonicity conditions for the sale probabilities x_1^{ij} and x_2^{ij}:

$$x_1^{HH} \geq x_1^{LH}, \quad x_1^{HL} \geq x_1^{LL}, \quad x_2^{HH} \geq x_2^{HL}, \quad x_2^{LH} \geq x_2^{LL}$$

In words, incentive compatibility requires that for either good the probability of getting it is (weakly) increasing with the buyer's valuation of that good. If these conditions do not hold, truthful revelation of types cannot be hoped for.

In the one-dimensional problem, whether we have two or more types, all incentive constraints except the downward adjacent ones can be ignored when the buyer's preferences have the single-crossing property and the monotonicity conditions hold (see Chapter 2). Unfortunately, this useful property does not extend to the multidimensional problem. Nevertheless, we shall begin by characterizing the solution to the seller's "relaxed problem," where only the downward incentive constraints, the monotonicity conditions, and the individual-rationality constraint for type LL are imposed. We then identify situations where the solution to the relaxed problem is the solution to the seller's problem. Finally, we characterize the solution to the seller's problem in situations where the relaxed problem is not valid.

In our two-dimensional problem, the downward incentive constraints are

$$R_{HL} \geq R_{LL} + x_1^{LL}\Delta_1$$

$$R_{LH} \geq R_{LL} + x_2^{LL}\Delta_2$$

$$R_{HH} \geq \max\{R_{LH} + x_1^{LH}\Delta_1, R_{HL} + x_2^{HL}\Delta_2, \ R_{LL} + x_1^{LL}\Delta_1 + x_2^{LL}\Delta_2\}$$

Given that the individual rationality constraint binds at the optimum for the relaxed problem ($R_{LL} = 0$), these incentive constraints can be simplified to

$$R_{HL} \geq x_1^{LL}\Delta_1$$

$$R_{LH} \geq x_2^{LL}\Delta_2$$

$$R_{HH} \geq x_1^{LL}\Delta_1 + x_2^{LL}\Delta_2 + \max\{(x_1^{LH} - x_1^{LL})\Delta_1, (x_2^{HL} - x_2^{LL})\Delta_2, 0\}$$

The seller's relaxed problem thus takes the form

$$\max_{\{x_1^{ij}, x_2^{ij}, R_{ij}\}} \sum_{ij} \beta_{ij}[x_1^{ij}(v_1^i - c_1) + x_2^{ij}(v_2^j - c_2)] - \sum_{ij} \beta_{ij} R_{ij}$$

subject to

$$R_{HL} = x_1^{LL}\Delta_1$$

$$R_{LH} = x_2^{LL}\Delta_2$$

$$R_{HH} = x_1^{LL}\Delta_1 + x_2^{LL}\Delta_2 + \max\{(x_1^{LH} - x_1^{LL})\Delta_1, (x_2^{HL} - x_2^{LL})\Delta_2, 0\}$$

$$x_1^{HH} \geq x_1^{LH}, \quad x_1^{HL} \geq x_1^{LL}, \quad x_2^{HH} \geq x_2^{HL}, \quad x_2^{LH} \geq x_2^{LL}$$

It is immediately apparent from this problem that the optimal contract for type (v_H, v_H) takes the form: $x_1^{HH} = x_2^{HH} = 1$, since lowering these probabilities of getting the goods would not relax any incentive constraint. In other words, there is no distortion of the consumption allocation for the highest type, just as in the one-dimensional problem. As we shall see, while this result is true generally in the one-dimensional problem, it holds for the relaxed problem only in the multidimensional case.

To characterize the optimal contracts for the other types, there are different cases to consider, depending on which of the downward incentive constraints for type (v_H, v_H) is binding. One case corresponds to a situation with no bundling and the others to (partial) bundling:

1. **No bundling**: The case with no bundling is that where $x_1^{LL} \geq x_1^{LH}$, $x_2^{LL} \geq x_2^{HL}$, so that the relevant incentive constraint for type (v_H, v_H) is

$$R_{HH} = x_1^{LL} \Delta_1 + x_2^{LL} \Delta_2$$

This is a situation with no bundling in that the probability of getting object i is not increasing in the valuation for object j ($x_i^{LL} \geq x_i^{LH}$). As our previous discussion indicates, bundling the two objects affects the buyer's choice of consumption only when she has a low valuation for one object and a high valuation for the other. In this case the buyer might want to buy only the high-value object if given a choice, but bundling forces her to buy both objects. Thus (partial) bundling is formally equivalent to raising the probability of selling object i when the value for object j is higher.

Substituting for the R_{ij}'s in the seller's objective function, the relaxed problem in the case of no bundling reduces to

$$\max_{\{x_1^{ij}, x_2^{ij}\}} \sum_{ij} \beta_{ij} [x_1^{ij}(v_1^i - c_1) + x_2^{ij}(v_2^j - c_2)] - \beta_H [x_1^{LL} \Delta_1 + x_2^{LL} \Delta_2]$$

subject to

$$x_1^{HH} \geq x_1^{HL}, \quad x_2^{HH} \geq x_2^{LH}, \quad x_1^{HL} \geq x_1^{LL}, \quad x_2^{LH} \geq x_2^{LL}, \quad \text{and}$$
$$x_1^{LL} \geq x_1^{LH}, x_2^{LL} \geq x_2^{HL}$$

where $\beta_H = \beta_{HH} + \beta$ denotes the marginal probability that the buyer's value for (either) one of the objects is high.

2. **Bundling**: When the relevant downward constraint for type (v_H, v_H) is either

$$R_{HH} = x_1^{LL} \Delta_1 + x_2^{LL} \Delta_2 + (x_2^{HL} - x_2^{LL}) \Delta_2$$

or

$$R_{HH} = x_1^{LL} \Delta_1 + x_2^{LL} \Delta_2 + (x_1^{LH} - x_1^{LL}) \Delta_1$$

there is some form of bundling, since then either $x_2^{HL} \geq x_2^{LL}$ or $x_1^{LH} \geq x_1^{LL}$ or both, so that the probability of getting good i is increasing in the valuation for good j. Substituting for the R^{ij} in the seller's objective function, we obtain the reduced problem:

$$\max_{\{x_1^{ij}, x_2^{ij}\}} \sum_{ij} \beta_{ij} [x_1^{ij}(v_1^i - c_1) + x_2^{ij}(v_2^j - c_2)] - \beta_H [x_1^{LL}\Delta_1 + x_2^{LL}\Delta_2]$$
$$- \beta_{HH} \max\{(x_2^{HL} - x_2^{LL})\Delta_2, (x_1^{LH} - x_1^{LL})\Delta_1\}$$

subject to

$$x_1^{HH} \geq x_1^{HL}, \quad x_2^{HH} \geq x_2^{LH}, \quad x_1^{HL} \geq x_1^{LL}, \quad x_2^{LH} \geq x_2^{LL}, \quad \text{and}$$
$$x_1^{LL} \leq x_1^{LH}, \quad x_2^{LL} \leq x_2^{LH}$$

6.1.3.1   Optimal Contract in the Symmetric Model

To proceed further, it is helpful to begin by imposing symmetry: $\Delta_1 = \Delta_2 \equiv \Delta$, $c_1 = c_2 \equiv c$, and $v_1^i = v_2^i \equiv v^i$ for $i = L, H$. The optimal contract is then also symmetric and simplifies to $\{x^{HH}, x^{LL}, x^{HL}, x^{LH}\}$, where $x^{HH} \equiv x_k^{HH}$, $x^{LL} \equiv x_k^{LL}$ for $k = 1, 2$, while $x^{HL} \equiv x_1^{HL} = x_2^{LH}$ (the probability of getting a good for which one has announced a high valuation while one has announced a low valuation for the other good), and similarly $x^{LH} \equiv x_1^{LH} = x_2^{HL}$ (the probability of getting a good for which one has announced a low valuation while one has announced a high valuation for the other good). In this case, the incentive constraint

$$R_{HH} = x_1^{LL}\Delta_1 + x_2^{LL}\Delta_2 + \max\{(x_1^{LH} - x_1^{LL})\Delta_1, (x_2^{HL} - x_2^{LL})\Delta_2, 0\}$$

becomes

$$R_{HH} = 2x^{LL}\Delta + \max\{(x^{LH} - x^{LL})\Delta, 0\}$$

so that the relaxed problem can be rewritten as

$$\max_{\{x^{ij}\}} 2[(\beta_{HH}x^{HH} + \beta x^{HL})(v^H - c) + (\beta x^{LH} + \beta_{LL}x^{LL})(v^L - c)]$$
$$- [2\beta x^{LL} + \beta_{HH}(2x^{LL} + \max\{(x^{LH} - x^{LL}), 0\})]\Delta$$

subject to

$$x^{HH} \geq x^{LH}, \quad x^{HL} \geq x^{LL}$$

Note that, in this program, it is suboptimal to set $x^{LH} < x^{LL}$: if this were to happen, the coefficient of x^{LH} in the seller's objective function would be positive and would lead to $x^{LH} = 1$, a contradiction. The relaxed problem is thus

$$\max_{\{x^{ij}\}} 2[(\beta_{HH} x^{HH} + \beta x^{HL})(v^H - c) + (\beta x^{LH} + \beta_{LL} x^{LL})(v^L - c)]$$
$$- [(2\beta + \beta_{HH})x^{LL} + \beta_{HH} x^{LH}] \Delta$$

subject to

$$x^{HH} \geq x^{LH}, \quad x^{HL} \geq x^{LL}, \quad x^{LH} \geq x^{LL}$$

What is more, when the condition $x^{HL} \geq x^{LH}$ is satisfied, it can be shown that the solution to the relaxed symmetric problem is actually the solution to the seller's optimal contracting problem.[1] To find this solution, all we need to determine is the sign of the coefficients of the x^{ij}:

- As is intuitive, the coefficients of x^{HH} and x^{HL} always have a positive sign, so that it is optimal for the seller to set $x^{HH} = x^{HL} = 1$.
- The coefficient of x^{LH} is $2\beta(v^L - c) - \beta_{HH}\Delta$; therefore, if

$$\frac{\Delta}{v^L - c} \geq 2\frac{\beta}{\beta_{HH}} \tag{6.3}$$

then it is optimal for the seller to minimize x^{LH} and to set $x^{LH} = x^{LL}$. If the opposite inequality holds, then the seller sets $x^{LH} = x^{HH} = 1$.
- The coefficient of x^{LL} is $2\beta_{LL}(v^L - c) - (2\beta + \beta_{HH})\Delta$; therefore, the seller wants to minimize $x^{LL} = x^{LH}$ if

$$\frac{\Delta}{v^L - c} \geq \frac{2\beta_{LL}}{2\beta + \beta_{HH}} = 2\frac{\beta_{LL}}{1 - \beta_{LL}}$$

Note that this inequality is implied by inequality (6.3) whenever

$$\frac{\beta_{LL}}{1 - \beta_{LL}} < \frac{\beta}{\beta_{HH}} \tag{6.4}$$

---

1. This result can be shown as follows: first, the fact that, in the relaxed problem, four downward incentive constraints (for types HL and LH with respect to type LL, and for type HH with respect to types HL and LH) are binding plus monotonicity ($x^{HH} \geq x^{LH}, x^{HL} \geq x^{LL}$) implies that the five upward incentive constraints are satisfied. Second, the fact that $x^{HL} \geq x^{LH}$ ensures that the last two constraints, involving types HL and LH, are also satisfied given that the downward and upward constraints are.

We thus have five cases: (i) when conditions (6.3) and (6.4) hold, it is optimal for the seller to set $x^{LL} = x^{LH} = 0$. If, on the other hand, (ii)

$$2\frac{\beta}{\beta_{HH}} \geq \frac{\Delta}{v^L - c} \geq 2\frac{\beta_{LL}}{1 - \beta_{LL}}$$

holds, then the seller sets $x^{LL} = 0$ and $x^{LH} = x^{HH} = 1$, while if (iii)

$$2\frac{\beta}{\beta_{HH}} \geq 2\frac{\beta_{LL}}{1 - \beta_{LL}} \geq \frac{\Delta}{v^L - c}$$

holds, then $x^{LL} = x^{LH} = x^{HH} = 1$. Finally, when condition (6.4) does not hold, then (iv) the seller's solution is given by $x^{LL} = x^{LH} = x^{HH} = 1$ if

$$\frac{\beta_L}{\beta} \geq \frac{\Delta}{v^L - c}$$

and (v) $x^{LL} = x^{LH} = 0$ otherwise.

To summarize, the key result in the symmetric model is the optimality for the seller to have pure bundling, where $x^{LL} = 0$ and $x^{LH} = x^{HL} = x^{HH} = 1$, when the buyer's valuations are not too positively correlated and when the informational rents are sufficiently high that it pays the seller to exclude type (v_L, v_L) but not so high that it is best to serve all other types. Indeed, the condition on valuations is condition (6.4) or, equivalently (remembering that $\beta_i = \beta_{ii} + \beta$ and that $\beta_{HH} + 2\beta + \beta_{LL} = 1$),

$$\frac{\beta_{LL}\beta_{HH} - \beta^2}{\beta_L\beta_H} < \frac{\beta_H}{1 - \beta}$$

The LHS of this inequality is the correlation coefficient linking the buyer's valuations for the two items. This inequality is always satisfied when the valuations are independent, since the RHS is always positive. This analysis thus confirms Adams and Yellen's intuition that bundling is an efficient screening device whenever "the correlation coefficient linking an individual's valuation of one good to his valuation of the other good is not strongly positive."

The other cases that we have detailed, where either $x^{LL} = x^{LH} = x^{HL} = x^{HH} = 1$ or $x^{LL} = x^{LH} = 0$ and $x^{HL} = x^{HH} = 1$, unfortunately are ambiguous, as they can be interpreted either as independent sales or as bundling. This is a limitation of the special setting with only two possible valuations for each item. The advantage of this simple formulation, however, is that it highlights exactly when and how the methodology for one-dimensional screening problems extends to multidimensional problems.

6.1.3.2 Optimal Contract in the Asymmetric Model

In the asymmetric problem where, without loss of generality, $\Delta_1 > \Delta_2$, the solution is similar to that in the symmetric problem whenever only downward incentive constraints are binding at the optimum. The only slight analytical complication is that now three different regions [depending on which downward incentive constraint for type (v_H,v_H) is binding] must be considered. Also, an interesting conceptual difference is that now the optimal menu of contracts may involve random allocations. To see this possibility, consider the example where there are only two equally likely types of buyers, buyer A with valuations $(v_1,v_2) = (1,2)$ and buyer B with $(v_1,v_2) = (3,1)$. Suppose moreover that the seller's costs are $c_1 = c_2 = 0$. Calling P_i the price of the bundle chosen in equilibrium by buyer type i, the seller's optimum is the result of

$$\max \ 0.5P_A + 0.5P_B$$

such that

$$x_1^A + 2x_2^A - P_A \geq 0$$

and

$$3x_1^B + x_2^B - P_B \geq \max\{0, 3x_1^A + x_2^A - P_A\}$$

Indeed, it can be checked that the relevant constraints concern participation by buyer type A as well as both participation and incentive compatibility for buyer type B. The result is that $x_1^B = x_2^B = 1$ (no distortion at the top), as well as $x_2^A = 1$ (since buyer A's valuation for good 2 is higher than buyer B's, lowering x_2^A below its efficient level only hurts incentive compatibility). The seller's problem thus becomes

$$\max \ 0.5P_A + 0.5P_B$$

such that

$$x_1^A + 2 - P_A = 0$$

and

$$4 - P_B = \max\{0, 3x_1^A + 1 - P_A\}$$

or

$$\max \quad 0.5\{x_1^A + 2\} + 0.5\{4 - \max[0, 2x_1^A - 1]\}$$

It is then optimal for the seller to set $0 = 2x_1^A - 1$ or $x_1^A = 0.5$. To summarize, the optimum implies giving both items for sure to type B and giving object 2 for sure but object 1 only with probability 0.5 to type A.

In general, in the asymmetric problem, other incentive constraints besides downward incentive constraints may be binding at the optimum. In that case the relaxed problem considered so far is no longer relevant. More precisely, when the buyer's valuations for the two items are negatively correlated and when Δ_1 is sufficiently larger than Δ_2, then some upward incentive constraints may be binding. In that case the optimal contract may distort the consumption allocation of the highest type (v_H, v_H). It thus appears that even the most robust result of the one-dimensional problem—no distortion at the top—does not survive in the multidimensional problem. However, even if the main conclusions of the one-dimensional problem do not extend in general to the multidimensional setting, the main methodological principles developed for the one-dimensional problem carry over to the more general setting.

6.1.4   Global Analysis for the General Model

The analysis for the 2×2 model seems to suggest that outside the symmetric model few general insights emerge about the multidimensional screening problem. It would thus seem that even less can be said in any generality about the general model with more than two items and a continuum of valuations. There is ground for optimism, however, for at least three reasons. First, a complete characterization of the general problem has been obtained by Armstrong (1996) and Rochet and Chone (1998). Second, as shown by Armstrong (1996), in the two-dimensional problem with a continuum of valuations a general insight emerges concerning the optimality of exclusion of the lowest valuation types. Third, as Armstrong (1999) has shown, when the number of items is large and the valuations for each item are independently distributed, the optimal contract can be approximated by a simple two-part tariff. We shall not attempt to provide the characterization of the general problem. We shall limit ourselves here to illustrating the latter two points.

6.1.4.1 The Optimality of Exclusion

To understand this result derived by Armstrong (1996), consider the problem with two items where v_i is uniformly distributed on the interval $[0, \theta + 1]$, $i = 1, 2$, and suppose that $c_i = 0$. Let P_i denote the price of item i and P_b the price of the bundle. Since the problem is symmetric, consider the symmetric contract $\{P_1 = P_2 = P, P_b\}$. The local analysis of MMW suggests that when valuations are independent, some bundling is optimal, so that $2P > P_b$. We shall solve here for the optimal prices P^* and P_b^* and show that in the two-dimensional problem it is always optimal to exclude the lowest valuations, while in the one-dimensional case all consumer types are served when $\theta \geq 1$.

Under mixed bundling, $\theta + 1 \geq P \geq \theta$ and $P_b \geq P + \theta$. Then all types with $v_2 \geq P$ and $v_1 \leq P_b - P$ consume only item 2; region Θ_2 in Figure 6.3 represents all those types. Similarly, all types with $v_1 \geq P$ and $v_2 \leq P_b - P$ consume only item 1; region Θ_1 in Figure 6.3 represents all those types. All types in region Θ_b purchase the bundle and have valuations $v_1 + v_2 \geq P_b$. Finally, all types in region Θ_0 are excluded. In this case, the seller's expected revenue from selling individual items is $2P(\theta + 1 - P)(P_b - P \quad 0)$, and his expected revenue

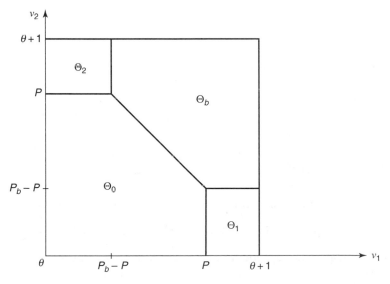

Figure 6.3
Exclusion under Mixed Bundling

from the bundle is $P_b(\theta+1-P)(\theta+1+P-P_b)+\frac{1}{2}P_b(2P-P_b)(2\theta+2-P_b)$, so that his profit is given by

$$2P(\theta+1-P)(P_b-P-\theta)$$

$$+P_b\left[(\theta+1-P)(\theta+1+P-P_b)+\frac{1}{2}(2P-P_b)(2\theta+2-P_b)\right]$$

Under pure bundling $P \geq P_b - \theta$, and for $2\theta + 1 \geq P_b \geq 2\theta$ the seller's expected profits are given by

$$P_b\left[1-\frac{1}{2}(P_b-2\theta)^2\right]$$

The seller's expected profit function is thus piecewise cubic in (P, P_b) and nonconcave. Solving the seller's unconstrained maximization problem, one obtains the result that pure bundling is optimal when $\theta > 0$ and the solution is given by

$$P_b = \frac{1}{3}(4\theta + \sqrt{4\theta^2 + 6}) \quad \text{with} \quad P \geq P_b - \theta$$

The fraction of types excluded from consumption is then

$$\frac{1}{18}(\sqrt{4\theta^2+6} - 2\theta)^2$$

This fraction is decreasing in θ, but it is strictly positive for all $\theta > 1$. In contrast, in the one-dimensional problem there is no exclusion for all $\theta \geq 1$. The intuition for this result is that by lowering P_b by ε the seller loses revenue ε from all those types that were already prepared to purchase the bundle and gains $P_b - \varepsilon$ from at most a fraction ε^2 of new consumers. Thus, at $P_b = \theta$, where no types are excluded, a small increase in price has a negligible effect on demand but a first-order effect on revenues. It is for this reason that some exclusion is always optimal in the two-dimensional problem. In the one-dimensional problem, in contrast, the fraction of new consumers is of order ε.

6.1.4.2   Approximating the Optimal Contract with a Two-Part Tariff

Extending the 2×2 model in a different direction, Armstrong (1999) shows that when the dimensionality of the seller's problem becomes large, the optimal contract can be approximated by a simple two-part tariff.

Consider the seller's problem when he can produce $n > 2$ items at a cost $c_i \geq 0$ for item i. The buyer's utility function is now

$$\sum_{i=1}^{n} v_i x_i - T$$

where $x_i \in [0,1]$ is the probability of getting good i, $v = (v_1, \ldots, v_n)$ is the buyer's type, and T is the payment from the buyer to the seller. Let $G(v)$ denote the seller's prior distribution over buyer types. The seller's optimal contracting problem then is to choose a payment schedule $T(x) = T(x_1, \ldots, x_n)$ to solve

$$\max E\left\{T[x(v)] - \sum_{i=1}^{n} c_i x_i\right\}$$

subject to

$$x(v) \in \arg \max_{x_i} \sum_{i=1}^{n} v_i x_i - T(x)$$

$$\sum_{i=1}^{n} v_i x_i(v) - T[x(v)] \geq 0$$

For some distributions of buyer types $G(v)$—in particular, when the valuations for the different items v_i are independently distributed—it is possible to approximate the optimal contract with a two-part tariff $P(x) = F + \Sigma_{i=1}^{n} c_i x_i$ when $n \to \infty$.

To see this possibility, let $S(v)$ denote the first-best social surplus obtained when the seller and the type-v buyer trade with each other, and let μ and σ^2 denote the mean and variance of $S(v)$. The seller's first-best expected profit is then equal to μ, and his second-best expected profits are necessarily such that $\pi^{SB} \leq \mu$.

If the seller offers a two-part tariff $P(x) = F + \Sigma_{i=1}^{n} c_i x_i$, then a type-$v$ buyer accepts this contract if and only if $S(v) \geq F$. Conditional on the buyer accepting the contract, the seller obtains a profit of F. Let π^P denote the maximum profit from the two-part tariff obtained by optimizing over F. If the seller sets $F = (1 - \varepsilon)\mu$, then

$$\pi^P \geq (1-\varepsilon)\mu \Pr\{S(v) \geq (1-\varepsilon)\mu\}$$
$$\geq (1-\varepsilon)\mu \ (1 - \Pr\{|S(v) - \mu| \geq \varepsilon\mu\})$$

But from Chebyshev's inequality,

$$\Pr\{|S(v) - \mu| \geq \delta\} \leq \frac{\sigma^2}{\delta^2}$$

so that

$$\pi^P \geq (1-\varepsilon)\mu\left(1 - \frac{\sigma^2}{\varepsilon^2 \mu^2}\right) \geq \mu\left[1 - \varepsilon - \frac{\sigma^2}{\varepsilon^2 \mu^2}\right]$$

or

$$\pi^P \geq \mu \left[1 - \kappa \left(\frac{\sigma}{\mu} \right)^{2/3} \right]$$

for $\varepsilon = [2(\sigma^2/\mu^2)]^{1/3}$ (while κ is a positive constant). Consequently,

$$\frac{\pi^P}{\pi^{SB}} \geq 1 - \kappa \left(\frac{\sigma}{\mu} \right)^{2/3}$$

so that the difference in profit between the optimal second-best contract and the optimal two-part tariff $P(x)$ is decreasing in σ/μ and vanishes when σ/μ tends to 0.

If the valuations for the individual items are independently distributed, and if we call μ_i and σ_i the mean and variance of $S_i(v_i)$, the first-best social surplus on item i for buyer type v, we have

$$\mu = \sum_{i=1}^{n} \mu_i \quad \text{and} \quad \sigma^2 = \sum_{i=1}^{n} \sigma_i^2$$

Substituting in the preceding inequality, one then obtains

$$\frac{\pi^P}{\pi^{SB}} \geq 1 - \kappa \left(\frac{\sqrt{\sum_{i=1}^{n} \sigma_i^2}}{\sum_{i=1}^{n} \mu_i} \right)^{2/3} \geq 1 - \kappa \left(\frac{\overline{\sigma}}{\underline{\mu}} \right)^{2/3} \frac{1}{\sqrt[3]{n}}$$

where $\overline{\sigma} = \max_i\{\sigma_i\}$ and $\underline{\mu} = \min_i\{\mu_i\}$.

Letting $n \to \infty$, one observes that the optimal two-part tariff contract $P(x)$ is approximately optimal when the seller has many items for sale (like a department store) and the buyer's valuations for these items are independently distributed. This is a rather striking result indicating that in complex environments simple contracts may be approximately optimal, a theme that will be illustrated again in Part IV, this time in the context of dynamic incomplete contracting. Note finally that this result is by no means dependent on the independence assumption: Armstrong (1999) shows that a similar result holds when valuations are correlated and when the seller can offer a menu of two-part tariffs.

6.2 Moral Hazard with Multiple Tasks

The classical moral hazard problem analyzed in Chapter 4 captures a fundamental aspect of contracting under uncertainty and hidden actions. It highlights the basic trade-off between risk sharing and incentives, and it reveals the importance of the likelihood ratio in estimating the agent's action choice and, thus, determining the shape of the optimal contract. Yet beyond these insights the general theory has limited practical interest unless more structure is imposed on the problem under consideration. Also, the general problem is too abstract to be able to capture the main features of an actual bilateral contracting problem with moral hazard. Specifically, in most real-world contracting problems, the agent's action set is considerably richer than the theory describes, and the variables the contract can be conditioned on are much harder to specify precisely in a contract or to observe.

To mention just one example, a CEO's job involves many dimensions and cannot adequately be reduced to a simple problem of effort choice. CEOs do not make only investment, production, and pricing decisions. They are also responsible for hiring other managers and employees, and for determining the overall strategy of the firm and the managerial structure inside the firm. They lay out long-term financial objectives and merger and acquisition plans, and they continually interact with the largest clients and investors. To capture the CEO's compensation problem, the classical principal-agent problem needs to be modified in a number of dimensions. At the very least her action set must include the range of different tasks he is responsible for, performance measures must be multidimensional, and the time dimension must be incorporated into the basic problem. In this subsection we shall mainly be concerned with the problem of multiple tasks and objectives. The time dimension is explored systematically in Part III.

When an agent is responsible for several tasks, the basic contracting problem can no longer be reduced to a simple trade-off between risk sharing and incentives. Now the principal must also worry about how incentives to undertake one task affect the agent's incentives to undertake other tasks. When a company's remuneration committee decides to tie the CEO's compensation to the firm's profit and stock price, it must consider how such a compensation package affects the CEO's various tasks that are not directly or immediately related to profit or stock price, such as employment and promotion decisions; mergers, acquisitions, and other forms of restructurings; and so on.

The same types of considerations arise in other job contexts. For example, with the hotly debated issue of incentive pay for teachers, and the proposal of linking teachers' pay to pupil performance in those standardized (multiple-choice) tests that are used for college admissions. The advantage of these tests is that they provide an independent measure of performance; their disadvantage is that they measure only part of what teachers are meant to teach to their pupils. If the rest (e.g., ability to write, to argue, to philosophize, to behave properly in the world) is not measured, there is a definite risk that incentive pay based on standardized tests would induce teachers to focus excessively on these tests and to neglect the other components of education.

At first sight it may appear that, as a result of enriching the agent's action set, the principal-agent problem is more intractable, and even less can be said about this problem in any generality than about the single-task problem. This is actually not the case. A moment's thought reveals that in fact the classic principal-agent problem considered in Chapter 4 is a general multitask problem, when the agent's action is defined to be a given probability distribution over outcomes rather than effort. Then, providing incentives to achieve a particular outcome may also be seen as affecting the agent's incentives to obtain other outcomes. Seen from this perspective, the main weakness of the classic problem is its excessive generality, and, indeed, the multitask principal-agent problems considered in the literature provide results beyond the classical ones precisely because they impose more structure on the classical problem. Thus the multitask principal-agent problem considered in Holmström and Milgrom (1991) focuses on the linear-contract, normal-noise, CARA-preferences model discussed in Chapter 4, and makes assumptions about the interconnection of the agent's different tasks in order to obtain predictions about high- or low-powered incentive schemes, job design, and various other employment practices in organizations. As we shall see, this approach is based on the competition between tasks that arises from the effort-cost function.

6.2.1 Multiple Tasks and Effort Substitution

The basic setup considered by Holmström and Milgrom is as follows: The agent undertakes at least two tasks a_i ($i = 1, \ldots, n; n \geq 2$), each task producing some measurable output q_i, where $q_i = a_i + \varepsilon_i$. The random component of output ε_i is assumed to be normally distributed with mean zero and variance-covariance matrix

$$\Sigma = \begin{pmatrix} \sigma_1^2 & \cdots & \sigma_{n1} \\ & \backslash & \\ \sigma_{1n} & \cdots & \sigma_n^2 \end{pmatrix}$$

where σ_i^2 denotes the variance of ε_i, and σ_{ij} is the covariance of ε_i and ε_j.

The agent has constant absolute risk aversion, and her preferences are represented by the utility function

$$u(w, a) = -e^{-\eta[w-\psi(a_1,\ldots,a_n)]}$$

where η is the coefficient of absolute risk aversion ($\eta = -u''/u'$), and $\psi(a_1, \ldots, a_n)$ is the agent's private cost of choosing actions $(a_1, \ldots, a_n)$. The principal is risk neutral and offers linear incentive contracts to the agent.

Within this setup, Holmström and Milgrom explore how the incentive contract varies with the shape of the cost function $\psi(a_1, \ldots, a_n)$, in particular how the choice of action level for one task affects the marginal cost of undertaking other tasks. They also ask how the incentive contract based on the subset of observable outputs q_i is affected by the nonobservability of the outputs of other tasks. This somewhat abstract line of questioning turns out to be pertinent for many employment situations in organizations, as the following example studied by Anderson and Schmittlein (1984) and Anderson (1985) illustrates.

The subject of these authors' study is employment contracts and job descriptions of salespeople in the electronic-components industry. The multiple activities of an individual salesperson in this industry can be classified into three categories of tasks: (1) selling the products of a manufacturer; (2) finding new customers; and (3) possibly selling the products of other manufacturers. In principle, these tasks could be undertaken as well by independent salespeople as by employees of a given manufacturer, but Anderson and Schmittlein find that in this industry most salespeople are employees rather than independent contractors. This observation is explained by Holmström and Milgrom as the efficient contractual outcome of a multitask principal-agent problem where the different tasks of the agent are substitutes and the outputs of some of the activities are not observable (or measurable).

More precisely, let a_1 represent selling activities for the principal, a_2 finding new customers, and a_3 selling on behalf of another manufacturer. Suppose in addition that the principal can observe only q_1, the volume of sales of its own components. Then, Holmström and Milgrom argue that if the principal is mostly concerned about the volume of sales q_1, it may be efficient to prevent the salesman from selling for other manufacturers. This purpose can be achieved by hiring the salesperson as an employee rather than an outside contractor who is free to choose how to organize his worktime. They explain:

Incentives for a task can be provided in two ways: either the task itself can be rewarded or the marginal opportunity cost for a task can be lowered by removing or reducing the incentives on competing tasks. Constraints are substitutes for performance incentives and are extensively used when it is hard to assess the performance of the agent. (Holmström and Milgrom, 1991, p. 27)

Thus, by imposing more structure on the classical principal-agent problem, the scope of incentive theory can be broadened to include aspects of incentive design (such as job description) other than simply the design of compensation contracts. We shall illustrate the core idea in Holmström and Milgrom's work by considering the simplest possible setting where the agent can undertake only two tasks ($n = 2$) whose outputs are independently distributed ($\sigma_{12} = 0$) and where the cost function takes the simple quadratic form $\psi(a_1, a_2) = \frac{1}{2}(c_1 a_1^2 + c_2 a_2^2) + \delta a_1 a_2$, with $0 \le \delta \le \sqrt{c_1 c_2}$. When $\delta = 0$, the two efforts are technologically independent, while when $\delta = \sqrt{c_1 c_2}$, they are "perfect substitutes," with no economies of scope between them. Whenever $\delta \ge 0$, raising effort on one task raises the marginal cost of effort on the other task, the so-called effort substitution problem.

With two observable outputs, the principal offers an incentive contract:

$$w = t + s_1 q_1 + s_2 q_2$$

to the agent. Under this contract the agent's certainty equivalent compensation is given by (see Chapter 4 for a definition and derivation)

$$t + s_1 a_1 + s_2 a_2 - \frac{\eta}{2}(s_1^2 \sigma_1^2 + s_2^2 \sigma_2^2) - \frac{1}{2}(c_1 a_1^2 + c_2 a_2^2) - \delta a_1 a_2$$

The agent chooses a_i to maximize this certainty equivalent compensation. The first-order conditions of the agent's problem equate the marginal return from effort and its marginal cost of effort:

$$s_i = c_i a_i + \delta a_j$$

for $i = 1, 2, j = 2, 1$. As in Chapter 4, this problem is simplified by the fact that the agent does not control the riskiness of her compensation, only its mean. With effort substitution, however, one has to take into account the fact that the marginal cost of effort on one task depends on the effort exerted on the other task. The unique solution to the agent's problem is given by

$$a_i = \frac{s_i c_j - \delta s_j}{c_i c_j - \delta^2}$$

In the following discussion we assume away corner solutions and focus on interior solutions, $a_i > 0$, which implies in particular $\delta < \sqrt{c_1 c_2}$: under perfect substitutability, the agent would perform only a single task, the one with the higher return, since she faces a single marginal cost of effort,

The principal's problem is then to choose $\{t; s_1; s_2\}$ to solve

$$\max a_1(1 - s_1) + a_2(1 - s_2) - t$$

subject to

$$a_1 = \frac{s_1 c_2 - \delta s_2}{c_1 c_2 - \delta^2}, \quad a_2 = \frac{s_2 c_1 - \delta s_1}{c_2 c_1 - \delta^2} \tag{IC}$$

$$t + s_1 a_1 + s_2 a_2 - \frac{\eta}{2}(s_1^2 \sigma_1^2 + s_2^2 \sigma_2^2) - \frac{1}{2}(c_1 a_1^2 + c_2 a_2^2) - \delta a_1 a_2 \geq \overline{w} \tag{IR}$$

At the optimum, the (IR) constraint is binding, so that we can substitute for t and (a_1, a_2) to obtain the unconstrained problem:

$$\max_{s_1, s_2} \left(\frac{s_1 c_2 - \delta s_2 + s_2 c_1 - \delta s_1}{c_1 c_2 - \delta^2} \right) - \frac{\eta}{2}(s_1^2 \sigma_1^2 + s_2^2 \sigma_2^2)$$

$$- \frac{1}{2} c_1 \left(\frac{s_1 c_2 - \delta s_2}{c_1 c_2 - \delta^2} \right)^2 - \frac{1}{2} c_2 \left(\frac{s_2 c_1 - \delta s_1}{c_2 c_1 - \delta^2} \right)^2 - \delta \left(\frac{s_1 c_2 - \delta s_2}{c_1 c_2 - \delta^2} \right) \left(\frac{s_2 c_1 - \delta s_1}{c_2 c_1 - \delta^2} \right)$$

The first-order conditions for this unconstrained problem yield

$$s_1 = \frac{c_2 - \delta + \delta s_2}{c_2 + \eta \sigma_1^2(c_1 c_2 - \delta^2)}$$

and

$$s_2 = \frac{c_1 - \delta + \delta s_1}{c_1 + \eta \sigma_2^2(c_1 c_2 - \delta^2)}$$

so that the solution is given by

$$s_1^* = \frac{1 + (c_2 - \delta)\eta \sigma_2^2}{1 + \eta c_2 \sigma_2^2 + \eta c_1 \sigma_1^2 + \eta^2 \sigma_1^2 \sigma_2^2(c_1 c_2 - \delta^2)}$$

and

$$s_2^* = \frac{1 + (c_1 - \delta)\eta \sigma_1^2}{1 + \eta c_2 \sigma_2^2 + \eta c_1 \sigma_1^2 + \eta^2 \sigma_1^2 \sigma_2^2(c_1 c_2 - \delta^2)}$$

Once again, let us focus here on interior solutions for the s_i^*'s. It is instructive to compare this solution to the one obtained when the two tasks are technologically independent and $\delta = 0$. In that case, the first-order conditions for the agent's problem reduce to $a_i = s_i/c_i$, and the optimal incentive contract for each task is the same as in the single-task problem considered in Chapter 4,

$$s_i^* = \frac{1}{1 + \eta c_i \sigma_i^2}$$

Thus, in the degenerate case of technological independence between tasks, optimal incentives for each task can be determined directly from the standard trade-off between risk sharing and incentives. This is no longer the case when tasks are substitutes.

Using the formulas for s_i^* we can indeed determine how the optimal (linear) incentive contract varies with the quality of output measures for each task. Assume, for example, that the measurability of task 2 worsens, that is, σ_2^2 increases. Then, as is intuitive, s_2^* goes down. But what is more interesting is that s_1^* also goes down. Indeed, the sign of the partial derivative of s_1^* with respect to σ_2^2 is the sign of $\delta \eta [\eta \sigma_1^2 (\delta - c_1) - 1]$,[2] which is negative since it has the sign opposite to that of s_2^*, which is positive. The key observation of this multitask approach is thus the *complementarity* between the s_i^*'s in the presence of effort-substitution problems.

Holmström and Milgrom push this logic to the limit and point out that, when the principal essentially cares about the task with unobservable output (task i with $\sigma_i^2 \to \infty$), then it may be best to give *no incentives at all* to the agent. Following Williamson, they define such a situation as one with "low-powered incentives." This is easiest to understand if we think of $a_i = 0$ as a normalization rather than a "true corner solution." It is indeed often natural to expect the agent, if she likes her job at all, to exert some effort even in the absence of any financial incentive (the effort choice of the agent will thus equate her marginal nonfinancial benefit with her marginal cost). In those situations, because of the effort-substitution problem, any incentives based on the observable output q_j may actually be counterproductive, since it will induce the agent to divert effort away from the task i valued by the principal.

---

2. Indeed, starting from the expression of s_1^*, the sign of its partial derivative with respect to σ_2^2 is the sign of $(c_2 - \delta)\eta[1 + \eta c_2 \sigma_2^2 + \eta c_1 \sigma_1^2 + \eta^2 \sigma_1^2 \sigma_2^2 (c_1 c_2 - \delta^2)] - [1 + (c_2 - \delta)\eta \sigma_2^2][\eta c_2 + \eta^2 \sigma_1^2 (c_1 c_2 - \delta^2)]$, which is equal to $\delta \eta [\eta \sigma_1^2 (\delta - c_1) - 1]$.

Another observation from this approach concerns the case where the principal may not be able to control all the dimensions of the incentive scheme. In the preceding analysis we assumed that both s_i^*'s were controlled by the principal. In reality, this may not be the case: for example, task 2 may refer to "outside work" that the agent could engage in. Then, clearly, if the market starts valuing such work more highly, so that s_2^* rises, the agent will divert effort away from task 1. To avoid this outcome, the principal will have to either raise s_1^* or prevent the agent from engaging in outside work (while compensating her so as to keep satisfying her participation constraint).

6.2.2   Conflicting Tasks and Advocacy

In the Holmström-Milgrom model that we just discussed, multitask problems arise because of the effort-substitution problem, that is, the fact that raising effort on one task raises the marginal cost of effort on the other tasks. In the absence of such an effect, we are back to the moral hazard problem of Chapter 4, where incentives on each task can be derived independently if individual outputs are independently distributed. This is not true anymore if there is a *direct conflict between tasks*. Think, for example,[3] about an agent/salesperson who has to try to sell two products made by a given principal/manufacturer, products 1 and 2, which are imperfect substitutes. For simplicity, assume that the level of sales on product i is $q_i \in \{0, 1\}$, and the q_i's are distributed independently with

$$\Pr(q_i = 1) = \alpha + \rho a_i - \gamma u_j \quad \text{for } i = 1, 2, j = 2, 1$$

Effort to promote product i is denoted by $a_i \in \{0, 1\}$. One unit of promotion effort on any given product costs an agent $\psi > 0$. Effort raises the probability of sale on the given product by ρ, but this comes partly at the expense of lowering the sale probability for the other product by γ. We assume that expending effort to promote both products is efficient in that $\rho - \gamma > \psi$.

We have explicitly ruled out here the effort-substitution problem stressed by Holmström and Milgrom, by assuming that the marginal cost of promotion effort a_i is independent of the level of a_j. The direct conflict between tasks, however, can make it expensive to induce $a_1 = a_2 = 1$ by a single agent. Indeed, assume agents are risk neutral but resource constrained; namely, their payoff equals their wage w minus their effort cost, and wages cannot be negative. If both products have to be promoted by

---

3. This example is based on Dewatripont and Tirole (2003).

a single agent, the principal can offer her a wage that is contingent on both q_i's, that is, a schedule w_{ij}. Given the symmetry of the problem, we have $w_{10} = w_{01}$, which we denote by w_1. Moreover, the principal clearly wants to set w_{00} equal to zero. Defining $\varphi = \alpha + \rho - \gamma$, the problem of the principal is thus

$$\min_{w_1, w_{11}} \varphi^2 w_{11} + 2\varphi(1 - \varphi)w_1$$

such that

$$\varphi^2 w_{11} + 2\varphi(1 - \varphi)w_1 - 2\psi \geq$$
$$(\varphi + \gamma)(\varphi - \rho)w_{11} + [(\varphi + \gamma) + (\varphi - \rho) - 2(\varphi + \gamma)(\varphi - \rho)]w_1 - \psi$$

and

$$\varphi^2 w_{11} + 2\varphi(1 - \varphi)w_1 - 2\psi \geq \alpha^2 w_{11} + 2\alpha(1 - \alpha)w_1$$

These two incentive constraints state respectively that the agent has to prefer exerting two efforts to exerting one or zero. It turns out that the optimal incentive scheme has $w_1 = 0$,[4] and that the binding incentive constraint is the second one,[5] which reduces to

$$\varphi^2 w_{11} - 2\psi \geq \alpha^2 w_{11}$$

---

4. Assume this is not the case, Then the LHS of the two incentive constraints is unchanged if we make the following change in the compensation schedule:

$$\Delta w_1 = -\frac{\varphi}{2(1-\varphi)}\Delta w_{11} < 0$$

Straightforward calculations show that this relaxes the RHS of both incentive constraints, and therefore allows us to improve the maximand by lowering expected compensation. This can be done until we reach $w_1 = 0$.

5. When $w_1 = 0$, and using the fact that $\varphi = \alpha + \rho - \gamma$, the two constraints can be rewritten as

$$\rho^2 + \gamma^2 + \alpha\rho - \alpha\gamma - \rho\gamma \geq \frac{\psi}{w_{11}}$$

and

$$\rho^2 + \gamma^2 + 2\alpha\rho - 2\alpha\gamma - 2\rho\gamma \geq \frac{2\psi}{w_{11}}$$

Since $\rho^2 + \gamma^2 > 0$, the second constraint implies the first.

At the optimum, we therefore have

$$w_{11} = \frac{2\psi}{\varphi^2 - \alpha^2}$$

This leaves the agent with a rent equal to $\alpha^2 w_{11}$ or

$$\frac{\alpha^2}{\varphi^2 - \alpha^2} 2\psi$$

Let us compare this outcome to the case where the principal hires two agents and asks each of them to promote one product. Assume that the principal offers each agent an incentive scheme and, if they both accept, they play a Nash equilibrium in effort choices. Once again, each agent's incentive scheme can be contingent on both q_i's. We can concentrate on a single agent, and by symmetry the other agent will receive the same incentive scheme. Clearly, the agent's wage will be positive only when she is successful in selling her own product. Once again, we thus have to determine w_{11} and w_{10}. The cost-minimizing incentive scheme that induces $a_1 = a_2 = 1$ is given by

$$\min_{w_{10}, w_{11}} \quad \varphi^2 w_{11} + \varphi(1-\varphi)w_{10}$$

such that

$$\varphi^2 w_{11} + \varphi(1-\varphi)w_{10} - \psi \geq (\varphi - \rho)[(\varphi + \gamma)w_{11} + (1 - \varphi - \gamma)w_{10}]$$

Since each agent undertakes only one task, there is only a single incentive constraint. Not exerting effort given that the other agent exerts effort lowers one's success probability from φ to $\varphi - \rho$ and raises the other agent's success probability from φ to $\varphi + \gamma$. The result is that the optimal incentive scheme has $w_{10} > 0$ but $w_{11} = 0$:[6] intuitively, the failure of the other agent is

---

6. Assume this is not the case. Then the LHS of the incentive constraint is unchanged if we make the following change in the compensation schedule:

$$\Delta w_{11} = -\frac{1-\varphi}{\varphi} \Delta w_{10} < 0$$

This relaxes the RHS of the incentive constraint, and therefore allows us to improve the maximand by lowering expected compensation. This can be done until we reach $w_{11} = 0$.

rewarded because it is itself an indication that the agent has exerted high effort. The optimum is therefore

$$w_{10} = \frac{\psi}{\varphi(1-\varphi)-(\varphi-\rho)(1-\varphi-\gamma)}$$

This leaves each agent with a rent equal to

$$\frac{(\varphi-\rho)(1-\varphi-\gamma)}{\varphi(1-\varphi)-(\varphi-\rho)(1-\varphi-\gamma)}\psi$$

In order to determine whether it is better to hire one or two agents, we have to compare the total rents they obtain. Remembering that $\varphi = \alpha + \rho - \gamma$, the rents left to one and two agents are, respectively,

$$\frac{\alpha^2}{(\alpha+\rho-\gamma)^2-\alpha^2}\psi$$

and

$$\frac{(\alpha-\gamma)(1-\alpha-\rho)}{(\alpha+\rho-\gamma)(1-\alpha-\rho+\gamma)-(\alpha-\gamma)(1-\alpha-\rho)}2\psi$$

Straightforward computations indicate that hiring a single agent is the better solution if and only if

$$2\frac{(\alpha+\rho-\gamma)^2}{\alpha^2} > \frac{(\alpha+\rho-\gamma)(1-\alpha-\rho+\gamma)}{(\alpha-\gamma)(1-\alpha-\rho)}+1$$

The LHS of this condition decreases in γ, which measures the intensity of conflict between tasks. Its RHS is increasing in γ.[7] For $\gamma = 0$, the LHS is

---

7. Indeed, the sign of the derivative of the RHS is the sign of

$$(\alpha-\gamma)(1-\alpha-\rho)[2(\alpha+\rho-\gamma)-1]+(\alpha+\rho-\gamma)[1-\alpha-\rho+\gamma](1-\alpha-\rho)$$

or the sign of

$$2(\alpha-\gamma)(\alpha+\rho-\gamma)+\rho[1-\alpha-\rho+\gamma]$$

which is positive.

bigger, so hiring a single agent is optimal.[8] However, for γ tending to α, the RHS tends to $+\infty$, and hiring two agents is optimal.

To sum up, we have considered a setting where, without any conflict between tasks, multitasking is beneficial for the principal, who prefers to hire a single agent to undertake both tasks rather than hiring one agent per task. However, introducing conflicts between tasks can change the result because, intuitively, agents take away rents from one another by exerting effort. In the limiting case where γ tends to α, the agent obtains no compensation whatsoever without exerting effort if the other agent does. This effect is not present with a single agent, who can coordinate her effort choices (it is for this reason that the binding incentive constraint is the one where he considers not exerting any effort at all).

Direct conflicts between tasks have been considered by Dewatripont and Tirole (1999) in a model where a principal has to hire one or two agents to search for information about the pros and cons of a decision under consideration by the principal. They assume that agents cannot be rewarded directly on the basis of the amount of information generated but only on the decision taken, which is itself positively related to the amount of "positive" information and negatively related to the amount of "negative" information. Therefore, there is a direct conflict between the task "searching for positive information" and the task "searching for negative information," and thus it may be optimal for the principal to hire two agents, one being asked to look for positive information and the other one for negative information, and to endow them with incentive schemes where they are "advocates," respectively, for and against the decision that is being considered. A natural example of this setting is the judicial system, whose goal is to have decisions made by judges—convicting a defendant, awarding damages to a plaintiff—based on the best possible information. Searching for this information is costly, and it is difficult to design incentive schemes based on the amount of information generated. However, decision-based rewards are common, whether they are explicit "contingency fees" or reputation-based delayed incentives (since court outcomes are easier to

---

8. Indeed, the condition then amounts to

$$2\frac{(\alpha+\rho)^2}{\alpha^2} > \frac{\alpha+\rho}{\alpha}+1$$

which is true.

remember than details about the information provided during the trial). In this setting, just as before, one can show that splitting the tasks between two agents and making them advocates of the defense and prosecution is the cost-minimizing way to reach informed judicial decisions.

6.3   An Example Combining Moral Hazard and Adverse Selection

Most contractual situations involve elements of both adverse selection and moral hazard. Often, however, one of these two incentive problems stands out as the key problem, so that the other problem can be ignored as a first approximation. In some cases it is not possible to decide a priori which of the two incentive problems is most important, or to disentangle the moral hazard from the adverse selection dimension. Many of these cases have been explored in the literature. One of the earliest models combining adverse selection with moral hazard is Laffont and Tirole (1986), who consider the problem of regulating a monopoly using cost observations. The monopoly may have a more or less efficient production technology (the adverse selection dimension) and may put in more or less effort in reducing cost (the moral hazard dimension). Several other models with this multidimensional incentive structure applied to other contexts have been developed since (see, for example, the book by Laffont and Tirole, 1993).

Recall that, in Chapter 2, we considered a simplified version of the Laffont-Tirole original setting, where the effort choice led to a deterministic cost realization. As a result, the key dimension of the analysis was adverse selection, even though moral hazard was also present. Here we shall extend the analysis to random performance, as in Chapter 4, and we shall detail the respective roles of moral hazard and adverse selection and the implications of their simultaneous presence.

To do so, we consider the problem of selling a firm or any other productive asset to a new owner-manager. This is an obvious example involving both adverse selection and moral hazard, since the new owner may be more or less able and she may put in more or less effort in running the firm. As we shall see, the prescriptions on the optimal sales contract for this problem depend in an essential way on whether only the adverse-selection or the moral-hazard aspect or both are explicitly taken into account. Although the problem we consider is highly stylized, it is relevant for determining how to structure corporate acquisition deals and privatization transactions.

The example we consider is based on a model considered by Bolton, Pivetta, and Roland (1997), but this problem has been explored more completely by Rhodes-Kropf and Viswanathan (2000) and Lewis and Sappington (2000; see also McAfee and McMillan, 1987b; Riley, 1985; Riordan and Sappington, 1987a). Consider the problem of a risk-neutral seller of a firm transacting with a risk-neutral buyer. The buyer can generate an uncertain revenue stream by running this firm. Suppose that there are only two possible revenue realizations: $X \in \{0, R\}$. The buyer may be more or less able at running this firm, and buyer ability here translates into a higher or lower probability of getting the high revenue outcome R. In addition, the buyer can raise the probability of getting R by working harder.

Let θ denote ability, and suppose that $\theta \in \{\theta_L, \theta_H\}$ with $\theta_L < \theta_H$. The seller does not know the buyer's type, and his prior is that the buyer has a high ability θ_H with probability β and a low ability θ_L with probability $(1 - \beta)$.

Let e denote effort here, and suppose that a buyer with ability θ who supplies effort e generates high revenues R with probability θe at a private cost of[9]

$$\psi(e) \equiv \frac{c}{2} e^2$$

Suppose for simplicity that the seller is determined to sell because he is unable to generate any revenue with the firm. The seller's problem then is to offer a menu of contracts (t_i, r_i) to maximize his expected return from the sale, where t_i denotes an up-front cash payment for the firm and r_i a repayment to be paid from the future revenues generated by the new buyer. Assume that the firm is a limited liability corporation so that $X \geq r_i \geq 0$. In that case there is no loss of generality in considering contracts of the form (t_i, r_i), where r_i is paid only if $X = R$.

The buyer's payoff under such a contract then takes the form

$$\theta_i e(R - r_i) - t_i - \frac{c}{2} e^2, \quad i = L, H \tag{6.5}$$

Her optimal choice of effort under a contract (t_i, r_i) is thus

$$e_i = \theta_i (R - r_i)/c \tag{6.6}$$

---

9. To ensure that we have well-defined probabilities, take c to be large enough that the buyer would never want to choose a level of effort e such that $\theta_H e \geq 1$.

and her maximum payoff under the contract is

$$\frac{1}{2c}[\theta_i(R-r_i)]^2 - t_i$$

As one might expect, the buyer's optimal choice of effort is independent of t_i but is decreasing in r_i.

The seller's program then is

$$\max_{(t_i, r_i)}\{\beta[t_H + \theta_H^2(R-r_H)r_H/c] + (1-\beta)[t_L + \theta_L^2(R-r_L)r_L/c]\}$$

subject to

$$\frac{1}{2c}[\theta_i(R-r_i)]^2 - t_i \geq \frac{1}{2c}[\theta_i(R-r_j)]^2 - t_j \quad \text{for all } j \neq i, \text{ and all } i = L, H$$

$$\frac{1}{2c}[\theta_i(R-r_i)]^2 - t_i \geq 0, \quad i = L, H$$

6.3.1   Optimal Contract with Moral Hazard Only

Suppose that the seller is able to observe the buyer's ability so that the only remaining incentive problem is moral hazard. Then the seller's problem can be treated separately for each buyer type i and reduces to

$$\max_{(t_i, r_i)}\{t_i + \theta_i^2(R-r_i)r_i/c\}$$

subject to

$$\frac{1}{2c}[\theta_i(R-r_i)]^2 - t_i \geq 0, \quad i = L, H$$

Since the participation constraint is binding, the problem becomes

$$\max_{r_i}\left\{\frac{1}{2c}[\theta_i(R-r_i)]^2 + \frac{1}{c}\theta_i^2(R-r_i)r_i\right\}$$

or equivalently

$$\max_{r_i} \frac{1}{2c}\theta_i^2(R^2 - r_i^2)$$

This problem has a simple solution: $r_H = r_L = 0$ and $t_i = \theta_i^2 R^2/(2c)$. To avoid the moral hazard problem the seller should sell the firm for cash only and not keep any financial participation in it. This simple yet striking result lies behind many privatization proposals suggesting that the state should sell off 100% of state-owned companies in order to minimize managerial incentive problems. The only reason why a seller might want to keep some financial participation in the pure moral-hazard case is that the buyer may be financially constrained and may not have all the cash available up-front (or the buyer may be risk averse).

6.3.2   Optimal Contract with Adverse Selection Only

Suppose now that the buyer's effort level is fixed at some level $\hat{e}$ but that the seller cannot observe the buyer's talent. The seller's program then is to

$$\max_{(t_i, r_i)}\{\beta(t_H + \theta_H \hat{e} r_H) + (1 - \beta)(t_L + \theta_L \hat{e} r_L)\}$$

subject to

$$\theta_i \hat{e}(R - r_i) - t_i \geq \theta_i \hat{e}(R - r_i) - t_j \quad \text{for all } j \neq 1, \text{ and all } i = L, H$$

$$\theta_i \hat{e}(R - r_i) - t_i - \frac{c}{2}\hat{e}^2 \geq 0; \quad i = L, H$$

This problem also has a simple solution: $r_H = r_L = R$ and $t_i = -c\hat{e}^2/2$. This contract minimizes the buyer's informational rent. In fact, it extracts all of it without inducing any distortions. Intuitively, in the absence of moral hazard, the best incentive-compatible way to extract rents from the buyer is to ask for 100% of the future return (and therefore no cash up-front).

6.3.3   Optimal Sales with Both Adverse Selection and Moral Hazard

The simplicity of the preceding solutions is of course driven by the extreme nature of the setup. It appears that neither extreme formulation is an adequate representation of the basic problem at hand and that it is necessary to allow for both types of incentive problems to have a plausible description of asset sales in practice.

Not surprisingly, the optimal menu of contracts when both types of incentive problems are present is some combination of the two extreme solutions that we have highlighted. Solving the problem of the seller can be done by relying on the pure adverse-selection methodology detailed in Chapter 2. Specifically, one can first note that only the individual-rationality constraint of the low buyer type and the incentive-compatibility constraint of the high buyer type will be binding. Indeed, (1) when the low type earns nonnegative rents, so will the high type, who can always mimic the low type; and (2) in the symmetric-information (that is, pure moral-hazard) optimum, the seller manages to leave the high type with no rents, but this outcome is what would induce her to mimic the low type. Therefore, the seller has to solve

$$\max_{(t_i, r_i)} \{\beta[t_H + \theta_H^2(R - r_H)r_H / c] + (1 - \beta)[t_L + \theta_L^2(R - r_L)r_L] / c\}$$

subject to

$$\frac{1}{2c}[\theta_H(R - r_H)]^2 - t_H = \frac{1}{2c}[\theta_H(R - r_L)]^2 - t_L$$

$$\frac{1}{2c}[\theta_L(R - r_L)]^2 - t_L = 0$$

Using the two binding constraints to eliminate t_H and t_L from the maximand, we obtain the usual efficiency-at-the-top condition $r_H = 0$ (as in the pure moral-hazard case). However, raising r_L allows the seller to reduce the informational rent enjoyed by the high buyer type, which is

$$\frac{1}{2c}(\theta_H^2 - \theta_L^2)(R - r_L)^2$$

The first-order condition with respect to r_L involves the usual trade-off between surplus extraction from the low buyer type and informational rent concession to the high buyer type, and leads to

$$r_L = \frac{\beta(\theta_H^2 - \theta_L^2)R}{\beta(\theta_H^2 - \theta_L^2) + (1 - \beta)\theta_L^2}$$

which is bigger than 0. The optimal menu of contracts is thus such that there is no effort-supply distortion for the high-ability buyer because she is a 100% residual claimant. But there is a downward effort distortion for the low-ability buyer that serves the purpose of reducing the informational rent of the high-ability buyer. The extent of the distortion, measured by the size of r_L, depends on the size of the ability differential $(\theta_H^2 - \theta_L^2)$ and on the seller's prior β: The more confident the seller is that he faces a high buyer type, the larger is his stake r_L and the larger is the up-front payment t_H.

6.4   Summary and Literature Notes

This chapter has first considered the multidimensional adverse selection paradigm, whose analysis was started by Adams and Yellen (1976) in the context of optimal selling strategies by a monopoly. A recurring theme in the literature has been to establish conditions under which mixed bundling (the simultaneous separate and joint sale of multiple products) is optimal. As shown by McAfee, McMillan, and Whinston (1989), mixed bundling is optimal when consumer valuations for the different goods are not strongly positively correlated, thereby extending Adams and Yellen's original insight.

The subsequent literature illustrates the difficulty of generalizing the analysis of the one-dimensional setting considered in Chapter 2 (see Armstrong, 1996, and Rochet and Choné, 1998, for general models, Armstrong and Rochet, 1999, for a complete solution of a simple case, and Rochet and Stole, 2003, for an overview). These studies have generated several new insights. In particular, Armstrong (1996) has established the prevalence of *exclusion* in optimal contracts: In the presence of multidimensional uncertainty, it typically becomes attractive to exclude buyers with the lowest valuation *for both products*, because the loss the seller incurs by excluding them is typically of second order relative to the gain he thereby makes in terms of rent extraction on the other buyer types. A second insight, illustrated in Armstrong (1999), concerns the optimality of simple contracts: A monopolist selling many items and facing consumers with independently distributed valuations can approximate the optimal contract with a simple two-part tariff.

We then turned our attention to multidimensional moral hazard. The core principle stressed here is the desirability of keeping a *balance* between incentives across tasks to avoid a form of "task arbitrage" by the agent that results in some tasks being neglected (when higher effort on one task raises the marginal cost of effort on the other task). Consequently, incentives on a given task should be reduced when a competing task becomes harder to monitor. In extreme cases, providing no incentives at all may be the optimum! An alternative route is to prevent the agent from undertaking the competing task altogether.

Our treatment of these issues has been based on Holmström and Milgrom (1991). Additional references include the following:

• Laffont and Tirole (1991) and Hart, Shleifer, and Vishny (1997) analyze the trade-off between incentives to cut costs and incentives to raise product quality.

• Laffont and Tirole (1988b) and Holmström and Tirole (1993) discuss incentives to improve short-term and long-term profits.

• Martimort (1996), Dixit (1996), and Bernheim and Whinston (1998a) analyze multiprincipal models (as we do in Chapter 13) and discuss the benefits of exclusivity, that is, of preventing the agent from dealing with more than one principal.

Multitask problems also arise in the absence of an effort-substitution problem when tasks are *directly in conflict*. In such a case, eliciting effort on both tasks from a single agent is more expensive for the principal because success on the second task directly undermines performance on the first task. This consideration leads to the optimality of hiring one agent per task and making them *advocates* for the task they are asked to perform, rather than having them internalize the overall objective function of the principal. This question has been investigated by Dewatripont and Tirole (1999), who analyze the optimality of organizing the judicial system (that is, the "pursuit of justice") as a competition between prosecution and defense lawyers (see also Milgrom and Roberts, 1986b; Shin, 1998). Another example of conflicting tasks concerns ex ante and ex post control of "illegal" behavior: Uncovering illegality ex post indicates a failure to have stopped it ex ante. Endowing the two tasks to separate agents then avoids "regulatory cover-ups," as discussed by Boot and Thakor (1993) and Dewatripont and Tirole (1994b).

Note finally that combining tasks can at times be good for incentives, by reducing adverse selection problems: see, for example, Riordan and Sappington (1987b) (and more generally Lewis and Sappington, 1989, on "countervailing incentives").

We concluded the chapter with an illustration of a model that combines adverse selection and moral hazard. Various models share this feature, including Laffont and Tirole (1986) and McAfee and McMillan (1987b) in the context of a problem of regulation of a natural monopoly; and Riley (1985), Riordan and Sappington (1987a), Lewis and Sappington (1997), and Caillaud, Guesnerie, and Rey (1992) in an agency setting. Crémer and Khalil (1992) also consider the related problem of an agent gathering information (at a cost) about the state of nature before signing a contract with the principal.

We have relied here on an application explored in Bolton, Pivetta, and Roland (1997) on the sale of a firm to a new risk-neutral owner-manager, which has been explored independently and more fully by Rhodes-Kropf and Viswanathan (2000) and Lewis and Sappington (2000). In this application, under pure moral hazard, the optimal strategy is to sell the firm to the manager for a fixed price in order to induce subsequent efficient managerial effort. Under pure adverse selection, the seller should instead ask for 100% of the future revenue of the firm, so as to leave no informational rent to the manager. In contrast to these two extreme solutions, when both information problems are present, the optimal contract resembles the contracts analyzed in Chapter 2, with efficient effort for one type and underprovision of effort for the other type.

II STATIC MULTILATERAL CONTRACTING

In this second part we consider static optimal contracting problems between $n \geq 3$ parties, or between one principal and two or more agents. The key conceptual difference between the bilateral contracting problems considered in the first part and the problems considered in this part is that the principal's contract-design problem is now no longer one of simply controlling a single agent's *decision problem,* but is a much more complex problem of designing a *game* involving the strategic behavior of several agents interacting with each other.

When it comes to game (or mechanism) design, one is confronted with a major new theoretical issue: predicting how the game will be played by the agents. Thus, a central question we shall have to address in this part is what are likely or reasonable outcomes of the game among agents defined by the contract. This is, of course, the central question that game theorists have been concerned with ever since the field of game theory was founded by von Neumann and Morgenstern (1944). Given that game theorists have proposed different approaches and equilibrium notions it should come as no surprise that contract theorists (often the same people wearing different hats) have also considered several different equilibrium notions for the games specified by a multilateral contract.

In many ways the most satisfactory approach is to design the games in such a way that each player has a unique dominant strategy. Then the outcome of the game is easy to predict. It is the unique dominant strategy equilibrium. Whenever it is possible to achieve the efficient outcome with such games, this is the most desirable way to proceed. But when it is not possible to achieve first-best efficiency with contracts where each party has a unique dominant strategy, it may be desirable to consider a larger class of contracts where the contracting parties are playing a game with a less clear-cut but hopefully more efficient outcome.[1]

In other words, it may be in the principal's best interest to accept that the contract creates a game situation with some inevitable uncertainty as to how the agents will play the game, if the most plausible outcome of play is

---

1. Situations where it is not possible to achieve first-best efficiency with contracts where each player has a well-defined dominant strategy are by no means uncommon. One of the main results in dominant strategy implementation due to Gibbard (1973) and Satterthwaite (1975) is an impossibility result akin to Arrow's impossibility theorem establishing that dominant strategy contracts cannot in general achieve first-best efficiency when there are at least three outcomes and when the players' domain of preferences is unrestricted.

more efficient. Now, although there is always some uncertainty as to how the parties play the game, it is not implausible that they will attempt to play some best response. Therefore it could be argued that a plausible outcome of play by the agents may be some Nash or (with incomplete information) Bayesian equilibrium of the game induced by the contract.

Most of the literature on contract and mechanism design theory takes this route and assumes that the set of outcomes of the game among agents is the set of Nash or Bayesian equilibria. As our purpose in this book is not to offer a crash course in game and mechanism design theory, we shall consider only optimal multilateral contracts with this equilibrium notion.[2]

The first chapter in this second part (Chapter 7) considers multilateral contracting problems under *hidden information*. Perhaps the leading example of such contracting problems is an *auction* involving a seller (the principal) and multiple buyers (the agents) with private information about their valuation of the goods for sale. The second chapter (Chapter 8) considers multilateral contracting problems under *hidden actions*. A classical example of such a contracting problem is the *moral hazard in teams* problem. More generally, this paradigm allows us to address many questions pertaining to the internal design of organizations.

---

2. For an overview of mechanism design under private information and other equilibrium notions we refer the interested reader to Mas-Colell, Whinston, and Green (1995, chap. 23), Fudenberg and Tirole (1991, chap. 7), and Palfrey (1992).

7 Multilateral Asymmetric Information: Bilateral Trading and Auctions

7.1 Introduction

In this chapter we consider optimal contracts when several contracting parties have private information. One central question we shall be concerned with is how trade between a buyer and a seller is affected by asymmetric information about both the buyer's value and the seller's cost. We shall also ask how a seller's optimal nonlinear pricing policy is affected by competition between several buyers with unknown value. We shall demonstrate that the general methodology and most of the core ideas developed in Chapter 2 carry over in a straightforward fashion to the general case of multilateral asymmetric information.

Consider $n \geq 2$ parties to a contract, each having private information about some personal characteristic. The game between these agents is generally referred to as a game of incomplete information. The accepted definition of a game with incomplete information since Harsanyi (1967–68) is as follows:

DEFINITION   A game of incomplete information $\mathbb{C} = (S, \Theta, \beta, u)$ is composed of the following:

• The strategy space $S = S_1 \times \ldots \times S_n$, with one strategy set S_i for each player $i = 1, \ldots, n$.

• The type space $\Theta = \Theta_1 \times \ldots \times \Theta_n$, with Θ_i denoting player i's set of possible types.

• The probability profile $\beta = \beta_1 \times \ldots \times \beta_n$, where $\beta_i \equiv \{\beta_i(\theta_{-i}|\theta_i)\}$ denotes player i's probability distribution over other players' types, $\theta_{-i} = (\theta_1, \ldots, \theta_{i-1}, \theta_{i+1}, \ldots, \theta_n)$, conditional on his own type θ_i. The β_i's are derived using Bayes' rule from $\beta^*(\theta)$, the joint distribution over the type space Θ.

• The utility profile $u = u_1 \times \ldots \times u_n$ where $u_i(s_{-i}, s_i|\theta_{-i}, \theta_i)$ denotes player i's von Neumann–Morgenstern utility as a function of the vector of strategies s and the vector of types θ.

The structure of $\mathbb{C}$ is assumed to be common knowledge among all the players in the game. That is, it is common knowledge that the distribution for θ is β^* and that β_i is simply the marginal distribution for θ_{-i} conditional on θ_i. For readers unfamiliar with these notions, an extensive exposition of games with incomplete information can be found in Fudenberg and Tirole (1991), Binmore (1992), or Myerson (1991).

The analogue of Nash equilibrium for games of incomplete information is the notion of Bayesian equilibrium defined as follows:

DEFINITION   A *Bayesian equilibrium* of a game with incomplete information $\mathbb{C}$ is a profile of best-response functions $\sigma = (\sigma_1, \ldots, \sigma_n) = (\sigma_{-i}, \sigma_i)$ where $\sigma_i : \Theta_i \to S_i$ is such that

$$\sum_{\theta_{-i} \in \Theta_{-i}} \beta_i(\theta_{-i}|\theta_i)u_i[\sigma_{-i}(\theta_{-i}), \sigma_i|\theta] \geq \sum_{\theta_{-i} \in \Theta_{-i}} \beta_i(\theta_{-i}|\theta_i)u_i[\sigma_{-i}(\theta_{-i}), s_i|\theta]$$

for all i, all θ, and all s_i.

In words, as for Nash equilibria in games with complete information, the profile of best-response functions is an equilibrium if no agent type gains by deviating from the prescribed best response, when all other agents are assumed to play according to the prescribed best-response functions.

Generally games with incomplete information have at least one equilibrium (possibly in mixed strategies) when strategy sets are compact and payoff functions are continuous. When the equilibrium is unique, there is little ambiguity, and the outcome of the game specified by the contract can be taken to be that equilibrium. When there are multiple equilibria, it is less clear what the outcome should be, but a case can be made for taking the most efficient equilibrium as the natural outcome.[1] In most applications in this chapter the optimal contract specifies a unique equilibrium, so that we do not need to confront this delicate issue. Nevertheless, it is important to bear in mind that even if an equilibrium is unique there is no guarantee that the outcome of the game is that equilibrium.[2]

With this word of caution we shall proceed and assume that the outcome of the game specified by the contract is the (unique) Bayesian equilibrium of that game. The contract is then described formally by $(\mathbb{C}, a)$ where $a = a[\sigma^*(\theta)]$ is the outcome function specifying an outcome for each type

1. On mechanisms that achieve unique equilibria, see Palfrey (1992).

2. In an interesting experiment Bull, Schotter, and Weigelt (1987) have indeed found that the variance in subjects' responses is considerably larger in contractual situations where the parties are effectively playing a game with incomplete information than in situations where they only have to solve a decision problem.

profile $\theta \in \Theta$ associated with the game $\mathbb{C}$. This outcome function simply maps the (unique) Bayesian equilibrium $\sigma^* = (\sigma_1^*, \ldots, \sigma_n^*)$ into an outcome for the game. What is done here is therefore simply to redefine utilities in terms of outcomes and types, instead of strategies and types: $u_i[\sigma^*(\theta)|\theta] \equiv u_i(a[\sigma^*(\theta)]|\theta)$.

The principal's contract design problem can then be described formally as follows: Let A denote the set of all possible outcomes, and let $V(\cdot): \Theta \rightarrow A$ denote some objective function of the principal. That is, $V(\theta)$ denotes an outcome favored by the principal when the profile of types is θ. The contract $(\mathbb{C}, a)$ is then said to implement $V(\cdot)$ if $a[\sigma^*(\theta)] = V(\theta)$. The principal's problem then is to achieve the most preferred objective $V(\cdot)$ by optimizing over the set of feasible contracts $(\mathbb{C}, a)$.

Although the general description of a game of incomplete information and of a Bayesian equilibrium looks rather daunting, in most applications in this book this description is both simple and natural. In particular, those applications where agents are assumed to be of only two possible types can be handled without too much difficulty.

In addition, although there is a very large set of contracts from which the principal can choose, many contracts will in fact be redundant. Just as in Chapter 2, it is possible to simplify the principal's problem by eliminating most irrelevant alternatives and restricting attention to a subset of so-called revelation contracts in which the players' strategy sets are simply their type set $S_i = \Theta_i$ and where players truthfully announce their type in the (unique) Bayesian equilibrium.

A revelation contract $(\mathbb{C}/\Theta, \hat{a})$, where S is replaced by Θ in $\mathbb{C}$, is said to truthfully implement $V(\cdot)$ if $\hat{a}[\sigma^*(\theta)] = V(\theta)$, where $\sigma^*(\theta) = [\theta_1(\theta), \ldots, \theta_n(\theta)]$ is the Bayesian equilibrium of the revelation game where each player truthfully reports his type. The revelation principle establishes that for every contract $(\mathbb{C}, a)$ that implements $V(\cdot)$ an alternative revelation contract $(\mathbb{C}/\Theta, \hat{a})$ can be found that also truthfully implements $V(\cdot)$.

THE REVELATION PRINCIPLE   Let $(\mathbb{C}, a)$ be a contract that implements $V(.)$; then a revelation contract $(\mathbb{C}/\Theta, \hat{a})$ can be found that truthfully implements $V(\cdot)$.

One can prove this result as follows: Let $\sigma^*(\theta)$ be the Bayesian equilibrium of the game $\mathbb{C}$, and define the composite function $\hat{a} = a \circ \sigma^*$. That is,

$\hat{a}(\theta) = a[\sigma^*(\theta)]$ for all $\theta \in \Theta$. To prove that $(\mathbb{C}/\Theta, \hat{a})$ truthfully implements $V(\cdot)$ it suffices to show that $\hat{\sigma}(\theta) = [\theta_1(\theta), \ldots, \theta_n(\theta)]$ is a Bayesian equilibrium of $(\mathbb{C}/\Theta, \hat{a})$. By construction we have

$$\sum_{\theta_{-i} \in \Theta_{-i}} \beta_i(\theta_{-i} | \theta_i) u_i \{a[\sigma^*(\theta)] | \theta\} \geq \sum_{\theta_{-i} \in \Theta_{-i}} \beta_i(\theta_{-i} | \theta_i) u_i \left\{a\left[\sigma^*_{-i}(\theta), s_i\right]\right\}$$

But, by definition of $\hat{a}$, we have $a[\sigma^*(\theta)] = \hat{a}(\theta)$ and $a[\sigma^*_{-i}(\theta), s_i] = \hat{a}(\theta'_i, \theta_{-i})$ for some type announcement $\theta'_i \neq \theta_i$. So we conclude that for all $i = 1, \ldots, n$ we have

$$\sum_{\theta_{-i} \in \Theta_{-i}} \beta_i(\theta_{-i} | \theta_i) u_i[\hat{a}(\theta) | \theta] \geq \sum_{\theta_{-i} \in \Theta_{-i}} \beta_i(\theta_{-i} | \theta_i) u_i[\hat{a}(\theta'_i, \theta_{-i}) | \theta]$$

as required, which proves the result.

Note that, in contrast to the result obtained in the single-agent problem, this result does not say that there is no loss of generality in restricting attention to revelation contracts, since it does not establish that there is necessarily a unique Bayesian-Nash equilibrium in the revelation contract $(\mathbb{C}/\Theta, \hat{a})$ constructed from the contract $(\mathbb{C}, a)$, even when the contract $(\mathbb{C}, a)$ admits only a unique equilibrium. In the transformation process from $(\mathbb{C}, a)$ to $(\mathbb{C}/\Theta, \hat{a})$, the players' strategy sets may well become smaller, and this may enlarge the equilibrium set (see Dasgupta, Hammond, and Maskin, 1979). In other words, in contrast to the single-agent problem, the restriction to revelation contracts may result in greater uncertainty concerning the outcome of the contract (a larger equilibrium set). Here, we choose to disregard this problem, which is treated at length in Palfrey (1992).

We shall consider in turn two classic pure exchange problems. The first is a bilateral trade problem under two-sided asymmetric information (about the seller's cost and the buyer's reservation value). The second is an auction setting where two (or more) buyers with private information about reservation values compete to purchase a good from a seller. As in Chapter 2, we begin our analysis of contracting under multilateral asymmetric information with a detailed exposition of the special case where each party has only two different types. This special case is more tractable and is sufficient to illustrate most economic insights. We then proceed to a more advanced analysis of the more general and elegant problem with a continuum of types.

7.2   Bilateral Trading

7.2.1   The Two-Type Case

In Chapter 2 we found that when an uninformed party (say, a seller, "he") makes a take-it-or-leave-it offer to an informed party (a buyer, "she"), then inefficient trade may result. For example, take a buyer with two possible valuations for a good: $v_H > v_L > 0$, and a seller who has a value of zero for the good. Let β denote the seller's prior belief that the buyer has a high valuation. Then the (risk-neutral) seller's best offer to the buyer is $P = v_H$ whenever $\beta v_H \geq v_L$. For such offers, there is (ex post) inefficient trade with probability $(1 - \beta)$ whenever the buyer's true value is v_L.

If instead the informed party (here, the buyer) makes the contract offer, then there is always ex post efficient trade. The buyer simply makes an offer $P = 0$ which the seller always accepts. Thus, if the objective is to promote efficient trade, there is a simple solution available in the case of unilateral asymmetric information: simply give all the bargaining power to informed parties.

This simple example highlights one obvious facet of the fundamental *trade-off between allocative efficiency and the distribution of informational rents:* If the bargaining power lies with the uninformed party, then that party attempts to appropriate some of the informational rents of the informed party at the expense of allocative efficiency. By implication, to reduce the allocative distortions associated with informational rent extraction, one should remove bargaining power from uninformed agents whenever it is possible to do so. Stated differently, if all bargaining power of uninformed agents can somehow be removed, one need no longer be concerned about allocative efficiency.

But this solution is not available when there is bilateral asymmetric information. An obvious question then is whether efficient trade is still attainable under bilateral asymmetric information if the surplus from trade can be distributed arbitrarily between the buyer and seller. It turns out that this question has a simple general answer. It has been elegantly put by Joseph Farrell (1987) as follows:

Suppose the problem is which of two people should have an indivisible object, a "seller" (who originally has it) or a "buyer." The efficient solution is that whoever in fact values it more should have it, with perhaps some payment to the other.

(That is, every Pareto-efficient outcome has this form.) The king can easily achieve this outcome using an incentive-compatible scheme if participation is compulsory: for example, he can confiscate the item from the "seller" and then auction it off, dividing the revenues equally between the two people. But this solution is not feasible with voluntary trade; the seller may prefer to keep the object rather than to participate and risk having to repurchase (or lose) something he already has. A lump sum payment to the seller could solve that problem, but then the buyer (who would have to make the payment) might prefer to withdraw. (p. 120)

As Farrell's explanation highlights, the difficulty here is not so much eliciting the parties' private information as ensuring their participation. We show in this section that efficient trade can (almost) always be achieved if the parties' participation is obtained *ex ante,* before they learn their type, while it cannot be achieved if the parties' participation decision is made when they already know their type. In other words, when the contracting parties already know their type, the extent to which the surplus from trade can be distributed arbitrarily between them while maintaining their participation is too limited to always obtain efficient trade.

Consider the situation where the seller has two possible costs $c_H > c_L \geq 0$ and the buyer's two possible valuations are such that $v_H > c_H > v_L > c_L$.[3] To simplify matters, assume that valuation and cost are independently distributed. Let the buyer's prior beliefs that the seller has low cost be γ. The principal's objective here is to achieve efficient trade. Let $x = 1$ denote "trade" and $x = 0$ denote "no trade."

Applying the revelation principle, the principal must find prices contingent on the buyer's value and seller's cost announcements, $P(\hat{v}, \hat{c})$, such that efficient trade, that is, $x(\hat{v}, \hat{c}) = 1$ if and only if $\hat{v} \geq \hat{c}$, is incentive compatible and individually rational for both buyer and seller. As we argued previously, the main difficulty here is not to find incentive-compatible prices: they can be found because efficient trades are *monotonic,* that is, the probability of trading under efficiency is increasing in the buyer's valuation and decreasing in the seller's cost. The problem is rather to find incentive-compatible prices that also satisfy both parties' individual-rationality constraints.

---

3. These are the values for which establishing efficient trade is most difficult. Indeed, suppose that instead we have $v_H > v_L > c_H > c_L$. In that case efficient trade is guaranteed by fixing a price $P \in [c_H, v_L]$. Alternatively, suppose that $c_H > v_H > v_L > c_L$. Then efficient trade is guaranteed by setting a price $P \in [c_L, v_L]$ and letting the seller decide whether he wants to trade at that price. Similarly, when $v_H > c_H > c_L > v_L$, efficient trade is established by setting $P \in [v_H, c_H]$ and letting the buyer decide whether to trade.

Whether efficient trade can be achieved will depend crucially on which individual-rationality constraints are relevant: *interim* or *ex ante* IR constraints. Interim constraints are relevant whenever the buyer and the seller know their type when signing the contract. Ex ante constraints are relevant when they sign the contract before knowing their exact cost or value realization. We begin by showing a general result—first established in the context of efficient public good provision by d'Aspremont and Gérard-Varet (1979)—that when ex ante individual-rationality constraints are relevant, then efficient trade can always be achieved despite the double asymmetry of information about costs and values.

7.2.1.1 Efficient Trade under Ex Ante Individual-Rationality Constraints

Suppose that the principal (say, a social planner) offers the buyer and seller, *before each one has learned his or her type,* the following bilateral trading contract: $\mathbb{C} = \{P(v_i,c_j) \equiv P_{ij}; x(v_i,c_j) \equiv x_{ij}; i = L, H; j = L, H\}$, where $x_{ij} = 1$ if $v_i \geq c_j$ and $x_{ij} = 0$ otherwise. The seller's incentive-compatibility (IC) and ex ante individual-rationality (IR) constraints then take the form

$$(1-\beta)[P_{LL} - c_L] + \beta[P_{HL} - c_L] \geq (1-\beta)P_{LH} + \beta[P_{HH} - c_L] \tag{7.1}$$

$$(1-\beta)P_{LH} + \beta[P_{HH} - c_H] \geq (1-\beta)[P_{LL} - c_H] + \beta[P_{HL} - c_H] \tag{7.2}$$

$$\gamma[(1-\beta)P_{LL} + \beta P_{HL} - c_L] + (1-\gamma)[(1-\beta)P_{LH} + \beta(P_{HH} - c_H)] \geq 0 \tag{7.3}$$

In these equations note that when the buyer has a low value v_L and the seller has a high cost c_H there is no trade, that is, $x_{LH} = 0$.

We therefore require the type-j seller to prefer truth telling given his type and *given that he expects the buyer to tell the truth about her type,* and to break even given that he himself expects to be of type L with probability γ.

Similarly, the buyer's (IC) and ex ante (IR) constraints are

$$\gamma[v_L - P_{LL}] - (1-\gamma)P_{LH} \geq \gamma[v_L - P_{HL}] + (1-\gamma)[v_L - P_{HH}] \tag{7.4}$$

$$\gamma[v_H - P_{HL}] + (1-\gamma)[v_H - P_{HH}] \geq \gamma[v_H - P_{LL}] - (1-\gamma)P_{LH} \tag{7.5}$$

$$\beta[v_H - \gamma P_{HL} - (1-\gamma)P_{HH}] + (1-\beta)[\gamma v_L - \gamma P_{LL} - (1-\gamma)P_{LH}] \geq 0 \tag{7.6}$$

In order to analyze this set of inequalities, let us call $\overline{P}$ the expected payment the buyer will have to make to the seller:

$$\overline{P} = \gamma[(1-\beta)P_{LL} + \beta P_{HL}] + (1-\gamma)[(1-\beta)P_{LH} + \beta P_{HH}]$$

Then the two (IR) constraints can be rewritten as

$$\beta v_H + (1-\beta)\gamma v_L \geq \overline{P} \geq \gamma c_L + (1-\gamma)\beta c_H$$

These constraints thus require the expected payment $\overline{P}$ to divide the expected first-best surplus, which is clearly positive, into two positive shares. This requirement implies a condition on the expected *level* of payments, which can be adjusted without any consequence on incentive constraints, which depend only on the *differences* of payments across realizations of costs and valuations. These incentive constraints can be redefined for the seller and buyer, respectively, as

$$(1-\beta)c_H \geq (1-\beta)[P_{LL} - P_{LH}] + \beta[P_{HL} - P_{HH}] \geq (1-\beta)c_L$$

and

$$(1-\gamma)v_H \geq \gamma[P_{HL} - P_{LL}] + (1-\gamma)[P_{HH} - P_{LH}] \geq (1-\gamma)v_L$$

The incentive constraints for the seller can be interpreted as follows: given truth telling by the buyer, if the seller announces a low cost, trade will take place with probability 1. Instead, if the seller announces a high cost, trade will take place only with probability β (that is, when the buyer has a high valuation). The increase in expected payment the seller will receive upon announcing low cost should thus cover the increase in expected production cost (due to trade taking place with probability 1 instead of β) if the seller's cost is c_L, but not if the seller's cost is c_H.

The idea is exactly the same for the buyer: given truth telling by the seller, if the buyer announces a high valuation, trade will take place with probability 1. Instead, if the buyer announces a low valuation, trade will take place only with probability γ (that is, when the seller has low cost). The increase in expected payment the buyer will incur upon announcing a high valuation should thus be lower than the increase in expected value of consumption (due to trade taking place with probability 1 instead of γ) if the buyer's valuation is v_H, but not if the buyer's valuation is v_L.

If constraints (7.1) to (7.6) are satisfied, both parties are happy to participate and truth telling results, so that we have implemented the ex post efficient allocation. The fact that payments exist such that all constraints are satisfied is easy to see. Indeed, the constraints can be satisfied recursively. First of all, note that the incentive constraints are not incompatible for any party, since $v_H > v_L$ and $c_H > c_L$. Second, consider any vector

$(P_{LL}, P_{LH}, P_{HL}, P_{HH})$ such that the incentive constraints of the seller are satisfied. It is easy to see that any change in (P_{LL}, P_{LH}) that keeps $(P_{LL} - P_{LH})$ unchanged will leave the incentive constraints of the seller unaffected. This observation provides a degree of freedom that can be used to satisfy the incentive constraints of the buyer. Finally, we have already observed that any change in $(P_{LL}, P_{LH}, P_{HL}, P_{HH})$ that involves an adjustment (upward or downward) of all four payments by the same amount leaves all incentive constraints unaffected. This fact provides another degree of freedom to set $\overline{P}$ to satisfy the participation constraints of the parties. This system of inequalities therefore admits a solution, and it is possible to find incentive-compatible and individually rational contracts that achieve efficient trade.

This result holds very generally. It holds, in particular, for public-goods problems with an arbitrary number of agents, each with an arbitrary number of independently distributed types, as d'Aspremont and Gérard-Varet (1979) have shown. But efficient trade can be achieved even when agents' types are correlated. This possibility is straightforward to establish in our simple example. In fact, correlation of types can make it easier to achieve efficiency, as we shall see when we consider auctions with correlated values.

A simple general explanation behind this result runs as follows: Assuming that one of the agents truthfully reveals her type, the other agent faces different odds depending on whether she tells the truth or not. This difference in odds can then be exploited to construct lotteries that have a negative net expected value when the agent lies, but a positive value when the agent truthfully reveals her type. Then, by ensuring that the ex ante compound lottery (the lottery over lotteries for each type) has a positive ex ante net expected value, the principal can make sure that both buyer and seller are willing to participate. Concretely, here, if for example the seller has cost c_H, then he (weakly) prefers the lottery requiring him to produce at a price P_{HH} with probability β, and not to produce and receive a transfer P_{LH} with probability $(1 - \beta)$. Similarly, if he has cost c_L, he prefers the lottery where he obtains $(P_{HL} - c_L)$ with probability β, and $(P_{LL} - c_L)$ with probability $(1 - \beta)$. As long as the compound lottery (composed of the lottery for type c_H and the lottery for type c_L) has a positive expected value, the seller is willing to accept the contract. And the same is true, mutatis mutandis, for the buyer.

A helpful economic intuition for this result, which is often given for problems of public-goods provision under asymmetric information, is that efficiency requires essentially that each agent appropriate the expected externality her actions impose on other agents. In this way, each agent is induced to internalize the whole collective decision problem and is effectively maximizing the social objective. Since the sum of all expected externalities is just the social surplus, trade can be implemented whenever it is efficient.

7.2.1.2 Inefficient Trade under Interim Individual-Rationality Constraints

Now suppose that the buyer and seller know their type before signing the contract. Then the ex ante participation constraints must be replaced by the following four interim constraints:

$$(1-\beta)P_{LL} + \beta P_{HL} - c_L \geq 0$$

$$(1-\beta)P_{LH} + \beta(P_{HH} - c_H) \geq 0$$

$$v_H - \gamma P_{HL} - (1-\gamma)P_{HH} \geq 0$$

$$\gamma v_L - \gamma P_{LL} - (1-\gamma)P_{LH} \geq 0$$

In fact, for some values of β and γ, these four constraints together with the incentive constraints (7.1), (7.2), (7.4), and (7.5) cannot all simultaneously hold. For example, let the probability of the seller facing a high-valuation buyer, β, tend to 1, then from conditions (7.1) and (7.2) we have $P_{HH} \simeq P_{HL}$, which we shall denote $\hat{P}$. Therefore, the interim participation constraints of the seller reduce to

$$\hat{P} - c_L \geq 0$$

$$\hat{P} - c_H \geq 0$$

In words, when the seller thinks the buyer is almost surely of type v_H, he knows he will have to produce with probability close to 1 whatever his type; as a result, the expected price $\hat{P}$ has to cover his cost, whether low or high.

In addition, when the probability of facing a high-valuation buyer, β, tends to 1 and $P_{HH} \simeq P_{HL} \equiv \hat{P}$, by condition (7.5), we have

$$v_H - \hat{P} \geq \gamma[v_H - P_{LL}] - (1-\gamma)P_{LH}$$

which says that, for the buyer, telling the truth about v_H and buying the good for sure at price $\hat{P}$ should be better than lying and getting v_H with probability γ (that is, when the seller has low cost) and paying the associated expected price. This condition together with $\beta \simeq 1$ implies that the interim participation constraints of the buyer reduce to

$$\hat{P} \le v_H$$

$$\hat{P} \le \gamma v_L + (1-\gamma)v_H$$

This expression says that the high-valuation buyer cannot be made to pay more than v_H, obviously, but also not more than $v_H - \gamma(v_H - v_L)$: this last term is the information rent the high-valuation buyer can obtain by pretending to have a low valuation and trading with probability γ at terms that give the low-valuation buyer zero rents.

Collecting all interim participation constraints together, we must have

$$\gamma v_L + (1-\gamma)v_H \ge c_H$$

But if the probability that the seller has a low cost, γ, tends to 1, this inequality does not hold: because the buyer believes that she is almost certainly facing a low-cost seller, it becomes very attractive for her to pretend to have a low valuation, since in any case the probability of trade is almost 1. To prevent the buyer from pretending this, we need $\hat{P} \le v_L$, but this is incompatible with $\hat{P} \ge c_H$, since we have assumed $c_H > v_L$ in order to make the problem interesting.

In other words, when prior beliefs are such that the seller thinks that he is most likely to face a high-value buyer and the buyer thinks that she is most likely to face a low-cost seller, then each one wants to claim a share of the surplus that is incompatible with the other party's claim, and trade breaks down.

Thus, when the optimal contract must satisfy both incentive-compatibility and interim individual-rationality constraints, efficient trade cannot always be obtained under bilateral asymmetric information. This result can be strengthened by considering the same setting with a continuum of types, as we shall see in section 7.2.2.

To summarize, bilateral trade may be inefficient when both buyer and seller have private information about their respective reservation prices and when this information is available before they engage in voluntary trade. The reason why trade may break down is that each party could attempt to obtain a better deal by misrepresenting his or her valuations. To avoid such misrepresentations, the high-value buyer and the low-cost seller must get informational rents, but the sum of the rents may exceed the surplus from trade in some contingencies, and with interim individual-rationality constraints, informational rents cannot be freely traded across contingencies.

The possibility of inefficient trade under these circumstances is an important theoretical observation because it provides one explanation for why rational self-seeking trading partners leave some gains from trade unexploited. It suggests that the Coase theorem may break down in voluntary trading situations with multilateral asymmetric information. It also points to the potential value of institutions with coercive power that can break interim participation constraints and secure participation at an ex ante stage.

7.2.2   Continuum of Types

Most of the analysis of the special 2×2 model can be straightforwardly extended to a model with a continuum of types by adapting the methodology outlined in section 2.3. In fact, an even sharper characterization of the main results can be obtained in the general problem.

The material of this section follows closely the model and analysis of Myerson and Satterthwaite (1983). They consider a bilateral trading problem where a single good is to be traded between two risk-neutral agents who have private, independently distributed, information about how much they value the item. Suppose, without loss of generality, that agent 1 is in possession of the item and that his privately known valuation v_1 has differentiable strictly positive density $f_1(v_1)$ on the interval $[\underline{v}_1, \bar{v}_1]$. Agent 2's privately known valuation v_2 has differentiable strictly positive density $f_2(v_2)$ on the interval $[\underline{v}_2, \bar{v}_2]$. As in section 7.2.1, the interesting case to consider is that where $\underline{v}_1 < \underline{v}_2 < \bar{v}_1 < \bar{v}_2$. In that case there are both situations where trade is (first-best) efficient and situations where trade is inefficient.

7.2.2.1   Inefficiency of Bilateral Trade with Interim Individual-Rationality Constraints

This section establishes that efficient trade cannot be achieved if contracting takes place at the interim stage. In order to prove this point, we first determine the set of implementable trades that satisfy interim individual rationality. We then show that efficient trading is not in this set.

Step 1: The Set of Implementable Trades   Applying the revelation principle, the principal's problem is to choose a revelation contract

$\{x(\hat{v}_1, \hat{v}_2); P(\hat{v}_1, \hat{v}_2)\}$—where $x(\hat{v}_1, \hat{v}_2)$ denotes the probability of trade and $P(\hat{v}_1, \hat{v}_2)$ the payment from agent 2 to agent 1 contingent on announcements $(\hat{v}_1, \hat{v}_2)$—which satisfies incentive-compatibility and individual-rationality constraints and maximizes the expected gains from trade.

Let us start with some definitions: In any truth-telling equilibrium, agent 1's expected net revenue is given by

$$P_1^e(v_1) = \int_{\underline{v}_2}^{\bar{v}_2} P(v_1, v_2) f_2(v_2) dv_2$$

and agent 2's expected payment by

$$P_2^e(v_2) = \int_{\underline{v}_1}^{\bar{v}_1} P(v_1, v_2) f_1(v_1) dv_1$$

Also, their respective expected probabilities of trade are given by

$$x_1^e(v_1) = \int_{\underline{v}_2}^{\bar{v}_2} x(v_1, v_2) f_2(v_2) dv_2$$

$$x_2^e(v_2) = \int_{\underline{v}_1}^{\bar{v}_1} x(v_1, v_2) f_1(v_1) dv_1$$

Therefore, each agent type's expected payoff under the contract can be written as

$$u_1(v_1) = P_1^e(v_1) - v_1 x_1^e(v_1)$$

$$u_2(v_2) = v_2 x_2^e(v_2) - P_2^e(v_2)$$

The incentive-compatibility and interim individual-rationality constraints for both agents are then given by

$$u_1(v_1) \geq P_1^e(\hat{v}_1) - v_1 x_1^e(\hat{v}_1) \quad \text{for all } v_1, \hat{v}_1 \in [\underline{v}_1, \bar{v}_1] \tag{IC1}$$

$$u_2(v_2) \geq v_2 x_2^e(\hat{v}_2) - P_2^e(\hat{v}_1) \quad \text{for all } v_2, \hat{v}_2 \in [\underline{v}_2, \bar{v}_2] \tag{IC2}$$

$$u_1(v_1) \geq 0 \qquad\qquad\qquad \text{for all } v_1 \in [\underline{v}_1, \bar{v}_1] \tag{IR1}$$

$$u_2(v_2) \geq 0 \qquad\qquad\qquad \text{for all } v_2 \in [\underline{v}_2, \bar{v}_2] \tag{IR2}$$

How can we reduce this set of constraints to a more manageable constrained optimization problem? As we learned in Chapter 2, when both agents' preferences satisfy the single-crossing condition

$$\frac{\partial}{\partial v}\left[-\frac{\partial u/\partial x^e}{\partial u/\partial P^e}\right] > 0$$

as they do here, we ought to expect the following:

1. Only the individual-rationality constraints for the lowest types may be binding: $u_1(\bar{v}_1) \geq 0$ and $u_2(\underline{v}_2) \geq 0$. Note here that the "lowest type" for agent 1 is $\bar{v}_1$. Indeed, since agent 1 is the owner of the item to begin with, his valuation should be interpreted as an opportunity cost, so that his rents will be lowest when his cost is highest.

2. Each agent's expected probability of trade must be monotonically increasing in his type: $x_2^e(v_2)$ is (weakly) increasing in v_2, and $x_1^e(v_1)$ is (weakly) decreasing in v_1.

3. Given monotonicity, only local incentive-compatibility constraints matter, so that each agent type's informational rent is simply the sum of the lowest type's rent and the integral of all inframarginal types' marginal rents:

$$u_1(v_1) = u_1(\bar{v}_1) + \int_{v_1}^{\bar{v}_1} x_1^e(y_1) dy_1$$

and

$$u_2(v_2) = u_2(\underline{v}_2) + \int_{\underline{v}_2}^{v_2} x_2^e(y_2) dy_2$$

This educated guess is indeed correct, as the following argument shows: From the (IC) constraints one observes that, since for any two $\hat{v}_1 > v_1$ we must have

$$u_1(v_1) \geq P_1^e(\hat{v}_1) - v_1 x_1^e(\hat{v}_1) = u_1(\hat{v}_1) + (\hat{v}_1 - v_1) x_1^e(\hat{v}_1)$$

and

$$u_1(\hat{v}_1) \geq P_1^e(v_1) - \hat{v}_1 x_1^e(v_1) = u_1(v_1) + (v_1 - \hat{v}_1) x_1^e(v_1)$$

It follows that

$$(\hat{v}_1 - v_1) x_1^e(v_1) \geq (\hat{v}_1 - v_1) x_1^e(\hat{v}_1)$$

This inequality then implies that x_1^e is weakly decreasing in v_1. Next, by dividing by $(\hat{v}_1 - v_1)$ and letting $\hat{v}_1$ tend to v_1, one obtains

$$u_1'(v_1) = -x_1^e(v_1)$$

which, by integrating with respect to v_1, is equivalent to

$$u_1(v_1) = u_1(\bar{v}_1) + \int_{v_1}^{\bar{v}_1} x_1^e(y_1) dy_1$$

Note that since $x(v_1, v_2) \in [0, 1]$ one can also observe that $u_1(v_1) \geq u_1(\bar{v}_1)$ for all $v_1 \in [\underline{v}_1, \bar{v}_1]$. One easily sees that exactly the same argument can be applied to agent 2's incentive constraints.

Thus, as in the situation with one-sided asymmetric information, we can reduce all the incentive constraints to essentially two conditions for each agent, a monotonicity condition and the first-order condition for each agent's optimization problem, which requires that the marginal increase in informational rent [$-u_1'(v_1)$ for agent 1 and $u_2'(v_2)$ for agent 2] be equal to the expected probability of trade [$x_1^e(v_1)$ for agent 1 and $x_2^e(v_2)$ for agent 2]. Also, at most one individual-rationality constraint will be binding for each agent.

The intuition for these results is straightforward. Agent 1 (the seller) gains by pretending that he is reluctant to sell so as to induce agent 2 (the buyer) to offer a higher price. Thus, other things equal, he would always claim to have the highest possible opportunity cost $\bar{v}_1$. To induce the seller to truthfully announce a valuation $v_1 < \bar{v}_1$, he must therefore be given some informational rent, and giving him this rent requires raising the likelihood of trade when he announces a lower opportunity cost v_1. A similar logic applies to the buyer, who wants to underestimate her valuation for the good. Thus any buyer with valuation $v_2 > \underline{v}_2$ must be given some rent to be induced to tell the truth, or equivalently the likelihood of trade must be increasing in the buyer's announced valuation.

Step 2: Efficient Trading Is Not Implementable   Can efficient trading be implemented? Efficient trading requires that trade take place with probability one whenever $v_1 \leq v_2$ and with probability zero when $v_1 > v_2$. Note first that this requirement does not conflict with monotonicity: the expected probability of trade will clearly be increasing in v_2 and decreasing in v_1. What does create a problem, however, is the sharing of rents: given the requirements of local incentive compatibility and interim individual rationality, efficient trading imposes a lower bound on the expected rents to be conceded to each party: for party 2, even assuming $u_2(\underline{v}_2) = 0$, we must have

$$u_2(v_2) = \int_{\underline{v}_2}^{v_2} F_1(y_2) dy_2$$

And for party 1, even assuming $u_1(\bar{v}_1) = 0$, we must have

$$u_1(v_1) = \int_{v_1}^{\bar{v}_1} [1 - F_2(y_1)] dy_1$$

Taking the expectations of these expressions with respect to v_2 and v_1 and summing them, it may well be that this lower bound on the expected rents to be given to the two parties more than exhausts the total surplus to be shared. And it turns out that indeed a contract imposing the first-best trade probabilities $[x^*(v_1, v_2) = 1$ for $v_1 \le v_2$ and $x^*(v_1, v_2) = 0$ for $v_1 > v_2]$ and satisfying all incentive–compatibility constraints inevitably leads to a violation of interim individual rationality.

To see this result, observe first that

$$P_1^e(v_1) = u_1(v_1) + v_1 x_1^e(v_1) = v_1 x_1^e + u_1(\bar{v}_1) + \int_{v_1}^{\bar{v}_1} x_1^e(y_1) dy_1$$

$$P_2^e(v_2) = v_2 x_2^e(v_2) - u_2(v_2) = v_2 x_2^e - u_1(\underline{v}_2) - \int_{\underline{v}_2}^{v_2} x_2^e(y_2) dy_2$$

For each expression $P_i^e(v_i)$, taking expectations with respect to v_i, integrating the last term by parts, and then substituting for the definitions of $P_i^e(v_i)$ and $x_i^e(v_i)$, one obtains, respectively,

$$\int_{\underline{v}_2}^{\bar{v}_2} \int_{\underline{v}_1}^{\bar{v}_1} P(v_1, v_2) f_1(v_1) f_2(v_2) dv_1 dv_2$$

$$= \int_{\underline{v}_2}^{\bar{v}_2} \int_{\underline{v}_1}^{\bar{v}_1} v_1 x(v_1, v_2) f_1(v_1) f_2(v_2) dv_1 dv_2 + u_1(\bar{v}_1) + \int_{\underline{v}_2}^{\bar{v}_2} \int_{\underline{v}_1}^{\bar{v}_1} x(v_1, v_2) f_1(v_1) f_2(v_2) dv_1 dv_2$$

$$= \int_{\underline{v}_2}^{\bar{v}_2} \int_{\underline{v}_1}^{\bar{v}_1} v_2 x(v_1, v_2) f_1(v_1) f_2(v_2) dv_1 dv_2 - u_2(\underline{v}_2)$$

$$- \int_{\underline{v}_2}^{\bar{v}_2} \int_{\underline{v}_1}^{\bar{v}_1} x(v_1, v_2) f_1(v_1) [1 - F_2(v_2)] dv_1 dv_2$$

Rearranging the last two expressions, one then obtains

$$u_1(\bar{v}_1) + u_2(\underline{v}_2) =$$

$$\int_{\underline{v}_2}^{\bar{v}_2} \int_{\underline{v}_1}^{\bar{v}_1} \left\{ \left[v_2 - \frac{1 - F_2(v_2)}{f_2(v_2)} \right] - \left[v_1 + \frac{F_1(v_1)}{f_1(v_1)} \right] \right\} x(v_1, v_2) f_1(v_1) f_2(v_2) dv_1 dv_2$$

This expected payoff must be nonnegative to satisfy both interim individual-rationality constraints. But substituting $x(v_1, v_2)$ in this expression with the first-best trading probabilities $x^*(v_1, v_2)$, we obtain

$$u_1(\bar{v}_1) + u_2(\underline{v}_2)$$

$$= \int_{\underline{v}_2}^{\bar{v}_2} \int_{\underline{v}_1}^{\min\{v_2, \bar{v}_1\}} [v_2 f_2(v_2) + F_2(v_2) - 1] f_1(v_1) dv_1 dv_2$$

$$- \int_{\underline{v}_2}^{\bar{v}_2} \int_{\underline{v}_1}^{\min\{v_2, \bar{v}_1\}} [v_1 f_1(v_1) + F_1(v_1)] f_2(v_2) dv_1 dv_2$$

$$= \int_{\underline{v}_2}^{\bar{v}_2} [v_2 f_2(v_2) + F_2(v_2) - 1] F_1(v_2) dv_2 - \int_{\underline{v}_2}^{\bar{v}_2} \min\{v_2 F_1(v_2), \bar{v}_1\} f_2(v_2) dv_2$$

where the last term is obtained after integration by parts.

Note, moreover, that $F_1(v_2) = 1$ for $v_2 \geq \bar{v}_1$, which means in particular that $\min\{v_2 F_1(v_2), \bar{v}_1\} = v_2 F_1(v_2)$ whenever $v_2 \leq \bar{v}_1$ and $\min\{v_2 F_1(v_2), \bar{v}_1\} = \bar{v}_1$ whenever $v_2 \geq \bar{v}_1$. Consequently, the preceding expression can be rewritten as

$$u_1(\bar{v}_1) + u_2(\underline{v}_2) = -\int_{\underline{v}_2}^{\bar{v}_2} [1 - F_2(v_2)] F_1(v_2) dv_2 + \int_{\bar{v}_1}^{\bar{v}_2} (v_2 - \bar{v}_1) f_2(v_2) dv_2$$

and, again integrating by parts,

$$u_1(\bar{v}_1) + u_2(\underline{v}_2) = -\int_{\underline{v}_2}^{\bar{v}_2} [1 - F_2(v_2)] F_1(v_2) dv_2 - \int_{\bar{v}_1}^{\bar{v}_2} [F_2(v_2) - 1] dv_2$$

Finally, since $F_1(v_2) = 1$ for $v_2 \geq \bar{v}_1$, this expression is equal to

$$= -\int_{\underline{v}_2}^{\bar{v}_1} [1 - F_2(v_2)] F_1(v_2) dv_2$$

This last expression, however, is strictly negative, since $\underline{v}_2 < \bar{v}_1$. This result establishes that the bilateral trading problem where both buyer and seller have private information at the time of trading *always* results in trade inefficiencies when each contracting party has a continuous distribution of types with strictly positive density on overlapping supports, as we have assumed here.

7.2.2.2 Second-Best Contract

If the first-best outcome is unattainable, the natural next question is, What is the second-best outcome? Remarkably, it turns out that the simple double auction first considered by Chatterjee and Samuelson (1983) is a second-best optimal contract here. We now show this result by first characterizing the second-best outcome and then showing that it can be implemented with the Chatterjee-Samuelson double auction.

Step 1: Characterizing the Second Best   Suppose for simplicity that each agent's value for the item is uniformly and independently distributed on the interval $[0, 1]$. The second-best ex ante optimal outcome maximizes the expected sum of utilities of the two parties subject to the incentive-compatibility and interim individual-rationality constraints for each agent. That is, formally the second-best outcome is a solution to the following constrained optimization problem:

$$\max_{x(v_1,v_2)} \int_0^1 u_1(v_1)dv_1 + \int_0^1 u_2(v_2)dv_2 = \int_0^1 \int_0^1 (v_2 - v_1)x(v_1, v_2)dv_1dv_2$$

subject to

$$\int_0^1 \int_0^1 (2v_2 - 1 - 2v_1)x(v_1, v_2)dv_1dv_2 \geq 0$$

The constraint is simply the expression for the participation constraint

$$\int_{v_2}^{\bar{v}_2} \int_{v_1}^{\bar{v}_1} \left\{ \left[v_2 - \frac{1 - F_2(v_2)}{f_2(v_2)} \right] - \left[v_1 + \frac{F_1(v_1)}{f_1(v_1)} \right] \right\} x(v_1, v_2)f_1(v_1)f_2(v_2)dv_1dv_2 \geq 0$$

when both v_i's are uniformly distributed on the interval $[0, 1]$.

Recall that when this condition holds, all incentive-compatibility and interim individual-rationality constraints are satisfied. The constraint must be binding at the optimum. Indeed, if it is not, then the solution to the unconstrained problem is simply the first-best rule, $x^*(v_1, v_2) = 1$ if $(v_2 - v_1) \geq 0$ and $x^*(v_1, v_2) = 0$ if $(v_2 - v_1) < 0$. But for this rule it is easily verified that

$$\int_0^1 \int_0^1 (2v_2 - 1 - 2v_1)x(v_1, v_2)dv_1dv_2 < 0$$

Next, pointwise optimization implies that the optimal $x(v_1, v_2)$ must take the general form

$$x(v_1, v_2) = \left\{ \begin{matrix} 1 & \text{if } (1+2\lambda)v_1 \leq (1+2\lambda)v_2 - \lambda \\ 0 & \text{otherwise} \end{matrix} \right\}$$

where λ is the Lagrange multiplier associated with the constraint. Thus the constraint can be rewritten as

$$\int_{\frac{\lambda}{1+2\lambda}}^{1} \int_{0}^{v_2 - \frac{\lambda}{1+2\lambda}} (2v_2 - 1 - 2v_1) dv_1 dv_2 = 0$$

After integration, this constraint reduces to the following simple expression:

$$\frac{3\lambda^2 + 2\lambda^3 - 1}{6(1+2\lambda)^3} = 0$$

so that, at the optimum, $\lambda = \frac{1}{2}$, and the second-best trading rule is given by

$$x^{SB}(v_1, v_2) = \begin{cases} 1 & \text{if } v_1 \leq v_2 - \frac{1}{4} \\ 0 & \text{otherwise} \end{cases}$$

Inefficient trade thus obtains whenever $v_2 - \frac{1}{4} \leq v_1 < v_2$. That is, under symmetric information it would be efficient to trade, but under the second-best efficient contract trade does not take place.

Step 2: Implementing the Second Best through a Double Auction Chatterjee and Samuelson (1983) consider the trading game where each agent simultaneously makes a bid for the item, b_i. If $b_1 \leq b_2$, agent 1 trades with agent 2 at a price $P = (b_1 + b_2)/2$. Otherwise, no trade takes place. There exists a Bayesian equilibrium of this double-auction game where agent 1 and agent 2, respectively, choose strategies

$$b_1 = \sigma_1(v_1) = \frac{1}{4} + \frac{2}{3}v_1$$

$$b_2 = \sigma_2(v_2) = \frac{1}{12} + \frac{2}{3}v_2$$

To check that this is indeed a Bayesian equilibrium, note that agent 1's and agent 2's best response functions of this double-auction game are given by the solutions to

$$\max_{b_1} \int_{b_1}^{1} \left(\frac{b_1 + b_2}{2} - v_1 \right) g_2(b_2) db_2$$

and

$$\max_{b_2} \int_{0}^{b_2} \left(v_2 - \frac{b_1 + b_2}{2} \right) g_1(b_1) db_1$$

Each party i is thus trying to maximize his surplus (which is nonzero only if $b_1 < b_2$) under the assumption that party j's bid is distributed according to the density $g_j(b_j)$. Denoting the cumulative density by $G_j(b_j)$ and using Leibniz's rule, one obtains the first-order conditions for these respective problems:

$$\frac{1}{2}[1 - G_2(b_1)] = (b_1 - v_1)g_2(b_1)$$

and

$$\frac{1}{2}G_1(b_2) = (v_2 - b_2)g_1(b_2)$$

In addition, for the candidate equilibrium strategies we have

$$G_2(b_1) = \Pr(b_2 \le b_1) = \Pr\left(v_2 \le \frac{3}{2}b_1 - \frac{1}{8}\right) = \frac{3}{2}b_1 - \frac{1}{8}$$

and thus

$$g_2(b_1) = G_2'(b_1) = \frac{3}{2}$$

and similarly

$$G_1(b_2) = \Pr(b_1 \le b_2) = \frac{3}{2}b_2 - \frac{3}{8}$$

and thus

$$g_1(b_2) = G_1'(b_2) = \frac{3}{2}$$

Substituting the values of $g_i(b_j)$ and $G_i(b_j)$ in the first-order conditions, one can check that we obtain the bidding functions we started with, that is,

$$b_1 = \sigma_1(v_1) = \frac{1}{4} + \frac{2}{3}v_1$$

and

$$b_2 = \sigma_2(v_2) = \frac{1}{12} + \frac{2}{3}v_2$$

which are indeed best-response functions to one another and thus form a Bayesian equilibrium. In this equilibrium, trade takes place as in the second best, that is, if and only if

$$\frac{2}{3}v_1 + \frac{1}{4} \le \frac{2}{3}v_2 + \frac{1}{12} \quad \text{or} \quad v_1 \le v_2 - \frac{1}{4}$$

Note, however, that there are other equilibria of this game, which are necessarily inefficient compared with the second best. The worst equilibrium is one where agent 1 always bids $b_1 = 1$ and agent 2 always responds with $b_2 = 0$. In that case trade never occurs. Unfortunately, it is not obvious a priori that the two agents would naturally choose to play the most efficient equilibrium. There could thus be gains to specifying a more complicated game where the set of Bayesian equilibria is smaller (possibly unique) so that the outcome of the game is more predictable.

7.2.2.3 Summary and Caveat

A central insight of the theory of optimal contracting under asymmetric information is that one should expect allocative inefficiencies to arise that are similar to the classic inefficiency associated with monopoly pricing. The novel lesson of the theory is that monopoly power is not just derived from monopoly ownership of a scarce resource, but also from the *informational monopoly rent* present in most contracting situations with asymmetric information. We began this chapter by pointing out that the potential allocative distortions, arising from the uninformed party's attempt to extract the informed party's informational rent, are reduced or even entirely eliminated if the bargaining power is shifted to the informed party. In more general contracting situations, however, where every party has private information at the time of contracting, there is no clearly identifiable "uninformed party" from whom the bargaining power is to be taken away. In such situations, all parties are "uninformed" with respect to the other parties' information, so to speak. One should therefore expect allocative inefficiencies to arise under optimal contracting that are driven by each party's attempts to extract the other party's informational rent. Conversely, as we have illustrated, when neither party has private information at the time of contracting (and therefore no informational rent), one should expect allocative efficiency to obtain, even if the contracting parties acquire private information at a later stage, which must be truthfully elicited to be able to implement the efficient allocation. In other (more abstract) words, allocative efficiencies are not attributable to the presence of incentive compatibility constraints per se, but rather to the combination of incentive compatibility and (interim) participation constraints.

We close this section with an important caveat to this general principle. The analysis of contracting under private information in Chapters 2 and 6 and section 7.2 has considered only asymmetric information about private values. When instead the informational advantage concerns common values, then allocative inefficiencies generally obtain even in simple situations where there is only one informed party. We illustrate this observation with the following simple example.

Consider the problem faced by a buyer (agent 1) and a seller (agent 2) of a painting with the following valuations as a function of the state of nature θ:

$$v_1(\theta) = a_1\theta - k_1$$

$$v_2(\theta) = a_2\theta - k_2$$

with

$$0 < a_1 < a_2$$

$$0 < k_1 < k_2$$

The state of nature might measure how fashionable the painting is likely to be. Suppose that only the seller observes $\theta \in [\underline{\theta}, \overline{\theta}]$, where

$$\underline{\theta} < \frac{k_2 - k_1}{a_2 - a_1} < \overline{\theta}$$

and that the buyer's prior belief is that θ is uniformly distributed on the interval $[\underline{\theta}, \overline{\theta}]$. Efficiency requires that the buyer acquire the good whenever

$$\theta \geq \frac{k_2 - k_1}{a_2 - a_1}$$

However, since only the seller knows the value of θ, it is not possible to induce him to give away the good only for high values of θ: the higher the θ, the more reluctant he will be to part with the good.[4] In fact, the most one

---

4. Applying the revelation principle, consider the set of contracts $\{x(\theta), P(\theta)\}$ over which the contracting parties can optimize, with $x(\theta) \in [0, 1]$ the probability that the sale takes place contingent on announcement θ by the seller and $P(\theta)$ the payment from the buyer to the seller contingent on announcement θ. Incentive compatibility requires that for any two θ and $\hat{\theta}$ we have

$$(a_1\theta - k_1)[1 - x(\theta)] + P(\theta) \geq (a_1\theta - k_1)\left[1 - x(\hat{\theta})\right] + P(\hat{\theta})$$

and

$$\left(a_1\hat{\theta} - k_1\right)\left[1 - x(\hat{\theta})\right] + P(\hat{\theta}) \geq \left(a_1\hat{\theta} - k_1\right)[1 - x(\theta)] + P(\theta)$$

or, combining these constraints,

can achieve is either no trade at all or unconditional trade for a given price (provided this does not violate IR constraints), depending on what generates a higher expected surplus.

This simple example illustrates how, when there is private information about common values, quite generally trade will be inefficient even if there is only one-sided asymmetric information.

7.3   Auctions with Perfectly Known Values

In the previous subsection we showed how in the presence of bilateral asymmetric information it may not always be possible to achieve efficient trade. In this subsection we show how the potential inefficiency resulting from bilateral asymmetric information can be reduced when there is competition among agents. We shall illustrate this general principle in the simplest possible example where a seller faces two risk-neutral buyers competing to buy one indivisible good (say, a house). As before, each buyer has two possible valuations for the good:

$$v_i = \begin{cases} v_H & \text{with probability } \beta_i \\ v_L & \text{with probability } 1 - \beta_i \end{cases}$$

where $v_H > v_L \geq 0$ and β_i denotes the seller's prior belief that buyer $i = 1, 2$ has a reservation value of v_H. To keep things as simple as possible, we shall assume here that $\beta_i = \beta$ and that each buyer's value is drawn independently.

When the seller (with cost normalized to 0) sets the terms of trade and there is a single buyer, he sets a price equal to v_H whenever $\beta v_H \geq v_L$, so that inefficient trade occurs with probability $(1 - \beta)$. With two buyers efficiency is improved even if the seller sticks to the same pricing policy, since inefficient trade now occurs only with probability $(1 - \beta)^2$. In other words, efficiency is improved with two buyers just because the likelihood of the seller facing a high-valuation buyer has increased. To some extent this improvement is an artifact of the simple structure of our example. The general reason why efficiency is improved with two buyers is that by getting

---

$$(\theta - \hat{\theta})[x(\hat{\theta}) - x(\theta)] \geq 0$$

It follows that any incentive-compatible contract must be such that $x(\theta)$ is (weakly) decreasing in θ.

the buyers to compete in an auction the seller can extract their informational rent with smaller trade distortions.

7.3.1   Optimal Efficient Auctions with Independent Values

The seller's optimal auction design problem in this example takes a very simple form. Since both buyers are identical ex ante, the seller can, without loss of generality, restrict attention to symmetric auctions, where both buyers are treated equally. Applying the revelation principle, an optimal auction then specifies the following:

• Payments from buyers to the seller contingent on their announced reservation values $\{P_{HH}, P_{HL}, P_{LH}, P_{LL}\}$.

• Contingent trades $\{x_{HH}, x_{HL}, x_{LH}, x_{LL}\}$, where x_{ij} denotes the probability of buyer i getting the good given announcements v_i and v_j.

These contingent payments and trades must satisfy the usual constraints:

1. *Feasibility*: $2x_{HH} \leq 1$; $2x_{LL} \leq 1$; $x_{HL} + x_{LH} \leq 1$.

2. *Buyer participation* for high- and low-valuation types, respectively:

$$\beta(x_{HH}v_H - P_{HH}) + (1 - \beta)(x_{HL}v_H - P_{HL}) \geq 0 \qquad \text{(IRH)}$$

and

$$\beta(x_{LH}v_L - P_{LH}) + (1 - \beta)(x_{LL}v_L - P_{LL}) \geq 0 \qquad \text{(IRL)}$$

3. *Incentive compatibility* for high- and low-valuation types, respectively:

$$\begin{aligned} \beta(x_{HH}v_H - P_{HH}) + (1 - \beta)(x_{HL}v_H - P_{HL}) \geq \\ \beta(x_{LH}v_H - P_{LH}) + (1 - \beta)(x_{LL}v_H - P_{LL}) \end{aligned} \qquad \text{(ICH)}$$

and

$$\begin{aligned} \beta(x_{LH}v_L - P_{LH}) + (1 - \beta)(x_{LL}v_L - P_{LL}) \geq \\ \beta(x_{HH}v_L - P_{HH}) + (1 - \beta)(x_{HL}v_L - P_{HL}) \end{aligned} \qquad \text{(ICL)}$$

An auction is efficient if and only if the item is allocated to the highest-value user. Since $v_H > v_L$, this statement means in particular $x_{HL} = 1$ and $x_{LH} = 0$. Since both buyers are identical ex ante, the seller can, without loss of generality, restrict attention to symmetric auctions, that is, cases where both buyers are treated equally. Therefore, efficiency also means $x_{HH} = x_{LL} = \frac{1}{2}$.

Here, we restrict attention to efficient auctions and characterize the one that maximizes the seller's expected revenue in this class. We know that, as in Chapter 2, constraint (IRH) will hold, given that (IRI) and (ICH) both hold. Moreover, (ICH) is likely to be binding at the optimum while (ICL) is likely to be slack. indeed, if the seller knew the type of the buyer, he would manage to extract all of her expected surplus. This possibility, however, would induce a high-valuation buyer to understate her valuation in order to limit this payment. Thus let us proceed under the assumption that only (IRL) and (ICH) bind. Observing that all parties are risk neutral, we can also express all payoffs in terms of the expected payments $P_L^e = \beta P_{LH} + (1 - \beta)P_{LL}$ and $P_H^e = \beta P_{HH} + (1 - \beta)P_{HL}$. Therefore, the efficient auction that maximizes the seller's expected revenue solves the following constrained optimization program:

$$\max_{P_i^e} 2[\beta P_H^e + (1 - \beta)P_L^e]$$

subject to

$$\beta \frac{1}{2}v_H + (1-\beta)v_H - P_H^e \geq (1-\beta)\frac{1}{2}v_H - P_L^e \qquad \text{(ICH)}$$

$$(1-\beta)\frac{1}{2}v_L - P_L^e \geq 0 \qquad \text{(IRL)}$$

At the optimum, the two constraints bind[5] and uniquely pin down the two choice variables; that is,

$$P_L^e = \frac{(1-\beta)v_L}{2} \quad \text{and} \quad P_H^e = \frac{v_H}{2} + \frac{(1-\beta)v_L}{2}$$

so that the seller's maximum net expected revenue from an efficient auction is

$$\beta v_H + (1-\beta)v_L \qquad (7.7)$$

---

5. This means that (ICL) will be satisfied:

$$\beta \frac{1}{2}v_H + (1-\beta)v_H - P_H^e = (1-\beta)\frac{1}{2}v_H - P_L^e$$

implies

$$\beta \frac{1}{2}v_L + (1-\beta)v_L - P_H^e \leq (1-\beta)\frac{1}{2}v_L - P_L^e$$

The seller obtains less revenue than the expected total surplus from trade, which equals $[1 - (1 - \beta)^2]v_H + (1 - \beta)^2 v_L$, because, just as in Chapter 2, the seller has to concede an informational rent to each high-valuation buyer, equal to $(1 - \beta)(v_H - v_L)/2$, the probability of the low-valuation buyer obtaining the object times the difference in valuations. In ex ante terms, this information rent costs the seller $2\beta(1 - \beta)(v_H - v_L)/2$, which is in fact the difference between the expected surplus from trade and the expected revenue of the seller in expression (7.7). In the next subsection we shall ask the question whether distortions from efficiency might be revenue enhancing for the seller, that is, whether, just as in Chapter 2, the seller might want the low-valuation buyers to have a lower probability of receiving the object, so as to reduce the informational rent of the high-valuation buyers.

Before dealing with that question, let us consider the case where the seller faces $n > 2$ buyers with independently and identically distributed valuations:

$$v_i = \begin{cases} v_H & \text{with probability } \beta \\ v_L & \text{with probability } 1 - \beta \end{cases}$$

As in the two-buyer case, the individual-rationality constraint (IRL) and the incentive constraint (ICH) together imply that

$$P_L^e = \frac{(1-\beta)^{n-1}}{n} v_L$$

and

$$P_H^e = \left[\sum_{i=0}^{n-1} \binom{n-1}{i} \frac{\beta^{n-i-1}(1-\beta)^i}{n-i} \right] v_H - \frac{(1-\beta)^{n-1}}{n}(v_H - v_L)$$

The first condition says that the low-valuation buyers obtain zero rents, since they pay v_L times the probability that they get the object (which is the probability that all other buyers are also low-valuation types, times $1/n$, since then the object is allocated at random). And the second condition says that the high-valuation buyers pay v_H times the probability that they get the object minus the information rent. The (somewhat involved) probability that they get the object depends on how many other high-valuation buyers there are, since the object is allocated at random among all of them. The key term, however, is the second one, that is, the information rent, which again is the probability that a low-valuation buyer gets the object, times the difference in valuations. But note that, as $n \to \infty$, thanks to competition, the information rent tends to zero, so that the seller is able to extract almost all the gains from trade as the number of bidders becomes large.[6] And since the object is then allocated almost for sure to a high-valuation bidder,[7] the seller's expected revenue converges to v_H.

7.3.2 Optimal Auctions with Independent Values

Let us return to the case with two buyers, where the seller has to concede a positive information rent to the high-valuation types. As said before, the seller may be able to increase expected revenue beyond the maximum revenue obtainable with an efficient auction, $\beta v_H + (1 - \beta)v_L$, by refusing to sell to low-value buyers. Just as inefficiently high pricing may be optimal for a seller facing a single buyer, inefficient auctions may yield a higher expected net revenue than efficient ones. Indeed, by reducing x_{LL} below $\frac{1}{2}$ the seller can relax the incentive constraint (ICH) and thus extract a higher payment from high-value buyers. We now turn to the analysis of optimal auctions and determine when it is optimal for the seller to set up an efficient auction.

Assuming again that only constraints (IRL) and (ICH) bind at the optimum, the seller's optimal choice of x_{ij} is given by the solution to the following optimization problem:

$$\max_{x_{ij}, P_i^e} 2[\beta P_H^e + (1 - \beta)P_L^e]$$

subject to

$$[\beta x_{HH} + (1 - \beta)x_{HL}]v_H - P_H^e = [\beta x_{LH} + (1 - \beta)x_{LL}]v_H - P_L^e \qquad \text{(ICH)}$$

$$[\beta x_{LH} + (1 - \beta)x_{LL}]v_L = P_L^e \qquad \text{(IRL)}$$

$$2x_{HH} \leq 1, \quad x_{HL} + x_{LH} \leq 1, \quad 2x_{LL} \leq 1 \qquad \text{(feasibility)}$$

Replacing P_H^e and P_L^e in the seller's objective function using the constraints (IRL) and (ICH), we obtain the reduced problem:

---

6. Each of the n buyers receives, with probability β, an information rent equal to

$$\frac{(1-\beta)^{n-1}}{n}(v_H - v_L)$$

And n times this expression tends to zero when $n \to \infty$.

7. It goes to a high-valuation buyer whenever there is at least one, that is, with probability $1 - (1 - \beta)^{n-1}$, which tends to 1 when $n \to \infty$.

$$\max_{x_{ij}} 2\beta\{[\beta x_{HH} + (1-\beta)x_{HL}]v_H - [\beta x_{LH} + (1-\beta)x_{LL}](v_H - v_L)\}$$
$$+ 2(1-\beta)[\beta x_{LH} + (1-\beta)x_{LL}]v_L$$

subject to

$$2x_{HH} \leq 1, \quad x_{HL} + x_{LH} \leq 1, \quad 2x_{LL} \leq 1 \qquad \text{(feasibility)}$$

The optimal values for x_{ij} can now be determined by evaluating the signs of the coefficients of x_{ij} in the seller's objective function:

• Consider first x_{HH}. Its coefficient is $2\beta^2 v_H$, which is strictly positive. It is therefore optimal for the seller to set $x_{HH} = \frac{1}{2}$.

• Next, note that the coefficient of x_{HL}, $2\beta(1 - \beta)v_H$, is always positive so that it is optimal to set $x_{HL} = 1 - x_{LH}$. Moreover, it is bigger than the coefficient of x_{LH}, $2[-\beta^2(v_H - v_L) + \beta(1 - \beta)v_L]$, so that it is optimal to set $x_{HL} = 1$ and $x_{LH} = 0$.

• Finally, the coefficient of x_{LL} is

$$2\left[-\beta(1-\beta)(v_H - v_L) + (1-\beta)^2 v_L\right]$$

so that it is optimal to set $x_{LL} = \frac{1}{2}$ if and only if $(1 - \beta)v_L \geq \beta(v_H - v_L)$; otherwise, it is optimal to set $x_{LL} = 0$.

The optimal auction thus again implies "efficiency at the top," that is, maximum probability of trade (subject to feasibility) for high-valuation buyers. When the seller faces two low-valuation buyers, the good is traded if $(1 - \beta)v_L \geq \beta(v_H - v_L)$, in which case the seller's expected payoff is $\beta v_H + (1 - \beta)v_L$. If instead $(1 - \beta)v_L < \beta(v_H - v_L)$, then the good is not traded and the seller's expected payoff is then $[\beta^2 + 2\beta(1 - \beta)]v_H$.

Note that when the seller faces only a single buyer, he decides to exclude the low-valuation buyer under the same condition $[(1 - \beta)v_L < \beta(v_H - v_L)]$, so that monopoly distortions are the same whether there is a single buyer or multiple buyers competing for the object. The only difference is that with multiple buyers the likelihood of inefficient exclusion of low-valuation buyers is lower. Interestingly, if a seller facing two buyers has the option of producing a second item at zero cost, then he will always want to produce the second item and sell both items at a price $P = v_L$ when $(1 - \beta)v_L \geq \beta(v_H - v_L)$, and when the opposite inequality holds at price $P = v_H$.

7.3.3   Standard Auctions with Independent Values

It is interesting to compare the optimal auction (from the point of view of the seller) with standard auctions frequently used in practice. There are at least four widely known and used auctions--the English auction, the Dutch auction, the Vickrey auction, and the first-price sealed-bid auction. Each of these auctions defines a game to be played by buyers (or bidders), where the strategies of the buyers are either bids (price offers) or continuation/exit decisions.

English Auction   The English auction is, perhaps, the best-known auction. The moves of each buyer at any stage of the auction are to announce a price offer that is higher than any previously announced bid, stay silent, or drop out. The auction ends when no new price offers are forthcoming. The good is sold to the highest bidder at the price offered by that bidder, provided that the highest bid exceeds the introductory price set by the seller. Even though this is in many ways a rather simple auction, it is sometimes useful to simplify its rules even further and to introduce an auctioneer who continuously raises the asking price. The buyers' moves then are simply to "continue" or to "exit."

Dutch Auction   The auctioneer starts the Dutch auction game by calling a very large asking price and continuously lowering the price until a buyer stops the process by accepting the last quoted asking price. Just as in the simplified English auction, bidders have only two moves: "stop" or "continue." The first buyer to stop the process gets the good at the last price quoted by the auctioneer.

Vickrey Auction   Here buyers simultaneously offer a price in a sealed envelope. The auctioneer collects all the bids and sells the good to the highest bidder at the second-highest price offer, provided that the second-highest offer is above the introductory price. If it is below the minimum price offer, but the highest bid is above it, then the highest bidder gets the good at the introductory price. If two or more bidders offer the highest price, then the good is allocated randomly to one of them at the highest price. In this auction buyers' strategies are simply price offers.

First-Price Sealed-Bid Auction   All the rules are the same as for the Vickrey auction, except that the good is sold at the highest price offer.

These four auctions seem rather different at first sight, and a seller facing the choice of any of these four auctions as the selling procedure for his good may be at a loss determining which is best for him.

If the seller and buyers are risk neutral and if the buyers' valuations are independently drawn from the same distribution, it turns out that it does not matter which of these auctions the seller chooses: as we will see, they all yield the same expected revenue. What is more, despite first appearances, the English auction and the Vickrey auction yield the same symmetric equilibrium outcome in this case. The Dutch and first-price sealed-bid auctions are strategically equivalent.

Consider first the English and Vickrey auctions, where each bidder has a unique (weakly) dominant strategy: In the English auction the dominant strategy is to "continue" until the ascending asking price process hits the reservation value of the bidder and then to "stop." This strategy clearly dominates any strategy involving "continuation" until after the asking price has been raised above the bidder's reservation value. It also dominates any strategy where the bidder "stops" before the asking price has hit her reservation value.

In the Vickrey auction each bidder's dominant strategy is to offer a price equal to her reservation value. With such an offer the bidder ends up getting the good at the second-highest bid—a price independent of her own announced offer—whenever she has made the highest offer. If a price equal to her reservation value is not the highest offer, then the good is necessarily sold at a price greater than or equal to her reservation value. Clearly, no bidder would want to acquire the good at such a high price. Thus the strategy of bidding her reservation value clearly dominates any strategy where the bidder offers a higher price. It also dominates price offers below the bidder's reservation value: such bids either do not affect the final outcome (when they remain the highest bid, so that the good is still sold to the highest bidder at the second-highest bid), or they adversely affect the outcome (when they are no longer the highest bid, so that the bidder loses the good to another bidder).

In sum, the equilibrium prices and the final allocations in the unique symmetric dominant-strategy equilibrium are the same under the English and Vickrey auctions, so that the seller ought to be indifferent between them. What is the seller's expected revenue? With probability β^2 both buyers have high valuations and offer v_H. In that case each buyer gets the good with probability $\frac{1}{2}$ at price v_H. With probability $2\beta(1 - \beta)$ one buyer has a high valuation and the other a low valuation. In this event the high-valuation buyer gets the good at the second-highest price v_L. Finally, with probability $(1 - \beta)^2$ both buyers have a low valuation. Then either buyer gets the good with probability $\frac{1}{2}$ at price v_L. Thus the expected revenue from the Vickrey and English auctions is

$$\beta^2 v_H + (1 - \beta^2) v_L$$

Also, the expected payoff of a v_L buyer is zero, while a v_H buyer gets an expected payoff of $(1 - \beta)(v_H - v_L)$.[8]

Consider now the Dutch and first-price sealed-bid auctions. They are equivalent in the sense that the strategy sets and the allocation rules are the same in both auctions. Indeed, in the Dutch auction, the game stops as soon as someone accepts a price, so that the strategy set can be thought of as a price one would be ready to pay given one's valuation. And the allocation rule in both auctions is that the good goes to the highest bidder at the highest offer.

In order to determine the outcome of these auctions, note first that, unlike in the Vickrey and English auctions, there is no dominant strategy for either player in the Dutch and first-price sealed-bid auctions. It is then less clear what the outcome of the game is likely to be for the latter two auctions. Ever since Vickrey's pioneering article appeared, the (symmetric) Bayesian equilibrium has been singled out as the most plausible outcome for these games.

More precisely, in each auction a player's strategy is given by $b_i(v)$, the bidding function chosen by player i. Because the distribution of valuations is discrete in our simple two-type model, we must allow for mixed strategies. The reason is the following: Suppose that bidder 1 chooses the pure strategy $b_1(v) = v$ [or $b_1(v) \leq v$ with $b_1(v_H)$ sufficiently close to v_H]; then bidder 2's best response is to set $b_2(v_L) = b_1(v_L) = v_L$ and $b_2(v_H) = b_1(v_L) + \varepsilon$ (with $\varepsilon > 0$ but arbitrarily small). If bidder 2 has a high valuation, she then

---

8. Note that there also exist asymmetric Bayesian equilibria in the Vickrey and English auctions. For example, bidder 1 may play a "preemptive" bidding strategy and always bid v_H. A best response of the other bidders is then to always bid v_L. But if all other bidders bid v_L, then one best response for bidder 1 is to bid v_H in the Vickrey auction and to "continue" until the price has reached v_H in the English auction.

As we discuss later in the chapter, these two auctions do not yield equivalent outcomes in general. For example, when bidders have imperfectly known (common) values, then the two auctions produce different outcomes.

gets an expected return of $(1 - \beta)(v_H - v_L - \varepsilon)$. But bidder 1's best response to bidder 2's pure strategy then is to set $b_1(v_H) = v_L + 2\varepsilon$, and so on. The point is that, since winning bidders must pay a price equal to the winning bid, they have an incentive to reduce their bid below their valuation even if they thereby run the risk of losing the good to the other bidder. Thus a high-valuation buyer may want to make a bid that is just marginally higher than v_L. But if her behavior is anticipated, another high-valuation bidder will outbid her. Thus high-valuation buyers must randomize to keep other bidders guessing. Since they must be indifferent between any bids they choose, they will, with positive probability, choose only bids in the interval $(v_L, \bar{b})$, where $\bar{b}$ solves the equation

$$(1 - \beta)(v_H - v_L) = (v_H - \bar{b})$$

As for low-valuation buyers, their equilibrium strategy is simply the pure strategy $b(v_L) = v_L$. To see this point, observe, first, that a bidder will never want to choose $b(v_L) > v_L$. Second, the best response to any pure strategy $b(v_L) < v_L$ is $b(v_L) + \varepsilon$. Finally, the best response to any mixed strategy with support $[b_L, v_L]$, where $b_L < v_L$, is to choose some (mixed) strategy with support $[\hat{b}_L, v_L]$, where $\hat{b}_L > b_L$. In sum, the game played by low-valuation bidders is essentially identical to a Bertrand price-competition game, which induces them to compete away all their rents.

Consequently, consider the symmetric (mixed strategy) Bayesian equilibrium, where $b(v_L) = v_L$ and $f(b|v_H)$ is the equilibrium distribution of bids of high-valuation buyers, with b belonging to the open interval $(v_L, \bar{b})$. By symmetry, the equilibrium probabilities of winning the auction for a low- and high-value buyer are, respectively, $(1 - \beta)/2$ and $\beta/2 + (1 - \beta)$. These are the same as in the English (and Vickrey) auction. In addition, low-valuation buyers get a net expected return of zero, just as in the English (and Vickrey) auction. As for high-valuation buyers, their expected return from bidding $b \approx v_L$ is approximately $(1 - \beta)(v_H - v_L)$. Since expected payoffs from any bid $b \in (v_L, \bar{b})$ must be the same in a mixed-strategy equilibrium, we can conclude that a high-valuation buyer's equilibrium expected payoff in the Dutch (and first-price sealed-bid) auction is $(1 - \beta)(v_H - v_L)$, the same as in the English (and Vickrey) auction. And given that, for each type, the bidders' equilibrium expected payoffs and probabilities of winning the auction are the same in all four auctions, we conclude that the seller's expected revenue must also be the same in all four auctions! This expected revenue is

$$\beta^2 v_H + (1 - \beta^2) v_L$$

Note that this expected revenue is lower than the revenue generated by the optimal efficient auction, which is

$$\beta v_H + (1 - \beta) v_L$$

The reason for this difference in revenue is that the high-valuation buyer obtains more rents in the standard auctions than in the optimal efficient auction; that is, her incentive constraint is not binding: she strictly prefers her own bidding strategy to the bidding strategy of the low-valuation buyer. This is not the case when the seller excludes the low-valuation type, that is, sets an introductory price of v_H. In this case, the standard auctions generate the same revenue as the optimal auction where one sets $x_{LL} = 0$. Therefore, exclusion of the low types is a more attractive option if one is restricted to standard auctions instead of being able to choose the optimal efficient auction.[9]

In the two-type case, therefore, we have revenue equivalence for the four standard auctions but not revenue equivalence between these four standard auctions and the optimal auction. It turns out that revenue equivalence is strengthened when we go from two types to a continuum of types, as the next section shows.

7.3.4 Optimal Independent-Value Auctions with a Continuum of Types: The Revenue Equivalence Theorem

Let us come back first to the bilateral contracting problem with one uninformed seller and one informed buyer considered in Chapter 2. Note that it can be extended in a straightforward manner to a situation with several buyers if the seller has an unlimited number of items for sale. In the extreme case where there is a very large number of buyers with identically, independently distributed types, all it takes then to adapt the one-buyer one-seller theory is to reinterpret the cumulative distribution function $F(\theta)$ as a population distribution indicating the fraction of buyers with preference types no greater than θ. If there is a smaller number of buyers with independently distributed types, the seller's problem can simply be

---

9. Remember that $x_{LL} = 0$ is part of an optimal auction if $(1 - \beta)v_L \leq \beta(v_H - v_L)$. Exclusion will thus occur if one is restricted to choosing a standard auction even in some cases where $(1 - \beta)v_L > \beta(v_H - v_L)$.

reformulated as the one-buyer problem by defining $F(\theta) = \Pi_{i=1}^{n} F_i(\theta_i)$, where $\theta = (\theta_1, \ldots, \theta_n)$.

However, if the seller has only a limited number of items for sale, the seller's problem is not just an optimal nonlinear pricing problem, but becomes an optimal multiunit auction problem. In this subsection we consider the *optimal multiunit auction problem with risk-neutral, independent-valuation buyers* of Maskin and Riley (1989) and show how it can be analyzed more or less as an optimal nonlinear pricing problem. This work extends the pioneering contributions of Myerson (1981) and Riley and Samuelson (1981) on revenue equivalence and on optimal auctions.

Suppose that the seller can sell only q_o units of a given good. There are n buyers ($n \geq 2$) with preferences defined as in Chapter 2: $u_i(q, T) = \theta_i v(q) - T$, where θ_i is distributed on $[\underline{\theta}, \bar{\theta}]$ with cumulative distribution function $F_i(\theta_i)$. Applying the revelation principle, the seller's problem is then to design a multiunit auction $\{q_i(\theta_i, \theta_{-i}), T_i(\theta_i, \theta_{-i})\}$, where $(\theta_i, \theta_{-i}) \equiv \theta$, q_i denotes the quantity of items obtained by buyer i, and T_i is buyer i's payment to the seller. Of course, the quantity of items sold cannot exceed the total quantity available, which we denote by q_o:

$$\sum_{i=1}^{n} q_i(\theta_i, \theta_{-i}) \leq q_o \text{ for all } (\theta_i, \theta_{-i})$$

Buyer i's expected payoff in a Bayesian equilibrium for this auction is then

$$\pi_i(\hat{\theta}_i, \theta_i) \equiv E_{\theta_{-i}}\{\theta_i v[q_i(\hat{\theta}_i, \theta_{-i})]\} - T_i(\hat{\theta}_i)$$

where $T_i(\hat{\theta}_i) = E_{\theta_{-i}}[T_i(\hat{\theta}_i, \theta_{-i})]$. Indeed, in a Bayesian equilibrium, each player expects the other players to play the equilibrium, that is, truth-telling, strategies, so that expectations of payoffs are computed using the *true type distributions* of the other players. Truth telling in the multiunit auction is incentive compatible if and only if

$$\pi_i(\theta_i, \theta_i) \equiv \max_{\hat{\theta}_i} \pi_i(\hat{\theta}_i, \theta_i)$$

One can check that, just as in Chapter 2 and in section 7.2.2, incentive compatibility is equivalent to the monotonicity of $E_{\theta_{-i}}\{q_i(\theta_i, \theta_{-i})\}$ with respect to θ_i plus local incentive compatibility, which after integration implies

$$\pi_i(\theta_i, \theta_i) = \pi_i(\underline{\theta}, \underline{\theta}) + E_{\theta_{-i}}\left[\int_{\underline{\theta}}^{\theta_i} v[q_i(y, \theta_{-i})]dy\right] \tag{7.8}$$

From the definition of $\pi_i(\hat{\theta}_i, \theta_i)$ and from equation (7.8) we thus have

$$T_i(\theta_i) = E_{\theta_{-i}} \left\{ \theta_i v[q_i(\theta_i, \theta_{-i})] - \pi_i(\underline{\theta}, \underline{\theta}) - \int_{\underline{\theta}}^{\theta_i} v[q_i(y, \theta_{-i})]dy \right\}$$

so that the seller's expected revenue from buyer i is given by

$$T_i^e = \int_{\underline{\theta}}^{\bar{\theta}} E_{\theta_{-i}} \left[\theta_i v[q_i(\theta)] - \pi_i(\underline{\theta}, \underline{\theta}) - \int_{\underline{\theta}}^{\theta_i} v[q_i(y, \theta_{-i})]dy \right] f_i(\theta_i)d\theta_i$$

Integrating the second term by parts, we get

$$T_i^e = \int_{\underline{\theta}}^{\bar{\theta}} E_{\theta_{-i}} \left[\theta v[q_i(\theta)] - \pi_i(\underline{\theta}, \underline{\theta}) - \frac{v[q_i(\theta)]}{h_i(\theta_i)} \right] f_i(\theta_i)d\theta_i$$

where $h_i(\theta_i) = f_i(\theta_i)/[(1 - F_i(\theta_i)]$ is the hazard rate. The seller's problem can now be expressed as

$$\max_{q_i(\theta)} \sum_{i=1}^{n} T_i^e = E_\theta \left\{ \sum_{i=1}^{n} \left[\theta_i v[q_i(\theta)] - \pi_i(\underline{\theta}, \underline{\theta}) - \frac{v[q_i(\theta)]}{h_i(\theta_i)} \right] \right\}$$

subject to

$$\sum_{i=1}^{n} q_i(\theta) \le q_0 \qquad \text{(feasibility)}$$

$$\pi_i(\underline{\theta}, \underline{\theta}) \ge 0 \quad \text{for all } i \qquad \text{(interim IR)}$$

$$E_{\theta_{-i}}\{q_i(\theta)\} \quad \text{nondecreasing in } \theta_i \qquad \text{(monotonicity)}$$

This reformulation of the problem shows that the expected revenue of the seller is *fully* determined by the rents granted to the lowest types of buyers, that is, $\pi_i(\underline{\theta}, \underline{\theta})$, as well as the allocation rule for the good, that is $q_i(\theta)$, and that all this is true *independently of the specific payments* made by the parties for each vector of types θ. This outcome is the result of incentive compatibility, which, in the case of a continuum of types {with $f_i(\theta_i) > 0$ for all θ_i's on $[\underline{\theta}, \bar{\theta}]$}, pins down uniquely the increase in rents of each type once $\pi_i(\underline{\theta}, \underline{\theta})$ and $q_i(\theta)$ have been chosen. This result is the *revenue equivalence theorem*, due to Myerson (1981) and Riley and Samuelson (1981). It does rely on the *independence* of valuations (which determines the way in which we have taken expectations) and on buyer *risk neutrality,* two assumptions we will relax in the examples that will follow. The preceding result, however, does not depend on any symmetry assumption in the distribution of valuations, but this assumption will be needed in order to compare the optimal auction with standard auctions (symmetry will be relaxed in an example in a subsequent section).

To compute the optimal auction and compare it with standard auctions, let us for simplicity restrict attention to the case where buyers have unit demands and their preferences are given by

$$\theta_i v(q_i) = \begin{cases} \theta_i q & \text{for } q \leq 1 \\ \theta_i & \text{for } q > 1 \end{cases}$$

Moreover, we assume that $F_i(\theta_i) \equiv F(\theta_i)$ and satisfies the regularity condition

$$J(\theta_i) \equiv \theta_i - \frac{1 - F(\theta_i)}{f(\theta_i)} \quad \text{is increasing in } \theta_i$$

so that we need not consider the possibility of bunching, and we can safely ignore the monotonicity condition, which will be automatically satisfied at the optimum. We refer the interested reader to Maskin and Riley (1989) for an exposition of the case where the regularity condition fails. It suffices to say here that the nature of the solution in this case is qualitatively similar to the solution in the one-buyer problem considered in Chapter 2.[10]

Given these assumptions we can rewrite the seller's optimization problem as

$$\max_{q_i(\theta)} E_\theta \left\{ \sum_{i=1}^{n} \left[\theta_i \min\{q_i, 1\} - \frac{\min\{q_i, 1\}}{h(\theta_i)} \right] \right\}$$

subject to

$$\sum_{i=1}^{n} q_i(\theta) \leq q_o$$

10. It is worth highlighting that the optimal auction problem we started out with, where each bidder has only two possible valuations for the item, is in fact the limit of a problem where each bidder has a continuous distribution of valuations on some interval, but where almost all the probability mass is centered on only two values. For such extreme distributions $J(\theta_i)$ is not increasing in θ_i, so that the optimal solution involves bunching. Bunching can be understood as a general form of conditional minimum bid restriction. It is generally possible for the seller to raise expected revenue by imposing such restrictions. It is for this reason that the optimal auction may yield strictly higher expected revenue than the four standard auctions in the two-types case (when the latter do not impose such minimum bid restrictions).

Note that this reformulation takes into account the fact that at the optimum $\pi_i(\underline{\theta}, \underline{\theta}) = 0$ for all i.

Substituting for $J(\theta_i)$, we have

$$\max_{q_i(\theta)} E_\theta \left\{ \sum_{i=1}^n [J(\theta_i)q_i(\theta)] \right\}$$

subject to

$$0 \le q_i(\theta) \le 1 \quad \text{and} \quad \sum_{i=1}^n q_i(\theta) \le q_o$$

Define $\tilde{\theta} = \inf\{\theta_i \mid J(\theta_i) \ge 0\}$. Under our assumption that $J(\theta_i)$ is increasing, we have $J(\theta_i) > 0$ if and only if $\theta_i > \tilde{\theta}$. Thus the optimal selling strategy is to sell up to q_o units to those buyers with the highest valuations in excess of $\tilde{\theta}$.

How does this optimal selling procedure compare with standard auctions? In an English auction and a Vickrey auction, if the seller sets an introductory price of $\tilde{\theta}$, this optimum will be reached, since it will mean that (1) buyers with valuations below $\tilde{\theta}$ will earn zero rents, and (2) the objects will be allocated to the highest-valuation buyers in excess of $\tilde{\theta}$. And the same will be true of the first-price sealed-bid auction and the Dutch auction with an introductory price of $\tilde{\theta}$, if we can show that bids are increasing with valuation (so that the objects will be allocated to the highest-valuation buyers in excess of $\tilde{\theta}$) in the symmetric Bayesian equilibrium. Let us show this result, for example, in the case where buyer valuations are uniformly distributed on $[0, 1]$ and where the seller faces two buyers and has a single object to offer. Let $g_i(b_i)$ be the probability that buyer i expects to obtain the object if she bids b_i. If her valuation is θ_i, she solves

$$\max(\theta_i - b_i)g_i(b_i)$$

Indeed, she trades off the probability of winning with the surplus upon winning. The first-order condition of this problem is

$$(\theta_i - b_i)g_i'(b_i) - g_i(b_i) = 0$$

Let us now look for a symmetric equilibrium where bids are increasing with the valuation, that is, $b_i(\theta_i)$ such that $db_i/d\theta_i > 0$. This means that the equilibrium probability of winning the object, $g(b_i)$, for somebody with valuation θ_i is in fact $g[b_i(\theta_i)] = \theta_i$ (given that the θ_i's are uniformly distributed on $[0, 1]$). Replacing θ_i by $g(b_i)$ in the preceding equation yields

$$[g(b_i) - b_i]g'(b_i) - g(b_i) = 0$$

The solution of this differential equation is $g(b_i) = 2b_i$, and since $\theta_i = g(b_i)$, this implies $b_i = \theta_i/2$: each buyer bids half her valuation, so that higher-valuation buyers get the object, thereby generating the same expected revenue for the seller (given the same introductory price, here normalized to zero) as the English or Vickrey auctions, and the same expected revenue as the optimal auction if the appropriate introductory price is chosen. And this result holds despite the fact that, for specific vectors of valuations, these auctions do not imply the same payments. (In particular, the English auction extracts more revenue when the two highest realized valuations happen to be "close by," and the Dutch auction extracts more revenue when the two highest realized valuations happen to be "far apart.")

All four standard auctions are therefore optimal if they set the appropriate introductory price, in this symmetric setup with risk-neutral buyers and independently drawn valuations. Let us now look at examples where this revenue equivalence may fail.

7.3.5   Optimal Auctions with Correlated Values

Let us now drop the assumption of independence of buyer valuations. As we shall see, relaxing this assumption has a crucial impact on the optimal auction. This can be seen in a two-type case, but is much more general, as shown by Crémer and McLean (1988). Denote by β_{ij} the probability that buyer 1 has valuation v_i and buyer 2 valuation v_j (where $i = L, H$ and $j = L, H$), and suppose that the buyers' valuations are correlated, so that $\beta_{HH}\beta_{LL} - \beta_{HL}\beta_{LH} \neq 0$ [instead, under independence, there exists β such that $\beta^2 = \beta_{HH}$, $(1 - \beta)^2 = \beta_{LL}$, and $\beta(1 - \beta) = \beta_{LH} = \beta_{HL}$].

What is the revenue of the four standard auctions in this case? Under the English (and Vickrey) auction the seller's expected revenue is $\beta_{HH}v_H + (1 - \beta_{HH})v_L$. It is straightforward to check that under the Dutch (and first-price sealed-bid) auction the seller obtains the same expected revenue. Indeed, in the latter two auctions a buyer with valuation v_L obtains an expected return of zero and a buyer with valuation v_H obtains $(1 - \beta_{HH})(v_H - v_L)$ just as in the English (or Vickrey) auction. Hence, the seller must also receive the same expected revenue.[11]

While correlation does not imply dramatic changes for the four standard auctions, the same is not true for the optimal one: the seller can now obtain an expected revenue of $\beta_{LL}v_L + (1 - \beta_{LL})v_H$, that is, extract all the surplus from the buyers! To see this result, consider the general contract (or auction) specifying the following:

• A payment P_{ij} from buyer 1 when her value is v_i and buyer 2's value is v_j (P_{ji} then denotes the payment from buyer 2).
• An efficient allocation of the good x_{ij}, that is, $x_{HH} = x_{LL} = \frac{1}{2}$, $x_{HL} = 1$, and $x_{LH} = 0$.

Such a contract extracts all the buyers' surplus if it is incentive compatible and if the buyers' individual-rationality constraints are binding for all types, or if

$$\beta_{LL}\left(\frac{v_L}{2} - P_{LL}\right) - \beta_{LH}P_{LH} \geq \beta_{LL}(v_L - P_{HL}) + \beta_{LH}\left(\frac{v_L}{2} - P_{HH}\right) \qquad \text{(ICL)}$$

$$\beta_{HH}\left(\frac{v_H}{2} - P_{HH}\right) + \beta_{HL}(v_H - P_{HL}) \geq -\beta_{HH}P_{LH} + \beta_{HL}\left(\frac{v_H}{2} - P_{LL}\right) \qquad \text{(ICH)}$$

and

$$\beta_{LL}\left(\frac{v_L}{2} - P_{LL}\right) - \beta_{LH}P_{LH} = 0 \qquad \text{(IRL)}$$

$$\beta_{HH}\left(\frac{v_H}{2} - P_{HH}\right) + \beta_{HL}(v_H - P_{HL}) = 0 \qquad \text{(IRH)}$$

Since correlation means that $\beta_{LL}\beta_{HH} - \beta_{LH}\beta_{HL} \neq 0$, we can in fact find P_{ij}'s such that these four conditions are satisfied. To see this point, first rewrite the two participation constraints as follows:

$$P_{LH} = \frac{\beta_{LL}}{\beta_{LH}}\left(\frac{v_L}{2} - P_{LL}\right) \qquad \text{(IRL)}$$

$$P_{HL} = v_H + \frac{\beta_{HH}}{\beta_{HL}}\left(\frac{v_H}{2} - P_{HH}\right) \qquad \text{(IRH)}$$

---

11. This revenue equivalence between the four auctions with correlated values is valid only in our special example with two possible valuations for each buyer. The appendix of this chapter (section 7.7) shows that it breaks down with three different valuations.

Next, define $\xi = (\beta_{HH}\beta_{LL})/(\beta_{HL}\beta_{LH})$, which differs from 1 because of correlation. Using the two preceding equations and the fact that the equilibrium surplus of each buyer is zero, we can rewrite the two incentive constraints as follows:

$$0 \geq \frac{\beta_{LH}}{2}(v_L - \beta v_H) - \beta_{LL}(v_H - v_L) + \beta_{LH}(\xi - 1)P_{HH} \tag{ICL}$$

$$0 \geq \frac{\beta_{HL}}{2}(v_H - \beta v_L) + \beta_{HL}(\xi - 1)P_{LL} \tag{ICH}$$

As we can see, it is possible to satisfy these incentive constraints and therefore to extract the entire first-best surplus for the seller whenever there is dependence between valuations, that is, whenever $\xi \neq 1$. In the case of positive correlation ($\xi > 1$), we just need to set P_{HH} and P_{LL} low enough. Intuitively, we deter deviations from truth telling by the high-valuation buyer by requiring from her a low enough P_{LL}, and therefore, by the participation constraint for the low-type (IRL), a high enough P_{LH}. This helps to satisfy the incentive constraint for the high-type (ICH) because, when a given buyer i has a high valuation, not telling the truth becomes costlier: the probability that the other buyer, j, has a high valuation too, and thus that the payment to be made is P_{LH} instead of P_{LL}, is higher than when buyer i has a low valuation. The same is true, mutatis mutandis, for a low-valuation buyer. And the same principle applies in the case of negative correlation ($\xi < 1$), but then it means setting P_{HH} and P_{LL} high enough: once again, the idea is to set the higher payments in the states of nature that are less probable under truth telling than under deviations from truth telling.

We have thus presented a mechanism that allows the seller to extract the full efficient surplus. Note, however, that it works under the double assumption that (1) the buyers are risk neutral, and (2) they have no resource constraints. Indeed, note that the payments will have to vary a lot across states of nature when correlation becomes small, that is, when $\xi \to 1$.

7.3.6   The Role of Risk Aversion

Let us now see what happens when we relax the assumption of risk neutrality. We shall limit ourselves here to considering a two-type example and comparing the performance of standard auctions. This approach, however, will give us the intuition of the role of risk aversion more generally.

Suppose for now that both buyers' preferences are represented by the strictly increasing and concave von Neumann–Morgenstern utility function $u(\cdot)$. How does risk aversion affect the buyers' bidding strategy? Note, first of all, that the buyers' bidding behavior in the English (and Vickrey) auction is unaffected by their attitudes toward risk. Whether a buyer is risk averse or not, it is always a best response to "continue" until the asking price hits the reservation value (or to bid the reservation value in the Vickrey auction). Thus the seller's expected revenue in these auctions is not affected by buyers' risk aversion.

In the Dutch (and first-price sealed-bid) auctions, however, risk aversion affects equilibrium bids. To see how, compare the high-value buyer's equilibrium (mixed) strategy under risk neutrality and risk aversion.[12] When the buyer is risk neutral, her expected payoff from a bid $b \in (v_L, \bar{b})$ is given by

$$[1 - \beta + \beta F(b)](v_H - b)$$

where $F(b)$ denotes the cumulative probability distribution function of bids of the high-value buyer

$$F(b) - \int_{v_L}^{b} f(y|v_H)dy$$

When the buyer offers $b \approx v_L$, her expected payoff is $(1 - \beta)(v_H - v_L)$, and since in a mixed-strategy equilibrium all bids that are made with positive probability must yield the same expected payoff, the following equation holds in equilibrium:

$$[1 - \beta + \beta F(b)](v_H - b) = (1 - \beta)(v_H - v_L) \tag{7.9}$$

When buyers are risk averse, this equation becomes

$$[1 - \beta + \beta \tilde{F}(b)]u(v_H - b) = (1 - \beta)u(v_H - v_L) \tag{7.10}$$

where $\tilde{F}(b)$ now denotes the cumulative probability distribution function of bids of the high-value buyer when she is risk averse. Rearranging equations (7.9) and (7.10) we obtain

$$1 + \frac{\beta F(b)}{(1 - \beta)} = \frac{v_H - v_L}{v_H - b}$$

---

12. Recall that for low-value buyers (whether they are risk averse or risk neutral), the equilibrium strategy is simply the pure strategy $b(v_L) = v_L$.

and

$$1 + \frac{\beta \tilde{F}(b)}{(1-\beta)} = \frac{u(v_H - v_L)}{u(v_H - b)}$$

Since $u(\cdot)$ is a strictly concave function, we know that

$$\frac{u(v_H - v_L)}{u(v_H - b)} < \frac{v_H - v_L}{v_H - b}$$

so that $\tilde{F}(b) \leq F(b)$, with $\tilde{F}(b) < F(b)$ for b belonging to the open interval $(v_L, \bar{b})$, or $1 - \tilde{F}(b) > 1 - F(b)$. In other words, a high-valuation risk-averse buyer is more likely to make high bids than a high-valuation risk-neutral buyer. Because she is risk averse, the high-valuation buyer wants to insure herself against the bad outcome of losing the item to the other buyer by raising her bid. Therefore, the Dutch (and first-price sealed-bid) auction raises a higher expected revenue than the English (and Vickrey) auction when buyers are risk averse.

It can be shown that a seller may be able to raise an even higher expected revenue from risk-averse buyers by charging a fee for participating in the auction (see Matthews, 1983; Maskin and Riley, 1984b). Such a fee amounts to a positive penalty on losers. This penalty has the effect of inducing risk-averse buyers to bid even higher so as to insure themselves against the bad outcome of losing.[13]

7.3.7 The Role of Asymmetrically Distributed Valuations

What happens when we drop the assumption of symmetry? Once again, let us start with the two-type case. Suppose that the two buyers have different probabilities of having a high valuation for the good. Without loss of generality, assume $\beta_2 > \beta_1$. Then the expected revenue of the seller in the English (and Vickrey) auction is given by $\beta_1 \beta_2 v_H + (1 - \beta_1 \beta_2) v_L$. Under the Dutch (and first-price sealed-bid) auction, however, expected revenues will be lower. To see this result, consider the equilibrium bidding strategies of the two players when they have low and high valuations for the good. We can say the following:

---

13. Note that (in contrast to the situation with a single buyer) this result holds irrespective of whether the buyer has preferences that exhibit decreasing or increasing absolute risk aversion. The point here is that while the penalty for losing lowers the equilibrium bid of a low-value buyer, this is only a second-order effect, while the resulting increase in the high-value buyer's bid is of first order.

- First, either buyer, when she has a low valuation, bids v_L, for the same reasons as in section 7.3.3. Therefore, by bidding just above v_L, buyer 1 obtains at least $(1 - \beta_2)(v_H - v_L) > 0$ when she has a high valuation, while buyer 2 obtains at least $(1 - \beta_1)(v_H - v_L) > 0$ when she has a high valuation.

- Second, each high-valuation buyer's equilibrium bidding strategy is again, as in section 7.3.3, a mixed strategy. And both buyers must have the same maximum bid, b_H ($< v_H$), in equilibrium: otherwise, since equilibrium strategies are correctly predicted, the buyer with the higher maximum bid can, without lowering her probability of winning, lower her maximum bid toward the maximum bid of her opponent. Moreover, this maximum bid cannot be chosen by either bidder with strictly positive probability: if one's opponent bids b_H with strictly positive probability, bidding b_H is dominated by bidding just above b_H: then one obtains the good for sure instead of with probability $\frac{1}{2}$. Consequently, whenever a bidder bids b_H, she obtains as payoff $v_H - b_H$.

- Third, obviously, each bid that is made with positive probability by one of the buyers in equilibrium must yield the same expected payoff to that buyer. Equating the payoffs between bidding b_H and bidding (just above) v_L, we obtain

$$v_H - b_H = (1 - \beta_1)(v_H - v_L) = (1 - \beta_2 + \beta_2\alpha)(v_H - v_L)$$

where α is the positive probability that buyer 2 bids v_L. Indeed, we need to have buyer 2 bidding less aggressively against the weaker buyer 1 in order to have both payoffs equal to $v_H - b_H$. This means that buyer 2 will bid with strictly positive probability like low-valuation buyers. Note that, under symmetry, $\alpha = 0$.

We are now ready to derive the seller's expected revenue. It is equal to the total surplus from trade minus the rents accruing to the buyers. Since the auction is efficient,[14] the expected total surplus equals

$$[1 - (1 - \beta_1)(1 - \beta_2)]v_H + (1 - \beta_1)(1 - \beta_2)v_L$$

Moreover, low-valuation buyers earn zero rents, while high-valuation buyers earn $(1 - \beta_1)(v_H - v_L)$. The sum of expected rents of the two buyers is therefore

---

14. "Efficiency" requires that if bids are equal, the higher-valuation buyer obtains the good: this in fact strengthens the result that the expected revenue here is lower than that of an English auction.

$$(\beta_1 + \beta_2)(1 - \beta_1)(v_H - v_L)$$

and the seller's expected revenue is

$$\beta_1^2 v_H + (1 - \beta_1^2)v_L$$

which is strictly less than the expected revenue under the English (and Vickrey) auction.

Intuitively, the reason why revenue equivalence breaks down when buyers' expected valuations differ is that in the first-price sealed-bid auction the extent of competition between bidders is determined by the weaker bidder. This result, however, is not very robust. For example, the Vickrey auction may yield lower expected revenue than the first-price sealed-bid auction when the two bidders' valuation supports differ. To see this possibility, suppose that the only difference between the two bidders is that $v_H^2 > v_H^1$; otherwise, $v_L^2 = v_L^1 = v_L$ and $\beta_1 = \beta_2 = \beta$. The seller's expected revenue in the Vickrey auction is then $\beta^2 v_H^2 + (1 - \beta^2)v_L$. But in the first-price auction expected revenue is strictly higher because the second buyer bids more aggressively when $v_H^2 > v_H^1$ than when $v_H^2 = v_H^1$. In fact, under asymmetry, there is no general result on the relative merits of first-price versus Vickrey auctions (see Maskin and Riley, 2000, for a more complete analysis of asymmetric auctions).

7.4   Auctions with Imperfectly Known Common Values

In many auctions, buyers may not have perfect information about the value of the item for sale. If all buyers are risk neutral and their valuation of the item is independent of other buyers' valuations, then the theory developed in the previous subsection is still relevant. The only change that is required is to replace the bidders' true value by their expected value.

However, if a buyer's final value depends on information other bidders may have, then the auction-design problem is fundamentally different. In this section we consider a simple example of an auction problem where buyers have imperfectly known common values. Many if not most auctions in practice are of this form. For example, art, treasury bill, or book auctions are effectively imperfectly known common-value auctions: most bidders do not know exactly how much the items to be auctioned are worth to others, and part or all of their own valuation for the item depends on what they believe to be the resale value of the item.

In our example the item for sale has a value $v \in \{H, L\}$, where $H > L > 0$. Nobody knows the true value of the item. The seller and two buyers have a prior belief $\frac{1}{2}$ that the item has a high value, H. The buyers receive an independent private estimate of the value or signal, $s_i \in \{s_H, s_L\}$, and thus have private information about the value of the item. When the value of the item is H, the probability of receiving signal s_H is $p > \frac{1}{2}$. Similarly, when the value is L, the probability of receiving signal s_L is $p > \frac{1}{2}$. Thus a buyer's expected value upon receiving the signal s_H is given by $v_H = E[v \mid s_H] = pH + (1-p)L$. Similarly, $v_L = E[v \mid s_L] = pL + (1-p)H$.

7.4.1 The Winner's Curse

The main change introduced by buyers' imperfect knowledge of their value is that the bidding process and the outcome of the auction may reveal information that induces bidders to revise their valuation of the item. One piece of information that is revealed to the winner of the auction—the highest bidder—is that she received an estimate of the value that was more favorable than the estimates of all other bidders. That information leads her to lower her valuation of the item. This phenomenon is known as the winner's curse: Winning is in a sense bad news, since it reveals that the winner overestimated the value of the item.

In our example the winner's curse takes the following form: Suppose that the seller puts the item up for sale in a Vickrey auction, and suppose that buyers behave as before and bid their expected reservation value v_H or v_L. Then the highest bidder wins and gets the item at the second-highest bid. When one buyer gets the signal s_H and the other the signal s_L, the winner gets the item at the price v_L, but her value conditional on winning—v_w—is now

$$v_w = E[v \mid (s_H, s_L)] = \frac{L+H}{2} < pH + (1-p)L = v_H$$

Even if winning brings about a downward revision of the value, the winner of the auction still makes a positive net gain, since

$$v_w = E[v \mid (s_H, s_L)] = \frac{L+H}{2} > pL + (1-p)H = v_L$$

When both buyers get the signal s_H, each one has a 50% chance of winning and paying the price v_H. In this case winning actually results in an upward revision of the value, and the winner's net payoff is strictly positive. In other words, in this event there is a "winner's blessing":

$$v_w = E[v \mid (s_H, s_H)] = \frac{p^2 H + (1-p)^2 L}{p^2 + (1-p)^2} > pH + (1-p)L = v_H$$

Finally, when both buyers get a signal s_L, the winner's net gain is negative, since

$$v_w = E[v \mid (s_L, s_L)] = \frac{p^2 L + (1-p)^2 H}{p^2 + (1-p)^2} < pL + (1-p)H = v_L$$

and in this case we have the winner's curse.

Several lessons can be drawn from this analysis. First, winning is not entirely bad news in the Vickrey auction, even if the winner may be led to revise her valuation downward. In fact, winning may even be a blessing if the second-highest bid (which is the price the winner must pay) reveals a high-value estimate from the other bidder. Second, winning is always bad for those bidding v_L. Consequently, buyers with a value v_L will bid below their ex ante value, so that bidding one's own (expected) value is no longer a dominant strategy. Third, the buyers with an ex ante value v_H are better off bidding above their value v_H. Indeed, this bid would not affect their final payoff in the event that the other bidder has a low-value estimate, but it would raise their probability of winning against a high-value buyer bidding v_H.

It should be clear at this point what the Bayesian equilibrium in the Vickrey auction is in our example:

1. Buyers receiving the signal s_L optimally bid

$$b_L = E[v \mid (s_L, s_L)] = \frac{p^2 L + (1-p)^2 H}{p^2 + (1-p)^2}$$

With any higher bid they would make a negative expected net gain, as we illustrated previously. The best response to any lower bid, $b < b_L$, is to raise the bid by $\varepsilon > 0$ so as to outcompete the other bidder in the classic Bertrand fashion.

2. Buyers receiving the signal s_H bid

$$b_H = E[v \mid (s_H, s_H)] = \frac{p^2 H + (1-p)^2 L}{p^2 + (1-p)^2}$$

Any higher bid would produce a negative expected net gain. And the best response to any lower bid, $b < b_H$, is again to raise the bid by $\varepsilon > 0$ in the classic Bertrand fashion.

Hence, the expected revenue from the Vickrey auction in our example is

$$\frac{1}{2}\left[p^2 - (1-p)^2\right](H-L) + \frac{p^2 L + (1-p)^2 H}{p^2 + (1-p)^2}$$

7.4.2   Standard Auctions with Imperfectly Known Common Values in the 2 × 2 Model

We saw that when buyers have perfectly known values for the item to be auctioned off, then the English and Vickrey auctions yield the same expected revenue and are in essence equivalent. The same is true of the Dutch and the first-price sealed-bid auction. Moreover, when the buyers' values are independent, these four auctions all yield the same expected revenue.

With imperfectly known buyer values, only the Dutch and first-price sealed-bid auction are equivalent in general. The equivalence between the English and Vickrey auctions breaks down with more than two buyers and more than two types, essentially because the English auction aggregates the dispersed estimates of the buyers more efficiently and, thus, reduces the winner's curse problem. Thus in the general model with $n > 2$ bidders and $N > 2$ types the Vickrey auction generates expected revenue no greater than the English auction. Also, the Vickrey auction generates a higher expected revenue than the Dutch auction when there are $N \geq 3$ types.

Unfortunately the 2 × 2 model (two bidders with two types) considered here provides a somewhat misleading picture, since in this special case revenue equivalence obtains even though bidders have imperfectly known common values. However, the virtue of this special case is to highlight the subtlety of the social-learning effects present in imperfectly known common-value auctions. The readers interested in seeing a general comparison of standard auctions when bidders have imperfectly known common values are referred to the classic paper by Milgrom and Weber (1982). In this chapter we consider only the 2 × 2 case.

We begin by showing that revenue equivalence obtains in the 2 × 2 case. We have already determined the seller's expected revenue in the Vickrey auction. Thus consider in turn the English and Dutch auctions (recall that the first-price sealed-bid auction is strategically equivalent to the Dutch auction).

· **English Auction:** It is a dominant strategy in the English auction for a buyer with ex ante value v_L to stay in the auction until the price hits the level

$$E[v \,|\, (s_L, s_L)] = \frac{p^2 L + (1-p)^2 H}{p^2 + (1-p)^2} \equiv v_{LL}$$

and to drop out when the price exceeds

$$E[v \,|\, (s_H, s_L)] = \frac{L+H}{2} \equiv v_{LH}$$

and for a buyer with ex ante value v_H to stay in the auction until the price hits the level v_{LH} and to drop out when the price reaches

$$E[v \,|\, (s_H, s_H)] = \frac{p^2 H + (1-p)^2 L}{p^2 + (1-p)^2} \equiv v_{HH}$$

Thus, given the dominant strategies of v_H buyers, it is a (weakly) dominant strategy for a v_L buyer to drop out when the price reaches v_{LL}. Assuming that this is the equilibrium bidding behavior of v_L buyers, one immediately infers from the fact that a buyer decides to stay in the auction when the price exceeds v_{LL} that this buyer has obtained a signal s_H.[15] Hence, when both buyers receive a signal s_H, they are able to infer each other's signal from their respective bidding behavior, and they stay in the auction until the price hits v_{HH}. Therefore, the seller's expected revenue in the English auction with only two bidders is the same as in the Vickrey auction.

· **Dutch Auction:** As in the case where buyers have perfectly known values, the equilibrium in the Dutch auction involves mixed strategies. It is easy to verify that in equilibrium $\underline{v}_L$ buyers bid v_{LL} and v_H buyers randomize over bids $b \in [v_{LL}, \bar{b}]$, where $\bar{b} < v_{HH}$. To verify that the equilibrium takes this form, note first that any mixed strategy $F_H(b)$ must satisfy the equation

$$\frac{1}{2}(v_{HL} - v_{LL}) = \frac{1}{2}(v_{HL} - b) + \frac{1}{2} F_H(b)(v_{HH} - b) \tag{7.11}$$

---

15. It is a straightforward exercise to show that a v_L buyer will never bid above v_{LL} in any equilibrium.

Hence, $\bar{b}$, which is given by the solution to

$$(v_{HL} - v_{LL}) = (v_{HL} - \bar{b}) + (v_{HH} - \bar{b})$$

is strictly less than v_{HH}. Next, note that given the v_H buyer's equilibrium strategy, it is a best response for a v_L buyer to bid v_{LL}. Indeed, any $b \in [v_{LL}, \bar{b}]$ would yield an expected payoff equal to

$$\frac{1}{2}(v_{LL} - b) + \frac{1}{2} F_H(b)(v_{HL} - b)$$

From equation (7.11) we have

$$\frac{b - v_{LL}}{v_{HH} - b} = F_H(b)$$

Substituting for $F_H(b)$, we can see that any bid $b \in [v_{LL}, \bar{b}]$ would yield a negative expected revenue for a v_L buyer:

$$\frac{1}{2}(v_{LL} - b)(v_{HH} - b) - \frac{1}{2}(v_{LL} - b)(v_{HL} - b) = \frac{1}{2}(v_{HH} - v_{HL})(v_{LL} - b) \le 0$$

Finally, just as in the case with independent (perfectly known) values, there is no pure best response for v_H buyers and the unique mixed strategy equilibrium has support $[v_{LL}, \bar{b}]$. Now, to see that the seller's expected revenue is the same as in the other standard auctions we have discussed, note simply that the payoffs of the two types of bidders are the same as in the other two auctions [v_L buyers get zero and v_H buyers get $(v_{HL} - v_{LL})/2$] and the equilibrium allocations are the same (v_L buyers get the item with probability $\frac{1}{4}$, and v_H buyers get the item with probability $\frac{3}{4}$). Therefore, the seller's expected revenue must be the same.

We have thus shown that revenue equivalence is maintained in the 2×2 model even though buyers have imperfectly known common values. It is worth pointing out that this equivalence extends to the $n \times 2$ model.[16] Also, the equivalence between the Vickrey and English auctions extends to the $2 \times N$ model. Indeed, the two bidders' symmetric equilibrium strategies in the English auction then simply take the form of a reservation price (conditional on the signal and history of play). The bidder with the highest reservation price then gets the item at the second-highest reservation price. With

---

16. We leave it as an exercise to show revenue equivalence in the $n \times 2$ model. This result can be established by adapting the arguments used in the 2×2 model.

two bidders there is no additional information generated in the English auction over the observation of the second-highest bid, so that the English auction is then informationally equivalent to the Vickrey auction. With more than two bidders, however, some information is lost in the Vickrey auction by observing only the second-highest bid, so that the English auction should be expected to generate more revenue. This conclusion is indeed what Milgrom and Weber (1982) establish.

7.4.3   Optimal Auctions with Imperfectly Known Common Values

Because the buyers' estimated values based on their private signals are correlated when there is a common (unknown) component to all buyers' valuations, it is possible for the seller to extract all the buyers' surplus in an optimal auction just as in section 7.3.5. On the one hand, since this is a common-value environment, maximizing the surplus simply means trading with probability one, while it does not matter who is allocated the good. On the other hand, buyers with a higher signal will be ready to pay more for receiving the good, so that it will be optimal to give it to them with a higher probability.

Specifically, let $\{P(\hat{s}_1, \hat{s}_2); x(\hat{s}_1, \hat{s}_2)\}$ denote an arbitrary (symmetric) contract offered by the seller to the two buyers where $P(\hat{s}_1, \hat{s}_2)$ denotes a payment from the buyer and $x(\hat{s}_1, \hat{s}_2)$ an allocation of the item to the buyer who has reported $\hat{s}_1$ conditional on the reported vector of signals $(\hat{s}_1, \hat{s}_2)$. Let us focus on $x(\hat{s}_1, \hat{s}_2)$ such that $x(s_H, s_H) = x(s_L, s_L) = \frac{1}{2}$, while $x(s_H, s_L) = 1$ and $x(s_L, s_H) = 0$. Call P_{ij} the payment to be made by a buyer who has announced signal i while the other buyer has announced signal j. Then the seller is able to extract all the buyers' surplus if both buyers' individual-rationality constraints are binding while both incentive-compatibility constraints are also satisfied:

$$-(1-p')P_{LH} + p'\left(\frac{1}{2}v_{LL} - P_{LL}\right) \geq (1-p')\left(\frac{1}{2}v_{LH} - P_{HH}\right) + p'(v_{LL} - P_{HL}) \quad \text{(ICL)}$$

$$p'\left(\frac{1}{2}v_{HH} - P_{HH}\right) + (1-p')(v_{HL} - P_{HL}) \geq -p'P_{LH} + (1-p')\left(\frac{1}{2}v_{HL} - P_{LL}\right) \quad \text{(ICH)}$$

$$-(1-p')P_{LH} + p'\left(\frac{1}{2}v_{LL} - P_{LL}\right) = 0 \quad \text{(IRL)}$$

$$p'\left(\frac{1}{2}v_{HH} - P_{HH}\right) + (1-p')(v_{HL} - P_{HL}) = 0 \quad \text{(IRH)}$$

where p' is the probability that a buyer who has received a low signal attributes to the other buyer having also received a low signal (see below).

The intuition behind these constraints is as follows. Take, for example, the first one, (ICL). On the LHS is the payoff of the buyer when she has received a low signal and tells the truth about it, while on the RHS is her payoff when she falsely claims to have received a high signal. In the first case, she receives the good with probability $\frac{1}{2}$ when the other bidder has also received a low signal, in which case she pays P_{LL} while the good has value v_{LL}. What is the probability of this outcome? It is

$$\Pr(s_L|s_L) = \Pr(s_L|L)\Pr(L|s_L) + \Pr(s_L|H)\Pr(H|s_L)$$
$$= p^2 + (1-p)^2 \equiv p'$$

which is lower than p but higher than $\frac{1}{2}$. Instead, when the other bidder has received a high signal [which happens with probability $(1 - p')$], the payment is P_{LH} and the other bidder gets the good for sure. The RHS of (ICL) takes the same probabilities p' and $(1 - p')$ and values for the object— that is, v_{LH} and v_{LL}—but the probabilities of trade and the payments correspond to the high announcement because the buyer lies about her signal.

Just as in section 7.3.5, we can first rewrite the two participation constraints as follows:

$$P_{LH} = \frac{p'}{(1-p')}\left(\frac{v_{LL}}{2} - P_{LL}\right) \tag{IRL}$$

$$P_{HL} = v_{HL} + \frac{p'}{(1-p')}\left(\frac{v_{HH}}{2} - P_{HH}\right) \tag{IRH}$$

Next, define $\xi = [p'/(1 - p')]^2$, which is greater than one. Using the two preceding equations and the fact that the equilibrium surplus of each buyer is zero, we can rewrite the two incentive constraints as follows:

$$0 \geq \frac{(1-p')}{2}(v_{LH} - \xi v_{HH}) - p'(v_{HL} - v_{LL}) + (1 - p')(\xi - 1)P_{HH} \tag{ICL}$$

$$0 \geq \frac{(1-p')}{2}(v_{HL} - \xi v_{LL}) + (1 - p')(\xi - 1)P_{LL} \tag{ICH}$$

Just as in section 7.3.5, it is possible to satisfy these incentive constraints and therefore to extract the entire surplus for the seller. Since this is a case of positive correlation, we need to set P_{HH} and P_{LL} low enough. Intuitively, we deter deviations from truth telling by the buyer who has received a good signal by requiring a low enough P_{LL} and, therefore, by the participation constraint (IRL) for the low type, a high enough P_{LH}. Doing so helps to satisfy the incentive constraint (ICH) for the high type because, when a given buyer i has received a high signal, not telling the truth becomes costlier: the probability that the other buyer, j, has a high signal too, and thus that the payment to be made is P_{LH} instead of P_{LL}, is higher than when buyer i has received a low signal. The same is true, mutatis mutandis, for a low-valuation buyer who has received a low signal.

We have thus presented a mechanism that allows the seller to extract the full surplus. Again, it works under the double assumption that (1) the buyers are risk neutral, and (2) they have no resource constraints. Beyond these assumptions, the full rent extraction result is very general, as has been shown by Crémer and McLean (1988). All that is required is some form of correlation between buyer valuations, which obtains naturally in settings where there is a common component to buyers' values. This result is yet another illustration of the fragility of the optimality of the four standard auctions considered in this chapter. On the whole, the conclusion that emerges—that the widely observed standard auctions are optimal only for a very narrow set of parameters—is disappointing for the theory of optimal contracts, for it suggests that some important considerations have been ignored that would explain why the English and sealed-bid auctions are used so often.

7.5 Summary

In this chapter we have considered two canonical static contracting problems with multilateral private information. The first problem is one where the contracting parties are complementary to each other and where, as a consequence, trade is fundamentally of a public-good nature. The second problem is one where some of the contracting parties (the buyers) are substitutable (at least partially) and compete with one another. A classic example of a problem of the second type, which we have focused on, is an auction organized by a seller. We have highlighted the fact that, in contrast to bilateral contracting problems (with one-sided asymmetric information), the outcome of optimal contracting is more difficult to predict, as the contracting parties are involved in a game situation that may have several equilibria. There is by now a large literature on *mechanism design* that is concerned with the question of how to structure contracts so that the game they induce results in a unique, hopefully dominant-strategy, equilibrium outcome (see Fudenberg and Tirole, 1991, chap. 7; Palfrey, 1992, for two extensive surveys of this literature). This literature is beyond the scope of this book, as it can be significantly more abstract and technical than the theories we have covered in this chapter. Rather than delve into this difficult topic, we have taken the shortcut followed by many and made the reasonable assumption that optimal contractual outcomes are given by the Bayesian equilibria of the game induced by the optimal contract.

Under that assumption, we have seen that key insights and methods developed in Chapter 2 extend to more general multilateral contract settings. For example, the revelation principle can be invoked to characterize second-best contracts without too much loss of generality. Similarly, under mild additional assumptions about preferences (the "single-crossing" condition) the set of binding incentive constraints takes an appealingly simple form.

Some fundamental ideas and results have emerged from our analysis in this chapter:

• We have learned that asymmetric information per se may not be a source of allocative inefficiency when hidden information is about *private values*. Rather, it is the combination of interim participation and incentive constraints that gives rise to allocative inefficiencies. There is an important lesson for policy in this basic insight—namely, that it may be desirable to make public decisions, and lock individuals in, before they learn their private information and can exploit their vested informational rents.

• Likewise, we have confirmed the basic general intuition that competition reduces informational monopoly power, at least when hidden information is about private values. Thus we have seen that in an auction the seller's expected revenue rises as more buyers compete for the item.

• A remarkable result of auction theory, which we have focused on in this chapter, is that several standard auction procedures, such as the English, sealed-bid, and Dutch auctions, yield the same expected revenue for the seller when bidders are risk neutral, have independently and identically distributed private values, and play the unique symmetric equilibrium in each bidding game. Furthermore, these auction procedures combined with minimum bid constraints may maximize the seller's expected revenue. As significant as this result is, however, we have also shown that *revenue equivalence* breaks down when any of these assumptions do not hold. Thus, when bidders are risk averse (or are budget constrained), the standard auctions do not generate the same expected revenue. What's more, none of the standard auctions are then optimal. Similarly, when bidders' hidden information is about common values, the standard auctions produce different expected revenues for the seller. A basic reason for the breakdown of revenue equivalence in this case is the *winner's curse,* which may induce excessively cautious bidding in the sealed-bid or Dutch auction relative to the English auction.

These are basic insights about auctions, which highlight the potential importance of the design of auction procedures. There is by now a large body of literature on auction design, which has been partly stimulated by government decisions in a number of countries to organize spectrum auctions, by the wave of privatization following the collapse of communism in the former Soviet Union, and, more recently, by the advent of the Internet and online auctions like eBay. It is clearly beyond the scope of this book to cover this literature in any systematic way. We refer the interested reader, for example, to Klemperer (2003), Krishna (2002), and Milgrom (2004).

7.6   Literature Notes

The theories covered in this chapter have a long ancestry. The founding article on auction theory and more generally the theory of contracting under multilateral asymmetric information is Vickrey (1961). Many of the ideas covered in this chapter are lucidly discussed in his article, which is highly recommended reading. One of the key insights in Vickrey's article—that it is a (weakly) dominant strategy for bidders to reveal their true values in a second-price auction—has found a useful later application to the problem of efficient provision of public goods, when the value of the good to individual agents is private information. Thus Clarke (1971), Groves (1973), and Groves and Ledyard (1977) have shown that in public-goods problems it may also be a dominant strategy for individuals to reveal their true values if their contribution to the cost of the public good is a form of second-price bid. This line of research has culminated in the major treatise on incentives in public-goods supply by Green and Laffont (1979). One weakness of what is now referred to as the Groves-Clarke mechanism is that generally the sum of the contributions required by all individuals to finance the public good and truthfully elicit their preferences (in dominant strategies) exceeds the cost of the public good. This finding prompted d'Aspremont and Gérard-Varet (1979) to show that it is possible to implement the efficient supply of public goods, obtain *budget balance,* and ensure truthful revelation of preferences, provided that one concentrates on the less demanding notion of Bayesian equilibrium rather than insisting on dominant-strategy equilibrium. d'Aspremont and Gérard-Varet require only ex ante participation constraints to hold. Moreover, they establish their result under the assumption that individual valuations are independently distributed, but later research by themselves, Crémer and McLean, and others has revealed that this result holds under much more general conditions. The final stage in this line of research has been reached with the contributions by Laffont and Maskin (1979) and Myerson and Satterthwaite (1983), who have shown that public-good provision under multilateral private information is generally inefficient when interim (or ex post) participation constraints must hold.

The public-good-provision problem is technically very similar to the bilateral-trading case we focused on in section 7.2, although the economic interpretation is different. This similarity has allowed us to illustrate in particular the contributions of d'Aspremont and Gérard-Varet (1979) and Myerson and Satterthwaite (1983), as well as the optimal double-auction mechanism of Chatterjee and Samuelson (1983), in this context.

Subsequent to this research on public goods, the 1980s and 1990s have witnessed a major revival in research on auction theory. Myerson (1981) and Riley and Samuelson (1981) provide the first general treatments of optimal auction design and rigorously establish the revenue-equivalence theorem for the first time. In later work, Matthews (1983) and Maskin and Riley (1984b) characterize optimal auctions with risk-averse bidders. Wilson (1977), Milgrom (1979), and Milgrom and Weber (1982) break new ground by analyzing equilibrium bidding behavior and information aggregation when bidders have private information on *common values* and their bidding is affected by the *winner's curse.* In related research, Crémer and McLean (1985, 1988) show how the seller can extract all the bidders' informational rent in an optimal auction when bidders' values are correlated.

More recently, the optimal auction design literature has explored asymmetric auctions (Maskin and Riley, 2000), auctions with budget-constrained bidders (Che and Gale, 1998), efficient auctions (Dasgupta and Maskin, 2000), multiunit auctions (Armstrong, 2000), and auctions with externalities (Jehiel, Moldovanu, and Stachetti, 1996), among several other topics (for a survey of the recent research on auctions see also Krishna, 2002, Klemperer, 2003, and Milgrom, 2004).

7.7   Appendix: Breakdown of Revenue Equivalence in a 2 × 3 Example

Although the English and Vickrey auctions are equivalent in the $2 \times N$ model, the equivalence between the Dutch and Vickrey (or first- and second-price) auctions breaks down under correlation, as the following example due to Maskin (1997) illustrates. In this example the two bidders have three possible types $\{v_L = 0, v_M = 1, v_H = 2\}$. The buyers have perfectly known correlated values: These values are pairwise positively correlated (that is, using the terminology of Milgrom and Weber (1982), they are *affiliated*). Specifically, the distribution of joint probabilities is given by

$$\Pr(v_L, v_L) = \Pr(v_H, v_H) = \frac{1}{3}$$

$$\Pr(v_L, v_M) = \Pr(v_M, v_L) = \Pr(v_M, v_H) = \Pr(v_H, v_M) = \frac{\alpha}{4}$$

$$\Pr(v_M, v_M) = \frac{1}{3} - \alpha$$

$$\Pr(v_L, v_H) = \Pr(v_H, v_L) = 0$$

where α is positive but small. The expected revenue in the Vickrey (second-price auction) is then given by

$$[\Pr(v_M, v_M) + \Pr(v_H, v_M) + \Pr(v_M, v_H)] + 2\Pr(v_H, v_H) =$$
$$\left[\left(\frac{1}{3} - \alpha\right) + \frac{\alpha}{2} + 2\frac{1}{3}\right] = \left[1 - \frac{1}{2}\alpha\right]$$

Thus at $\alpha = 0$ the derivative of expected revenue with respect to α is $-\frac{1}{2}$.

Consider now the expected revenue in the Dutch (first-price) auction. Recall that in this auction the (symmetric) equilibrium is in mixed strategies, at least for types v_M and v_H. Thus let types v_M and v_H, respectively, randomize over bids in the supports $[0, b_M]$ and $[b_M, b_H]$ with the cumulative distribution functions F_M and F_H. Then the seller's expected revenue is given by

$$\frac{\alpha}{2}\int_0^{b_M} b\, dF_M(b) + \left(\frac{1}{3} - \alpha\right)\int_0^{b_M} b\, d[F_M(b)]^2 +$$
$$\frac{\alpha}{2}\int_{b_M}^{b_H} b\, dF_H(b) + \frac{1}{3}\int_{b_M}^{b_H} b\, d[F_H(b)]^2 \qquad (7.12)$$

where $F_M(b)$ is given by the indifference condition

$$\left[\frac{\alpha}{4}(1-b)+\left(\frac{1}{3}-\alpha\right)F_M(b)(1-b)\right]=\frac{\alpha}{4}$$

for all $b \in [0, b_M]$. Hence,

$$F_M(b)=\frac{3\alpha b}{(4-12\alpha)(1-b)} \quad \text{and} \quad b_M=\frac{4-12\alpha}{4-9\alpha} \tag{7.13}$$

Similarly, $F_H(b)$ is given by the indifference condition

$$\frac{\alpha}{4}(2-b)+\frac{1}{3}F_H(b)(2-b)=\frac{\alpha}{4}(2-b_M)$$

for all $b \in [b_M, b_H]$. Hence,

$$F_H(b)=\frac{3\alpha}{4(2-b)}(b-b_M) \quad \text{and} \quad b_H=\frac{8+3\alpha b_M}{4+3\alpha} \tag{7.14}$$

Substituting equations (7.13) and (7.14) into expression (7.12), one obtains the rather unwieldy expression for the seller's expected revenue

$$\frac{\alpha}{2}\int_0^{\frac{4-12\alpha}{4-9\alpha}}\left(\frac{3\alpha b}{(4-12\alpha)(1-b)^2}\right)db+\left(\frac{1}{3}-\alpha\right)\int_0^{\frac{4-12\alpha}{4-9\alpha}}\left(\frac{(9\alpha^2)(2b^2)}{(4-12\alpha)^2(1-b)^3}\right)db+$$

$$\frac{\alpha}{2}\int_{\frac{4-12\alpha}{4-9\alpha}}^{\frac{8+3\alpha\left(\frac{4-12\alpha}{4-9\alpha}\right)}{4+3\alpha}}\left(\frac{\frac{3\alpha b}{4}\left(2-\frac{4-12\alpha}{4-9\alpha}\right)}{(2-b)^2}\right)db+ \tag{7.15}$$

$$\frac{1}{3}\int_{\frac{4-12\alpha}{4-9\alpha}}^{\frac{8+3\alpha\left(\frac{4-12\alpha}{4-9\alpha}\right)}{4+3\alpha}}\left(\frac{\frac{9\alpha^2 b}{8}\left(b-\frac{4-12\alpha}{4-9\alpha}\right)\left(\frac{4-6\alpha}{4-9\alpha}\right)}{(2-b)^3}\right)db$$

Now the derivatives with respect to α of the first and third terms of expression (7.15) at $\alpha = 0$ are finite. However, the derivatives of the second and fourth terms are both infinitely negative, as

$$\lim_{\alpha\to 0}\left(\frac{\left(\frac{1}{3}-\alpha\right)(9\alpha^2)\left(2\left(\frac{4-12\alpha}{4-9\alpha}\right)^2\right)}{(4-12\alpha)^2\left(1-\left(\frac{4-12\alpha}{4-9\alpha}\right)\right)^3}\right)\frac{d}{d\alpha}\left(\frac{4-12\alpha}{4-9\alpha}\right)=-\infty$$

and

$$
\lim_{\alpha \to 0} \frac{\frac{1}{3}(9)\left(\frac{8+3\alpha\left(\frac{4-12\alpha}{4-9\alpha}\right)}{4+3\alpha}\right)\alpha^2\left(\frac{8+3\alpha\left(\frac{4-12\alpha}{4-9\alpha}\right)}{4+3\alpha}-\frac{4-12\alpha}{4-9\alpha}\left(\frac{4-6\alpha}{4-9\alpha}\right)\right)}{8\left(2-\frac{8+3\alpha\left(\frac{4-12\alpha}{4-9\alpha}\right)}{4+4\alpha}\right)^3} = -\infty
$$

Moreover, at $\alpha = 0$ expected revenues from the first-price and second-price auctions are both 1, as can be seen from expressions (7.12) and (7.15). Since the derivative of the seller's expected revenue with respect to α is infinitely negative for the first-price auction but finite for the second-price auction, the latter must generate strictly more revenue for α near zero.

This example is an illustration of the general result of Milgrom and Weber (1982) that the Dutch (and first-price sealed-bid) auction generates no more expected revenue than the Vickrey auction when buyer's valuations are affiliated. One accepted intuition for this result is that the Vickrey auction provides more information to the winning bidder than the Dutch auction (the highest and second-highest bid as opposed to the highest bid only).

As a consequence, bidders are encouraged to bid more aggressively in the Vickrey auction.[17]

17. Note that Milgrom and Weber show only that expected revenue in the Dutch auction cannot exceed expected revenue in the Vickrey auction (Theorem 15). They are silent on when or whether the Vickrey auction provides strictly higher revenues than the Dutch auction. Maskin's example thus provides a reassuring illustration of the breakdown of revenue equivalence in the case where bidders' values are affiliated.

In this chapter we consider contracting situations where a principal inter-acts with multiple agents, each taking hidden actions. This extension takes us from the general topic of optimal incentive provision, studied in Chapter 4, to the field of organization design and the theory of the firm. The main issues we shall be concerned with here are the extent to which competition or cooperation among agents should be fostered, how agents should be supervised or monitored, how to deal with corruption or collusion, and how hierarchical an organization of multiple agents should be. Though the main economic questions addressed in this chapter are different from those studied in Chapter 4, the core ideas and general methodology are the same.

As between Chapters 2 and 7, a key difference between the single-agent contracting situation covered in Chapter 4 and the multiagent situation covered here is that in the former case the principal's problem is one of designing an optimal incentive *contract,* while in the latter his problem is to design a whole *organization* of multiple agents that strategically interact with each other in a game. As in Chapter 7, we shall limit our analysis here to the most common equilibrium notions of these games considered in the literature: the Nash and Bayesian equilibria. We again refer the reader interested in other solution concepts to the surveys by Moore (1992) and Palfrey (1992).

In an important article Alchian and Demsetz (1972) proposed that a firm is in essence an organization that is set up to deal with a *moral-hazard-in-teams* problem. That is, a firm is an organization (or a multilateral contract) set up to mitigate incentive problems arising in situations involving multi-ple agents. The specific setting that Alchian and Demsetz consider is one involving a team of workers where each worker wants to rely on the others to do the work. As in situations involving public-goods provision under private information mentioned in Chapter 7, each worker wants to *free ride* on the work of others. The employer's role in Alchian and Demsetz's view is then one of supervising employees and making sure that they all work. Interestingly, to ensure that the employer himself has the right incentives to monitor his team, Alchian and Demsetz argue that he should be the residual claimant on the firm's revenues and that workers should be paid only fixed wages.

Alchian and Demsetz's perspective on the firm is the starting point of this chapter. In another important contribution, Holmström (1982b) pro-vides a first formalization of Alchian and Demsetz's moral-hazard-in-teams problem and derives an optimal multilateral incentive contract for the team when only the team's aggregate output is observable. We begin by examining his model and his main conclusion that incentive efficiency requires a *budget breaker*—that is, an individual who holds some claims on the output of the team but is otherwise not involved in production.

We then proceed to analyze optimal incentive contracts and the role of competition between agents when individual performance is observable. Firms often provide incentives to their employees by comparing their individual performance and promoting the better performers to higher ranks or more desirable jobs. We detail in particular the contributions by Lazear and Rosen (1981) and Green and Stokey (1983) and examine the rationale and optimal design of such *tournaments*. In particular, we evaluate in detail both the benefits of such tournaments, in terms of reducing the overall risk agents are exposed to, and the costs, in terms of reducing *cooperation* among agents (as stressed by Holmström and Milgrom, 1990, among others).

A potential factor limiting the effectiveness of tournaments is collusion among agents. We examine collusion both between competing agents and between agents and their supervisors. Following the important paper by Tirole (1986), we derive in particular the optimal *collusion-proof* contract and consider how the organization can be structured to reduce the potential for collusion.

We close the chapter by touching on the fundamental question of the boundaries of the firm. As Alchian and Demsetz, and before them Kaldor (1934), have plausibly argued, a natural limit on the size of firms would appear to be the employer's diminishing ability to monitor effectively a larger group of employees. However, as Calvo and Wellisz (1978) have shown, a firm may still be able to grow infinitely large if the employer sets up an efficient internal hierarchy composed of supervisors, who monitor other supervisors, who monitor workers. Their theory provides a simple rationale for the existence of hierarchies but raises the difficult question of what limits the size of the firm if it is not the CEO's limited ability to supervise. Following Qian (1994), we show how this challenge can be resolved if, as Williamson (1967) has argued, there is a greater and greater loss of control of the top the deeper is the hierarchy (that is, the more layers it has).

8.1   Moral Hazard in Teams and Tournaments

Consider a principal engaged in a contractual relation with n agents. The principal is assumed to be risk neutral, and each of the $i = 1, \ldots, n$ agents has the usual utility function separable in income and effort

$$u_i(w_i) - \psi_i(a_i)$$

where $u_i(\cdot)$ is strictly increasing and concave, $\psi_i(\cdot)$ is strictly increasing and convex, and $a_i \in [0, \infty)$.

The agents' actions produce outputs, which in the most general form can be written as a vector of random individual outputs:

$$q = (q_1, \cdots, q_n)$$

with joint conditional distribution

$$F(q \,|\, a)$$

where

$$a = (a_1, \cdots, a_n)$$

denotes the vector of actions taken by the agents.

Following Holmström (1982b), we shall consider in turn two diametrically opposite cases. In the first case, the output produced by the agents is a single aggregate output Q with conditional distribution $F(Q|a)$. This is the pure case of *moral hazard in a team*. Contributions by multiple agents are required, but a single aggregate output is obtained. In the second case, each agent produces an individual random output q_i, which may be imperfectly correlated with the other agents' outputs. In this second case we shall assume that the principal cares only about the sum of the individual agents' outputs.

To offer a concrete example, in the first case the aggregate output might be the revenue generated by a multiagent firm, while in the second case the individual outputs might be the crops of individual farmers, or the sales generated by individual marketers or traders.

When only aggregate output is observed, the n agents basically face a problem of private provision of a public good: each agent contributes a costly action to increase a common output. All agents benefit from an increase in the effort of any one of them. As Holmström (1982b) points out, optimal effort provision can then be obtained only when one breaks *the budget constraint of the team*, that is, the requirement that the sum of individual output-contingent compensations must be equal to the aggregate output. Or, to use the language of Alchian and Demsetz, optimal effort is provided only if there is also a residual claimant on the output after all agents have been compensated. This argument is developed in detail in section 8.1.1.

Holmström's argument is very general, but it relies on limited information used by the principal. Indeed, Legros and Matsushima (1991) and Legros and Matthews (1993) have shown that it may be possible to achieve or approximate incentive efficiency without breaking the budget constraint of the team by relying on the statistical information about the agents' choice of individual actions contained in the realized output. That is, as in the single-agent case, it is possible to achieve first-best efficiency just by relying on the *informativeness principle*. We cover several examples illustrating such incentive schemes in section 8.1.2.

We then move to the opposite case where individual performance levels are observable and contractible. The novel issue to be considered in this case is how the principal might benefit by basing individual agents' compensation on their relative performance rather than only on their absolute performance. Section 8.1.3 addresses this question by considering situations where individual agents' outputs are imperfectly correlated in a simple CARA utility function, normally distributed output, and linear-contract framework, where the optimal incentive scheme can easily be computed. This simple formulation allows us to highlight two related ideas: first, relative performance evaluation serves the purpose of filtering out common output shocks, and there is otherwise no point in making agents compete with each other; second, by reducing the overall uncertainty agents face, the use of relative performance evaluation induces more effort provision in equilibrium, so that relative performance evaluation is positively correlated with equilibrium effort levels.

Section 8.1.4 considers a simple and widely used form of relative performance evaluation: *tournaments*. This classical form of relative performance compensation has the particularity of using only an *ordinal* ranking of performance. As Lazear and Rosen (1981) first pointed out, when agents are risk neutral, tournaments can be seen as an alternative to piece-rate contracts in achieving first-best levels of effort. They involve a lottery with a probability of winning that each agent can influence through her effort level. While the prize the winner obtains seems unrelated to her marginal productivity ex post and thus seems arbitrary, from an ex ante perspective it can be reconciled with optimal incentive provision. When agents are risk averse, however, tournaments are generally suboptimal relative-performance compensation contracts, as they do not optimally trade off risk sharing and incentives. However, as Green and Stokey (1983) have shown, the efficiency of a tournament increases with the number of participants, as the law of large numbers helps reduce the uncertainty in compensation generated by the opponents' random performance.

8.1.1 Unobservable Individual Outputs: The Need for a Budget Breaker

Consider the situation where $n \geq 2$ agents form a partnership to produce some deterministic (scalar) aggregate output

$$Q = Q(a_1, a_2, \cdots, a_n)$$

by supplying a vector of individual hidden actions (or efforts) $a = (a_1, \ldots, a_n)$. Suppose that the output production function is a strictly increasing and concave function of the vector of actions $a = (a_1, \ldots, a_n)$:

$$\frac{\partial Q}{\partial a_i} > 0, \qquad \frac{\partial^2 Q}{\partial a_i^2} < 0, \qquad \frac{\partial^2 Q}{\partial a_i \partial a_j} \geq 0$$

and the matrix of second derivatives $\mathbf{Q}_{ij}$ is negative definite.

Suppose also that all agents are risk neutral:

$$u_i(w) = w$$

Formally, we define a *partnership* to be a vector of output-contingent compensations for each agent, $\mathbf{w}(Q) = [w_1(Q), w_2(Q), \ldots, w_n(Q)]$ such that

$$\sum_{i=1}^{n} w_i(Q) = Q \quad \text{for each } Q$$

For the sake of argument, we take each $w_i(Q)$ to be differentiable almost everywhere.

We focus here on the externality that arises in a *team* of self-interested individuals when effort levels are unobservable and no measure of individual performance is available. In such a situation rewarding an agent for raising aggregate output means rewarding her higher effort and also the higher effort of the other agents! Thus the difficulty for a principal trying to motivate several agents is now compounded by free riding among the agents.

As we know from Chapter 4, a risk-neutral individual agent will supply first-best effort, given that all other agents supply first-best effort, if she is compensated with the full marginal return of her effort. We shall take it that the first-best vector of actions $a^* = (a_1^*, a_2^*, \ldots, a_n^*)$ is uniquely defined by the first-order conditions

$$\frac{\partial Q(a^*)}{\partial a_i} = \psi_i'(a_i^*), \quad \text{for each } i$$

Consider an arbitrary partnership contract $\mathbf{w}(Q)$. Under this contract each agent i independently chooses her action a_i to maximize her own utility given the other agents' actions $a_{-i} = (a_1, \ldots, a_{i-1}, a_{i+1}, \ldots, a_n)$. Thus agent i will choose an effort a_i to satisfy the first-order condition

$$\frac{dw_i[Q(a_i, a_{-i})]}{dQ} \frac{\partial Q(a_i, a_{-i})}{\partial a_i} = \psi_i'(a_i)$$

If all agents get the full marginal return from their effort, at least locally, it appears possible that a Nash equilibrium where all agents supply first-best effort levels might exist. Proceeding with this lead, the first-best output level may then be achieved in a Nash equilibrium if each agent i gets a compensation contract $w_i[Q(a_i, a_{-i})]$ providing her with the full marginal return from her effort, when all other agents also supply the first-best effort level

$$\frac{dw_i[Q(a_i, a_{-i}^*)]}{dQ} = 1$$

But this condition amounts to setting $w_i(Q) = Q$ (up to a constant). Obviously this cannot be done for every agent in the partnership if we must also satisfy the budget constraint

$$\sum_{i=1}^{n} w_i(Q) = Q \quad \text{for each } Q$$

As Holmström (1982b) notes, however, it is possible to specify such a compensation scheme for all agents if one introduces a *budget breaker* into the organization. That is, if a third party agrees to sign a contract with all n

agents offering to pay each of them $w_i(Q) = Q$. It is straightforward to check that if a budget breaker agrees to sign such a contract with the n agents, then there indeed exists a Nash equilibrium where all agents supply their first-best action and where the budget breaker pays out $nQ(a^*)$ in equilibrium.

This would be a profitable contract for a budget breaker and each of the n agents if the n agents also agree to hand over the entire output to the budget breaker and make an up-front payment z_i to the budget breaker such that

$$\sum_{i=1}^{n} z_i + Q(a^*) \geq nQ(a^*)$$

and

$$z_i \leq Q(a^*) - \psi_i(a_i^*)$$

Because at the first best we have

$$Q(a^*) - \sum_{i=1}^{n} \psi_i(a_i^*) > 0$$

it is straightforward to check that there is a vector of transfers $z = (z_1, \ldots, z_n)$ that satisfies these conditions. Obviously the up-front payment z_i will not affect an individual agent's incentives to supply effort.

Holmström's observation that a team facing a multiagent moral-hazard problem requires a budget breaker has been very influential. It has been seen as a fundamental reason why a firm needs a residual claimant and why a firm needs to seek outside financing to be able to break its budget constraint. Note, however, that Holmström's budget breaker is very different from Alchian and Demsetz's residual claimant, who holds equity in the firm to induce him to monitor the team's agents effectively. At first glance, the budget breaker also looks very different from any claimants on firms we see in reality. One feature of the budget breaker's contract in particular seems odd: he would lose money if the firm (or team) performs better. Indeed, the budget breaker's payoff $w_{BB}(Q)$ under the preceding contract satisfies

$$\frac{dw_{BB}(Q)}{dQ} = -(n-1)Q \quad \text{at } Q(a^*)$$

Interestingly, Holmström's logic is entirely based on the idea that a risk-neutral agent's incentives are optimized when she is a residual claimant. But we know from Chapter 4 that there may be other ways to provide first-best incentives by exploiting the information about action choice contained in realized output. In the contracting situation we have considered, each agent may, for example, be compensated with a *Mirrlees contract,* which rewards each agent with a bonus b_i if output level $Q(a^*)$ is realized, and be punished with a penalty k to be paid to the budget breaker if any other output is obtained. If the bonuses b_i and k are such that

$$b_i \geq \psi_i(a_i^*) - k$$

for all i, then there indeed exists a Nash equilibrium where all agents supply their first-best action under this contract as well. In addition, this contract may not require a budget breaker to sustain it in equilibrium if

$$Q(a^*) \geq \sum_{i=1}^{n} b_i$$

It does, however, require a budget breaker off the equilibrium to collect all the penalties nk.

It is not uncommon for firms to pay their employees bonuses when certain profit targets are reached. These bonus schemes may thus be seen as efficient incentive schemes to solve a moral-hazard-in-teams problem.

Another possible interpretation of the Mirrlees contract is debt financing by the firm. Under this interpretation the firm commits to repay total debts of

$$D = Q(a^*) - \sum_{i=1}^{n} b_i$$

and salaries b_i to each employee. If the firm fails to meet its obligations, it is forced to default, the creditors collect whatever output the firm has produced, and the employees pay a bankruptcy cost of k.

Although both the bonus and the debt financing schemes appear to be more realistic than Holmström's proposed incentive scheme, they are vulnerable to an important weakness. These schemes generally give rise to multiple equilibria in agents' action choice. For example, another equilibrium under these schemes besides $a^* = (a_1^*, \ldots, a_n^*)$ may be for all agents to do nothing. Indeed, if all other agents do nothing $[a_{-i} = (0, \ldots, 0)]$, agent

i's best reply is to also do nothing, since on her own she cannot meet the output target $Q(a^*)$ at a reasonable effort cost. That is, if all other agents do nothing, we have

$$b_i - \psi_i(\hat{a}_i) \leq -k$$

where $\hat{a}_i$ is such that

$$Q(0, \cdots, \hat{a}_i, \cdots, 0) = Q(a^*)$$

To rule out this inaction equilibrium the incentive scheme would have to set punitive penalties k [so that $b_i - \psi_i(\hat{a}_i) > -k$], but then it is easy to check that these penalties would support equilibria where some agents shirk.

In contrast, Holmström's scheme supports a unique efficient equilibrium. To see this point, observe that if all other agents do nothing, agent i chooses a_i to solve

$$\max_{a_i} Q(0, \cdots, a_i, \cdots, 0) = \psi_i(a_i)$$

so that her best response is some $a_i > 0$. But since $\partial^2 Q / \partial a_i \partial a_j \geq 0$, this induces all other agents to best respond with higher actions. Iterating best responses in this way, it is easy to see that when the first-best vector of actions $a^* = (a_1^*, a_2^*, \ldots, a_n^*)$ is uniquely defined by the first-order conditions

$$\frac{\partial Q(a^*)}{\partial a_i} = \psi_i'(a_i)$$

as we have assumed, then $a^* = (a_1^*, a_2^*, \ldots, a_n^*)$ is a unique Nash equilibrium under the Holmström scheme.

Note, however, that the fact that the Mirrlees contract we have described may support multiple equilibria, some of which are highly inefficient, is not a fatal objection to the application of these schemes to solve moral-hazard-in-teams problems. First, the efficient equilibrium under these schemes may be a natural *focal point*. Second, as the next section illustrates, these schemes can be easily adapted to ensure that the efficient equilibrium is unique. In addition, these schemes can also be adapted to satisfy budget balance on and off the equilibrium path.

8.1.2 Unobservable Individual Outputs: Using Output Observations to Implement the First Best

In Chapter 4 we pointed out that when some output realizations are impossible if the agent chooses the right action, then the first-best outcome can be implemented through a form of *forcing contract,* where the agent is punished severely for output realizations that are not supposed to arise. In multiagent situations such simple contracts are less easily applied because it is not always possible to identify the culprit among the agents who did not do what she was supposed to do. Legros and Matsushima (1991) and Legros and Matthews (1993), however, have shown that it is often possible to implement small deviations from the first-best action profile, which let the principal identify more easily the agent responsible for a unilateral deviation. What is more, they show that it is then possible to implement or approximate the first-best action profile with incentive schemes that always satisfy budget balance.

We now illustrate the basic ideas behind these incentive schemes in three simple examples. The first two examples (based on Legros and Matthews, 1993) assume that aggregate output is deterministic, so that shirking by any of the agents is perfectly detected. These examples rely on the idea that, upon observing a deviation from the required aggregate output, the principal may be able to identify at least one agent who did not shirk. The principal is then able to preserve budget balance by imposing penalties on the other agents (who are presumed to have shirked) to be paid to the non-shirking agent. The third example (based on Legros and Matsushima, 1991) considers a situation where aggregate output is random, so that detection of shirking is imperfect. This example builds on ideas similar to those of Crémer and McLean (1985), discussed in Chapter 7, and extends the two previous ones by exploiting differences in probability distributions over output realizations that arise when different agents shirk.

Example 1: Deterministic Output with Finite Action Space   Consider the situation where three agents work together in a team. Each agent has a binary action set and can either supply effort ($a_i = 1$) or shirk ($a_i = 0$). Supplying effort is costly [$\psi_i(1) > \psi_i(0)$], but it is first-best efficient for all three agents to supply effort: $a_1^* = a_2^* = a_3^* = 1$.

The first-best output is denoted Q^*, while the output level when only agent i shirks [where $a_i = 0$ and $a_{-i} = (1, 1)$] is denoted Q_i. Legros and Matthews argue that in most cases one has $Q_1 \neq Q_2 \neq Q_3$ (they argue that this assumption is true generically). When this is the case, a single shirker is identifiable and can be punished. It is easy to check that a forcing contract can then be used to implement $a*$ while preserving budget balance.

Legros and Matthews point out that it is also possible to implement the first-best outcome while maintaining budget balance, as long as a non-shirker can be identified and rewarded. Thus in our example it is also possible to implement the first-best outcome when $Q_1 = Q_2 \neq Q_3$. The only situation where the first best is not implementableuniquely occurs when $Q_1 = Q_2 = Q_3$ (we leave it to the reader to verify these observations).

Example 2: Deterministic Output with Approximate Efficiency   It is much harder to identify a deviating agent when agents' action sets are large and allow for many possible deviations. The deviating agent can then more easily select an action that prevents the principal from identifying the deviator. Legros and Matthews show, however, that in such situations it may still be possible to approximate the first best. Here is the argument: Consider a team of two agents who can each pick an action $a_i \in [0; +\infty)$. Suppose that the team's aggregate output is given by

$$Q = a_1 + a_2$$

and let the effort cost for each agent be

$$\psi_i(a_i) = a_i^2/2$$

so that the first-best action profile is given by

$$a_1^* = a_2^* = 1$$

The incentive scheme proposed by Legros and Matthews is based on the idea that one agent—for example, agent 1—randomizes her action choice and chooses $a_1 = 0$ with a small positive probability ε. This randomization lets the principal detect a deviation by agent 2 with probability ε and thus allows the principal to approximate the first best. To see this result, consider the incentive scheme

1. For $Q \geq 1$,

$$w_1(Q) = (Q-1)^2/2 \quad \text{and} \quad w_2(Q) = Q - w_1(Q)$$

2. For $Q < 1$,

$$w_1(Q) = Q + k \quad \text{and} \quad w_2(Q) = 0 - k$$

This incentive scheme supports a Nash equilibrium where agent 2 chooses $a_2 = 1$ with probability 1, and agent 1 randomizes by choosing $a_1 = 1$ with probability $(1 - \varepsilon)$ and $a_1 = 0$ with probability ε.

To see that this is indeed a Nash equilibrium, note the following points:

• Given action choice $a_2 = 1$, agent 1's best response is given by the solution to

$$\max_{a_1}\left[w_1(a_1 + 1) - \frac{a_1^2}{2}\right] = \max_{a_1}\left[\frac{a_1^2}{2} - \frac{a_1^2}{2}\right] = 0$$

In other words, agent 1 is indifferent between any action a_1, so that a choice of $a_1 = 1$ with probability $(1 - \varepsilon)$ and $a_1 = 0$ with probability ε is a best response for agent 1.

• As for agent 2, a choice of $a_2 \geq 1$ guarantees an aggregate output that is no less than 1: $Q \geq 1$. Since $w_1(Q)$ is increasing in a_2 when $Q \geq 1$, a choice of $a_2 = 1$ is optimal in the action subset $[1, +\infty)$ and gives agent 2 a payoff

$$(1 - \varepsilon)\left[2 - \frac{1}{2}\right] + \varepsilon[1 - 0] - \frac{1}{2} = 1 - \frac{\varepsilon}{2}$$

A choice of $a_2 < 1$, however, implies that $Q < 1$ with probability ε. This gives agent 2 a payoff of

$$(1 - \varepsilon)\left[1 + a_2 - \frac{a_2^2}{2}\right] - \varepsilon k - \frac{a_2^2}{2} \leq 1 + a_2 - a_2^2 - \varepsilon k$$

which is maximized at $a_2 = \frac{1}{2}$. At $a_2 = \frac{1}{2}$, agent 2's payoff is then

$$\frac{5}{4} - \varepsilon k$$

Therefore, $a_2 = 1$ is optimal if

$$k \geq \frac{1}{2} + \frac{1}{4\varepsilon}$$

The incentive scheme thus works as follows: If aggregate output is too low, agent 2 is punished and agent 1 is rewarded (to maintain budget balance). But, given that agent 1 gets to collect the fine k, she has an incentive to try to lower aggregate output as much as possible. It is for this reason that the penalty is imposed on agent 2 only when aggregate output is below

$Q(0, 1)$. Then the agent who is punished for low output is deterred from underproviding effort, and the agent collecting the fine is prevented from strategically lowering output. Thus a critical assumption in this example is that at least one agent has a finite lowest action.

Under this incentive scheme, agent 1 effectively acts like a monitor who randomly inspects agent 2. The monitoring cost is then the loss of output that agent 1 could have contributed. But, oddly, here the monitor does not see anything directly. She can only infer agent 2's action indirectly from the realized output.

This is undoubtedly an ingenious scheme, but it seems too fragile and special to be applied in practice. For one thing, the principal must know exactly what each agent's effort cost is. In addition, it is not clear how easily this scheme can be generalized and applied to teams with three or more agents. Finally, this scheme breaks down when aggregate output is random.

However, when aggregate output is random, as shown by Legros and Matsushima (1991), other incentive schemes are available akin to the Crémer and McLean lottery mechanisms discussed in the previous chapter.

Example 3: Random Aggregate Output   Consider a team of two agents. As in the first example, each agent has a binary action set, $a_i \in \{0, 1\}$, and first-best efforts are given by $a^* = (1, 1)$. In contrast to the first example, however, there are now three possible aggregate output realizations, $Q_H > Q_M > Q_L$.

Aggregate output is increasing in the agents' effort choices. We shall suppose that when both agents shirk, aggregate output is Q_L with probability 1, and that the conditional probability distributions over output satisfy first-order stochastic dominance. Specifically, we shall suppose that the conditional probability distributions are as follows:

$$
\begin{array}{c}
 \quad Q_H \ \ Q_M \ \ Q_L \\
\begin{array}{l}
a_1 = a_2 = 1 \\
a_1 = 0, a_2 = 1 \\
a_1 = 1, a_2 = 0
\end{array}
\begin{pmatrix}
\frac{1}{3} & \frac{1}{3} & \frac{1}{3} \\
\frac{1}{6} & \frac{1}{3} & \frac{1}{2} \\
\frac{1}{6} & \frac{1}{6} & \frac{2}{3}
\end{pmatrix}
\end{array}
$$

Note that each output level can occur with positive probability under the three action profiles, $(1, 1)$, $(1, 0)$, $(0, 1)$. But when one of the agents shirks, the highest output is less likely. Moreover, the probability distribution is worse when agent 2 shirks. With the knowledge of Crémer and McLean schemes it is easy to see that this difference in distributions, depending on who shirks, can be exploited to implement the first-best pair of effort levels

a^*. What is more, the first best can be implemented with an incentive scheme that satisfies budget balance.

Concretely, consider the incentive scheme with transfers $t_i(Q)$ defined as deviations from equal shares of output, $t_i(Q) = w_i(Q) - Q/2$, and such that $t_1(Q) + t_2(Q) = 0$ for each output level. Let $\psi_i \equiv \psi_i(1) > \psi_i(0) = 0$ denote the effort cost of action $a_i = 1$. Then, preventing shirking by any agent requires

$$\frac{1}{6}[t_1(Q_H) - t_1(Q_L)] \geq \psi_1$$

and

$$\frac{1}{6}[t_2(Q_H) + t_2(Q_M)] - \frac{1}{3}t_2(Q_L) \geq \psi_2$$

It is straightforward to check that we can find transfers t_i that satisfy these incentive constraints while also maintaining budget balance:

$$t_1(Q_H) + t_2(Q_H) = t_1(Q_M) + t_2(Q_M) = t_1(Q_L) + t_2(Q_L) = 0$$

For example, if

$$t_1(Q_L) = t_2(Q_L) = 0$$

$$t_1(Q_H) = 6\psi_1 = -t_2(Q_H)$$

and

$$t_2(Q_M) = 6(\psi_1 + \psi_2) = -t_1(Q_M)$$

then all the constraints are satisfied.

As in the Crémer and McLean schemes, the idea is to reward each agent in the output realizations where her effort contribution makes the greatest difference. Here agent 1 is disproportionately rewarded when Q_H is realized, while agent 2 is disproportionately rewarded when Q_M is realized. Interestingly, under this scheme, payments to each agent are nonmonotonic even though the probability distributions over output satisfy MLRP.

To summarize, these three examples illustrate that it is often possible to provide first-best incentives to a team without having to break budget balance and without requiring that all agents be made residual claimants on aggregate output. Thus Holmström's initial insight that participation of third parties (or outside financing of the team) is essential to provide adequate incentives to teams needs to be qualified. Often the role of the outside party can be played by one of the team members, whose incentive problem is easy to isolate, and often the information contained in output realizations can be used to design effective incentive schemes, as in the single-agent moral-hazard problems. However, the schemes we have discussed here, as ingenious as they may be, may not be easily implemented in reality and indeed are not commonly observed.

8.1.3 Observable Individual Outputs

When moving from a situation where only aggregate output of a team of agents is observable to one where individual agent outputs are observable, one moves from a problem of eliciting cooperation, or avoiding free riding among agents, to a problem of harnessing competition between agents. This statement is actually somewhat of an oversimplification, as we shall see, but the basic point remains that the core issue becomes one of controlling competition among agents.

Relative performance evaluation is a widely used incentive scheme in multiagent moral-hazard settings. Whether at school, at work, or in sports, individual agent performances are regularly ranked. These rankings are used to select and promote agents, or generally to reward the best performers. A very common relative performance evaluation scheme is the so-called *rank-order tournament,* which measures only ordinal rankings of performance. That is, it takes into account only the rankings of individual outputs from the highest to the lowest (or only the sign of the difference between any two individual outputs) and otherwise ignores the information contained in the value of the difference in outputs. We shall be interested in the efficiency properties of these schemes and ask when there is no loss in efficiency in ignoring the levels of individual outputs. To take an example from sports, when is it efficient to take account of only the rank of the racers at the finish line, as in sailing regattas or Formula 1 races, and when is it efficient to also take account of absolute time (or distance) performance, as in most track-and-field events, where record speeds or distances are also rewarded?

Before analyzing tournaments in detail, we set off by considering a simple setting involving relative performance evaluation of two agents. Following Holmström (1979, 1982b), we can apply the informativeness principle of Chapter 4 and begin by determining when an optimal (linear) incentive scheme for agent i also takes account of agent j's performance ($j \neq i$). In other words, we ask when agent i's compensation also depends on her performance relative to agent j. We carry through this exercise in the somewhat special setting that proved so tractable in the single-agent problem, where both agents have CARA risk preferences, where their individual outputs are normally distributed random variables, and where their respective incentive contracts are linear in output.

Consider the multiagent situation with two identical agents, each producing an individual output q_i by supplying effort a_i, where

$$q_1 = a_1 + \varepsilon_1 + \alpha\varepsilon_2$$

$$q_2 = a_2 + \varepsilon_2 + \alpha\varepsilon_1$$

The random variables ε_1 and ε_2 are independently and normally distributed with mean zero and variance σ^2. Relative to the single-agent problem considered in Chapter 4, the only innovation is the parameter α. When $\alpha \neq 0$, the two outputs are correlated. As one would expect from the informativeness principle, when the outputs are correlated it should be optimal to base an individual agent's compensation on both output realizations, as both provide information about an individual agent's action choice.

We shall take the principal to be risk neutral, but both agents are risk averse and have CARA risk preferences represented by the negative-exponential utility function

$$u(w, a) = -e^{-\eta[w - \psi(a)]}$$

where a denotes the agent's effort, η the coefficient of absolute risk aversion, and $\psi(\cdot)$ the agent's effort cost, which we assume to be a quadratic function:

$$\psi(a) = \frac{1}{2}ca^2$$

Finally, we restrict attention to linear incentive schemes of the form

$$w_1 = z_1 + v_1 q_1 + u_1 q_2$$

$$w_2 = z_2 + v_2 q_2 + u_2 q_1$$

where the z_i are fixed compensation payments, and the v_i and u_i are variable performance-related compensation coefficients.

The absence of relative performance evaluation here is equivalent to setting $u_i = 0$. Given the symmetry of the principal's problem, we need only to solve for an individual optimal scheme (a_i, w_i). A principal trying to maximize his expected payoff in his relation with agent 1 will then solve

$$\max_{a_1, z_1, v_1, u_1} E(q_1 - w_1)$$

subject to

$$E[-e^{-\eta[w_1 - \psi(a_1)]}] \geq u(\overline{w})$$

and

$$a_1 \in \arg\max_a E[-e^{-\eta[w_1 - \psi(a)]}]$$

where $u(\overline{w})$ is the default utility level of the agent and $\overline{w}$ is her certain monetary equivalent outside wealth.

As we highlighted in Chapter 4, maximization of the agent's expected utility with respect to a is equivalent to maximizing the agent's certainty equivalent wealth $\hat{w}_1(a)$ with respect to a, where $\hat{w}_1(a)$ is defined by

$$-e^{-r\hat{w}_1(a)} = E\{-e^{-r[w_1 - \psi(a)]}\}$$

Thus, as

$$Var[v_1(\varepsilon_1 + \alpha\varepsilon_2) + u_1(\varepsilon_2 + \alpha\varepsilon_1)] = \sigma^2\left[(v_1 + \alpha u_1)^2 + (u_1 + \alpha v_1)^2\right]$$

the agent's optimization problem is to choose a to maximize her certainty-equivalent wealth:

$$\max_a\left\{z_1 + v_1 a + u_1 a_2 - \frac{1}{2}ca^2 - \frac{\eta\sigma^2}{2}\left[(v_1 + \alpha u_1)^2 + (u_1 + \alpha v_1)^2\right]\right\}$$

Note that, in the Nash equilibrium of the two agents' effort provision game, each agent correctly anticipates the effort choice a_j of the other agent.

As in the one-agent problem, the solution of the agent's problem here is easily obtained:

$$a_1 = \frac{v_1}{c}$$

Substituting for a_i in each agent's certainty-equivalent wealth formula, we obtain each agent's equilibrium payoff. For agent 1 this equilibrium payoff is given by

$$z_1 + \frac{1}{2}\frac{v_1^2}{c} + \frac{u_1 v_2}{c} - \frac{\eta\sigma^2}{2}\left[(v_1 + \alpha u_1)^2 + (u_1 + \alpha v_1)^2\right]$$

The principal's problem then reduces to solving the following constrained maximization problem for each agent:

$$\max_{z_1, v_1, u_1} \left\{ \frac{v_1}{c} - \left(z_1 + \frac{v_1^2}{c} + \frac{u_1 v_2}{c} \right) \right\}$$

subject to

$$z_1 + \frac{1}{2} \frac{v_1^2}{c} + \frac{u_1 v_2}{c} - \frac{\eta \sigma^2}{2} \left[(v_1 + \alpha u_1)^2 + (u_1 + \alpha v_1)^2 \right] = \overline{w}$$

Or, substituting for z_1,

$$\max_{v_1, u_1} \left\{ \frac{v_1}{c} - \frac{1}{2} \frac{v_1^2}{c} - \frac{\eta \sigma^2}{2} \left[(v_1 + \alpha u_1)^2 + (u_1 + \alpha v_1)^2 \right] \right\}$$

The principal's problem can be solved sequentially:

1. For any given v_1, u_1 is determined to minimize risk.

2. The variable v_1 is then set to optimally trade off risk sharing and incentives.

Proceeding in this way and minimizing the variance

$$\frac{\eta \sigma^2}{2} \left[(v_1 + \alpha u_1)^2 + (u_1 + \alpha v_1)^2 \right]$$

of agent 1's payoff with respect to u_1, keeping v_1 fixed, yields the formula

$$u_1 = -\left(\frac{2\alpha}{1 + \alpha^2} \right) v_1$$

One learns from this formula that the optimal u_1 is negative when the two agents' outputs are positively correlated, or $\alpha > 0$ (assuming, as we shall verify, that the optimal v_1 is positive). In other words, one learns from this expression that under the optimal incentive scheme an individual agent is *penalized* for a better performance by the other agent.

Why should an individual agent be penalized for the other agent's good performance? The reason is that a better performance by agent 2 is likely to be due to a high realization of ε_2, which also positively affects agent 1's output. In other words, both agents' high output is then partly due to good luck. Therefore, by setting a negative u_1, the optimal incentive scheme reduces agent 1's exposure to a *common shock* affecting both agents' output, and thus reduces the variance of agent 1's compensation. If both agents' performance outcomes were negatively correlated, u_1 would instead be positive to reduce each agent's exposure to an exogenous shock.

From this formula we thus learn that the real reason why an agent's optimal incentive scheme is based in part on the other agent's output realization (in other words, the reason for introducing a form of *relative performance evaluation*) is to reduce each agent's risk exposure by *filtering out the common shock* contribution to each agent's output. That is, as stressed by Holmström (1982b), the reason behind relative performance evaluation is not to induce agents to compete but to use competition among agents (i.e., relative performance evaluation) to reward each agent's effort while exposing agents to less risk. We also see from the preceding equation that relative performance evaluation is used if and only if individual outputs are not independent ($\alpha \neq 0$).

In our second step we substitute for the optimal u_1 in the principal's objective and solve for the optimal v_1:

$$\max_{v_1}\left\{\frac{v_1}{c} - \frac{v_1^2}{2c} - \frac{\eta\sigma^2}{2}v_1^2\frac{(1-\alpha^2)^2}{1+\alpha^2}\right\}$$

Differentiating with respect to v_1 and solving the first-order condition then yields the formula

$$v_1 = \frac{1+\alpha^2}{1+\alpha^2+\eta c\sigma^2(1-\alpha^2)^2}$$

Note that when $\alpha = 0$ this formula reduces to the familiar formula at the end of section 4.2 of Chapter 4. The change introduced by the correlation in the two agents' outputs is to reduce the overall risk exposure of any individual agent and thus to enable the principal to give stronger incentives to both agents. Remarkably, when α approaches 1 (or -1), then each agent's output is almost entirely affected by a single, common source of noise. By filtering out this common shock, the optimal incentive scheme can then almost eliminate each agent's exposure to risk and thus approximate first-best incentives by letting v_1 tend to 1.

Finally, it is worth highlighting that although the true reason for relative performance evaluation is not to induce competition—and through greater competition to induce more effort provision—the end result is still higher effort provision. But the reason why equilibrium effort is higher is lower risk exposure.

8.1.4   Tournaments

We now turn to the analysis of perhaps the most prevalent form of relative performance evaluation encountered in reality, tournaments. As we have already pointed out, tournaments do not make use of all the output information available, since they base compensation only on an ordinal ranking of individual agents' outputs. One obvious advantage of tournament schemes is that ordinal rankings of output are easy to measure and hard to manipulate. Perhaps, most importantly, the principal has little incentive to manipulate the outcome of a tournament, as he has to reward a winner no matter who wins (that is, unless the principal can secretly collude with one agent, promising to favor her in deciding who the winner is and extracting some surplus from her against this promise). However, when compensation is based on output levels, the principal has a strong incentive to cheat and to report output levels that require lower payments to the agent. Therefore, in situations where the principal is best placed to measure output and is able to massage output data, tournaments are well suited for reducing the principal's incentives to manipulate reported output. As Fairburn and Malcomson (2001) have argued, one situation where this issue is likely to be important is incentive compensation of employees by midlevel managers. They argue that a midlevel manager's ability to manipulate performance measures of his underlings is an important reason why a tournament, which rewards the best employees with bonuses and job promotions, is an efficient incentive scheme.

In situations where output is easily measured and is difficult to manipulate, however, it is less clear that tournaments are optimal incentive schemes. As one might expect from the analysis in Chapter 4, when agents are risk neutral, tournaments (among other incentive schemes) may allow the principal to achieve first-best efficiency. This is indeed the case, as the article by Lazear and Rosen (1981) confirms. We begin our analysis of tournaments with their article not so much to highlight this point, which is after all not too surprising, as to discuss some interesting economic implications they draw from their analysis.

8.1.4.1   Tournaments under Risk Neutrality and No Common Shock

Lazear and Rosen (1981) consider the situation where two risk-neutral agents produce individual outputs that are independently distributed (no common shock). Based on our preceding analysis, there would appear to be no reason why tournaments would be efficient incentive schemes in this setting. However, Lazear and Rosen show that the first-best outcome can be implemented using a tournament.

Specifically, they assume that

$$q_i = a_i + \varepsilon_i$$

where the random variables ε_i are identically but independently distributed with cumulative probability distribution $F(\cdot)$, with mean 0 and variance σ^2. Agents have effort cost $\psi(a_i)$, and the first-best effort level for each agent is given by the first-order condition

$$1 = \psi'(a^*)$$

Lazear and Rosen compare two methods of payment: purely individual performance-related pay (say, *piece rates*) and relative-performance-based pay, *tournaments*. The first method implements the first best when pay is set as follows:

$$w_i = z + q_i$$

and

$$z + E[q_i] - \psi(a^*) = z + a^* - \psi(a^*) = \bar{u}$$

where $\bar{u}$ is the agents' reservation utility.

The tournament is structured as follows: The agent with the higher output gets a fixed wage z plus a prize W, while the agent with the lower output gets only the wage payment z. Under the tournament the expected payoff for an agent i exerting effort a_i, when agent j exerts effort a_j, is then

$$z + pW - \psi(a_i)$$

where p is the probability that agent i is the winner. That is, p is given by

$$p = \Pr(q_i > q_j) = \Pr(a_i - a_j > \varepsilon_j - \varepsilon_i) = H(a_i - a_j)$$

where $H(\cdot)$ is the cumulative distribution of $(\varepsilon_j - \varepsilon_i)$, which has zero mean and variance $2\sigma^2$. The best response for an agent under the tournament is then given by

$$W \frac{\partial p}{\partial a_i} = \psi'(a_i)$$

or

$$Wh(a_i - a_j) = \psi'(a_i)$$

where $h(\cdot)$ is the density of $(\varepsilon_j - \varepsilon_i)$.

In a symmetric equilibrium, effort levels by both agents are identical. Thus, in order to implement the first-best action choice $a*$ in a symmetric equilibrium of the tournament game, the tournament must specify a prize:

$$W = \frac{1}{h(0)}$$

The fixed wage z can then be set to satisfy each agent's individual rationality constraint:

$$z + \frac{H(0)}{h(0)} - \psi(a*) = \bar{u}$$

We see here that a tournament can do as well as a piece-rate system in implementing the first best under risk neutrality. The mechanisms by which the first best is achieved, however, look very different. Under the piece-rate scheme, it looks like the agent has direct control over her compensation, up to a random shock: she is directly controlling the mean of her compensation. Instead, in a symmetric tournament, both agents choose the same effort level, and it is solely chance that determines who the winner is! Incentives to work under the tournament, however, are driven by each agent's ability to control the *probability of winning*. The optimal tournament chooses the level of the prize so as to provide exactly the same marginal expected return from effort as in the piece-rate system.

One common form of tournament is promotions in firms. One is at times surprised to see promoted individuals obtain very high raises: why should that be, given that the individual remains the same from one day to another? Has her marginal productivity risen so much from one job to the other? The preceding simple tournament example shows how compensation can be divorced from marginal productivity because of lottery features that look ex post like pure randomness but can be justified for ex ante incentive reasons. In particular, this example shows how a *winner-take-all* incentive-based system may actually reflect ex ante expected productivity-related pay.

The example can also be easily extended to situations with more than two agents to show why prizes must be increasing in each round of elimination of a tournament (see Rosen, 1986). To illustrate the basic logic of the argument, consider a tournament among two pairs of agents where, just as in tennis, the two best agents are picked in a first round of elimination and move on to a second round to compete for the number-one slot. Let W_1 and W_2, respectively, denote the prizes of the first- and second-placed agents following the two rounds of competition. As before, agents get paid a fixed wage z plus these prizes, and we solve for a symmetric equilibrium in each of the three tournaments: the first two tournaments to pick the best two performers and the subsequent "final" to select the overall winner.

Proceeding by backward induction, we begin by solving for the optimal latter tournament. Based on the preceding analysis, it is easy to see that we must have

$$(W_1 - W_2) = \frac{1}{h(0)}$$

Moving back to the first round of elimination, we then see that the expected payoff for an agent i exerting effort a_i, given the other agent $j \neq i$ effort a_j, is then

$$z + p_1 V_W - \psi(a_i)$$

where p_1 is the probability that agent i wins in the first round, and

$$V_W = H(0)(W_1 - W_2) + W_2 - \psi(a^*)$$

is agent i's expected continuation payoff of "moving to the final," and the best response for an agent in the first round is then given by

$$\frac{\partial p_1}{\partial a_i} = \psi'(a_i)$$

or

$$[H(0)(W_1 - W_2) + W_2 - \psi(a^*)]\frac{\partial p_1}{\partial a_i} = \psi'(a_i)$$

Thus, in order to implement the first-best action choice a^* in a symmetric equilibrium of the first round, the tournament must specify a prize structure such that

$$\left[W_2 + \frac{H(0)}{h(0)} - \psi(a^*)\right]h(0) = 1$$

In this expression, $h(0)$ is, as before, the partial derivative of the probability of winning with respect to effort, given symmetric equilibrium effort levels, while

$$\frac{H(0)}{h(0)} - \psi(a^*)$$

is the expected equilibrium reward from competing in the final. Since this reward is positive, it means that

$$W_2 < \frac{1}{h(0)} = W_2 - W_1$$

That is, the difference in prizes between the first and second agents must be strictly higher than the difference in prizes between the second agent and the last two. The reason why the rewards for winning must be increasing in each round of elimination of the tournament is that after passing a round the remaining competitors actually lose the option value of surviving. Thus, to preserve their incentives to work, they need to be compensated with higher monetary rewards.

8.1.4.2   Tournaments with Risk-Averse Agents and Common Shocks

We have just seen that when agents are risk neutral and when their outputs are independent, piece rates and tournaments are equally efficient incentive schemes. In this subsection we discuss the analysis of Green and Stokey (1983), who show that this equivalence breaks down when agents are risk averse. They establish that tournaments are then dominated by piece-rate schemes when agents' outputs are independent, but tournaments may dominate piece rates when a common shock affects agents' performance. Tournaments are then also approximately second-best optimal incentive schemes when the number of agents is large. The reason why a tournament's efficiency improves as the number of agents in play increases is that the sophistication of the tournament increases with the number of agents: it can specify finer rankings and a richer reward structure $\{W_i\}$ based on those rankings. With a large number of agents, the *distribution* of individual performances, for a given realization of the common shock, converges to a *fixed distribution*. Each agent then controls her expected ranking by choosing her effort level. Thus, in the limit, the tournament system is like a piece-rate system that has filtered out the common shock.

We illustrate these ideas in our simple example with two output levels $q_i \in \{0, 1\}$. Each agent i can increase the probability of success ($q_i = 1$) by exerting more effort. We model this idea by letting the probability of success be given by

$$\Pr(q_i = 1) = \xi a_i$$

where $\xi \in (0, 1]$. The common shock affecting all agents' output is thus introduced by letting all agents' output be zero ($q_i = 0$) with probability $(1 - \xi)$. As we have done many times, we shall take the cost-of-effort function to be a simple quadratic function:

$$\psi(a_i) = \frac{c}{2} a_i^2$$

We begin by considering the situation with two identical risk-averse agents with utility function

$$u(w) - \psi(a)$$

where $u(\cdot)$ is a strictly increasing, concave function.

We shall compare the two incentive schemes by evaluating the cost to the principal of implementing a given effort profile for both agents (a_1, a_2).

We begin by considering the second-best contract in the artificial single-agent problem where one observes (1) whether output was affected by a common shock (in which case a wage w_c is paid), (2) the individual agent's output realization $q_i \subset \{0, 1\}$, and (3) a reference output realization $q_j \in \{0, 1\}$ on which the single-agent contract may be based. In this situation a feasible contract thus has five components: $w = \{w_{00}, w_{10}, w_{01}, w_{11}, w_c\}$ where, in the absence of the common shock, agent i receives wage w_{ij} when her own output is i and the reference output is j.

We also let

$$\Pr(q_j = 1) = \xi a_2$$

As we have shown in Chapter 4, when an individual agent's output can take only two values, then the agent's incentive constraint

$$a_1 \in \arg\max_a \Big\{ \xi[a(1 - a_2)u(w_{10}) + a a_2 u(w_{11})$$

$$+ (1 - a)(1 - a_2)u(w_{00}) + (1 - a)a_2 u(w_{01})] + (1 - \xi)u(w_c) - \frac{1}{2}ca^2 \Big\}$$

can be replaced without loss of generality by the first-order condition of the agent's problem:

$$\xi[(1-a_2)u(w_{10})+a_2u(w_{11})-(1-a_2)u(w_{00})-a_2u(w_{01})]=ca_1$$

Thus, assuming that the principal wants to implement action a_1, his cost-minimization problem reduces to

$$\min_{\{w_{00},w_{10},w_{01},w_{11},w_c\}} \kappa(w) = \{\xi[a_1(1-a_2)(w_{10})+a_1a_2w_{11}+(1-a_1)(1-a_2)w_{00}$$
$$+(1-a_1)a_2w_{01}]+(1-\xi)w_c\}$$

subject to

$$\xi[a_1(1-a_2)u(w_{10})+a_1a_2u(w_{11})+(1-a_1)(1-a_2)u(w_{00})+(1-a_1)a_2u(w_{01})]$$
$$+(1-\xi)u(w_c)\geq\frac{1}{2}ca_1^2 \qquad\qquad\text{(IR)}$$

and

$$\xi[(1-a_2)u(w_{10})+a_2u(w_{11})-(1-a_2)u(w_{00})-a_2u(w_{01})]=ca_1 \qquad\qquad\text{(IC)}$$

Denoting by λ and μ the Lagrange multipliers of the (IR) and (IC) constraints, the first-order conditions of the principal's constrained minimization problem then are

$$\frac{\partial\kappa}{\partial w_{10}}=0$$

which implies

$$\xi a_1(1-a_2)=\xi(1-a_2)[\lambda a_1+\mu]u'(w_{10})$$

and

$$\frac{\partial\kappa}{\partial w_{11}}=0$$

which implies

$$\xi a_1a_2=\xi a_2[\lambda a_1+\mu]u'(w_{11})$$

Therefore, the optimal contract must set

$$w_{10}=w_{11}$$

and, similarly,

$$w_{00}=w_{01}$$

We are thus able to draw the following observations from this problem:

1. When either the common shock can be filtered out ($w_c \neq w_{ii}$) or there is no common shock ($\xi = 1$), then any relative-performance evaluation scheme, which would result in either $w_{10} \neq w_{11}$ or $w_{00} \neq w_{01}$ or both, is suboptimal. Only a piece-rate scheme is then optimal. As we have already emphasized in Chapter 4, the reason is simply that a relative-performance-evaluation scheme would then only increase the agent's risk exposure without improving her incentives.

2. If a general relative-performance-evaluation scheme is suboptimal, then a fortiori a tournament is suboptimal. Indeed, a tournament would specify a reward structure such that $w_{11} = w_{00} = w_c = T$ (where T stands for "tie"), $w_{10} = W$ (where W stands for "winner"), and $w_{01} = L$ (where L stands for "loser"). Unless $L = T = W$, this reward structure could not satisfy the preceding optimality conditions. But when $L = T = W$, then the agent obviously has no incentive to put in any effort.

3. In the presence of a common shock ($\xi < 1$), a simple piece rate is suboptimal. Indeed, the optimal contract must satisfy

$$\frac{\partial \kappa}{\partial w_c} = 0$$

which implies

$$(1 - \xi) = \lambda(1 - \xi)u'(w_c)$$

and

$$\frac{\partial \kappa}{\partial w_{00}} = 0$$

which implies

$$\xi(1 - a_1)(1 - a_2) = \xi(1 - a_2)[\lambda(1 - a_1) + \mu]u'(w_{00})$$

These conditions thus require that $w_{00} \neq w_c$ whenever $\mu \neq 0$, while a simple piece-rate scheme would be such that $w_{00} = w_c$.

4. In the presence of a common shock, a tournament may dominate a piece-rate scheme. To see this possibility, suppose that the first-best outcome for the principal is to implement the action profile $a_1 = a_2 = 1$, so that success ($q_i = 1$) is guaranteed for both agents in the absence of a common (negative) shock (this is the first-best outcome whenever the agents' effort

cost parameter c is low enough).

Consider the principal's problem of providing agent 1 with incentives to choose action a_1 under a tournament scheme when agent 2's action choice $a_2 = 1$ is secured. Then the principal chooses the tournament's reward structure $\{L, T, W\}$ to solve the problem

$$\min_{T,W,L} \xi a_1 T + \xi(1-a_1)L + (1-\xi)T$$

subject to

$$\xi a_1 u(T) + \xi(1-a_1)u(L) + (1-\xi)u(T) - \frac{1}{2}ca_1^2 \geq 0$$

and

$$\xi[u(T) - u(L)] = ca_1$$

Thus, to implement action $a_1 = 1$, the principal sets

$$u(T) = u(L) + \frac{c}{\xi}$$

As can be immediately seen, in that case the agent gets T for sure and is perfectly insured. In other words, the tournament then implements the first-best outcome. That is, it implements a Nash equilibrium where both agents set $a_i = 1$ and are both perfectly insured in equilibrium.

However, under the optimal piece-rate scheme that implements the action profile $a_1 = a_2 = 1$, each agent's compensation is such that

$$w_{11} = w_{10} > w_{01} = w_{00} = w_c$$

In other words, each agent's compensation is risky, as w_c is paid with probability $1 - \xi > 0$ whenever a negative common shock occurs.

This extreme case thus illustrates how, by filtering out the common shock, the tournament may expose agents to less risk than a piece-rate scheme. It is for this reason that tournaments may dominate piece-rate schemes when agents' outputs are affected by a common shock.

Having shown that a tournament can dominate an optimal piece-rate scheme in the presence of common shocks, we now turn to the last major result established by Green and Stokey—that a tournament may approximate a second-best relative-performance-evaluation scheme when the number of agents grows large.

Suppose that $n + 1$ identical risk-averse agents participate in a tournament, so that each agent competes with n other agents. Green and Stokey's insight is that, as n grows large, each agent's relative position in the output rankings will become almost entirely a function of her own effort supply. Indeed, by the law of large numbers, the distribution of the other agents' outputs conditional on the vector of actions (a_i, a_{-i}) and on the realization of the common shock converges to a fixed limit distribution as n grows large. A relative-performance-evaluation scheme can then filter out the common shock almost perfectly.

To see this result, consider the following simple tournament: (1) if all agents produce the same output, everybody receives T; (2) otherwise, those who are successful receive W, and the others receive L. Assuming that all other agents choose effort level a_*, an agent choosing effort a_i obtains

T with probability $\quad (1 - \xi) + \xi a_i a_*^n + \xi (1 - a_i)(1 - a_*)^n$

W with probability $\quad \xi a_i (1 - a_*^n)$

and

L with probability $\quad \xi(1 - a_i)\left[1 - (1 - a_*)^n \right]$

From the preceding argument we know that a tournament is first-best optimal when $a_i = a_* = 1$. Thus, consider the situation where $a_i = a_* < 1$. Then, as $n \to \infty$, $a_*^n \to 0$, and $(1 - a_*)^n \to 0$, so that the tournament tends to the second-best contract, in which agent i gets

$w_c = T$ with probability $(1 - \xi)$

$w_1 = W$ with probability ξa_i

and

$w_0 = L$ with probability $\xi(1 - a_i)$

To summarize, we have learned in this section that tournaments are suboptimal when a small number of risk-averse agents compete. They are dominated by piece-rate schemes, which do not base compensation on any form of relative performance evaluation, when agents' individual outputs are not affected or are barely affected by a common shock. When common shocks are a large component of individual outputs, however, relative performance schemes strictly dominate any piece-rate schemes, but tournaments are generally dominated by more general relative performance schemes, which fully exploit all the information about action choices contained in output realizations. Only when there are a large number of agents involved do tournaments approximate the second-best optimal contract.

8.2   Cooperation or Competition among Agents

The good side of relative-performance-evaluation schemes is that they help reduce agents' risk exposure by filtering out common shocks that affect their individual performance. But there may also be a dark side to these schemes, as Lazear (1995) and others have suggested. By fostering competition among agents, tournaments and relative-performance-based incentive schemes may undermine cooperation among agents and in extreme cases even foster destructive behavior such as "sabotage" of other agents' outputs. We take up this issue in this section and ask how a principal may be able to induce agents to cooperate or help each other accomplish their tasks when such cooperation is desirable. We shall cover two different approaches to modeling cooperation that have been considered in the literature. In the first approach, cooperation takes the form of agent i helping agent j accomplish a task. In the second approach, cooperation is in the form of coordination through contracting of agents' action choices. In this latter approach, when the principal tries to elicit cooperation among agents, he lets the agents form a partnership (or firm), and only contracts with the firm as a whole, as opposed to contracting with each individual agent separately.

8.2.1   Incentives to Help in Multiagent Situations

The first approach to fostering help among agents has been explored in Itoh (1991). We shall illustrate his analysis and main findings in the by-now-familiar and highly tractable setting where agents' individual output can take only two values: $q_i \in \{0, 1\}$. We shall consider a situation with a risk-neutral principal and only two risk-averse agents, $i = 1, 2$. The new feature in Itoh's setup is that each agent now has a two-dimensional action set. That is, each agent must now choose a pair

$$(a_i, b_i) \in [0, +\infty) \times [0, +\infty)$$

where a_i represents agent i's effort on her own task and b_i represents her help on the other agent's task. Each agent's utility function takes the usual separable form

$$u_i(w) - \psi_i(a_i, b_i)$$

where u_i is strictly increasing and concave, and ψ_i is strictly increasing and convex. In our illustration we shall also assume the following functional forms:

$$u_i(w) = \sqrt{w}$$

and

$$\psi_i(a_i, b_i) = a_i^2 + b_i^2 + 2ka_ib_i$$

where $k \in [0, 1]$.

As for the probability distribution over each agent's output, we shall assume that there are no common shocks affecting individual outputs and that outputs are independently distributed, with

$$\Pr(q_i = 1) = a_i(1 + b_j)$$

These assumptions imply that the two agents' efforts a_i and b_j are complements and that, therefore, there may be benefits in inducing cooperation among the two agents. When $k > 0$, however, each agent bears an additional cost in not specializing entirely in her own task and in helping the other agent.

The question we shall be concerned with is determining when or whether it is desirable to encourage mutual help despite the fact that the sharing in each other's output required may also induce agents to free ride on each other.

The principal can induce cooperation by giving each agent a stake in the other agent's output. That is, the principal can offer each agent a contract

$$w_i = \{w_{00}^i, w_{01}^i, w_{10}^i, w_{11}^i\}$$

where w_{mn}^i denotes the payment to agent i when $q_i = m$ and $q_j = n$. The only restriction on the contracts the principal can offer to each agent is, of course, that all payments must be nonnegative ($w_{mn}^i \geq 0$). Given that the two agents are identical, we can without loss of generality restrict attention to symmetric contracts, $w = \{w_{00}, w_{01}, w_{10}, w_{11}\}$.

We set off by deriving equilibrium payoffs when the principal does not attempt to induce any cooperation among the two agents ($b_i = 0$). This is the case whenever the contract offered to each agent is such that $w_{00} = w_{01}$ and $w_{10} = w_{11}$. We then compare these payoffs to those that can be obtained under cooperation ($b_i > 0$).

8.2.1.1 No Help

When the principal does not attempt to elicit any cooperation, he offers each agent a simple piece-rate contract rewarding output $q_i = 1$ with a payment w_1 and output $q_i = 0$ with a payment w_0. As we know from Chapter 4, it is then optimal to set $w_0 = 0$ and to set w_1 to maximize

$$a_i(1 - w_1)$$

subject to

$$a_i = \frac{1}{2}\sqrt{w_1} \qquad \text{(IC)}$$

and

$$a_i\sqrt{w_1} - a_i^2 = \frac{w_1}{4} \geq 0 \qquad \text{(IR)}$$

Substituting for w_1, the principal's problem reduces to choosing a_i to maximize the payoff

$$a_i - 4a_i^3$$

The optimum is then reached for

$$a_i = \sqrt{\frac{1}{12}}$$

and the principal's payoff is then

$$\frac{2}{3}\sqrt{\frac{1}{12}}$$

8.2.1.2 Inducing Help

Consider now contracts that induce agents to help each other ($b_i > 0$). Optimal contracts that induce help are necessarily such that

$$w_{11} > w_{10} \quad \text{and} \quad w_{01} > w_{00} = 0$$

That is, agent i gets a higher reward when agent j is successful. Only such an increase in rewards can encourage agent i to help agent j. Note that by conditioning agent i's pay on agent j's output in this way, such contracts expose agent i to greater risks and require that the principal pay a higher risk premium. The question for the principal then is whether the higher output obtained through cooperation pays for the higher risk premium. To be able to determine whether that is the case, we need to solve for the symmetric Nash equilibrium in action choice (a, b) induced by a contract of the form $w_{11} > w_{10}$ and $w_{01} > w_{00} = 0$.

In equilibrium, (a,b) must be a best response for each agent and solve the individual agent problem

$$\max_{a,b} a_j(1+b)a(1+b_j)\sqrt{w_{11}} + a_j(1+b)[1-a(1+b_j)]\sqrt{w_{01}}$$
$$+ a(1+b_j)[1-a_j(1+b)]\sqrt{w_{10}} - a^2 - b^2 - 2kab$$

Differentiating with respect to b and a, we obtain the first-order conditions at $(a_j,b_j) = (a,b)$:

$$a^2(1+b)(\sqrt{w_{11}} - \sqrt{w_{10}}) + a[1 - a(1+b)]\sqrt{w_{01}} = 2(b+ak) \qquad (8.1)$$

and

$$a(1+b)^2(\sqrt{w_{11}} - \sqrt{w_{01}}) + (1+b)[1 - a(1+b)]\sqrt{w_{10}} = 2(a+bk) \qquad (8.2)$$

These first-order conditions yield the answers to our main question:

1. When $k > 0$, there is a minimum threshold in help $b^* > 0$ such that any lesser help b (for which $0 < b < b^*$) yields a strictly lower payoff to the principal than no help at all ($b = 0$). In other words, when $k > 0$, it pays to induce either a lot of cooperation or none at all. This observation may help explain why we often see in organizations a culture of either strong cooperation or none at all.

To see why the preceding first-order conditions yield this result, note first that under no help the optimal contract exposes each agent to minimum risk by setting $w_{11} - w_{10} = w$, say, and $w_{01} = w_{00} = 0$.

Now, as can be seen from condition (8.1) [with a RHS equal to $2(b + ak)$ and $a > 0$], when $k > 0$, any $b > 0$ requires a significant deviation from the contract $w_{11} - w_{10} = w$ and $w_{01} = w_{00} = 0$. Such a discontinuous deviation from optimal risk sharing cannot be optimal if only a very small change in output is obtained (that is, when b is close to zero). Only a significant change in output, induced by a significant level of b, can justify the increased risk exposure for the agents required under any contract seeking to induce positive cooperation.

2. When instead $k = 0$, contracts that induce help are always strictly optimal. In fact, raising helping effort b above zero is certainly optimal if effort on the own task a were to remain fixed, since, with $k = 0$, the mar-

ginal cost of raising b at 0 is zero. Consequently, to establish the result, we just have to make sure a does not fall in the process. This property can be checked from the first-order conditions (8.1) and (8.2), as follows. Start from the corner solution where $b = 0$, $w_{11} = w_{10} = w$, and $w_{01} = w_{00} = 0$; then raise $\sqrt{w_{11}}$ and $\sqrt{w_{01}}$ by du, while keeping $\sqrt{w_{10}}$ constant; let da and db denote the changes in a and b induced by this change in compensation. From the first-order conditions (8.1) and (8.2) we then observe that

$$(a+da)^2(1+db)du + (a+da)[1-(a+da)(1+db)]du = 2db$$

which implies $(a+da)du = 2db > 0$ ....(i)

and

$$(a+da)(1+db)^2\sqrt{w} + (1+db)[1-(a+da)(1+db)]\sqrt{w} = 2(a+da)$$

which implies $(1+db)\sqrt{w} = 2(a+da)$ ....(ii)

Since da, db, and du are small, equation (i) implies that $2db \approx adu > 0$. In addition, at $b = 0$ we have $\sqrt{w}/2 = a$, so that equations (i) and (ii) together imply that

$$2da = db\sqrt{w} > 0$$

which establishes the result.

Itoh's analysis thus highlights another reason why in multiagent situations it may be optimal to base an agent's compensation also on the other agents' performance. This approach is meant to induce cooperation among agents. By giving individual agents a stake in other agents' output, it is possible to elicit more cooperation. But this may come at the cost of more risk exposure for individual agents. One difficulty with this basic logic is that it might predict much more cooperation than we see in reality. It is at this point that Itoh's emphasis on the potential cost in terms of lack of specialization (when $k > 0$) becomes relevant. When there are gains to specialization, then it is worthwhile to encourage cooperation only when it makes a significant difference.

Note that when a common shock affects individual agents' outputs, then it is no longer obvious that inducing cooperation necessarily implies that agents have a greater risk exposure. In the presence of common shocks it may, however, be more expensive to elicit cooperation if it means abstaining from a relative-performance-evaluation incentive scheme that filters out the common shock. The next section considers cooperation in the presence of common shocks but in a somewhat different setting.

8.2.2   Cooperation and Collusion among Agents

The second approach to cooperation among agents (taken in Holmström and Milgrom, 1990, Varian, 1990, Macho-Stadler and Perez-Castrillo, 1993, Ramakrishnan and Thakor, 1991, and Itoh, 1993) does not allow agents to help each other directly to accomplish their tasks, but lets them sign contracts to coordinate their actions. The important and obvious question in this setup is, Why does the principal gain by letting agents jointly determine their effort supply through contracts? Pursuing the logic of the revelation principle, why can the principal not do as well or better by contracting directly with the agents? What does he gain by allowing for a stage of indirect contracting?

The answer to these questions proposed in the literature rests on the general idea that when agents may be able to observe action choices that the principal cannot see, then there may be gains to letting agents write side contracts that coordinate their action choices. Interestingly, however, these gains are not available if agents' individual outputs are affected by common shocks, for then it is best to filter out the common shock through a relative performance incentive scheme, which induces agents to compete. Cooperation would undermine competition under such a scheme and thus prevent the filtering out of the common shock.

We follow here the analysis of Holmström and Milgrom (1990), and consider the situation involving two risk-averse agents, each producing a random output

$$q_i = a_i + \varepsilon_i$$

by supplying effort a_i. Suppose also that the random variables ε_i are normally distributed with mean zero and variance-covariance matrix

$$\begin{pmatrix} \sigma_1^2 & \sigma_{12} \\ \sigma_{12} & \sigma_2^2 \end{pmatrix}$$

so that the correlation coefficient between the two variables is $\rho = \sigma_{12}/(\sigma_1 \sigma_2)$.

Finally, as is by now familiar, suppose also that the two agents have CARA risk preferences with coefficient η_i represented by the negative exponential utility function

$$u_i(w_i, a_i) = -e^{-\eta_i[w_i - \psi_i(a_i)]}$$

where $\psi_i(a_i)$ is the strictly increasing, convex, monetary-cost-of-effort function.

We shall consider in turn the contracting situations with no cooperation, where the principal contracts with each agent separately and agents respond by playing a noncooperative game in action choices (*no side contracting*), and the situation with cooperation, where the principal contracts with the team of agents that contractually coordinate their action choices (*full side contracting*). In each situation we restrict attention to linear contracts of the form:

$$w_1 = z_1 + v_1 q_1 + u_1 q_2$$

$$w_2 = z_2 + v_2 q_2 + u_2 q_1$$

8.2.2.1 No Side Contracting

Under linear incentive contracts we obtain the simple formula for the agents' certainty equivalent wealths:

$$CE_1(a_1, a_2) = z_1 + v_1 a_1 + u_1 a_2 - \psi_1(a_1) - \frac{\eta_1}{2}(v_1^2 \sigma_1^2 + u_1^2 \sigma_2^2 + 2v_1 u_1 \sigma_{12})$$

and

$$CE_2(a_1, a_2) = z_2 + v_2 a_2 + u_2 a_1 - \psi_2(a_2) - \frac{\eta_2}{2}(v_2^2 \sigma_2^2 + u_2^2 \sigma_1^2 + 2v_2 u_2 \sigma_{12})$$

A risk-neutral principal, contracting separately with each agent, then chooses $\{z_i, v_i, u_i\}$ $(i = 1, 2)$ to maximize expected net profits:

$$(1 - v_1 - u_2)a_1 + (1 - u_1 - v_2)a_2 - z_1 - z_2$$

subject to the incentive constraints that the action choices of the two agents (a_1, a_2) form a Nash equilibrium in effort levels:

$$a_i = \arg\max_{\hat{a}_i} CE_i(\hat{a}_i, a_j) \quad i = 1, 2, j = 2, 1$$

and the individual-rationality constraints

$$CE_i(a_i, a_j) \geq 0 \quad i = 1, 2, j = 2, 1$$

As is by now familiar, the equilibrium action choices a_i are tied down entirely by the agent's share in own output v_i through the first-order condition of the agent's problem:

$$v_i = \psi_i'(a_i) \quad i = 1, 2$$

Consequently, the shares u_i in the other agent's output should be set to minimize risk exposure for each agent. That is

$$u_i = -v_i \frac{\sigma_i}{\sigma_j} \rho \quad \text{for } i \neq j$$

As we have already noted, when outputs are positively correlated ($\rho > 0$), the optimal linear contract penalizes each agent for a good performance by the other agent.

Substituting for u_i in the agents' certainty-equivalent wealth formulas, we find that the total risk exposure of the two agents for a given own incentive (v_1, v_2) is

$$\sum_{i=1}^{2} \eta_i [v_i^2 \sigma_i^2 (1 - \rho^2)] \tag{8.3}$$

We shall compare this expression with the total risk exposure under full side contracting *at the same* (a_1, a_2).

8.2.2.2 Full Side Contracting

The type of team the principal faces when he allows for side contracting between the two agents before signing on the team of agents depends on what the agents themselves can contract on. The literature considers two situations: one, where the agents do not observe each other's effort choices and can contract only on output; and the other, where they can also contractually specify their actions. We now consider each one in turn and highlight the following general observations, derived by Holmström and Milgrom (1990):

1. *If the agents can contract only on their respective output levels, then side contracting by the agents can only make the principal worse off.*[1]
Here the agents do not bring any new contracting possibilities to the principal. They can only use their side contracting at the expense of the principal. Indeed, note that all the agents can do here under side contracting is to specify a transfer $(\phi q_1 + \chi q_2)$ from agent 1 to agent 2. The principal can always undo any such transfer by resetting

---

1. See also Varian (1990).

v_1 to $v_1 - \phi$

u_2 to $u_2 + \phi$

u_1 to $u_1 - \chi$

and

v_2 to $v_2 + \chi$

and restrict himself to "coalition-proof contracts." But this approach forces the principal into a more restricted problem than the no-side-contracting problem. Therefore, by letting agents write such side contracts he may be made worse off. We will see this same point again in the next section when we discuss side contracting between an agent and a supervisor.

2. When the two agents can contract on both their effort levels and their respective outputs, then when they are faced with a given incentive scheme (v_i, u_i) for $i = 1, 2$, they respond by maximizing their joint surplus:

$$\max_{\phi, \chi, a_i} (v_1 + u_2)a_1 + (v_2 + u_1)a_2 - \psi_1(a_1) - \psi_2(a_2)$$

$$- \frac{\eta_1}{2}\left[(v_1 - \phi)^2 \sigma_1^2 + (u_1 - \chi)^2 \sigma_2^2 + 2(v_1 - \phi)(u_1 - \chi)\sigma_{12}\right]$$

$$- \frac{\eta_2}{2}\left[(v_2 + \chi)^2 \sigma_2^2 + (u_2 + \phi)^2 \sigma_1^2 + 2(v_2 + \chi)(u_2 + \phi)\sigma_{12}\right]$$

As can be seen from this problem, a given incentive scheme (v_i, u_i) by the principal then maps into a pair of effort levels and a risk-sharing scheme: (ϕ, χ, a_1, a_2). Since we have transferable utility, we can think of the principal as maximizing total surplus, optimizing over (v_i, u_i), $i = 1, 2$, and anticipating the (ϕ, χ, a_1, a_2) that follows. This formulation of the principal's problem under this form of side contracting brings out the following useful observation:

The principal's optimal contract is the same whether the agents can contract only on (a_1, a_2) or on both (a_1, a_2, q_1, q_2).

This insight can be understood intuitively as follows: For a fixed action pair (a_1, a_2) the two agents do not add any new risk-sharing opportunities through their side contract. Therefore, once the agents have contracted on (a_1, a_2) they cannot improve the contracting outcome by also writing a side contract on (q_1, q_2).

3. This observation leads to the next useful remark:

The principal's optimal contracting problem under side contracting with the two agents can be reduced to a single-agent contracting problem, where he faces a single agent with coefficient of risk aversion

$$1/\eta = 1/\eta_1 + 1/\eta_2$$

supplying effort (a_1, a_2) with cost-of-effort function[2]

$$\psi(a_1, a_2) = \psi_1(a_1) + \psi_2(a_2)$$

To establish this claim, we need to do a little algebra and derive the optimal (ϕ, χ) for a given incentive scheme (v_i, u_i), $i = 1, 2$. We can then compute the optimal total risk exposure of the two agents.

Once the agents' supply of effort corresponding to the incentive (v_i, u_i) has been fixed in the side contract, the side transfer $(\phi q_1 + \chi q_2)$ can be set to minimize the agents' total risk exposure. Then,

$$\frac{\partial(CE_1 + CE_2)}{\partial \phi} = 0$$

implies

$$\eta_1[(v_1 - \phi)\sigma_1^2 + (u_1 - \chi)\sigma_{12}] = \eta_2[(u_2 + \phi)\sigma_1^2 + (v_2 + \chi)\sigma_{12}] \tag{8.4}$$

and

$$\frac{\partial(CE_1 + CE_2)}{\partial \chi} = 0$$

implies

$$\eta_1[(u_1 - \chi)\sigma_2^2 + (v_1 - \phi)\sigma_{12}] = \eta_2[(v_2 + \chi)\sigma_2^2 + (u_2 + \phi)\sigma_{12}] \tag{8.5}$$

Multiplying both sides of equation (8.5) by σ_{12}/σ_2^2 and subtracting it from equation (8.4) then yields

$$\eta_1(v_1 - \phi) = \eta_2(u_2 + \phi)$$

Similarly, multiplying equation (8.5) by σ_1^2/σ_{12} and subtracting it from equation (8.4) yields

$$\eta_1(u_1 - \chi) = \eta_2(v_2 + \chi)$$

Both conditions then imply

---

2. This result is due to Wilson (1968).

$$\phi = \frac{\eta_1 v_1 - \eta_2 u_2}{\eta_1 + \eta_2}$$

$$\chi = \frac{\eta_1 u_1 - \eta_2 v_2}{\eta_1 + \eta_2}$$

and therefore

$$v_1 - \phi = \frac{\eta_2}{\eta_1 + \eta_2}(v_1 + u_2)$$

$$u_1 - \chi = \frac{\eta_2}{\eta_1 + \eta_2}(u_1 + v_2)$$

$$v_2 + \chi = \frac{\eta_1}{\eta_1 + \eta_2}(u_1 + v_2)$$

$$u_2 + \phi = \frac{\eta_1}{\eta_1 + \eta_2}(v_1 + u_2)$$

Thus the optimal total risk exposure for the two agents for a given incentive (v_i, u_i) is

$$\frac{\eta_1}{2(\eta_1 + \eta_2)^2}\left[\eta_2^2(v_1 + u_2)^2 \sigma_1^2 + \eta_2^2(u_1 + v_2)^2 \sigma_2^2 + 2\eta_2^2(v_1 + u_2)(u_1 + v_2)\sigma_{12}\right]$$

$$+ \frac{\eta_2}{2(\eta_1 + \eta_2)^2}\left[\eta_1^2(u_1 + v_2)^2 \sigma_2^2 + \eta_1^2(v_1 + u_2)^2 \sigma_1^2 + 2\eta_1^2(u_1 + v_2)(v_1 + u_2)\sigma_{12}\right]$$

which is equal to

$$\frac{1}{2}\left(\frac{\eta_1 \eta_2^2 + \eta_2 \eta_1^2}{(\eta_1 + \eta_2)^2}\right)\left\{(v_1 + u_2)^2 \sigma_1^2 + (u_1 + v_2)^2 \phi_2^2 + 2(u_1 + v_2)(v_1 + u_2)\sigma_{12}\right\} \tag{8.6}$$

Finally, we can then define

$$\frac{\eta_1 \eta_2^2 + \eta_2 \eta_1^2}{(\eta_1 + \eta_2)^2} = \frac{\eta_1 \eta_2}{\eta_1 + \eta_2} = \eta \quad \left(\text{since } \frac{1}{\eta} = \frac{1}{\eta_1} + \frac{1}{\eta_2}\right)$$

Therefore, the total risk exposure for the two agents can be reinterpreted as that of a single agent with absolute risk aversion η, facing a contract $(v_1 + u_2, u_1 + v_2)$.

4. With this simplification in hand, we are, at last, able to confirm our

central conjecture, derived by Holmström and Milgrom (1990) and also Ramakrishnan and Thakor (1991):

Full side contracting dominates no side contracting if and only if $\rho \leq \bar{\rho}$.

To establish this result, observe that to implement the same pair of effort levels (a_1, a_2) under both contracting regimes (with and without side contracting) we must have the same pair of incentive levels (v_1, v_2) under both regimes. Under side contracting, in addition, we have $u_1 = u_2 = 0$ and (ϕ, χ) set, as before, to minimize risk exposure. Comparing the respective formulas for the risk exposures under no side contracting and side contracting on actions, equations (8.3) and (8.6), we then observe that (1) the risk exposure (8.3) starts above (8.6) for $\rho = 0$, and is equal to 0 for $\rho = 1$; and (2) the risk exposure (8.6) is below (8.3) at $\rho = 0$, but is positive and grows with ρ. The result then follows from these two observations.

The intuition for this result is as follows: At $\rho = 0$ cooperation between agents can only be good: it simply means that they work harder by monitoring each other. For $\rho > 0$, however, cooperation also undermines relative performance evaluation, which results in a higher cost for the principal the higher the correlation ρ.

We end this section on a note of caution made by Itoh (1993) about the approach taken here to the problem of cooperation among agents. As is well known from mechanism design, when one allows for more general mechanisms than we have here, the principal ought to be able to always do (weakly) better than letting agents collude with a side contract, by eliciting the hidden information about agents' effort levels directly through reports from individual agents. The principal could, for example, elicit the agents' information in an efficient, incentive-compatible way by designing a Maskin-type message game (we review Maskin schemes in Chapter 12). One example of a model taking this approach is that of Ma (1988). The theory of collusion discussed previously thus seems to be vulnerable, as there appear to be optimal contractual solutions that do not involve any collusion.

However, Maskin schemes are rarely observed in reality. An obvious question then is, What makes them nonoperational in reality? The only limited answer we shall offer for now is that the Maskin message games would be powerless if the agents could also collude in sending reports and if utility were transferable. The reason is that, as the only goal of the principal here is to extract informational rents from the agents through a message game, a coordinated action by all agents ought to be able to defeat that purpose, as in the model of collusion of Tirole (1986) to which we turn next.

8.3 Supervision and Collusion

One important cost of having agents monitor each other, which we did not consider in the previous section, is that monitoring distracts agents from their production activities. If there are returns to specialization, then it may be more efficient to have some agents specialize in monitoring or supervision activities while others specialize in production. Indeed, many organizations are structured this way in practice. However, as our discussion on collusion among agents in the previous section indicates, the efficiency of monitoring and supervision by specialized monitors may be constrained by the possibility of collusion between the supervisor and the supervisee. In this section we turn to the analysis of collusion in vertical organizational structures, which in their simplest form involve one principal, one supervisor, and one agent.

Such vertical structures are ubiquitous, and collusion in these structures is a fundamental concern. Whether in auditing, tax collection, law enforcement, or regulation, a major concern is that monitoring activities are weakened or subverted by collusion between the supervisor and the agent. A fundamental question concerning these structures then is how the incentives of supervisor and agent ought to be structured to maximize the effectiveness of monitoring activities and to minimize the risk of collusion. We now turn to the analysis of this broad question. To keep the analysis as transparent as possible, we shall limit our discussion to situations where, as in Chapter 5, the information about the agent produced by the monitor is hard, verifiable information. In such a setting, as in a typical auditing problem, collusion between the supervisor and agent takes the particularly simple form of suppressing damaging information about the agent.

8.3.1 Collusion with Hard Information

The basic problem we shall consider involves three risk-neutral parties: principal, supervisor, and agent. The supervisor obtains information about the agent and provides it to the principal. The latter hires the agent and supervisor under a contract that bases each of their compensation on the supervisor's verifiable reports on the agent's productivity. An example of such a situation is the shareholders of a firm (collectively acting as the principal) hiring an auditing firm to produce and certify the firm's annual income statements, on which the firm manager's compensation is based. Clearly, a concern shareholders ought to have in such a situation is that the auditor and firm manager might collude and "manipulate" the firm's accounts, for example by underreporting losses or instead by overstating costs.

This simple three-tier contracting relation was first analyzed in an influential paper by Tirole (1986). He allows for an extreme form of collusion between the auditor and the manager: collusion that is enforceable through side contracts between the supervisor and agent, albeit at a higher cost than normal contracts. In the presence of such collusion, Tirole shows that the principal will design an optimal contract for the two parties that is *collusion-proof*. That is, the principal can without loss of generality restrict attention to contracts that do not involve any collusion in equilibrium. This observation is akin to the *revelation principle* discussed in Chapter 2, which states that the principal can restrict attention to contracts that do not involve any lying by the agent under the contract.

One consequence of restricting attention to collusion-proof contracts is that the principal will have to dull the agent's incentives relative to a situation where collusion is not possible, so as to reduce the agent's incentives to collude with the auditor. As obvious as this observation is, it has apparently not been taken sufficient note of by compensation committees in large U.S. firms that have granted such high-powered incentives to their CEOs that they have given them strong incentives to manipulate reported earnings. At the same time, by letting accounting firms engage in both auditing and consulting activities, U.S. financial regulators have given these CEOs the means to "bribe" auditing firms with the prospect of lucrative consulting contracts.

We begin our analysis of this contracting problem by characterizing first the outcome under no collusion. The contracting problem between the principal and agent takes the following simple form: the principal buys a service from the agent that he values at $V > 1$. The agent produces this service at (unobservable) cost $c \in \{0, 1\}$. The agent knows the value of c, and the principal's prior beliefs about the agent's costs are $\Pr(c = 0) = \frac{1}{2}$. The principal can hire a monitor to get a better estimate of the agent's cost. Consider the extreme case where by paying a fee z to a supervisor the principal can obtain exact proof of the agent's true costs with probability p when $c = 0$

and otherwise no proof at all of the agent's cost [more explicitly, the monitor sees nothing with probability 1 when $c = 1$, and with probability $(1 - p)$ when $c = 0$]. When would the principal want to hire such a supervisor?

If the principal does not hire a supervisor, he faces a standard screening problem and offers the agent a price $P = 1$ for the service if $V - 1 > V/2$ and $P = 0$ otherwise. For the remainder of the analysis we shall take it that $V > 2$, so that the price $P = 1$ is indeed optimal. In that case, the principal's payoff is simply $(V - 1)$. If the principal hires a monitor at cost z, and if there is no collusion, then, when $c = 0$, the principal gets to see the agent's cost with probability p and can offer the agent a price $P = 0$. When he gets no information from the supervisor, the principal now has even more reason to believe that the agent has high costs ($c = 1$) and then optimally offers the agent a price $P = 1$. This contract gives the principal a payoff of

$$\frac{1}{2}pV + \left(1 - \frac{1}{2}p\right)(V - 1) - z$$

We shall assume that z is small enough that

$$\frac{1}{2}pV + \left(1 - \frac{1}{2}p\right)(V - 1) - z > V - 1$$

In that case the principal is better off hiring a supervisor to monitor the agent.

How is this contract affected by the possibility of collusion between the monitor and agent? The supervisor and agent can gainfully collude under this contract when the agent's cost is $c = 0$ and the supervisor has obtained proof of the agent's low costs. In that case the agent will obtain only a price $P = 0$ if her costs are revealed by the supervisor, while if the supervisor pretends he has not obtained any proof the agent gets a price $P = 1$ for her services. Supervisor and agent can then share a potential rent of 1 by suppressing the information.

A self-interested supervisor colludes with the agent only if he benefits from such behavior. Consider the following collusion technology: if the agent offers the supervisor a transfer T for suppressing his information, the supervisor obtains a benefit of kT, where $k \leq 1$. The idea is that, since the agent's transfer to the supervisor must be hidden (through, say, some complex financial transactions in a tax haven on some Caribbean island), the supervisor ends up getting less than what the agent paid.

To avoid such collusion, the far-sighted principal has to promise the supervisor a reward w for proving that $c = 0$. This reward must be high enough so that the following collusion-proofness or *coalition-incentive-compatibility constraint* is satisfied:

$$w \geq k \tag{CIC}$$

When this constraint holds, the agent cannot gain by inducing the supervisor to suppress information, since she would have to pay the supervisor more than 1 to get him to suppress the information.

The principal would not incur higher expected costs from hiring the supervisor if he can subtract from the supervisor's pay the amount $\frac{1}{2}pw$ when the supervisor reports no information. Then the only consequence for the principal of the possibility of collusion between the supervisor and agent is that he has to incentivize the supervisor by adding a "bounty" to his pay for delivering valuable information. This is not a very surprising finding. Nevertheless, it is worth pausing and pointing out that the remuneration of auditing firms in reality is far from resembling this structure. Typically, auditing firms are not rewarded for exposing accounting irregularities. Instead, their incentives to perform come from the penalties they face if they are found to collude with the firm's manager. Unfortunately, these latter incentives are effective only if the probability of detection of collusion is sufficiently high.

When, moreover, as Tirole assumes, the supervisor has a limited wealth constraint, so that $\frac{1}{2}pw$ cannot be entirely subtracted from his pay when he does not report any information, then collusion raises the principal's costs of hiring a supervisor whenever $\frac{1}{2}pk > z$. In that case, the principal's payoff when hiring a supervisor under a collusion-proof contract is

$$\tfrac{1}{2}p(V - k) + (1 - \tfrac{1}{2}p)(V - 1)$$

This simple example captures the essence of Tirole's analysis. It highlights in a stark way that the principal could not gain from allowing collusion to take place in equilibrium. Collusion could occur in equilibrium only if the supervisor's limited wealth constraint is binding, if k is a random variable, and if most of the time the realizations of k are small. In other words, collusion could occur in equilibrium in his model only if it would not pay the principal to attempt to deter the rare cases where collusion might be profitable for the supervisor and agent because they happen to have access to a cheap enforcement technology. If, for example, the principal thinks that $k = \frac{1}{2}$ with probability $1 - \varepsilon$ and $k = 1$ with probability ε, where ε is small, then setting $w = \frac{1}{2}$ is optimal, and equilibrium collusion occurs with probability ε.

Our simple example also highlights how the possibility of collusion increases the costs of monitoring for the principal. Interestingly, in a somewhat richer example it can be shown that when it is costly for the principal to pay a reward w to the supervisor, it may pay the principal to slightly dull the agent's incentives so as to reduce the collusion rent between the supervisor and agent. We leave it to the reader to extend our simple setup to allow for this possibility.

8.3.2   Application: Auditing

Tirole's basic three-tier structure with collusion has been applied to an auditing problem and extended further by Kofman and Lawarrée (1993). Their starting point is the observation that, in reality, firms and their external auditors are themselves subject to random audits by supervisory authorities. The basic theory of collusion we have just outlined suggests that the supervisory authorities, or external auditors (as Kofman and Lawarrée denote them), can serve as a control mechanism not only on the firm's managers but also on their auditors.

Kofman and Lawarrée consider the situation where external auditors are more expensive than internal ones but are immune to collusion. This is a plausible description of financial regulation in the United States, where SEC staff are reputed to be incorruptible but resources are so stretched that SEC staff can investigate only a small fraction of listed firms at any time (this fraction has at times been so small that SEC supervision has sometimes been referred to as the SEC roulette).

Kofman and Lawarrée's model is built on the following simple principal-agent structure:

A risk-neutral manager produces output (or profits) with the following technology:

$$q = \theta + a$$

where $\theta \in \{\theta_1, \theta_2\}$ is the firm's type, with $\theta_1 < \theta_2$ and $\Pr(\theta_1) = \frac{1}{2}$. The manager has a convex cost-of-effort function given by $\psi(a) = a^2/2$. A risk-neutral principal contracts with the agent. The principal's first-best problem, when he can observe both θ and a, is thus to choose type-contingent transfers T_i and actions a_i to maximize his expected profit:

$$\max_{a_i, T_i} \frac{1}{2}(\theta_1 + a_1 - T_1) + \frac{1}{2}(\theta_2 + a_2 - T_2)$$

subject to

$$T_i \geq \frac{a_i^2}{2} \quad \text{for } i = 1, 2 \tag{MIRi}$$

where (MIRi) denotes the individual rationality constraint of the manager when her firm is of type i. The solution to this problem is clearly to set $a_i = 1$ and $T_i = \frac{1}{2}$.

The principal's second-best problem (when θ_i is private information), in the absence of any supervision, is to maximize the same payoff but with an additional incentive constraint:

$$T_2 - \frac{a_2^2}{2} \geq T_1 - \frac{(\max\{0, a_1 - \Delta\theta\})^2}{2} \tag{MIC2}$$

(As we know from Chapter 2, only one of the two incentive incentive constraints will bind at the optimum.) We also know from Chapter 2 that the second-best contract specifies efficient effort provision for type θ_2, under-provision of effort for type θ_1, and positive informational rents for type θ_2 only.

For simplicity, suppose that $\Delta\theta = \theta_2 - \theta_1 = 1$. Since effort a_1 is no greater than 1, this assumption means that type θ_2 is able to produce q_1 at zero effort. Using this observation, the incentive constraint can be written in the simpler form

$$T_2 - \frac{a_2^2}{2} \geq T_1 \tag{MIC2}$$

Combining constraints (MIR1) and (MIC2), substituting for T_i in the objective, and maximizing with respect to a_i then yields the second-best solution $a_1 = \frac{1}{2}$ and $a_2 = 1$.

8.3.2.1 Supervision

How can auditing improve on this outcome? Kofman and Lawarrée model auditing by assuming that the auditor observes an imperfect signal y_i of managerial productivity. As before, we assume that this signal is hard information. This assumption simplifies the auditing problem, in particular by ruling out the possibility that the auditor blackmails or extorts the manager by threatening to fabricate damaging reports. As in Tirole's problem, the only concern with auditing is the possibility of collusion between the auditor and the manager. Kofman and Lawarrée allow for both type-1 and type-2 errors and assume that the signals observed by the auditor are such that

$$\Pr(y_i|\theta_i) = \zeta > \tfrac{1}{2} > 1 - \zeta = \Pr(y_j|\theta_i)$$

Again, to avoid any complicating issue relating to the threat of extortion, assume that both the manager and the auditor(s) observe the signal y_i.

We now turn to the interaction of internal and external auditors. To see how the threat of an external audit can be used to reduce the risk of collusion between the internal auditor and the manager, it is helpful to proceed in three steps. These steps also allow us to cover other important contributions on optimal incentive contracting with auditing on which Kofman and Lawarree's analysis builds. In a first step we analyze the optimal contracting problem between the manager, an honest-but-costly auditor, and the principal. In a second step we consider optimal contracting between a cheap-but-corruptible auditor, the manager, and the principal. Finally, in a third step we consider the optimal contracting problem when both types of auditors are combined.

Honest-but-Costly Supervisor

The contracting problem involving an honest-but-costly supervisor is similar to the auditing problem in Baron and Besanko (1984). It involves the following four stages:

1. The manager learns her firm's type θ_i.

2. The principal offers contracts to the manager and auditor.

3. The manager optimizes her payoff under these contracts by choosing her hidden action.

4. The contract the principal has signed with the auditor specifies an output-contingent audit probability and triggers a stochastic audit after realized profits q_i are observed.

As in Tirole's setup, the objective for the principal is to reduce the informational rent of the efficient manager. This can be achieved with a punishment to be imposed on the efficient manager if she is found underproviding effort. That is, the optimal contract imposes a penalty on the manager when output is low, but the signal received by the auditor is the one that is positively correlated with the efficient type.

Let γ be the probability of an audit when output is low, and let K denote the penalty imposed on the manager when signal y_2 is observed. Let the cost of sending the supervisor be z as before, and let K^* denote the maximum penalty the principal can impose on the manager.

The principal's contracting problem then takes the form

$$\max_{a_i, T_i, \gamma, K} \frac{1}{2}\{\theta_1 + a_1 - T_1 + \gamma[(1-\zeta)K - z]\} + \frac{1}{2}(\theta_2 + a_2 - T_2)$$

subject to

$$T_1 - \gamma(1-\zeta)K \geq \frac{a_1^2}{2} \tag{MIR1}$$

$$T_2 \geq \frac{a_2^2}{2} \tag{MIR2}$$

$$T_2 - \frac{a_2^2}{2} \geq T_1 - \gamma\zeta K \tag{MIC2}$$

In comparison with the second-best problem without supervision, three new effects arise: First, the principal faces new auditing costs: sending the auditor with an ex ante probability $\gamma/2$ costs $\gamma z/2$. Second, auditing comes with a type-1 error: the inefficient manager is wrongly punished with probability $(1 - \zeta)$. As the manager is risk neutral, this effect washes out: it involves a reward for the principal that is exactly compensated by a rise in the transfer T_1. Third, supervision reduces the information rent of the efficient manager, who is punished more often than the inefficient one if she chooses to produce low output. To see this result, note that when constraints (MIR1) and (MIC2) are combined, then

$$T_2 - \frac{a_2^2}{2} \geq \frac{a_1^2}{2} - \gamma(2\zeta - 1)K \tag{MIC2'}$$

Interestingly, when the penalty K is high enough, the second individual-rationality constraint (MIR2) may also be binding. When this is the case, the efficient manager's informational rent will have been eliminated.

Another straightforward, but nevertheless important, observation is that the benefit of an audit rises with K, so that *maximum deterrence* is optimal. In other words, it is optimal to set $K = K^*$. This observation dates back at least to the early economic analyses of crime by Becker (1968). In his original contribution Becker showed that maximum deterrence is efficient when there are no type-1 errors, as it minimizes the probability of apprehension of criminals needed to deter crime, and therefore law enforcement costs. As the analysis here indicates, this logic extends to the situation where auditors may make type-1 errors.[3] As is intuitive, the benefit of maximum deterrence also rises in ζ, the accuracy of the audit signal.

The overall trade-off facing the principal involves rent extraction from the efficient manager versus the audit cost z. As can be easily verified, the optimal contract for a given cost z has the following features:

1. When the signal has low accuracy and/or the maximum punishment of the manager is low, there is no audit at all and $a_1 = \frac{1}{2}$.

2. When the signal has somewhat higher accuracy and/or the maximum punishment of the manager is higher, an audit is worthwhile. Given the linearity of the contracting problem, the audit takes place with probability 1 when a low output is observed. The audit reduces the informational rent of the efficient manager, but as long as she still retains positive rents, the effort choice of the inefficient manager remains at $\frac{1}{2}$.

3. When the accuracy of the signal ζ is very high or the punishment K^* is large, the efficient manager's informational rent vanishes [and (MIR2) is binding]. At that point the inefficient manager gradually raises effort a_1 up to the first-best level (as ζ or K^* increases). The reason is that it takes lower-effort distortions to reduce the informational rent of the efficient manager.

4. Once the first-best effort has been reached for the inefficient manager, further increases in signal accuracy or punishment make it possible to start reducing the probability γ of an audit.

A number of important insights for the regulation of audits are contained in this simple analysis. In particular, this analysis highlights how the optimal frequency of audits depends in a nonmonotonic way on the accuracy of audits and the level of punishments for accounting fraud. We now turn to the analysis of optimal audits in the presence of collusion.

Cheap-but-Corruptible Auditor

The contracting situation involving a cheap-but-corruptible auditor is quite similar to Tirole's setup. It differs from the previous one in two respects:

---

3. Interestingly, maximum deterrence may even be efficient in the presence of type-1 errors when the agent is risk averse. The reason is that maximum deterrence may actually reduce the agent's overall risk exposure if it results in a sufficiently low probability of audit (see Bolton, 1987).

First, collusion can now take place between the supervisor and the manager once low output has been chosen and the "high-productivity signal" y_2 has been observed. As in Tirole's model, we let the two parties write enforceable side contracts that maximize their joint payoff. To avoid collusion, the principal must again reward the auditor for revealing incriminating evidence on the agent. Let w be the reward the auditor obtains when revealing the signal y_2 to the principal. This reward must then be set to satisfy the collusion-proofness constraint:

$$w \geq K \tag{CIC}$$

The second difference from the previous problem is that now audits come for free, so that the principal pays no cost z. However, if we assume that the auditor is resource constrained and thus cannot be punished for failing to reveal the signal y_2, the principal still faces an expected audit cost of $\gamma w(1 - \zeta)/2$. That is, as before, the audit takes place only when q_1 is observed (which happens with probability $\frac{1}{2}$ in equilibrium), and then the audit is triggered only with probability γ. In addition, the auditor then gets the signal y_2 only with probability $(1 - \zeta)$.

The contracting problem the principal faces is thus similar to the previous one, except that now $w(1 - \zeta)$ replaces z in the principal's objective function, and an additional constraint (CIC) is imposed on the principal.

Note that the principal's audit cost is now increasing in the agent's punishment K. Thus the principal now faces the following trade-off between audit costs and informational rent extraction: in expected terms, the auditor gets

$$\gamma(1-\zeta)\frac{K}{2}$$

which results in a reduction of the manager's rent, again in expected terms, by

$$\gamma(2\zeta-1)\frac{K}{2}$$

as can be verified from constraint (MIC2'). Therefore, the principal now calls an audit if and only if $2\zeta - 1 \geq 1 - \zeta$, or $\zeta \geq \frac{2}{3}$.

When the accuracy of the signal is sufficiently high that this condition holds, there will be an audit when q_1 is observed and, as before (and as can be easily verified), the optimal outcome will depend on the value of the maximum punishment K^* that can be imposed on the agent.

If K^* is small, effort provision by both types of agents will be the same as without monitoring, but the manager's information rent will be reduced. For higher values of K^*, the informational rent vanishes, and the low-productivity manager gradually raises her effort level up to its first-best level.

One fundamental difference from the previous problem, however, is that *maximum deterrence* ceases to be strictly optimal here. When the efficient manager's informational rent has been eliminated and first-best effort levels have been reached, a further rise in the punishment K brings no additional benefits, as the rise in the punishment is entirely offset by a rise in the auditor's reward, w. In the previous problem this was not the case. Indeed, the probability of a costly audit, γ, could be reduced while γK was kept constant. Here, instead, the rent of the collusive supervisor depends on γK, and this cost does not decrease with K. It is for this reason that adding an additional honest auditor can help, even if he is costly. The honest auditor can play a useful role in monitoring collusion and thereby helping reduce the reward that must be given to the corruptible auditor.

Once again, this simple contracting problem has yielded an important insight—that Becker's principle of maximum deterrence emphasized so much in the law and economics literature breaks down when the monitor and agent can collude.

Cheap-but-Corruptible and Honest-but-Costly Supervisors

Finally, consider the contracting problem where both types of auditors may be hired. Again, an audit takes place here only when output q_1 has been observed. This problem is somewhat more complex, as the principal has a choice between a number of different audit patterns. We need to introduce new notation to describe this problem.

As before, γ denotes the probability of a (cheap-but-corruptible) internal audit. Let K_i denote the manager's punishment when the internal auditor reveals signal y_2, let φ denote the probability of an (honest-but-costly) external audit *instead* of an internal one, and let K_e denote the manager's punishment when the external auditor reveals signal y_2. Finally, let υ denote the probability of an external audit when the internal audit results in a reported signal y_1. In this event, if the reported signal y_1 is due to collusion between the internal auditor and the agent, then collusion is detected for sure by the external auditor and the respective punishments K_{ie} and S_i are imposed on the manager and the internal auditor.

Most of the difficulty in analyzing this contracting situation lies in the definition of the new contracting variables. Once these have been defined, the principal's problem can be straightforwardly set up in the usual form:

$$\max_{a_i, T_i, \gamma, \varphi, \upsilon, w, K_j} \frac{1}{2}(\theta_1 + a_1 - T_1 + \gamma[(1 - \zeta)(K_i - w) - \zeta \upsilon z] + (1 - \gamma)\varphi[(1 - \zeta)K_e - z])$$

$$+ \frac{1}{2}(\theta_2 + a_2 - T_2)$$

subject to

$$T_1 - (1 - \zeta)[\varphi(1 - \gamma)K_e + \gamma K_i] \geq \frac{a_1^2}{2} \qquad \text{(MIR1)}$$

$$T_2 \geq \frac{a_2^2}{2} \qquad \text{(MIR2)}$$

$$T_2 - \frac{a_2^2}{2} \geq T_1 - \zeta[\varphi(1 - \gamma)K_e + \gamma K_i] \qquad \text{(MIC2)}$$

and

$$w \geq K_i - \upsilon(K_{ie} \mid S_i) \qquad \text{(CIC)}$$

Note that the probability of an audit when output q_1 is realized is now $[\gamma + \varphi(1 - \gamma)]$ instead of γ. As before, the efficient manager must be compensated for being unfairly punished in equilibrium with probability $(1 - \zeta)$. This observation explains the form of the constraint (MIR1).

There are now two potential benefits of external audits. Besides the usual benefit of reducing managerial rents, there is the added benefit of deterring or reducing the benefit of collusion between the internal auditor and the manager.

Next, note that maximum deterrence continues to be optimal under external audits, so that $K_e = K_{ie} = K^*$ and $S_i = S_i^*$, where S_i^* denotes the maximum punishment that can be imposed on the internal auditor.

What do we learn from this problem about the optimal frequency of external audits, that is, about υ and φ? Consider first the optimal choice of υ. When the internal auditor starts with no resources, we can rewrite the collusion-proofness constraint as

$$w = \max\{0, K_i - \upsilon(K^* + S_i^*)\} \qquad \text{(CIC)}$$

Given that the principal already relies on an internal audit, the net expected benefit of an external audit policy υ is then

$$(1-\zeta)(K_i-w)-\zeta\upsilon z$$
$$=(1-\zeta)\min\{K_i,\upsilon(K^*+S_i^*)\}-\zeta\upsilon z$$
$$=\min\{(1-\zeta)K_i-\zeta\upsilon z,\upsilon[(1-\zeta)(K^*+S_i^*)-\zeta z]\} \tag{8.7}$$

Thus the choice of υ, which has no impact on the individual-rationality or incentive constraints of the manager, is driven by the following considerations: Either

$$(1-\zeta)(K^*+S_i^*)-\zeta z<0$$

in which case it is optimal to set $\upsilon=0$, or

$$(1-\zeta)(K^*+S_i^*)-\zeta z\geq 0$$

and equation (8.7) implies that the optimal υ is given by

$$\upsilon=\frac{K_i}{K^*+S_i^*}$$

For this value of υ, in turn, it is optimal to set $K_i=K^*$, which means that $w=0$: whenever an external audit takes place with positive probability, the cost of the internal audit is reduced to zero (and therefore $\gamma=1$ is optimal). Since, moreover, external audits do not occur with probability one when q_1 is realized and an internal audit is triggered, this result implies that the overall audit costs for the principal are reduced compared with the situation where he could rely only on the external auditor. Note that this analysis also implies that $\varphi=0$ is optimal; that is, it is inefficient for the principal to rely only on a costly external audit.

The Kofman and Lawarrée analysis thus rationalizes the simultaneous use of internal and external auditing, where internal audits take place on a continuing basis, while external audits occur only intermittently on a random basis. This application highlights the richness of the principal-supervisor-agent framework when potential collusion is introduced.

Note, however, that this approach leaves open the issue of the enforcement of side contracts. Several attempts have been made to address this issue. First, in Tirole (1992) and Martimort (1999) collusion is possible through self-enforcing side contracts when auditor and agent interact repeatedly over time. An interesting implication of that analysis is that the principal may gain by forcing frequent rotation of auditors to preserve their independence and undermine collusion. Regular rotation of auditors has been proposed as a new regulatory requirement in the United States in the wake of the accounting scandals of 2001 and is mandated in Italy. Second, in Leppamaki (1998) and Laffont and Meleu (1997) collusion is modeled as an exchange of favors, with the supervisor suppressing damaging information about the agent in exchange for the agent suppressing harmful information about the supervisor.

8.4 Hierarchies

Much of the theory of organizations covered so far in this chapter is mostly applicable to small-scale firms. We now address one of the most difficult and least well understood questions in economics: What accounts for large organizations, firms with more than 100,000 employees, say? What is their role? Why do they exist? And how should they be organized internally?

The representative firm in micro- or macroeconomic textbooks is still the small business of the preindustrialization era. Yet, as many economic historians have documented (most notably Chandler, 1962, 1977, 1990), much of the economic development of the industrialization and postindustrialization eras has been driven by large-scale organizations, such as the large railroads of the 19th century (some with more than 100,000 employees) or large automobile manufacturers like General Motors (with more than 700,000 employees).

Despite the enormously important role these organizations play, formal economic theories of large firms and their internal organization are still few and far between. In this section we cover theories of hierarchies and large-scale firms that build on the basic multiagent moral-hazard paradigm discussed in this chapter. In our summary of the chapter we shall also point to the other recent formal theories of hierarchies, which are not based on a basic agency relation.

We shall be concerned with the following questions: Why do hierarchies exist? How are efficient hierarchical organizations designed? What determines the number of layers (or tiers) in a hierarchy, the pay structure, and employees' incentives along the hierarchical ladder?

Much of this section builds on the model by Qian (1994), which itself integrates several earlier models by Williamson (1967), Beckmann (1977), Rosen (1982), and, most importantly, Calvo and Wellisz (1978, 1979). The Calvo and Wellisz approach to hierarchies builds on the basic efficiency-wage model discussed in Chapter 4 and adds monitoring by hierarchical supervisors. The models by Williamson and others formalize the notion of *loss of control* in large multilayer firms—that is, the idea that monitoring and management of employees becomes more difficult as the number of layers that separate the manager from his employees becomes higher. As we shall see, when one adds the notion of loss of control to a model of hierarchies à la Calvo and Wellisz, as Qian does, one can formulate a theory of the optimal size and internal organization of firms.

Consider a hierarchy composed of M layers or tiers. For notational convenience, our convention will be to denote the highest tier, occupied by the principal, as tier number 0, and the bottom layer of workers as tier number M. For simplicity, we shall also ignore potential integer problems and assume that the identical number of subordinates for any given manager in any given tier (obtained by dividing the number of employees in tier $l + 1$ by the number of employees in tier l) is always an integer number. We shall refer to this number as the *span of control* of the managers in a given tier. Thus, let x_l be the number of agents in tier l and m_{l+1} the span of control in tier l; then the number of agents in tier $l + 1$ is given by $x_l m_{l+1}$. Also, in what follows we assume that there are N workers in the bottom layer: $x_M = N$.

With this notation in hand, let the total output of the hierarchy be

$\theta N q_M$

where θ denotes the profitability of the business, N the number of productive workers, or scale of the business, and q_M the effective output per productive worker in an M-layered hierarchy. Following Qian, we model loss of control by assuming that

$q_l = a_l q_{l-1}, \quad \text{where } a_l \leq 1$

so that

$q_M = a_M a_{M-1} \cdots a_1 a_0$

There is, thus, a lower loss of control the higher are the a_l's. In a first-best world the organization would have no loss of control because all the layers would set $a_l = 1$. However, loss of control arises in a second-best world as the variables a_l are hidden actions chosen by each employee in layer l. In the second-best problem Qian analyzes only the principal faces no incentive problem and sets $a_0 = 1$. For all other layers, $a_l \leq 1$, and an efficiency wage determines the level of a_l as follows: Each (risk-neutral) employee's payoff in layer l is given by a fixed wage, w_l, which is paid if she is found not to be shirking, minus her cost of effort $\psi(a_l)$. Each employee's effort provision is monitored by her supervisor with probability p_l. If the employee is found to be shirking, then she gets no compensation. Therefore, as we have seen in Chapter 4, an employee's maximum level of effort given the wage w_l and the probability of monitoring p_l is determined by the incentive constraint

$$w_l - \psi(a_l) = (1 - p_l)w_l$$

where the RHS denotes the employee's expected payoff when she shirks and sets $a = 0$.

The probability of monitoring any given agent in layer l, in turn, is determined as follows: When a supervisor has m_l agents to monitor, she can only supervise each agent in her span of control with probability

$$p_l = \frac{1}{m_l}$$

In other words, the time a supervisor can spend checking on a subordinate is inversely related to the number of subordinates under her control. This relation is quite intuitive. Substituting for p_l, we obtain the following fundamental equation linking pay to span of control and performance:

$$w_l = \psi(a_l)m_l$$

From this equation we can see the fundamental trade-off that shapes the form of the organization and the number of hierarchical layers. Suppose there were only two layers, layer 0 occupied by the principal and layer 1 filled by N productive workers. Then, to achieve a level of effort a_M for all the workers, the principal might have to pay a large wage

$$w_M = \psi(a_M)N$$

when N is large. The principal might then be better off setting up a three-layer hierarchy with an intermediate layer of supervisors, each with a span of control of m_1 workers. Setting up such an intermediate layer would reduce the principal's own span from N to N/m_1 and would increase the probability of inspection of each worker from $1/N$ to $1/m_1$. The benefit of such a deepening of the organization is that now a level of effort a_M for any worker can be elicited with a much lower wage of

$$w_M = \psi(a_M)m_1$$

The cost of this deepening, however, is that now the principal must also pay a wage w_1 to N/m_1 supervisors. In addition, these supervisors must each be incentivized to reduce the loss of control resulting from the addition of the intermediate layer. Thus, if the principal wants to have no loss of control whatsoever, he needs to remunerate his supervisors at an efficiency wage of

$$w_1 = \psi(1)\frac{N}{m_1}$$

Thus the principal's organization-design problem when moving from a two- to a three-layer hierarchy is to determine the optimal span of control in the middle layer and the optimal loss of control at the two bottom layers. If he gets more supervisors, he can reduce his own span of control and thus reduce both the wage per supervisor and the loss of control in the middle layer. However, he has to pay more supervisors.[4]

More generally, the principal's organization-design problem for an exogenous scale N takes the following form:

$$\underset{m_l, a_l, x_l, M}{Max} \left\{ \theta N q_M - \sum_{l=1}^{M} \psi(a_l) m_l x_l \right\}$$

subject to

$$x_l = x_{l-1} m_l$$

$$q_l = q_{l-1} a_l$$

$$x_0 = q_0 = 1$$

$$x_M = N$$

and

$$0 \le a_l \le 1 \quad \text{for all } l$$

As is easy to see, this is a rather complex optimization problem, involving both integer variables (the number of tiers) and continuous variables.

---

4. Note that Qian specifies two separate activities in middle layers, supervision of employees on the one hand and reduction of loss of control on the other. Moreover, only one of these activities involves an incentive problem. Supervision of employees in his model is a purely mechanical activity. Other, perhaps more natural, models specify a single supervisory activity in middle layers, which, however, involves an incentive problem. This is the approach taken in Calvo and Wellisz (1978), for example. The advantage of Qian's formulation, however, is that it leads to a more tractable optimization problem.

Unfortunately, optimization problems involving the design of hierarchies are inherently difficult ones. This is, perhaps, an important reason why hierarchies have not been studied more by economists. Progress in characterizing optimal hierarchies has been made in the literature either by formulating a problem that is sufficiently regular so that an explicit solution to a difference equation can be found (see, for example, Radner, 1993) or, as Qian has chosen to do, by taking M, the number of layers in the hierarchy, to be a continuous variable, so that the optimal hierarchy can be characterized using calculus of variations.[5]

Rather than attempt to provide a more technically involved discussion of the solution to the general continuous problem considered by Qian, we shall limit ourselves here to a simple example of hierarchies with only two or three tiers ($M = 1$ or $M = 2$).

Consider first the case of a two-tier hierarchy with $M = 1$. Recalling that $w = \psi(a)N$, which is paid to N agents, the principal's optimization problem for this hierarchy is fairly simple:

$$\max_{a}\{\theta Na - \psi(a)N^2\}$$

subject to

$$0 \leq a \leq 1$$

The first-order condition for this problem is given by

$$\psi'(a) = \frac{\theta}{N}$$

It is convenient to take the following functional form for the effort cost function:

$$\psi(a) = a^3$$

For this functional form, the first-order condition yields the simple expression

$$a = \left(\frac{\theta}{3N}\right)^{1/2}$$

5. As Van Zandt (1995) points out, however, formulating a continuous problem as Qian has done is not without conceptual problems. He shows that, as much as continuous approximations can be justified with respect to x_l, they are not necessarily valid with respect to M.

We shall take θ to be low enough so that the optimal a is always strictly less than one.[6] We can also back out the formula for the efficiency wage,

$$w = \left(\frac{\theta}{3}\right)^{3/2} N^{1/2}$$

to observe that productivity per worker is decreasing with the number of workers, while at the same time wages are increasing in the number of workers.

Consider now the three-tier hierarchy with $M = 2$. The principal's problem is now the much more complex problem

$$\max_{a_1, a_2, x_1, m_1, m_2} \{\theta N a_1 a_2 - \psi(a_1) m_1 x_1 - \psi(a_2) m_2 N\}$$

subject to

$$N = x_1 m_2$$

$$x_1 = m_1$$

$$a_1 \leq 1$$

and

$$a_2 \leq 1$$

Substituting for m_1 and m_2, we obtain the unconstrained problem,

$$\max_{a_1, a_2, x_1} \left\{\theta N a_1 a_2 - \psi(a_1) x_1^2 - \psi(a_2) \frac{N^2}{x_1}\right\}$$

which can be solved in the following three steps:

First Step: Take a_1 and a_2 as Given, and Optimize with Respect to x_1. With the functional form $\psi(a_i) = a_i^3$ the first- and second-order conditions with respect to x_1 reduce to

$$a_2^3 \left(\frac{N}{x_1}\right)^2 = a_1^3 2 x_1$$

and

$$-a_1^3 2 - 2 a_2^3 N^2 / x_1^3 < 0$$

6. Notice that for simplicity we have suppressed the principal's own effort cost in setting $a_0 = 1$.

From the first-order condition we therefore obtain that

$$x_1 = \frac{a_2}{a_1} N^{2/3} 2^{-1/3} \tag{8.8}$$

Second Step: Substitute for the Value of x_1 in Equation (8.8) into the Objective Function and Maximize with Respect to a_1. The reduced maximand now is

$$\max_{a_1, a_2} \{ \theta N a_1 a_2 - a_1 a_2^2 N^{4/3} (2^{-2/3} + 2^{1/3}) \}$$

or

$$\max_{a_1, a_2} \{ \theta N a_1 a_2 - a_1 a_2^2 \kappa N^{4/3} \}$$

where

$$\kappa = (2^{-2/3} + 2^{1/3}) \approx (6.75)^{1/3} < 2$$

From this maximand, it is easy to see that the principal's objective is linear in a_1, so that $a_1 = 1$ is optimal given that

$$\theta N a_2 - a_2^2 \kappa N^{4/3}$$

must be positive at the optimal a_2.

Third Step: Substitute for $a_1 = 1$ in the Principal's Objective and Solve for a_2. The principal's objective now is

$$\max_{a_2} \{ \theta N a_2 - a_2^2 N^{4/3} \kappa \}$$

subject to

$$0 \le a_2 \le 1$$

and the first-order condition to this problem yields the solution

$$a_2 = \frac{\theta}{2\kappa} N^{-1/3}$$

Again, we shall take θ to be small enough that $a_2 < 1$.

This procedure provides a complete characterization of the solution, and we are now ready to compare the two hierarchies with $M = 1$ and $M = 2$.

A first observation is that optimal effort provision is lower at lower tiers in the hierarchy: $a_2 \le a_1$. That is, agents work harder the higher up in the hierarchy they are. This is a general observation that is valid in the general problem considered by Qian. There is a fundamental economic reason for this result: the higher up in the hierarchy one is, the more worker outputs one's effort enters into. Since supervisors' effort enters multiplicatively into each worker's output, the marginal return of each supervisor's effort is magnified by the span of control of that supervisor, while the marginal cost of the supervisor's effort is the same as for workers. It follows that supervisors should work harder the higher up the ladder they are.

A second observation is that the three-tier hierarchy ($M = 2$) is more likely to dominate the two-tier hierarchy ($M = 1$) when θ and/or N increases. To see this relation, note that, after substituting for the optimal efforts and control spans in each hierarchy, we obtain the following expressions for the principal's profit under both hierarchies:

$$Na(\theta - a^2 N) = (2 \cdot 3^{-3/2})\theta^{3/2} N^{1/2}$$
$$\approx 0.5 \, \theta^{3/2} N^{1/2}$$

for $M = 1$, and

$$Na_2(\theta - a_2 N^{1/3}\kappa) = (4\kappa)^{-1}\theta^2 N^{2/3}$$
$$\approx 0.15 \, \theta^2 N^{2/3}$$

for $M = 2$. Therefore, $M = 2$ dominates $M = 1$ when $\theta^{1/2}N^{1/6} \geq 3$. Again, this observation is valid for the general problem. When the scale of the firm increases, it becomes profitable to add more layers to the hierarchy. And the depth of the hierarchy grows faster with scale when the overall productivity of the firm is higher.

This latter observation is easy to understand when combined with the third observation that in each hierarchy effort increases with θ and decreases in N. This is intuitive and again a general conclusion: When θ increases, the return on effort is higher, and since the cost-of-effort function is strictly convex, it pays more to introduce an intermediate layer at higher efforts to cut down on wage costs at lower layers. Similarly, an increase in N reduces the level of supervision in hierarchy $M = 1$ and, as we have shown, results in a cut in effort. Consequently, a rise in N increases the gain of an intermediate layer, to save on wages at the bottom layer.

Our final observation about wages in hierarchy $M = 2$ is that w_1 increases with both θ and N, while w_2 increases with θ but decreases with N. Indeed, for the optimal three-tier hierarchy we have

$$w_1 = \psi(a_1)x_1 = x_1 = a_2 N^{2/3} 2^{-1/3} = \frac{\theta}{2\kappa} N^{1/3} 2^{-1/3}$$

and

$$w_2 = \psi(a_2)\frac{N}{x_1} = a_2^2 N^{1/3} 2^{1/3} = \left(\frac{\theta}{2\kappa}\right)^2 N^{-1/3} 2^{1/3}$$

The intuition for these results is that a rise in θ makes higher effort optimal at the bottom, which requires a higher wage w_2 and therefore more supervision. But when adding more supervisors the principal's span of control rises, and to compensate for the resulting supervision loss the principal must pay higher wages w_1 to his supervisors. In contrast, while a higher N results in a higher wage for supervisors, to compensate for the supervision loss in the middle tier, it results in a lower wage at the bottom layer as supervision at that level improves with the addition of more supervisors. Interestingly, therefore, when N increases there is an increase in wage inequality in the organization—that is, a rise in w_1/w_2.[7]

To sum up, Qian's theory as illustrated in this simple example yields many empirically consistent predictions about organizations: (1) The prediction that effort decreases when one goes down the hierarchical ladder is broadly consistent with casual observation on how hard employees in large firms work. (2) The prediction that the optimal number of tiers of the organization increases with profitability and scale also appears to be in step with reality. (3) The conclusion that, for a given number of tiers, wages increase as the profitability of the organization increases is consistent with reality, and more interestingly, the prediction that wages at the bottom layer decrease with scale, which at first sight seems contradictory, also appears to be borne out in reality. (4) The result that for the three-tier organization (and more generally for organizations with more than three tiers) wage inequality within the organization increases as its scale of operation increases is also in step with casual observation on how pay scales in firms vary with size.

---

7. Note that when $N \geq 4$, we have $w_1 \geq w_2$ as $a_2 \leq 1$.

Finally, an important result in Qian, which we have not been able to illustrate in our simple example, is that, when the firm can optimize over the number of workers N, then in general there is a determinate optimal finite size of the firm, which is increasing in θ. The main reason why the optimal size of the firm is finite is that the principal has to incur a loss of control as he adds more layers. Thus Qian's model articulates and extends Kaldor's theory for why firms eventually face decreasing returns to scale—because they are unable to perfectly duplicate the scarce managerial input of the top manager. As compelling as this explanation is, it unfortunately does not fully resolve the question of the optimal size of firms. In Qian's model loss of control is assumed and not fully explained. In particular, Qian remains silent on the question of why firms would be unable to avoid loss of control through selective intervention by top management. To be able to articulate rigorous answers to this fundamental question, we need to move to Part IV, dealing with incomplete contracts and control.

8.5 Summary

In this chapter we have introduced the main approaches to the theory of the firm that are based on a multiagent moral-hazard contracting problem. We have seen how the introduction of competition between agents can improve their incentive contract and how competition can be undermined by collusion among agents, but also how competition itself may undermine cooperation among agents. We have pursued the analysis of collusion further in the context of a principal-supervisor-agent relation and analyzed how auditors' incentives must be structured to minimize collusion or corruption. Finally, we have explored how a theory of firm size and internal hierarchical structure can be built on the idea of monitoring and limited attention.

The main insights of our analysis for the internal organization of firms are the following:

• As Alchian and Demsetz (1972) first proposed, the main purpose of a firm may be to mitigate incentive problems arising in situations involving multiple agents. A firm may be described in simple terms as involving a boss who supervises workers' effort provision, possibly assisted by a group of supervisors.

• As Holmström (1982b) first pointed out, to maximize incentives for all team members it may be efficient for the firm to write a financial contract with a third party, the *budget breaker*. Interestingly, this contract may resemble a debt contract. Thus the theory of moral hazard in teams may provide yet another rationale for debt financing.

• When agents' individual performance is observable it may be efficient to base their compensation in part on their relative performance, as is done for example in *tournaments*, studied by Lazear and Rosen (1981) and Green and Stokey (1983), in particular. As stressed by Holmström (1982b), the main advantage of relative performance schemes is that they expose risk-averse agents to less risk when agents' individual performance is subject to common shocks. The strength of tournaments as a particular relative-performance-evaluation scheme is that they reduce the principal's incentive to manipulate the outcome ex post, as he must pay out the prizes to some winners anyway.

• The main drawback of relative-performance evaluation schemes is that they may foster destructive competitive behavior, such as sabotage of other agents' output, and generally undermine cooperation among agents. Thus, as detailed, for example, by Holmström and Milgrom (1990), in situations where cooperation is likely to bring large benefits and where agents' individual performance is only subject to small common shocks, it may be optimal to move away from relative-performance schemes and instead have agents share the returns of their actions. It may then even be worth letting the agents collude.

• In vertical principal-supervisor-agent structures, however, it is generally not optimal to let the agent collude with the supervisor. As detailed by Tirole (1986), collusion-proof incentive schemes in such structures generally result in dulled incentives for the agent, relative to situations where collusion is not feasible, but enhanced incentives for the supervisor (or auditor). The analysis of optimal incentive contracting to prevent collusion in these structures yields a number of important insights on how incentives of the accounting and auditing industry ought to be structured.

These are some of the main lessons to be drawn from this chapter. There is a rapidly growing literature on organizations and the multiagent moral-hazard perspective on firms. We have covered only some of the foundational studies in this chapter. For a more wide-ranging treatment of the themes discussed here we refer the reader to the book on the economics of organization by Milgrom and Roberts (1992) and the survey on the theory of the firm by Holmström and Tirole (1989).

8.6   Literature Notes

As we have already emphasized, the founding articles on the multiagent moral-hazard perspective on the firm are by Alchian and Demsetz (1972) and Holmström (1982b). We have already discussed many of the subsequent contributions they have spurred in the body of the chapter. An important related general analysis that we have not covered in the chapter is Mookherjee (1984), which considers a more general framework than Holmström (1982b).

We have also not had the space to cover several different interesting areas of application of contracting with multi-agent moral hazard. Thus, one set of applications is sharecropping, partnerships, and franchise contracts, which all have been modeled as contracting problems with multi-agent moral hazard (see, in particular, Eswaran and Kotwal, 1985, for an early such model of sharecropping; Mathewson and Winter, 1985, and Lal, 1990, for models of franchising contracts; Demski and Sappington, 1991, and Bhattacharya and Lafontaine, 1995, for models of partnership contracts with double-sided moral hazard). Another important area of application, which we have not been able to cover, is joint ventures and in particular research joint ventures (see, in particular, Bhattacharya, Glazer, and Sappington, 1992, for a model of multi-agent moral hazard and disclosure of information in a research joint venture). A third large area of application is the auditing and accounting literature (see, for example, Demski and Sappington, 1984, 1987, and Melumad, Mookherjee, and Reichelstein, 1995). Finally, an important omission from the chapter, and which possibly might be the culmination of this approach, is the contribution of Holmström and Milgrom (1994) on the firm viewed as an incentive system.

Two areas on which there is now a substantial body of economic literature and on which we have barely touched are, first, collusion in organizations and, second, hierarchies. Following the original article on collusion in principal-supervisor-agent structures by Tirole (1986), the literature has grown in a number of interesting directions. Laffont and Martimort (1997, 2000) have explored collusion under asymmetric information and dealt with issues relating to the modeling of mechanism design of side contracts. Felli (1996), Strausz (1997), Baliga and Sjostrom (1998), Laffont and

Martimort (1998), and Macho-Stadler and Perez-Castrillo (1998) explore the idea that delegation to the supervisor or decentralization may be a way of reducing the scope for collusion. The difficult problem of collusion with soft information has also been explored by Baliga (1999) and Faure-Grimaud, Laffont, and Martimort (2003).

Similarly, the economic literature on hierarchies includes a number of alternative approaches besides moral hazard and loss of control, that Calvo and Wellisz (1978, 1979), Williamson (1967), and Qian (1994) have emphasized. Optimal hierarchies to minimize the costs of information processing and communication have been analyzed in Keren and Levhari (1979, 1983), Radner (1992, 1993), Bolton and Dewatripont (1994), Van Zandt (1998, 1999), Prat (1997), and Vayanos (2003). Another approach to the design of hierarchies by Crémer (1980), Aoki (1986), Geanakoplos and Milgrom (1991), and Marschak and Reichelstein (1995, 1998) is based on bounded rationality and the limited attention of managers. Another role of hierarchies explored in Garicano (2000) and Beggs (2001) is the facilitation of the handling and allocation of more or less specialized tasks to generalists and specialists. Finally, Sah and Stiglitz (1986) explore the question of the optimal decision structure (hierarchical or polyarchical) for the approval of risky projects by firms, when managers can make mistakes in their project evaluations. Hart and Moore (2000) also deal with the issue of the optimal allocation of decision rights in an organization and explore the idea of hierarchies as precedence rules.

All these approaches attest to the richness of the economic question of the internal organization of firms. They point to the complementary role of hierarchical institutions to markets, and also to the richness of alternative ways of allocating tasks, goods, and services besides trading in organized markets.

REPEATED BILATERAL CONTRACTING

The third part of this book deals with ongoing, or repeated, contractual relations between two parties. New conceptual issues arise here that relate to *renegotiation* of long-term contracts and the inability of contracting parties to always *commit* to or enforce long-term contractual agreements.

The fact that a contractual relation may be enduring affects incentive provision and information revelation in fundamental ways. For example, in the early stages of a contractual relation the agent may hold back on revealing information that could be used against her in later stages of the relation. Alternatively, the agent may engage in *reputation building* activities to enhance her future value to the principal. In short, repeated interaction opens up a whole variety of new incentive issues, but it also permits more refined contractual responses.

In principle, long-term contracts could be ever increasing in complexity as the contractual relation persists and optimal contracting problems could become increasingly intractable. This is all the more to be expected if the contracting parties may renegotiate the contract along the way. We shall explain, however, that paradoxically, optimal long-term contracts could actually take a simpler form in an ongoing relation than in a one-shot relation. They may, for example, specify a simple linear relation between output performance and compensation, or they may just specify simple performance targets.

At a more conceptual level, a major difference with the static optimal contracting problems analyzed in Part I is that in repeated contracting situations the *revelation principle* no longer generally applies. As a result, the characterization of optimal long-term contracts under asymmetric information is often significantly more complex. However, if the revelation principle no longer applies, there is nevertheless a closely related general principle that helps in determining the optimal form of the contract: The *renegotiation-proofness principle*. According to this principle optimal long-term contracts take the form of contracts that will not be renegotiated in the future. The determination of optimal renegotiation-proof contracts then generally involves solving an optimization problem where the by now familiar incentive constraints are replaced by tighter renegotiation-proofness constraints.

The first chapter in this third part (Chapter 9) considers optimal long-term contracts under *hidden information*. The second chapter (Chapter 10) considers optimal long-term contracts under *hidden actions*. Much of the material in these two chapters draws on fairly recent research and is synthesized here for the first time. Unlike the material in Part I, the concepts and methods explored in this part are not as well digested and may well evolve significantly in response to future research breakthroughs.

Dynamic Adverse Selection

In this chapter we consider repeated interactions between two contracting parties under one-sided asymmetric information. We analyze two opposite cases: one where the agent's type is drawn once and remains fixed over time; the other where there is a new independent draw every period. In the first situation, dynamic contracting issues arise because of the gradual elimination of the informational asymmetry over time. The second situation leads to questions of intertemporal distribution of allocative distortions as a way to reduce the agent's informational rent. We begin by considering the case where the agent's type remains fixed over time. As in Chapter 3, the game-theoretic concept we rely upon is perfect Bayesian equilibrium.

9.1 Dynamic Adverse Selection with Fixed Types

The basic issue at the heart of dynamic-adverse-selection models with fixed types can be understood with the following example, which considers a seller facing a buyer whose valuation he does not know. As seen in Chapter 2, in a static setting, the seller may want to set a price so high that he does not sell with probability one, even if his production cost is below the lowest possible buyer valuation. This is an example of the classic trade-off between allocative efficiency and informational rent extraction under adverse selection.

What happens, however, once the buyer has made her buying decision? If she did not buy, the seller now *knows* that her valuation is low. The information revealed through the execution of the contract therefore opens up a new trading opportunity, at a lower price. While this opportunity is Pareto-improving ex post, it ends up hurting the seller from an ex ante point of view, because high-valuation buyers will anticipate that an initial unwillingness to trade will prompt the seller to lower his price. Recontracting thus limits the ability of the contract to rely on ex post allocative inefficiency for rent extraction purposes; to put it differently, this is a case where sequential optimization differs from overall ex ante optimization.

This commitment problem under adverse selection is relevant in a variety of settings that we shall consider. In fact, *mutually efficient renegotiation* arises whenever the uninformed party has an interest in becoming "softer" with the informed party. It happens, as we have stressed, with monopolists facing buyers with uncertain valuations (*bargaining/durable-good monopoly problem*). It also arises with creditors who do not want to terminate entrepreneurs with bad projects because of previously sunk expenses (*soft-budget-constraint problem*). More generally, the issue of renegotiation arises whenever the parties are protected by a *long-term contract* but cannot commit against sequential, mutually profitable, alterations of this contract.

A second commitment problem in dynamic-adverse-selection settings concerns *unilateral contractual* gains: When the parties can sign only short-term contracts, ex post opportunism can also arise because of information revealed by contract execution. This is the case of the *ratchet effect,* by which the uninformed party offers the informed party "tougher" contracts if it learns that its productivity or valuation is higher. The mechanics of short-term contracting is somewhat different from that of long-term contracting with renegotiation. Once again, however, what is an ex post unilateral gain for the uninformed party turns out to be detrimental from an ex ante point of view, because it is anticipated by the informed party.

How can the uninformed party mitigate these two commitment problems? Several ideas have been explored in the literature:

• First, one can design contracts whose execution limits the amount of information revealed about the informed party's type, that is, contracts with (partial) pooling in the allocative choices of the informed party. This approach limits ex post recontracting opportunities.

• A more extreme version of this idea is to make it impossible for the uninformed party to observe in timely fashion the contract choices of the informed party, by not investing in the appropriate monitoring systems. This leads to "simpler" and more "rigid" contracts than the optimal static counterparts.

• More generally, the literature obviously stresses the benefits of signing *long-term contracts*, even if the parties cannot commit not to engage in future Pareto-improving renegotiation. While a long-term contract protects each party against ex post opportunistic behavior by the other party, short-term contracts can instead help alleviate excessive uninformed-party softness. For example, making it hard for an initial creditor to provide refinancing can limit the soft-budget-constraint problem mentioned earlier.

In section 9.1.1 we first detail a dynamic buyer-seller problem and discuss the consequences of the two potential problems facing an uninformed seller, that is, lack of commitment to engage in Pareto-improving renegotiation of long-term (or sale) contracts and lack of commitment not to engage in opportunistic behavior under short-term (or rental) contracting. We then turn to various other applications. Section 9.1.2 considers the renegotiation of insurance contracts and discusses the desirability of restricting the information available to the uninformed party about the behavior of the informed party. Section 9.1.3 turns to credit markets and the soft budget constraint, and the optimality of relying on a sequence of uninformed parties to alleviate commitment problems. Finally, section 9.1.4 revisits these insights in a much-studied application, the regulation of a monopolist with private information on its intrinsic productivity.

9.1.1 Coasian Dynamics

An important potential effect of repeated interactions is to reduce monopoly power by creating intertemporal competition between current and future incarnations of the monopolist. This effect has been noted first in durable-goods markets, where it has been observed that a monopoly seller may face competition from old buyers who sell the good in secondhand markets. A related point has been articulated by Coase (1972), who conjectured that a monopolist selling a perfectly durable good in a world with no discounting would be forced to sell essentially at marginal cost. The logic behind his conjecture is that early buyers would not accept monopoly prices if they anticipate that future prices will decline following their purchase of the durable good. The expected price decline would indeed follow if there is a fixed total demand for the durable good. Coase's basic logic is relevant more generally to any dynamic contracting situation where the agent's type is fixed over time, as emphasized by Stokey (1981), Bulow (1982), Fudenberg and Tirole (1983), Gul, Sonnenschein, and Wilson (1986), and Hart and Tirole (1988). In this section, we follow the analysis of Hart and Tirole (1988), who have detailed the comparison between short-term and long-term contracts.

We consider a problem of a buyer and seller ("she" and "he," respectively) with bilateral risk neutrality, two periods, two buyer types, and a single unit of good to exchange. We then briefly extend the analysis to three periods.

Specifically, assume a buyer that has valuation v_i per period of consumption of the good [with $0 < v_L < v_H$ and, initially, $\Pr(v_H) = \beta$, which is common knowledge] while the seller has zero valuation for the good. The seller maximizes the net present value of his expected revenue, while the buyer maximizes the net present value of her consumption minus her payment to the seller. Both parties have a common discount factor $\delta \leq 1$.

Finally, we call x_{it} the probability that the type-i buyer consumes the good in period t.

9.1.1.1   Full Commitment Solution

Consider first what the seller could achieve by making a single take-it-or-leave-it two-period contract offer. Let us define net present values as follows: $\Delta = \delta^0 + \delta^1 = 1 + \delta$, $X_i = x_{i1} + \delta x_{i2}$, and T_i is the net present value of the payment of the buyer of type i to the seller.

Under full commitment, because buyer types are fixed, the seller's problem reduces to the static problem. Indeed, the seller offers the buyer a menu $\{(X_L, T_L), (X_H, T_H)\}$ that solves

$$\max_{X_i, T_i}(1 - \beta)T_L + \beta T_H$$

subject to

$$v_i X_i - T_i \geq 0 \quad i = L, H$$

$$v_i X_i - T_i \geq v_i X_j - T_j \quad i, j = L, H$$

and

$$0 \leq X_i \leq \Delta \quad i = L, H$$

As explained in Chapter 2, at the optimum the participation constraint for $i = L$ and the incentive constraint for $i = H$ and $j = L$ are binding, so that the seller's problem reduces to

$$\max_{X_i}(1 - \beta)v_L X_L + \beta[v_H X_H - (v_H - v_L)X_L]$$

The solution is $X_H = \Delta$, and $X_L = \Delta$ if

$$\beta < \frac{v_L}{v_H} \equiv \beta'$$

in which case $T_L = v_L = T_H = v_L$. Indeed, selling to both types means collecting the low valuation only. Instead, if $\beta > \beta'$, that is, if the probability of facing a low-valuation buyer is low enough, it is best to exclude her and set $X_L = 0 = T_L$, which allows the seller to set $T_H = v_H$. This is the trade-off highlighted in Chapter 2. Since the problem here is linear, we thus have either ex post efficiency or a corner solution with zero consumption.

To make things interesting, we now assume $\beta > \beta'$. This assumption makes a difference after the period-1 choice by the buyer: once she has declined to consume, the seller knows that her valuation is v_L. It will then be in his interest to lower the price in period 2. This response, however, will be anticipated by the buyer initially.

9.1.1.2   Selling without Commitment: The Durable-Good Monopoly Problem

If, at each period t, the seller can make only *spot-contracting* offers to the buyer, that is, offers to buy the good in period t at price P_t, what is the perfect Bayesian equilibrium of this game?

If the buyer buys in period 1, the game is over. If the buyer does not buy in period 1 after a price offer P_1, call $\beta(P_1)$ the probability assessment by the seller that he is facing a type-H buyer. This assessment has to be compatible with Bayes' rule.

The continuation equilibrium in period 2 has to be $P_2 = v_H$ if $\beta(P_1) > \beta'$ and $P_2 = v_L$ otherwise, by sequential rationality. In any case, the type-L buyer is left with zero surplus in period 2. This buyer thus accepts a period-1 offer if and only if

$$P_1 \leq v_L \Delta$$

What about the type-H buyer? If she expects $P_2 = v_H$, she is getting zero surplus in period 2 and accepts a period-1 offer if and only if

$$P_1 \leq v_H \Delta$$

If instead she expects $P_2 = v_L$, she is more reluctant in period 1 and accepts an offer if and only if

$$P_1 \leq v_H \Delta - \delta(v_H - v_L) = v_H + \delta v_L \equiv P'$$

The seller is thus faced with three choices in period 1:

• First, he can set a price $P_1 \leq v_L \Delta = v_L(1 + \delta)$ and sell with probability 1 in period 1. The maximum revenue he can obtain in this range is by setting the highest such price. His revenue is then $v_L(1 + \delta)$.

• Second, he can sell in period 2 to the consumer of type L. Then the second period price will be v_L. Consequently, the highest possible first-period price is P', and the seller's revenue is

$$(1 - \beta)\delta v_L + \beta P' = (1 - \beta)\delta v_L + \beta(v_H + \delta v_L) = \beta v_H + \delta v_L$$

Since we have assumed that $\beta > v_L/v_H$, this option is better for the seller than the first one.

• Third, the seller can set a first-period price higher than P', but less than or equal to $v_H(1 + \delta)$. In this case, the continuation equilibrium has to be in mixed strategies: for $P_2 = v_L$, the type-H buyer does not want to buy in period 1, so $P_2 = v_L$ cannot be a continuation equilibrium; and for $P_2 = v_H$, the type-H buyer wants to buy in period 1, so $P_2 = v_H$ cannot be a continuation equilibrium either. In order to make the seller indifferent between setting his second-period price at v_L or at v_H, we must have $v_L = \beta(P_1)v_H$. This means having the type-H buyer accept the first-period offer with probability γ such that

$$\beta' \equiv \frac{v_L}{v_H} = \frac{\beta(1-\gamma)}{\beta(1-\gamma)+(1-\beta)}$$

or

$$\gamma = \frac{\beta - \beta'}{\beta(1-\beta')}$$

In turn, the buyer has to be indifferent between accepting and rejecting P_1, implying that the probability that $P_2 = v_H$ given P_1, which we call $\sigma(P_1)$, has to satisfy

$$v_H(1+\delta) - P_1 = \delta[1 - \sigma(P_1)](v_H - v_L)$$

which means

$$\sigma(P_1) = 1 - \frac{v_H(1+\delta) - P_1}{\delta(v_H - v_L)}$$

A first-period price P_1 thus leads to randomization by the type-H buyer, with (constant) probability γ of accepting the seller offer, and second-period randomization by the seller, with probability $\sigma(P_1)$ of offering the high second-period price and probability $[1 - \sigma(P_1)]$ of offering the low second-period price. The expected revenue of the seller is then

$$\beta\gamma P_1 + [\beta(1-\gamma)+(1-\beta)]\delta v_L$$

which is maximized for the highest possible price in this range, that is, for $P_1 = v_H(1 + \delta)$ and for $\sigma(P_1) = 1$. The seller's revenue is then

$$\beta\gamma v_H(1+\delta)+[\beta(1-\gamma)+(1-\beta)]\delta v_L$$

which, using the value of γ we computed earlier, equals

$$\frac{\beta-\beta'}{1-\beta'}v_H(1+\delta)+\left(1-\frac{\beta-\beta'}{1-\beta'}\right)\delta v_L$$

This expected revenue has to be compared with the seller's revenue under the second pricing strategy where he sells for sure to the type-H buyer only in period 1, that is, $\beta v_H + \delta v_L$. The preceding expression is increasing in β: for $\beta \to \beta'$, selling for sure is better than randomizing, because randomizing means selling with a very small probability in period 1. Instead, for $\beta \to 1$, selling for sure in period 1 is worse than randomizing, because by randomizing the seller can sell with a high probability at the high price v_H in period 1. There is thus a cutoff value of β above which randomizing is preferred and below which selling for sure to type-H is preferred.

Lack of commitment thus means that the seller cannot refrain from cutting prices when he becomes more pessimistic about the valuation of the buyer. Selling to the high-valuation buyer for sure in period 1 thus means having to settle for a lower first-period price than under commitment, because the buyer understands the price will be low in period 2. And keeping prices high means accepting that a sale will be less likely in period 1. This last strategy is profitable when the seller cannot hope to get much revenue from a low-valuation buyer in period 2, because the probability that he is facing such a buyer is low.

9.1.1.3   Renting without Commitment: The Ratchet Effect

The preceding analysis assumed a sale, that is, consumption with probability 1 in periods 1 *and* 2 by a buyer who had made her decision to buy in period 1. Another strategy is *spot rental*; that is, the buyer pays R_1 in period 1 just to consume in period 1, and the seller makes a new offer R_2 in period 2.

As is known from the durable-good-monopoly literature, renting could be an attractive alternative to selling for the monopolist (see, for example, Tirole, 1988). This result, however, relies on the assumption of *buyer anonymity:* the firm is supposed to face a continuum of anonymous buyers. Under a sale, the firm first serves the top part of the demand curve and cannot commit not to subsequently lower the price, thereby making high-valuation consumers reluctant to buy early, just as before. Instead, a rental solution gets around this problem because the seller faces the same demand curve period after period and *because he cannot keep track of who has already bought.*

If we assume instead that the seller faces a nonanonymous buyer, things change dramatically: In the case of a sale, the only problem for the seller in the previous situation was his inability to commit not to *lower* the price in period 2 when he thinks he is facing a type-*L* buyer. Now, a second problem is the seller's inability to commit not to *raise* the rental price in period 2 when he thinks he is facing a type-*H* buyer. This *ratchet effect* will also be taken into account by the type-*H* buyer.

What is the perfect Bayesian equilibrium? In period 2 it is the same as before for a given $\beta(R_1)$: $R_2 = v_H$ if $\beta(R_1) > \beta'$ and $R_2 = v_L$ otherwise. What about period 1? As in the previous section, we have three cases:

• Note that the type-*L* buyer does not accept any R_1 above v_L. One option for the seller is thus to set $R_1 = v_L$, rent to both types in period 1, and set $R_2 = v_H$ (because $\beta > v_L/v_H \equiv \beta'$). His revenue is then $v_L + \delta\beta v_H$.

• In a fully separating equilibrium, the highest first-period rental price the type-*H* buyer accepts is such that

$$v_H - R_1 \geq \delta(v_H - v_L)$$

Indeed, separating by renting in period 1 implies obtaining no surplus in period 2 ($R_2 = v_H$), while not renting in period 1 means obtaining the low rental price in period 2 ($R_2 = v_L$). In this case, the revenue for the seller is

$$\beta[v_H - \delta(v_H - v_L)] + \delta[\beta v_H + (1 - \beta)v_L]$$

This equals

$$\beta v_H + \delta v_L$$

which is higher than the expected revenue under the first strategy for $\delta \leq 1$, since $\beta > v_L/v_H \equiv \beta'$. This outcome is the same as the one obtained with full separation when the buyer is offered a sale contract. Note, however, that here the constraint on R_1 is

$$R_1 \leq (1 - \delta)v_H + \delta v_L$$

This means that separation is possible only for $\delta \leq 1$.

• Finally, the seller can induce semiseparation. As in the previous subsection, this means inducing the type-H buyer to rent with probability

$$\gamma = \frac{\beta - \beta'}{\beta(1 - \beta')}$$

in order to make the seller indifferent between setting $R_2 = v_L$ and $R_2 = v_H$ after a rejection of R_1. In turn, the buyer has to be indifferent between accepting and rejecting R_1. Since accepting means getting no surplus in period 2, the seller must set $R_2 = v_H$ with probability $\sigma(R_1)$ to satisfy the equation

$$v_H - R_1 = \delta[1 - \sigma(R_1)](v_H - v_L)$$

to keep the buyer indifferent between accepting or rejecting R_1. This means that

$$\sigma(R_1) = 1 - \frac{v_H - R_1}{\delta(v_H - v_L)}$$

Once again, the best such outcome for the seller is the highest possible rental price, that is, $R_1 = v_H$. In this case, the seller's revenue is

$$\beta \gamma v_H (1 + \delta) + [\beta(1 - \gamma) + (1 - \beta)]\delta v_L$$

which, using the value of γ we computed previously, equals

$$\frac{\beta - \beta'}{1 - \beta'} v_H + \left(1 - \frac{\beta - \beta'}{1 - \beta'}\right)\delta v_L$$

With two periods, we thus obtain the same outcome as with a sale. This result ceases to be true, however, with more than two periods, as we now show.

9.1.1.4   More Than Two Periods: On the Suboptimality of Renting without Commitment

With more than two periods, the ratchet effect can make the rental solution strictly worse than the sale solution, because the combination of dynamic incentive problems faced by the seller—his desire to lower the rental price for the type-L buyer and to raise it for the type-H buyer—limits the separation of types that can occur. Indeed one can show that, as a result of the seller's dynamic incentive problems, the type-H buyer cannot be made to accept early separating rental offers in equilibrium with probability 1.

To be specific, call β_t the seller's period-t probability assessment that the buyer has a high valuation given that she has rejected his offers in periods $1, 2, \ldots, t-1$ (we thus have $\beta_1 = \beta$). Then we have the following result: In a T-period rental problem, if $\delta + \delta^2 \geq 1$, we have $\beta_t \geq \beta'$ for all $t \leq T - 1$. This result can be proved by contradiction. Take the first period $t \geq 2$ such that $\beta_t < \beta'$. If $t \leq T - 1$ and the buyer has rejected the previous offers, the seller has an incentive to set the rental price equal to v_L from t on. If the buyer has accepted the previous offer, the seller from then on sets the rental price equal to v_H. For a type-H buyer to accept the offer at $t - 1$, we must therefore have

$$v_H - R_{t-1} \geq (v_H - v_L)(\delta + \ldots + \delta^{T-t+1}) \geq (v_H - v_L)(\delta + \delta^2)$$

But this implies $R_{t-1} \leq v_L$, which means that both types of buyers take the R_{t-1} offer, a contradiction with $\beta_{t-1} \geq \beta' > \beta_t$.

In the rental case, there is thus a limited amount of revelation of types that is possible before the last two periods. This limitation implies in particular that, when full separation is optimal in the two-period problem (which is the case for β close enough to β'), the sale outcome is strictly better than the rental outcome in the three-period problem. Indeed, in the latter problem, the seller could sell in period 1 to the type-H buyer at a price

$$P_1 = v_H + (\delta + \delta^2)v_L$$

and in period 2 to the type-L buyer at a price

$$P_2 = (1 + \delta)v_L$$

In contrast, in the rental outcome, he only has the following two choices:

• First, set $R_1 > v_L$, so as to have $\beta_2 = \beta'$. The continuation payoff as of period 2, however, is only $(1 + \delta)v_L$ (because the seller randomizes and thus gains nothing when he sets a rental price different from v_L). Moreover, in period 1, we have $R_1 \leq v_H$ and a probability of renting strictly less than the probability of facing the type-H buyer. This outcome is thus worse than the sale outcome.

• Second, set $R_1 = v_L$, so as to have the two-period full-separation outcome starting in period 2. But this is like the sale outcome, with period 2 replacing period 1. This is worse again, however, because $\delta < 1$ and $\beta v_H > v_L$.

The suboptimality of renting with nonanonymous buyers relative to selling illustrated in this three-period example is a general phenomenon, as shown by Hart and Tirole (1988). To summarize, in the durable good monopoly problem renting dominates sales if buyers remain anonymous, but otherwise sales dominate renting.

9.1.1.5   Long-Term Contracts and Renegotiation

The previous subsections contrasted the full-commitment solution and the no-commitment, spot-contracting solution. In between these two cases is the case where long-term contracts are feasible but the seller cannot commit not to offer the buyer a new contract at the beginning of period 2 that would replace the initial contract *if the buyer finds it acceptable*. This case differs from the full-commitment solution, where the seller is assumed to be able to refrain not only from engaging in *opportunistic* behavior (the ratchet effect) but also from making *Pareto-improving* offers (cutting the price to sell at mutually agreeable terms).

This intermediate case is very realistic. Indeed, by contractual enforcement, we typically mean protection against opportunistic contract violations that hurt a contracting party. Contractual enforcement is limited to situations where one party complains about a violation and does not prevent the parties from simultaneously agreeing to tear up the agreement and sign a new one.[1] Pareto-improving renegotiation is a concern because, once again, what is Pareto optimal as of period 2 may not be Pareto optimal as of period 1.

What is the optimal long-term sale contract without commitment not to renegotiate? Sequential Pareto optimality means that the seller has to set a second-period price that is sequentially optimal, that is, $P_2 = v_H$ if $\beta(P_1) > \beta'$ and $P_2 = v_L$ otherwise. This is exactly the same constraint as in subsection 9.1.1.2. Indeed, there is no way the seller can do better than the "no-commitment outcome" under sales.

Under a long-term contract with renegotiation, one way of implementing the outcome under sales is as follows:

• In the "full-separation case," the buyer can be offered in period 1 a long-term contract with two options: she can consume either in both periods at a price of $v_H + \delta v_L$ or only in period 2 at a first-period price of δv_L.

---

1. One could try to prevent voluntary renegotiation by including a third party in the contract that would receive a large sum of money were the contract to be renegotiated. This plan will not work, however, unless this third party has exogenous commitment powers. Indeed, the third party will understand that, unless it accepts to renegotiate its payment downward, Pareto-improving renegotiation will not take place. If there exists a Pareto-improving renegotiation, it will then accept it in order to receive a share of the positive surplus it generates.

• In the "semiseparation case," the buyer can be offered in period 1 a long-term contract with three options in total: in period 1, she has to choose between consuming and not consuming the good; if she consumes in period 1, she is to consume in period 2 also, and to pay $v_H(1 + \delta)$ overall (in period-1 money); if she does not consume in period 1, she then has a second choice in period 2: either she does consume and pays δv_H overall, or she does not consume and pays nothing.

This is an illustration of the *renegotiation-proofness principle:* In both cases, we implement the solution through a renegotiation-proof contract. This implementation can be accomplished quite generally, because *the result of future (anticipated) renegotiation can always be included in the initial contract.* The preceding contracts are indeed renegotiation-proof: Under full separation, renegotiation entails consumption for both types, which is ex post efficient and thus not susceptible to Pareto improvements; and in the semiseparating case, strict Pareto improvements are also ruled out, provided the high-valuation buyer chooses to consume in period 1 with probability

$$\gamma = \frac{\beta - \beta'}{\beta(1 - \beta')}$$

In this case, while a high price in period 2 is of course not ex post efficient, it is *interim efficient:* Given that only the buyer knows her type, there is no way the seller can raise his payoff by offering a new contract. Inducing more consumption would indeed mean lowering the price to v_L, which would not strictly improve the seller's second-period profit relative to the initial contract.

While there is no difference between spot contracting and long-term contracting with renegotiation in the case of a sale, this is not true in the rental case. Indeed, long-term contracting gets rid of the ratchet effect, and the preceding long-term contract can easily be reinterpreted as a renegotiation-proof long-term rental contract:

• In the "full-separation case," the buyer can be offered in period 1 a long-term contract with two options: she can consume either in both periods at a rental price of v_H in period 1 and v_L in period 2, or only in period 2 at a rental price of v_L.

• In the "semiseparation case," the buyer can be offered in period 1 a long-term contract with three options in total: in period 1, she has to choose between consuming and not consuming the good; if she consumes in period 1, she is to consume in period 2 also, and pays a rental price of v_H each period; if she does not consume in period 1, she then has a second choice in period 2: either she does consume, and pays a rental price of v_H; or she does not consume, and pays nothing.

This solution is exactly like the preceding one, once we properly discount what the buyer pays. We thus have two results here:[2] First, with long-term contracts and renegotiation, the sale and rental outcome coincide both with one another and with the spot-contracting sale outcome. Second, optimal long-term contracts with renegotiation can be computed as renegotiation-proof contracts without loss of generality. This renegotiation-proofness principle should not be interpreted too literally: While optimal outcomes can be achieved in this setting without equilibrium renegotiation, they can often also be reached through contracts that are renegotiated along the equilibrium path. The renegotiation-proofness principle seems nonetheless at odds with reality, where contract renegotiation often "looks unavoidable." Accounting for this idea, however, requires imposing limits on the set of initial contracts, a road that has been taken by "incomplete contract theory," and a topic we shall discuss in Part IV.

9.1.2 Insurance and Renegotiation

This section revisits the insights of the previous one in the case of insurance contracts. Here, ex post mutually profitable renegotiation limits the ability of the contract to rely on allocative inefficiency in order to improve insurance. As in the case of Coasian dynamics, imperfect information revelation emerges as an optimal contractual response to this commitment problem. This application also allows us to show how simple, less informative contracts reduce the room for renegotiation and may thereby improve upon contracts that rely on the observation of more numerous choice variables taken by the informed party.

Consider a simple model, adapted from Dewatripont and Maskin (1990; see also Dewatripont, 1989), where a risk-averse firm seeks insurance from a risk-neutral insurer. The sequence of events is as follows: first, an insurance contract is signed; second, the firm privately learns its profitability;

---

2. These results are general in the T-period version of this game, as emphasized by Hart and Tirole (1988).

third, the firm makes publicly observable input choices, and the contract is executed. The profit of the firm, π, equals

$$\pi = \theta Q(k, l) - rk - wl$$

where k is capital, with rental rate r; l is labor, with wage rate w; $\theta Q(k, l)$ is revenue, with $Q(\cdot)$ increasing and concave in inputs; $\theta \in \{\theta_L, \theta_H\}$, where $\theta_L < \theta_H$ and both θ_i's are equiprobable ex ante; and k and l are contractible, but θ and revenue are not.

Ex post efficiency can now be defined as follows: l_i^* and k_i^* are the ex post efficient input choices if and only if $\theta_i Q_k(k_i^*, l_i^*) = r$ and $\theta_i Q_l(k_i^*, l_i^*) = w$ [where $Q_k(\cdot)$ and $Q_l(\cdot)$ are the first derivatives of output with respect to k and l, respectively]. Suppose that the payoff of the firm is $v(\pi + I)$, where I is the insurance payment to the firm and v is an increasing concave function.

9.1.2.1   Second-Best Contracting (No Renegotiation)

The commitment optimum is the solution to

$$\max_{k_i, l_i, I_i} \frac{1}{2} \sum_{i=L}^{H} v[\theta_i Q(k_i, l_i) - rk_i - wl_i + I_i]$$

subject to the participation (or zero-profit) constraint of the insurer

$$\frac{1}{2} \sum_{i=L}^{H} I_i \leq 0$$

and the incentive constraints

$$\theta_i Q(k_i, l_i) - rk_i - wl_i + I_i \geq \theta_i Q(k_j, l_j) - rk_j - wl_j + I_j \quad i, j = L, H$$

The first best involves ex post efficiency and full insurance for the firm, that is, $\pi_L + I_L = \pi_H + I_H$. This equation, however, violates incentive compatibility when $\theta = \theta_H$, so, as seen in Chapter 2, the second best involves setting

$$k_H = k_H^*, \qquad l_H = l_H^*$$

and

$$k_L < k_L^*, \qquad l_L < l_L^*$$

Indeed, we have efficiency at the top, in state θ_H, but $\theta_L Q_k(k_L, l_L) > r$ and $\theta_L Q_l(k_L, l_L) > w$, that is, underutilization of both inputs in state θ_L, in order to improve risk sharing.

9.1.2.2 Sequential Input Choice with Renegotiation

What if input choices are now sequential; say, capital has to be set first and labor second, with the possibility of a take-it-or-leave-it offer by the insurer to the firm after the first input has been chosen? Once again, without loss of generality, we can consider a renegotiation-proof contract.

Focusing first on *contracts with pure strategies*, renegotiation-proofness implies one of two possible constraints: either pooling, that is, $k_L = k_H$, or separation followed by ex post efficiency, that is, $\theta_L Q_l(k_L, l_L) = w$. Indeed, if $k_L = k_H$, there is no room for renegotiation, since the insurer has not learned anything from the choice of capital, so the labor-input choice is not constrained by renegotiation. But if $k_L \neq k_H$, there is symmetric information after capital has been chosen, so the insurer can make the firm an offer to renegotiate away any employment level l_L such that $\theta_L Q_l(k_L, l_L) \neq w$. That is, the insurer can offer to move to ex post efficient employment (given θ_L and k_L) while pocketing the efficiency gain.

Renegotiation hurts ex ante welfare, since it limits the ex post inefficiency that the contracting parties would like to commit to ex ante in order to improve risk sharing.

What about *mixed-strategy* contracts, which entail partial and gradual information revelation? Intuitively, having *some* underemployment of labor in state θ_L requires at least *some* pooling of capital levels. Consider the following contract:

$$\begin{pmatrix} k_H\, l_H\, I_H \\ k_L\, l'_H\, I'_H \\ k_L\, l'_L\, I_L \end{pmatrix}$$

where the first two rows of the contract matrix are chosen when $\theta = \theta_H$ and with respective probabilities $1 - \gamma$ and γ, while the third row is chosen when $\theta = \theta_L$. The first column of the contract matrix concerns the choice made by the firm in the first stage, that is, the capital-choice stage; the second column concerns the (second-stage) labor choice; and the third column concerns the net payment by the insurer associated with each capital-labor pair. In the first stage, state θ_H is thus only partially revealed by the choice of k, since, with probability γ, the firm in that state chooses the capital level associated with θ_L. The goal of this partial pooling is the desire to maintain at least some level of underemployment of labor for state θ_L in order to improve risk sharing.

Indeed, renegotiation-proofness requires

$$\gamma(\theta_H - \theta_L)Q_l(k_L, l_L) \geq \theta_L Q_l(k_L, l_L) - w \tag{RP}$$

This condition can be understood as follows: Start from an inefficiently low l_L from an ex post perspective. If $\theta = \theta_L$, raising employment by Δl generates an ex post efficiency gain equal to

$$[\theta_L Q_l(k_L, l_L) - w]\Delta l \tag{9.1}$$

But what if $\theta = \theta_H$ [note that, if k_L is chosen, the relative probability of θ_H becomes $\left(\frac{\gamma}{2} / \frac{1}{2}\right) = \gamma$]? It is optimal not to induce the firm to choose l_L in this case instead of l'_H. Since the insurer has, by assumption, full bargaining power in the renegotiation, it can retain the full benefit of the efficiency gain (9.1). Doing so still leaves a net gain of

$$(\theta_H - \theta_L)Q_l(k_L, l_L)\Delta l$$

for the firm if $\theta = \theta_H$, which has to be conceded through a higher insurance payment in order to keep the firm from choosing l_L if $\theta = \theta_H$. This result explains why, if (RP) is satisfied, the insurer does not find it profitable to raise employment above l_L through renegotiation.

The optimal renegotiation-proof contract thus solves:[3]

$$\max_{k_i, l_i, I_i, l'_H, I'_H} \frac{1}{2} \sum_{i=L}^{H} v[\theta_i Q(k_i, l_i) - rk_i - wl_i + I_i]$$

such that

$$\frac{1}{2}I_L + \frac{1}{2}[\gamma I'_H + (1-\gamma)I_H] \leq 0$$

$$\theta_H Q(k_H, l_H) - rk_H - wl_H + I_H = \theta_H Q(k_L, l'_H) - rk_L - wl'_H + I'_H \geq$$

$$\theta_H Q(k_L, l_L) - rk_L - wl_L + I_L$$

and the renegotiation-proofness constraint (RP).

What can we say about the optimal contract? It is easy to first show that optimality implies efficiency at the top, that is, $k_H = k_H^*$ and $l_H = l_H^*$, but also a level l'_H such that $\theta_H Q_l(k_L, l'_H) = w$. Second, note that optimal insurance means trying to have a high I_L, a low I_H, and a low I'_H. The cost of pooling at $k_L < k_H^*$ when $\theta = \theta_H$ is that it raises I'_H which, by the individual-rationality constraint, limits the level of I_L. However, the benefit of pooling

---

3. Note that, since the firm randomizes between k_L and k_H in the capital-choice stage when $\theta = \theta_H$, it has the same payoff under (k_L, l'_H, I'_H) and (k_H, l_H, I_H), and thus the same maximand as without renegotiation.

at k_L when $\theta = \theta_H$ is that it allows sustaining a lower l_L, as shown by (RP): if $\gamma = 0$, $\gamma l'_H$ disappears from the individual-rationality constraint, but ex post efficiency is imposed on l_L, as shown by (RP). Dewatripont and Maskin (1990, 1995a) show that, if $|Q_{ll}/Q_l|$ is not too large, the optimal contract involves $\gamma > 0$, that is, imperfect information revelation. Intuitively, $Q(\cdot)$ should not be too concave, so that sustaining some underemployment of labor does not require too high a γ.

Beyond imperfect information revelation, what are the other insights from imposing renegotiation-proofness? A first immediate consequence concerns the existence of benefits from "contract rigidity": if adjusting employment is hard after the beginning of the relationship, renegotiation-proofness could become trivially satisfied. This insight is part of the general idea that, with fixed types, there is a benefit from commitment.

A more interesting consequence of renegotiation-proofness is the existence of benefits from "limited observability" and thus from "simple contracts." Here, observing k for the insurer has a benefit (to obtain l_L, the insuree has to set both l_L and k_L), but also a cost, because of renegotiation-proofness. When is observing k worse than not observing it? Dewatripont and Maskin (1995a) provide sufficient conditions for this insight. Here is a simple example: assume k can take only two values: $k \in \{\underline{k}, \bar{k}\}$, and assume the second best involves $\underline{k}$ and $l_L^{**} < l_L^*$ for θ_L and $\bar{k}$ and l_H^* for θ_H. Add the following assumption:

$$\theta_H Q\left(\underline{k}, l_L^{**}\right) - r\underline{k} > \theta_H Q\left(\bar{k}, l_L^{**}\right) - r\bar{k}$$

that is, if the firm can have only l_L^{**} as employment level, $\underline{k}$ is the profit-maximizing capital choice even if $\theta = \theta_H$. Then, under this assumption, the second best can be achieved if the choice of capital level by the firm is not observable by the insurer, but not if it is. The intuition is as follows: under this assumption, controlling labor is sufficient to "control" capital too, while simultaneously getting rid of renegotiation. Instead, for $l_L^{**} < l_L^*$, renegotiation is problematic, since the choice of $\underline{k}$ leads the insurer to offer to renegotiate away all ex post inefficiency in labor choice. Consequently, a "simple" contract where only the level of labor enters the insurance contract dominates a more complex contract with more observability. Note that

---

4. We also need the assumption that the insurer does not know exactly *when* capital is chosen; otherwise, it would be enough to know that capital has been chosen for sure to make renegotiation profitable (see Dewatripont and Maskin, 1995a, and also Fudenberg and Tirole, 1990, in a dynamic-moral-hazard context).

this result begs the question of how the insurer can commit not to observe capital choices.[4] One idea is that observing such choices requires *ex ante information systems,* which could be hard to set up during the relationship. The insurer could thus decide not to adopt such systems even if they are free ex ante, since their informational value is negative at that point, because of the commitment problem induced by renegotiation.

9.1.3   Soft Budget Constraints

"Soft budget constraints"—the refinancing of loss-making state-owned enterprises—have been portrayed as a major inefficiency in centrally planned economies, most notably by Janos Kornai (1979, 1980). But the notion of the potential lack of credibility of the termination threat of loss-making projects is also seen as a pervasive problem in corporate finance. As Dewatripont and Maskin (1995b) have highlighted,[5] soft budget constraints can be seen as resulting from a dynamic incentive problem: they represent an inefficiency in the sense that the funding source would like to commit ex ante not to bail out firms but knows that it will be tempted to refinance the debtor ex post because the initial injection of funds is sunk. In such a world, hardening the budget constraint requires finding a commitment device that makes refinancing ex post unprofitable. The literature on transition from plan to market has analyzed several transition strategies as ways to harden budget constraints.[6] In this section we focus on one of them, the decentralization of credit, as an illustrative commitment device against soft budget constraints.

Soft budget constraints arise because the uninformed party cannot commit to remain tough enough with the informed party (just like the seller who cannot commit not to lower his price in the future). It is thus the mirror image of the ratchet problem where the planner cannot commit not to be excessively tough with the firm it controls. The originality of this section lies in the specific device considered to get around this commitment problem, namely, the reliance on a *sequence* of uninformed parties as a way to limit the amount of information generated in the course of the relationship.

9.1.3.1   Soft Budget Constraints as a Commitment Problem

Consider the following adverse selection problem: A (private or state-

---

5. See also Schaffer (1989).

6. See, for example, Dewatripont, Maskin, and Roland (1999) and especially the book by Roland (2000).

owned) creditor faces a population of (private or state-owned) firms, each needing one unit of funds in initial period 1 in order to start its project. A proportion β of these projects are of the "good, quick" type: after one period, the project is successfully completed and generates a gross (discounted) financial return $\pi_G > 1$. Moreover, the entrepreneur managing the firm obtains a positive net (discounted) private benefit E_G. In contrast, there is a proportion $(1 - \beta)$ of bad and slow projects that generate no financial return after one period. If a project is terminated at that stage, the entrepreneur obtains a private benefit E_T. Instead, if refinanced, each project generates after two periods a gross (discounted) financial return π_B^* and a net (discounted) private benefit E_B. Initially, β is common knowledge, but individual types are private information. A simple result easily follows: if $1 < \pi_B^* < 2$ and $E_B > 0$, refinancing bad projects is sequentially optimal for the creditor, and bad entrepreneurs, who expect to be refinanced, apply for initial financing. The creditor would, however, be better off if he were able to commit not to refinance bad projects, since he would thereby deter entrepreneurs with bad projects from applying for initial financing, provided $E_T < 0$.

Termination is here, by assumption, a discipline device that allows the uninformed creditor to turn away bad types and finance only good ones.[7] The problem is that termination is not sequentially rational if π_B^* is bigger than one: once the first unit has been sunk into a bad project, its net continuation value is positive, so that, in the absence of commitment, the soft-budget-constraint syndrome arises. In this setup, because irreversibility of investment is such a general economic feature, the challenge is to explain why hard budget constraints prevail rather than why budget constraints are soft in the first place. The next subsection focuses on the decentralization of credit as a reason behind hard budget constraints.

9.1.3.2 Decentralization of Credit

The setup of the previous subsection is compatible with a π_B^* that reflects pure profit-maximization motives. Indeed, in the presence of sunk costs, sequential profit maximization can be inferior to ex ante profit maximization. To avoid such an inferior outcome, the decentralization of credit may be helpful, working through a reduction in π_B^*.

---

7. This differs from a static problem à la Stiglitz and Weiss (1981) where creditors can at best finance all types, and at worst finance only bad types (see Chapter 2).

To be specific, assume that the continuation value of bad projects depends on a monitoring effort level a to be exerted by the initial creditor. Specifically, assume that the gross (discounted) financial return of a bad project that is refinanced is either 0 or $\bar{\pi}_B$ and that the probability of $\bar{\pi}_B$ is a. Finally, assume a to be private information to the initial creditor, who incurs effort cost $\psi(a)$, assumed to be increasing and convex in a.

In this case, *centralization* of credit means that the initial creditor is also the one refinancing a bad firm, so that the chosen effort level a^* fully internalizes the benefit of monitoring:

$$\pi_B^* \equiv \max_a \{a\bar{\pi}_B - \psi(a)\} \quad \text{which implies} \quad \bar{\pi}_B = \psi'(a^*)$$

Under *decentralization* of credit, the initial creditor is liquidity constrained, and refinancing has to be performed by a new creditor who, by assumption, has not observed monitoring effort. Assume also limited initial resources for the firm as well as the initial creditor, so that the new creditor has to be paid exclusively out of the return of the project. Call $\hat{a}$ the expectation of monitoring effort a by the new creditor. Under perfect competition among new creditors, the refinancing contract will grant the new creditor $1/\hat{a}$ in case the project is successful and generates $\bar{\pi}_b$. For a given $\hat{a}$, the initial creditor will solve

$$\max_a \{a[\bar{\pi}_B - 1/\hat{a}] - \psi(a) + 1\} \equiv \pi_b^{**}$$

In equilibrium, the chosen effort level a^{**} is equal to $\hat{a}$, and satisfies $\bar{\pi}_B = \psi'(a^{**}) + 1/a^{**}$. Consequently, a^{**} is lower than a^*, and the associated continuation value of the project π_B^{**} is lower than π_B^*. If $\pi_B^{**} < 1 < \pi_B^*$, decentralization of credit, as defined previously, hardens the budget constraint of the firm.

The general insight behind this result is that decentralized finance may lead to externalities that reduce the attractiveness of refinancing and thus harden budget constraints. This suggests that (more decentralized) bond or equity finance is typically associated with a harder budget constraint than (more centralized) bank finance, a point also stressed by von Thadden (1995).

Note that, in this setup, if π_B^{**} is bigger than 1, decentralization of credit is *worse* than centralization: The refinancing of bad projects is not prevented but occurs with inefficiently low monitoring. If, however, one interprets a market economy as one where creditor size is endogenous (that is, allowing for centralized as well as decentralized credit), one can show that in this setup efficient creditor size arises in equilibrium (see Dewatripont and Maskin, 1995b). While the market system is then unambiguously better than exogenous centralization, this conclusion is not always true under alternative model specifications, as the next section indicates.

9.1.3.3   Budget Constraints and Risk Taking

While hard budget constraints can deter bad entrepreneurs from starting projects, von Thadden (1995) and Dewatripont and Maskin (1995b) have pointed out that they can induce short-termism among good entrepreneurs. Specifically, introduce into the preceding framework the ability for good entrepreneurs to choose between their good, quick project, which yields $\pi_G > 1$ and E_G after one period, and a *good but slow* project, which yields a financial return of 0 after one period (and private benefit E_T if terminated) but a gross financial return $\pi_{LT} > 2$ and a positive private benefit E_{LT} if refinanced. This good but slow project thus has a positive net present value even though, at the end of period 1, it cannot be distinguished from bad projects.

The presence of the good but slow project can introduce a *coordination problem* among good entrepreneurs. To see this, consider again the case where decentralization of credit is necessary and sufficient for a hard budget constraint, that is, $\pi_B^{**} < 1 < \pi_B^*$. In this case, it is easy to see that (1) there always exists an equilibrium where credit is decentralized, the budget constraint is hard, and all good entrepreneurs choose short-run projects; (2) for π_{LT} sufficiently large, there also exists an equilibrium where credit is centralized, the budget constraint is soft, and all good entrepreneurs choose long-run projects; and (3) when it exists, the second equilibrium Pareto-dominates the first one.

Intuitively, when $\pi_B^{**} < 1 < \pi_B^*$, decentralized financing is the only way to deter bad projects from being started. Expectations by creditors that all long-term projects are bad are self-fulfilling, since good entrepreneurs expect termination if they do not choose quick projects. Another equilibrium is possible, however, if the financing of all long-term projects, good and bad, is more profitable than financing solely good, quick projects. In that case, creditors' expectations that all good entrepreneurs choose long-term projects are also self-fulfilling. In this setting, which allows for good but slow projects, the hard budget constraint equilibrium induces "short-termist" behavior that more than offsets the gain from deterring bad long-term projects from being started. It is therefore Pareto-dominated by the soft-budget-constraint equilibrium.

9.1.4 Regulation

Just as the threat of termination of inefficient projects by creditors may lack credibility, the same may be true of a regulator's attempt to commit to a price cap or a given required rate of return. This strategy can indeed be frustrated either by lobbying from the regulated firm for price increases or by public pressure to lower prices.

We illustrate the dynamic incentive problems faced by a regulator of a natural monopoly in the framework popularized in the book by Laffont and Tirole (1993), discussed in Chapter 2. There, we considered a natural monopoly with an exogenous cost parameter $\theta \in \{\theta_L, \theta_H\}$ and $\Delta\theta = \theta_H - \theta_L > 0$. The firm's cost of producing the good is $c = \theta - e$, where e stands for effort, with associated cost $\psi(e) = [\max\{0, e\}]^2/2$, increasing and convex in e. The government wants the good to be produced for the lowest possible payment $P = s + c$ (where s is the subsidy paid to the firm in excess of accounting cost c). The payoff of the firm is $P - c - \psi(e) = s - \psi(e)$, which has to be nonnegative for the firm to be willing to participate. If the government observes the value of the cost parameter θ, we have as first-best outcome $e^* = 1$ and $s^* = 0.5$.

Chapter 2 considered the one-period problem where the government cannot observe the cost parameter of the firm, but has prior belief $\Pr(\theta = \theta_L) = \beta_1$. Calling (s_L, c_L) the contract chosen by type θ_L (with associated effort $e_L = \theta_L - c_L$), and (s_H, c_H) the contract chosen by type θ_H (with associated effort $e_H = \theta_H - c_H$), the government solves

$$\min\{\beta_1(s_L - e_L) + (1 - \beta_1)(s_H - e_H)\}$$

such that

$$s_L - [\max\{0, e_L\}]^2/2 \geq 0$$

$$s_H - [\max\{0, e_H\}]^2/2 \geq 0$$

$$s_L - [\max\{0, e_L\}]^2/2 \geq s_H - [\max\{0, e_H - \Delta\theta\}]^2/2$$

$$s_H - [\max\{0, e_H\}]^2/2 \geq s_L - [\max\{0, e_L + \Delta\theta\}]^2/2$$

Assuming away corner solutions and noting that the two relevant constraints are

$$s_L - e_L^2/2 = s_H - (e_H - \Delta\theta)^2/2$$

$$s_H - e_H^2/2 = 0$$

we obtained in Chapter 2 the following first-order conditions:

$$e_L = 1$$

and

$$e_H = 1 - \frac{\beta_1}{1 - \beta_1}\Delta\theta$$

We thus have ex post allocative efficiency at the top, as well as underprovision of effort for the inefficient type, in order to reduce the rent of the efficient type [which equals $e_H^2/2 - (e_H - \Delta\theta)^2/2$].

9.1.4.1   Two Periods and Full Commitment

Assume now that the government faces a two-period problem, with a constant cost parameter θ, an identical technology $c_t = \theta - e_t$, and an identical effort-cost function $\psi(e_t)$ in each period $t = 1, 2$. Normalize to 1 the length of the first period, and call δ the length of the second period. Under full commitment, the government offers two-period contracts $(s_{H1}, c_{H1}, s_{H2}, c_{H2})$ and $(s_{L1}, c_{L1}, s_{L2}, c_{L2})$ simply to minimize the expected sum of actual costs under the participation and incentive constraints of the firm; these state that, for each type of firm, (1) the sum of subsidies covers at least the sum of effort costs, and (2) the two-period contract corresponding to its own type is more attractive than the two-period contract corresponding to the other type. As observed in earlier sections, in this stationary environment, the best the government can do is to replicate the one-period contract described previously. Indeed, observe first that the first best is to replicate the one-period first-best contract. In this solution, it is the incentive constraint of the efficient type that is violated under adverse selection, so we have ex post efficient effort for the efficient type ($e_{L1} = e_{L2} = 1$) and underprovision of effort for the inefficient type. Could it be optimal to have $e_{H1} \neq e_{H2}$? In fact, no: consider the following contract change: replace (e_{H1}, e_{H2}) by a unique effort level $\hat{e}$ such that

$$(1 + \delta)\hat{e} = e_{H1} + \delta e_{H2}$$

while keeping the inefficient type's payoff unchanged:

$$s_{H1} - e_{H1}^2/2 + \delta(s_{H2} - e_{H2}^2/2) = (1+\delta)(\hat{s} - \hat{e}^2/2)$$

where $\hat{s}$ is the per-period subsidy paid to the inefficient type. By the convexity of the effort-cost function, this contract change allows the government to reduce its total payment: while the expected overall level of effort remains constant by construction, the expected total subsidy goes down, since the stabilization of the effort level over time reduces total effort cost. The only question remaining concerns the incentive the efficient type might have to mimic the inefficient type. The efficient type's payoff from mimicking the inefficient type when $e_{H1} \neq e_{H2}$ is

$$s_{H1} - (e_{H1} - \Delta\theta)^2/2 + \delta\left[s_{H2} - (e_{H2} - \Delta\theta)^2/2\right]$$

which equals

$$s_{H1} - e_{H1}^2/2 + \delta(s_{H2} - e_{H2}^2/2) + \Delta\theta(e_{H1} + \delta e_{H2}) - (\Delta\theta)^2(1+\delta)/2$$

Similarly, under the constant $\hat{e}$, it is

$$(1+\delta)(\hat{s} - \hat{e}^2/2) + \Delta\theta(1+\delta)\hat{e} - (\Delta\theta)^2(1+\delta)/2$$

Since, by the construction of $(\hat{s}, \hat{e})$, the payoff of the inefficient type stays unchanged after this contract change, then so does the incentive of the efficient type to mimic the inefficient type. The result—that stabilizing the effort of the inefficient type while keeping its payoff constant is worthwhile for the principal—comes from the convexity of the effort-cost function, that is, from its positive *second* derivative. As for the result that such a move preserves the incentive constraint of the *efficient* type, it can be shown that this relies on the nonnegativity of the *third* derivative of this effort-cost function (see Laffont and Tirole, 1993). This condition is (just) satisfied here, since a quadratic effort cost has a zero third derivative.

9.1.4.2   Pareto-Improving Renegotiation

What if, after the firm has made its period-1 choice, the government came back and made a new contract offer at the beginning of period 2? Assume that the initial contract remains the default contract; that is, the firm can reject the new contract offer and stick to the original contract terms. As in earlier sections, the firm's period-1 contract choice reveals the firm's type. This knowledge can provide the government with an opportunity to make a renegotiation offer that is Pareto improving as of period 2 but that exacerbates incentive-compatibility problems. In particular, the full commitment optimum cannot be reached anymore.

As in earlier sections, there is no loss of generality in restricting attention to renegotiation-proof contracts, and three types of contracts are possible: *separating, pooling,* and *semiseparating* contracts.

• *Separating contracts:* When $(s_{H1}, c_{H1}) \neq (s_{L1}, c_{L1})$, period-2 outcomes have to be allocatively efficient for both types. The government thus solves

$$\min\{\beta_1(s_{L1} - e_{L1} + \delta[s_{L2} - e_{L2}]) + (1 - \beta_1)(s_{H1} - e_{H1} + \delta[s_{H2} - e_{H2}])\}$$

subject to

$$s_{H1} - e_{H1}^2/2 + \delta[s_{H2} - e_{H2}^2/2] = 0$$

$$s_{L1} - e_{L1}^2/2 + \delta[s_{L2} - e_{L2}^2/2] = s_{H1} - (e_{H1} - \Delta\theta)^2/2 + \delta\left[s_{H2} - (e_{H2} - \Delta\theta)^2/2\right]$$

and

$$e_{L2} = e_{H2} = 1$$

While $e_{L2} = 1$ also obtains in the full commitment optimum, $e_{H2} = 1$ does not and is therefore a binding renegotiation-proofness constraint. Optimization with respect to first-period efforts yields the same outcome as in a one-period problem, namely $e_{L1} = 1$, and

$$e_{H1} = 1 - \frac{\beta_1}{1 - \beta_1}\Delta\theta$$

Type θ_L obtains more rents than in the full-commitment outcome thanks to a higher level of e_{H2}, which is anticipated when the first-period contract choice is made. This rent concession is costly for the government. However, the cost is proportional to δ, the length of the second period, so that this contract approximates the full commitment optimum for δ tending to zero.

• *Pooling contracts:* When $(s_{H1}, c_{H1}) = (s_{L1}, c_{L1}) \equiv (s_1, c_1)$ (with associated effort levels $e_{H1} = \theta_H - c_1$ and $e_{L1} = \theta_L - c_1$) at the beginning of period 2, the belief of the government is still $\Pr(\theta = \theta_L) = \beta_1$, and sequential optimality is in fact not a constraint on the optimal contract. Specifically, the government solves

$$\min\{\beta_1(s_1 - e_{L1} + \delta[s_{L2} - e_{L2}]) + (1 - \beta_1)(s_1 - e_{H1} + \delta[s_{H2} - e_{H2}])\}$$

subject to

$$s_1 - e_{H1}^2/2 + \delta[s_{H2} - e_{H2}^2/2] = 0$$

$$\delta[s_{L2} - e_{L2}^2/2] = \delta\left[s_{H2} - (e_{H2} - \Delta\theta)^2/2\right]$$

This problem can be solved period by period. In period 2, we have

$$e_{L2} = 1$$

$$e_{H2} = 1 - \frac{\beta_1}{1 - \beta_1}\Delta\theta$$

as in the full commitment optimum, and this relation holds because the government has an unchanged belief about the firm's distribution of types. Concerning period 1, lowering the actual cost c_1 for *both* types means lowering effort levels one for one. This requires raising s_1, to keep the participation constraint of type θ_L satisfied, by an amount e_{H1}. Optimality thus implies $e_{H1} = 1$ and $e_{L1} = 1 - \Delta\theta$: here, first-period underprovision of effort occurs for the *efficient* type. The optimal pooling contract minimizes the rent that is conceded to type θ_L. The loss for the government relative to the full-commitment optimum is due to the first-period misallocation of effort, and it consequently tends to the full-commitment optimum when this period becomes relatively short (that is, when $1/\delta$ tends to zero).

• *Semiseparating contracts:* In order to reduce the period-1 underprovision of effort of type θ_L that occurs in the pooling contract, one can reduce the pooling probability. Doing so, however, raises the rents that have to be conceded to type θ_L. Specifically, assume that type θ_L mixes between (s_{L1}, c_{L1}) with probability $1 - \gamma$ and (s_{H1}, c_{H1}) with probability γ, while type θ_H chooses (s_{H1}, c_{H1}) with probability 1. Call (s_{L2}, c_{L2}) the continuation contract after (s_{L1}, c_{L1}) has been chosen, and $\{(s_{H2}, c_{H2}), (s_{HL2}, c_{HL2})\}$ the continuation *menu* after (s_{H1}, c_{H1}) has been chosen [where (s_{HL2}, c_{HL2}) is chosen in period 2 by type θ_L and (s_{H2}, c_{H2}) by type θ_H]. In this latter case, the regulator's posterior is

$$\Pr(\theta_L|c_{H1}) = \frac{\gamma\beta_1}{\gamma\beta_1 + (1 - \beta_1)} \equiv \beta_2$$

The sequentially optimal period-2 contract entails $e_{HL2} = 1$ and

$$e_{H2} = 1 - \frac{\beta_2}{1 - \beta_2}\Delta\theta = 1 - \gamma\frac{\beta_1}{1 - \beta_1}\Delta\theta$$

for the efficient and inefficient types, respectively. As before, only the requirement on e_{H2} is a constraint, whenever $\beta_2 \neq \beta_1$. The optimum is thus the result of

$$\min \beta_1 \{(1-\gamma)(s_{L1} - e_{L1} + \delta[s_{L2} - e_{L2}]) +$$
$$\gamma(s_{H1} - [e_{H1} - \Delta\theta] + \delta[s_{HL2} - e_{HL2}])\} + (1-\beta_1)\{s_{H1} - e_{H1} + \delta(s_{H2} - e_{H2})\}$$

subject to

$$s_{H1} - e_{H1}^2/2 + \delta[s_{H2} - e_{H2}^2/2] = 0$$

$$s_{HL2} - e_{HL2}^2/2 = s_{H2} - (e_{H2} - \Delta\theta)^2/2$$

$$s_{L1} - e_{L1}^2/2 + \delta[s_{L2} - e_{L2}^2/2] = s_{H1} - (e_{H1} - \Delta\theta)^2/2 + \delta[s_{HL2} - e_{HL2}^2/2]$$

and

$$e_{H2} = 1 - \gamma \frac{\beta_1}{1 - \beta_1} \Delta\theta$$

The first constraint is the participation constraint of type θ_H; the second one is the incentive constraint of type θ_L for period 2, given that it has chosen (s_{H1}, c_{H1}) in period 1; the third one states that type θ_L is indifferent between $(s_{L1}, c_{L1}, s_{L2}, c_{L2})$ and $(s_{H1}, c_{H1}, s_{HL2}, c_{HL2})$, a necessary condition for mixing to be optimal; and the fourth one is the renegotiation-proofness constraint. As before, it is optimal to set the allocatively efficient effort level for type θ_L whenever it is not pooling with the other type, which implies in particular $e_{L2} = e_{HL2}$. After straightforward substitutions, one can rewrite the optimization problem as

$$\min \left\{ \beta_1 \left(\frac{e_{L1}^2}{2} - e_{L1} + \delta \left[\frac{e_{L2}^2}{2} - e_{L2} \right] + \frac{e_{H1}^2}{2} - \frac{1}{2}(e_{H1} - \Delta\theta)^2 \right. \right.$$
$$\left. + \delta \left[\frac{e_{H2}^2}{2} - \frac{1}{2}(e_{H2} - \Delta\theta)^2 \right] + \frac{\gamma}{2} \left[(e_{H1} - \Delta\theta)^2 - (e_{H1} - \Delta\theta) - \left(\frac{e_{L1}^2}{2} - e_{L1} \right) \right] \right)$$
$$\left. + (1-\beta_1) \left[\frac{e_{H1}^2}{2} - e_{H1} + \delta \frac{e_{H2}^2}{2} - \delta e_{H2} \right] \right\}$$

subject to

$$e_{H2} = 1 - \gamma \frac{\beta_1}{1 - \beta_1} \Delta\theta$$

The maximand is the same as under full commitment, except for the efficiency loss from pooling in period 1 for type θ_L, which comes from setting effort level $(e_{H1} - \Delta\theta)$ instead of e_{L1}, with ex ante probability $\beta_1\gamma$. Solving this optimization problem yields, as before,

$$e_{L1} = e_{L2} = e_{HL2} = 1$$

while

$$e_{H1} = 1 - \frac{\beta_1(1-\gamma)}{1 - \beta_1 + \beta_1\gamma}\Delta\theta$$

Effort e_{H1} thus rises with γ, since it is an inefficiently low effort for type θ_L. More interesting is the optimality condition on γ and e_{H2}. Taking the derivative of the maximand with respect to γ while having e_{H2} move with γ, and equating it to zero, yields

$$[\beta_1\delta\Delta\theta + (1-\beta_1)\delta(e_{H2} - 1)]\frac{\beta_1}{1-\beta_1}\Delta\theta =$$

$$\beta_1\frac{1}{2}\left[(e_{H1} - \Delta\theta)^2 - (e_{H1} - \Delta\theta) - \left(\frac{e_{L1}^2}{2} - e_{L1}\right)\right]$$

The RHS of this equation is positive: It represents the allocative loss from pooling in period 1 for type θ_L. Therefore, the LHS of the equation has to be positive too; that is, e_{H2} has to be higher than $1 - \beta_1\Delta\theta/(1 - \beta_1)$. But this result can be sequentially optimal only if $\beta_2 < \beta_1$, so that *full pooling is never optimal.* Pooling becomes asymptotically optimal only when $\delta \to \infty$, that is, when the cost of pooling goes to zero in relative terms. Otherwise, the idea is that, at effort level

$$e_{H2} = 1 - \frac{\beta_1\Delta\theta}{1-\beta_1}$$

(which can be sustained only through full pooling), a rise in this effort level brings only a second-order loss, while any cut in γ (from the value of 1) brings a first-order gain.

9.1.4.3   Short-Term Contracts and the Ratchet Effect

Assume now that the parties can sign only one-period contracts, that is, neither the regulator nor the firm can commit in advance to an outcome (s_2, c_2). What changes in comparison with the previous subsection? Sequential optimality still induces the same second-period effort, that is, an effort of 1 for the efficient type and an effort equal to

$$1 - \frac{\beta_2}{1 - \beta_2} \Delta \theta$$

for the inefficient type under the belief that $\Pr(\theta_L) = \beta_2$. As before, beliefs depend on the period-1 outcome, and thus on whether the contract involves full separation, full pooling, or partial separation. The key difference between long-term renegotiation-proof contracts and short-term contracts concerns payments to the firm: the government cannot commit to giving the firm more rents than the participation and incentive constraints require. In particular, under full separation the government knows exactly which type it faces at the beginning of period 2. Consequently, as in the previous subsection, unit effort is offered at that point. But, unlike in the previous subsection, the government offers to give *both* types of firms exactly zero rents in period 2.

The two incentive constraints for the firm are now

$$s_{L1} - \frac{e_{L1}^2}{2} \geq s_{H1} - \frac{1}{2}(e_{H1} - \Delta\theta)^2 + \delta\left[\frac{e_{H2}^2}{2} - \frac{1}{2}(e_{H2} - \Delta\theta)^2\right]$$

and

$$s_{H1} - \frac{e_{H1}^2}{2} \geq s_{L1} - \frac{1}{2}(e_{L1} + \Delta\theta)^2$$

The first constraint is the usual incentive constraint for the efficient type, with two differences from the full-separation contract of the previous subsection: (1) since the government gives the firm zero rents in period 2 (that is, chooses $s_{L2} = e_{L2}^2/2$), rents can only be given in period 1, through s_{L1}; and (2) if the inefficient firm receives zero rents, the efficient firm obtains the sum over the two periods of the effort-cost differentials at (e_{H1}, e_{H2}); however, the government may now be forced to give the inefficient type positive rents. Indeed, the rise in s_{L1} described previously may induce the inefficient firm to "take the money and run," that is, pretend to be the efficient firm in period 1 [even if that implies an effort level of $(e_{L1} + \Delta\theta)$], while not producing at all in period 2. Laffont and Tirole show that indeed the optimal contract may, under some parameter values, require *both* incentive constraints to be binding. In comparison with long-term renegotiation-proof contracts, more pooling may be optimal, and full pooling can in particular be an optimum. The general insight from this model, as from models of long-term renegotiation-proof contracts, is that information revelation through contract execution has a cost from an ex ante point of view. Institutional features that limit the consequences of information revelation can therefore be desirable. This is the case with "regulatory lags," whereby the regulatory scheme is reconsidered only infrequently by the regulatory authorities: While the government or the regulated firm might wish otherwise ex post, ex ante social welfare can be enhanced by limiting the frequency of regulatory reviews. Of course, a key assumption behind this insight is the fact that we have concentrated on purely constant types: In reality, the environment may change over time, leading to the need for somewhat flexible regulatory schemes. For more on this issue, see the book by Laffont and Tirole (1993).

9.2   Repeated Adverse Selection: Changing Types

One lesson emerging from our analysis of repeated adverse selection with fixed types is that there are no gains from an enduring relationship when the informed party's type is fixed. More precisely, the uninformed party's maximum average per-period payoff is lower when the two parties interact over time than when they engage in one-time spot contracting in an anonymous market. The best the uninformed party can hope to achieve in a repeated relation is to repeat the optimal static contract.

In contrast, when the agent's type changes over time, there are substantial gains to be obtained for the uninformed party from a long-term relationship. First, when the agent's type changes over time, the agent is less concerned about revealing her type in any given period because doing so does not necessarily undermine her bargaining position in future periods. Moreover, the gains from trade to be shared from future contracting provide an additional instrument to screen agent types in early periods.

The classic example of a dynamic contracting problem under adverse selection with changing types is that of an individual household (or firm) facing privately observed income or preference shocks over time and determining how best to consume dynamically thanks to financial contracting. We cast the analysis of our dynamic contracting problem in the context of this application. As will become clear, this somewhat abstract formulation of intertemporal consumption (or investment) in the presence of transitory shocks can shed considerable light on two fundamental economic issues: (1)

the effect of liquidity shocks on consumption and investment; and (2) the implications for long-run wealth distribution of repeated partially insurable income (or preference) shocks.

We begin by formulating and analyzing the optimal long-term contracting problem, then compare it to two benchmark situations: (1) no contracting (or autarky) and (2) borrowing and lending in a competitive securities market. The optimal contract can be thought of as an efficient arrangement between a financial intermediary and households subject to liquidity needs. By comparing this institutional arrangement with the equilibrium outcome obtained through trading in a competitive securities market, we are able in particular to contrast, at an admittedly abstract level, the strengths and weaknesses of institution-based financial systems versus market-based financial systems (to borrow terminology introduced by Allen and Gale, 2000). In one sentence, one important trade-off between these two systems that emerges from this analysis is that the former may provide better intertemporal risk sharing or consumption smoothing, but at the risk of creating financial instability through banking crises.

In this section, we treat three successive problems. The first has a two-period horizon where the individual learns in period 1 whether she would rather consume immediately or is happy to wait until period 2 for her consumption. This problem, first analyzed by Diamond and Dybvig (1983), thus considers a single preference shock, an assumption that simplifies the analysis and already delivers quite a number of insights. The second problem we consider also has a two-period horizon but with two independently distributed income shocks. This problem, pioneered by Townsend (1982), allows us to consider a more general comparison between simple debt contracts and insurance contracts. It also serves as starting point for the third problem, which considers an infinite horizon.

9.2.1 Banking and Liquidity Transformation

It is often argued that one of the main economic roles of banks is to transform illiquid long-term investments into liquid savings. The basic idea is the following: Investments with the highest return are often long-term projects that generate positive net revenues only after a few years. An example of such a project would be a dam (together with a hydroelectric plant), which typically takes more than a decade to complete. Most individuals would shy away from such projects, despite their high final return, because they cannot afford to tie up their savings for such a long period. In practice such long-term projects are financed by banks (when they are not undertaken by governments), who themselves obtain the funds from their depositors. The banks act as intermediaries between the depositors and the debtor by providing a liquidity transformation service: they allow depositors to benefit from the future returns of the project before these are realized, by allowing depositors to withdraw their savings at any time. Banks are able to offer this liquidity-transformation service by relying on the statistical regularity that not all depositors wish to withdraw their funds at the same time.

One of the first explicit analyses of the demand for liquidity and the transformation function of banks is due to Diamond and Dybvig (1983). Their paper builds on the general methodology of optimal contracting under asymmetric information outlined in Chapter 2. We consider a slightly more general version of their model, which consists in an economy with a continuum of ex ante identical consumers who live for two periods. These consumers have one dollar to invest at date zero in one of two projects:

• A short-term project, which yields a gross return $r \geq 1$ in period 1. This investment can be rolled over to yield r^2 in period 2.

• A long-term project with the following cash flow over periods 1 and 2:

$$
\begin{array}{ccc}
t=0 & t=1 & t=2 \\
-1 & 0 & R > r^2
\end{array}
$$

The long-term project can also be liquidated at date 1 and generate a liquidation value of L.

At date zero, consumers are uncertain about their future preferences. They can be of two different types in the future: type-1 consumers ($\theta = \theta_1$) are "impatient" and prefer to consume in period 1; type-2 consumers ($\theta_1 = \theta_2$), are "patient" and are willing to postpone their consumption if it is worth doing so. These preferences are represented by the following type-contingent utility function:

$$
U(c_1, c_2; \theta) = \begin{cases} u(c_1 + \eta c_2) & \text{when } \theta = \theta_1 \\ u(\mu c_1 + c_2) & \text{when } \theta = \theta_2 \end{cases}
$$

where

• $\eta < 1$ and $\mu < 1$ are parameters representing the loss in utility from, respectively, late consumption for type 1 and early consumption for type 2.

- $u(\cdot)$ is twice continuously differentiable, strictly increasing, and concave.[8]

The uncertainty about preferences is resolved in period 1. Each consumer learns exactly what her type is at that point. Naturally, this information remains private.

Consumers have independently, identically distributed preference shocks; the ex ante probability of being a type-1 consumer is given by $\Pr(\theta = \theta_1) = \gamma$. Given that there is a continuum of ex ante identical consumers, there will be a proportion γ of impatient and $(1 - \gamma)$ of patient consumers at date 1. A bank will be able to take advantage of this statistical regularity to invest in the long-term project despite the preference risk consumers face at date zero.

The general-resource-allocation problem in this economy is to determine the optimal mix of investments and the optimal revenue-sharing rule to insure consumers against their preference uncertainty. This problem can be represented as an optimal contracting problem under asymmetric information. The problem is to maximize a representative consumer's expected utility at date zero, subject to a resource constraint and incentive-compatibility constraints.

As usual, it is helpful to begin by solving the *first-best problem,* where a consumer's type is assumed to be common knowledge. This problem consists in determining the amount $x \in [0, 1]$ to invest in the short-term project and the consumption of each type. We denote by c_{it} the amount of period t consumption of a type-i consumer, $t = 1, 2, i = 1, 2$. Given each type's preferences, it is obvious that a first-best optimal consumption allocation c_{it}^* for $t = 1, 2$ and $i = 1, 2$ must specify

$$c_{12}^* = c_{21}^* = 0$$

The optimal mix of investment is also easy to see: On the one hand, if $r \leq L$, then everything should be invested in the long-term project, and an amount

$$y = \frac{c_{11}^* \gamma}{L}$$

8. Diamond and Dybvig make the stronger assumption that

$$-c\frac{u''(c)}{u'(c)} > 1$$

should be liquidated in period 1.[9] On the other hand, if $r > L$ (and $r^2 < R$), then a fraction

$$x = \frac{c_{11}^* \gamma}{r}$$

should be invested in the short-term project and the remainder in the long-term project. We proceed with the assumption that $r > L$.

Finally, optimal insurance requires the equalization of the marginal rate of substitution between period-1 and period-2 consumption with the marginal rate of transformation, or

$$ru'\left(c_{11}^*\right) = Ru'\left(c_{22}^*\right)$$

The first-best contract is not attainable in general in a second-best world. To be feasible, this contract must satisfy the following incentive compatibility constraints:

$$u\left(c_{11}^*\right) \geq u\left(\eta c_{22}^*\right)$$

and

$$u\left(c_{22}^*\right) \geq u\left(rc_{11}^*\right)$$

The first constraint ensures that an impatient consumer is not better off pretending to be patient so as to obtain a higher return on her investment. Similarly, the second constraint ensures that a patient consumer cannot gain by pretending to be impatient. Note the important difference between these two constraints. A patient consumer need not consume in period 1 when mimicking an impatient consumer; she can simply withdraw her funds from the bank in period 1 and reinvest her savings in the short-term project.

The two incentive constraints are satisfied only if

$$1 \geq \eta r$$

It is obvious that this condition does not always hold. But, even if it does hold, the first-best contract is not always attainable. Suppose, for example, that $\eta = 0$, so that the first incentive constraint is always satisfied. Then the first-best contract satisfies the second incentive constraint only if $c_{22}^* \geq rc_{11}^*$. But this assumption implies that

---

9. Diamond and Dybvig assume that $r = L = 1$, and therefore their solution is such that all the consumers' savings are invested in the long-term project.

$$ru'\left(c_{11}^{*}\right) \le Ru'\left(rc_{11}^{*}\right)$$

and this inequality cannot hold, for example, if the utility function has decreasing relative risk aversion.[10] This observation establishes that the first-best contract is not always feasible in a second-best world. Consequently, the second-best contract may provide imperfect insurance against preference shocks. It can be shown in particular that it may result in an ex post inefficient allocation of consumption such that $c_{21} > 0$.

Four important economic insights follow from the preceding analysis:

1. As stressed first by Diamond and Dybvig (1983), the second-best optimal allocation, $(c_{11}^{SB}, c_{12}^{SB}, c_{21}^{SB}, c_{22}^{SB})$ (which may or may not coincide with the first-best allocation c_{it}^{*}) can be implemented by a bank investing the consumers' savings in a suitable portfolio of projects and offering them demand-deposit contracts, such that the consumers are free to determine in period 1 whether to choose a consumption pattern $(c_{11}^{SB}, c_{12}^{SB})$ or $(c_{21}^{SB}, c_{22}^{SB})$. In other words, financial intermediation may emerge endogenously in this economy to provide a (constrained) efficient liquidity transformation service.

2. As stressed first by Jacklin (1987), the same allocation can be achieved by setting up a publicly traded firm issuing equity to consumers at date zero and paying dividends

$$\gamma c_{11}^{SB} + (1 - \gamma)c_{21}^{SB}$$

in period 1. Impatient and patient consumers then trade dividends for ex-dividend shares in the secondary stock-market in period 1. Thus an institutional setup where consumers invest in mutual funds, and where these funds hold shares in publicly traded firms, is in principle as efficient at transforming liquidity as a bank.

---

10. Indeed, the inequality

$$ru'(c) \le Ru'(rc)$$

implies that

$$-c\frac{u''(c)}{u'(c)} \le -rc\frac{u''(rc)}{u'(rc)}$$

With $r \ge 1$ this inequality implies that the utility function $u(\cdot)$ has increasing relative risk aversion.

3. The second-best allocation is in general strictly better when consumers cannot reinvest the funds they withdraw in period 1. To see this point, it suffices to compare the two incentive constraints

$$u(\mu c_{21}^{SB} + c_{22}^{SB}) \geq u(\mu c_{11}^{SB} + c_{12}^{SB})$$

and

$$u(\mu c_{21}^{SB} + c_{22}^{SB}) \geq u(r c_{11}^{SB} + c_{12}^{SB})$$

The first constraint applies if the reinvestment option is not available. The second one allows for reinvestment and is therefore more demanding. As Jacklin (1987), Diamond (1997), and Allen and Gale (2000), among others, have argued, a bank-based financial system may be able to prevent reinvestment of savings in period 1 and thus be able to provide a better form of insurance against liquidity shocks than mutual funds holding shares in publicly traded firms and operating in the secondary market. In other words, it is optimal to provide insurance with nontraded instruments.

4. As stressed by Diamond and Dybvig (1983), however, the optimal demand-deposit contract offered by a bank may give rise to bank runs. The basic idea here is that if all type-2 consumers decide to mimic type-1 consumers, then there may not be enough money in the bank to meet all withdrawal demands. When such an event happens, the bank fails, and the anticipation of such a failure is precisely what may trigger a run on the bank by all type-2 consumers. To the extent that the secondary market solution is run-proof, it (weakly) dominates the solution with financial intermediation, where depositors are allowed to reinvest their savings in the short-term investment in period 1.

9.2.2   Optimal Contracting with Two Independent Shocks

We now extend the previous analysis by assuming that the consumer faces two independent income shocks rather than one preference shock at the beginning of period 1. We closely follow the treatment in Townsend (1982).

Consider the dynamic contracting problem between two parties: a risk-averse consumer and a risk-neutral bank. The consumer's time-separable utility function is $u(c_1) + u(c_2)$, where c_t denotes consumption in period $t = 1, 2$. We assume for now only that $u(\cdot)$ is strictly increasing and strictly concave and that $u'(0) = +\infty$. Later we consider specific functional forms to obtain closed-form solutions. The consumer faces random income shocks.

Her income is independently and identically distributed in the two periods and takes the value $w = 1$ with probability p and $w = 0$ with probability $(1 - p)$. The bank has sufficient wealth to be able to lend to the consumer whatever is required. For simplicity we set the equilibrium interest rate to zero. In this setup the optimal contract takes the form of an endowment-contingent transfer $\{b_1(w_1); b_2(w_1;w_2)\}$. Let $w^1 = (w_1)$ and $w^2 = (w_1;w_2)$; then the first-best problem is the solution of

$$\max_{b_t(w^t)} E\{u[w_1 + b_1(w^1)] + u[w_2 + b_2(w^2)]\}$$

subject to the individual-rationality constraint

$$E[b_1(w^1) + b_2(w^2)] \leq 0$$

Since interest rates are equal to zero, the individual-rationality constraint reduces to a condition that net expected transfers from the bank to the consumer should be nonpositive. Assigning Lagrange multiplier λ to the individual-rationality constraint and differentiating with respect to $b_t(w^t)$, we obtain the following first-order conditions:

$$u'[w_t + b_t(w^t)] = \lambda \quad \text{for } t = 1,2$$

so that, unsurprisingly, the optimal consumption stream of the risk-averse consumer must be constant:

$$w_t + b_t(w^t) = p$$

which implies

$$\begin{cases} b_1(0) = b_2(w_1;0) = p \\ b_1(1) = b_2(w_1;1) = p - 1 \end{cases}$$

Besides the fact that the first-best contract involves perfect insurance for the consumer, the other important property is that there appears to be no gain from writing a long-term contract. The repetition of the static contract—that is, spot contract $[b(0) = p$ and $b(1) = p - 1]$—achieves the same allocation.

Suppose now that the income realization w_t is private information to the consumer. It is clear then that the first-best spot contract is no longer feasible, since a consumer with income realization $w_t = 1$ would have an incentive to claim $\hat{w}_t = 0$ in order to hold on to her endowment and receive a positive net transfer $b_t(\hat{w}_t) = p$.

If the first best is not implementable through a sequence of spot contracts, what can be implemented through such a sequence? The answer to this question leads to a striking insight: the only incentive-compatible sequence of spot contracts is no insurance. To see this, begin with the last period. Any difference in net transfers $b_2(0) \neq b_2(1)$ would lead to a violation of incentive compatibility, the consumer having a strict incentive to always collect the higher net transfer. Hence, there can be no insurance at date $t = 2$. Working backward to period 1, it is straightforward to observe that there cannot be any difference in net transfers in period 1 either. Does this observation imply that there cannot be any scope for insurance when income shocks are privately observed? Fortunately no: Some insurance is possible when the consumer and the bank can write a long-term contract.

To show this possibility, Townsend first considers a simple debt contract with zero interest, that is, $b_2(w_1;w_2) = -b_1(w_1)$. Faced with such a contract, the consumer chooses $b_1(w_1)$ to solve

$$\max_{b_1(w_1)} u[w_1 + b_1(w_1)] + E\{u[w_2 - b_1(w_1)]\}$$

The optimal $b_1(w_1)$ then satisfies a familiar Euler equation:

$$u'[w_1 + b_1(w_1)] = E\{u'[w_2 - b_1(w_1)]\}$$

In general, the solution to this equation is such that $b_1(1) < 0 < b_1(0)$, so that, through this borrowing and lending behavior, the consumer ends up "purchasing partial insurance" in period 1. This insurance, however, comes at the expense of forgoing some *intertemporal consumption smoothing,* in the following sense: The consumer strictly prefers more intraperiod insurance in period 1 to an equal expected consumption across periods.

Townsend's next important insight is that simple borrowing/lending arrangements with $b_2(w_1;w_2) = -b_1(w_1)$ are not second-best efficient in general. To see this, note that, by revealed preference and the strict concavity of $u(\cdot)$, the consumer's incentive constraints

$$u[1 + b_1(1)] + E\{u[w_2 - b_1(1)]\} > u[1 + b_1(0)] + E\{u[w_2 - b_1(0)]\}$$

and

$$u[b_1(0)] + E\{u[w_2 - b_1(0)]\} > u[b_1(1)] + E\{u[w_2 - b_1(1)]\}$$

are both slack. Therefore, it is possible to find a better long-term contract than a simple borrowing/lending contract $b_2(w_1;w_2) = -b_1(w_1)$.

To characterize the second-best long-term contract, note first that any incentive-compatible long-term contract requires a net transfer in period 2 that is independent of the consumer's type:

$$b_2(w_1;0) = b_2(w_1;1) \equiv b_2(w_1) \quad \text{for } w_1 = 0,1$$

As pointed out previously, the consumer otherwise has an incentive to misreport period-2 income. Therefore, the second-best contracting problem reduces to

$$\max_{b_t(w_1)} p\{u[1+b_1(1)] + [pu(1+b_2(1)) + (1-p)u(b_2(1))]\} +$$
$$(1-p)\{u[b_1(0)] + [pu(1+b_2(0)) + (1-p)u(b_2(0))]\}$$

subject to

$$u[1+b_1(1)] + \{pu[1+b_2(1)] + (1-p)u[b_2(1)]\} \geq$$
$$u[1+b_1(0)] + \{pu[1+b_2(0)] + (1-p)u[b_2(0)]\} \tag{IC1}$$

$$u[b_1(0)] + \{pu[1+b_2(0)] + (1-p)u[b_2(0)]\} \geq$$
$$u[b_1(1)] + \{pu[1+b_2(1)] + (1-p)u[b_2(1)]\} \tag{IC0}$$

and

$$p[b_1(1)+b_2(1)] + (1-p)[b_1(0)+b_2(0)] \leq 0 \tag{IR}$$

An educated guess suggests that only (IC1) is likely to be binding at the optimum.

We have already established that an optimal second-best contract is not of the form of a simple borrowing/lending contract such that $b_2(w_1) = -b_1(w_1)$. This simple contract form is optimal only conditional on the realization of w_1 and does not provide sufficient coverage of income risk in period 1.

To see how the optimal second-best contract can improve risk sharing by trading off intraperiod risk at date 1 against intertemporal consumption smoothing, it is helpful to consider the following simple example proposed by Townsend: Let

$$u(w) = w - \gamma w^2$$

with $\gamma < \frac{1}{2}$. Let $p = \frac{1}{2}$, and consider the class of contracts with balanced transfers accross income states such that

$$b_t(1) + b_t(0) = 0 \quad \text{for } t = 1,2$$

This class of contracts, where the (IR) constraint is always satisfied, introduces some flexibility not available under a simple borrowing/lending scheme by removing the requirement that transfers over time must net out $[b_1(w_1) + b_2(w_1) = 0]$. It is, however, more restrictive than a simple borrowing/lending contract in that it requires transfers to balance out across income states within a period. Note that while this contract class can be shown to improve upon the simple borrowing/lending scheme considered earlier, it is not necessarily second-best optimal.

As it turns out, the complete characterization of the second-best optimal contract is rather involved and not particularly insightful, even if the consumer is assumed to have a simple quadratic utility function. We therefore limit ourselves here to showing that the contract with balancedness across income states dominates the contract with intertemporal balancedness.

Letting $b_2 = -\alpha b_1$ with $0 \leq \alpha \leq 1$ and assuming balancedness across states, the consumer optimization problem reduces to

$$\max_{b_1, \alpha} \left\{ 1 - b_1 - \gamma(1-b_1)^2 + \frac{1}{2}\left[1 + \alpha b_1 - \gamma(1+\alpha b_1)^2 + \alpha b_1 - \gamma(\alpha b_1)^2\right] \right\} + \left\{ b_1 - \gamma(b_1)^2 + \frac{1}{2}\left[1 - \alpha b_1 - \gamma(1-\alpha b_1)^2 - \alpha b_1 - \gamma(-\alpha b_1)^2\right] \right\}$$

subject to

$$1 - b_1 - \gamma(1-b_1)^2 + \frac{1}{2}\left[1 + \alpha b_1 - \gamma(1+\alpha b_1)^2 + \alpha b_1 - \gamma(\alpha b_1)^2\right] = 1 + b_1 - \gamma(1+b_1)^2 + \frac{1}{2}\left[1 - \alpha b_1 - \gamma(1-\alpha b_1)^2 - \alpha b_1 - \gamma(-\alpha b_1)^2\right]$$

This assumes that constraint (IC0) is not binding. Differentiating the Lagrangean with respect to b_1 and α then yields, after straightforward computations,

$$\alpha = \frac{1-2\gamma}{1-\gamma} < 1 \quad \text{and} \quad b_1 = \frac{1}{2(1+\alpha^2)}$$

Instead, under a simple borrowing/lending scheme, the consumer could chooses how much to borrow after the first income realization. After being unlucky in period 1, the consumer's problem is

$$\max_{b_1} b_1 - \gamma(b_1)^2 + \frac{1}{2}\left[1 - b_1 - \gamma(1-b_1)^2 - b_1 - \gamma(-b_1)^2\right]$$

which yields $b_1 = \dfrac{1}{4}$. After being lucky in period 1, the consumer's problem is

$$\max_{b_1} 1 - b_1 - \gamma(1 - b_1)^2 + \tfrac{1}{2}\Big[1 + b_1 - \gamma(1 + b_1)^2 + b_1 - \gamma(b_1)^2\Big]$$

which once again yields $b_1 = \tfrac{1}{4}$. With quadratic utility, the consumer therefore saves as much after being lucky as she borrows after being unlucky. Her behavior therefore satisfies balancedness across income states, and is a special case of the previous contract, with $\alpha = 1$ by construction, and $b_1 = \tfrac{1}{4}$. It is now immediately clear why simple borrowing and lending is suboptimal: It provides less than optimal insurance against period 1 income risk:

$$\frac{1}{4} < \frac{1}{2(1 + \alpha^2)}$$

since

$$\alpha = \frac{1 - 2\gamma}{1 - \gamma} < 1$$

when $\gamma < \tfrac{1}{2}$.

Intuitively, when balancedness across time is not required, the consumer ends up consuming more in period 1 after an unlucky income realization, since part of this consumption is "compensated" by lower consumption in period 1 after the lucky income realization and not solely by lower period-2 consumption (whether or not period-2 income is high). Insurance, however, is only partial in period 1 (and this remains true for second-best insurance): For period-1 insurance to be incentive compatible, it must still be accompanied by some "compensating transfers" in period 2, which (because of incentive compatibility again) cannot depend on the realization of period-2 income. Since these transfers destabilize period-2 consumption, they involve a cost and therefore make full period-1 insurance unattractive.

To summarize, the analysis of the two-period problem highlights how second-best risk sharing requires trading off more intertemporal consumption smoothing for intratemporal risk sharing than under a simple borrowing/lending scheme. This analysis echoes and complements Diamond and Dybvig's observations discussed earlier. It illustrates in a simple and striking way that equilibrium risk sharing obtained by trading debt claims in a competitive securities market results in suboptimal risk sharing in general. That is, better risk sharing is obtainable by nontradable claims issued by a financial intermediary that is free to impose any rate of intertemporal transformation that is desirable.

Another conclusion emerging from this simple two-period problem is that, given that second-best insurance is only partial, endogenous income inequalities emerge in this setup between those consumers that had a lucky run of income shocks and those that were less lucky. A natural question raised by this analysis is how the income distribution evolves under second-best risk sharing as the number of periods is increased beyond $t = 2$. We turn to this question in the next subsection by extending Townsend's contracting problem to an infinite-horizon setting.

9.2.3   Second-Best Risk Sharing between Infinitely Lived Agents

As the analysis of the two-period problem makes clear, it is difficult to obtain sharp characterizations of the optimal contract for general concave utility functions $u(\cdot)$. This difficulty is compounded in the infinite-horizon contracting problem. We therefore limit attention to the most tractable functional form for the agent's utility function and assume that the infinitely lived consumer has CARA risk preferences represented by the utility function

$$u(c) = -e^{-rc}$$

We closely follow the treatment of this problem in Green (1987) and Thomas and Worrall (1990) [see Atkeson and Lucas, 1992, for the technically more involved analysis of this problem when the consumer has CRRA risk preferences represented by a utility function of the form $u(c) = (c^{1-r} - 1)/(1 - r)$].

The risk-neutral financial intermediary and the risk-averse consumer have the common discount factor $\delta \in (0, 1)$. As in the two-period problem considered earlier, this consumer is faced with an i.i.d. binomial income process, such that in any given period her income is $w = 1$ with probability p and $w = 0$ with probability $(1 - p)$. The consumer can sign a long-term insurance contract with the risk-neutral bank. If income is observable, then the bank would break even by offering the consumer a constant consumption flow of p and taking on all the residual income risk. Hence, the first-best flow utility level attainable by the consumer is given by $u(p) = -e^{-rp}$, and the first-best discounted present value of this steady consumption stream is given by

$$v_{FB} = -\frac{1}{(1-\delta)} e^{-rp}$$

The worst outcome for the consumer is autarky, where no insurance is obtained. In that case the expected flow utility of consumption is given by

$$-[pe^{-r} + (1-p)]$$

and the present discounted value of the random consumption stream under autarky is

$$v_A = -\frac{1}{(1-\delta)}[pe^{-r} + (1-p)]$$

Note that an important implicit assumption here is that income takes the form of a perishable good.

Even if income shocks are private information, we know from the previous section that it is possible for the consumer to improve expected flow utility of consumption by writing a long-term incentive-compatible insurance (or loan) contract. Let $S^t = \{0, 1\}^t$ denote the set of sample paths of income from period $\tau = 0$ to $\tau = t$ and let $h^t = (w_0; w_1; \ldots; w_t) \in S^t$ represent a history of income realizations up to time t; then a long-term contract is a sequence of contingent net transfers $b_t(h^t)$ for $t = 0, \ldots, \infty$. Although solving for an optimal incentive-compatible long-term contract is a potentially daunting problem, it is possible to obtain a reasonably simple characterization of the optimal contract in the special setting considered here by exploiting the stationarity of the underlying problem.

In the previous section we formulated the optimal contracting problem as a constrained maximization problem for the consumer. In the infinite-horizon problem it turns out that the dual problem of maximizing the bank's expected return subject to incentive-compatibility constraints and an individual-rationality constraint for the consumer is more tractable. Denote the consumer's outside option by v. The consumer's individual-rationality constraint can then be written as

$$E\left[\sum_{t=0}^{\infty} \delta^t \{u[b_t(h^t) + w_t]\}\right] \geq v$$

As one might expect, this constraint is always binding at the optimum. Turning to the consumer's incentive-compatibility constraints, denote by $b_1(\hat{h}^{t-1})$ and $b_0(\hat{h}^{t-1})$ the transfer from the bank to the consumer in period t when the consumer has reported a history of income realizations up to period $t-1$ of $\hat{h}^{t-1}$ and reports income realization 1 and 0, respectively, at date t. Since the consumer's income is identically and independently distributed over time, the expected future discounted value of the contract at time t can depend only on past transfers based on reported history and not the actual history h^t. Indeed, since income is perishable, the only intertemporal link here concerns the transfers the consumer can expect to receive in the future, and these transfers depend only on past reported history of income realizations. We can, therefore, write the consumer's continuation value under the contract at date t as, respectively, $v_1(\hat{h}^{t-1}) \equiv v[b_1(\hat{h}^{t-1})]$ and $v_0(\hat{h}^{t-1}) \equiv v[b_0(\hat{h}^{t-1})]$, so that the consumer's incentive compatibility constraints are

$$u[b_1(\hat{h}^{t-1})+1]+\delta v_1(\hat{h}^{t-1}) \geq u[b_0(\hat{h}^{t-1})+1]+\delta v_0(\hat{h}^{t-1})$$

and

$$u[b_0(\hat{h}^{t-1})]+\delta v_0(\hat{h}^{t-1}) \geq u[b_1(\hat{h}^{t-1})]+\delta v_1(\hat{h}^{t-1})$$

for all $\hat{h}^{t-1} \in S^{t-1}$ and all $t \geq 0$. It is instructive to stress the similarity between these incentive constraints and (IC1) and (IC0) in the previous subsection.

Having determined the bank's constraints, the next step is to describe the bank's objective. We can define the bank's continuation value under the contract as

$$-E\left[\sum_{t=0}^{\infty} \delta^t b_t(h^t)\right]$$

In other words, the bank's payoff is the expected present discounted value of future repayments. Taking advantage of the recursive structure of the underlying contracting problem, we can define the bank's value function to be the unique solution of the Bellman equation

$$C(v) = \min_{\{(b_1,v_1);(b_0,v_0)\}} \{p[b_1+\delta C(v_1)]+(1-p)[b_0+\delta C(v_0)]\}$$

subject to

$$p[u(b_1+1)+\delta v_1]+(1-p)[u(b_0)+\delta v_0] = v \qquad \text{(IR)}$$

and

$$u(b_1+1)+\delta v_1 \geq u(b_0+1)+\delta v_0 \qquad \text{(IC1)}$$

$$u(b_0) + \delta v_0 \geq u(b_1) + \delta v_1 \tag{IC0}$$

When the income process is observable to the bank, so that incentive constraints can be ignored, a flow utility level u (less than 0) can be guaranteed at minimum cost to the consumer by choosing net transfers b_0^{FB} and b_1^{FB} such that

$$-e^{-r(b_1^{FB}+1)} = -e^{-rb_0^{FB}} = u$$

or

$$1 + b_1^{FB} = -\frac{1}{r}\log(-u) = b_0^{FB}$$

Therefore, the flow cost to the bank of guaranteeing utility level u equal to $(1 - \delta)v$ (less than 0) is given by

$$pb_1^{FB} + (1-p)b_0^{FB} = -\frac{1}{r}\log(-u) - p = -\frac{1}{r}[\log(1-\delta) + \log(-v)] - p$$

Hence, the first-best discounted expected cost to the bank is

$$\frac{1}{1-\delta}[pb_1^{FB} + (1-p)b_0^{FB}] = -\left[\frac{\log(1-\delta) + \log(-v) - rp}{(1-\delta)r}\right] \equiv C^{FB}(v)$$

When the income process is unobservable, the bank cannot offer an incentive-compatible contract that perfectly insures the consumer. Its cost is then higher because it needs to pay an extra insurance premium to maintain the same level of flow utility u. The incentive constraints (IC1) and (IC0) can be rewritten in slightly more convenient form as follows:

$$e^{-r}u_1 + \delta v_1 \geq e^{-r}u_0 + \delta v_0$$

and

$$u_0 + \delta v_0 \geq u_1 + \delta v_1$$

where $u_0 = -e^{-rb_0}$ and $u_1 = -e^{-rb_1}$. The two constraints can be rewritten as

$$u_0 - u_1 \geq \delta(v_1 - v_0) \geq e^{-r}(u_0 - u_1)$$

Note that, just as in Townsend's setting, we expect to have at the optimum

$$u_1 < u_0 \quad \text{and} \quad v_0 < v_1$$

that is, the consumer receives a net transfer when unlucky, but, to guarantee incentive compatibility, it comes at the cost of a lower continuation utility. Both constraints are therefore unlikely to be binding simultaneously at the second-best optimum. Moreover, since $b_1^{FB} < b_0^{FB}$, it appears that the relevant incentive constraint is (IC1), the one preventing the high-income type from mimicking the low-income type,

$$-e^{-r}(u_1 - u_0) = \delta(v_1 - v_0)$$

Consequently, the bank's optimal-contract-design problem becomes

$$C(v) = \min_{\{(u_1,v_1);(u_0,v_0)\}} \left\{ p\left[-\frac{1}{r}\log(-u_1) - 1 + \delta C(v_1) \right] + (1-p)\left[-\frac{1}{r}\log(-u_0) + \delta C(v_0) \right] \right\}$$

subject to

$$v = p(e^{-r}u_1 + \delta v_1) + (1-p)(u_0 + \delta v_0)$$

and

$$-e^{-r}(u_1 - u_0) = \delta(v_1 - v_0)$$

The form of the first-best cost function $C^{FB}(v)$ suggests that a likely form of the second-best cost function $C(v)$ is

$$C(v) = k - \frac{\log(-v)}{(1-\delta)r}$$

where k is a constant that remains to be determined. Indeed, substituting for this functional form in the preceding Bellman equation, we obtain

$$C(v) = \min\left\{ p\left[-\frac{1}{r}\log(-u_1) - 1 + \delta\left(k - \frac{\log(-v_1)}{(1-\delta)r} \right) \right] \right.$$
$$\left. + (1-p)\left[-\frac{1}{r}\log(-u_0) - 1 + \delta\left(k - \frac{\log(-v_0)}{(1-\delta)r} \right) \right] \right\}$$

or, after some manipulations,

$$C(v) = \min\left\{ \delta k - 1 - \frac{1}{r}\left[p\left(\log\left(\frac{u_1}{v}\right) + \left(\frac{\delta}{1-\delta}\right)\log\left(\frac{v_1}{v}\right) \right) \right.\right.$$
$$\left.\left. + (1-p)\left(\log\left(\frac{u_0}{v}\right) + \left(\frac{\delta}{1-\delta}\right)\log\left(\frac{v_0}{v}\right) \right) \right] - \frac{\log(-v)}{(1-\delta)r} \right\}$$

Letting

$$f(k,v,v_i,u_i) \equiv \delta k - 1 - \frac{1}{r}\left\{ p\left[\log\left(\frac{u_1}{v}\right) + \left(\frac{\delta}{1-\delta}\right)\log\left(\frac{v_1}{v}\right) \right] \right.$$
$$\left. + (1-p)\left[\log\left(\frac{u_o}{v}\right) + \left(\frac{\delta}{1-\delta}\right)\log\left(\frac{v_0}{v}\right) \right] \right\}$$

it is then apparent that the solution to the Bellman equation has the required functional form

$$C(v) = \min\left\{f(k,v,v_i,u_i) - \frac{\log(-v)}{(1-\delta)r}\right\}$$

Since $C(v)$ is now expressed in terms of utilities relative to v, that is, in terms of ratios u_i/v and v_i/v, it is convenient to further simplify the bank's problem by denoting[11]

$$v_i \equiv a_i v \quad \text{and} \quad u_i \equiv g_i v$$

Note that all utilities are negative, so that the a_i's and g_i's are positive. The bank chooses $(a_1; g_1; a_0; g_0)$ to solve

$$\min_{\substack{(a_1;g_1);\\(a_0;g_0)}} -\frac{1}{r}\left\{p\left[\log g_1 + \left(\frac{\delta}{1-\delta}\right)\log a_1\right] + (1-p)\left[\log g_0 + \left(\frac{\delta}{1-\delta}\right)\log a_0\right]\right\}$$

subject to

$$\delta(a_1 - u_0) = -e^{-r}(g_1 - g_0) \tag{IC1}$$

and

$$p(e^{-r}g_1 + \delta a_1) + (1-p)(g_0 + \delta a_0) = 1 \tag{IR}$$

Note that the solution of this convex minimization program is independent of k. Moreover, it can be checked that the optimal solution entails

$$a_1 < a_0 \quad \text{and} \quad g_0 < g_1$$

which, since the utilities are negative, implies $u_1 < u_0$ and $v_0 < v_1$. This solution also satisfies (IC0), the other incentive constraint:[12]

---

11. Since the consumer has a CARA utility function, one can summarize the value of the contract in terms of certainty equivalent. In other words, one can write $v(b_i) = u(b_i + \pi)$ (where π denotes the risk premium). This means here that

$$v_i = \frac{a_i}{g_i}u_i$$

12. This constraint can be written as

$$g_0 v + \delta a_0 v \geq g_1 v + \delta a_1 v$$

Since v is negative, this is equivalent to

$$\delta(a_0 - a_1) \leq (g_1 - g_0)$$

which is true, given the binding incentive constraint (IC1).

$u_0 + \delta v_0 \geq u_1 + \delta v_1$

As in the two-period problem, the consumer can thus obtain intraperiod insurance against adverse income shocks ($u_0 > u_1$) at the expense of intertemporal consumption smoothing ($v_0 < v_1$). A number of other striking implications emerge from this analysis. First, since $v_1 > v_0$, the inequality in welfare between *lucky* consumers, who have high income shocks, and *unlucky* consumers grows over time. Second, if we denote by v_t the consumer's utility at the beginning of period t, then v_t converges to $-\infty$ almost surely (see Thomas and Worrall, 1990). The proof of this result relies on the observation that $C'(v_t)$ is a martingale or, in other words, that

$E[C'(v_{t+1})] = C'(v_t)$

Hence, by the martingale convergence theorem, $C'(v_t)$ converges almost surely to some limit. Thomas and Worrall show that this limit must be zero and therefore that $\lim_{t \to \infty} v_t \to -\infty$. Intuitively, the reason why the limit must be $-\infty$ is that any finite limit can occur only with probability zero because future v_i's would always *spread out* from that point. One way of understanding the economic logic behind this striking result it to think of the infinitely lived consumer as living permanently *above her means* when she has a negative income shock and continually postponing the pain of having to repay her accumulated debts to the future. Such behavior makes sense when the consumer discounts the future. A compounding effect comes from the convexity of $C(v)$. Other things equal, the bank's cost is higher the more spread out are the v_i's (to maintain incentive compatibility), but the curvature of $C(v)$ is flatter at low values of v. Therefore, the cost of maintaining a spread between v_1 and v_0 is lower, the lower is v—hence the incentive for the bank to let v_t drift downward. There are two potential constraints on the second-best optimal process v_t. First, as debts accumulate, the consumer may be tempted to default. To avoid default the bank will limit the amount of debt the consumer can accumulate and thus limit her ability to *consume above her means*. As a result, there would be less intraperiod insurance and more intertemporal consumption smoothing. Second, if there was competition between multiple banks, and consumers could switch at any time between banks, then banks would also be limited in the extent to which they can trade off intertemporal consumption smoothing to increase intraperiod insurance. Indeed, the downward drift in v_t would be reduced by banks' attempts to steal away previously unlucky consumers by offering them better savings terms.

9.3   Summary and Literature Notes

This chapter has first dealt with dynamic adverse selection models with constant types. Lack of commitment can arise in "mild" form when *long-term contracts* protect each party against unilateral violations but the parties cannot commit not to engage in future *Pareto-improving* renegotiations; it arises in more severe form when only *short-term contracts* are available (for example, because the principal is a government that cannot commit not to unilaterally change the law). In the first case, the principal cannot commit not to be *too soft* with the agent in the future (this is the *durable-good-monopoly problem* or the *soft-budget-constraint problem*), while in the second he can also not commit not to be *too tough* (this is the *ratchet effect*). In both cases, the principal is hurt because outcomes he finds sequentially optimal are not ex ante optimal.

Commitment problems arise because information revealed through contract execution leads to recontracting opportunities that hurt the principal from an ex ante point of view. A general lesson from this literature therefore concerns the desirability of limiting the information revealed in the course of contract execution, that is, of signing contracts with (partial) pooling. The form of optimal contracts has been analyzed in detail by Freixas, Guesnerie, and Tirole (1985) and Laffont and Tirole (1988a) for the case of short-term contracting, by Dewatripont (1989) for the case of long-term contracting with renegotiation (and the *renegotiation-proofness principle*), and by Hart and Tirole (1988) and Laffont and Tirole (1990) for both cases simultaneously. For further theoretical developments, see in particular (1) Beaudry and Poitevin (1993) for an analysis of instantaneous renegotiation in signaling games, (2) Rey and Salanie (1996) for a discussion of the possibility of achieving long-term commitment through a sequence of (renegotiated) two-period contracts, (3) Bester and Strausz (2001) for a generalization of the revelation principle to the case of imperfect commitment (where "truth telling" occurs only with probability less than one, due to equilibrium pooling); and (4) Bajari and Tadelis (2001) for an analysis of imperfect commitment and costly renegotiation.

The chapter has also looked at specific applications, the most influential being the regulation setting due to Laffont and Tirole (see their 1993 book). In terms of contract theory, we have stressed several economic insights:

- In the case of a buyer-seller model ("Coasian dynamics"), the optimality of sale contracts over rental contracts, to avoid the ratchet effect (Hart and Tirole, 1988). This is in contrast with the result obtained under buyer anonymity, where renting is a way of avoiding *all* commitment problems, by making the problem of the seller stationary (on this version of the durable-monopoly problem, see, for example, Stokey, 1981; Bulow, 1982, or Gul, Sonnenschein, and Wilson, 1986).

• The potential optimality of exogenously restricting the observability of contract execution for the principal. While this is never optimal in the absence of commitment problems, because it worsens incentive-compatibility constraints, it can be desirable as a way to limit the harm caused by limited commitment. This problem has been analyzed by Dewatripont and Maskin (1995a) in the context of insurance contracts. A related insight is due to Crémer (1995), who stresses the benefits of "arm's length" relationships. He considers a dynamic model where a principal hires an agent who has private information about her intrinsic productivity. The agent's output depends on this productivity and also on her effort. The principal would like to incentivize the agent by threatening to fire her in case of low past effort. This threat may not be credible, however, because Crémer assumes that, once effort has been chosen, the principal's benefit from not firing the agent solely depends on her intrinsic productivity, not on her past effort. If the principal observes effort or productivity and cannot commit in advance to a firing rule, the agent then knows she will not be penalized for low effort and therefore shirks. Keeping the agent "at arm's-length" is useful in this case: Since the principal observes only output and not effort or productivity, he may rationally attribute low output to low intrinsic productivity, which makes the firing rule credible. This is thus another case where reducing observability alleviates commitment problems.

• Reduced observability also helps alleviate the soft-budget-constraint problem, that is, the refinancing of loss-making projects. As argued by

---

13. For a comprehensive treatment of the soft-budget-constraint literature, see the survey by Kornai, Maskin, and Roland (2003). This issue has received a fair amount of attention in the "transition economics" literature (see Roland, 2000). Note that dynamic adverse selection models have also been used to analyze aspects of the *political economy of transition,* namely, the question of optimal industrial restructuring under political constraints (see Dewatripont and Roland, 1992, which builds on Lewis, Feenstra, and Ware, 1989). An interesting feature of this setting is that political constraints represent an intermediate form of long-term contracting between a government and its electorate: Prior agreements remain in force as long as a majority of the electorate refuses to change them. An agenda-setting reform-minded government, however, will try to undo them by endogenously targeting specific groups of the population that can form a proreform majority.

Dewatripont and Maskin (1995b), this problem can naturally arise when initial investments are sunk by the time the creditor realizes the project has a negative net present value.[13] In this setting, making it necessary to have the refinancing performed by a new, less well informed creditor may harden the budget constraint and improve overall efficiency. As stressed by Dewatripont and Maskin (1995b) and von Thadden (1995), however, this gain comes at the expense of long-run risk taking. The connection between the number of creditors and the probability of refinancing with commitment problems has also been analyzed by Bolton and Scharfstein (1996).

The main driving factor of dynamic-adverse-selection models with constant types is the information revealed through contract execution. When types are independent across periods, things change drastically, and the main focus is the trade-off between intraperiod risk sharing and intertemporal consumption smoothing. Three cases were considered:

• First, a simple two-period consumption model where the agent learns at the beginning of period 1 that he needs to consume in period 1 or can wait until period 2. This simple model of liquidity shocks, put forward by Diamond and Dybvig (1983), allows one to highlight the benefits of banking and of deposit contracts—but also, as stressed first by Jacklin (1987) concerning equity/bond contracts—as a way to pool independently distributed individual liquidity shocks. These latter instruments seem to be preferable, since they are not subject to bank runs, a potential equilibrium phenomenon in the Diamond-Dybvig setting. However, one can argue that a "bank-based setting" may be able to allow for potentially more risk sharing, by limiting the reinvestment opportunities of agents who consider withdrawing their funds early while they need to consume only later on. This issue has been stressed, for example, by Diamond (1997) and Allen and Gale (2000). The Diamond-Dybvig model has in fact generated a large literature on banking and liquidity provision; see Bhattacharya and Thakor (1993) and Freixas and Rochet (1997) for surveys.

• The second case we considered is that of two independently distributed income shocks. Pioneered by Townsend (1982), this case has allowed us to stress the trade-off between insurance and intertemporal consumption smoothing. Specifically, in a static setting, there is no way to induce separation of types, since the agent would always report the income realization that allows her to receive the highest net transfer. Instead, with two income shocks, one can make the (constant) second-period transfer contingent on the income reported in period 1. In case of a negative (positive) period-1 income realization, the agent then optimally receives a positive (negative) transfer, which then leads to a negative (positive) transfer in period 2. This transfer is beneficial because, in the case of a negative (positive) income shock in period 1, the agent's period-1 marginal utility is higher (lower) than her expected period-2 marginal utility. Note that some of this protection against temporary income shocks can be obtained by simple borrowing and lending. Townsend shows, however, that optimal long-term contracts go beyond pure borrowing/lending to allow for more intraperiod insurance, at the expense of intertemporal consumption smoothing. As one might have guessed, the distinction between situations with preference shocks and income shocks is somewhat artificial. Indeed, the banking model of Haubrich and King (1990) highlights how these two cases give rise to fundamentally similar economic problems.

• The third case we considered extends the Townsend model to an infinite horizon. Intuitively, as in the two-period model, agents who experience negative income shocks receive positive net transfers at the cost of lower expected future consumption. Green (1987), Thomas and Worrall (1990), and Atkeson and Lucas (1992) have provided infinite-horizon extensions of the Townsend model. We have seen how to compute a stationary solution of this problem. This solution leads to increasing wealth dispersion over time. Moreover, as shown by Thomas and Worrall, the probability of reaching zero wealth tends to 1 in the long run! Lucas (1992) discusses the relevance of these predictions. Let us stress here that it is natural to think that limits to contract enforcement (e.g., the possibility of default) would partially call into question these limit results (see, Kocherlakota, 1996, and Ligon, Thomas, and Worrall, 2002, for analyses of the implication of limited contractual enforcement).

10 Dynamic Moral Hazard

In reality most principal-agent relationships are repeated or long-term. Repetition of the relation can affect the underlying incentive problem in three fundamental ways. First, repetition can make the agent less averse to risk, since she can engage in "self-insurance" and offset a bad output shock in one period by borrowing against future income. More generally, repetition introduces the possibility of intertemporal risk sharing. Second, repeated output observations can provide better information about the agent's choice of action. Both of these effects ameliorate the incentive problem and increase the flow surplus from the contract. A third countervailing effect, however, is that repetition increases the agent's set of available actions. She can now choose when to work, and she can offset a bad performance in one period by working harder the next period.

As one can easily imagine, the interaction of these three effects results in a considerably more complex contracting problem than the one-shot problem. As we saw in Chapter 4, the one-shot problem is already too sensitive to the underlying environment to be able to predict in a robust way the simple spot contracts (such as piece-rate or commission contracts) that are observed in practice. However, although repetition increases the complexity of the optimal contracting problem, it can paradoxically result in simpler optimal contracts in some special settings, as we shall see.

In general, optimal long-term contracts can unfortunately be considerably more complex than simple one-shot contracts. Indeed, the optimal contract will depend in general on the entire history of output realizations and not just on some aggregate measure of performance over some fixed interval of time. When an output outcome affects the agent's current compensation, it will also affect her future rewards under an optimal contract. In light of this potential added complexity, it is all the more pertinent to inquire whether there are plausible conditions under which optimal long-term contracts are simple. We shall devote significant space to this question.

Following the characterization of the optimal long-term contract in a general setting, where the one-shot contracting problem is repeated twice, we shall determine the conditions under which a series of short-term incentive contracts, which regulate the agent's savings, can replicate the optimal long-term contract. We then proceed to inquire under what conditions simple incentive contracts such as linear contracts or efficiency-wage-type contracts are optimal or nearly optimal. Next, we consider renegotiation of long-term contracts with moral hazard, when the agent's actions have persistent effects on output. Finally, having considered partial deviations from full-commitment contracts with renegotiation, we shall consider the case of no commitment where implicit as well as explicit incentives are important in affecting the agent's choice of actions.

Unfortunately, the literature on repeated moral hazard does not consider a common framework. In particular, different assumptions about when the agent consumes, access to credit, and control of savings are made, and as a result it is difficult to relate the different papers to one another. We base part of this chapter on the unifying treatment proposed by Chiappori, Macho, Rey, and Salanié (1994).

10.1   The Two-Period Problem

Suppose that the one-shot contracting problem considered in Chapter 4 is repeated twice. That is, at the beginning of period $t = 1, 2$ the agent privately chooses an action $a \in A$. This action then maps into n possible output realizations in period t. The probability distribution of output q_i^t in period t is given by $p_i(a_t)$, where a_t denotes the agent's action choice in period t and $i = 1, \ldots, n$. As in Chapter 4, we assume that $p_i(a) > 0$ for all $a \in A$. Since the probability distribution over output outcomes in any given period depends only on the action chosen by the agent in that period, and since the action set is the same in both periods, the two periods can be thought of as technologically independent. The only possible link between the two periods is through changes in preferences of principal and agent in response to output outcomes or action choice in the first period. Only in such a setup is it possible that a series of two spot contracts may be optimal.

To maintain this separation between periods, we assume that the principal's and agent's preferences are time separable. In each period the agent's objective function is, as before,

$$u(c) - \psi(a)$$

where c denotes the monetary value of consumption. As in Chapter 4, we assume that $u(\cdot)$ is strictly increasing and concave and $\psi(\cdot)$ is strictly increasing and convex. We also assume that $\lim_{c \to \underline{c}} u(c) = -\infty$ for some $\underline{c} > -\infty$. Moreover, the agent has an identical reservation utility in both periods $\bar{u}$. The principal's objective function is $V(q - w)$, where w is the wage paid to the agent. Again, $V(\cdot)$ is strictly increasing and weakly concave. That is, the principal can be risk averse or risk neutral.

The timing of the contracting game between the principal and agent is as follows:

- At the beginning of period $t = 1$ the principal makes a take-it-or-leave-it offer of a long-term contract to the agent. This contract specifies an action for the first period a_1 and an action plan for the second period $a_2(q_i^1)$, as well as a contingent wage schedule $w_1(q_i^1)$ and $w_2(q_i^1, q_i^2)$.

- The agent can accept or reject the offer. If the agent rejects, the game ends. If the agent accepts, she proceeds to choose an action plan a_1 in the first period.

- Following the realization of first-period output, the long-term contract can be renegotiated and replaced by a new continuation contract specifying an action $\hat{a}_2$ and compensation $\hat{w}_2(q_i^2)$. Again, the principal makes a take-it-or-leave-it offer and the new contract replaces the old one only if both principal and agent are strictly better off under the new contract.

As we shall see, the optimal long-term contract offered at the beginning of period 1 will be "renegotiation-proof" under fairly general conditions. Also, under similar conditions the optimal long-term contract can be implemented by a sequence of short-term contracts (which regulate the agent's savings), where the principal makes a take-it-or-leave-it offer in period 1 of a short-term contract $\{a_1, w_1(q_i^1)\}$, followed by another offer in period 2 of a contract $\{a_2, w_2(q_i^2)\}$.

SOME DEFINITIONS   To be more precise, we provide the following definitions:

A long-term contract is *renegotiation-proof* if, at every contracting date, the continuation contract is an optimal solution to the continuation contracting problem for the remaining periods.

A long-term contract is *spot implementable* if and only if there exists a perfect Bayesian equilibrium of the spot-contracting game, the outcome of which replicates the long-term contract.

A contract exhibits *memory* if second-period wages depend on first-period output outcomes.

A new issue arising in repeated-moral-hazard problems is the agent's borrowing/saving decisions and consumption smoothing. If the agent is better off smoothing her consumption over time, then the optimal long-term contract might provide some intertemporal risk sharing. Also, if the agent's attitude toward risk depends on wealth, then the principal must be able to track the evolution of the agent's wealth after consumption to determine the agent's risk preferences. What is more, the principal may want to control the agent's saving decisions so as to provide better incentives. We shall consider in turn three different scenarios.

In the first, the agent has *no access to credit markets* and must rely on the principal to transfer wealth over time. Although this scenario may appear somewhat unrealistic, it provides a useful benchmark. In the second scenario, the agent has *access* to credit, but we let the principal *monitor* the agent's saving behavior. Finally, in the third scenario the principal does not observe the agent's saving decisions.

10.1.1   No Access to Credit

The results detailed in this section have been first derived by Rogerson (1985b). Assume here that the agent has no access to credit markets. In other words, the agent is forced to consume whatever she earns in any period.

The optimal long-term contract then specifies $n + n^2$ contingent consumption levels, where

$w_i \equiv$ wage associated with q_i^1 in period 1

$w_{ij} \equiv$ wage associated with (q_i^1, q_j^2) in period 2

The agent responds by choosing the action plan:[1]

$a_1 \equiv$ action in period 1

$a_i \equiv$ action in period 2 contingent on q_i^1

Assuming away discounting, the optimal long-term contract then solves the following program:

$$
\begin{cases}
\displaystyle \max_{(w_i),(w_{ij}),a_1,(a_i)} \sum_{i=1}^{n} p_i(a_1) \left[V(q_i^1 - w_i) + \sum_{j=1}^{n} p_j(a_i) V(q_i^2 - w_{ij}) \right] \\[2ex]
\text{subject to} \\[1ex]
[a_1,(a_i)] \in \displaystyle \arg\max_{\tilde{a}_1,(\tilde{a}_i)} \sum_{i=1}^{n} p_i(\tilde{a}_1) \left[u(w_i) - \psi(\tilde{a}_1) + \sum_{j=1}^{n} p_j(\tilde{a}_i) u(w_{ij}) - \psi(\tilde{a}_i) \right] \\[2ex]
\text{and} \\[1ex]
\displaystyle \sum_{i=1}^{n} p_i(a_1) \left[u(w_i) - \psi(a_1) + \sum_{j=1}^{n} p_j(a_i) u(w_{ij}) - \psi(a_i) \right] \geq 2\overline{u}
\end{cases}
$$

---

1. Note the slight abuse of notation here: The action in period 1 a_1 is not the same as the action in period 2 contingent on q_i^1, even though it is also called a_1.

As is apparent from this program, the two-period optimal contracting problem is significantly more complex than the one-shot problem. Nevertheless, by considering marginal intertemporal transfers for every given first-period output realization q_i^1, a fundamental relationship between contingent wages across periods can be established (we drop time superscripts because at any time the output distribution only depends on effort):

$$\frac{V'(q_i - w_i)}{u'(w_i)} = \sum_{j=1}^{n} p_j(a_i) \left[\frac{V'(q_j - w_{ij})}{u'(w_{ij})} \right] \tag{10.1}$$

Or, more strikingly, if the principal is risk neutral, this equation reduces to a form of Euler equation,

$$\frac{1}{u'(w_i)} = \sum_{j=1}^{n} p_j(a_i) \left[\frac{1}{u'(w_{ij})} \right]$$

The optimal contract smoothes the agent's consumption so as to equate (the inverse of) her marginal utility in the first period with the expected (inverse) marginal utility in the second period.

To see why this relationship between contingent wages across periods must hold, suppose to the contrary that the optimal contract $[(w_i), (w_{ij})]$ is such that equation (10.1) does not hold, and consider the modified contract $[(\hat{w}_i), (\hat{w}_{ij})]$ such that, for all (i, j),

$$u(\hat{w}_i) = u(w_i) - \varepsilon_i$$

and

$$u(\hat{w}_{ij}) = u(w_{ij}) + \varepsilon_i$$

This new contract provides the agent with the same level of expected utility as the old contract (for any action plan chosen by the agent) for every first-period output realization q_i^1. Therefore, the agent accepts this contract and chooses the same action plan as before. But the new contract changes the principal's payoff by

$$\sum_{i=1}^{n} p_i(a_1) \left[V(q_i - \hat{w}_i) - V(q_i - w_i) + \sum_{j=1}^{n} p_j(a_i)[V(q_j - \hat{w}_{ij}) - V(q_j - w_{ij})] \right]$$

Now, for small ε_i's, we have, approximately,

$$w_i - \hat{w}_i = \varepsilon_i / u'(w_i)$$

and

$$w_{ij} - \hat{w}_{ij} = -\varepsilon_i / u'(w_{ij})$$

so that the net benefit to the principal is approximately

$$\sum_{i=1}^{n} p_i(a_1) \left[\left(\frac{V'(q_i - w_i)}{u'(w_i)} \right) - \sum_{j=1}^{n} p_j(a_i) \left(\frac{V'(q_i - w_{ij})}{u'(w_{ij})} \right) \right] \varepsilon_i \qquad (10.2)$$

The principal can thus increase his payoff by choosing small ε_i's of the same sign as the term in brackets. In other words, unless the term in brackets is equal to zero [so that equation (10.1) holds] there are profitable deviations from the contract (w_i, w_{ij}). Therefore, equation (10.1) is one of the conditions characterizing the optimal long-term contract.

Another important observation emerging from expression (10.2) is that in general the optimal second-best contract has "memory." It is easy to see this fact by applying an argument almost identical to the preceding one.

Suppose by contradiction that the optimal contract is memoryless and takes the form (w_i, w_j), so that the second-period wage is independent of first-period output. This contract is optimal only if

$$\frac{V'(q_i - w_i)}{u'(w_i)} = \sum_{j=1}^{n} p_j(a_i) \frac{V'(q_j - w_j)}{u'(w_j)} \quad \text{for all } i$$

But note that under the memoryless contract, a_i is independent of the first-period outcome q_i, so that the right-hand side of the above equation is a constant independent of q_i. But

$$\frac{V'(q_i - w_i)}{u'(w_i)} = \kappa \quad \text{constant}$$

implies that the agent enjoys first-best insurance in period 1. This contract cannot be optimal in general, for then the agent has inadequate incentives to supply effort in period 1.

A somewhat disappointing implication of this observation is that in general the optimal long-term contract will be very complex. This complexity is difficult to reconcile with the simplicity of long-term incentive contracts observed in reality. Long-term employment (or incentive) contracts observed in practice do not appear to fine-tune the agent's intertemporal consumption to the extent predicted by the theory.

As we shall discuss in later chapters, long-term contracts observed in reality also appear to be simple in part because they leave many aspects of the long-term relation unspecified or implicitly specified in an informal agreement among the parties. In other words, the explicit part of observed long-term contracts is often highly incomplete. A difficult question for the theory is then to explain what is left implicit and what is written explicitly into the contract.

Before tackling this difficult issue, however, it is important to understand the general structure of optimal long-term contracts and to ask whether there are plausible environments in which optimal long-term contracts have a simple structure.

One important insight about optimal long-term contracts emerging from the fundamental relationship between contingent wages across periods in equation (10.1) is that it is always in the principal's interest to try to "front-load" the agent's consumption. In other words, it is optimal to force the agent to consume more in earlier periods than she would like ex post and to reduce her savings. Intuitively, by keeping her continuation wealth low, the principal can ensure that the agent's marginal utility of money remains high. He can thus reduce his cost of providing the agent with effective monetary incentives.

To show that the optimal long-term contract has this property, we shall hypothetically let the agent borrow or save (at zero interest, as we assume no discounting) after the realization of the first-period outcome. We shall use condition (10.1) to show that the agent never wants to consume more than what she earns under the contract in that period and if anything wants to save some of her first-period income.

To see this result, note first that the agent's marginal expected utility with respect to savings following the realization of q_i is

$$\sum_{i=1}^{n} p_j(a_i)u'(w_{ij}) - u'(w_i)$$

Substituting for $u'(w_i)$ using condition (10.1) (and assuming for simplicity that the principal is risk-neutral), this becomes

$$\sum_{j=1}^{n} p_j(a_i)u'(w_{ij}) - \frac{1}{\displaystyle\sum_{j=1}^{n} \frac{p_j(a_i)}{u'(w_{ij})}}$$

Now, since $1/x$ is a convex function of x, by Jensen's inequality we have

$$\frac{1}{\displaystyle\sum_{j=1}^{n} \frac{p_j(a_i)}{u'(w_{ij})}} \leq \sum_{j=1}^{n} p_j(a_i)u'(w_{ij})$$

so that

$$\sum_{j=1}^{n} p_j(a_i) u'(w_{ij}) - u'(w_i) \geq 0$$

In words, under the optimal long-term contract the agent's marginal expected utility with respect to savings is always nonnegative, so that the agent would like to save more at the margin than the contract allows her.

One important simplification one might hope for is that the optimal long-term contract be implementable by a sequence of spot contracts, for then the one-shot model of moral hazard considered in Chapter 4 might easily be adapted to the repeated contracting problem. Unfortunately, spot implementation requires that the optimal long-term contract be memoryless if the agent has no access to a savings technology. We shall see, however, that if the agent can save her income independently and if the principal can monitor her savings, then spot implementation is feasible under fairly general conditions. This approach is possible under monitored access to savings, since then the principal can separate the consumption-smoothing part (by controlling the agent's savings decision) from the standard incentives-versus-risk-sharing part of the contract.

10.1.2   Monitored Savings

Under the monitored-savings scenario, the agent has *access* to credit, but the principal can *monitor* the agent's savings. To be consistent, we also let the agent monitor the principal's savings. A long-term contract can now specify not only a profile of output-contingent wage payments but also output-contingent savings for the principal and agent, respectively t_i and s_i. Therefore, the optimal contracting problem now takes the form

$$
\left\{
\begin{array}{l}
\displaystyle \max_{\substack{(w_i),(w_{ij}),(s_i),(t_i) \\ a_1,(a_i)}} \sum_{i=1}^{n} p_i(a_1) \left[V(q_i - w_i - t_i) + \sum_{j=1}^{n} p_j(a_i) V(q_j - w_{ij} + t_i) \right] \\[2ex]
\text{subject to} \\[1ex]
\displaystyle [a_1, (a_i)] \in \arg\max_{\tilde{a}_1,(\tilde{a}_i)} \sum_{i=1}^{n} p_i(\tilde{a}_1) \left[u(w_i - s_i) - \psi(\tilde{a}_1) + \sum_{j=1}^{n} p_j(\tilde{a}_i) u(w_{ij} + s_i) - \psi(\tilde{a}_i) \right] \\[2ex]
\text{and} \\[1ex]
\displaystyle \sum_{i=1}^{n} p_i(a_1) \left[u(w_i - s_i) - \psi(a_1) + \sum_{j=1}^{n} p_j(a_i) u(w_{ij} + s_i) - \psi(a_i) \right] \geq 2\bar{u}
\end{array}
\right.
$$

Observe that only total savings $(s_i + t_i)$ are determined at the optimum, since the principal can always undo the agent's saving decision through an adequate choice of (w_i), (w_{ij}), and (t_i). Therefore, we can set the savings of one of the parties to zero without loss of generality.

When we set t_i equal to zero and compare the preceding program with the optimization problem in the "no access" scenario, it appears that the situation where the agent's savings decisions can be monitored is equivalent to the no-access scenario. The only difference now is that the optimal contract can exhibit "memory of consumption" without requiring any "memory of wages." Indeed, by setting s_i so that

$$c_{ij}^* = w_{ij} = w_j + s_i$$

and

$$w_i = c_i^* - s_i$$

the long-term contract can implement a consumption plan by controlling savings directly rather than indirectly through history-dependent wage plans. In other words, when savings can be monitored, a long-term contract with memory is now in principle spot-implementable. In fact, the principal may now solve the optimal long-term contract by separating the consumption-smoothing part from the standard static incentive-contracting problem. This central observation has been made independently by Malcomson and Spinnewyn (1988), Fudenberg, Holmström, and Milgrom (1990), and Rey and Salanié (1990).

We shall illustrate this separability property more explicitly under the simplifying assumption that the principal is risk neutral.

Suppose that the agent saves s in the first period. Then the spot contract in period 2 is the solution to

$$\begin{cases} \max_{(w_j),a} \sum_{j=1}^{n} p_j(a)(q_j - w_j) \\ \text{subject to} \\ a \in \arg\max_{\tilde{a}} \sum_{j=1}^{n} p_j(\tilde{a})u(w_j + s) - \psi(\tilde{a}) \\ \sum_{j=1}^{n} p_j(a)u(w_j + s) - \psi(a) \geq u(\bar{c} + s) - \psi(\bar{a}) \end{cases}$$

where $(\bar{c}, \bar{a})$ are the outside option consumption level and action, such that $u(\bar{c}) - \psi(\bar{a}) = \bar{u}$.

Now, given any realization q_i in period 1, the optimal long-term contract must solve the following continuation problem:

$$
\begin{cases}
\max_{(\hat{w}_j),a} \sum_{j=1}^{n} p_j(a)(q_j - \hat{w}_j) \\
\text{subject to} \\
a \in \arg\max_{\tilde{a}} \sum_{j=1}^{n} p_j(\tilde{a})u(\hat{w}_j) - \psi(\tilde{a}) \\
\sum_{j=1}^{n} p_j(a)u(\hat{w}_j) - \psi(a) \geq \sum_{j=1}^{n} p_j(a_i^*)u(c_{ij}^*) - \psi(a_i^*)
\end{cases}
$$

To replicate the solution to this continuation problem with an optimal period-2 spot contract, it thus suffices to set period-1 savings s_i such that

$$
u(\overline{c} + s_i) - \psi(\overline{a}) = \sum_{j=1}^{n} p_j(a_i^*)u(c_{ij}^*) - \psi(a_i^*)
$$

Note that a solution s_i to this equation always exists if the agent's utility function $u(\cdot)$ is unbounded below.

To summarize, when the principal can monitor the agent's savings, it is possible to implement the optimal long-term contract with a sequence of spot contracts even if the optimal contract has "memory of consumption." The reason is simply that with monitored savings the principal can separate the consumption-smoothing problem by controlling the agent's savings separately.

This observation is important for at least three reasons. First, it provides a rationale for short-term incentive contracting. As long as the principal can control the agent's savings, there is no value in committing to a long-term contract. Second, it pinpoints the main source of gain from a repeated relation: the opportunities created for intertemporal risk sharing. Third, it leads to a simple recursive structure for the long-term contracting problem. With spot implementation, the principal's problem can be formulated as a dynamic-programming problem, where the principal maximizes the sum of his current-flow payoff and the expected discounted value of future spot contracting by offering spot contracts to the agent, which the latter can accept or reject.

The result that optimal long-term contracts are spot implementable under monitored savings extends to any finitely repeated contracting problem if the agent's preferences are additively or multiplicatively separable. This conclusion has been established in Fudenberg, Holmström, and Milgrom (1990). Besides additive (or multiplicative) separability of the agent's preferences, several other assumptions that we have made implicitly here are important to obtain this result. These assumptions guarantee that there is no asymmetric information between the principal and agent at recontracting dates. Thus, to ensure that there is common knowledge of production possibilities and preferences at each recontracting date, we have not only assumed that the agent's savings can be monitored by the principal but also that each production period is time separable, so that the agent's action choice in any given period affects only that period's output and has no impact on the agent's future action sets or future costs of taking particular actions.

An important corollary of spot implementation is that when it is spot-implementable the optimal long-term contract is also renegotiation-proof. In other words, at every recontracting date, the continuation contract is an optimal solution for the remaining periods. This conclusion follows immediately from the observation that once contingent savings s_i have been determined, the second-period optimal spot contract is always an optimal continuation contract. We shall see in the next section how spot implementation or renegotiation-proofness breaks down when there is asymmetric information between the principal and agent at recontracting dates.

10.1.3 Free Savings and Asymmetric Information

The principal may not always be able to observe and monitor the agent's savings. In that case the continuation contracting problem may involve some asymmetric information. All the issues considered under dynamic adverse selection then become relevant. In particular, the optimal long-term contract may no longer be renegotiation-proof or spot-implementable.

We shall illustrate this statement with an example involving a single action choice in period 2 but (hidden) consumption by the agent in both periods.

Example The agent only supplies effort in period 2.

- $a \in \{H, L\}$ with $\psi(H) = 1$ and $\psi(L) = 0$
- $q \in \{0, 1\}$ with $p_1(H) \equiv p_H > p_1(L) \equiv p_L > 0$

We restrict attention to parameter values such that it is optimal to induce the agent to choose action H. A long-term contract then simply specifies second-period output-contingent wages (w_0, w_1).

We shall denote by c_1^H the agent's first-period consumption if she plans to choose $a = H$ and by c_1^L her first-period consumption when she plans to choose action $a = L$. That is, for $j = H, L$, c_1^j maximizes

$$u(c) + p_j u(w_1 - c) + (1 - p_j) u(w_0 - c)$$

The agent's (binding) incentive constraint in period 1 is

$$u(c_1^H) + p_H u(w_1 - c_1^H) + (1 - p_H) u(w_0 - c_1^H) - 1$$
$$= u(c_1^L) + p_L u(w_1 - c_1^L) + (1 - p_L) u(w_0 - c_1^L)$$

but by revealed preference and strict concavity of $u(\cdot)$ we know that

$$u(c_1^L) + p_L u(w_1 - c_1^L) + (1 - p_L) u(w_0 - c_1^L)$$
$$> u(c_1^H) + p_L u(w_1 - c_1^H) + (1 - p_L) u(w_0 - c_1^H)$$

so that in period 2 we have

$$u(c_1^H) + p_H u(w_1 - c_1^H) + (1 - p_H) u(w_0 - c_1^H) - 1$$
$$> u(c_1^H) + p_L u(w_1 - c_1^H) + (1 - p_L) u(w_0 - c_1^H)$$

In other words, in period 2 the agent's incentive constraint is *slack*. There is therefore an opportunity for both parties to renegotiate the initial contract at that point. Note that if the principal could monitor the agent's consumption (or savings), this problem would not arise, for then the principal could impose a particular consumption choice on the agent in period 1 such that the incentive constraint in period 2 would remain binding. It is the principal's inability to monitor the agent's consumption that creates a renegotiation problem in period 2.

There is one special case, however, where the principal's inability to monitor the agent's savings is not problematic, namely, when the agent's optimal savings are independent of her choice of action. This property of the agent's savings behavior obtains when she has CARA risk preferences. With such preferences wealth effects are absent and history can no longer affect the agent's savings behavior. Fudenberg, Holmström, and Milgrom (1990) show that with CARA risk preferences the optimal long-term contract (with no monitored savings) is then spot implementable and renegotiation-proof.

10.2   The T-period Problem: Simple Contracts and the Gains from Enduring Relations

The previous section has highlighted the importance of intertemporal risk sharing as a benefit of long-term contracting. Two other sources of gains from long-term contracting have been suggested in the literature: better monitoring of the agent's actions and more "punishment" options for poor performance. For instance Radner (1986a) identifies the gains from enduring relations under moral hazard as follows:

These repetitions give the principal an opportunity to observe the results of the agent's actions over a number of periods, and to use some statistical test to infer whether or not the agent was choosing the appropriate action. The repetitions also provide the principal with opportunities to "punish" the agent for apparent departures from the appropriate action. (p. 27)

A possible countervailing effect of repeated interactions may also be to worsen the incentive problem the principal faces, for now the agent has more opportunities to shirk, try her luck, and make up for bad outcomes by working harder. In other words, in an enduring relation the agent's action set is richer, and the principal's incentive problem may be worse as a result. This effect has been emphasized by Holmström and Milgrom (1987) and has led to the idea that with repetition incentive contracts may become simpler even though the underlying incentive problem grows in complexity.

Much of the literature on repeated moral hazard, which allows for infinitely many periods, has been concerned with approximation results of the first-best outcome with simple incentive contracts under no (or almost no) discounting. In particular, Radner (1981, 1985), Rubinstein (1979), Rubinstein and Yaari (1983), Fudenberg, Holmström, and Milgrom (1990), and Dutta and Radner (1994), among others, provide such results. There are small differences in the types of simple contracts considered and in their interpretation. All contracts share the feature that as long as the agent's accumulated wealth is above a given threshold, the agent either maintains a given mean level of per-period consumption or continues to be employed. Should the agent's wealth fall below that threshold, then depending on the contract considered, the agent cuts down on her consumption in order to build up her stock of wealth, or the contract is terminated. These contracts are interpreted to be a form of either employment contract or bankruptcy contract or, alternatively, as self-insurance schemes for the agent. Although the basic underlying argument and method of proof are similar, the intuitive explanations given for the approximation results differ substantially from one paper to another. One strand of the literature (e.g., Fudenberg, Holmström, and Milgrom, 1990) argues that the gains from the (infinitely) repeated relation stem exclusively from self-insurance by the agent, while the other (e.g., Radner, 1986a) also emphasizes the benefits from enhanced statistical inference and punishments.

In order to disentangle the relative importance of these factors, we shall attempt to isolate each one by repeating only some elements of the principal-agent relationship and not others. We thus distinguish five special cases in increasing order of complexity:

Case 1: Repeated Output   In the special case of repeated output, the agent makes a single action choice, but there are multiple output realizations. Moreover, the agent consumes only at the end of the repeated relation. Here the only benefit of repetition is better statistical inference. This special case can be seen as a simple representation of a problem where the agent must be given adequate incentives to undertake a risky investment.

Case 2: Repeated Actions   In the case of repeated actions, only the agent's action choice is repeated. There is a single output realization, and consumption takes place at the end. This case can be seen as an intertemporal analogue of a multitask problem. The benefit (or cost) of repeated action choice is that the agent may be able to spread her effort over time more efficiently.

Case 3: Repeated Consumption   Again, in the case of repeated consumption, the agent makes a single action choice, and there is a single output realization. But now the agent may consume in several periods. In this case the only potential benefits from long-term contracting arise from consumption-smoothing opportunities. We shall not discuss this case below because the example considered in subsection 10.1.3 already provides the intuition for this special case. As the example highlights, the gains from long-term contracting depend to a large extent on whether the agent's intertemporal consumption can be monitored by the principal. If it cannot, then the opportunities for consumption smoothing open to the agent may worsen the underlying incentive problem—so much so that the gains from intertemporal insurance may be outweighed by the greater costs of providing incentives to the agent. Thus unmonitored consumption smoothing may come at the expense of the incentive efficiency of the contract.

Case 4: Repeated Actions and Output   In this case both action choices and output are repeated, but consumption takes place only at the end. This is the setup considered by Holmström and Milgrom (1987). The focus here will be not so much on the benefits of an enduring relation as on the form of the optimal long-term contract.

Case 5: Infinitely Repeated Actions, Output, and Consumption   The case of infinitely repeated actions, output, and consumption is the most general case considered in the literature. Here, as in the previous case, we investigate to what extent simple contracts can be approximately optimal.

10.2.1   Repeated Output

In the repeated-output case we let the agent choose an action only once, at $t = 0$. We shall suppose that there are only two possible output outcomes in any given period: $q \in \{0, 1\}$ and $p(a) = \Pr(q = 1|a)$, with $p(a)$ strictly increasing in a.

We shall contrast two extreme scenarios. One, where there is a single output realization at date $t = 0$, was considered in Chapter 4. In this scenario we have seen that the second-best contract, in general, cannot approximate the first-best outcome.

In contrast, in the other extreme scenario, where there are infinitely many independent increments in output, a second-best contract can approximate the first-best outcome arbitrarily closely. To see this point, consider the situation where there are infinitely many independent, binomial increments in output over a finite interval of time T. That is, consider the situation where, over the interval of time T, cumulative output follows a Brownian motion:

$$dq = a \cdot dt + \sqrt{\sigma} \cdot dZ$$

where $a \in A$ denotes the drift of output, σ is a constant volatility parameter, and dZ is a standard Wiener process. The drift is chosen by the agent at time $t = 0$. Even if the principal and agent can observe only final accumulated output $Q(T)$ and can write a contract contingent only on $Q(T)$, they can now approximate the first-best outcome. Indeed, as $Q(T)$ is normally distributed with mean $a \cdot T$ and variance $\sigma \cdot T$, a Mirrlees-type contract—where the principal chooses $\underline{Q}$ such that for all $Q(T) < \underline{Q}$ the agent gets punished and otherwise she gets a sure payment of w^*—can approximate the first-best outcome (see Chapter 4).

This example captures in a simple and stark way the idea that more precise statistical inference is made possible by the observation of the sum of repeated independent output observations. Here we have made heavy use of the fact that the normal distribution approximates the sum of independently, identically, and binomially distributed random variables. But the general point that repeated observation of independently distributed output outcomes improves statistical inference does not depend on this construction. To the extent that an ongoing principal-agent relation involves more frequent output observations than action choices, there is a statistical inference effect that ameliorates the efficiency of the contract.

10.2.2 Repeated Actions

Take $T = 2$ and suppose now that there are n possible output outcomes at the end of period 2 and that the probability of outcome q_i is given by $p_i(a_1 + a_2)$, where a_t denotes the agent's action choice in period $t = 1, 2$. That is, here the agent can choose two effort levels in succession, and the probability distribution over output is influenced by the sum of the agent's efforts. In all other respects the static principal-agent problem considered in Chapter 4 remains the same. Under this scenario the principal's optimal contracting problem becomes

$$
\begin{cases}
\displaystyle\max_{(w_i, a_1, a_2)} \sum_{i=1}^{n} p_i(a_1 + a_2)V(q_i - w_i) \\[2mm]
\text{subject to} \\[2mm]
(a_1, a_2) \in \displaystyle\arg\max_{\tilde{a}_1, \tilde{a}_2} \sum_{i=1}^{n} p_i(\tilde{a}_1 + \tilde{a}_2)u(w_i) - \psi(\tilde{a}_1) - \psi(\tilde{a}_2) \\[2mm]
\text{and} \\[2mm]
\displaystyle\sum_{i=1}^{n} p_i(a_1 + a_2)u(w_i) - \psi(a_1) - \psi(a_2) \geq \bar{u}
\end{cases}
$$

In the first-best problem there is an obvious benefit from letting the agent spread her effort over time. Since the effort-cost function $\psi(\cdot)$ is strictly increasing and convex, it is optimal to supply an equal amount of effort in each period. When the agent can spread her effort over time, the overall cost of inducing a total effort supply of a is then reduced by

$$\psi(a) - 2\psi\left(\frac{a}{2}\right)$$

Does this benefit from lower costs translate into an improved second-best contract? Unfortunately, it is not clear that it will. The reason is that when the agent can spread her effort over time, the principal may face worse incentive constraints. Clean comparative statics results on the effects of a change in the agent's effort cost on the second-best outcome are not obtainable. Grossman and Hart (1983a) provide examples where a reduction in the agent's cost of effort makes the principal worse off. They are able to show only a limit result that the first-best outcome is approached in the limit when the agent's (marginal) cost of effort goes to zero (see their proposition 17).

10.2.3 Repeated Actions and Output

The previous two special cases have highlighted, first, that if an ongoing principal-agent relation involves more frequent output observations than action choices, there is a statistical inference effect that ameliorates the efficiency of the contract; second, that if the frequency of output observations is less than the frequency of action choices, then the optimal long-term contract may produce a worse outcome than if the frequencies of action choices and output observations were constrained to be equal.

In this subsection we first explore the issue of the relative benefits and costs of a higher frequency of output observations and revision of actions more systematically by considering an insightful example of a repeated principal-agent relation adapted from the repeated partnership game of Abreu, Milgrom, and Pearce (1991).

In a second step we shall also explore the important theme that as the agent's action set gets richer (with more frequent action choices), this process leads to a simpler optimal incentive contract, since, with more incentive constraints potentially binding, the principal's flexibility in designing the contract is reduced. This general idea was first explored by Holmström and Milgrom (1987), who suggested that in some special settings the agent's opportunities for shirking over time may be so varied that an optimal response is to provide the agent with incentives that are linear in output, so that the agent is subjected to a constant incentive pressure no matter how her performance evolves over time.

10.2.3.1   Repeated Actions and Output: Richer Action Set versus More Frequent Information

This example is best interpreted as a machine (or asset) maintenance problem, where the agent must continuously exert effort to keep the machine in good running order. The machine yields a flow payoff of $\pi > 0$ to the principal as long as it is well maintained by the agent. However, if the agent shirks, the principal's flow payoff is zero. The agent has only two actions available, $a = 1$ ("maintain") and $a = 0$ ("shirk") at any time τ. She incurs a flow cost $0 < \psi < \pi$ when she chooses $a = 1$, but no cost when $a = 0$.

Both principal and agent are assumed to be risk neutral and to discount future payoffs at rate $r > 0$. For simplicity we assume that principal and agent can sign only *efficiency-wage* contracts such that the agent gets a flow wage payment $w \geq \psi$ as long as she remains employed. Otherwise, she gets a flow payoff of zero.

The principal-agent relation is modeled in continuous time, but principal and agent are assumed to be able to revise their actions only after a fixed interval of time t has elapsed, so that effectively the problem is a discrete-time one. The question we shall investigate is how the efficiency of the contract is affected when we vary t or r.

Perfect Information

Suppose to begin with that the principal observes perfectly his accumulated flow payoff at the end of each interval of time t. Then, as long as the agent has chosen to maintain the machine ($a = 1$), his mean flow payoff over the interval of time t is given by

$$r \int_0^t e^{-r\tau} \pi \, d\tau = \pi(1 - e^{-rt})$$

The optimal efficiency-wage contract then takes the simple form that the principal continues to employ the agent at wage w as long as his mean flow payoff is $\pi(1 - e^{-rt})$ and otherwise fires the agent.

Under such a contract the agent's incentive constraint takes the form

$$w(1 - e^{-rt}) \leq w - \psi$$

The RHS represents the agent's mean flow payoff when she never shirks. The LHS is her payoff when she shirks and is fired at the expiration of the time interval t. The optimal wage w is then set so that the incentive constraint is binding. It is instructive to rewrite the incentive constraint as follows:

$$rt = \log\left(\frac{w}{\psi}\right)$$

It is clear from this expression that an increase in the frequency of revision of the contract (a reduction in t) has the same beneficial effect as a reduction in the discount rate r. We shall see, however, that when the principal cannot observe perfectly his accumulated flow payoff at the end of each interval of time t, it is possible that a greater frequency of revision can make things worse. The reason is that more frequent revisions provide not only the principal with more scope to fine-tune the incentive contract but also the agent with greater opportunities for shirking. As we shall illustrate, if greater frequency of revisions entails a reduction in the quality of information obtained by the principal at the end of each interval of time t, then the incentive problem may well be worse when information is available more often. Then, as in the example by Dewatripont and Maskin (1995a) described in Chapter 9, it may be preferable to choose an information technology where performance measures are available less frequently.

Imperfect Information

Suppose now that the principal can no longer perfectly determine whether the agent maintained the machine over the interval of time t. Suppose that the principal can observe only machine breakdowns or failures over the interval and that the Poisson arrival rate of a breakdown per unit time is $\lambda > 0$ when the agent maintains the machine or $\mu > \lambda$ when the agent shirks. The probability distribution of k breakdowns over the interval of time t is then given by

$$p_k(t) = \frac{e^{-\lambda t}(\lambda t)^k}{k!}$$

when the agent maintains the machine and

$$q_k(t) = \frac{e^{-\mu t}(\mu t)^k}{k!}$$

when she shirks.

The efficiency-wage contract must now condition the principal's firing decision on the number of observed failures. This is an imperfect signal because failures can occur even when the agent maintains the machine. The higher the number of observed failures over the interval of time t, the more likely it is that the agent shirked, since $\mu > \lambda$. This relationship can be seen more formally by observing that

$$\frac{q_k}{p_k} = e^{(\lambda - \mu)t}\left(\frac{\mu}{\lambda}\right)^k$$

is increasing in the number of failures k.

It is therefore intuitively plausible that an optimal efficiency-wage contract will choose some cutoff number of failures $\hat{k}$ such that the agent is retained for all $k < \hat{k}$ but is fired whenever the number of failures is equal to or greater than $\hat{k}$. We shall show that this is indeed the case.

The fundamental difficulty with shortening the time interval t is now apparent. The shorter the interval, the lower the probability that a significant number of failures occur, which would give the principal a sufficiently accurate signal that the agent has shirked. In other words, the shorter the time interval, the worse the quality of the information available to the principal to base the incentive contract on. Therefore, in this example, increasing the rate at which the principal and agent receive information can make the incentive problem worse.

More formally, let $\alpha = (\alpha_1, \alpha_2, \ldots, \alpha_k, \ldots, \alpha_K)$ denote the principal's firing probability as a function of observed failures k. Under such a firing policy and a wage rate w, the agent's payoff v if she always maintains the machine is given by

$$v = (1 - e^{-rt})(w - \psi) + e^{-rt}v\left[\sum_{k=1}^{K} p_k(1 - \alpha_k)\right]$$

or

$$v(1 - e^{-rt}) = (1 - e^{-rt})(w - \psi) - e^{-rt}v\left[\sum_{k=1}^{K} p_k \alpha_k\right] \tag{10.3}$$

since $\sum_{k=1}^{K} p_k = 1$.

If, however, the agent shirks over an interval t, her payoff is

$$w(1-e^{-rt})+e^{-rt}v\left[\sum_{k=1}^{K}q_{k}(1-\alpha_{k})\right]$$

so that the agent's incentive constraint is now

$$w(1-e^{-rt})+e^{-rt}v\left[\sum_{k=1}^{K}q_{k}(1-\alpha_{k})\right]\leq v \tag{10.4}$$

Indeed, if this inequality is satisfied, a one-time deviation does not pay. At the optimum, the wage rate w is set so that constraint (10.4) binds. Combining equations (10.3) and (10.4), the incentive constraint and the agent's payoff under the contract take the following simple form

$$\psi(1-e^{-rt})=e^{-rt}v(\mathcal{L}-1)\left[\sum_{k=1}^{K}\alpha_{k}p_{k}\right] \tag{IC}$$

and

$$v=w-\psi-\frac{\psi}{\mathcal{L}-1}$$

where

$$\mathcal{L}=\frac{\sum_{k=1}^{K}\alpha_{k}q_{k}}{\sum_{k=1}^{K}\alpha_{k}p_{k}}$$

denotes the likelihood ratio under the firing policy α.

Note that relative to the case of perfect information the agent's payoff is reduced by $\psi/(\mathcal{L}-1)$. As can be seen from the expression for v, the principal's objective is now to try to choose a firing policy α to maximize the likelihood ratio $\mathcal{L}$ subject to satisfying the agent's incentive constraint.

This objective is achieved by choosing the lowest possible $\hat{k}$ compatible with the incentive constraint (IC), such that $\alpha_{k}=1$ for all $k\geq\hat{k}$ and $\alpha_{k}=0$ for all $k<\hat{k}$. To see this point, note simply that the solution to the unconstrained problem

$$\max_{\alpha} \frac{\sum_{k=1}^{K} \alpha_k q_k}{\sum_{k=1}^{K} \alpha_k p_k}$$

is given by $\alpha_k = 0$ for all $k \leq K - 1$ and $\alpha_k = 1$ for $k = K$. If this solution violates the constraint

$$\psi e^{rt}(1 - e^{-rt}) = v(\mathcal{L} - 1)\left[\sum_{k=1}^{K} \alpha_k p_k\right] \qquad \text{(IC')}$$

then obviously the principal must find the highest $\hat{k}$ such that constraint (IC') holds.

As we shall now illustrate, it is possible that when the time interval t is short there may not exist any $\hat{k}$ that satisfies condition (IC') for $w \leq \pi$. But note first that the LHS of condition (IC') is an increasing function of r and that the RHS is independent of r. Therefore, a reduction in r allows the principal to improve the contract by lowering v (or w) and increasing $\mathcal{L}$. Thus, as in the case of perfect information, a lower discount rate allows the principal to improve the incentive contract by imposing scaled-up punishments on the agent if the number of observed failures is greater than a given threshold. In the limit as $r \to 0$, the LHS is zero, so that the optimal contract with imperfect monitoring can let $v \to 0$. In other words, in the limit when there is no discounting, the optimal contract with imperfect monitoring approximates the optimal contract with perfect monitoring. Note that this statement is true for any time interval t.

We shall now show that a reduction in the time interval t does not necessarily improve the incentive problem in contrast to the case of perfect information. The comparative statics with respect to t are significantly more delicate than with respect to r, as changes in t affect both the LHS and RHS of condition (IC'). To sidestep the difficulties involved in this exercise, we shall instead consider a feasible contracting situation with t bounded away from zero and show that for t close to zero this situation is no longer feasible.

Consider a time interval t bounded away from 0 and a discount rate $\hat{r}$ low enough (but also bounded away from zero) so that an efficiency wage contract with $w \leq \pi$ is feasible. Note that such a contract exists if

$\pi > \psi$, since the solution with perfect information can be approximated when $r \to 0$.

Now, let t shrink. In the limit, as $t \to 0$, the likelihood ratio $\mathcal{L} = \mu/\lambda$, since the only events of order t are that no failure or one failure occurs. Moreover, when $t \to 0$, the agent's mean flow payoff v under the contract is approximately

$$r\int_0^\infty (w - \psi)e^{-r\tau}e^{-\alpha_1 \lambda \tau}dt = \frac{r(w - \psi)}{r + \alpha_1 \lambda}$$

Therefore, the incentive constraint reduces to

$$r\psi = \left[\frac{r(w - \psi)}{r + \alpha_1 \lambda}\right]\alpha_1(\mu - \lambda)$$

as $t \to 0$. Now, if

$$\psi > \frac{(\mu - \lambda)(\pi - \psi)}{r + \lambda}$$

it is not possible to satisfy the incentive constraint with a wage payment $w \leq \pi$ when $t \to 0$. Note that for μ close to λ this inequality can hold for $\psi < \pi$, so that a contract can be feasible for t bounded away from zero but not for a t arbitrarily close to zero. In other words, this example illustrates that a high frequency of revision of actions for the agent can worsen the incentive problem to such an extent that a feasible contract no longer exists. The problem for the principal is that when the time interval is very short, he no longer has a sufficiently accurate signal to be able to deter one-time deviations from the efficient action by the agent. In other words, when the agent can revise her action choice more and more frequently, her opportunities for shirking increase faster than the quality of the principal's signal about her action choice.

10.2.3.2   Repeated Actions and Output: Richer Action Sets and Simple Incentive Contracts

We now explore the idea that as the agent's action set gets richer (with more frequent action choices), a simpler, possibly linear optimal incentive contract may be the result. This general idea has been explored by Holmström and Milgrom (1987), who consider an example with T periods, where in each period $t = 1, \ldots, T$ the agent chooses an action $a^t \in A$.

This action affects only the probability distribution $p_i(a^t)$ over the n possible output outcomes at the end of that period. To keep things simple, we shall allow for only two possible output outcomes in each period, $n = 2$. We denote by $p(a^t)$ the probability of a high-output outcome q_H, and by $[1 - p(a^t)]$ the probability of a low outcome q_L, $(q_H > q_L)$. With this simplification the agent's action can be taken to be directly the choice of probability $p^t = p(a^t)$, and her action set the interval $[0,1]$. Consumption by the principal or agent takes place only at the end of period T.

Since consumption takes place at the end and the T production periods are technologically independent from one another, there appear to be benefits neither from consumption-smoothing opportunities nor from improved statistical inference.

The only possible intertemporal link between periods here may be through the wealth accumulation of the principal and agent, which may alter their respective risk preferences. However, even this link is assumed away in the Holmström and Milgrom setup with the assumption that both principal and agent have CARA risk preferences represented by the respective negative exponential utility functions

$$V(y) = -e^{-Ry}$$

for the principal and

$$u(y) = -e^{-ry}$$

for the agent.

Therefore, there appear to be no benefits from long-term contracting in this example. There may, however, potentially be a cost, since the agent may be able to modulate her actions in any period $t > 1$ on the observed realized history of output up to t, $Q^{t-1} = (q^1, \ldots, q^{t-1})$.

The point of this example is not so much to identify the benefits of long-term contracting as to highlight how in this potentially complex repeated-moral-hazard problem the optimal long-term contract may have a very simple structure, namely, that it is linear in final cumulative output.

It is important to emphasize at the outset that a critical assumption for this striking result is the assumption of CARA risk preferences. Without this assumption Holmström and Milgrom's aggregation and linearity result would not obtain. Under more general risk preferences, the principal and agent's attitudes toward risk would evolve with their accumulated wealth, so that the optimal long-term contract (or sequence of spot contracts) would be a nonlinear function of the history of output. With CARA risk preferences, however, the optimal spot-incentive contract is independent of the agent's wealth, as we shall illustrate.

The principal's one-shot optimal-contracting problem here takes the form

$$
\begin{cases}
\max_{(p,s_1,s_2)} p \cdot V(q_H - s_H) + (1-p)V(q_L - s_L) \\
\text{subject to} \\
p \in \arg\max_{\hat{p}} \{\hat{p}u[s_H + w - \psi(\hat{p})] + (1-\hat{p})u[s_L + w - \psi(\hat{p})]\} \\
\text{and} \\
pu[s_H + w - \psi(p)] + (1-p)u[s_L + w - \psi(p)] \geq u(w)
\end{cases}
$$

where w denotes the agent's initial wealth and s_i the agent's output-contingent compensation, $i = H, L$.

As we know from Chapter 4, we can replace the agent's incentive constraint with the first-order conditions of the agent's optimization problem

$$
u[s_H + w - \psi(p)] - u[s_L + w - \psi(p)] - pu'[s_H + w - \psi(p)]\psi'(p)
$$
$$
- (1-p)u'[s_L + w - \psi(p)]\psi'(p) = 0
$$

or

$$
-e^{-r[s_H + w - \psi(p)]} + e^{-r[s_L + w - \psi(p)]} + p\psi'(p)e^{-r[s_H + w - \psi(p)]} + (1-p)\psi'(p)e^{-r[s_L + w - \psi(p)]} = 0
$$

Multiplying through by e^{rw}, we then note that the agent's incentive constraint is independent of w:

$$
-e^{-r[s_H - \psi(p)]} + e^{-r[s_L - \psi(p)]} + p\psi'(p)e^{-r[s_H - \psi(p)]} + (1-p)\psi'(p)e^{-r[s_L - \psi(p)]} = 0 \quad (10.5)
$$

Substituting for the functional form of $u(\cdot)$, the individual-rationality constraint can also be written as

$$
p(-e^{-r[s_H + w - \psi(p)]}) + (1-p)(-e^{-r[s_L + w - \psi(p)]}) \geq -e^{-rw}
$$

or, multiplying through by e^{rw},

$$
p(-e^{-r[s_H - \psi(p)]}) + (1-p)(-e^{-r[s_L - \psi(p)]}) \geq 1 \quad (10.6)
$$

Combining condition (10.5) with condition (10.6) now makes it apparent that the optimal contract $\{s_L^*, s_H^*\}$ is independent of the agent's wealth w. In other words, with CARA risk preferences, changes in w do not affect $\Delta = s_H^* - s_L^*$, so that the optimal long-term contracting problem between the principal and agent is effectively stationary. With this observation in mind, we can now turn to the T-period version of the problem.

Since in any period $t \leq T$ of this problem, the agent can observe the entire history of output realizations up to t, her strategy of play over the contracting period is given by $p^t(Q^{t-1})$. That is, she can condition her action choice in period t, p^t, on the history of realized outputs up to t, Q^{t-1}.

Thus a long-term contract specifies an incentive-compatible history-contingent action plan $p^t(Q^{t-1})$ and a history-dependent compensation $s(Q^T)$.

When the contract expires, the agent's accumulated wealth is then given by

$$s(Q^T) - \sum_{t=1}^{T} \psi(p^t)$$

and the principal's accumulated wealth is

$$\sum_{t=1}^{T} q^t - s(Q^T)$$

The T-period problem thus takes the form

$$
\begin{cases}
\max_{(\{p^t(Q^{t-1})\}, s(Q^T))} E\left[V\left\{\sum_{t=1}^{T} q^t - s(Q^T)\right\}\right] \\
\text{subject to} \\
p^t(Q^{t-1}) \in \arg\max_{\hat{p}^t(Q^{t-1})} E\left[u\left\{w + s(Q^T) - \sum_{t=1}^{T} \psi[\hat{p}^t(Q^{t-1})]\right\}\right] \\
\text{and} \\
E\left[u\left\{w + s(Q^T) - \sum_{t=1}^{T} \psi[p^t(Q^{t-1})]\right\}\right] \geq u(w)
\end{cases}
$$

Given a contract $\{p^t(Q^{t-1}), s(Q^T)\}$, we can define the value of the contract for the agent to be

$$v_0 = \max_{\{p^t(Q^{t-1})\}} E\left[u\left\{s(Q^T) - \sum_{t=1}^{T} \psi[p^t(Q^{t-1})]\right\}\right]$$

and the continuation value at any date t to be

$$v_t(Q^{t-1}) = \max_{\{p^\tau(Q^{\tau-1})\}} E\left[u\left\{s(Q^T) - \sum_{\tau=t}^{T} \psi[p^\tau(Q^{\tau-1})] | Q^{t-1}\right\}\right]$$

Note that the continuation value excludes all the effort costs accumulated by the agent up to time t, $\sum_{\tau=1}^{t-1} \psi[p^\tau(Q^{\tau-1})]$. The reason is, first, that these costs are sunk by then and, second, that with CARA risk preferences the sunk effort costs enter multiplicatively into the agent's objective function, so that they can be factored out.

Given the contract $\{p^t(Q^{t-1}), s(Q^T)\}$, we can also define the agent's certainty-equivalent wealth, $w_t(Q^{t-1})$, in any period t by solving the equation

$$u(w_t) = v_t(Q^{t-1})$$

Using the agent's certainty-equivalent wealth, we can rewrite the agent's optimization problem given any history Q^{t-1} in the following simple way: We can take $p^t(Q^{t-1})$ to be the solution to the problem

$$\max_p \{pu[w_{t+1}(Q^{t-1}; q_H) - \psi(p)] + (1-p)u[w_{t+1}(Q^{t-1}; q_L) - \psi(p)]\}$$

Note that this problem has exactly the same form as the single-period problem considered earlier. Therefore, the solution to the agent's optimization problem depends only on the difference

$$w_{t+1}(Q^{t-1}; q_H) - w_{t+1}(Q^{t-1}; q_L)$$

and not on the agent's certainty-equivalent wealth $w_t(Q^{t-1})$. We can therefore define a spot contract $s_t(Q^t)$ to induce the action choice p^t by the agent

$$s_t(Q^{t-1}; q^t) = w_{t+1}(Q^{t-1}; q^t) - w_t(Q^{t-1})$$

such that the first-order condition holds:

$$-e^{-r[s_t(Q^{t-1}; q_H) - \psi(p^t)]} + e^{-r[s_t(Q^{t-1}; q_L) - \psi(p^t)]} + p^t \psi'(p^t) e^{-r[s_t(Q^{t-1}; q_H) - \psi(p^t)]}$$
$$+ (1-p^t)\psi'(p^t) e^{-r[s_t(Q^{t-1}, q_L) - \psi(p^t)]} = 0 \tag{10.7}$$

Aggregating over all periods, we can then write the agent's final wealth as

$$w_T(Q^T) = s(Q^T) = \sum_{t=1}^{T} s_t(Q^t) + w_0$$

where w_0 denotes the agent's certainty-equivalent wealth at the time of signing the contract.

Or, denoting by A_L^t (and, respectively, A_H^t) the number of realizations q_1 (respectively, q_2) up to period t, we can rewrite $s(Q^T)$ as follows:

$$s(Q^T) = \sum_{t=1}^{T} [s_t(Q^{t-1}; q_H)(A_H^t - A_H^{t-1}) + s_t(Q^{t-1}; q_L)(A_L^t - A_L^{t-1})] + w_0$$

Thus the principal's problem reduces to choosing $\{p^t, s_t\}$ and w_0 to maximize

$$E\left\{ V\left[\sum_{t=1}^{T} q^t - s_t(Q^{t-1}; q^t) \right] - w_0 \right\}$$

subject to equation (10.7) and

$$u(w_0) \geq u(w)$$

Given that the long-term contracting problem is stationary, one might expect that the optimal strategy for the principal is also stationary. That is, the principal chooses

$$p^t(Q^{t-1}) = p^*$$

and, therefore,

$$s_t(Q^{t-1}; q_L) = s_L^* \quad \text{and} \quad s_t(Q^{t-1}; q_H) = s_H^*$$

for (s_L^*, s_H^*) such that

$$-e^{-r[s_H^* - \psi(p^*)]} + e^{-r[s_L^* - \psi(p^*)]} + p^* \psi'(p^*) e^{-r[s_H^* - \psi(p^*)]} + (1-p^*)\psi'(p^*)e^{-r[s_L^* - \psi(p^*)]} = 0$$

This is indeed the case and can be seen from the following induction argument: When $T = 1$, the principal's optimal strategy is obviously p^* and (s_1^*, s_2^*). Suppose now that the principal's strategy is stationary for the repeated problem with $T = \tau$, and let V_T^* denote the value for the T-problem when $w_0 = 0$. Then, by the exponential form of V, the principal's payoff for the problem with $T = \tau + 1$ is given by

$$-e^{Rw_0} E\left[V(q^1 - s_L) E\left\{ V\left[\sum_{t=2}^{\tau+1} (q^t - s_L)|Q^1 \right] \right\} \right]$$

$$\leq -e^{Rw_0} E\left[V(q^1 - s_L)V_\tau^* \right] \leq -e^{Rw_0} V_1^* V_\tau^*$$

The first inequality follows from the assumed optimality of the stationary strategy p^* and (s_L^*, s_H^*) for the repeated problem with $T = \tau$. Since V_τ^* enters as a constant in the remaining one-period problem, it does not affect the solution to this problem, which is again p^* and (s_L^*, s_H^*). Thus the solution to the principal's T-period problem is stationary.

We can therefore write

$$s(Q^T) = \sum_{t=1}^{T} [s_H^* \cdot A_H^T + s_L^* \cdot A_L^T] + w_0$$

In other words, the solution to the optimal long-term contracting problem is linear in aggregate final output.

The T-period problem considered by Holmström and Milgrom is special in a number of respects. The most important restriction is that both principal and agent are assumed to have CARA risk preferences. We have also assumed that output follows a binomial process, but their aggregation and linearity result extends to the multinomial case where $q^t \in \{q_1, q_2, \ldots, q_n\}$.

The logic behind their result is thus the following: When both principal and agent have CARA risk preferences (as well as time-independent utility functions and cost of effort) the T-period problem is stationary, so that all dynamics have been removed from the problem. With CARA risk preferences it is possible to break up the dynamic optimization problem into a succession of identical static problems. Next, if output is binomial, the static contract is linear by construction. Finally, given the time-independent nature of the T-period problem, it is possible to dispense with disaggregate information on the output path and to write the contract as a linear function of aggregate output only.

While conceding that the optimality of linear contracts is obtained under strong assumptions, Holmström and Milgrom have argued that it provides a justification for concentrating on linear contracts in the "normal-noise, CARA-preference" case. As seen in Chapters 4, 6, and 8, this case has proved very attractive in applications.

10.2.4 Infinitely Repeated Actions, Output, and Consumption

The previous example with repeated actions and output provides one illustration of how optimal incentive contracts in repeated-moral-hazard problems can take a simple form: with (binomial) i.i.d. increments in output and CARA risk preferences, the optimal incentive contract was shown to be linear (or affine) in final accumulated output.

In this subsection, we provide another illustration of the optimality of simple contracts in a repeated-moral-hazard problem. We illustrate how a simple no-insurance contract, where the agent is made a residual claimant, may be approximately optimal in a general infinitely repeated principal-agent relationship with little discounting.

Suppose that for any given action chosen by the agent the distribution of output q_t has a compact support, and let $\underline{q}(a)$ denote the lowest possible output outcome under any given action choice a. Also denote by a^* the first-best action, by $q^* = E[q|a^*]$ the mean output when the agent chooses the first-best action, by $\underline{q}$ the lower bound under the first-best action, and by w_t the agent's accumulated wealth up to period t.

Suppose that the principal can perfectly monitor the agent's borrowing/saving decisions and that, for simplicity, he does not allow the agent to borrow. However, the agent is allowed to save as she pleases otherwise.

Consider the cutoff for the discount factor $\bar{\delta} < 1$. Then, for any $\delta > \bar{\delta}$, a feasible strategy for the agent is to choose the first-best action a^* in every period and to consume

$$c = q^* - \theta\delta + (1-\delta)w_t \quad \text{if } w_t \geq \frac{q^* - \underline{q}}{\bar{\delta}}$$

where $\theta \in (0, q^* - \underline{q})$ and

$$c = \underline{q} + (1-\delta)w_t \quad \text{if } w_t < \frac{q^* - \underline{q}}{\bar{\delta}}$$

Thus, as long as the agent's accumulated wealth remains above a given threshold, $w_t \geq (q^* - \underline{q})/\bar{\delta}$, she consumes approximately her mean output plus the interest earned on her accumulated wealth $(1 - \delta)w_t$, when θ is close to 0.

Let $h^t = (w_0, w_1, \ldots, w_t)$ denote the sample path of the agent's accumulated wealth under this action choice and consumption plan. Then the agent's conditional expected wealth in period $t + 1$ (under this first-best action choice and consumption plan) is given by

$$E[w_{t+1}|h^t] = \begin{cases} w_t + \theta & \text{if } w_t \geq \dfrac{q^* - \underline{q}}{\bar{\delta}} \\[2ex] w_t + \dfrac{q^* - \underline{q}}{\delta} & \text{if } w_t < \dfrac{q^* - \underline{q}}{\bar{\delta}} \end{cases}$$

Thus, since

$$E[w_{t+1}|h^t] \geq w_t + \min\left\{\theta, \frac{q^* - \underline{q}}{\delta}\right\}$$

$\{w_t\}$ is a submartingale with drift bounded away from zero. In other words, the agent's accumulated wealth grows on average over time.

Moreover, the increments in wealth are uniformly bounded for $\delta > \bar{\delta}$ (since the distribution for q_t has compact support). Therefore, there is a finite time horizon $T(\varepsilon)$ for $\varepsilon \in (0, 1)$ such that

$$\Pr\left\{w_t \geq \frac{q^* - \underline{q}}{\bar{\delta}} \text{ for all } t \geq T(\varepsilon)\right\} \geq 1 - \varepsilon$$

In other words, the probability that the agent will be able to consume her mean output plus the interest in every period after time $T(\varepsilon)$ is greater than or equal to $1 - \varepsilon$. Therefore, the agent's flow payoff under this plan is at least

$$(1 - \varepsilon)\delta^{T(\varepsilon)}[u(q^* - \theta\delta) - \psi(a^*)] + [1 - (1 - \varepsilon)\delta^{T(\varepsilon)}][u(\underline{q}) - \psi(a^*)]$$

Hence, as $\varepsilon \to 0$ and $\delta \to 1$, the agent's flow payoff tends to the first-best payoff $u(q^*) - \psi(a^*)$ when θ is close to zero.

In other words, the contract where the agent is made residual claimant is approximately first-best efficient when there is little discounting.

Note that we have not referred to the agent's individual-rationality constraint in this argument. It should be clear that the preceding argument can be adapted to allow for an adequate flow lump-sum transfer from the agent to the principal to satisfy the agent's (IR) constraint.

The simple contract where the agent is made residual claimant is not the only contract that is approximately efficient. Another approximately efficient contract is one resembling an efficiency-wage contract. Under this contract the agent is paid a fixed wage s per period above her reservation flow utility as long as accumulated performance $Q_t = Q_{t-1} + q_t - s$ remains above a given threshold $\bar{Q}$. Should Q_t fall below this threshold, the agent is fired and replaced by another agent. Using a limit argument similar to the preceding one, it can be shown that when there is little discounting, this contract is approximately first-best efficient (see Radner, 1986a).

10.3   Moral Hazard and Renegotiation

In the previous sections, dynamic considerations arose because of repeated effort and output realizations. As this section indicates, dynamic issues can arise even in the case of a single effort choice and output realization. Indeed, when there is a substantial lag between the time when the agent's costly action is sunk and the time when output is realized, there is scope for renegotiation of the initial incentive contract. Once the action is sunk, there is no need to expose the agent to further risk. An opportunity then arises to improve risk sharing. In particular, if the principal is risk neutral and the agent is risk averse, it is optimal to fully insure the agent once her action (or investment) is sunk. Of course, if the agent anticipates renegotiation after her action has been chosen, her incentives may be altered. Two cases can be distinguished:

• If the effort choice is not observed by the principal, the anticipation of renegotiation is problematic: the incentives of the agent may be reduced or even eliminated.

• If instead the effort choice is observed by the principal (although still non-contractable), dynamic contracting can tackle sequentially the two problems of inducing proper effort (through initial contracting) and providing optimal insurance (at the renegotiation stage).

We cover these two cases in turn in the next two subsections.

10.3.1   Renegotiation When Effort Is Not Observed by the Principal

When the effort choice is not observed by the principal, the anticipation of renegotiation may eliminate all incentives for the agent. To prevent this result, the outcome of full insurance once the action is sunk must somehow be avoided. Avoiding this outcome is possible only if the principal remains unsure about which action the agent chose. Indeed, if the principal knows for sure what the agent chose to do, he can determine exactly the expected value of the underlying investment and insure the agent at actuarially fair terms. However, if the agent is randomizing her choice over several actions, the principal is put in a position of an asymmetrically informed insurer in the renegotiation phase. As we learned from Chapter 2, the optimal insurance contract in this case does not allow for full coverage in general, so that the agent may remain exposed to some risk.

In this subsection we shall consider this basic dynamic contracting problem under the assumption that the principal (who remains uninformed about the agent's choice of action) makes a take-it-or-leave-it offer of a menu of contracts to the agent. This case has been analyzed by Fudenberg and Tirole (1990) and Ma (1991). Under an alternative assumption, considered by Ma (1994) and Matthews (1995), it is the agent who makes a new contract offer, the form of which may convey information about her action choice. We discuss this case at the end of this subsection, and we stress that the problems discussed when the uninformed party makes the offer can be eliminated under an informed-party offer.

We focus here on the analysis of Fudenberg and Tirole (1990). The simplest possible setup in which their problem can be formally analyzed is the two-outcomes model considered in Chapter 4. In this problem, output is high, q_H, with probability $p(a)$ and low, q_L, with probability $[1 - p(a)]$. Suppose, in addition, that the agent's action set contains only two elements $a \in A = \{0, 1\}$, and let $p_1 = p(1)$ and $p_0 = p(0)$, with $p_1 > p_0$. Also, let the cost of effort $\psi(1) = \psi > 0$ and $\psi(0) = 0$.

The dynamic contracting game between the principal and agent unfolds as follows: The principal begins by offering an initial (menu of) contract(s) C_0 to the agent. The latter accepts or rejects (one of) the contract(s) (in the menu). If the agent decides to reject the contract, the game ends and the agent gets her reservation utility $\bar{u} = 0$. If she accepts, she selects action $a = 1$ with probability x and action $a = 0$, with probability $(1 - x)$.

Once the action is sunk and before the outcome is realized, the principal is allowed to make a new offer of a menu of contracts $\{[w_L(1), w_H(1)]; [w_L(0), w_H(0)]\}$, which consists of two pairs of output-contingent wages, being more attractive after a choice of $a = 1$ and a choice of $a = 0$ respectively. The agent can select either of the two contracts on the menu or reject both. If she rejects the new offer, the old contract is enforced, and if she accepts, the new contract is enforced. Finally, output is realized and wage payments are made.

Note that by the revelation principle, we can restrict attention to an incentive-compatible menu of contracts $\{[w_L(1), w_H(1)]; [w_L(0), w_H(0)]\}$ in the renegotiation phase.

As in the case of dynamic contracting under adverse selection, we can restrict attention at the initial contracting stage to "renegotiation-proof" contracts. Formally, an initial contract $C_0 = \{[w_L(1), w_H(1)]; [w_L(0), w_H(0)]\}$ is renegotiation-proof for the mixed action choice x if it solves the principal's compensation-cost minimization problem

$$\min_{[\hat{w}_L(i);\hat{w}_H(i)]} x[p_1\hat{w}_H(1)+(1-p_1)\hat{w}_L(1)]+(1-x)[p_0\hat{w}_H(0)+(1-p_0)\hat{w}_L(0)]$$

subject to the incentive constraints

$$p_1u[\hat{w}_H(1)]+(1-p_1)u[\hat{w}_L(1)] \geqslant p_1u[\hat{w}_H(0)]+(1-p_1)u[\hat{w}_L(0)]$$

$$p_0u[\hat{w}_H(0)]+(1-p_0)u[\hat{w}_L(0)] \geqslant p_0u[\hat{w}_H(1)]+(1-p_0)u[\hat{w}_L(1)]$$

and the participation constraints

$$p_1u[\hat{w}_H(1)]+(1-p_1)u[\hat{w}_L(1)] \geqslant p_1u[w_H(1)]+(1-p_1)u[w_L(1)]$$

$$p_0u[\hat{w}_H(0)]+(1-p_0)u[\hat{w}_L(0)] \geqslant p_0u[w_H(0)]+(1-p_0)u[w_L(0)]$$

Two important observations must be made about this problem: First, note that the agent's cost of effort does not appear in the problem. It is because the agent's action is sunk at the renegotiation stage. Second, both types' individual-rationality constraints may be binding here.

To see why the principal can restrict attention to "renegotiation-proof" contracts, imagine that the principal offered a contract C_0 that was not renegotiation-proof. This contract would then be replaced by a new contract C, which solves the preceding compensation-cost minimization problem.

The new contract C provides at least the same payoff to the agent as the old contract, C_0, but it strictly improves the principal's payoff. Moreover, since the agent anticipates renegotiation, her action choice x remains the same whether she is offered C_0, which gets renegotiated into C, or whether she is offered C directly. Hence there is no loss in restricting attention to "renegotiation-proof" contracts.

Just as in a standard adverse selection problem the principal's choice of an optimal menu of contracts to solve the compensation-cost-minimization problem, given some anticipated action choice x by the agent, boils down to a problem of extracting the informational rent of "type $a = 0$"—who always wants to pretend to be "type $a = 1$," other things equal—by distorting the efficient allocation of type $a = 1$. Hence we would expect the optimal menu of contracts to be such that type $a = 0$ gets full insurance (no distortion at the top) but type $a = 1$ gets less than full insurance. In other words, only contracts that offer full insurance to type $a = 0$ are renegotiation-proof, so that we must have $w_L(0) = w_H(0) = w^*$. As long as an action $x > 0$ is optimal, we must also have $w_L(1) < w_H(1)$. Finally, and not surprisingly given

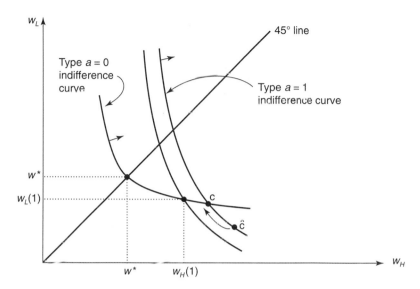

Figure 10.1
Menu of Renegotiation-Proof Contracts

what we learned in Chapter 2, the interim incentive-compatibility constraint for type $a = 0$ must be binding, so that

$$u(w^*) = p_0 u[w_H(1)] + (1 - p_0)u[w_L(1)] \tag{IIC}$$

It is instructive to represent the menu of renegotiation-proof contracts in a diagram, as seen in Figure 10.1. The indifference curve for type $a = 1$ is steeper than the curve for type $a = 0$ because $p_1 > p_0$, so that type $a = 0$ values insurance more than type $a = 1$.

If the interim incentive constraint were not binding, as at outcome $\hat{c}$, the principal could offer more insurance to type $a = 1$ without violating incentive compatibility.

The menu of contracts such that type $a = 0$ is fully insured and such that $w_L(1) \leq w_H(1)$, with $u(w^*) = p_0 u[w_H(1)] + (1 - p_0)u[w_L(1)]$, is not necessarily renegotiation-proof. It is renegotiation-proof only if the agent's action choice, x, is not too high. To see this point, consider again the diagram depicting the menu of renegotiation-proof contracts and consider the deviation shown in Figure 10.2.

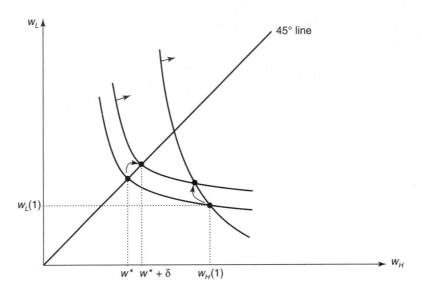

Figure 10.2
Profitable Deviation for Small x

Suppose that the principal offers to raise w^* to $w^* + \delta$. This change increases the wage bill by $(1 - x)\delta$ but allows the principal to offer more insurance to type $a = 1$.

Let $\delta w_H < 0$ and $\delta w_L > 0$ denote the change in type $a = 1$'s compensation scheme that keeps her indifferent:

$$p_1 \delta w_H u'(w_H) + (1 - p_0)\delta w_L u'(w_L) = 0$$

The expected gain in the wage bill of type $a = 1$ resulting from better insurance is then

$$x[p_1 \delta w_H + (1 - p_1)\delta w_L]$$

Hence for the contract to be renegotiation-proof we must have

$$x[p_1 \delta w_H + (1 - p_1)\delta w_L] \leqslant (1 - x)\delta$$

so that x cannot be too high.

Having established that the principal can restrict attention to renegotiation-proof contracts, we now turn to the derivation of the optimal ex ante renegotiation-proof contract. We shall take it that the principal wants to induce a choice $1 > x > 0$, in which case the agent's ex ante incentive constraint is given by

$$p_1 u[w_H(1)] + (1 - p_1) u[w_L(1)] - \psi = u(w^*) \tag{AIC}$$

Anticipating no renegotiation, the agent is indifferent between actions $a = 1$ and $a = 0$, and is then happy to choose the prescribed x. If the principal expects the agent to choose the prescribed x, he will not renegotiate the ex ante contract, so that the agent cannot gain by deviating from the prescribed action in order to induce renegotiation.

The two constraints (AIC) and (IIC) uniquely tie down $w_H(1)$ and $w_L(1)$ as a function of $u(w^*)$. Similarly, for any w^*, the principal wants to induce the highest possible choice of x compatible with renegotiation, $x(w^*)$, given by

$$x(w^*)[p_1 w_H(w^*) + (1 - p_1) w_L(w^*)] = 1 - x(w^*)$$

Hence the principal's ex ante problem reduces to

$$\max_{w^*} x(w^*)\{p_1[q_H - w_H(w^*)] + (1 - p_1)[q_L - w_L(w^*)]\}$$
$$+ [1 - x(w^*)][p_0 q_H + (1 - p_0) q_L - w^*]$$

To determine the optimal choice of w^*, we thus need to investigate how $x(w^*)$ varies with w^*. Fudenberg and Tirole (1990) establish that the sign of dx/dw^* may be positive if the agent's risk preferences exhibit decreasing absolute risk aversion. But if the agent has constant or increasing absolute risk aversion, then dx/dw^* is negative. The intuition for this result is that, by increasing the agent's wealth w^*, the principal may be able to reduce the agent's demand for insurance sufficiently so that he gains from it.

This analysis of moral hazard with renegotiation (through uninformed party offers), while somewhat abstract, may provide some insights into some contractual clauses of executive compensation contracts. For example, an executive who has made important long-run investments or strategic decisions should be offered the option of scaling up or down her risk exposure. Similarly, an executive's compensation after retirement may be substantially less sensitive to the firm's performance (even if this performance conveys important information about the executive's actions), if the CEO prefers this option. In practice, CEOs have a lot of discretion in structuring their incentive packages. Also, they have the option of forfeiting their stock options when they retire. This is consistent with the theory of moral hazard with renegotiation.

Let us end this subsection with a brief discussion of the case where the informed party, that is, the agent, makes a take-it-or-leave-it renegotiation offer to the principal after effort has been chosen. This case, analyzed by Ma (1994) and Matthews (1995), differs from the one we have just discussed in that the renegotiation offer can act as a *signal* about the effort chosen by the agent. Instead, in the case where the principal makes an offer, his belief about effort is obviously independent of his offer. In the agent-offer case, low effort followed by full insurance for the agent can be avoided if the principal's belief about effort becomes more "optimistic" when the agent makes a renegotiation offer that is riskier for her. While this game has a multiplicity of perfect Bayesian equilibria, as is typical in signaling games, Ma and Matthews both show that the second-best outcome, that is, the outcome of the moral-hazard model when renegotiation is impossible, can be sustained as a unique equilibrium under appropriate refinements. Specifically, Ma assumes that, if an effort is optimal for the agent both for the initial contract proposed by the principal and for the renegotiated contract offered by the agent, then this is the effort the principal believes the agent has taken. And, in a similar vein, Matthews also rules out beliefs about effort where the agent would have played some types of dominated strategies.[2]

The lessons one can draw from these results are as follows: (1) the idea analyzed by Fudenberg and Tirole (1990) and Ma (1991)—that the anticipation of efficient risk sharing once effort has been chosen reduces effort incentives—is quite intuitive; (2) its impact on equilibrium effort and insurance depends, however, on the details of the renegotiation game; and (3) under some assumptions, this impact can be completely eliminated, but this requires strong assumptions.

10.3.2   Renegotiation When Effort Is Observed by the Principal

When, after effort is chosen by the (risk-averse) agent, the effort is *observed by the (risk-neutral) principal before the uncertainty about output is realized,* Hermalin and Katz (1991) show that the optimal contract can achieve the

---

2. This approach amounts, in game-theoretic parlance, to a relatively weak form of *forward induction,* which allows selecting the best subgame equilibrium for the agent.

first best: the initial contract can make the agent residual claimant, thereby inducing first-best effort, then renegotiation can offer full insurance to the agent. Full insurance here does *not* destroy incentives to exert effort, in contrast with either the model without renegotiation or the model with renegotiation but unobserved effort by the principal. Indeed, here, the principal offers the agent a fixed wage that depends on her level of effort, since he has observed it. The initial contract thus determines a reservation utility for the agent that depends positively on her effort level.

Dewatripont, Legros, and Matthews (2003) add to this problem the monotonicity and limited-liability conditions of Innes,[3] detailed in Chapter 4. Innes showed that these conditions led to the optimality of debt contracts in a principal-agent model with bilateral risk neutrality, because debt was the effort-maximizing contract. Such a contract, however, is not very good in terms of insurance for the agent in the case where she is risk averse. In a Hermalin and Katz setup, however, this problem disappears thanks to renegotiation, even though the optimal contract cannot be achieved when the Innes constraints are introduced.

To provide intuition for this result, let us focus on an example with three output or revenue outcomes:

$$0 = q_L < q_M < q_H$$

Denoting by r_i the repayments to the investor/principal given outcome q_i, the agent/entrepreneur's limited liability constraint requires that $r_L = 0$, while monotonicity of the investor's payoff requires[4]

$$r_L \leq r_M \leq r_H$$

In this case, a debt contract is defined by

$$r_M < q_M \Rightarrow r_H = r_M$$

or

either $r_H = r_M$ or $r_M = q_M$

---

3. Before them, Matthews (2001) performed the same exercise for the case where effort is not observable by the principal (see the discussion below).

4. Remember that, among the four constraints, it is the limited liability of the entrepreneur/agent and the monotonicity of the payoff of the principal/investor that matter in the case considered by Innes. The same is true in this case.

We now establish the optimality of a debt contract in the following example, where the entrepreneur's utility function is given by

$$2\sqrt{w_i} - a$$

The agent's utility is thus the square root of the entrepreneur's monetary payoff, $w_i = q_i - r_i$, minus the effort cost, which is assumed to be linear in effort. Concerning the productivity of effort, we make for simplicity the following assumptions on the probability $p_i(a)$ of q_i (on top of MLRP; see Chapter 4):

$$p'_M(a) > 0 \quad \text{and} \quad p''_M(a) < 0$$

and

$$p'_H(a) > 0 \quad \text{and} \quad p''_H(a) < 0$$

10.3.2.1   First-Best Contracts

The first-best contract involves a constant monetary payoff w for the entrepreneur and is the solution to

$$\max_{w,a} 2\sqrt{w} - a$$

subject to

$$\sum_i p_i(a)(q_i - w) \geq I$$

where I is the investment cost that the investor has to provide. Substituting the constraint (which is binding at the optimum) into the maximand yields

$$\max_a 2\sqrt{\sum_i p_i(a)q_i - I} - a$$

This is a concave problem (remember that $q_L = 0$), whose first-order condition is

$$\frac{\sum_i p'_i(a)q_i}{\sqrt{\sum_i p_i(a)q_i - I}} =$$

Since

$$\sum_i p_i(a)q_i - I = w$$

this can also be rewritten as

$$w = \left[\sum_i p_i'(a)q_i \right]^2$$

Calling a^* the first-best effort level, we thus see that the entrepreneur's payoff is increasing in effort up until effort level a^*.

10.3.2.2   Second-Best Contracts

The second-best contract sets the r_i's ex ante. Given the effort choice of the agent, this determines the expected payoff of the investor. Assuming a take-it-or-leave-it offer by the entrepreneur after effort choice, this investor's expected payoff remains the same, but the entrepreneur asks for a constant monetary payoff at that stage. This payoff w is determined by

$$\sum_i p_i(a)q_i - w = \sum_i p_i(a)r_i$$

while the second-best contract is the solution of

$$\max_{r_i,a} 2\sqrt{w} - a$$

subject to

$$\sum_i p_i(a)r_i \geq I, \quad \text{with } r_L = 0 \leq r_M \leq r_H$$

and thus

$$w = \sum_i p_i(a)(q_i - r_i)$$

What the entrepreneur offers initially is thus $\{r_L, r_M, r_H\}$, so that her problem after the investor has accepted the offer is

$$\max_{r_i,a} 2\sqrt{\sum_i p_i(a)(q_i - r_i)} - a$$

This is once again a concave problem (remember that $q_L = r_L = 0$) whose first-order condition is

$$\frac{\sum_i p_i'(a)(q_i - r_i)}{\sqrt{\sum_i p_i(a)(q_i - r_i)}} = 1 \tag{10.8}$$

Since $\sum_i p_i(a)(q_i - r_i) = w$, this can also be rewritten as

$$w = \left[\sum_i p_i'(a)(q_i - r_i)\right]^2$$

Just like the first-best contract, the second-best contract allows the investor to recoup the initial investment I but implies a different pair (w, a). Specifically, since $q_L = r_L = 0$ and moreover $p_M'(a) > 0$, $p_M''(a) < 0$, $p_H'(a) > 0$, and $p_H''(a) < 0$, the second-best contract must imply a lower constant wage w and a lower effort level than in the first-best contract. Indeed, in equilibrium, we have $\sum_i p_i(a)r_i = I$, which means that, for $a = a^*$, the denominator of the LHS of equation (10.8) would be the same as in the first-best contract. Instead, its numerator is smaller [since $p_M'(a) > 0$ and $p_H'(a) > 0$, and since $q_M > r_M$ and $q_H > r_H$]. A reduction of effort below level a^* restores equality, since the denominator is increasing in effort while the numerator is decreasing in effort [given $p_M''(a) < 0$ and $p_H''(a) < 0$].

The second-best contract thus suffers from insufficient effort. The best contract is consequently the one that maximizes effort. This is the debt contract, as can be shown by contradiction. Indeed, assume it is not the case; that is, assume the optimal contract implies $r_H > r_M$ and $r_M < q_M$. Call its associated effort level $\hat{a}$. Then consider the following change in the contract:

$$dr_M = -\frac{p_H(\hat{a})}{p_M(\hat{a})} dr_H > 0$$

Such a change will leave the payoff of the investor unchanged at unchanged effort $\hat{a}$. Moreover, given the initial contract, this change can be made without violating either the monotonicity or limited-liability constraint. Finally, given MLRP, this change will lead to a (Pareto-improving) increase in effort: at effort level $\hat{a}$, the denominator of equation (10.8) is unchanged, while the change in the numerator is

$$p_M'(\hat{a})\frac{p_H(\hat{a})}{p_M(\hat{a})} dr_H - p_H'(\hat{a})dr_H = -dr_H\left[\frac{p_H'(\hat{a})}{p_H(\hat{a})} - \frac{p_M'(\hat{a})}{p_M(\hat{a})}\right]p_H(\hat{a}) > 0$$

At effort level $\hat{a}$, the incentive to invest is thus higher than 1, so that equation (10.8) can be restored only by an increase in equilibrium effort. This proves that any nondebt contract can be improved upon.

The intuition of the result is clear: just as in Innes (1990), a debt contract maximizes incentives to exert effort subject to the limited-liability and

monotonicity constraints. And just as in Hermalin and Katz (1991), renegotiation after both parties have observed the effort choice but before the
realization of output allows one to combine maximum effort incentives and
optimal insurance. The difference with Hermalin and Katz is that the first
best is here unattainable. Dewatripont, Legros, and Matthews (2003) show
that message-contingent contracts cannot improve upon simple debt contracts given the constraint imposed by renegotiation-proofness, at least
when one restricts attention to pure-strategy implementation.

The preceding result has an obvious parallel with the earlier result of
Matthews (2001), which shows that limited liability plus monotonicity
implies the optimality of an initial debt contract in the same model but
without observability of the effort choice by the principal. Matthews (2001)
in fact adds the Innes (1990) constraints to the informed-party-offer model
of Matthews (1995). The result here is simpler, since renegotiation takes
place under symmetric information, so that no refinement of perfect
Bayesian equilibrium is needed.

Furthermore, the results of Dewatripont, Legros, and Matthews (2003)
and Matthews (2001) provide a simple theory of the dynamics of the capital
structure of firms: this theory fits, for example, very well the case of an entrepreneur who first obtains debt finance from a bank and then goes public,
that is, moves to equity finance. Such a pattern is well documented (see, for
example, Diamond, 1991b). Here, it results from the fact that the effort of
the entrepreneur is especially crucial in the initial stage of the business.
Note also that, here, the entrepreneur has a constant wage, and therefore
no equity stake ex post, because she is the only risk-averse party. If both
parties were risk averse, we would have coinsurance after renegotiation,
which could be reinterpreted as giving the entrepreneur some equity in the
firm.

10.4   Bilateral Relational Contracts

So far in this chapter we have restricted attention to court-enforceable contracts. These are the only enforceable contracts when the relation between
the contracting parties is finite. But when the principal and agent are
engaged in a repeated, open-ended relationship, they may be able to extend
any formal court-enforced contract with informal self-enforced provisions.
Informal agreements are self-enforcing when some credible future

punishment threat in the event of noncompliance induces each party to stick to the agreed terms. A classic example of an informal self-enforced provision in employment contracts is a promise of a bonus payment or a promotion as a reward for good performance. Most employment relations have such informal promises. Even though employers have full discretion in whether to make the promised bonus payment, they generally tend to honor their promises. One reason why they do not renege on their promise is that they fear that disgruntled employees may leave or shirk. Another example is dividend payments by corporations. These are entirely discretionary payments, but corporations are reluctant to renege on their promises out of fear that the stock price will drop substantially following the announcement of the dividend cut. In Chapter 3 we saw that initiation of dividend payments may be a way of signaling expected high future earnings. We pointed out that one weakness of the signaling theory is that it assumes that firms will not renege on their promise. Thus one way of explaining why they would stick to their promised payments is to see dividend payments as self-enforcing provisions in a relational contract.

The early literature on relational contracts confines attention to contracting situations with symmetric information (see, for example, Klein and Leffler, 1981; Shapiro and Stiglitz, 1984; Bull, 1987). The most complete analysis of relational contracts under symmetric information is given by MacLeod and Malcomson (1989).

In this section we provide an analysis of optimal relational contracts under hidden actions and information in a bilateral contracting problem. For simplicity and for expositional reasons we shall restrict attention to situations where both principal and agent are risk neutral. We shall also assume that the performance measure on which the relational contract is conditioned is observable by both parties even if it is not verifiable by a court. This section is based on the treatments of MacLeod and Malcomson (1989) and Levin (2003).

We shall consider a sequence of spot contracts between an infinitely lived risk-neutral principal and agent. Both have the same discount factor $\delta < 1$. In each period t the principal's and agent's reservation utilities are, respectively, $\overline{V}$ and $\overline{u}$. If they engage in a spot contract, the agent privately chooses an action $a \in A$. This action results in n possible output realizations at the end of period t, which we rank in order of increasing output: $q_1 < q_2 < \ldots < q_n$. The probability distribution of output q_i^t in period t is given by $p_i(a_t)$, where a_t denotes the agent's action choice in period t and $i = 1, \ldots, n$. As usual, we assume that $p_i(a) > 0$ for all $a \in A$ and that the likelihood ratio $p_i'(a)/p_i(a)$ is increasing in output q_i (that is, MLRP holds; see Chapter 4). Following the output realization, the principal makes a payment W_t to the agent. This payment may comprise an explicit contractually agreed payment w_t and a discretionary bonus b_t. Following the payment, the principal's end-of-period flow payoff is

$$q_i^t - W_t$$

and the agent's payoff is

$$W_t - \psi(a_t, \theta_t)$$

where θ_t denotes a privately observed cost parameter. For simplicity again, we shall assume that θ_t takes two values, $\theta_t \in [\theta_L, \theta_H]$ with $\theta_L \leq \theta_H$. We shall also assume that θ_t is an i.i.d. variable with $\beta = \Pr(\theta_t = \theta_H)$. As before, we assume that $\psi(\cdot)$ is strictly increasing and convex in a. We also assume that $\psi(0, \theta) = 0$ and that $\psi_\theta \geq 0$ and $\psi_{a\theta} > 0$.

In a first-best situation the agent would choose $a \in A$ to maximize

$$\sum_{i=1}^{n} p_i(a) q_i - \psi(a, \theta)$$

Suppose that there is a uniquely defined first-best action $a^{FB}(\theta)$. To ensure that we have an interesting problem, we shall, of course, assume that

$$\sum_{i=1}^{n} p_i(a^{FB}) q_i - \psi(a^{FB}, \theta) > \bar{s} \equiv \bar{V} + \bar{u}$$

It is also convenient to make the additional mild assumption that

$$\sum_{i=1}^{n} p_i(0) q_i - \psi(0, \theta) \leq \bar{s}$$

We are now in a position to define the relational contracting problem. A relational contract is a perfect Bayesian equilibrium of an infinite-horizon game, where the players' moves in each stage game (or each period) are the following:

• A participation decision and an action choice (subject to participation) for the agent a_t

• A participation decision and an output-contingent bonus payment decision (subject to participation and following the output realization) for the principal $b_t(q_i^t)$

Let σ^a and σ^p denote a strategy for the agent and principal, respectively, over the infinite-horizon game. A strategy specifies the agent's and principal's move at any time t as a function of observed history of play and output realizations. More precisely, the principal and agent condition their respective moves at date t on the history of output realizations and past transfers. In other words, they condition their moves on the same observed past history. The agent does not condition her move on her past actions when her action choice is not observable to the principal, as action costs incurred in the past are sunk and past actions do not affect the principal's continuation play in any way.

The players' flow payoffs are determined partly by a court-enforced payment plan ζ^w—which specifies a payment from the principal to the agent at each date t as a function of *verifiable* history of play and output realizations—and by a self-enforced discretionary payment plan ζ^b—which specifies a bonus payment at each date t as a function of *observable* history of play and output realizations. For simplicity we shall assume that output realizations are observable but not verifiable, and that past payments are observable and verifiable.

A perfect Bayesian equilibrium of the infinite-horizon game is such that the players' moves following any history are best responses.

The (normalized) payoff at any point in time t under a relational contract $(\sigma, \zeta) = (\sigma^a, \sigma^p, \zeta^w, \zeta^b)$ is then given by

$$V_t = (1-\delta)E_{t|(\sigma,\zeta)}\sum_{\tau=t}^{\infty}\delta^{t-1}[\Lambda(q_\tau - W_\tau) + (1-\Lambda)\overline{V}]$$

for the principal, and

$$u_t = (1-\delta)E_{t|(\sigma,\zeta)}\sum_{\tau=t}^{\infty}\delta^{t-1}\{\Lambda[W_\tau - \psi(a_\tau, \theta_\tau)] + (1-\Lambda)\overline{u}\}$$

for the agent, where Λ is an indicator variable taking value one if both parties decide to participate, and zero if one of the parties opts out.

Since opting out of the relationship is one of the moves available to each party at any time, any relational contract must give each party a payoff greater than or equal to his or her outside option:

$$V_t \geq \overline{V} \quad \text{and} \quad u_t \geq \overline{u}$$

Also, if a relational contract generates a total surplus $s_t > \overline{s}$, then it is possible to enforce any division $(u_t, s_t - u_t)$ of the surplus such that $u_t \geq \overline{u}$ and $(s_t - u_t) \geq \overline{V}$ as a relational contract by specifying a suitable fixed transfer w_t between principal and agent. Indeed, the fixed transfer affects only each party's participation decision and not any other moves. As long as $u_t \geq \overline{u}$ and $(s_t - u_t) \geq \overline{V}$, participation is clearly preferable, so that $(u_t, s_t - u_t)$ is clearly also a relational contract. Hence, a relational contract (σ, ζ) at date $t = 0$ is optimal if it maximizes the joint surplus s_0. Another implication of the result that it is possible to enforce any division $(u_t, s_t - u_t)$, such that $u_t \geq \overline{u}$ and $(s_t - u_t) \geq \overline{V}$, as a relational contract is that one can restrict attention to stationary contracts without loss of generality to characterize the joint payoff under an optimal relational contract.

DEFINITION   A relational contract (σ^*, ζ^*) is stationary if in every period on the equilibrium path $a_t = a(\theta_t)$, $b_t = b(q_i^t)$, and $w_t = w$.

We leave the proof of the above observation as an exercise. The argument involves showing that one can average out nonstationary transfers and actions to obtain a stationary contract with the same payoff.

Dynamic programming can be used to obtain a simple characterization of an optimal stationary relational contract. Let u^* and $s^* - u^*$ denote the agent's and principal's payoff under the stationary contract (σ^*, ζ^*), let w^* and $b^*(q_i)$ denote the court-enforced transfer and discretionary bonus under the stationary contract (σ^*, ζ^*), and let $a^*(\theta)$ denote the agent's action choice; then the joint value of the contracting relation s^* is given by

$$s^* = \max_{a(\theta)}(1 - \delta)E_{\theta,q}[q - \psi[a(\theta),\theta] | a(\theta)] + \delta E_{\theta,q}[s^* | a^*(\theta)]$$

subject to

$$a^*(\theta) \in \arg\max_{a \in A}\left\{E_q\left[w^* + b^*(q_i) + \frac{\delta}{1-\delta}u^* | a\right] - \psi(a, \theta)\right\} \tag{IC}$$

$$b^*(q_i) + \frac{\delta}{1-\delta}u^* \geq \frac{\delta}{1-\delta}\overline{u} \tag{PCA}$$

and

$$-b^*(q_i) + \frac{\delta}{1-\delta}(s^* - u^*) \geq \frac{\delta}{1-\delta}\overline{V} \qquad \text{(PCP)}$$

The first constraint ensures that the agent has the correct incentive to stick to the prescribed action plan $a^*(\theta)$. The second constraint ensures continued participation of the agent. Implicit in the constraint is the assumption that when the agent quits, she quits forever. There is no loss of generality in making this assumption. In fact the threat of a permanent quit is the strongest possible threat for the agent and is the one that allows for the largest possible set of self-enforcing contracts. The third constraint ensures continued payment of the discretionary bonus by the principal. If the principal were to withhold the bonus payment $b^*(q_i)$ in any period, he would receive only the flow payoff $\delta\overline{V}/(1-\delta)$ in the future, as the agent would quit forever following such a move. If the principal complies, the agent does not quit and he gets the flow payoff $\delta(s^* - u^*)/(1-\delta)$ in the future. The third constraint thus ensures that complying with the bonus payment results in a weakly higher payoff for the principal.

Several questions immediately arise concerning this contract. First, is it clear that the agent's strategy of participating and supplying action $a^*(\theta)$ in period t as long as the history of output and payments has been $\{[q^{t-1}, w^* + b^*(q^{t-1})]\}$ in every period and otherwise quitting forever, and the principal's strategy of participating and paying $w^* + b^*(q_i^t)$ as long as the history of output and payments has been $\{[q^{t-1}, w^* + b^*(q^{t-1})]\}$ in every period and otherwise quitting forever, are mutually best responses following any history? If the principal decides to quit forever following a deviation from the history of outputs and payments $\{[q^{t-1}, w^* + b^*(q^{t-1})]\}$, then obviously a best response for the agent is also not to participate, and vice versa. Therefore, if conditions (IC), (PCA), and (PCP) are satisfied, the contract (σ^*, ζ^*) does indeed support a perfect Bayesian equilibrium.

Second, following a deviation by one party, is there not scope for renegotiation? It turns out that (stationary) relational contracts such that $u^* > \overline{u}$ and $(s^* - u^*) > \overline{V}$ can easily be made renegotiation-proof. The reason is again related to the possibility of enforcing any division $(u_t, s^* - u_t)$, such that $u_t \geq \overline{u}$ and $(s^* - u_t) \geq \overline{V}$, as a relational contract. If renegotiation precludes enforcement of inefficient punishments such that $s_\tau < s^*$ following a deviation in period $t < \tau$, a relational contract can still be enforced with jointly efficient punishments by changing the division of the surplus s^* following a deviation. Thus the following contract can be specified: the principal promises payments w^* and $b^*(q_i)$ unless one party deviates. If the agent deviates, switch to a continuation contract with payments $\hat{w} + \hat{b}(q_i)$ such that $\hat{u} = \bar{u}$ (and $\hat{V} = s^* - \hat{u}$) following the deviation, and if the principal deviates, switch to a continuation contract with payments $\tilde{w}$ and $\tilde{b}(q_i)$ such that $\tilde{V} = \bar{V}$. If further deviations occur, treat them similarly. This expanded relational contract is obviously renegotiation-proof because it lies on the constrained Pareto frontier. It should also be clear that, since continuation payoffs are the same for the deviating party as when continuation involves nonparticipation, this expanded contract can enforce the same optimal joint payoff s^*.

Third, is it clear that an optimal stationary contract (σ^*, ζ^*) actually exists? When θ and q take on a finite number of values, as we have assumed here, existence can be established using similar arguments as used for static-adverse-selection and moral-hazard problems (see Levin, 2003, for a proof of existence).

Interestingly, discretionary payments $b^*(q_i)$ may be positive or negative depending on how the net surplus from the relational contract $(s^* - \bar{s})$ is divided between the principal and agent. If the agent gets a small share of the net surplus, then discretionary payments $b^*(q_i)$ must be positive. Indeed, only large positive discretionary payments, which may be necessary to give the agent adequate incentives to supply effort [or costly actions $a(\theta)$], can satisfy the agent's participation constraint (PCA) when $(u^* - \bar{u})$ tends to zero. In this case the relational contract can be interpreted as a "performance pay" contract. At the other extreme, when the principal gets a small share of the net surplus, discretionary payments $b^*(q_i)$ must be negative. In this case the relational contract resembles an "efficiency-wage" contract.

The main difference between a relational contract and the fully enforceable contracts we have seen in Chapters 2, 4, and 6 comes from the additional self-enforcement constraints (PCA) and (PCP). Letting $\bar{b}$ and $\underline{b}$ denote the highest and lowest discretionary bonus payments, respectively, these two constraints can be combined into the following single self-enforcement constraint.

$$(\bar{b} - \underline{b}) \le \frac{\delta}{1-\delta}(s^* - \bar{s}) \tag{SEC}$$

When this constraint is binding, relational contracts provide less high-powered incentives than fully enforceable contracts. We now illustrate how this constraint can modify the form of the optimal contract in the two polar opposite cases of pure moral hazard and pure adverse selection.

10.4.1   Moral Hazard

The case of pure moral hazard arises here when $\theta_L = \theta_H = \theta$. As we saw in Chapter 4, an optimal incentive contract under risk neutrality takes a very simple form: when there is no gain to sharing output risk, it is optimal to make the agent a residual claimant. More precisely, the optimal contract specifies an output-contingent payment to the agent of

$$W(q_i) = w + q_i$$

where w is a fixed payment such that

$$w = \bar{u} - \max_{a \in A}\{E_q[q \mid a] - \psi(a, \theta)\}$$

This contract is not self-enforcing if

$$(q_n - q_1) > \frac{\delta}{1 - \delta}[E_q[q \mid a^{FB}] - \psi(a^{FB}, \theta) - \bar{s}]$$

Whenever the self-enforcement constraint (SEC) is violated under the residual claims contract, it is optimal to specify a relational contract such that

$$b(q_i) = \bar{b} \quad \text{for } q_i \geq q_k$$

$$b(q_i) = \underline{b} \quad \text{for } q_i < q_k$$

for some $q_1 \leq q_k \leq q_n$. This result follows immediately from the MLRP assumption. We leave it as an exercise for the reader to prove. A useful hint here is the analogy that can be drawn between this relational contract under pure moral hazard and risk neutrality and the fully enforceable moral-hazard problem under limited liability considered by Innes (1990). Thus self-enforcing constraints act like limited-liability constraints.

10.4.2   Adverse Selection

The case of pure adverse selection arises when the agent's action choice a_t is observable to the principal, but not the agent's cost type θ. As in Chapter

2, we can apply the revelation principle to characterize the optimal stationary relational contract. Observe also that the Spence-Mirrlees condition

$$\frac{\partial}{\partial \theta}\left(\frac{\partial[W - \psi(a, \theta)]}{\partial a}\right) < 0$$

is satisfied under our assumptions about the agent's cost-of-effort function $\psi_{a\theta} > 0$). Therefore, the optimal contract can be characterized as the solution to the following program:

$$s^* = \max_{a(\theta), W(\theta)} (1 - \delta)E_{\theta,q}[q - \psi(a(\theta), \theta)|a(\theta)] + \delta E_{\theta,q}[s^*|a^*(\theta)]$$

subject to

$$b(\theta_L) - \psi[a(\theta_L), \theta_L] \geq b(\theta_H) - \psi[a(\theta_H), \theta_L]$$

$$b(\theta_H) - \psi[a(\theta_H), \theta_{II}] \geq \bar{u}$$

and

$$|b(\theta_H) - b(\theta_L)| \leq \frac{\delta}{1 - \delta}(s^* - \bar{s})$$

As we showed in Chapter 2, the optimal contract under full court enforcement would have "no distortion at the top," which here means, on the one hand, that the high-cost type provides an efficient level of effort. That is, $a(\theta_H)$ satisfies

$$\sum_{i=1}^{n} p_i'[a(\theta_H)]q_i = \psi'[a(\theta_H), \theta_H]$$

On the other hand, the low-cost type underprovides effort. This is a distortion imposed by the principal to reduce the low-cost type's informational rent.

Now, the basic "no distortion at the top" property does not hold generally under an optimal relational contract, since the bonus schedule $b(\theta)$ associated with the second-best contract under full enforceability may violate the self-enforcement constraint (SEC). In that case, all cost types underprovide inputs. In other words, the self-enforcement constraint puts an overall limit on the total incentives that can be given to the agent. Levin (2003) shows that when there are more than two cost types (say, a continuum), then not only does the optimal relational contract result in underprovision of inputs for all cost types, but also "bunching" of cost types (that is, equal input provision for different cost types; see Chapter 2) is more likely.

10.4.3   Extensions

In this section we have considered only pure relational contracts. But the framework can be extended to allow for both contractually explicit incentives and implicit incentives. Several articles take a stab in this direction. Bernheim and Whinston (1998b) consider a model where the contracting parties can write more or less complete incentive contracts supplemented by implicit incentives. They show that it can be in the parties' interest to rely less on formal incentives than they could in order to exploit implicit incentives as much as possible. Similarly, Baker, Gibbons, and Murphy (1994) and Pearce and Stachetti (1998) explore a model with risk-averse agents combining both explicit and implicit incentives. Finally, MacLeod (2003) extends the setup considered here and analyzes a relational contracting problem between a risk-averse agent and a risk-neutral principal, where the performance measures of each party are subjective and imperfectly correlated. Interestingly, he shows that in an optimal relational contract the agent's compensation does not depend on her own performance evaluation, while her cooperation does. If according to her own evaluation the agent feels that she is unfairly treated, then she stops cooperating.

10.5   Implicit Incentives and Career Concerns

In this section we consider relational contracts in multilateral settings and analyze how the agent responds to both *explicit* contractual incentives and *implicit* market-driven incentives. In most long-term contracting problems with moral hazard in reality, agents' incentives are driven by a combination of formal contractual rewards and *career concerns*. This observation is especially true of executive compensation, as Gibbons and Murphy (1992) have emphasized, but it is also true of most employment contracts. In contrast to contractual incentives, market incentives are not easily controlled and can often be excessively strong.

Holmström (1982a) provides the classic treatment of incentives driven by career concerns. The simplest version of the model he considers is as follows: There are two periods, $t = 1, 2$. The agent's output performance in each period is given by

$$q_t = \theta + a_t + \varepsilon_t$$

where θ denotes the agent's unknown ability, a_t is the agent's unobservable effort, and ε_t is white noise (a normally distributed random variable with mean zero and variance σ^2). A key departure from earlier models (and, as we shall see, a key simplification) is that the agent's ability is assumed to be initially unknown to everybody, whether the agent or the principal. Only the prior distribution over θ is commonly known and shared by all contracting parties ex ante. Therefore, contracting at date 1 takes place under symmetric information. Effort a_t is observed only by the agent, who incurs the usual hidden effort cost $\psi(a_t)$.

Holmström assumes that although output performance q_t is observable by everyone, no explicit contract contingent on the realization of q_t can be written. All the principal can do is pay the agent a fixed wage w_1 in period 1 and w_2 in period 2. With fixed wages it would seem that the agent has no incentive to supply effort. However, although the agent has no explicit contractual incentives, she has market-driven incentives that operate through changes in market wages in period 2 that follow from the observation of first-period output.

Holmström takes the second-period market wage $w_2(q)$ to be set by competition among principals for the agent's services and to be equal to the market's beliefs about the agent's expected productivity conditional on the realization of first-period output: $E(\theta|q_1)$. Since high first-period output is more likely for a high θ, the market updates prior beliefs about the agent's ability upward whenever a high output is observed. This result gives the agent incentives to supply effort in the first period, so as to raise her first-period output and thus her second-period wage.

If δ is the discount factor between the two periods, the (risk-neutral) agent maximizes

$$w_1 - \psi(a) + \delta w_2(q)$$

In a pure-strategy equilibrium, where the market anticipates that the agent will put in effort a^* in the first period, we thus have

$$w_2(q) = q - a^* = \theta + a - a^*$$

and so

$$\psi'(a^*) = \delta$$

Notice, on the one hand, that when $\delta > 1$ the agent puts in more effort than is first-best optimal in the first period. The first-best-optimal effort level indeed is given by $\psi'(a^{FB}) = 1$. On the other hand, the agent puts in $a_2 = 0$ in the second period, as she does not gain anything from exerting herself at that point. In other words, the agent may respond to market incentives by exerting herself too much early on, in an attempt to build a reputation for high ability, but then rests on her laurels later on in her career. (Notice, however, that the market is not fooled by the agent in equilibrium and correctly anticipates and discounts her first-period effort choice a^*.) Holmström generalizes this model in a multiperiod setting and shows how, quite generally, the agent's equilibrium effort provision is excessive early on and insufficient in later stages of an agent's career.

Following these preliminary observations, we shall generalize the one-shot career-concerns model following Dewatripont, Jewitt, and Tirole (1999a, 1999b), and we shall compare the career-concerns paradigm with the explicit-incentives one.

We denote the agent's vector of actions or efforts by $a = (a_1, \ldots, a_N) \in \mathbb{R}^N$, which implies a cost $\psi(a)$. The market observes a vector of performance variables $q = (q_1, \ldots, q_M) \in \mathbb{R}^M$, which lead to a reward w for the agent, whose utility is then

$$w - \psi(a)$$

The reward w reflects the market's expectation of an unknown (scalar) talent parameter θ conditional on the observable q. Let $f(\theta, q|a)$ denote the joint density of talent and performance variables given effort vector a. Let

$$\hat{f}(q|a) = \int f(\theta, q|a)d\theta$$

denote the marginal density of the performance variables. The agent's reward for performance variables q and equilibrium actions a^* (anticipated by the market) is thus

$$w = E(\theta|q, a^*) = \int \theta \frac{f(\theta, q|a^*)}{\hat{f}(q|a^*)} d\theta$$

The agent therefore chooses a so as to maximize her expected utility:

$$\max E[E(\theta|q, a^*)] - \psi(a)$$

where the first expectation is with respect to performance and the second with respect to talent.

It is helpful to derive a general first-order condition for this problem. Assuming an interior solution, this first-order condition for an equilibrium is

$$\frac{d}{da}\left[\int\left(\int\theta\frac{f(\theta,q|a^*)}{\hat{f}(q|a^*)}d\theta\right)\hat{f}(q|a)dq\right]\Bigg|_{a=a^*}=\psi_a(a^*)$$

or

$$\int\int\theta f(\theta,q|a^*)\frac{\hat{f}_a(q|a^*)}{\hat{f}(q|a^*)}dqd\theta=\psi_a(a^*)$$

where ψ_a and $\hat{f}_a$ denote the gradients with respect to effort of the agent's effort-cost function and of the marginal distribution. Using the fact that the (multidimensional) likelihood ratio has zero mean $[E(\hat{f}_a/\hat{f})=0]$, we can rewrite the equilibrium condition as

$$\text{cov}\left(\theta,\frac{\hat{f}_a}{\hat{f}}\right)=\psi_a(a^*) \tag{10.9}$$

where "cov" denotes the covariance of two random variables.[5] The vector $\text{cov}(\theta,\hat{f}_a/\hat{f})$ describes the agent's *marginal incentives*. It expresses the link between performance and expected talent for a given equilibrium effort a^*. We now consider more specific applications of this general formulation.

10.5.1   The Single-Task Case

Consider the following generalization of the additive-normal model of Holmström: assume a single task and a single performance variable ($N = M = 1$), and suppose that performance is given by

$$q=\theta(\mu a+\phi)+\gamma a+\varepsilon$$

---

5. Condition (10.9) for an *implicit* incentive scheme can be compared with the standard formula for *explicit* incentive schemes (Mirrlees, 1999; Holmström, 1979; Jewitt, 1988). Suppose the agent receives an explicit transfer $t(q)$ contingent on performance q and has utility $u(t)$ from income t. Then the first-order condition for the agent is

$$\text{cov}\left(u[t(q)],\frac{\hat{f}_a}{\hat{f}}\right)=\psi_a(a^*)$$

where μ, γ, and ϕ are positive known constants, while θ and ε are independently distributed random variables with Gaussian distribution

$$\theta \sim \mathcal{N}(\bar{\theta}, \sigma_\theta^2) \quad \text{and} \quad \varepsilon_i \sim \mathcal{N}(0, \sigma_\varepsilon^2)$$

Holmström's additive-normal model assumes that $\mu = 0$ (and $\phi = \gamma = 1$). A positive μ implies a *complementarity* between talent and effort (a *pure multiplicative-normal* model implies $\mu \neq 0$ and $\phi = \gamma = 0$). In this case, talent matters more, the higher the effort; that is, it makes a difference especially when the agent "tries to make things happen." This complementarity can then lead to multiple equilibria: If the market puts a lot of weight on the agent's performance, she is induced to work hard; in turn, her hard work leads the market to pay attention to her performance. The converse is true in the case of low effort.

We can apply condition (10.9) to obtain, for a given expected effort $\hat{a}$,

$$\frac{\bar{\theta}\mu + \gamma}{(\mu\hat{a} + \phi) + \dfrac{\sigma_\varepsilon^2}{(\mu\hat{a} + \phi)\sigma_\theta^2}} = \psi'(\hat{a})$$

The marginal cost of effort (the RHS) is assumed to be increasing in $\hat{a}$. The covariance between θ and the likelihood ratio (the LHS) depends on $\hat{a}$ only when $\mu \neq 0$. Indeed, in the pure additive case ($\mu = 0$), we obtain as RHS (assuming also for simplicity $\phi = \gamma = 1$):

$$\frac{\sigma_\theta^2}{\sigma_\varepsilon^2 + \sigma_\theta^2}$$

that is, the signal-to-noise ratio, which is independent of effort. With a multiplicative effect ($\mu > 0$) the derivative of the denominator of the covariance with respect to effort becomes

$$\mu\left[1 - \frac{\sigma_\varepsilon^2}{\sigma_\theta^2(\mu\hat{a} + \phi)^2}\right]$$

which is increasing in $\hat{a}$. There exists therefore a level of $\hat{a}$, which we can call $\tilde{a}$, such that this derivative is positive for all $\hat{a} > \tilde{a}$. Depending on parameter values, $\tilde{a}$ is strictly positive or not. For σ_ε^2 small enough, the covariance between θ and the likelihood ratio is always decreasing in effort. Take, for example, the pure multiplicative model without noise: $q = \theta\hat{a}$. For a given a^*, the market estimates θ as q/a^*, so that a given increase in expected effort

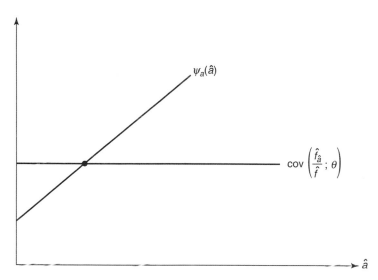

Figure 10.3
Additive Case ($\mu = 0$)

by the agent leads to a weaker upward revision of the market's estimate of talent. For positive σ_ε^2, however, there is another, opposite effect: higher expected effort leads the market to put more weight on talent relative to noise when observing good performance. In fact, for $\phi = 0$, when the market expects $\hat{a} = 0$, it attributes good performance *solely* to good luck, which is not the case when it expects positive effort. For low $\hat{a}$'s, this second effect can dominate the first one for ϕ small enough or $\sigma_\varepsilon^2/\sigma_\theta^2$ high enough. And for $\hat{a}$'s high enough, the first effect always dominates.

Figure 10.3 shows the unique equilibrium in the additive case ($\mu = 0$). Figure 10.4 shows the unique equilibrium when $\mu > 0$ and ϕ large or $\sigma_\varepsilon^2/\sigma_\theta^2$ low. Finally, the last case is depicted in Figure 10.5, where two stable equilibria may coexist (the intermediate one being unstable).

10.5.2   The Multitask Case

Let us now consider a generalization of the preceding analysis to look at the connection between effort incentives and the set of (symmetric) activities pursued by the agent. Assume that performance on task $i \in \{1, \ldots, N\}$ is given by

$$q_i = \theta(\mu a_i + \phi) + \gamma a_i + \varepsilon_i$$

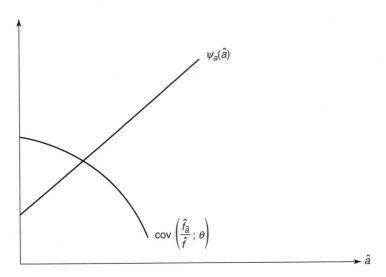

Figure 10.4
Weak Multiplicative Factor ($\mu > 0$; ϕ large or $\sigma_\varepsilon^2/\sigma_\theta^2$ small)

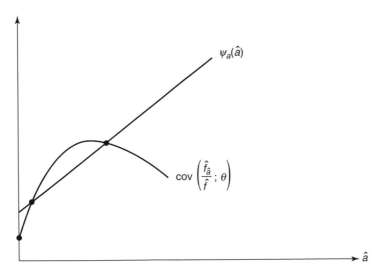

Figure 10.5
Strong Multiplicative Factor ($\mu > 0$; ϕ small or $\sigma_\varepsilon^2/\sigma_\theta^2$ large)

where μ, γ, and ϕ are positive known constants, $a_i \geq 0$ is effort expended on task i, and, as earlier, θ and ε_i are independently distributed random variables:

$$\theta \sim \mathcal{N}(\overline{\theta}, \sigma_\theta^2) \quad \text{and} \quad \varepsilon_i \sim \mathcal{N}(0, \sigma_\varepsilon^2)$$

Let us distinguish between the (exogenous) number of potential tasks (N) and the number of tasks actually pursued (n) for which $a_i > 0$. Suppose that the principal cares only about the aggregate output

$$Q = \sum_{i=1}^{N} q_i$$

so that only the total level of effort matters, not its distribution across individual tasks. Similarly, assume away any economies or diseconomies of scope, so the cost function can be written as a function, $\psi(\hat{a})$, of total effort $\hat{a} \equiv \sum_{i=1}^{N} a_i$ [with $\psi' > 0$, $\psi'' > 0$, $\psi'(0) \geq 0$]. We can now analyze the relationship between the *number* of tasks the agent pursues and total effort.

Consider first the case where only the total performance on a subset I of tasks

$$Q_I = \sum_{i \in I} q_i$$

is observed by the market. We are then back to the single-task case. Whatever the set of tasks the agent could work on, if the market observes only Q_I, the agent expends effort solely on the tasks included in I. As for total effort, $\hat{a}$, if I includes n tasks,

$$Q_I = \theta(\mu\hat{a} + n\phi) + \gamma\hat{a} + \sum_{i \in I} \varepsilon_i$$

This expression implies that[6]

$$\mathrm{cov}_n\left(\theta, \frac{\hat{f}_{\hat{a}}}{\hat{f}}\right) = \frac{(\overline{\theta}\mu + \gamma)}{(\mu\hat{a} + n\phi) + \dfrac{n\sigma_\varepsilon^2}{(\mu\hat{a} + n\phi)\sigma_\theta^2}}$$

---

6. Since all ε_i's are uncorrelated, the distribution of Q_I is normal with mean $\overline{\theta}(\mu\hat{a} + nb) + \gamma\hat{a}$ and variance $\sigma_\theta^2(\mu\hat{a} + nb)^2 + n\sigma_\varepsilon^2$. Consequently,

$$\frac{\hat{f}_{\hat{a}}(Q_I)}{\hat{f}(Q_I)} = \frac{[(\theta - \overline{\theta})(\mu\hat{a} + nb) + \sum_{i \in I} \varepsilon_i][\overline{\theta}\mu + \gamma]}{\sigma_\theta^2(\mu\hat{a} + nb)^2 + \sigma_\varepsilon^2}$$

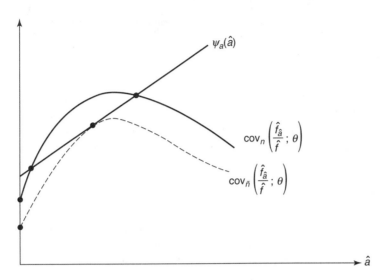

Figure 10.6
No High-Effort Equilibrium Beyond $\bar{n}$

Positive equilibrium levels of effort are those which equate this covariance with $\psi'(\hat{a})$. An increase in n lowers the covariance between talent and the likelihood ratio, and thus equilibrium effort, in all three cases depicted in Figures 10.3–10.5. The most interesting one concerns Figure 10.5, where, for n large enough, the high-effort equilibrium disappears, as shown in Figure 10.6.

In the (Holmström) additive-normal model, $\hat{a}$ decreases continuously with n, which may not be the case when a multiplicative effect is introduced: As Figure 10.6 shows, there is then a maximum n, call it $\bar{n}$, that allows for the high-effort equilibrium; beyond that value, $\hat{a}$ can only be zero.

The intuition for why total effort decreases with n can be most easily understood by focusing on the pure additive case ($\mu = 0$) and the pure multiplicative case ($\phi = \gamma = 0$). For simplicity, moreover, assume $\phi = \gamma = 1$ in the pure additive case and $\mu = 1$ in the pure multiplicative case. Consider first the "noiseless case" $\sigma_\varepsilon^2 = 0$, where the pure additive and the pure multiplicative models become, respectively,

$$Q_I = \theta_n + \hat{a}$$

$$Q_I = \theta \hat{a}$$

In the pure multiplicative case, n does not affect $\hat{a}$. Instead, in the pure additive case, incentives to expend effort go down when n goes up, since the market infers the following θ from a performance Q_I given effort expectation $\hat{a}^*$:

$$\frac{Q_I - \hat{a}^*}{n} = \theta + \frac{\hat{a} - \hat{a}^*}{n}$$

There is, moreover, a second effect of an increase in n on effort, similar in both cases: the variance of $\sum_{i=1}^{n} \varepsilon_i$, namely, $n\sigma_\varepsilon^2$, increases with n. In total, effort thus goes down when n increases.

Summing up, when the market can observe only the aggregate performance on n tasks, the higher the number of tasks n, the lower the equilibrium total effort. Moreover, in the presence of a multiplicative effect ($\mu > 0$) and for $\psi'(0) > 0$, there is a value of n beyond which the high-effort equilibrium disappears altogether.[7]

In the preceding analysis we have restricted public information to the observation of aggregate performance Q_I. Suppose now that individual performances are observed:

$$S_I = \{q_i | i \in I\}$$

The results are then as follows:

1. In the pure additive case, Q_I is a sufficient statistic for S_I as far as updating θ is concerned, so observing S_I or Q_I makes no difference. Consequently, the unique equilibrium effort $\hat{a}^*$ is the same whether aggregate performance (Q_I) or disaggregated performance (S_I) is observed.

2. In the pure multiplicative case, we instead obtain a multiplicity of equilibria, since the agent will want to focus on the tasks the market expects her

---

7. Concerning the robustness of these results, note that one could object, in the additive case, to the role of a rise in n in increasing the link between talent and performance Q_I: if it means splitting the agent's total working time into more slices, one might want to have, in the "noiseless" case,

$$Q_I = \frac{\theta}{n} n + \hat{a} = \theta + \hat{a}$$

However, in this case, the results are again valid: for $\sigma_\varepsilon^2 = 0$, raising n leaves total effort unaffected, and for $\sigma_\varepsilon^2 > 0$, it lowers total effort.

to focus on![8] Specifically, when a_i is expected to be equal to 0, q_i is considered as pure noise and disregarded by the market, making $a_i = 0$ optimal for the agent. For each $I' \subseteq I$, there is thus an equilibrium where $a_i = 0$ for $i \notin I'$, and a_i is positive and constant across i's $\in I'$, and where total effort is the same as that when only $Q_{I'} = \sum_{i \in I'} q_i$ is observed.

Following this analysis of multidimensional career concerns, we are now in a position to ask: What results rely on career concerns, as opposed to explicit incentives? The earlier result of a negative link between the number of tasks n and total effort when only aggregate performance is observable would also hold in a simple linear explicit-incentive-scheme context with CARA preferences, since a rise in n means more noise. It is therefore our "technological assumptions" that generate a benefit of focus under aggregate performance observability. Under explicit incentive schemes, the roles of θ and ε, however, are more symmetric than under career concerns, as the next subsection will make clear. But here, the difference between career concerns and explicit incentives lies in the case where S_I is observed, since (1) under explicit incentive schemes, the multiplicity of equilibria is not a concern, and (2) in the additive case, which has a unique equilibrium, expanding S_I lowers total effort, while with pure explicit incentives, one can always disregard additional information, which is at best irrelevant.

A general lesson of the preceding analysis is that there is a benefit of "focus." Indeed, a principal interested in maximizing $Q = \sum_{i=1}^{N} q_1$ and thus indifferent with respect to the *distribution* of individual performances (the q_i's) should try to induce focus. As for the agent, in the case of an exogenous date-1 financial compensation she prefers a broad mission, so as to reduce effort; indeed, she realizes she will fool no one by working in equilibrium and sees a broad mission as a commitment not to expend effort. If, instead, the agent is able to obtain ex ante a wage equal to expected productivity, committing to a focused mission through the observability of a single q_i maximizes her wage.

The idea of giving agents "focused missions" is a celebrated theme in the analysis of government bureaucracies—for example, in the book by Wilson (1989), which details how successful government agencies are the ones that

---

8. In the absence of economies of scope in the effort-cost function, multitask equilibria are in fact unstable: Were the market to put slightly more weight on any given task, the agent would "react" by concentrating her efforts solely on that task! However, the presence of economies of scope can ensure the local stability of these equilibria.

have managed to translate very broad objectives into well-focused missions. Another important theme in that literature is the idea that missions have to be not only focused but also "clear." This can be translated in this model by looking at equilibria with random allocation of effort across tasks by the agent. In this case, Dewatripont, Jewitt, and Tirole (1999b) show that, in the presence of multiplicative effects, effort goes down, ceteris paribus, when one moves from a pure-strategy equilibrium to a mixed-strategy equilibrium. The intuition is that the market may now have to infer from the vector of performance levels not only talent but also which task(s) was (were) pursued. Consequently, a given variation in performance will lead to less updating of the talent parameter in a mixed-strategy equilibrium than in a pure-strategy equilibrium.

10.5.3   The Trade-off between Talent Risk and Incentives under Career Concerns

Let us finally consider task-specific productivity and ask how effort is related to the specific bundle of tasks given to the agent.

Consider the additive-normal model, where performance for task $i = 1, 2$, is

$$q_i = \theta_i + a_i + \varepsilon_i$$

where θ_i and ε_i are normally distributed:

$$\theta_i \sim \mathcal{N}(\overline{\theta}, \sigma_\theta^2) \quad \text{and} \quad \varepsilon_i \sim \mathcal{N}(0, \sigma_\varepsilon^2)$$

with ε_1 and ε_2 independently distributed from one another and from the two dimensions of talent; but the latter may be imperfectly correlated (until now, we had assumed perfect correlation). Assume prospective employers care about $\theta_1 + \theta_2$. How is total effort $a_1 + a_2 = \hat{a}$ related to the correlation coefficient ρ between θ_1 and θ_2? Aggregate performance

$$q_1 + q_2 = (\theta_1 + \theta_2) + \hat{a} + \varepsilon_1 + \varepsilon_2$$

has a normal distribution with mean $2\overline{\theta} + \hat{a}$ and variance $2(1 + \rho)\sigma_\theta^2 + 2\sigma_\varepsilon^2$, so that

$$\frac{\hat{f}_{\hat{a}}(q_1 + q_2)}{\hat{f}(q_1 + q_2)} = \frac{(\theta_1 + \theta_2 - 2\overline{\theta}) + (\varepsilon_1 + \varepsilon_2)}{2(1 + \rho)\sigma_\theta^2 + 2\sigma_\varepsilon^2}$$

and

$$\text{cov}\left(\theta_1 + \theta_2, \frac{\hat{f}_{\hat{a}}}{\hat{f}}\right) = \frac{2(1+\rho)\sigma_\theta^2}{2(1+\rho)\sigma_\theta^2 + 2\sigma_\varepsilon^2}$$

Therefore, in equilibrium, total effort will be higher, the higher the ρ: since the mean of $\theta_1 + \theta_2$ is unchanged, a higher ρ implies a higher signal-to-noise ratio, because it means a higher initial uncertainty about talent relative to pure noise in performance.

This observation implies that, if one has to allocate N tasks in total to agents who can each do only n tasks, effort will be maximized by grouping tasks that require "similar" talents. Consider, for example, four tasks that must be performed, with two agents, A and B, that can each be given two tasks. Assume the output in task i to be

$$q_i = \theta_{i\kappa} + a_i + \varepsilon_i$$

for $\kappa \in \{A, B\}$ if agent κ is allocated to task i, has task-specific talent $\theta_{i\kappa}$, and expends effort a_i on task i. Assume that the $\theta_{i\kappa}$'s have identical mean $\bar{\theta}$ and variance σ_θ^2 and all ε_i's have zero mean and variance σ_ε^2. Assume also that tasks 1 and 2, and 3 and 4, respectively, are thus related in that $\theta_{1\kappa}$ and $\theta_{2\kappa}$ are positively correlated and the same is true for $\theta_{3\kappa}$ and $\theta_{4\kappa}$, while other dimensions of talent are otherwise uncorrelated. Suppose further that the market cares only about $\sum_{i \in I(\kappa)} \theta_{i\kappa}$, where $I(\kappa)$ is the set of the two tasks allocated to agent κ. In this case, incentives are maximized by allocating tasks 1 and 2 to one agent and tasks 3 and 4 to the other.[9]

This "specialization result" is specific to the career-concern paradigm: In a model where the agent cares solely about monetary incentives, as in Holmström and Milgrom (1991), allocating tasks should reduce the total variance due both to pure noise and talent risk, and, by doing so, effort can be increased, since the trade-off between effort and risk has been improved. This positive correlation between effort and talent risk in career-concern models, a feature reversed in explicit-incentive-scheme models, is a key insight that helps one to understand the importance of "focus" in the literature that tries to explain government agencies' performance.

---

9. In a more general model, there may be costs to creating focus by clustering related tasks in this way, resulting, for example, from complementarities between unrelated tasks in the principal's objective function, or from agent risk aversion (specialization will increase risk). These costs have to be weighed against the beneficial incentive effect of specialization.

10.6 Summary

In this chapter, we have first extended the classical moral hazard model to the case of repeated effort, consumption, and output realizations. We have isolated three potential gains from long-term contracting with moral hazard. First, the agent may be willing to take more risk, as she can partially self-insure against a bad outcome by smoothing consumption over time. Second, the principal may gain more information about the agent's action choice from repeated observation of the agent's performance. Third, an optimal long-term contract can improve over repeated spot contracting by monitoring the agent's savings and by forcing the agent to consume more in earlier periods.

Offsetting these potential gains, however, is the fact that the agent has a richer action set in a repeated relation. The agent chooses a whole action plan in a repeated relation, which can be contingent on observed cumulative output performance. By adjusting her effort to past performance, the agent can then "slack off" in more sophisticated and less visible ways. This greater flexibility in effort supply over time constrains the principal's ability to extract the gains from self-insurance or other sources of gains from an enduring relation with the agent.

In extreme situations we have seen that the agent's action set may be so rich that the best the principal can do is to offer the agent a simple incentive contract that is linear in both output increments and cumulative output. In other settings, simple efficiency-wage contracts or debt contracts may also be approximately optimal. However, in general, the optimal contract predicted by the theory can be extremely complex—too complex to be descriptive or prescriptive for incentive contracting in reality.

One of the reasons why most long-term contracts observed in reality are relatively simple is that enforcement costs are likely to escalate significantly with contractual complexity. Disagreements and litigation are more likely for more complex contracts, and judges are more likely to make mistakes in interpreting and enforcing complex contracts. In reality, formal long-term contracts are often written in vague terms, partly because it is often more efficient to rely on self-enforcement than on legal enforcement. We have seen how the theory of optimal contracting can be extended to such *relational contracts*. In bilateral settings, the only difference with legally enforced optimal long-term contracts is that some actions and transfers are constrained by a self-enforcement constraint. But otherwise the structure of the optimal contract is unchanged. However, in settings where there is competition for the agent's services, implicit incentives or *"career concerns"* may lead to substantial distortions, with the agent excessively responding to market incentives early on and later resting on her laurels.

Another limit to the gains achievable through optimal long-term contracting is the inability of the contracting parties to commit not to *renegotiate* the contract in the future. We have, thus, seen how ex post renegotiation can undermine ex ante incentives. This issue has gained particular prominence in debates on executive compensation. Many critics of executive compensation have singled out the common practice of lowering the strike price on out-of-the-money options granted to executives, following a drop in stock price. The resetting of the strike price obviously benefits the company by restoring incentives ex post, but the anticipation of such moves undermines ex ante incentives.

By introducing relational contracts, implicit incentives, and renegotiation of long-term contracts, this chapter naturally paves the way toward the fourth major part of this book, on incomplete contracts. The trade-off between ex ante and ex post incentives will take even sharper forms in the context of incomplete contracts, as contracting parties have even less room to commit to ex post inefficiencies.

10.7   Literature Notes

Most of the material in this chapter is based on recent research that has not yet found its way into textbooks. While we have offered our own perspective on the literature, we have stressed the following strands of work.

First, on moral hazard with multiple effort and output realizations, we have detailed the pioneering papers by Rogerson (1985b) and by Radner (1981), and the subsequent work by Malcomson and Spinnewyn (1988), Fudenberg, Holmström, and Milgrom (1990), Rey and Salanié (1990), on the one hand, and Rubinstein and Yaari (1983), Radner (1985), and Dutta and Radner (1994), on the other. The surveys by Chiappori, Macho, Rey, and Salanié (1994) and Radner (1986a) discuss much of this literature. A large related literature on repeated partnership games also deals with many of the issues in this chapter (see, most notably, Radner, 1986b; Abreu,

Pearce, and Stacchetti, 1990; Fudenberg, Levine, and Maskin, 1994; Kandori and Matsushima, 1998; and Compte, 1998). Finally, an extensive literature on long-term insurance contracts covers similar ground (see, e.g., Dionne, 2000).

Second, on the role of the frequency of effort and output realizations, we have stressed the contribution of Abreu, Milgrom, and Pearce (1991) and especially that of Holmström and Milgrom (1987) on the optimality of linear contracts under CARA preferences. As seen in Chapters 4, 6, and 8, such incentive schemes have proved very attractive in applications.

We have then turned to the issue of renegotiation of moral hazard contracts. Pioneering contributions in this literature include Fudenberg and Tirole (1990) and Ma (1991) when the principal does not observe the agent's effort choice, and Hermalin and Katz (1991) when he does. Subsequent work includes Ma (1994) and Matthews (1995, 2001) in the first case and Dewatripont, Legros, and Matthews (2003) in the second. One case we have not covered here is the one where the agent cannot commit not to unilaterally breach the contract, e.g., because of legal "no-slavery" provisions. In a simple insurance problem without hidden actions or adverse selection, such lack of commitment leads to interesting dynamics when the contract plays an insurance role, as shown by Holmström (1983) or Harris and Holmström (1982).

The literature on bilateral relational contracts, which we discussed next, is quite large. Early work includes Klein and Leffler (1981), Shapiro and Stiglitz (1984), and Bull (1987). In this chapter, we have in particular stressed the work of MacLeod and Malcomson (1989) and Levin (2003). Note that MacLeod and Malcomson (1988) extend the setting to multilayer organizations, while Bernheim and Whinston (1998b), Baker, Gibbons, and Murphy (1994), and Pearce and Stacchetti (1998) combine explicit and implicit incentives. Finally MacLeod (2003) allows for subjective, imperfectly correlated performance measures observed by the principal and the agent.

Finally, the literature on career concerns was pioneered by Holmström (1982a). Extensions include Gibbons and Murphy (1992), who have added explicit incentives to the picture; Meyer and Vickers (1997), who have also allowed for relative performance evaluation; and Dewatripont, Jewitt, and Tirole (1999a, 1999b), who have considered a multitask setting. Finally, Stein (1989) and Scharfstein and Stein (1990) have applied Holmström's paradigm, respectively, to the questions of short-termism and herd behavior.

IV INCOMPLETE CONTRACTS

With this fourth part of the book we take yet another important step toward reality. Recall that the first stage of contract theory—as studied by Edgeworth—was concerned with the characterization of efficient exchange contracts in situations involving no uncertainty and no asymmetric information. It was only in the 1950s that a second stage was reached, with the explicit consideration of uncertainty. At that time, problems of optimal coinsurance, optimal risk diversification, and portfolio choice became the main focus of attention.

About two decades later a third stage was reached—considering contractual situations with asymmetric information. This has led to the introduction of incentive constraints alongside participation constraints and to the elaboration of a rich theory of incentive contracting. Parts I and II attempted to provide a comprehensive coverage of this theory.

Following a decade or so of intense research, the field reached yet another stage in the 1980s—concerned with issues of repeated or dynamic contracting. Issues of commitment and renegotiation were systematically explored in that decade and later. This latest development has led to the introduction of "renegotiation-proofness" constraints alongside incentive and participation constraints. Part III covered the main ideas emerging from this new wave of research.

The final stage of development is taken up in Part IV. As in Part III, this stage is concerned with long-term contracts. However, the orientation is entirely different. Rather than optimizing over a general contract set that is subject to incentive, renegotiation-proofness, and participation constraints, long-term contracts are taken to be of a prespecified (incomplete) form, and the control variables become instead ownership titles, control rights, decision-making rules, discretion, tasks, authority, and the like, to be allocated among contracting parties. Part IV discusses this methodology, as well as, in Chapter 12, its relationship with the "complete contract" methodology.

11 Incomplete Contracts and Institution Design

11.1 Introduction: Incomplete Contracts and the Employment Relation

The introduction of incomplete contracts involves both a substantive and a methodological break. The substantive change can be illustrated with a concrete example, the conduct of monetary policy. A central problem in macroeconomic research over the past two decades, as well as a major political issue, has been the question of central bank independence. This is an issue involving both incentive and commitment considerations. If one takes a dynamic-contracting approach as outlined in Part III, one is inevitably led to focus on the problem of financial compensation of the central banker. The main issue becomes how to structure the central banker's compensation package to induce him to run monetary policy according to the objectives stated in the law (e.g., price stability). Some of the literature on the subject has indeed taken such a turn. For example, Walsh (1995) and others have proposed compensation contracts for central bankers contingent on the rate of inflation. Some countries—most notably New Zealand--have even considered implementing such contracts.

If, however, one takes an incomplete-contracting perspective, then other aspects besides central bankers' compensation become relevant, such as the bank's decision-making procedures, discretion versus rules, and central bank accountability. As this example illustrates, the substantive change brought about by the introduction of contractual incompleteness is to shift the focus away from issues of compensation contingent on outcomes to procedural and institutional-design issues.

The analysis of institutions is clearly of fundamental importance, and an incomplete-contracting approach offers a vehicle to explore these issues systematically. The fourth stage of research in contract theory is thus a natural development, which should eventually produce an economic theory of institutions as rich as the theory of incentives developed in the past three decades.

The introduction of contractual incompleteness also involves a methodological break. Most of the literature assumes a particular form of contractual incompleteness and does not explain the form of the contract as the outcome of some optimization problem. Optimization is confined to the choice of institution: the design of decision-making rules and the allocation of control rights. Typically, contractual incompleteness is explained by a limitation in contractual language—the inability to describe accurately certain events before the fact, even when these events and their implications are easily recognized after the fact. It has been a matter of debate how restrictive this constraint is in theory and in practice. We provide an extensive discussion of this debate in Chapter 12. For now, we shall simply assume that the inability to describe certain future events is a binding constraint and explore the implications for institution design of this form of contractual incompleteness.

11.1.1   The Employment Relation

Perhaps the first formal model with incomplete contracts is Simon's (1951) theory of the employment relation. In that model Simon compares two long-term contracts, one where the service to be provided by a seller at some point in the future is precisely specified in a contract, the other where the service is left to the discretion of the buyer within some contractually specified limits referred to as the "acceptance set." Simon identifies the former contract as a "sales contract" and the latter as an "employment relation." The choice of contract is then determined by the degree of uncertainty at the time of contracting about precisely which service the buyer would prefer in the future, as well as the degree of indifference of the seller to providing a specific service within the "acceptance set." Simon's theory raises several difficult questions. Perhaps the most important one is, Why must the buyer and seller agree to a trade before the uncertainty is realized? Why not wait for the uncertainty to be resolved and then write a spot contract? A second question relates to the extreme form of the sales contract: Why can't the buyer and seller agree to some form of state-contingent delivery contract? Why is it cheaper to write a contract specifying an "acceptance set" than a contract specifying a state-contingent delivery plan?

It is possible to address most of these questions and to provide an updated theory of the employment relation by introducing a "holdup" problem as in Klein, Crawford, and Alchian (1978) and more generally taking Williamson's transactions-cost perspective (Williamson, 1975, 1979, 1985). As a way of introducing the main ideas of the incomplete-contracts approach to institution design, we shall begin by providing such an updated theory.

Suppose that the buyer can undertake an (unobservable) investment today that raises her payoff from the service to be provided by the seller in the future. This investment is sunk by the time buyer and seller negotiate over service provision in a spot contract, so that the buyer may be "held up" by the seller, to use a term favored by Klein, Crawford, and Alchian. The need for a long-term contract then arises as a way of protecting the buyer's ex ante investment against ex post "opportunism" by the seller (a term favored by Williamson). But prior to the investment stage the buyer does not know which type of service she may need, and it is not possible to describe under what precise circumstances she needs a particular service. The contract can specify only the nature of a service to be provided under all circumstances, or a menu of services that the seller agrees to provide at predetermined terms (the latter arrangement can also be thought of as a general option contract).

Williamson has argued that the incompleteness of contracts inevitably induces contracting parties to attempt to interpret the contract to their own advantage ex post and that this behavior can lead to both ex ante and ex post inefficiencies. The contracting parties not only may make inefficient ex ante investments, if investment is not observable or verifiable and they anticipate ex post opportunism, but also may get involved in inefficient contractual disputes ex post. Williamson sees key institutional arrangements in market economies, such as authority relations, to be responses designed to overcome the potential inefficiencies in long-term relations governed by incomplete contracts. An employment relation, which leaves much to the discretion of the employer, is valuable if it can reduce the scope for ex post haggling or allow the employer to appropriate the rents created by her ex ante investments.

In an attempt to simplify the formal analysis, most of the recent literature abstracts from ex post inefficiencies resulting from contractual disputes and focuses entirely on ex ante investment inefficiencies. We shall take the same approach in developing our updated theory of the employment relation. The first formal model of inefficient ex ante investment resulting from ex post opportunism is due to Grout (1984). Later the property-rights theory of the firm formulated by Grossman and Hart (1986) and Hart and Moore (1990) built on this general idea also developed informally by Klein, Crawford, and Alchian (1978) and Williamson (1975, 1985). We shall discuss this theory in the next subsection.

11.1.2   A Theory of the Employment Relation Based on Ex Post Opportunism

Consider a risk-neutral buyer and a risk-neutral seller, neither of whom has alternative contractual opportunities. There are n types of service that the seller can provide denoted by $a_i (i = 1, \ldots, n)$. The buyer needs only one of these services ex post. Provision of the service is observable and verifiable, so that a contract can be written specifying a payment contingent on execution of the service. Suppose that in the event of no trade both parties get zero, and if they trade service a_i at price P_i they get, respectively,

$$U(a_i, \theta_l) - P_i$$

for the buyer, and

$$P_i - \psi(a_i, \theta_l)$$

for the seller, where θ_l denotes a state of nature. Suppose that there are $N \geq n$ states of nature $(l = 1, \ldots, N)$. Thus both buyer and seller payoffs can vary with the underlying state of nature.[1]

The buyer can increase U by increasing her ex ante investment I. That is, let $U = U(a_i, \theta_l, I)$, with $\partial U/\partial I > 0$ and $\partial^2 U/\partial I^2 < 0$. The cost of investment is taken to be simply $\kappa(I) = I$. To keep the analysis as simple as possible, assume that

$$U(a_i, \theta_l, I) \in \{0, \phi(I), \Phi(I)\}$$

and

$$\psi(a_i, \theta_l) \in \{0, c, C\}$$

with

$$0 < \Phi(I) - C < \phi(I) - c < \Phi(I) - c < \Phi(I) \quad \text{for all } I \geq 0$$

Furthermore, assume that in any given state θ_l

$$U(a_i, \theta_l, I) = 0 \implies \psi(a_i, \theta_l) = 0$$

$$U(a_i, \theta_l, I) = \phi(I) \implies \psi(a_i, \theta_l) = c$$

$$U(a_i, \theta_l, I) = \Phi(I) \implies \psi(a_i, \theta_l) = C$$

In other words, in any given state θ_l, any valuable service is costly, and the high-value service is also the high-cost service.

---

1. A slightly more general contract could specify a payment P_0 to the buyer in case of no trade. This payment could be interpreted as a penalty clause. As will become clear, there is no loss of generality in setting $P_0 = 0$ here. However, in other settings the optimal penalty is nonzero, as we show in Chapter 12.

Suppose also that for any realized state of nature θ_l, there is always at least one service ex post $a_i(\theta_l)$ such that $U(a_i, \theta_l, I) = \phi(I)$ so that the maximum surplus $\phi(I)$ can be realized. Then the efficient level of ex ante investment I^* is given by maximizing

$$\max_{I \geq 0}\{\phi(I) - I\}$$

and is characterized by the first-order conditions

$$\phi'(I^*) = 1$$

However, suppose in addition that in any realized state of nature θ_j, there are other services available $a_j(\theta_l)$ and $a_k(\theta_l)$ ($j \neq i; k \neq i$) such that $U(a_j, \theta_l, I) = \Phi(I)$ and $U(a_k, \theta_l, I) = 0$.

We shall assume that there is a basic technological constraint that prevents the buyer and seller from writing an ex ante contract contingent on the realized state of nature. In other words, a precise description of each state would be so costly that it would outweigh all the benefits from writing such a fine-tuned contract. Given that contracts cannot be made contingent on the state of nature, there are four basic options available to the contracting parties:

• They can wait until the state is realized and write a spot contract.

• They can write a sales contract, which specifies a single service to be provided ex post at prespecified terms.

• They can write a buyer-employment contract specifying a menu of services from which the buyer can choose ex post. This service must then be delivered at prespecified terms.

• They can write a seller-employment contract specifying a menu of services from which the seller can choose ex post. This service must then be delivered at prespecified terms.[2]

Consider each type of contract in turn.

11.1.2.1 Spot Contract

If buyer and seller negotiate over a service ex post, we shall assume that they divide equally the gains from trade. These gains are maximized by

---

2. Note that these four options do not provide a fully exhaustive list of feasible contracts. In particular, one can envision hybrid forms of employment contracts, where one of the parties is randomly selected ex post to pick a service within her prespecified menu of services. As interesting as these contractual forms are, we shall not pursue them here in order to save space.

choosing a service $a_i(\theta_l)$ such that $U(a_i, \theta_l, I) = \phi(I)$ and $\psi(a_i, \theta_l) = c$. Thus buyer and seller each get $[\phi(I) - c]/2$ ex post, so that the buyer chooses her ex ante investment I^s to maximize

$$\frac{\phi(I) - c}{2} - I$$

and underinvests. The level of investment is then given by

$$\phi'(I^s) = 2$$

11.1.2.2   Sales Contract

If buyer and seller write a sales contract of the form $\{a_i, P_i\}$, where a_i denotes the service to be delivered and P_i the price, then ex post the realized state is such that either

1. $U(a_i, \theta_l, I) = \phi(I)$ and $\psi(a_i, \theta_l) = c$,
2. $U(a_i, \theta_l, I) = \psi(a_i, \theta_l) = 0$, or
3. $U(a_i, \theta_l, I) = \Phi(I)$ and $\psi(a_i, \theta) = C$.

If the state of nature is such that $U(a_i, \theta_l, I) = \phi(I)$ and $\psi(a_i, \theta_l) = c$, then the contract is executed, and buyer and seller get, respectively, $\phi(I) - P_i$ and $P_i - c$. If, however, the other configurations of payoffs obtain, then the parties are better off *renegotiating* the contract and switching to another action a_j such that $U(a_i, \theta_l, I) = \phi(I)$ and $\psi(a_j, \theta_l) = c$.

Renegotiation involves bargaining over the surplus $[\phi(I) - c - (\Phi(I) - C)]$ if $U(a_i, \theta_l, I) = \Phi(I)$ and $\psi(a_i, \theta_l) = C$, and over the surplus $(\phi(I) - c)$ if $U(a_i, \theta_l, I) = \psi(a_i, \theta_l) = 0$. Assuming, as before, that this surplus is divided equally among the parties, their respective payoffs in this event are

$$\Phi(I) - P_i + \frac{1}{2}[\phi(I) - c - \Phi(I) + C] \quad \text{and} \quad P_i - C + \frac{1}{2}[\phi(I) - c - \Phi(I) + C]$$

if

$$U(a_i, \theta_l, I) = \Phi(I) \quad \text{and} \quad \psi(a_i, \theta_l) = C$$

and

$$-P_i + \frac{1}{2}[\phi(I) - c] \quad \text{and} \quad P_i + \frac{1}{2}[\phi(I) - c]$$

if

$$U(a_i, \theta_l, I) = 0 \quad \text{and} \quad \psi(a_i, \theta_l) = 0$$

To proceed further we need to impose more structure on this example. Suppose now that there are $N = n$ equiprobable states of nature, and that service a_l is the uniquely efficient action in state θ_l. In other words, $U(a_l, \theta_l, I) = \phi(I)$ and $\psi(a_l, \theta_l) = c$ in state θ_l, and for $i \neq l$ either

$$U(a_i, \theta_l, I) = \Phi(I) \quad \text{and} \quad \psi(a_i, \theta_l) = C$$

or

$$U(a_i, \theta_l, I) = 0 \quad \text{and} \quad \psi(a_i, \theta_l) = 0$$

Moreover, all other services are equally likely to be a high-cost service a_k or a worthless service a_j.

Given this probability distribution over action-state realizations, the buyer's ex ante payoff is given by

$$\frac{1}{n}[\phi(I) - P_i] + \left(\frac{n-1}{2n}\right)\left\{\Phi(I) - P_i + \frac{1}{2}[\phi(I) - c - \Phi(I) + C]\right\}$$
$$+ \left(\frac{n-1}{2n}\right)\left\{-P_i + \frac{1}{2}[\phi(I) - c]\right\} - I$$

so that the buyer's optimal level of investment under this contract is given by the solution to the first-order condition

$$\phi'(I^S)\left(\frac{n+1}{n}\right) + \Phi'(I^S)\left(\frac{2n-1}{n}\right) = 2$$

Note that the price P_i is determined ex ante so as to split the overall expected surplus from the transaction—$[\phi(I^S) - c]$.

11.1.2.3 Buyer-Employment Contract

Now consider the case where buyer and seller write a buyer-employment contract of the form $\{A, P(a) \,|\, a \in A\}$, where A is a subset of services—Simon's acceptance set—from which the buyer can choose, and $P(a)$ are the predetermined terms for supplying service a. The main point of writing such a contract is to give the buyer some flexibility to choose the most desired service ex post. The cost of writing such a contract, however, is that it puts the seller in a position where he agrees to provide a service that may be very costly ex post. Because there are both costs and benefits in writing such a contract, it is unclear a priori whether this contract dominates a sales contract.

Since all services are symmetric ex ante, it is obvious that the acceptance set should contain all possible services a_i, and that there is no loss of generality in setting $P(a) = P$. Under such an employment contract, the buyer would always choose a service that maximizes

$$\max_a [U(a, \theta_l, I) - P]$$

In other words, the buyer would always choose an inefficient action yielding a payoff of $U(a_j, \theta_l, I) = \Phi(I)$ and imposing a cost C on the seller. Of course, both parties will renegotiate away from this inefficient outcome ex post and agree on a new contract to supply service a_l in state θ_l. The surplus from renegotiation is again divided equally, so that the buyer's and seller's respective payoffs become

$$\Phi - P + \frac{1}{2}[\phi(I) - c - \Phi(I) + C]$$

and

$$P - C + \frac{1}{2}[\phi(I) - c - \Phi(I) + C]$$

Under this contract the buyer chooses her ex ante investment I^{BE} to solve

$$\max_I \left\{ \frac{1}{2}[\phi(I) + \Phi(I)] - I \right\}$$

Thus the level of investment under the buyer-employment contract is given by the solution to the first-order condition

$$\phi'(I^{BE}) + \Phi'(I^{BE}) = 2$$

Again, the terms of trade P are set so as to divide equally the ex ante expected surplus from trade $[\phi(I^{BE}) - c]$.

11.1.2.4   Seller-Employment Contract

Finally, consider the case where buyer and seller write a seller-employment contract, where the seller now chooses the service in the acceptance set A. As before, the acceptance set should contain all possible services a_i, and since all services are symmetric ex ante, $P(a) = P$ for all $a \in A$. Under this employment contract, the seller's optimization problem is

$$\max_a\{P - \psi(a, \theta_l)\}$$

so that the seller always selects the least costly action a_j such that $\psi(a_j, \theta_l) = 0$.

As under the buyer-employment contract, buyer and seller would then renegotiate away from this inefficient ex post outcome. The surplus from renegotiation would again be divided equally, so that the buyer's and seller's respective payoffs become

$$-P + \frac{1}{2}[\phi(I) - c]$$

and

$$P + \frac{1}{2}[\phi(I) - c]$$

The buyer then chooses her ex ante investment under the seller-employment contract I^{SE} to solve

$$\max_I\left\{\frac{1}{2}[\phi(I) - c]\right\}$$

so that the level of investment under the seller-employment contract is the same as under ex post spot contracting.[3]

11.1.2.5   Which Contract Is Better?

Given that under each contract the ex ante expected surplus from trade is $[\phi(I^k) - c]$ (with $k = s, S, BE, SE$), the best contract is the one that induces the most efficient investment level by the buyer. It is easy to see that, as long as $\phi'(I) \geq \Phi'(I) \geq 0$, the spot contract is (weakly) dominated by the sales and buyer-employment contracts, since the latter two contracts induce higher investment and since there is no overinvestment under any contract.[4] The buyer-employment contract dominates the sales contract when

$$\frac{1}{n}[\phi'(I^S) - \Phi'(I^S)] > 0$$

---

3. Note that this need not always be the case. For example, if the least-cost service has a strictly positive value, then the two investment levels would differ in general.

4. When $\Phi'(I) > \phi'(I)$ the buyer may actually overinvest under the buyer-employment or the sales contract. In that case, spot contracting could actually dominate these two contracts.

Interestingly, the comparison between sales and buyer-employment contracts involves different considerations from those Simon had in mind. The difference stems from the absence of ex ante investment and ex post renegotiation in his theory. For Simon the comparison between the two contracts is only in terms of ex post efficiency. The buyer-employment contract tends to induce trade of excessively costly services, while the sales contract induces trade of services that do not maximize net surplus ex post. Depending on the extent of uncertainty and the variance in costs across services and states of nature, one or the other contract may dominate in his setup.

Here, instead, the contracts are evaluated in terms of ex ante efficiency—that is to say, in terms of their effects on the buyer's incentives to invest. If the marginal return on investment for the costly (inefficient) action is higher than for the efficient action—$\Phi'(I^S) > \phi'(I^S)$—then the sales contract may dominate the buyer-employment contract. Otherwise, the employment contract is preferable. Note, however, that as n grows large, the difference between the two contracts becomes negligible. Thus, when one allows for renegotiation, the comparison between the two contracts is more subtle than the simple trade-off between "flexibility" and "exploitation" emphasized by Simon.

While some important objections to Simon's model of the employment relation can be addressed by introducing ex ante (nonobservable) investment by the buyer, other criticisms are harder to dispose of. One important criticism by Alchian and Demsetz (1972) of the notion of master-servant relation implicit in the employment contract has been that there is no difference between an employer ordering an employee around and a customer ordering a grocer to deliver a basket of goods. One difference that we have highlighted is that the employment contract is a commitment to serve in the future as opposed to a spot contract to sell goods to a customer. While this is an important distinction, it is probably not the only defining one.

11.2   Ownership and the Property-Rights Theory of the Firm

Just as an employment contract gives the employer the right to determine what the employee should do (subject to remaining within the law), an ownership title on a property or asset gives the owner the right to dispose of the property as she sees fit. Some limits can be put on the owner's rights by law, and other limits may be agreed on contractually, but unless these are explicitly specified, the owner can do what she wants with the asset. In other words, the owner has "residual rights of control" over the asset, to use terminology introduced by Grossman and Hart (1986). In addition, an ownership title gives the owner the right to all revenues generated by the asset that have not been explicitly pledged to a third party.

It is instructive to contrast Grossman and Hart's definition of ownership—based on residual rights of control—with Alchian and Demsetz's and Jensen and Meckling's—which defines the owner of a firm only in terms of cash-flow rights (the owner being the "residual claimant" on the cash flow)—to appreciate the importance of the departure of the incomplete-contracts approach from standard incentive theory.

Given the similarities between employment contracts and ownership titles, it is not too surprising that the next set of formal models with incomplete contracts were concerned with ownership and residual rights of control. The models of Grossman and Hart (1986) and Hart and Moore (1990) explore the issue of the value of ownership and residual rights of control in situations where parties write incomplete contracts.

According to their theory, the owner of a firm has the right in particular to exclude others from using the firm's assets. This right serves as a protection against ex post opportunism. In its simplest form the theory predicts that ownership of productive assets is allocated to the party requiring the most protection against ex post opportunism. The following simple example illustrates the basic theory.

Consider a situation with at most two separate firms or productive assets. Grossman and Hart take the example of a publisher and a printer. Say firm 1 is a printing press producing copies of books or journals for firm 2, a publishing company. If the two firms are owned separately, they may write long-term supply contracts, which are assumed to be incomplete. In other words, under these contracts there may be events requiring new decisions not prespecified in the contract. In that case it is assumed that the printer and publisher will negotiate a new ex post efficient contract.

The ex post negotiating position will differ from the ex ante situation, in which the two firms have written the initial long-term contract, if in the meantime either firm (or both) has taken actions or made investments that are costly to reverse (or to switch to another supply relation). In other words, the ex post negotiating position of one of the parties may have worsened if that party is locked into the supply relation as a result of its previous actions. For example, if the printing firm has spent vast sums customizing its software to fit the special needs of the publisher, it will have put itself in a position where it has little choice but to deal with the publisher ex post. Recognizing this fact, the publisher may be able to extract better terms ex post than ex ante when it was in competition with other publishers.

If the printing firm anticipates that it may end up in a weaker negotiating position ex post by making publisher-specific investments, it may refrain from making these investments even if they are efficient.

In contrast, if firms 1 and 2 were integrated, so that the printer was the sole owner of both the printing press and the publishing business, then his ex post negotiating position with the publisher (who is now his employee) would likely be less affected by his ex ante specific investments. In fact, it is conceivable that under this ownership allocation the printer might be able to appropriate all the gains from ex post negotiations. If that were the case, the printer would of course be inclined to make any ex ante specific investments that are efficient.

But if the printer is the sole owner of both assets, then presumably the publisher would have less incentive to invest than under nonintegration or under vertical integration with the publisher owning the integrated firm.

The property-rights theory of the firm predicts that any ownership allocation can arise in equilibrium depending on the relative value of each party's ex ante specific investments. If investments in customized software are most valuable, then it makes sense for the printer to own both printing press and publishing business. If investments in authors, agents, or marketers are most valuable, then it makes sense for the publisher to own the publishing business as well as the printing press. Finally, if both types of investment are important, it may be best to have nonintegration.

This is in a nutshell the theory outlined for two firms in Grossman and Hart (1986). The important contribution of the property-rights theory of the firm is to both explain the value of ownership and delineate the costs and benefits of integration. We now turn to a more formal exposition of the theory.

11.2.1 A General Framework with Complementary Investments

It is relatively straightforward to provide a formal treatment of the property-rights theory in a simple setting with only two agents and two assets. But how can the theory be applied to a large corporation with multiple divisions and thousands of employees and suppliers?

Hart and Moore (1990) take a first stab at this question as follows. Just as in the two-firm case considered by Grossman and Hart, one can envision a first stage where I agents make ex ante investment x_i at a cost $\psi(x_i)$ (these investments may be more or less specific to some subset of assets A in the set of all productive assets available in the economy, $\overline{A}$). Then, in a second stage, the ex ante investments of a subset of agents $S \subseteq I$ combined with the subset of assets $A \subseteq \overline{A}$ can generate an ex post surplus from trade $V(S; A \mid x)$, where $x = (x_1, x_2, \ldots, x_I)$ denotes the vector of all agents' ex ante investments.

To simplify matters, Hart and Moore assume an extreme form of contractual incompleteness: no long-term contracts specifying future trade can be written ex ante. Only trade in ownership titles can take place ex ante. As in the case with two firms, the division of the surplus from trade among the S agents depends on who owns which subset of assets.

The main modeling difficulty when considering a general setup with I agents is determining how the ex post surplus $V(S; A \mid x)$ gets divided up among the contracting parties in multilateral negotiations—in other words, how the terms of trade get determined. Hart and Moore's proposed solution is to envision a centralized marketplace where all the negotiations get done simultaneously ex post. They assume that the outcome of multilateral negotiations is ex post efficient under any ownership allocation and that the surplus is divided according to the *Shapley value*. Thus, as in the case with two firms, the only way ownership affects the final outcome is through the division of ex post surplus and its impact on ex ante investment incentives. As emphasized earlier, the assumption that all ex post negotiations are efficient—in other words, that the Coase theorem applies ex post—is mainly a simplifying assumption. By considering in turn the case where there is no renegotiation, which may involve extreme ex post inefficiencies, and the case of perfect renegotiation, one is exploring two natural polar cases. Most contractual situations in practice are likely to be a combination of these two extreme cases.

11.2.1.1   The Shapley Value

The Shapley value assigns a payoff to an agent i possibly involved in a transaction with S agents who together own or control $\omega(S)$ assets.

DEFINITION: OWNERSHIP ALLOCATION   Let $\mathbb{S}$ denote the set of all possible subsets of agents I, and $\mathbb{A}$ the set of all possible subsets of assets in $\overline{A}$. Then the mapping $\omega(S)$ from $\mathbb{S}$ to $\mathbb{A}$ denotes the subset of assets owned by the subset of agents S.

Hart and Moore assume that each asset can be controlled by at most one of the groups of agents S or its complement $I \setminus S$. In addition, they assume that the assets controlled by some subgroup $S' \subseteq S$ must also be controlled by the whole group S. In effect, when a group of agents S decides to form a firm, they agree to pool all the assets owned by any of the group members. Formally these assumptions translate into the following properties for the mapping $\omega(S)$:

$$\omega(S) \cap \omega(I \setminus S) = \emptyset \ \text{ and } \ \ \omega(S') \subseteq \omega(S) \ \text{ so that } \ \ \omega(\emptyset) = \emptyset$$

DEFINITION: THE SHAPLEY VALUE   Given an ownership allocation $\omega(S)$, a vector of ex ante investments x, and the associated ex post surplus for any given group of agents S, $V[S, \omega(S)|x]$, the Shapley value specifies the following expected ex post surplus for any agent i:

$$B_i(\omega \mid x) \equiv \sum_{S|i \in S} p(S)\{V[S; \omega(S) \mid x] - V[S \setminus \{i\}; \omega(S \setminus \{i\}) \mid x]\} \tag{11.1}$$

where

$$p(S) = \frac{(s-1)!(I-s)!}{I!} \tag{11.2}$$

and $s = |S|$ is the number of agents in S.

In words, the Shapley value is an expected payoff, where expectations are taken over all possible subgroups S that agent i might join ex post. That is, each agent looks at ex post group formation like a random process where any order in which groups get formed is equally likely. It is for this reason that the probability distribution $p(S)$ is as specified in equation (11.2). Given any ex post realization of a group, S, the Shapley value assigns to each agent i in the group the difference in surplus obtained with the entire group S and with the group excluding agent i:

$$V[S; \omega(S) \mid x] - V[S \setminus \{i\}; \omega(S \setminus \{i\}) \mid x]$$

In other words, the Shapley value assigns to each agent i the expected contribution of that agent to the overall ex post surplus obtained through multilateral trade between all agents.

11.2.1.2   Example 1: Printer-Publisher Integration

Suppose that $I = 2$ and $\overline{A} = \{a_1, a_2\}$, as in Grossman and Hart's example of the printer (agent 1) and the publisher (agent 2). Each agent can make ex ante investments x_i in a first stage, and trade takes place in a second stage.

In this simple setup only the following three ownership allocations are possible:[5]

Nonintegration: $\omega(1) = \{a_1\}, \quad \omega(2) = \{a_2\}$

Publisher integration: $\omega(1) = \emptyset, \quad \omega(2) = \{a_1, a_2\}$

Printer integration: $\omega(1) = \{a_1, a_2\}, \quad \omega(2) = \emptyset$

The Shapley Value

Nonintegration   Suppose that no ex post surplus can be generated without combining both assets. Then under nonintegration the ex post surplus that can be generated with only one agent is

$$V(\{1\}; \{a_1\} \,|\, x) = V(\{2\}; \{a_2\} \,|\, x) = 0$$

where $x = (x_1, x_2)$.[6]

If, however, both agents form a group by trading access to their respective assets, they generate a strictly positive surplus

$$V(\{1, 2\}; \{a_1, a_2\} \,|\, x) \equiv V(x) > 0$$

Under nonintegration, the Shapley value then assigns an expected payoff to each agent of

$$B_1(NI \,|\, x) = B_2(NI \,|\, x) = \frac{1}{2} V(x)$$

(where NI stands for nonintegration), since there are only two equally likely orderings of group formation, $\{1, 2\}$ and $\{2, 1\}$—so that $p(\{1, 2\}) = p(\{2, 1\}) = \frac{1}{2}$—and

$$V(\{1, 2\}; \{a_1, a_2\} \,|\, x) - V(\{j\}; \{a_j\} \,|\, x) = V(x)$$

Printer Integration   Under printer integration, it may be possible for the printer to generate an ex post surplus on his own, since he owns both assets. The publisher cannot generate any surplus on his own, as under

5. Actually there is a fourth possible ownership allocation, where under nonintegration the printer owns the publishing business and the publisher owns the printing press. Under this ownership allocation, each agent holds the other agent's "tools" as a "hostage." In the simple example considered here, this ownership allocation is equivalent in terms of equilibrium payoffs and investments to nonintegration with the reverse asset ownership.

6. This is a simplifying assumption. Grossman and Hart (1986) actually allow for a positive but lower ex post surplus when both assets are not combined. As a result, nonintegration is more likely to be an efficient ownership allocation in their setup than in this example.

nonintegration. Even if the printer can generate a positive surplus on his own, it seems plausible that he might be able to do even better by hiring the publisher, so that the ex post surplus that can be generated with only one agent is likely to be as follows:

$$V(\{2\}; \emptyset \mid x) = 0, \qquad V(\{1\}; \{a_1, a_2\} \mid x) = \Phi_1(x_1)$$

with $\Phi(x_1) < V(x)$.

The Shapley value under printer integration is then given by

$$B_1(PI \mid x) = \frac{1}{2}[V(x) - \Phi_1(x_1)] + \Phi_1(x_1) \quad \text{for agent 1}$$

$$B_2(PI \mid x) = \frac{1}{2}[V(x) - \Phi_1(x_1)] \qquad\qquad \text{for agent 2}$$

where PI stands for printer integration.

Publisher Integration   Similarly, one can take publisher integration to be the mirror image of printer integration, so that the Shapley value under publisher integration becomes

$$B_1(pI \mid x) = \frac{1}{2}[V(x) - \Phi_2(x_2)] \qquad\qquad \text{for agent 1}$$

$$B_2(pI \mid x) = \frac{1}{2}[V(x) - \Phi_2(x_2)] + \Phi_2(x_2) \quad \text{for agent 2}$$

where pI stands for publisher integration.

Ex Ante Investments

Suppose that $V(x)$ is strictly increasing and concave in $x = (x_1, x_2)$, that $\Phi_i(x_i)$ is increasing and concave in x_i, and that the investment-cost functions $\psi_i(x_i)$ are strictly increasing and convex in x_i. Under each ownership allocation, agents choose their ex ante investment noncooperatively to maximize their respective expected payoff:

$$\max_{x_i}\{B_i[\omega(S) \mid x_1, x_2] - \psi_i(x_i)\}$$

Investments are chosen *noncooperatively*, either because they are not observable, as in the employment relation considered earlier, or because they are difficult to verify by a third party. In either case it would be costly or impossible to write an enforceable performance contract specifying the level of investment each party must undertake. Note that if investments are not observable, the ex post payoffs generated by those investments are still assumed to be observable. These are central assumptions in the property-rights theory of the firm, which have generated some controversy. The conceptual issues involved here are discussed extensively in the next chapter.

Suffice it to say here that if ex ante investments could be specified contractually, then the allocation of ownership titles would not serve any role in providing incentives to invest. The Coase theorem, stating that efficiency can be obtained through private contracting no matter how ownership titles are allocated (provided that ownership rights are completely determined), would then again obtain. In other words, the allocation of ownership rights would be irrelevant for efficiency.

Proceeding under the assumption that investments are chosen non-cooperatively, the property-rights theory of the firm predicts that each ownership allocation results in Nash-equilibrium investment levels. These equilibrium investment levels can be obtained from the first-order conditions of each party's optimization problem (assuming that it is concave):

$$\frac{\partial B_i[\omega(S) \,|\, x_1, x_2]}{\partial x_i} = \psi_i'(x_i)$$

Thus, under nonintegration, equilibrium investment levels (x_1^{NI}, x_2^{NI}) are given by

$$\frac{1}{2}\frac{\partial V(x_1^{NI}, x_2^{NI})}{\partial x_1} = \psi_i'(x_1^{NI})$$

$$\frac{1}{2}\frac{\partial V(x_1^{NI}, x_2^{NI})}{\partial x_2} = \psi_2'(x_2^{NI})$$

$$(11.3)$$

Under printer integration, (x_1^{PI}, x_2^{PI}) are given by

$$\frac{1}{2}\frac{\partial V(x_1^{PI}, x_2^{PI})}{\partial x_1} + \frac{1}{2}\Phi_1'(x_1^{PI}) = \psi_1'(x_1^{PI})$$

$$\frac{1}{2}\frac{\partial V(x_1^{PI}, x_2^{PI})}{\partial x_2} = \psi_2'(x_2^{PI})$$

$$(11.4)$$

Finally, under publisher integration, (x_1^{pI}, x_2^{pI}) are given by

$$\frac{1}{2}\frac{\partial V(x_1^{pI}, x_2^{pI})}{\partial x_1} = \psi_1'(x_1^{pI})$$

$$\frac{1}{2}\frac{\partial V(x_1^{pI}, x_2^{pI})}{\partial x_2} + \frac{1}{2}\Phi_2'(x_2^{pI}) = \psi_2'(x_2^{pI})$$

$$(11.5)$$

As can be seen by comparing conditions (11.3), (11.4), and (11.5), the printer has greater incentives to invest for any given level of the publisher's investment x_2 under printer integration than he has under nonintegration and publisher integration provided that $\Phi_1'(x_1) > 0$. Similarly, the publisher has greater incentives to invest given x_1 under publisher integration than he has under nonintegration and printer integration when $\Phi_2'(x_2) > 0$. If, however, $\Phi_2'(x_2) \leq 0$, integration may have no effect or a negative effect on investment.

Thus the property-rights theory of the firm proposes a simple analysis of the costs and benefits of integration. Starting from a position of nonintegration, the benefit of printer integration may be to induce more specific investment by the printer, but the cost of integration is then necessarily a lower investment by the publisher.

Equilibrium Ownership Structures

The property-rights theory predicts an equilibrium ownership structure that is ex ante efficient. The reasoning is that, while contracts on future trade of inputs and services may not be feasible or may be too costly to write, contracts exchanging ownership titles are simple and easy to enforce. Two strong underlying assumptions of the theory are, first, that each contracting party has enough resources to buy any ownership title that it values the most (there are no wealth constraints) and, second, that once an efficient ownership allocation has been achieved, there are no further gains to retrading ownership titles. We shall relax each of these assumptions later and consider the implications for equilibrium ownership allocations. For now, however, we shall stick with these two underlying assumptions and identify situations where, respectively, nonintegration, printer integration, and publisher integration are optimal.

Nonintegration is the equilibrium ownership structure if and only if

$$V(x_1^{NI}, x_2^{NI}) - \psi_1(x_1^{NI}) - \psi_2(x_2^{NI}) \geq$$
$$\max\{V(x_1^{PI}, x_2^{PI}) - \psi_1(x_1^{PI}) - \psi_2(x_2^{PI}); V(x_1^{pI}, x_2^{pI}) - \psi_1(x_1^{pI}) - \psi_2(x_2^{pI})\}$$

Otherwise, either printer or publisher integration obtains depending on which one yields the higher total net surplus. In determining which ownership allocation is optimal, it is helpful to begin by characterizing the socially efficient level of investments (x_1^*, x_2^*). A social planner maximizing the total net ex ante surplus would choose (x_1^*, x_2^*) to satisfy the following first-order conditions:

$$\frac{\partial V(x_1^*, x_2^*)}{\partial x_1} = \psi_1'(x_1^*)$$

$$\frac{\partial V(x_1^*, x_2^*)}{\partial x_2} = \psi_2'(x_2^*)$$

(11.6)

Assuming that the social planner's optimization problem is concave, these are necessary and sufficient conditions characterizing the socially efficient level of investments. If the two parties' investments are *complementary*, then $\partial^2 V(x_1, x_2)/\partial x_2 \partial x_1 \geq 0$. In that case, by comparing conditions (11.3), (11.4), and (11.5), we can observe the following:

1. If $\Phi_i'(x_i) > 0$, printer integration results in higher investment levels for both printer and publisher than under nonintegration.

Indeed, the printer invests more, since

$$\frac{1}{2}\frac{\partial V(x_1^{NI}, x_2^{NI})}{\partial x_1} + \frac{1}{2}\Phi_1'(x_1^{NI}) > \frac{1}{2}\frac{\partial V(x_1^{NI}, x_2^{NI})}{\partial x_1}$$

and the publisher invests as much as or more than under nonintegration, since $\partial^2 V(x_1, x_2)/\partial x_2 \partial x_1 \geq 0$.

Similarly, publisher integration results in higher investment levels for both parties. Therefore, when $\Phi_i'(x_i) > 0$, nonintegration induces lower investment levels than either printer or publisher integration.

2. If $\Phi_i'(x_i) \leq 0$, nonintegration results in (weakly) higher investment levels than under either mode of integration. In that case nonintegration is the efficient ownership allocation, since it induces the smallest underinvestment of all three allocations.

Note that situations where $\Phi_i'(x_i) \leq 0$ are not implausible. Anytime specialized investments (such as customized software) adapted to the special skills of agent j are made, these investments could turn out to be counterproductive when agent j is not hired ex post. In other words, any customization toward agent j weakens the bargaining position of agent i (even if he is the owner of all assets). In that case integration is counterproductive, since it discourages agent i's investment (by weakening his ex post bargaining position) and thus in turn discourages agent j's investment.

Whether one of the integration modes is efficient when $\Phi_i'(x_i) > 0$ cannot be determined from conditions (11.3), (11.4), and (11.5) alone. Indeed, if $\Phi_i'(x_i)$ is large, either form of integration may result in overinvestment, in which case it is not obvious that integration dominates nonintegration.[7] Depending on the specific functional form of $V(x)$ and $\Phi_i(x_i)$, nonintegration or either integration mode can be optimal.

However, if $0 < \Phi_i'(x_i) \le [\partial V(x_i, x_j)]/\partial x_i$ for all x_j, then integration always dominates nonintegration. In other words, if marginal returns on investment are always highest under ex post trade between the two agents, then vertical integration dominates nonintegration.

To summarize, this example illustrates that some form of integration is optimal when marginal returns on investment are highest when all assets and agents are combined in trade ex post, and when the marginal return on investment remains positive if the owner of all assets does not hire the other agent.

11.2.1.3   Equilibrium Investment Levels and Ownership Allocations in the General Framework

Extrapolating from the bilateral example, there appear to be several simple characterizations of equilibrium investments and ownership allocations in a general setting. The example suggests that all ownership allocations might result in underinvestment if marginal returns on investment are higher when more assets and/or agents are combined in trade ex post. Similarly, the example suggests that if a subset of assets are worth more when combined together, then they should be owned by one party. Such characterizations and others are indeed possible if a number of strong assumptions are made about the underlying model.

Hart and Moore (1990) assume the following properties for $V(S; A \mid x)$, $\partial[V(S; A \mid x)]/\partial x_i \equiv V^i(S; A \mid x)$, and $\psi_i(x_i)$:

A1. The function $\psi_i(x_i)$ is nonnegative, strictly increasing, and convex, $\lim_{x_i \to 0} \psi_i'(x_i) = 0$, and $\lim_{x_i \to \bar{x}} \psi_i'(x_i) = \infty$ for some $0 < \bar{x} < \infty$.

---

7. The idea that ownership may result in overinvestment incentives has been noted in different contexts by Bolton and Whinston (1993), Rajan and Zingales (1998), DeMeza and Lockwood (1998), and Bolton and Xu (2001). The general idea that these papers have in common is that overinvestment is the result of the owner's attempt to get a better deal for himself in ex post bargaining. He will be prepared to engage in socially wasteful investment if this allows him to work out a better deal ex post.

A2. The function $V(S; A \mid x)$ is an increasing and concave function of x, so that $V^i(S; A \mid x) \geq 0$; moreover, $V(S; A \mid x) \geq 0$ and $V(\emptyset; A \mid x) = 0$.

A3. $V^i(S; A \mid x) = 0$ if $i \notin S$.

A4. $\partial[V^i(S; A \mid x)]/\partial x_j \geq 0$ for all $j \neq i$.

Assumption A4 implies that all agents' investments are complements.

A5. For all subsets $S' \subseteq S, A' \subseteq A$,

$$V(S; A \mid x) \geq V(S'; A' \mid x) + V(S \setminus S'; A \setminus A' \mid x)$$

Assumption A5 is a superadditivity assumption implying that a group of agents controlling a collection of assets can always create as much surplus as or more surplus than the sum of the surpluses obtainable by subdividing the group and assets.

A6. For all subsets $S' \subseteq S, A' \subseteq A$,

$$V^i(S; A \mid x) \geq V^i(S'; A' \mid x)$$

Assumption A6 is critical. As will become clear, it basically rules out the possibility of overinvestment under any given ownership allocation. When applied to the bilateral example considered previously, it implies in particular that $\Phi_i'(x_i) \leq [\partial V(x_i, x_j)]/\partial x_i$ for all x_j.

When these six assumptions hold, Hart and Moore (1990) show that the following two-part proposition can be obtained:

1. For any ownership allocation $\omega(S)$ there is underinvestment. That is, the unique Nash equilibrium investment levels $x^e(\omega)$ satisfy $x_i^e(\omega) \leq x_i^*$ for each i, where x_i^* is the socially efficient investment level.

2. If marginal returns on investment are higher for all agents under ownership allocation $\hat{\omega}$ than ω, that is,

$$\frac{\partial}{\partial x_i} B_i(\hat{\omega} \mid x) \geq \frac{\partial}{\partial x_i} B_i(\omega \mid x) \quad \text{for all } x$$

then equilibrium investment levels are higher under $\hat{\omega}$ than ω,

$$x_i^e(\hat{\omega}) \geq x_i^e(\omega)$$

and total ex post surplus increases,

$$W[x^e(\hat{\omega})] \geq W[x^e(\omega)]$$

where $W(x)$ is defined by

$$W(x) \equiv V(\overline{S}, \overline{A} \mid x) - \sum_{i=1}^{I} \psi_i(x_i)$$

This proposition provides a simple method for evaluating the efficiency of different ownership allocations. All that is required is to rank the different allocations by the level of investments they induce. If allocation $\hat{\omega}(S)$ induces higher investments for all agents than allocation $\omega(S)$, then it is clearly a more efficient allocation.

It is instructive to see why this result obtains. As it is somewhat complex it may help to skip the following sketch of proof on first reading.

Given assumptions A1 and A2, Nash equilibrium investments $x^e(\omega)$ are given by the first-order conditions

$$\frac{\partial}{\partial x_i} B_i(\omega \mid x)\Big|_{x=x^e(\omega)} = \sum_{S \mid i \in S} p(S) V^i(S; \omega(S) \mid x^e(\omega)) = \psi_i'(x^e(\omega))$$

for all $i = 1, \ldots, I$. Or, using more compact notation, Nash equilibrium investment levels are characterized by

$$\nabla g(x, \omega)\big|_{x=x^e(\omega)} = 0 \tag{11.7}$$

where

$$g(x, \omega) \equiv \left[\sum_{S} p(S) V[S; \omega(S) \mid x] - \sum_{i=1}^{I} \psi_i(x_i) \right] \tag{11.8}$$

Ex ante efficient investment levels, however, are obtained by maximizing

$$W(x) \equiv V(\overline{S}, \overline{A} \mid x) - \sum_{i=1}^{I} \psi_i(x_i)$$

and are characterized by

$$V^i(\overline{S}, \overline{A} \mid x) = \psi_i'(x_i)$$

for all $i = 1, \ldots, I$.

Now consider a change from allocation ω to $\hat{\omega}$ such that

$$\frac{\partial}{\partial x_i} B_i(\hat{\omega} \mid x) \geq \frac{\partial}{\partial x_i} B_i(\omega \mid x)$$

for all x, and define

$$f(x, \lambda) \equiv \lambda g(x, \hat{\omega}) + (1 - \lambda) g(x, \omega)$$

for some $\lambda \in [0,1]$. Let $x(\lambda)$ be the solution to

$$\nabla f(x, \lambda) = 0 \tag{11.9}$$

Totally differentiating equation (11.9), we then obtain

$$H(x, \lambda) dx = -[\nabla g(x, \hat{\omega}) - \nabla g(x, \omega)] d\lambda$$

where $H(x, \lambda)$ is the Hessian of $f(x, \lambda)$ with respect to x (matrix of second derivatives).

Now, by the concavity assumptions A1 and A2, $H(x, \lambda)$ is negative definite. Moreover, by assumption A4, the off-diagonal elements of $H(x, \lambda)$ are nonnegative. Together these properties imply that $H(x, \lambda)^{-1}$ is a nonpositive matrix.[8] Therefore,

$$\frac{dx(\lambda)}{d\lambda} \geq 0$$

so that

$$x^e(\hat{\omega}) \geq x^e(\omega)$$

Next, define

$$h(x, \lambda) \equiv \lambda W(x) + (1 - \lambda) g(x, \omega)$$

---

8. To see why $H(x, \lambda)^{-1}$ is a nonpositive matrix, it is helpful to consider the following 2×2 example:

$$Z = \begin{pmatrix} z_{11} & z_{12} \\ z_{21} & z_{22} \end{pmatrix}$$

where $z_{11} < 0$, $z_{22} < 0$, $z_{12} = z_{21} \geq 0$, and $z_{11}z_{22} - z_{21}z_{12} > 0$, by assumptions A1, A2, and A4. By Cramer's rule we then have

$$Z^{-1} = \frac{1}{\det Z} \begin{pmatrix} z_{22} & -z_{12} \\ -z_{21} & z_{11} \end{pmatrix}$$

a nonpositive matrix. In the general $I \times I$ case, Cramer's rule can also be used to establish this result.

By assumption A6

$$\nabla W(x) \geq \nabla g(x, \omega)$$

for all x, and therefore, replicating the argument made before with $f(x, \lambda)$, one can show that

$$x^* \geq x^e(\omega)$$

for all ownership allocations ω.

Finally, since $W(x)$ is increasing and concave and since

$$\nabla W[x^e(\hat{\omega})] \geq \nabla g[x^e(\hat{\omega}), \hat{\omega}] \quad \text{and} \quad x^e(\hat{\omega}) \geq x^e(\omega)$$

it follows that $W[x^e(\hat{\omega})] \geq W[x^e(\omega)]$.

A number of simple implications immediately follow from this proposition

1. If only one agent invests ex ante, that agent should be the owner of all assets. This observation follows from the fact that the marginal return from investing is increasing in the number of assets owned and by the proposition.

2. Any asset must be owned by either group S or its complement $I \backslash S$. This observation follows again from assumption A6 and the proposition. It has the important implication that ownership allocations where more than one agent has veto power over an asset are inefficient. In other words, joint ownership of assets is inefficient.

3. Strictly complementary assets should be owned together. Two assets are said to be strictly complementary if access to one asset generates no value without access to another asset. Formally, assets a_k and a_l are strictly complementary if

$$V^i(S; A \backslash \{a_k\} \mid x) = V^i(S; A \backslash \{a_l\} \mid x) = V^i(S; A \backslash \{a_k, a_l\} \mid x)$$

Again this implication follows straightforwardly from assumption A6 and the proposition. Another way of putting it is that separating the ownership of two complementary assets is like giving veto power to more than one agent over the combined assets.

11.2.1.4 Example 2: A Printer-Publisher-Bookseller Example

Example 1 and the accompanying general framework provide the simplest possible illustration of the property-rights theory of the firm. They show

how the ownership allocation inducing the highest level of investments emerges as an equilibrium ownership allocation. We now provide an example that illustrates how the Shapley value can be derived when three agents are bargaining. It also illustrates how the simple prediction of the property rights theory—that the equilibrium ownership structure is the one inducing the highest level of investments—can break down in a simple three-agent, three-asset extension.

Suppose now that $I = 3$ and that $\overline{A} = \{a_1, a_2, a_3\}$, with agent 1 as the printer, agent 2 as the publisher, and agent 3 as the bookseller. Only the publisher and printer need to make ex ante investments x_i in the first stage, but trade in the second stage now requires all three parties.[9] Any book or journal can be sold only through a bookseller. The latter purchases books ex post from the publisher, who may or may not be integrated with the printer.

Suppose that integration with the bookseller is either too costly or not possible for regulatory reasons, so that the only integration decision is, as before, between the printer and publisher.[10] We shall only briefly illustrate the Shapley value in this three-agent example and discuss how the integration decision between the publisher and printer may be altered by the presence of the bookseller.

Suppose again that no ex post surplus can be generated without combining all three assets. Then, under nonintegration,

$$V(\{1\}; \{a_1\} \mid x) = V(\{2\}; \{a_2\} \mid x) = V(\{3\}; \{a_3\} \mid x) = 0$$

and

$$V[\{1, 2\}; \{a_1, a_2\} \mid x] = V[\{1, 3\}; \{a_1, a_3\} \mid x] = V[\{2, 3\}; \{a_2, a_3\} \mid x] = 0$$

If, however, all three agents form a group by trading access to their respective assets, they generate a strictly positive surplus from trade

$$V[\{1, 2, 3\}; \{a_1, a_2, a_3\} \mid x] \equiv V(x) > 0$$

Under nonintegration, the Shapley value then assigns an expected payoff to each agent of

9. Ex ante investments are physical investments. There are no investments in human capital here for simplicity.

10. Suppose, in addition, that the courts would find it difficult to enforce a contract between the bookseller and the other parties promising a payment to one or both other parties if they integrate.

$$B_1(NI \mid x) = B_2(NI \mid x) = B_3(NI \mid x) = \frac{1}{3}V(x)$$

since (1) there are six equally likely orderings of group formation,

$$\{1, 2, 3\}, \{1, 3, 2\}, \{2, 1, 3\}, \{2, 3, 1\}, \{3, 2, 1\}, \text{and} \{3, 1, 2\}$$

(2) each agent is last in two out of six orderings, and (3) only the last agent in the ordering makes a positive marginal contribution:

$$V[\{1, 2, 3\}; \{a_1, a_2, a_3\} \mid x] - V[\{i, j\}; \{a_i, a_j\} \mid x] = V(x)$$

In other words, when two out of three agents have already given access to their assets, it is only the third agent that makes it possible to generate a surplus of $V(x)$ by also giving access to his own asset.

Under either printer or publisher integration the number of firms shrinks to two. Now bargaining over access to all three assets is again bilateral (between the integrated firm $\{1, 2\}$, which can grant access to assets $\{a_1, a_2\}$, and the bookseller 3). Therefore, the Shapley value assigns an expected payoff to the integrated publisher $\{1, 2\}$ and the bookseller 3 of, respectively,

$$B_{1,2}(I \mid x) = B_3(I \mid x) = \frac{1}{2}V(x)$$

(where I stands for integration). Indeed, under integration there are again only two equally likely orderings of group formation, $(\{1, 2\}; 3)$ and $(3; \{1, 2\})$.

Thus, under printer or publisher integration, the printer's and publisher's combined share of the ex post surplus is reduced from $\frac{2}{3}V(x)$ to $\frac{1}{2}V(x)$. Clearly, it would not be in the publisher's and printer's interests to merge if merging weakened their ex post negotiating position to such an extent, unless, of course, they were able to significantly increase the ex post surplus by inducing significantly higher levels of investment.

To illustrate this point, suppose that only the printer invests ex ante. Then the printer would invest more and generate a higher surplus under printer integration than under nonintegration, since $\frac{1}{2}V'(x_1) > \frac{1}{3}V'(x_1)$. However, printer integration would not occur in equilibrium if

$$\frac{1}{2}V(x_{PI}) - \psi(x_{PI}) < \frac{2}{3}V(x_{NI}) - \psi(x_{NI})$$

Thus the equilibrium ownership allocation in this example is not the socially efficient allocation (see Heavner, 1999, for an extensive analysis of this point).

11.2.1.5 Summary

The property-rights theory of the firm thus provides simple elements that explain how ownership affects economic decisions and what the costs and benefits of integration are. Ownership is mainly viewed as a bargaining chip in ex post multilateral negotiations. Synergies in mergers are mainly explained as resulting from higher investments induced by the merger. Importantly, the property-rights theory of the firm does not view a merger as resulting in a different form of transacting between the merged entities—as a shift from negotiation-based transactions to command-based transactions. All transactions take place in the same centralized marketplace under any ownership allocation. Only the terms of trade (the Shapley value) vary with the ownership allocation.

Another limitation of the theory is that it is mainly a theory of entre-preneurial firms run by owner-managers. As we highlighted earlier, the theory predicts that ownership of assets by shareholders who are not in any way related to the underlying business of the firm is inefficient. Ownership should go only to agents who make ex ante investments, and it should not be shared.

We shall return to these important limitations in section 11.3. Before turning to the modifications and extensions to the property-rights theory required to widen the scope of application of the theory, we briefly turn to a discussion of ownership and integration with substitutable investments.

11.2.2 A Framework with Substitutable Investments

With substitutable investments, higher levels of investment by agent j may discourage investment by agent i. We shall illustrate how this result can occur in a simple setup with three agents first considered by Bolton and Whinston (1993). In this setup there is one upstream firm supplying scarce inputs to two downstream firms. The ex ante investments of the two downstream firms are substitutable because the two firms compete for inputs. When inputs are in scarce supply, only the highest bidders (with the highest ex post values) get to purchase the inputs. Therefore, an increase in investment by firm j, which tends to raise its ex post value for the input, may have the effect of lowering the ex post profit of firm i, and thus discouraging firm i from investing.

As we now illustrate, one then can no longer determine equilibrium ownership allocations simply by looking at the level of ex ante investments.

Moreover, equilibrium ownership allocations may be inefficient. This finding is not entirely surprising, since under imperfect competition, concentrated ownership may serve the dual role of strengthening market power and providing protection against ex post opportunism.

The setup considered in Bolton and Whinston differs from the Hart and Moore framework in two main respects.

First, ex post surplus from trade is assumed to be random: downstream firm D_i, having made ex ante investments x_i, can generate an ex post surplus by teaming up with upstream firm U of $V_i(x_i, \theta)$, where θ is a random variable with distribution $\mu(\theta)$ $(i = 1, 2)$. The random shocks are such that under some realizations $\tilde{\theta}$, $V_1(x_1, \tilde{\theta}) > V_2(x_2, \tilde{\theta})$, and under other realizations $\hat{\theta}$, $V_2(x_2, \hat{\theta}) > V_1(x_1, \hat{\theta})$ (see Figure 11.1).

Second, the ex post multilateral bargaining solution is not the Shapley value but something closer to a second-price auction. That is, Bolton and Whinston show how noncooperative bargaining with outside options à la Binmore, Rubinstein, and Wolinsky (1986, see also Sutton, 1986) results in equilibrium terms of trade for inputs identical to those obtained in a second-price auction, when

$$|V_i(x_i, \theta) - V_j(x_j, \theta)| > \frac{1}{2}\min\{V_i(x_i, \theta), V_j(x_j, \theta)\} \qquad (11.10)$$

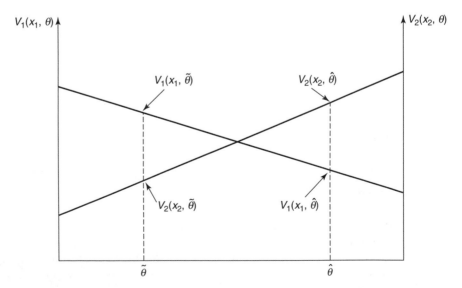

Figure 11.1
Ex-Post Surplus from Trade with Downstream Firms, D_1 and D_2

When condition (11.10) holds, the upstream firm sells the input(s) to the highest bidder at a bid equal to the second-highest value $V_i(x_i, \theta)$. Although Bolton and Whinston also consider cases where condition (11.10) does not hold, as well as cases where there is no scarcity of inputs ex post, we shall for the sake of brevity restrict attention to situations where inputs are always scarce and condition (11.10) is always satisfied. These are situations of extreme competition for inputs by downstream firms, where the Bertrand (or Vickrey) equilibrium outcome, $P = \min\{V_i(x_i, \theta), V_j(x_j, \theta)\}$ is a better reflection of the one-sided nature of negotiations than the Shapley value, which gives the lower-value bidder a strictly positive ex post surplus.

Suppose that only downstream firms make ex ante investments (such as promotion or advertising of their respective final products) and that the cost of investment, as before, is given by $\psi_i(x_i)$. Suppose, in addition, that subsection 11.2.1.3's conditions in assumption A1 hold for $\psi_i(x_i)$ and in assumption A2 hold for $V_i(x_i, \theta)$ and $V_j(x_j, \theta)$. Let Θ_1 denote the subset of realizations of θ such that $V_1(x_1, \theta) > V_2(x_2, \theta)$ and Θ_2 the subset of realizations of θ such that $V_2(x_2, \theta) \geq V_1(x_1, \theta)$.

11.2.2.1 Socially Optimal Investment Levels

The ex ante optimal investment levels (x_1^*, x_2^*) maximize the expected ex ante net surplus given by

$$\int_{\Theta_1} V_1(x_1, \theta)d\mu(\theta) - \psi_1(x_1) + \int_{\Theta_2} V_2(x_2, \theta)d\mu(\theta) - \psi_2(x_2)$$

Given our assumptions on $\psi_i(x_i)$ and $V_i(x_i, \theta)$, this is a concave objective function, so that the ex ante efficient investment levels are characterized by the first-order conditions

$$\int_{\Theta_i} \frac{\partial V_i(x_i, \theta)}{\partial x_i} d\mu(\theta) = \psi_i'(x_i) \tag{11.11}$$

11.2.2.2 Equilibrium Investment Levels under Nonintegration

Remarkably, equilibrium investment levels under nonintegration satisfy exactly the same conditions and are therefore efficient. To see this result, we need to start from the ex post bargaining outcome and move backward to the investment stage. The ex post bargaining outcome under nonintegration is that the downstream firm with the highest value gets the inputs at a price equal to the second-highest value. Thus ex post payoffs for downstream firm D_i are given by

$$\max\{0, V_i(x_i, \theta) - V_j(x_j, \theta)\}$$

and ex ante expected payoffs are

$$\int_{\Theta_i} [V_i(x_i, \theta) - V_j(x_j, \theta)] d\mu(\theta) - \psi_i(x_i)$$

Hence, Nash-equilibrium investment levels $x^{NI} = (x_1^{NI}, x_2^{NI})$ under nonintegration are characterized by the first-order conditions

$$\int_{\Theta_i} \frac{\partial V_i(x_i^{NI}, \theta)}{\partial x_i} d\mu(\theta) = \psi_i'(x_i^{NI}) \tag{11.12}$$

It is immediately apparent that equations (11.11) and (11.12) are the same and therefore that equilibrium investment levels under nonintegration are ex ante efficient. There is a basic economic logic for this result. Each downstream firm gets to appropriate exactly its entire ex post rent when it is positive (the amount by which its value exceeds that of its rival). So each downstream firm seeks to maximize the expected ex post rent, which is the same as the social objective.

Since nonintegration induces efficient equilibrium investments in this example, it is tempting to conclude that nonintegration is necessarily the equilibrium ownership allocation. This is not the case, however. The basic reason, as mentioned earlier, is that the upstream firm U and one of the downstream firms D_i can strengthen their combined market power at the expense of the other downstream firm by vertically integrating. Or, to use the terminology in Bolton and Whinston, vertical integration provides anticompetitive gains in the form of partial (or total) *foreclosure* of the unintegrated downstream firm.

To see this point, start again from the ex post bargaining outcome and suppose that downstream firm D_1 is vertically integrated with U.

11.2.2.3 Equilibrium Investment Levels under Vertical Integration $\{D_1, U\}$

The integrated firm's ex post payoff is

$$\min\{V_1(x_1, \theta), V_2(x_2, \theta)\} + \max\{0, V_1(x_1, \theta) - V_2(x_2, \theta)\}$$

where the first term is U's payoff and the second D_1's payoff. This expression is equal to

$$V_1(x_1, \theta)$$

Thus the integrated firm's ex ante expected payoff is

$$\int_{\Theta} V_1(x_1, \theta)d\mu(\theta) - \psi_1(x_1)$$

and its equilibrium investment level is characterized by the first-order conditions

$$\int_{\Theta} \frac{\partial V_1(x_1^{VI}, \theta)}{\partial x_1} d\mu(\theta) = \psi_1'(x_1^{VI})$$

In other words, the integrated firm now overinvests, since it gets to appropriate not only its entire expected ex post rent but also part of the other downstream firm's ex post rent, as Figure 11.2 highlights. Since the vertically integrated firm overinvests, the unintegrated firm D_2 now underinvests, since the set of states Θ_2 in which it gets a positive rent is now smaller (see Figures 11.2 and 11.3 for an illustration).

As a result of the integrated firm's overinvesting, firms U and D_1 gain by integrating, while firm D_2 loses (see Figure 11.3 for an illustration of the increased ex ante expected payoff under vertical integration)

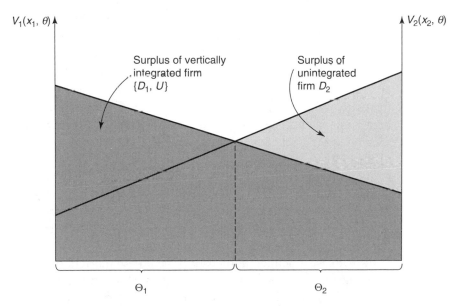

Figure 11.2
Expected Surplus from Trade for $\{D_1, U\}$ and D_2

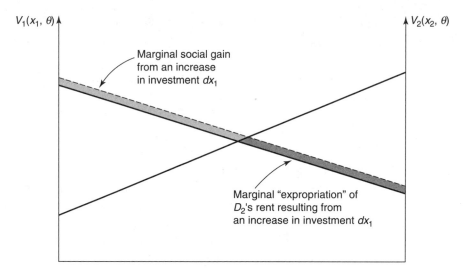

Figure 11.3
Marginal Expected Gain from Investment for $\{D_1, U\}$

Therefore, nonintegration cannot be an equilibrium outcome here even though it supports an efficient investment outcome. The three contracting parties must be able to enforce an agreement ex ante not to engage in any retrading of assets to ensure the stability of nonintegration. Agreements preventing any future retrading of assets, however, are rarely seen and appear to be impractical. In reality, an owner may need to trade his asset for many different reasons, and a wholesale ban on future trades may be highly inefficient. The only possible alternative then is to write a contract specifying the contingencies when an asset can be sold and those when it cannot. However, the same reasons that make it too costly to write contingent long-term contracts on future trade of inputs or other commodities would appear to make it prohibitively costly to write a long-term contingent contract specifying future trades of assets. To be consistent, it is reasonable to assume that it is simply not possible to write contracts regulating future trade of assets.

In that case, nonintegration cannot be an equilibrium ownership allocation, since the upstream firm and one of the downstream firms can achieve a higher joint payoff by deviating and vertically integrating.

11.2.2.4   Equilibrium Ownership Allocations

So far we have not formally defined the notion of equilibrium for owner-ship allocations. A new difficulty arising from the possibility for future retrades of assets is that the desirability of the current trade depends in part on parties' expectations on future retrades. To deal with this issue in a general way, Bolton and Whinston introduce a weak notion of stability by imposing strict conditions on feasible future retrades. Specifically, they define an equilibrium (or quasi-stable) ownership allocation to be such that there do not exist any deviating trades that are guaranteed to strictly raise the payoffs of all parties to that trade. A payoff increase for an agent is guaranteed if it is obtained regardless of whether any future trades occur that do not involve that agent.

According to that equilibrium notion, nonintegration is clearly not stable, since, for example, U and D_1 can guarantee a higher joint payoff by verti-cally integrating. Their payoff increase is guaranteed because no other trade of assets without U and D_1 is feasible.

However, vertical integration by U and D_1 is an equilibrium allocation, since D_1 is not guaranteed a higher payoff by reverting back to noninte-gration. If it does so, D_1 individually exposes itself to a retrade resulting in the integration of U and D_2. Similarly, if U and D_1 deviated by purchasing D_2's asset, they would lower their joint payoff, since then D_2 would have no incentives to invest ex ante.

To summarize, the analysis in Bolton and Whinston points to an important difference in the predictions of the property-rights theory of the firm as they apply to settings in which investments are complementary, or settings where firms are in competition so that their investments may be substitutes. Roughly speaking, in situations where there is little or no competition ex post, ownership primarily serves the role of providing a valuable bargaining chip to protect ex ante investments. However, in situations where firms compete ex post, concentrated ownership serves the dual role of strength-ening market power and providing protection against ex post opportunism. In that case, equilibrium ownership allocations may well be inefficient.

11.3   Financial Structure and Control

The property-rights theory of the firm provides the first formal elements of an answer to the fundamental question posed by Coase (1937) of why there are firms, what they do, and why there are organizations directing production and the allocation of goods or services outside the marketplace.

However, it does not account for the basic observation associated with the names of Berle and Means (1932) that in most corporations ownership is separated (at least partially) from control. Professional managers (with minimal ownership stakes in their firms) rather than shareholders run most large corporations. As we saw in Part I, this separation of ownership and control creates a fundamental agency problem. Though we have considered the problem of how to optimally trade off risk sharing and incentives, we have not addressed the issue of why control is separated from ownership and what the implications of this separation are for the theory of the firm.

Besides risk aversion and the desire to diversify risk, an obvious reason why ownership is separated from control is that the agents who benefit the most from the protection of ownership do not always have the means to acquire these valuable ownership rights. They are wealth constrained. To become owners they must then raise the funds necessary to purchase the assets from wealthy third parties. These third parties will have no special connection with the firm's business, but nevertheless will insist on getting protections of their own to ensure that their investments are repaid. These protections may be in the form of voting or veto rights if they become equity owners, or collateral and other debt collection rights if they become creditors. Thus managers' wealth constraints provide a simple immediate explanation for the separation of ownership and control observed in most corporations.

How does the answer to the question of who should own a set of productive assets change when the agent or agents who need access to these assets are wealth constrained? We shall begin by considering this question in the simplest possible setup, with only one productive asset and two agents, the manager and the financier. This setup was first considered by Aghion and Bolton (1992), who have pointed out that debt financing can be seen as a way of allocating control in a "state-contingent" fashion, with equity holders or managers retaining control in nondefault states and creditors taking control in default states. Aghion and Bolton assume that financial contracts are incomplete only to the extent that they cannot be made fully contingent on all future states of nature. In particular, financial contracts can be a function of realized profits, as in standard agency models. A stronger assumption is made in Bolton and Scharfstein (1990, 1996) and Hart and Moore (1989, 1994, 1998), where financial contracts cannot be based on realized profits, as cash flows are either not observable to the financier or not verifiable by a court. We shall illustrate how the weaker assumption in Aghion and Bolton provides a richer theory of optimal (state-contingent) control allocations. In contrast, the stronger assumption of nonverifiability of cash flows in Bolton and Scharfstein, and Hart and Moore, gives rise to a dynamic theory of debt.

11.3.1   Wealth Constraints and Contingent Allocations of Control

Consider the start-up financing problem, where a risk-neutral wealth-constrained entrepreneur E needs funds $K > 0$ to start a venture. These funds can be obtained from a risk-neutral investor (say a venture capitalist) I, who has unlimited resources.

Once the venture is up and running, some event θ may occur affecting the future profitability of the project and requiring new actions a to be undertaken. These actions involve private costs or benefits to the entrepreneur, $h(a, \theta)$, which may vary with the realized event. Once these actions have been taken, some time elapses, returns r are realized, and the venture is wound down. The utility function over income and actions of the entrepreneur is

$$U_E(y_E, a) = y_E + h(a, \theta)$$

The entrepreneur values monetary returns from the project y_E as well as other dimensions of her job, such as personal satisfaction from completing a project she created, her reputation, the benefits of being her own boss, the ability to take time off when she wants, the benefits of retaining the business in the family, and so on. We label all these other dimensions as "private benefits."

The investor, however, cares only about money, since he does not take an active part in the business. Therefore, his utility function is simply

$$U_I(y_I, a) = y_I$$

This is the basic setup considered by Aghion and Bolton (1992).[11]

Because the entrepreneur values other things besides money, conflicts of interest may arise between the two contracting parties. Situations may arise

---

11. Note that there are no ex ante "noncontractable" investment decisions in this framework. Here control allocation is driven by considerations of ex post inefficiency and not by ex ante investment inefficiencies.

where the entrepreneur wants to take an action that does not maximize the monetary return from the project. To some extent these conflicts of interest can be resolved contractually ex ante or ex post. However, as we shall see, contractual incompleteness together with the entrepreneur's limited wealth constraint makes it impossible to completely resolve all conflicts contractually. As a result, the allocation of control—who gets to make the critical decisions—is an important dimension of the financial contract.

As simple as this basic setup is, there is nevertheless a fairly complex set of financial contracts over which the parties can optimize. Hence, to keep things as simple as possible, Aghion and Bolton allow for only two possible events, a "good" and a "bad" one, $\theta \in \{\theta_B, \theta_G\}$. In addition, only two courses of action can be considered, say, "liquidation" or "continuation," following the realization of the event θ, $a \in \{a_L, a_C\}$. Finally, realized revenues can take only two values, $r \in \{0, 1\}$. The ex ante probability of a "good" event is given by

$$\Pr(\theta = \theta_G) = p \in [0, 1]$$

and the probability of a high return conditional on event θ_i $(i = B, G)$ and action a_j $(j = L, C)$ is given by

$$y_j^i \equiv \Pr(r = 1 \mid \theta = \theta_i; a = a_j)$$

Also, it is convenient to write

$$h(\theta_i, a_j) \equiv h_j^i$$

To have an interesting problem, the required action must, of course, vary with the realized event. The convention is that continuation is more efficient in the good state, while liquidation is better in the bad state, so that

$$y_C^G + h_C^G > y_L^G + h_L^G$$

and

$$y_L^B + h_L^B > y_C^B + h_C^B$$

Finally, the project must obviously yield a high enough expected return so that the investor is willing to put up money, so that

$$p y_C^G + (1 - p) y_L^B > K$$

11.3.1.1 Financial Contracts, Bargaining, and Renegotiation

Financial contracts are assumed to be incomplete only to the extent that repayments to the investor and future action choice cannot be made contingent on the realization of the event θ. The contract can, however, prescribe an action plan contingent on a signal ζ correlated with θ—$a(\zeta)$—as well as repayments contingent on the signal ζ, the realized return r, and the prescribed action a—$t(\zeta, r, a)$.

Consistent with other simplifying assumptions, the signal can take only two values, $\zeta \in \{\zeta_G, \zeta_B\}$, with

$$p^G = \Pr(\zeta = \zeta_G \mid \theta = \theta_G) > \tfrac{1}{2}$$

and

$$p^B = \Pr(\zeta = \zeta_B \mid \theta = \theta_B) > \tfrac{1}{2}$$

Note that the distance

$$d = (|1 - p^G| + |1 - p^B|)$$

can then be taken to be a measure of the degree of incompleteness of the contract.

Although Aghion and Bolton allow for general contracts contingent on actions, it is both simpler and more realistic to restrict attention to contracts that cannot prescribe future actions or specify payments contingent on action choice. This would be the case if the action chosen were unobservable to the other party, as in a standard setting with moral hazard. Hence, we shall consider only contracts that allocate control rights (but do not prescribe specific actions), and specify only repayments $t(\zeta, r)$ (independent of action choice). Since there are only two possible return realizations, $r \in \{0, 1\}$, we can also restrict attention to affine transfers lower than or equal to r given the entrepreneur's wealth constraint

$$t(\zeta, r) = t_\zeta r + k_\zeta \le r$$

Given that contracts are incomplete, it is possible that the contract agreed on initially may result in an inefficient action choice after the realization of θ. In that case the contracting parties would want to renegotiate the initial contract.

We shall suppose that the entrepreneur can make take-it-or-leave-it offers both at the initial contracting stage and at the renegotiation stage. This assumption reflects a situation of extreme ex post opportunism by the entrepreneur: once the investor has handed over the money and the investment has been sunk, he is at the mercy of the entrepreneur. He can rely only on legal enforcement of the initial financial contract to get his money back.

11.3.1.2   Entrepreneur Control

Under entrepreneur control, actions are chosen to maximize the entrepreneur's payoff

$$a_E^i = \arg\max_{a_j}\{y_j^i(1-t_l)-k_l+h_j^i\}$$

where $i \in \{G, B\}$ refers to the state of nature θ_i, $l \in \{G, B\}$ to the signal, and $j \in \{C, L\}$ to the chosen action. Given that the entrepreneur gets both monetary returns and private benefits, she may not always choose the action with the highest expected return y_j^i. She is more likely to choose an action with a low y_j^i to the extent that her share of monetary returns is lower. If she were a 100% claimant on the project's return, she would always choose the ex post efficient action. However, in that case the investor would get no compensation for his investment. Therefore, even under an optimal initial contract it may not be possible to induce the entrepreneur to choose the ex post efficient action for all realizations of ζ and θ. However, we shall show now that even if the optimal ex ante contract induces the entrepreneur to choose an inefficient action for some realizations of the signal ζ and the state θ, ex post renegotiation will result in an efficient action choice.

To see this result, consider, for example, the situation where the optimal ex ante contract induces the entrepreneur to continue (that is, choose $a = a_C$) when $\zeta = \zeta_G$ and $\theta = \theta_G$,

$$y_C^G(1-t_G)+h_C^G \geq y_L^G(1-t_G)+h_L^G$$

but not when when $\zeta = \zeta_B$ and $\theta = \theta_G$,

$$y_L^G(1-t_B)+h_L^G \geq y_C^G(1-t_B)+h_C^G$$

In that case the entrepreneur and investor would renegotiate the contract when $\zeta = \zeta_B$ and $\theta = \theta_G$. That is, the entrepreneur would make a take-it-or-leave-it offer to the investor to choose a_C instead of a_L in exchange for a new transfer of

$$y_C^G + h_C^G - (y_L^G + h_L^G) - y_L^G t_B$$

which leaves the investor with the same payoff as in the initial contract under choice of action a_L. This renegotiation offer allows the entrepreneur to appropriate the entire gain from renegotiation

$$y_C^G + h_C^G - (y_L^G + h_L^G)$$

and to attain a strictly higher payoff:

$$y_C^G - y_L^G t_B + h_C^G > y_L^G (1 - t_B) + h_L^G$$

since, by assumption, $y_C^G + h_C^G > y_L^G + h_L^G$.

It is easy to verify that under any initial contract, renegotiation will always lead to an efficient action choice. In other words, entrepreneur control always achieves efficiency (possibly following renegotiation). The general principle here is that, since the investor has unlimited wealth, he can always bribe the entrepreneur to take the ex post efficient action.

The problem under entrepreneur control thus is not inefficient investment but inadequate investor protection. The basic reason why the investor may not be adequately protected under entrepreneur control is that even if the entrepreneur does the right thing, the investor does not get to share the returns from renegotiation. Venture capitalists and other investors are well aware of this problem. It is for this reason that they generally insist on veto rights or majority control as a condition for investment (see Kaplan and Stromberg, 2003, for empirical evidence).

To see when the investor does not get sufficient protection under entrepreneur control, suppose that

$$h_C^G > h_L^G \quad \text{but} \quad h_L^B < h_C^B$$

In that case the entrepreneur is led to choose the ex post inefficient action of continuing in the bad state unless she gets a sufficiently large financial stake in the firm.

Let

$$\Delta^B \equiv (y_L^B + h_L^B) - (y_C^B + h_C^B)$$

denote the difference in total payoffs in the bad state (between liquidation and continuation), and let

$$\Delta_y^B \equiv y_L^B - y_C^B$$

denote the difference in monetary returns in the bad state.

Now the investor and entrepreneur have three possible contractual strategies to get the entrepreneur to choose liquidation over continuation in the bad state:

1. They can *rely entirely on ex post renegotiation;* in that case, the contract providing the highest return to the investor is the one giving all future revenue streams to the investor, $t_\zeta = 1$ and $k_\zeta = 0$ for $\zeta = \zeta_G, \zeta_B$. The investor's ex ante expected payoff is then

$$\Pi_R = p y_C^G + (1-p) y_C^B$$

Note that the investor's payoff is no more than Π_R because he gets no additional gain from renegotiation in state θ_B.

2. They can *write a renegotiation-proof contract* giving the entrepreneur the right financial incentives to choose liquidation over continuation in the bad state: the renegotiation-proof contract providing the highest return to the investor while maintaining the entrepreneur's incentives is such that

$$1 - t_\zeta = \frac{\Delta_y^B - \Delta^B}{\Delta_y^B} \quad \text{for } \zeta = \zeta_G, \zeta_B \text{ (and } k_\zeta = 0)$$

The investor's ex ante expected payoff under this contract is

$$\Pi_{NR} = [p y_C^G + (1-p) y_L^B] t_\zeta$$

or

$$\Pi_{NR} = [p y_C^G + (1-p) y_L^B] \frac{\Delta^B}{\Delta_y^B}$$

3. They can write a contract that is *partially renegotiation-proof* in the bad state. Such a contract would set

$$t_B = \frac{\Delta^B}{\Delta_y^B} \quad \text{and} \quad t_G = 1 \quad \text{(with } k_\zeta = 0)$$

The investor's ex ante expected payoff under this contract is then

$$\Pi_{PR} = p y_C^G \left[p^G + (1 - p^G) \frac{\Delta^B}{\Delta_y^B} \right] + (1-p) \left[(1 - p^B) y_C^B + p^B y_L^B \frac{\Delta^B}{\Delta_y^B} \right]$$

Interestingly, renegotiation-proof contracts do not always give the best protection to the investor. The reason is that, to avoid renegotiation, the investor must give up a large financial stake. Such a concession is excessive in the good state. The investor can therefore do better by attempting to target a large financial return for the entrepreneur only in the bad state.

In sum, entrepreneur control always results in an efficient investment policy, but, unfortunately, it does not provide sufficient investor protection when

$$\max\{\Pi_R, \Pi_{PR}, \Pi_{NR}\} < K$$

11.3.1.3 Investor Control

By giving control to the investor the contract can ensure that the action maximizing monetary returns gets chosen without having to bribe the entrepreneur. Control thus gives added protection to the investor and ensures that he will invest in the venture. The investor's ex post payoff is

$$y_j^i t_l + k_l$$

so that he will want to choose the action maximizing y_j^i if and only if $t_l \geq 0$.

Although a financial contract with $t_l < 0$ is feasible, the contracting parties would never gain by having $t_l < 0$ under investor control. Indeed, the investor would then at best act like the entrepreneur by choosing actions that minimize y_j^i. He would then get a lower payoff than under entrepreneur control. Therefore, we can restrict attention to $t_l \geq 0$ under investor control. The investor will then always choose the action with the highest expected monetary return y_j^i.

By doing so, the investor does not necessarily choose an ex post efficient action (he maximizes only monetary returns but not overall returns). For example, if

$$y_L^G > y_C^G$$

the investor may choose to liquidate in the good state even though it is ex post efficient to continue. This scenario is not implausible. Indeed, one often hears entrepreneurs and managers complain that investors are excessively "short-termist"—that they do not put enough value on preserving the firm as a going concern. This example provides a simple illustration of this conflict.

Now it would seem that if the initial contract induces the investor to choose an inefficient action ex post, then—as under entrepreneur control—ex post renegotiation would lead to an efficient choice of action. This is, however, not the case. The reason is that the entrepreneur is wealth constrained and does not necessarily have the financial resources to bribe the investor to continue rather than liquidate. The entrepreneur would be unable to effectively bribe the investor whenever

$$y_C^G(1-t_l)-k_l < t_l(y_L^G - y_C^G)$$

The LHS represents the entrepreneur's total pledgeable wealth in state θ_G under the renegotiated action choice a_C, and the RHS represents the minimum bribe required to get the investor to switch from liquidation to continuation.

Thus ex post efficiency under investor control is assured only if

$$t_l \leq \frac{y_C^G - k_l}{y_L^G} \tag{11.13}$$

Setting $t_l = (y_C^G - k_l)/y_L^G$, the investor's ex ante expected payoff is then given by

$$p[p^G y_C^G + (1-p^G)y_C^G]+$$
$$(1-p)\left\{p^B\left[\left(\frac{y_C^G - k_B}{y_L^G}\right)y_L^B + k_B\right] + (1-p^B)\left[\left(\frac{y_C^G - k_G}{y_L^G}\right)y_L^B + k_G\right]\right\}$$

Now, if the liquidation value is lower in the bad than in the good state, $y_L^B \leq y_L^G$ (which seems reasonable), then it is straightforward to see that the investor's ex ante expected payoff is strictly increasing in k_G and k_B. Hence, the optimal compensation scheme (ensuring ex post efficiency) under investor control is to maximize k_l subject to the constraints that $t_l \geq 0$ and $k_l \leq 0$ (the latter constraint is simply the entrepreneur's ex post limited wealth constraint when $r = 0$).

Assuming that $y_L^B \leq y_L^G$ (a sufficient condition), we conclude that the optimal ex post efficient compensation contract is such that $k_l = 0$. In other words, under investor control the optimal ex post efficient compensation contract is an equity contract with an equity stake for the investor of $t = y_C^G/y_L^G$. The investor's maximum ex ante expected payoff under an ex post efficient contract is then

$$\Pi_I = [p y_L^G + (1-p) y_L^B] \frac{y_C^G}{y_L^G}$$

Note that the result that equity is an optimal contract is not robust. Indeed, if we were to relax the entrepreneur's ex post wealth constraint from $k_i \le 0$ to $k_i \le w$ (where $w > 0$), then the optimal compensation contract would be a combination of equity $[t = (y_C^G - w)/y_L^G]$ and (collateralized) debt ($k = w$). The larger the entrepreneur's initial wealth w is, the more (collateralized) debt she would incur. This result is not entirely surprising. By lowering the equity stake of the investor, the optimal contract is giving lower-powered incentives to the investor and thus minimizing his ex post opportunism.

Unfortunately, even the best ex post efficient contract for the investor may not provide a sufficient return to cover the investment outlay K. In that case, the contracting parties may be forced to write an ex post inefficient contract—one that sometimes lets the investor liquidate rather than continue in the good state. If a contract with $t_i \le y_C^G/y_L^G$ for both realizations of the signal $l \in \{\zeta_B, \zeta_G\}$ is not feasible, then the next best contract is the one where $t_B = 1$ and $t_G = y_C^G/y_l^G$. This contract induces an ex post efficient outcome when the more likely signal ζ_G is realized in state θ_G and an inefficient action choice when ζ_B is realized. The investor's ex ante payoff under this contract is then

$$\hat{\Pi}_I = p[p^G y_C^G + (1-p^G) y_L^G] + (1-p)\left[p^B y_L^B + (1-p^B) \frac{y_C^G}{y_L^G} y_L^B \right]$$

Note that the maximum achievable payoff for the investor here is obtained by maximizing the ex post inefficiency in state θ_G and setting both t_B and t_G equal to 1. The investor's ex ante payoff under this contract is $\hat{\Pi}_I = p y_L^G + (1 - p) y_L^B$. This highly inefficient contract is always feasible, since

$$p y_L^G + (1-p) y_L^B \ge p y_C^G + (1-p) y_L^B > K$$

11.3.1.4 Contingent Control

To summarize our analysis so far, we have found that entrepreneur control is always efficient but may not be feasible, while investor control is always feasible but may not be efficient. We now show that when only inefficient investor control is feasible, a more desirable or efficient control allocation may be available that allocates control to the entrepreneur only when ζ_G is realized and to the investor when ζ_B occurs.

Suppose that

$$y_L^G > y_C^G \quad \text{and} \quad h_L^B < h_C^B$$

so that the entrepreneur and investor have conflicting objectives in both states of nature. Under this assumption about underlying cash flows and private benefits, the entrepreneur is always in favor of continuation, while the investor is always in favor of liquidation. It is only efficient to continue in the good state, so that an efficient state-contingent control allocation would be to give the entrepreneur control in the good state and the investor control in the bad state. Since state-contingent control allocations are not feasible, the best approximation to this allocation is to have the signal-contingent allocation that we described previously.

Consider this signal-contingent allocation, and suppose that $t_l = 1$ and $k_l = 0$ for $l = \zeta_B, \zeta_G$. Under this financial structure the investor's and entrepreneur's ex ante payoffs are, respectively,

$$\Pi_{SC} = p[p^G y_C^G + (1 - p^G)y_L^G] + (1 - p)[p^B y_L^B + (1 - p^B)y_C^B]$$

and

$$\pi_{SC} = p[p^G h_C^G + (1 - p^G)h_L^G] + (1 - p)[p^B h_L^B + (1 - p^B)(y_L^B - y_C^B + h_L^B)]$$

Indeed,

1. In the event (θ_G, ζ_G) (which occurs with probability pp^G) the entrepreneur has control and chooses the ex post efficient action a_C. This choice yields ex post payoffs of y_C^G for the investor and h_C^G for the entrepreneur (given the cash-flow-sharing rule $t_l = 1$ and $k_l = 0$ for $l = \zeta_B, \zeta_G$).

2. In the event (θ_G, ζ_B) [probability $p(1 - p^G)$] the investor has control and chooses the inefficient action a_L (given the sharing rule $t_B = 1$ and $k_B = 0$, this outcome cannot be renegotiated). The ex post payoffs are then, respectively, y_L^G for the investor and h_L^G for the entrepreneur.

3. In the event (θ_B, ζ_B) (probability $(1 - p)p^B$) the investor has control and chooses the efficient action a_L. The ex post payoffs are then, respectively, y_L^B for the investor and h_L^B for the entrepreneur.

4. In the event (θ_B, ζ_G) [probability $(1 - p)(1 - p^B)$] the entrepreneur has control, threatens to choose the inefficient action a_C in the absence of rene-

gotiation, and obtains a renegotiation rent of $y_L^B - y_C^B$. The ex post payoffs are therefore y_C^B for the investor and $y_L^B - y_C^B + h_L^B$ for the entrepreneur.

In contrast, the entrepreneur's payoff under investor control (with $t_B = 1$ and $t_G = y_C^G/y_L^G$) is

$$\hat{\pi}_I = p[p^G h_C^G + (1-p^G)h_L^G] + (1-p)\left\{p^B h_L^B + (1-p^B)\left[y_L^B\left(1-\frac{y_C^G}{y_L^G}\right) + h_L^B\right]\right\}$$

Comparing π_{SC} with $\hat{\pi}_I$, it is straightforward to check that $\pi_{SC} > \hat{\pi}_I$ whenever

$$\frac{y_C^B}{y_L^B} < \frac{y_C^G}{y_L^G}$$

Similarly, a comparison of the investor's ex ante payoffs under the two control allocations, Π_{SC} and $\hat{\Pi}_I$, yields that $\Pi_{SC} > \hat{\Pi}_I$ whenever

$$\frac{y_C^G}{y_L^G} < \frac{y_C^B}{y_L^B} \tag{11.14}$$

That is, contingent control (with $t_I = 1$ and $k_I = 0$) gives the investor a higher payoff than investor control (with $t_B = 1$ and $t_G = y_C^G/y_L^G$) whenever the difference in monetary returns between liquidation and continuation is higher in the good state than in the bad state. Vice versa, when the opposite inequality holds, contingent control is preferred over investor control by the entrepreneur.

We can summarize the analysis of contingent control as follows. When $y_C^B/y_L^B < y_C^G/y_L^G$ and only investor and contingent control are feasible, then contingent control is the preferred choice of the entrepreneur. When $y_C^B/y_L^B > y_C^G/y_L^G$, then contingent control (with $t_B = 1$ and $t_G = y_C^G/y_L^G$) is the equilibrium outcome only if neither entrepreneur nor investor control is feasible. There may indeed be some investments with high setup costs K that are feasible under the contingent-control allocation but not under investor control (with $t_B = 1$ and $t_G = y_C^G/y_L^G$).

Comparing contingent control with entrepreneur control, note that in the limit as $p^G \to 1$ and $p^B \to 1$, we have

$$\Pi_{SC} \to py_C^G + (1-p)y_L^B > \max\{\Pi_R, \Pi_{NR}\}$$

Also, it is straightforward to check that $\Pi_{SC} > \Pi_{PR}$. Therefore, as $p^G \to 1$ and $p^B \to 1$, there are values of the setup cost K such that

$$\Pi_{SC} > K > \max\{\Pi_R, \Pi_{PR}, \Pi_{NR}\}$$

For those values of K, contingent control is the contracting outcome either when $y_C^B/y_L^B < y_C^G/y_L^G$ or when $y_C^B/y_L^B > y_C^G/y_L^G$ and $K > \hat{\Pi}_I$.[12]

11.3.1.5 Comments

The Aghion and Bolton model provides one answer to the question of who should control a firm when the agents who set up the firm are wealth constrained. Their answer is consistent with the result of Hart and Moore (1990) that the most efficient ownership or control allocation is to give all control rights to those agents making ex ante investments or those agents having an essential role in production. In the Aghion and Bolton model the most efficient allocation is entrepreneur control. However, their analysis points out that this allocation may not be feasible when these critical agents are wealth constrained. Control must then be shared with investors.

Under some circumstances, the equilibrium-control allocation is a contingent-control allocation. This situation can be interpreted as a form of debt financing or, perhaps more plausibly, as a form of venture-capital financing. The venture-capital interpretation was first suggested by Berglöf (1994). More recently Kaplan and Stromberg (2003) have argued that the contingent-control allocation describes quite accurately some key features of venture-capital investment contracts. Their empirical analysis, which is based on 200 venture-capital deals by 14 venture-capital partnerships with 118 firms, stresses that cash-flow rights are generally allocated separately from voting or board rights and that future financing and control rights are often contingent on observable measures of firm performance. Generally, the venture-capital lead partner obtains full control if the firm performs poorly, and if the firm performs well the entrepreneur can increase her control rights.

11.3.2 Wealth Constraints and Optimal Debt Contracts when Entrepreneurs Can Divert Cash Flow

The Aghion and Bolton analysis can explain different forms of outside financing when entrepreneurs are wealth constrained. In their model,

---

12. Some readers may note that the analysis of contingent control here is somewhat different from Aghion and Bolton (1992). The reason is that the comparison between the two control structures in that paper is incomplete (but see Vauhkonen, 2002, for a more complete comparison).

outside investors may take a controlling equity position, may hold non-voting shares (which give them no control rights whatsoever), or may write a financial contract that gives them contingent-control rights. The last type of financial contract can take different forms. It could be a contingent veto right, an option contract like a warrant, or a debt contract.

Debt is a special form of financial contract inducing a special form of contingent-control allocation. First, debt is generally a fixed repayment claim on the firm, which is independent of realized cash flow. Second, debt involves a transfer of control from the entrepreneur to the creditor(s) only in states of nature where the entrepreneur is unable or unwilling to honor her fixed repayment claim. In that case the entrepreneur is said to be in default of her debt obligation. Third, when the entrepreneur defaults on her debt repayment, the creditor(s) generally have the right to seize the firm's cash flow up to the point when the repayment is fully met.

To be able to explain why debt financing is an efficient financial contract, one needs to introduce other features into the Aghion and Bolton framework besides their form of contractual incompleteness. If one makes the additional assumption that realized cash flows are either private information to the entrepreneur or nonverifiable to third parties, then debt can be an optimal financial contract. The reason is that with unobservable (or unverifiable) cash flows it is easy for the entrepreneur to engage in self-dealing by diverting cash flow from the firm. The investor's only responses then are to threaten to foreclose on the firm's assets or to cut off future lending if the entrepreneur does not meet a fixed repayment.

The first models with unobservable or unverifiable cash flow that derive an optimal investment contract with the three main characteristics of debt—a fixed repayment claim, a right to foreclose on the firm's assets in case of default, and priority repayment in case of default—are due to Bolton and Scharfstein (1990) and Hart and Moore (1989, 1998). We shall consider a simple model of debt financing with nonverifiable cash flow, which is a special case of both the Hart and Moore (1998) and Bolton and Scharfstein (1990) models.

To set the stage, we begin by briefly discussing the earlier literature on the optimality of debt as a financial contract. As discussed in Chapter 5, the first models of optimal debt are due to Townsend (1979), Diamond (1984), and Gale and Hellwig (1985). Cash flow is assumed to be private information to the entrepreneur in these models, and investors are assumed to only observe realized cash flow at a cost. There is a positive monitoring cost, which the risk-neutral contracting parties will attempt to minimize. It is efficient to only monitor (or inspect the books) for a subset of reported earnings. Over the set of reported earnings for which there is no inspection, incentive-compatible truthful reporting of earnings requires that repayments to investors must be independent of reported earnings. This requirement explains why it is optimal to have a fixed repayment claim, the first characteristic of debt. Then, in order to minimize monitoring costs, it is optimal to inspect only low reported earnings and to have creditors claim the full realized cash flows. This fact explains a second characteristic of debt—that creditors have priority in default. However, the third characteristic—the right to foreclose on the firm's assets in case of default—cannot be adequately explained with this approach.[13] Other models of debt as an optimal financial contract, based on moral hazard with or without renegotiation (Innes, 1990, Matthews, 2001, or Dewatripont, Legros, and Matthews, 2003), do not account for creditor foreclosure rights either.

11.3.2.1 A Simple Two-Period Problem

We now turn to the analysis of a simple dynamic investment problem where a critical feature of the optimal financial contract is the investor's right to foreclose on the firm's assets in case of default. Consider a risk-neutral entrepreneur with an investment project requiring an investment outlay $K > 0$ in period 0 and returning a random cash flow $r \in \{0, r^H\}$ in period 1. The probability that the high-cash-flow outcome is realized is given by $\Pr(r = r^H) = p \in [0, 1]$. Suppose for simplicity that there is no discounting and that the equilibrium interest rate is zero. We shall assume that p and r^H are large enough so that the investment has a positive net expected return and is worth undertaking:

$$pr^H > K$$

Suppose that the entrepreneur has no initial wealth and turns to a wealthy, risk-neutral financier to fund the project. If cash flow r is observable to both parties and verifiable by a judge, the wealthy financier will agree to lend any amount L to the entrepreneur such that

$$pr^H \geq L \geq K$$

in return for an r^H-contingent repayment $t^H(L) \geq L/p$.

---

13. As stressed in Chapter 5, the optimality of debt in these models hinges critically on the assumed risk neutrality of the parties. Also, to obtain the type of inspection policy that can be interpreted as a risky debt contract with bankruptcy costs, random inspection and renegotiation must be ruled out. Finally, it is technically difficult to extend the result of optimality of debt to multiperiod settings (see Gale and Hellwig, 1989; Chang, 1990; Webb, 1992).

If, however, cash flow r is privately observed by the entrepreneur, or is not verifiable in court, then this one-period project cannot get any outside funding. Indeed, if r is privately observed by the entrepreneur, she will never disclose the realization of r^H, and the investor would never get his money back. Similarly, if r^H is observable to both parties but not verifiable in court, the entrepreneur would refuse to pay $t^H(L)$ when r^H is realized, and the investor would not be able to enforce payment in court. Either way, an extreme form of credit rationing obtains because of the inability to enforce repayment in high-cash-flow states.

This extreme form of inefficiency, however, obtains only in the special case of one-period-lived projects. For multiperiod projects, where cash flows occur repeatedly over time, it can be substantially reduced. The basic reason is that when investment projects generate cash flows repeatedly over time, the investor can induce her to make repayments either by threatening to foreclose on the entrepreneur's assets in case of nonpayment (as in Hart and Moore, 1998) or by threatening to withhold future funding (as in Bolton and Scharfstein, 1990).

To see how this threat works, consider the same investment problem as before but now twice repeated. That is, the first investment project with an outlay of $K > 0$ in period 0 generates a random cash flow $r \in \{0, r^H\}$ in period 1. The second project also requires an outlay of $K > 0$ in period 1 and generates an identically and independently distributed cash flow $r \in \{0, r^H\}$ in period 2.[14]

In this longer-horizon investment problem, a long-term investment contract specifies the following:

1. The size of the initial loan, $L_0 \geq K$.

2. The size of the loan commitment in period 1 contingent on a high repayment $t^H(L_0)$—L_1^H.

3. The size of the loan commitment in period 1 contingent on a low repayment $t^L(L_0)$—L_1^L.

Since there are only two possible cash-flow outcomes in period 1, there is no need to specify a richer deterministic loan commitment menu in that

---

14. Note that these two consecutive projects can also be seen as a single project with an outlay of $K > 0$ in period 0, a random cash flow $r_1 \in \{l, r^H - K\}$ in period 1, and second-period cash flow $r_2 \in \{0, r^H\}$. The cash flow $r_1 = l$ is given by $l = -K$ if the second project is undertaken even after a low-cash-flow outcome in period 1. It is given by $l = 0$ if the second project is not undertaken. Hart and Moore (1998) consider a single project with two cash-flow rounds, while Bolton and Scharfstein (1990) consider two identical consecutive projects.

period.[15] Also, since cash flows are either private information or nonverifiable, it will not be possible to extract any payment from the entrepreneur in period 2, as we have seen. Thus any long-term investment contract is characterized by the five variables $\{L_0, L_1^H, t^H, L_1^L, t^L\}$.

Suppose for now that the parties can commit not to renegotiate this contract. In its most basic form, we shall describe a debt contract to be a long-term investment contract such that

$$L_1^H \geq K - (r^H - t^H)$$

and

$$L_1^L < K + t^L$$

In other words, a debt contract is such that the entrepreneur is granted sufficient additional funding to be able to undertake the second project when she repays t^H, but is denied adequate further funding when she does not meet her repayment obligation t^H in period 1. The debt contract can also be interpreted as giving the creditor the right to foreclose, or "pull the plug," on the entrepreneur's project when she defaults on the fixed repayment obligation t^H. Note that this contract has the important property that investment in period 1 is positively correlated with realized cash flow.

We shall now show why long-term investment contracts must be debt contracts and why the risk-neutral investor may be willing to invest in the firm in period 0 under such a contract. Applying the revelation principle, we observe that loan commitments in any long-term contract must satisfy the incentive-compatibility constraint requiring that the entrepreneur truthfully report cash flow r^H when it is realized:

$$r^H - t^H + L_1^H + \gamma^H (pr^H - K) \geq r^H - t^L + L_1^L + \chi^H (pr^H - K) \tag{11.15}$$

where, γ^H and χ^H are indicator functions. The function γ^H takes the value $\gamma^H = 1$ when

$$r^H - t^H + L_1^H \geq K$$

that is, when the entrepreneur has enough accumulated funds to finance the new project. Otherwise, $\gamma^H = 0$. Similarly, $\chi^H = 1$ when $r^H - t^L + L_1^L \geq K$, and otherwise $\chi^H = 0$.

---

15. Bolton and Scharfstein (1990) allow for a menu of stochastic loan commitments such that contingent on a repayment $t^i(L_0)$ the investor commits to finance the new project with probablity β^i, where $i = L, H$.

The other incentive-compatibility constraint—that the entrepreneur truthfully report cash flow $r^L = 0$ when it is realized—always holds here, as the entrepreneur does not have the funds available to mimic a high-cash-flow outcome when realized cash flow is $r^L = 0$. The reader might wonder why the entrepreneur cannot borrow funds from another lender to be able to mimic r^H. The reason is simply that no lender would be foolish enough to lend to the entrepreneur knowing that she would never repay the new loan.

Besides the preceding incentive-compatibility condition, any long-term investment contract must also satisfy the investor's individual-rationality constraint

$$-L_0 + p(t^H - L_1^H) + (1-p)(t^L - L_1^L) \geq 0 \tag{11.16}$$

as well as the wealth constraints

$$t^H \leq r^H + L_0 - K \tag{11.17}$$

and

$$t^L < L_0 - K \tag{11.18}$$

An optimal long-term investment contract then maximizes the entrepreneur's expected payoff

$$L_0 - K + p(r^H - t^H + L_1^H + \gamma^H[pr^H - K]) \\ + (1-p)(-t^L + L_1^L + \chi^L[pr^H - K]) \tag{11.19}$$

(where $\chi^L = 1$ when $-t^L + L_1^L \geq K$ and otherwise $\chi^L = 0$) subject to constraints (11.15), (11.16), (11.17), and (11.18).

To find the solution to this constrained optimization problem, note first that a long-term investment contract cannot satisfy the individual-rationality constraint (11.16) if both γ^H and χ^H equal 1. To see this point, note that the incentive constraint (11.15) and the limited-wealth constraint (11.18) imply that

$$t^H - L_1^H \leq t^L - L_1^L \leq L_0 - K - L_1^L$$

when $\gamma^H = 1$ and $\chi^H = 1$. But then constraint (11.16) cannot hold. A similar argument establishes that long-term contracts such that $\gamma^H = 0$ and $\chi^H = 0$, or such that $\gamma^H = 0$ and $\chi^H = 1$, are also not feasible. Thus the only feasible long-term contract is such that $\gamma^H = 1$ and $\chi^H = \chi^L = 0$. In words, a long-term contract is feasible only if it is a debt contract, where the investor commits to refinance when the entrepreneur repays t^H, but not when the repayment is only t^L. In particular, note that financing the project with outside equity is not feasible here, whether or not the investor gains control of the project. Indeed, neither form of equity financing involves a commitment to invest in the new project if and only if the first-period cash-flow realization is r^H.

Finally, note that financing the first project with a long-term debt contract is feasible whenever

$$-K + p(r^H - K) \geq 0$$

or

$$pr^H \geq K(1+p)$$

When this condition is satisfied, the investor is willing to finance the first project with a long-term debt contract such that $L_0 = K$, $t^H = r^H$, $L_1^H = K$, and $t^L = L_1^L = 0$. In addition, this contract is incentive compatible for the entrepreneur.

Thus credit rationing can be substantially reduced for multiperiod projects where cash flows occur repeatedly over time. In the preceding example, financing of the first project through long-term debt is feasible provided the project's present value is sufficiently larger than the setup cost. Moreover, renewed financing of the second project is guaranteed if the first project pays off. The reason why financing is possible when the project is repeated twice is that the lender can now use the threat of foreclosure or termination to induce repayment of r^H in period 1.

This analysis raises a number of questions about the robustness of the result of the optimality of debt as a financial contract. First, does debt remain an optimal financial contract if the parties are allowed to renegotiate the long-term investment contract? Second, is debt an optimal contract if there are more than two cash-flow outcomes in any given period or when cash flows are autocorrelated? Third, is long-term debt an optimal contract when there are more than two iterations in investment? Also, does debt remain optimal in a wider class of (message-game) contracts? We turn to a discussion of each of these questions in the following subsections.

11.3.2.2 Renegotiation

Notice first that a commitment to terminate the investment in period 1 following a low-cash-flow realization, $r = 0$, is credible. Indeed, the investor would have no reason to rescind the contract in that case because he can only lose money by reinvesting at that point. Similarly, the commitment to continue the investment in period 1 following a high-cash-flow realization, $r = r^H$, is also credible. Indeed, the continuation contract at that point is Pareto efficient, so that no mutually beneficial renegotiation is obtainable.

Does this conclusion mean that the preceding long-term debt contract is renegotiation-proof? Interestingly, as Hart and Moore (1989) first noted, the answer is no. The reason is that when r^H is realized the entrepreneur may be able to successfully negotiate down the potentially onerous terms in the initial contract under which she can get refinancing in period 1. To see how this process works, suppose that the initial long-term contract is such that $L_0 = K$, $t^H = r^H$, $L_1^H = K$, $t^L = 0$, and $L_1^L = 0$. If the entrepreneur decided to repay t^L when the cash flow was r^H, she would not be able to get new financing for the second project under the initial contract.

Does this mean that she will not be able to undertake the new project? Not necessarily, since her retained earnings at that point $(r^H - t^L) = r^H$ are sufficient to finance the entire setup cost K on her own. It is, however, reasonable to suppose that investment in the new project in period 1 by the entrepreneur would be sufficient evidence in court to prove that the realized cash flow in period 1 was r^H. As under existing law, it would then be feasible for the investor to block any new investment by the entrepreneur at that point. Note that if the investor could not stop the entrepreneur from investing on her own following default on the long-term debt contract, then the contract would no longer be feasible, since the entrepreneur would always default following the realization of r^H.

Suppose that unless the contract is renegotiated following default the entrepreneur would not be able to invest in the new project. Hart and Moore (1989) observe that following default (that is, a repayment of t^L even though realized cash flow is r^H) the entrepreneur and investor can actually find a mutually beneficial renegotiation. Indeed, if they do not renegotiate, their respective payoffs are r^H and 0. But if they do renegotiate, they gain the additional surplus $[pr^H - K] > 0$, which they can divide between themselves.

Hart and Moore (1989, 1998) and most of the subsequent literature on optimal long-term debt contracting assume that bargaining in renegotiation always results in an efficient outcome. This assumption is not unreasonable if there is only one creditor negotiating with the entrepreneur. We shall take the bargaining solution in our simple example to be any $(\alpha, 1 - \alpha)$ split of the renegotiation surplus, where $1 > \alpha > 0$ denotes the entrepreneur's share of the renegotiation surplus.[16] The bargaining problem in our simple example with twice-repeated investment is a standard problem, and the bargaining solution does not require any special justification. As we shall see, however, in more general multiperiod problems the bargaining solution in renegotiation is less obvious and is sensitive to specific assumptions about the parties' rights while they are negotiating.

Under our assumed bargaining solution, a long-term debt contract is renegotiation-proof only if the following condition holds:

$$L_0 - K + r^H - t^H + L_1^H + (pr^H - K) \geq r^H + \alpha[pr^H - K] \tag{11.20}$$

The RHS of expression (11.20) denotes the entrepreneur's payoff when (1) realized cash flow is r^H, (2) she repays only t^L, and (3) the original contract is renegotiated. If this payoff is less than what she would get by repaying t^H, then the contract is renegotiation-proof. Notice that when $\alpha = 0$, incentive compatibility of the long-term debt contract guarantees renegotiation-proofness. But when $\alpha > 0$ the renegotiation-proofness constraint (11.20) may bind before the incentive compatibility constraint (11.15). In that case, the optimal renegotiation-proof contract is obtained by maximizing expression (11.19) subject to constraints (11.20), (11.16), (11.17), and (11.18).

As can be easily checked, the optimal renegotiation-proof contract then is still a debt contract. The only difference with the case of full commitment concerns the feasibility of debt financing. A long-term debt contract is now feasible if and only if

$$-K + p(1 - \alpha)(pr^H - K) \geq 0$$

Note that the repayment t^H can also be interpreted as the purchase price for the entrepreneur of the right to continue investing in the project, which is sold to her by the investor. As long as this price is set optimally by the investor, there will be no room for further renegotiation.

11.3.2.3   General Cash Flows

In the preceding example we have allowed for only two cash-flow outcomes in each period, with $r \in \{0, r^H\}$. The analysis is almost the same if one

---

16. Note that since $r^H > [pr^H - K]$, any division of the surplus from renegotiation is feasible following the realization of r^H.

assumes that $r \in \{r^L, r^H\}$ with $r^L > 0$, as in Bolton and Scharfstein (1990). They assume that r^L is pledgeable but not $(r^H - r^L)$, so that cash flows are in effect partially observable (or verifiable). One difference with the preceding analysis is that under the new assumption, $r^L > 0$, it may be possible to have projects that are worth funding, yet that do not allow the entrepreneur to self-finance in period 1 following a high-cash-flow realization, because the inequalities

$$-K + pr^H + (1-p)r^L \geq 0$$

and

$$r^H - r^L < K$$

are compatible. In that case, the investor is able to block any new investment by the entrepreneur in period 1 without having to enforce any legal rights to block new investments.

In fact, the analysis is, if anything, strengthened if one allows for correlation in cash flows. Let $E[r \mid r_1]$ denote expected period-2 cash flows conditional on period-1 cash-flow realization r_1. With positive serial correlation, $E[r \mid r^H] > E[r \mid r']$. Now the entrepreneur's expected payoff in period 2 is greater when period-1 cash flow is r^H, so that she stands to lose more if she is not refinanced. This outcome reduces her incentive to underreport cash flow in period 1 and strengthens the investor's threat of termination. We leave it as an exercise to show that the optimal long-term contract remains a debt contract.

The analysis also extends with minor modifications to a situation where cash flow is distributed continuously on the interval $[r^L, r^H]$, with $r^L \geq 0$, $r^H < +\infty$, and density functions $f_1(r)$ and $f_2(r)$ in periods 1 and 2, respectively. As shown in Faure-Grimaud (2000) and Povel and Raith (2004), when the entrepreneur can make a take-it-or-leave-it offer to an investor, the optimal long-term investment contract under full commitment takes the form that the entrepreneur can refinance the project if she repays $D \leq E[r_2]$ in period 1 (where $E[r_2]$ denotes expected cash flow in period 2). If she repays only $t < D$, then she is only allowed to refinance the project with probability

$$\xi(t) = 1 - \frac{D-t}{E[r_2]}$$

The probability of refinancing is such that the entrepreneur's incentive is to repay $t = r$, whenever $r < D$. Thus the optimal contract is as if the investor always had higher priority and the entrepreneur did not get any return in period 1 until the investor had been repaid in full. The optimal contract is depicted in Figure 11.4. With a continuum of cash-flow realizations, it is even more striking how the optimal contract resembles a standard debt contract.

Note that Hart and Moore (1998) consider the related problem where there is a single up-front investment $K > 0$ in period 0 followed by two

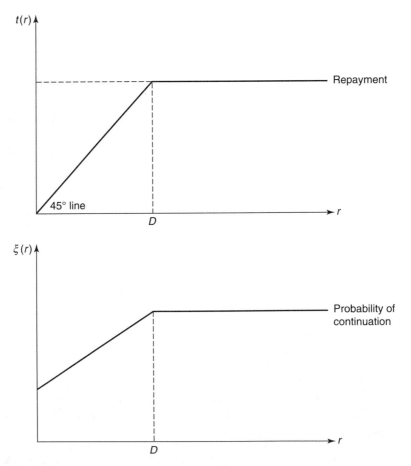

Figure 11.4
Repayment and Probability of Continuation under the Optimal Contract

observable but not verifiable (random) cash-flow realizations, $r_1 \in [r^L, r^H]$ and $r_2 \in [r^L, r^H]$. Their framework is almost identical to the one we have considered, with one important difference: They assume that all uncertainty about cash flows is realized in period 1. In this slightly different investment problem, they explore three additional extensions:

First, they allow the entrepreneur to borrow more than is needed to fund the project. If the amount borrowed is B, then the surplus available to the entrepreneur is $T = B - K$. It is assumed that when the entrepreneur saves T, *it cannot be seized by the investor*. The entrepreneur can use T in period 1 either to meet repayments to the investor or to reinvest in the project. If he reinvests in the project, then she gets a (random) unit return π, where for all π, $1 \le \pi \le E[r_2]$. In this problem the entrepreneur may want to carry forward $T > 0$ as a way of hedging against bad cash-flow outcomes in period 1.

Second, they allow for random verifiable cash flows (or liquidation value) r^L.

Third, they consider more general contracts where the investor may have the option to buy the new project from the entrepreneur in period 1. When the investor becomes the owner of the project in this way, he becomes the recipient of the cash flow.

Restricting attention to standard debt contracts (T, D, r^L), where D is the required repayment in period 1 and r^L is the liquidation value in case of default, Hart and Moore first ask which of two types of debt contracts is optimal, a *fastest* debt contract with $T = 0$ or a *slowest* debt contract with $D > T + r^H$. Note that for any T there is a unique D such that the creditor's individual-rationality constraint binds. Also, the more the entrepreneur borrows (that is, the higher is T) the more she needs to repay (the higher is D) to keep the creditor on his break-even constraint. Thus, the two debt contracts—fastest and slowest— are the two extreme feasible contracts.

Under the slowest contract $(D > T + r^H)$, the entrepreneur engages in maximal hedging but is always forced to default in period 1. Under this contract she effectively "rents" the project from the creditor from period 0 to period 1. Under the fastest contract $(T = 0)$ the entrepreneur borrows the minimum amount and does not engage in any hedging.

Hart and Moore find, on the one hand, that, when the unit return on reinvesting cash in period 1 is low $(\pi = 1)$ and only r_1 is random, then the slowest debt contract is optimal. In other words, maximum hedging of period 1 cash flow is optimal. On the other hand, if only period-2 cash flow, r_2, is random, then the fastest debt contract is optimal. When only r_2 is random, hedging is unnecessary. In addition, under this stochastic structure the entrepreneur faces a potentially high cost of termination when r_2 is high. To eliminate this cost, the optimal debt contract is such that the entrepreneur is always able to repay D in period 1. We leave it as an exercise to derive these two results.

The second question Hart and Moore address is, When are standard debt contracts optimal financial contracts? They show that when the unit return on reinvesting cash in period 1 is high ($\pi = E[r_2]$) and r^L, r_1 and r_2 are positively serially correlated, then the fastest debt contract is optimal in a larger class of message-game (or option-to-buy) contracts. This debt contract is optimal because it maximizes the likelihood of continuation of the project in the cash-flow states where continuation is most desirable.

11.3.2.4   More Than Two Investment Rounds

The analysis and results of the dynamic problem with two rounds of investment also extend to situations with more than two rounds. In particular, debt contracts with foreclosure rights in the event of default remain optimal. Also, the basic life cycle of investment, with a development phase followed by a cash-flow-extraction phase—which holds by construction in the two-period problem—can now be derived as an optimal policy in the multiperiod problem.

The main qualitative change in problems with more than two rounds of investment concerns renegotiation and the credibility of the investor's threat of termination in the event of default. We shall illustrate this change by considering a problem with three rounds of investment first analyzed in Gromb (1994). Consider the same investment problem as before but now repeated three times. That is, each of the three investment projects has an outlay of $K > 0$ in period $t = 0, 1, 2$ and generates an identically and independently distributed cash flow $r \in \{0, r^H\}$ in periods $t + 1$.

To keep the analysis as simple as possible, it is convenient to assume now that the investor has all the bargaining power both in the initial contracting stage and in subsequent renegotiations. Thus we shall assume that the investor begins by making a take-it-or-leave-it contract offer and that he can at any time propose to renegotiate the contract with the entrepreneur.

Consider first the optimal contract under full commitment. This contract must now specify contingent loan commitments in periods 1 and 2. Proceeding by backward induction, it is easy to see that there should be no refinancing in period 2 following a low-cash-flow outcome. It is, however, less clear whether there should be no refinancing in period 1 following a low-cash-flow outcome. On the one hand, no refinancing in period 1 following default is an even more effective threat than before, since now two rounds of investment are passed up. On the other hand, the cost of passing up valuable investments is greater. Indeed, two more rounds of investment remain in period 1. Our preceding analysis shows that the optimal continuation contract at that point is to renew investment for one round and to make a loan commitment on another round contingent on no default.

Gromb (1994) shows that it is (weakly) optimal to undertake the first project. Indeed, the investor cannot do worse than passing up the first project because he can always replicate the outcome in the two-investment-round problem by committing to never finance the third project. When $p \le \frac{1}{2}$, it is optimal to cut off new lending for both remaining rounds of investment in period 1 following a bad cash-flow realization $r_1 = 0$, but to also commit to finance both remaining projects following a high-cash-flow realization $r_1 = r^H$. The logic behind this extreme contract is that the investor can get the entrepreneur to make a maximum repayment following a high-cash-flow realization in period 1 equal to the present expected value of the two remaining projects:

$$t^H = 2pr^H$$

Since the entrepreneur stands to lose access to both continuation projects if she reports a low-cash-flow outcome in period 1, she is willing to pay as much as the whole continuation value of the two projects for the free access to the two continuation projects. Note that when $p \le \frac{1}{2}$, she is also able to pay t^H following a high-cash-flow realization $r_1 = r^H$. Note also that the investor cannot extract more than $2pr^H$ from the entrepreneur under any long-term contract, since she will always run away with the money in the last period.

The other alternative for an optimal long-term contract would be to continue to finance both remaining projects following a high-cash-flow realization, but also to finance one project following a bad cash-flow realization. However, under this contract the investor would have a higher investment outlay and could hope to get a total repayment of at most $2pr^H$.

As one might expect, the optimal full commitment contract is not renegotiation-proof. But, more importantly, the threat to cut off any future funding following default in period 1 is now no longer credible. Indeed, as we have pointed out, it is optimal for the investor to make a renegotiation offer following default in period 1 renewing investment for one round and making a loan commitment for another round contingent on no default in period 2. Anticipating such an offer, the entrepreneur would never make any repayment in period 1. Thus the investor's future monopoly rents undermine his present power to extract rents by making his threat of termination not credible.

There are two possible renegotiation-proof contracts that the investor might then select. Under one contract, the investor would simply pass up the first round of investment and then offer the entrepreneur the same continuation contract as in the problem with two rounds of investment.[17] This contract would yield a net expected return of

$$p(pr^H - K) - K \qquad (11.21)$$

Under the other contract, the investor would fund the first project, commit to fund both remaining projects if the entrepreneur repays $t^H = pr^H$ in period 1, commit to fund the second project if the entrepreneur does not repay anything in period 1, and commit to fund the third project if the entrepreneur repays $t^H = pr^H$ in period 2. This contract would yield a net expected return of

$$p(pr^H - 2K) + (1-p)p(pr^H - K) - K$$

or

$$[p + p(1-p)](pr^H - K) - K(1+p) \qquad (11.22)$$

Comparing expressions (11.21) and (11.22), we find that the latter contract is optimal if and only if

$$K \le (1-p)(pr^H - K)$$

The analysis of this simple example with three investment rounds highlights an important principle. If the future relationship is profitable, the investor has little incentive to terminate it following default. This fact, in turn, undermines his ability to extract payments from the entrepreneur. In the limit, when there is an infinite number of possible investment rounds,

---

17. Note that since the investor has all the bargaining power, the two-period contract where he commits to renew funding only if the entrepreneur repays $t^H = r^H$ is renegotiation-proof.

Gromb (1994) shows that even a monopoly lender cannot make a net positive return on investment in a renegotiation-proof long-term investment contract. Indeed, any renegotiation-proof contract cannot rely on strictly Pareto-dominated termination threats. When lending is terminated, both investor and entrepreneur get a continuation value of zero. Therefore, if the investor were to obtain a strictly positive return under the long-term contract, the termination threat would be Pareto-dominated.

Admittedly, this extreme result may be sensitive to underlying assumptions on the bargaining process under renegotiation. Hart and Moore (1994), for example, assume that when the entrepreneur defaults, the investor takes control of the assets and can collect the project's cash flow for that period. This ability, of course, significantly increases the investor's power to extract payments from the entrepreneur.

The multiperiod problem considered in Gromb (1994) has been extended in several different directions by DeMarzo and Fishman (2002). They allow for investments of varying size, more general return distributions, consumption and reinvestment of accumulated cash flow, correlation in returns, and different bargaining and liquidation scenarios. Their model encompasses Bulow and Rogoff (1989), Gromb (1994), and Hart and Moore (1994) as special cases. Remarkably, they show that the optimal renegotiation-proof long-term investment contract is a debt financing contract combining a bond with a long-term coupon payment and a line of credit that the entrepreneur can draw on in the event of bad cash-flow outcomes. Only when the line of credit has been exhausted will the entrepreneur be forced to default and transfer control to the investor.

11.4 Summary

In this chapter we have introduced exogenous limits on contracting, which restrict the contracting parties to write incomplete contracts. The introduction of these exogenous constraints is a major break from the earlier chapters in the book. It is a methodological break, which allowed us to focus on and formulate other key notions of organizations and firms, such as authority or employment relations, ownership, and control rights. We began with Simon's theory of authority when long-term contracts are incomplete, which is essentially a theory of flexibility: by delegating authority to an agent, the contracting parties let the agent make efficient choices in response to changing circumstances. These choices will be made with the interests of the controlling party in mind, but if the other contracting parties have aligned interests, they will on average prefer the efficient choices of the controlling agent to a narrow and inflexible, contractually specified outcome. We argued that much of Simon's theory rests on the assumption that long-term contracts cannot be renegotiated easily and that the theory must be supplemented with a holdup problem to explain why it is preferable to write long-term contracts in the first place.

The introduction of a holdup problem led us next to the theory of ownership articulated by Grossman, Hart, and Moore, that ownership is a *residual right of control*. This theory makes a fundamental break with earlier notions of ownership articulated by Alchian and Demsetz (1972) and Jensen and Meckling (1976), among others, that ownership is only a *right to residual returns*. We showed how Grossman, Hart, and Moore were able to develop a theory of the boundaries of firms and the costs and benefits of integration based on this notion of ownership rights. We also highlighted how vertical integration decisions could be socially inefficient and could result in monopolization and reduced competition.

The notion of ownership as a residual right of control can be refined by introducing financial contracts. We saw how investments financed through debt basically give rise to a *contingent ownership allocation*. Control of the investment project remains in the hands of the founder if all debts are repaid and is transferred to creditors when the entrepreneur is unable to repay her debts. We determined conditions under which a contingent-control allocation induced by debt financing dominates any other form of shared ownership or control arrangement. Basically, when investors need protections mostly in particular circumstances, and when the borrower's inability to repay is a signal that is closely correlated with these states of nature, then contingent control is efficient. Thus venture capital contracts generally involve contingent-control allocations, as Kaplan and Stromberg (2003) have documented, because control in the hands of the venture capitalist is more valuable in early stages, when success of the venture is still uncertain. Once success is assured, the venture capitalist's role is less important, so that it is generally efficient to commit to relinquishing control in those circumstances.

Finally, we closed the chapter with a further refinement of contingent-control allocations through debt financing in situations where the borrower may be able to divert money from the firm, or may abscond with the loan and/or the proceeds of the investment. In the presence of such a *willingness-to-repay problem*, lending for investment is feasible only if the lender can brandish the threat of cutting off the borrower from further loans in the event of a default. We argued that such a threat is effective only if the lender has an exclusive relation with the borrower or is able to secure collateral and can foreclose the firm's assets in the event of default. In addition, it must also be in the lender's interest to shut out the firm from further lending or liquidate its assets for the threat to be credible. All in all, this incomplete-contracts perspective combined with the notion of limited enforcement of repayment gives rise to a rich theory of debt financing and *creditor rights*—one that brings us closest to real debt contracts and to the main issues that debtor-creditor law and bankruptcy law are concerned with.

11.5   Literature Notes

Many of the ideas developed in this chapter find their origin in Coase's classic (1937) article on the theory of the firm. This article points out that most of the economic activity that takes place in firms is not regulated by complete, explicit contracts. All this activity takes place outside a market environment by choice, and an explanation is required to show why such economic transactions are superior to market transactions. Markets cannot be omniefficient, for otherwise there would be no firms. Similarly, economic activity in firms cannot be omniefficient, for otherwise there would be no markets. What determines whether an activity should be a market transaction or an authority transaction was in Coase's mind a fundamental microeconomic question that remained unanswered in his day.

The first attempt at developing a formal theory that could address this basic question is due to Simon (1951). But, undoubtedly, the economist who has done most in taking up Coase's challenge and in articulating a full-fledged economic theory of the firm and organizations is Williamson. In several books (1975, 1985) and classic articles (1971, 1979), he has developed what is now commonly referred to as *transactions cost economics*.

Interestingly, although Williamson's theory is based on the notion of incomplete contracts, which is the starting point for the property-rights theory of Grossman, Hart, and Moore discussed in this chapter, it provides a different perspective on firms. In his mind, firms are long-term *governance structures* designed to dull the different contracting parties' drive to pursue their self-interest. Firms thus are able to achieve more efficient outcomes through better cooperation, where market-based transactions are likely to break down due to excessive haggling and excessively high bargaining costs.

Another classic article, which explores the consequences for the theory of the firm of *holdup problems* (a notion first articulated in Goldberg, 1976) that arise when contracts are incomplete, is Klein, Crawford, and Alchian (1978). Together with Williamson's transactions cost economics, it provides the main notions that have given rise to the more modern formal theories discussed in this chapter.

Much of the rapidly growing economics literature on the theory of the firm subsequent to Grossman and Hart (1986) and Hart and Moore (1990) is discussed in the survey article by Holmström and Tirole (1989), the Clarendon lectures by Hart (1995), a book by Hansmann (1996), and perspective articles by Holmström and Roberts (1998) and Bolton and Scharfstein (1998).

As discussed in this chapter, financial contracting has been a particularly fruitful application, following the contributions of Aghion and Bolton (1992), Bolton and Scharfstein (1990), and Hart and Moore (1989, 1994, 1998). Beyond the work discussed in this chapter, let us also mention the articles by Berglöf and von Thadden (1994) and Dewatripont and Tirole (1994a) that provide finer predictions on the optimal capital structure of the firm (see Section 12.4.1.2 in Chapter 12 on this).

In the last few years there has also been an explosion of research on the implications of incomplete contracting for the design of economic institutions such as ownership, governance, and the internal organization of the firm. The most recent literature has explored the link between self-enforcing (relational) contracts and asset ownership (see, in particular, Baker, Gibbons, and Murphy, 2002; Halonen, 2002; and Stole and Zwiebel, 1996a, 1996b). Another major line of research has explored the question of the governance of larger firms or organizations with potentially a large number of owners (or voters) and also an administrative structure with multiple managers (see, in particular, Gertner, Scharfstein, and Stein, 1994, and Inderst and Muller, 2003, on internal capital markets in conglomerate firms; Hart and Moore, 2000, Hart and Hölmstrom, 2002, Rajan and Zingales, 2001, and Wernerfelt, 1997, on internal hierarchies of large and growing firms; and Bolton and Rosenthal, 2003, and Aghion and Bolton, 2003, on constitution design, majority voting, and political intervention).

Foundations of Contracting with Unverifiable Information

12.1 Introduction

The literature on incomplete contracts presented in the previous chapter has allowed us to analyze a number of important economic issues that had been left untouched in the earlier parts of this book, which were devoted to "classical" or "complete" contract theory. This latter brand of contract theory, however, has also analyzed the paradigm of mutually observable but unverifiable information through the lens of mechanism design. This approach has led to a literature on Nash implementation, similar to the Bayesian implementation paradigm considered in Chapter 7.

In the Nash implementation paradigm, Maskin (1977) has made the point that it is in principle easy for a mutually observed piece of information, say, a state of nature θ, to be made verifiable and thus contractable to a third party: just ask the parties that are known to have observed θ to announce it, and punish them heavily if they disagree in their announcements. This type of mechanism will generate truth telling about θ as a Nash equilibrium.

This reasoning, however, is subject to several criticisms: (1) While truth telling is a Nash equilibrium, so is coordination of announcements on a single state of nature *that is not the true one*. (2) The punishment of all agents is clearly not in their collective interest: What if the agents decided to tear up the contractual mechanism after a unilateral deviation from truth telling, that is, what if they decided to renegotiate? (3) More fundamentally perhaps, this type of mechanism is not one that is observed in practice.

The implementation literature has mainly focused on issue 1, that is, the uniqueness problem. This abundant literature (surveyed in Moore, 1992) is succinctly covered in the next section, with special emphasis on Maskin's theorem and on its most successful extension, subgame-perfect implementation, due to Moore and Repullo (1988). While this literature has been quite successful at characterizing general implementation results, it is fair to say, however, that it has not really addressed criticism 3.

Issue 2, that is, renegotiation, has been addressed in a general implementation context by Maskin and Moore (1999). It has also been introduced in a number of applications of the observable-but-unverifiable-information paradigm that have focused on the "holdup" problem in bilateral transactions with relation-specific investment (following Goldberg, 1976; Klein, Crawford, and Alchian, 1978; and Williamson, 1975, 1985). As we highlighted in the previous chapter, this problem has been at the heart of the preoccupations of incomplete-contract theorists. Taking a mechanism-design perspective with ex post renegotiation has in fact generated a number of interesting results: As shown in section 12.3, it allows one, first, to rely on implementation techniques to define which outcomes can be implemented and, second, to take advantage of equilibrium renegotiation to show that the optimum can be achieved through a simple initial contract that is later renegotiated.

A central issue raised by incomplete-contract theory is the importance not only of observable-but-unverifiable information but also of ex ante noncontractable actions. This issue has been addressed in the mechanism-design perspective by Maskin and Tirole (1999a, 1999b), who have argued that ex ante noncontractability of actions does not restrict implementability under certain conditions. This question, together with the response by Hart and Moore (1999), based on Segal's (1999a) work, is also summarized in section 12.3.

We then go on to argue, in section 12.4, that another route to address the concerns of incomplete contract theory is to assume not only ex ante but also *ex post* noncontractability of actions. While at first glance this analysis seems to go very much "the incomplete contract route," it is quite standard: the effort variable in a classical moral-hazard model is exactly an action that is noncontractable both ex ante and ex post! One implication of ex post noncontractability of actions, moreover, is that this assumption leads to a theory of authority, provided one is able to contract on "who can take the action." Section 12.4 details the type of results one can obtain under these assumptions, in the context of financial contracting and of delegation of authority.

Finally, we conclude the chapter by looking at a repeated-game setting with ex post unverifiable payoffs that provides an alternative foundation for the notion of authority: While spot-market transactions cannot take advantage of punishment strategies involved in repeated interaction, this statement is not true for an authority relation—where one party "follows orders" and is compensated "fairly" for executing orders. It is shown in section 12.5 that such a relation may dominate spot transactions in relations that are durable enough.

12.2 Nash and Subgame-Perfect Implementation

12.2.1 Nash Implementation: Maskin's Theorem

The key theorem that started the literature on implementation with unverifiable information is due to Maskin (1977). Since in his framework individuals are all assumed to know the state of nature and there is thus no private information between them, implementation is *in Nash equilibrium*. Maskin starts with a set of states of nature Θ and a function/correspondence $f(\theta)$ to be implemented for each state of nature $\theta \in \Theta$. The implementation problem is then the design of a game or mechanism M [with strategies, or messages m_i for each player i and outcomes $g(m_1, \ldots, m_i, \ldots)$, belonging to a set of outcomes Y] that is to be played by the agents and for which *all* Nash equilibria of the game belong to $f(\theta)$. This is particularly challenging if $f(\theta)$ is a function, thereby allowing only one acceptable outcome for each state of nature θ.

Maskin's theorem focuses on two properties of functions/correspondences $f(\theta)$ to be implemented. The first one is *monotonicity:* $f(\theta)$ is said to be monotonic if, for each pair θ and $\tilde{\theta}$ belonging to Θ and for each $y \in Y$ such that $y \in f(\theta)$, we have also $y \in f(\tilde{\theta})$ whenever, for each player i and each outcome $z \in Y$, if y is (weakly) preferred to z by player i in state θ, y is also (weakly) preferred to z by player i in state $\tilde{\theta}$.

At first glance, monotonicity seems like a very natural property for functions/correspondences to be implemented: It says that if an outcome y belongs to the acceptable set $f(\theta)$ for state θ, it also belongs to $f(\tilde{\theta})$, the acceptable set for any state $\tilde{\theta}$ for which, relative to state θ, outcome y never "goes down" in the ranking of any individual relative to any other outcome z. But while this is indeed a natural efficiency condition, the next subsection will indicate that it is in fact quite restrictive in terms of distributional objectives.

The second property of functions/correspondences $f(\theta)$ to be implemented is referred to as *weak no-veto power* (WNVP): $f(\theta)$ satisfies WNVP if, for each state θ, outcome y must be in the acceptable set $f(\theta)$ whenever at most one agent does not have outcome y as his or her preferred outcome in Y.

This property is a weak form of nondictatorship, applying to the case where all agents but one agree on the most preferred outcome. It is much less restrictive than monotonicity, and, in particular, in the presence of a private good, such as money, it is trivially satisfied. Indeed, there is no allocation of money that is "the best one" for more than one agent at a time if they all value money.

We are now ready to state Maskin's theorem, which consists in two parts:

(i) *Necessary condition:* If $f(\theta)$ is Nash implementable, then it is monotonic.

(ii) *Sufficient condition:* With at least three agents, if $f(\theta)$ is monotonic and satisfies WNVP, then it is Nash implementable.

Let us first establish the necessary part (i) by contradiction. If $f(\theta)$ is not monotonic, then there exists a pair of states of nature θ, $\tilde{\theta}$ and an outcome y such that $y \in f(\theta)$ and $y \notin f(\tilde{\theta})$ even though, for each agent i and each outcome $z \in Y$, if y is (weakly) preferred to z by agent i in state θ, y is also (weakly) preferred to z by agent i in state $\tilde{\theta}$.

However, saying that $f(\theta)$ is implementable and that y belongs to $f(\theta)$ means that there exists a mechanism M whose Nash equilibrium set for state θ includes outcome y. But this statement means that outcome y is also a Nash equilibrium in state $\tilde{\theta}$: Saying that y is a Nash equilibrium for state θ, with equilibrium vector of messages m^*, means that outcome y is preferred to any other outcome $g(m_i, m^*_{-i})$ for each agent i and message m_i; however, given our assumption on y, θ, and $\tilde{\theta}$, outcome y must also be preferred to any other outcome $g(m_i, m^*_{-i})$ for each agent i and message m_i in state $\tilde{\theta}$. Consequently, outcome y is also a Nash equilibrium in state $\tilde{\theta}$; that is, $y \in f(\tilde{\theta})$, a contradiction which proves claim (i).

Let us now prove the sufficient condition (ii). This can be proved by construction: Take a mechanism M where the set of messages for agent i is $\{(\theta, y, n) \mid \theta \in \Theta, y \in Y, n \in N\}$, with the following properties: (1) If all announcements concerning θ and y are identical across agents and $y \in f(\theta)$, then the outcome $g(\cdot) = y$; (2) if all agents but i announce the same θ and the same $y \in f(\theta)$, while agent i announces a state $\tilde{\theta}$ and an outcome z, then the outcome of the mechanism is z if agent i (weakly) prefers y to z in state θ, and the outcome of the mechanism is y otherwise; and (3) in all other cases, the outcome of the mechanism is $\tilde{y}$ where outcome $\tilde{y}$ is the one announced by the agent who has announced the highest positive integer n.

Clearly, for each state θ and outcome $y \in f(\theta)$, y is a Nash equilibrium outcome. The key question is, Can an outcome $\tilde{y} \notin f(\theta)$ also be a Nash equilibrium? It cannot, as may be seen as follows:

• First, assume that everybody announces a state $\tilde{\theta}$ and an outcome $\tilde{y}$, such that $\tilde{y} \in f(\tilde{\theta})$ but $\tilde{y} \notin f(\theta)$. Then, by monotonicity, there exist an agent i and an outcome z such that i (weakly) prefers $\tilde{y}$ to z in state $\tilde{\theta}$ but strictly prefers z to $\tilde{y}$ in state θ. Consequently, by property (2), i can deviate and impose z, so that $\tilde{y}$ is not a Nash equilibrium.

• Second, if $\tilde{y}$ is the result of nonunanimous announcements about state θ and outcome $\tilde{y}$, then, by property (3), there is at most one agent who cannot, by deviating alone, impose his or her preferred outcome. (This would be the agent facing other agents who *all* play the same strategy.) All other agents can do it, by announcing their preferred outcome and announcing an integer higher than the equilibrium announcements of the other agents. Consequently, for $\tilde{y}$ to be a Nash equilibrium, by WNVP, it must belong to $f(\theta)$.

• Third, by property (3), the argument just made also applies in the case of unanimous announcements about a state of nature $\tilde{\theta}$ and an outcome $\tilde{y} \notin f(\tilde{\theta})$. Claim (ii) has thus been established.

The intuition for Maskin's result is as follows. Consider first the necessary condition (i). It simply says that, if an outcome $y \in f(\theta)$ is a Nash equilibrium of a mechanism in state θ, so will it be in any state $\tilde{\theta}$ for which this outcome remains as attractive relative to other outcomes as in state θ. The sufficiency part (ii) is much less immediate. It shows how to construct a mechanism that uniquely implements any monotonic function/correspondence that satisfies WNVP.

The idea of the construction is to get rid of undesired Nash equilibria by appropriately enriching the strategy space the agents have at their disposal. First, it gets rid of the possibility that all agents agree on a state θ and an outcome $y \in f(\theta)$ in the case that the true state of nature is not θ. This is taken care of by allowing any single agent to impose another outcome *that he or she is known not to prefer to outcome y if the true state is really θ*. By monotonicity of $f(\theta)$, this exactly gets rid of all undesired outcomes. Second, the mechanism prevents other equilibria where all agents either agree on a θ and a $y \notin f(\theta)$ or fail to agree unanimously. Here, the trick used to get rid of this equilibrium is to allow agents to single-handedly impose their favorite outcome by "naming the largest integer of all the integers chosen by the agents." This "integer game" works because any candidate equilibrium involves prespecified strategies, and thus prespecified integers, so that a deviation can always involve a larger integer than these candidate strategies.[1] Equilibria thus fail to exist because the agents have been endowed with *unbounded strategy sets*.

---

1. And it works in all possible cases because of WNVP.

12.2.2   Subgame-Perfect Implementation

Maskin's theorem has generated a whole literature about unique implementation under unverifiable information. For a very good survey, see Moore (1992). Some studies make the implementation problem more difficult by excluding unrealistic mechanisms, for example, those that include integer games as a way to eliminate undesirable equilibria. Other studies instead make the implementation problem less difficult by considering approximate (or "virtual") implementation or by considering a subset of Nash equilibria. Among these, subgame-perfect implementation, pioneered by Moore and Repullo (1988), is particularly noteworthy, because it shows that most desirable outcomes are in fact uniquely implementable as subgame-perfect equilibria.

As an illustration, we focus here on a public-good example with two agents, $i = 1, 2$, and a decision $y \in \{0, 1\}$; $y = 1$ means that the public good is produced, while $y = 0$ means it is not. The decision rule can also specify associated net transfers $(t_1, t_2) \in R^2$. Agent i's preference depends on a parameter θ_i, with the state of nature $\theta = (\theta_1, \theta_2) \in \Theta$. Specifically, agent 1's payoff is $\theta_1 y + t_1$, and agent 2's payoff is $\theta_2 y + t_2$. Parameters θ_1 and θ_2 are interpreted here as the utilities the agents derive from the public good *net of its production cost*.

A decision rule can be defined as a triple $[y(\theta), t_1(\theta), t_2(\theta)]$. The monotonicity assumption is very restrictive here, in preventing distributional concerns from being taken care of. Indeed, note that the allocatively efficient decision involves $y(\theta) = 1$ if and only if $\theta_1 + \theta_2 \geq 0$. If one takes a state of nature (θ_1, θ_2) where the decision is to produce the good and where the transfers are $[t_1(\theta), t_2(\theta)]$, we cannot rule out this outcome from the decision correspondence for any other state where, for example, the only difference with (θ_1, θ_2) is that parameter θ_1 has increased. Indeed, in this new state of nature, the outcome $[y(\theta), t_1(\theta), t_2(\theta)]$ has not gone down in any individual ranking of outcomes relative to state of nature θ. However, distributional concerns would imply that one would naturally want agent 1 to receive a lower net transfer, since his or her utility from the decision to produce the good has increased.

The strength of subgame-perfect implementation is that the monotonicity assumption is not required anymore: In fact any outcome rule $[y(\theta), t_1(\theta), t_2(\theta)]$ can be easily implemented as a unique subgame-perfect equilibrium using the following two-stage mechanism:

• *Stage 1:* (*a*) agent 1 announces a parameter θ_1; (*b*) agent 2 "agrees," in which case one goes to stage 2, or "challenges," that is, announces a parameter $\tilde{\theta}_1 \neq \theta_1$; (*c*) when challenged, agent 1 then has to choose between two options (and that choice is then implemented): either an outcome ($x, t_x - \Delta t$, $-t_x - \Delta t$) or an outcome ($z, t_z - \Delta t, -t_z + \Delta t$), such that Δt is very large and

$$\theta_1 x + t_x > \theta_1 z + t_z$$

and

$$\tilde{\theta}_1 x + t_x < \tilde{\theta}_1 z + t_z$$

• *Stage 2* (if agent 1 has not been challenged): same as stage 1, but with the roles reversed: agent 2 first announces θ_2, then if agent 1 agrees, outcome $[y(\theta_1, \theta_2), t_1(\theta_1, \theta_2), t_2(\theta_1, \theta_2)]$ is implemented; otherwise, move to a step (*c*) similar to the one in stage 1.

The idea of the mechanism is as follows: Each agent is asked in turn to reveal his or her preference parameter, and each is deterred from lying because, by being challenged, he or she then has to pay the principal an amount Δt that is chosen to be very large. However, the challenged agent has the possibility to "get back" at the challenger, by "sticking to the initial choice," that is, choosing decision x instead of decision z. In this case, the challenger also has to pay the principal Δt, while if the challenged agent "concedes," by choosing decision z, the challenger pockets Δt. The mechanism induces truth telling because, for each pair of parameters $\theta_i \neq \tilde{\theta}_i$, there exist x, z, t_x, t_z satisfying the conditions of step (*c*) of stage 1 (this can be done by choosing $x = 1$ and $z = 0$ if $\theta_i > \tilde{\theta}_i$, and $x = 0$ and $z = 1$ otherwise). And if the set of states of nature Θ is finite, there exists an amount Δt large enough to simultaneously prevent deviations from truth telling and ludicrous challenges.

The strength of subgame perfection is that, in comparison with Nash implementation, we add an off-equilibrium possibility of checking individual preferences: We need only to find *any outcome pair* for which there is a preference reversal between the parameter θ_i announced by agent i and the parameter $\tilde{\theta}_i$ announced by the challenger. This requirement is typically easy to satisfy in economic applications. The mechanism has several additional attractive properties: (1) It is balanced in equilibrium if for each state θ we have $t_1(\theta) + t_2(\theta) = 0$; (2) if we had at least three agents, we could have balancedness even out of equilibrium, because in the case where both the challenged agent and the challenger have to pay Δt, they could pay it to a third agent; finally (3), for the mechanism to work, for each agent i, we need to identify only one other agent beyond i that has observed para-meter θ_i.

Note, however, that the preceding mechanism relies to a great extent on the uncompromising faith in rationality of all players that underlies subgame-perfect equilibrium: If in step (a) of stage 1, agent 1 deviates from truth telling, agent 2 decides to challenge in step (b) *because he or she has faith in the fact that agent 1 will make a payoff-maximizing decision in step* (c). This reasoning is the key behind equilibrium truth telling in step (a). However, under this reasoning, a deviation from truth telling is sure to cost agent 1 a very large amount Δt. It then takes quite some confidence for agent 2 to think that agent 1 will "come back to his or her senses" in step (c) and optimize over a stake that is typically much smaller. This is in fact a general problem with subgame-perfect equilibrium in games where players take actions repeatedly: Deviations are always considered to be "one-shot deviations from rationality" that do not shatter the faith players have in the subsequent rationality of their opponents. However, here, in contrast to standard game theory, we have specifically *designed* a game instead of analyzing one whose rules are derived from economic stylized facts. And we have specifically chosen the cost of the initial deviation to be very large in case a challenge occurs, and as a result, it is really the move in step (a) that is the crucial one for agent 1. Therefore, the preceding criticism of subgame perfection is particularly relevant here.

A second criticism of the preceding mechanism is that, once an agent has been challenged, the continuation equilibrium may involve ex post inefficient outcomes, so that it is subject to the renegotiation critique. In the next section we present models that address this critique. We do it in the context of a specific bilateral investment setting.

12.3   The Holdup Problem

The notion of "hold-up problem" has first been defined and addressed in the seminal article by Goldberg (1976). It has been developed further by Klein, Crawford, and Alchian (1978) and Williamson (1975, 1985). Here we consider the formulation of the contracting problem giving rise to a hold-up problem due to Hart and Moore (1988): Two contracting parties, a prospective buyer and a prospective seller, can enter a relationship in which they can end up trading a quantity $q \in [0, 1]$ at a price P. The utility they obtain from trading depends on the buyer's valuation v and the seller's production cost c. These utilities are uncertain at the time of contracting and can be influenced by specific investments made by each party at an earlier date. Specifically, we make the following assumptions:

$$v \in \{v_L, v_H\}, \quad \text{with } v_L < v_H \quad \text{and} \quad \Pr(v_H) = j$$

where investment j costs the buyer $\psi(j)$, and

$$c \in \{c_L, c_H\}, \quad \text{with } c_L < c_H \quad \text{and} \quad \Pr(c_L) = i$$

where investment i costs the seller $\phi(i)$. Assume that the two investment-cost functions are increasing and convex, and that they are *sunk* whatever the ex post level of trade. The ex post payoff levels are thus

$$vq - P - \psi(j)$$

for the buyer and

$$P - cq - \phi(i)$$

for the seller. The timing is as follows. First, the parties contract; second, they simultaneously choose their investment levels i and j; third, they *both* learn the state of nature $\theta = (v, c)$; fourth, they execute the contract.

What is the first-best outcome? Assume for simplicity that

$$c_H > v_H > c_L > v_L$$

Under this assumption, the *ex post efficient* level of trade is $q = 1$ if $\theta = (v_H, c_L)$ and 0 otherwise. As for ex ante efficiency, since the parties are assumed to be risk neutral, it is equivalent to investment efficiency; that is, i and j must result from

$$\max_{i,j} \{ij(v_H - c_L) - \psi(j) - \phi(i)\}$$

Assuming an interior solution, the first-order conditions give us the optimal investment levels i^* and j^*:

$$i^*(v_H - c_L) = \psi'(j^*)$$

and

$$j^*(v_H - c_L) = \phi'(i^*)$$

The contracting problem the literature has analyzed is one where the state of nature $\theta = (v, c)$ and the investment levels i and j are not contractable, although θ is observable to both contracting parties ex post. If there is spot contracting ex post, after θ is realized and investments i and j are sunk, and if the gains from trade at that point are evenly divided between buyer and seller, there will be underinvestment in equilibrium as we have already noted and as Figure 12.1 below illustrates. The solid curves represent the optimal investment functions i^* and j^* while the dashed curves represent the best response functions under spot contracting:

$$\frac{1}{2} i(v_H - c_L) = \psi'(j^{br})$$

and

$$\frac{1}{2} j(v_H - c_L) = \phi'(i^{br})$$

The difficulty faced by the contracting parties ex ante is how to formulate an optimal long-term contract that is independent of θ, which mitigates

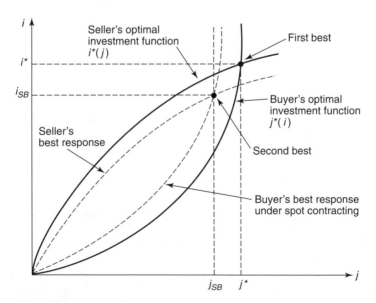

Figure 12.1
Underinvestment with a Holdup Problem

this underinvestment problem. As explained in the next subsections, the contributions in the literature differ in the following respects:

• First, they make different assumptions on the extent to which the level of trade is contractable: Chung (1991), Aghion, Dewatripont, and Rey (1994, hereafter ADR), and Noldeke and Schmidt (1995) allow for "specific-performance contracts," where the contract can specify a given level of trade that parties can request ex post, whether it is efficient or not. Instead, Hart and Moore (1988) focus on "contracting at will," where courts only enforce price schedules contingent on the level of trade, without being able to identify who was responsible for the possible failure to trade. This issue will prove crucial for the ability of the contract to achieve first-best outcomes or not.

• Second, while all contributions assume that the parties cannot commit not to undertake ex post Pareto-improving renegotiations, they differ in their assumptions about the ability to contractually influence the renegotiation process. ADR go furthest in contractual "renegotiation design," by assuming that relative bargaining powers in renegotiation can be contractually chosen. While they focus on specific exogenous bargaining games, Chung, Noldeke-Schmidt, and Hart-Moore end up with the same (one-sided) distribution of bargaining powers as ADR. Instead, Edlin and Reichelstein (1996) assume simple Nash bargaining powers in the renegotiation process. It turns out, however, that assumptions about bargaining powers are not as important as the distinction between specific performance and contracting at will.

• Finally, whereas all the preceding contributions rule out direct externalities, that is, any direct effect of the buyer's investment on the seller's cost or of the seller's investment on the buyer's valuation, Che and Hausch (1999) allow for such externalities. They show that not only is the first best not generally reachable anymore, but *the null contract* may be the optimal contract. And Segal (1999a) obtains a similar result without such direct externalities but for environments that are very "complex."

12.3.1   Specific Performance Contracts and Renegotiation Design

Let us first assume that the contract can specify "default options" that parties can request whenever trade is possible. In this case, one can define the level of trade $\tilde{q}$ such that

$$\tilde{q}(c_H - c_L) = \phi'(i^*)$$

and one can consider the following contractual mechanism: Once θ has been realized, the parties play the following game: in stage 1, the buyer can make an offer (P, q) to the seller; in stage 2, the seller accepts the offer (and trade takes place at these terms), or rejects it, in which case $\tilde{q}$ is traded, at a prespecified price $\tilde{P}$ designed to share the ex ante surplus according to initial bargaining strengths.

This mechanism implements the first best. Indeed, note first that the buyer has full bargaining power in the two-stage game. She will thus offer to trade the ex post efficient quantity while leaving the seller indifferent between this trade and his default-option payoff. While ex post efficiency is guaranteed, what about investment efficiency? The seller will anticipate obtaining his default option payoff whatever the ex post level of trade, so that he will solve

$$\max \{\tilde{P} - ic_L\tilde{q} - (1-i)c_H\tilde{q} - \phi(i)\}$$

By the construction of $\tilde{q}$, investment level i^* is the seller's optimal choice, whatever the buyer's investment may be. Finally, since the buyer has full bargaining power, she is residual claimant on her investment and solves

$$\max\{i^* j(v_H - c_L) - [\tilde{P} - i^* c_L\tilde{q} - (1-i^*)c_H\tilde{q}] - \psi(j)\}$$

She thus maximizes total surplus minus the payoff of the seller (which does not depend on her investment) and minus her cost of investment. Consequently, she chooses $j = j^*$ if the seller chooses $i = i^*$.

The preceding mechanism thus induces efficient *bilateral* investment and circumvents the "moral-hazard-in-teams" problem à la Holmström (1982b), that we discussed in Chapter 8. For the buyer, efficient investment is achieved simply by making her a residual claimant. More intriguing is the case of the seller, who has the appropriate incentive to invest *despite having no bargaining power at all*. His incentive to invest comes from his being able to request the default option, whose attractiveness rises when his production cost goes down. This option makes the seller's payoff sensitive to his investment, and, through this second instrument, both parties can have proper incentives to invest.

The preceding mechanism is in the spirit of subgame-perfect implementation, as it is a multistage mechanism with a unique subgame-perfect equilibrium (where stage 1 could be reinterpreted as having the buyer "announce θ"). Moreover, in this game each party acts only once, so that, in comparison with the Moore-Repullo example, the reliance on backward induction is less objectionable. Still, the mechanism relies on the ability of the parties to commit to ex post inefficient outcomes: If in stage 1 the buyer has made a "crazy offer," the seller may face two ex post inefficient possibilities and no way out of this suboptimal choice.

ADR, however, provide a reinterpretation of this mechanism that involves a much-weakened ability of the parties to commit not to engage in Pareto-improving renegotiations: Assume that, in the absence of a contract, the parties bargain—starting at a date t after θ has been observed—about the terms of trade in an alternating-offer bargaining game à la Rubinstein (1982). As is well known, in state $\theta = (v_H, c_L)$ there is a unique stationary subgame-perfect equilibrium of this game for any pair of discount factors $\delta_B < 1$ for the buyer and $\delta_S < 1$ for the seller. Indeed, when it is her turn to make an offer P^B, the buyer solves

$$\min P^B \text{ such that } P^B - c_L \geq \delta_S (P^S - c_L)$$

Similarly, when it is his turn to make an offer P^S, the seller solves

$$\max P^S \text{ such that } v_H - P^S \geq \delta_B (v_H - P^B)$$

Since at the optimum these two inequalities are binding, uniqueness follows (with trade taking place immediately at time t). If the seller makes the first offer, the price is

$$P^S = \frac{1-\delta_B}{1-\delta_B\delta_S} v_H + \delta_B \frac{1-\delta_S}{1-\delta_B\delta_S} c_L$$

If instead the buyer can make the first offer, the price is

$$P^B = \delta_S \frac{1-\delta_B}{1-\delta_B\delta_S} v_H + \frac{1-\delta_S}{1-\delta_B\delta_S} c_L$$

Since discount factors are less than 1 and $v_H > c_L$, the price offered by the buyer is lower than the price offered by the seller. If, however, both discount factors are equal and tend to 1, then both prices tend to $(v_H + c_L)/2$, so that gains from trade are shared equally. But if one party becomes very patient relative to the other ($\delta_k \to 1$ while δ_l remains bounded away from 1), he or she obtains the entire surplus from trade.

How can the contract influence the bargaining process? First assume that the contract can specify a default option $(\tilde{P}, \tilde{q})$ that each party can enforce when it is his or her turn to react to the offer by the other party: Beyond accepting or waiting one period to be able to make an offer, it can request the default option. This action turns the bargaining game into an alternating-offer game with an "outside" option, which has been studied by Binmore, Rubinstein, and Wolinsky (1986), who have defined the so-called *outside-option principle:* Call $(\tilde{U}_B, \tilde{U}_S)$ the parties' payoffs associated with the outside option. Call (U_B^*, U_S^*) the parties' (ex post efficient) payoffs in the bargaining game *without* the outside option. Then, if (U_B^*, U_S^*) Pareto-dominates $(\tilde{U}_B, \tilde{U}_S)$, the equilibrium payoffs of the game with the outside option are (U_B^*, U_S^*). If (U_B^*, U_S^*) does not Pareto-dominate $(\tilde{U}_B, \tilde{U}_S)$, the outcome of the game with outside option is ex post efficient and gives party k for whom $\tilde{U}_k > U_k^*$ his or her outside option payoff.

In order to limit the seller to his default-option payoff, one has to make sure this payoff is better for him than the outcome of bargaining without the default option. This outcome can be ensured by introducing a *penalty for delayed trade* that the seller would have to pay the buyer. If this penalty is big enough, the seller will immediately accept any offer (P, q) that is better for him than $(\tilde{P}, \tilde{q})$, in order to avoid delay.

The first-best outcome can thus be implemented. Moreover, it can be achieved in a "light" way, that is, through a relatively simple contract, consisting in a default option and a penalty for delayed trade. Simplicity is in fact achieved because the contract allows for *equilibrium renegotiation* and only *supplements* the underlying bargaining structure the agents have at their disposal in the absence of contracting.

One important assumption, however, is that renegotiation stops whenever the default option has been chosen by one party. This is reasonable if there is, for example, a fixed cost to be incurred whenever the seller produces, so that multiple trades over time would be excessively costly. In such a case, "requesting the default option" simply means that the seller unilaterally decides to produce. In some environments, however, the technology may allow the parties, after the default level of trade has occurred, to keep bargaining if the ex post efficient trade is higher than the default trade. This possibility would undermine the preceding results, as section 12.3.2.2 will show.

12.3.2 Option Contracts and Contracting at Will

The original holdup model of Hart and Moore (1988) did not introduce renegotiation design, but instead considered the following bargaining game (which we present in simplified form, following Noldeke and Schmidt,

1995): After θ has been realized, the parties can simultaneously send one another new written trading offers. Assume now that trade can take only the values 0 and 1, so that an offer consists in at most two prices, since it can concern only "trade" and "no trade." Assume the initial contract was a pair (P_0, P_1) (for no trade and trade, respectively) and call the new offers by the buyer and seller (P_0^B, P_1^B) and (P_0^S, P_1^S). Once the stage where the parties exchange new offers is over, trade does or does not take place (in a way that we will specify) and a payment is made, possibly after the intervention of courts. These are assumed to be able to observe whether trade has taken place or not and to enforce the corresponding payment. This payment is the original one, that is, P_k if a quantity k was exchanged ($k = 0, 1$), unless a party finds it in his or her interest to show the court a new written offer made by the other party. These assumptions guarantee that the initial contract protects each party against unilateral violations while allowing for Pareto-improving renegotiations.

In equilibrium, the only offers ever shown to the court are those sent by the buyer to the seller saying she accepts a *higher* price and those sent by the seller to the buyer saying he accepts a *lower* price. Why would such offers ever be written? Because they may be the only way to ensure that the other party accepts the ex post efficient trade.

The outcome of this game depends on the ability to enforce default options, as we now show.

12.3.2.1 Option Contracts

Noldeke and Schmidt (1995) allow for specific performance contracts, as in ADR. They consider option contracts, where the seller receives a price P_0 if the good is not delivered, and has the option to deliver the good and receive an additional payment K (so that $P_1 = P_0 + K$).

How does renegotiation proceed in this setting? Three cases have to be distinguished:

• First, consider the case $K < c_L$. Barring renegotiation, the seller never has an incentive to deliver the good in this case. This is ex post efficient whenever the buyer's valuation is low or the seller's cost is high (or both), in which case no trade takes place and the equilibrium payment made by the seller is P_0. But what happens in state $\theta = (v_H, c_L)$, where trade is efficient? Achieving trade requires raising the premium the seller receives for delivery at least up to c_L. In fact, the buyer can make sure not to have to raise it further: By sending a letter offering $P_1^B = P_0 + c_L$, the buyer induces the seller to deliver the good and knows the seller has the incentive to show this letter to the court. Indeed, otherwise the enforced price would be the lower P_1. Moreover, any letter sent by the seller requiring a higher price would simply not be shown to the court by the buyer. Consequently, just as in ADR, one party has full bargaining power: In this game, the party who behaves in equilibrium in a way that is suboptimal *at the initial contract prices* has no bargaining power at all. And since here it is only the seller that makes the trade decision (unlike in the next subsection), it is always the buyer who has full bargaining power.

- Second, consider the case $c_L < K < c_H$. Barring renegotiation, ex post inefficiency occurs when both the seller's cost and the buyer's valuation are low, since the seller would find it profitable to deliver the good although $v_L < c_L$. Once again, the buyer can extract the full surplus from renegotiation, by sending a letter agreeing to a higher price for no trade, that is, $P_0^B = P_1 - c_L$.

- Finally, when $c_H < K$, the seller always wants to deliver the good, and this case is inefficient when the buyer's valuation is low or the seller's cost is high (or both). As before, the buyer can extract the full surplus from renegotiation by sending a letter agreeing to a higher price for no trade, that is, $P_0^B = P_1 - c$, where c is the realized cost of the seller.

This mechanism is similar to the one presented in the previous subsection: The buyer has full bargaining power, while the seller receives his initial contract payoff, which depends on the value of his cost even in cases where trade may not take place ex post. Let us focus on the case where $c_L < K < c_H$, where the seller obtains P_0 when his cost is high, and $P_1 - c_L = P_0 + K - c_L$ when his cost is low. He thus chooses his investment to solve

$$\max \{i(K - c_L) - \phi(i)\}$$

To ensure an appropriate investment choice, K has to be chosen so that

$$K - c_L = \phi'(i^*)$$

This implies $K < c_H$, since from the definition of the first-best outcome, we have

$$\phi'(i^*) = j^*(v_H - c_L) < v_H - c_L < c_H - c_L$$

Given the choice of K, it is optimal for the seller to make the first-best investment choice, whatever the investment decision of the buyer. As for the buyer, as in the previous subsection, she is residual claimant with respect to her investment choice—having full bargaining power in the renegotiation—so she chooses $j = j^*$ when the seller chooses $i = i^*$. The first-best outcome is implemented again, this time with a simple option contract $(P_0, P_1 = P_0 + K)$.

12.3.2.2 Contracting at Will

Assume now, as in the original Hart-Moore (1988) model, that specific performance contracts cannot be enforced by courts. Think, for example, that, were the seller to deliver the good, the buyer could always claim it is not of "appropriate" quality. If quality is unverifiable, the court can only observe whether trade took place and enforce quantity-contingent price schedules, but cannot distinguish who is responsible for the lack of trade. In this setup, trade takes place only if *both* parties want it to happen. Hart and Moore use the following model: After θ has been realized, the parties can exchange written messages with new price offers. Then both parties simultaneously decide whether they want to go ahead with trade. Only if both agree does trade take place, followed by the same associated payments as before.

Consider a simple contract (P_0, P_1). Under these terms, trade takes place if and only if $v \geq P_1 - P_0 \geq c$. If this condition is not met, at least one party prefers not to trade, and no trade is the outcome. This is ex post efficient unless $\theta = (v_H, c_L)$, in which case we have the following two possibilities:

• If $P_1 - P_0 > v_H > c_L$, although trade is efficient, the buyer finds it too expensive. In this case, it is the seller who has full bargaining power, since he can ensure trade by sending the buyer a letter agreeing to $P_1^S = P_0 + v_H$. With this offer, the buyer is ready to trade and is unable to induce the seller to agree to any lower price.

• If $v_H > c_L > P_1 - P_0$, it is now the seller who finds trade too costly for the price difference. The buyer now has full bargaining power, being able to induce trade by agreeing to $P_1^B = P_0 + c_L$. As before, the full bargaining power goes to the party who would benefit from trading at the initial contracting prices.

The preceding reasoning indicates that in this example there is no loss of generality in choosing P_0 and P_1 such that $v_H \geq P_1 - P_0 \geq c_L$, since price differences that do not satisfy these inequalities are renegotiated so as to (just) satisfy them. How much investment does such a renegotiation-proof contract generate? The key idea with at-will contracting is that, in case of disagreement, the starting point of renegotiation is always no trade, so that the parties benefit from their own investment only when it is efficient to trade. The payoffs are therefore

$$i j[v_H - (P_1 - P_0)] - P_0 - \psi(j)$$

for the buyer, and

$$P_0 + i j[(P_1 - P_0) - c_L] - \phi(i)$$

for the seller. Consequently, the classical moral-hazard-in-teams problem arises, with underinvestment as the outcome. Hart and Moore thus provide foundations to the arguments of Goldberg, Klein, Crawford, and Alchian, and Williamson that underinvestment is likely when long-term contracts are incomplete.

Note finally that the preceding result assumes that the parties sign a simple contract (P_0, P_1). Could they improve upon it using message games? Hart and Moore show that they cannot, so that, just as in subsections 12.3.1 and 12.3.2.1, the optimum is achieved through a simple contract that relies on equilibrium renegotiation.

12.3.3   Direct Externalities

Let us now introduce direct investment externalities, as done by Che and Hausch (1999). For simplicity, assume that only the seller can profitably invest in the relationship. Assume, moreover, that the seller's investment has an impact not only on his production cost but also on the quality of the product. Specifically, the seller's investment influences not only his cost in that $\Pr(c_L) = \beta i$ but also the buyer's valuation in that $\Pr(v_H) = \gamma i$. The first best is then the result of

$$\max\{\beta \gamma i^2 (v_H - c_L) - \phi(i)\}$$

Assuming an interior solution, the first-order condition implies

$$2\beta \gamma i^* (v_H - c_L) = \phi'(i^*)$$

As shown by Che and Hausch, direct externalities can dramatically affect the efficiency properties of contracts. To illustrate, assume the parties can initially sign a simple specific-performance contract $(\tilde{P}, \tilde{q})$. Following Edlin and Reichelstein (1996), assume also that the renegotiation that follows the investment choice and the realization of θ can be represented by generalized Nash bargaining, leading to ex post efficiency with a share

α of the surplus from renegotiation going to the seller and a share $(1 - \alpha)$ going to the buyer. The seller's expected payoff from the contract $(\tilde{P}, \tilde{q})$ is his default payoff plus a share α of the surplus from renegotiation, that is,

$$E_{(v,c)|i}\{\tilde{P} - c\tilde{q} + \alpha[(v - c)q^* - (v - c)\tilde{q}]\} - \phi(i)$$

where q^* is the first-best level of trade [that is, 0 unless $\theta = (v_H, c_L)$]. This expression is therefore equal to

$$\tilde{P} + \alpha\beta\gamma i^2(v_H - c_L) - [(1 - \alpha)E_{(v,c)|i}(c\tilde{q}) + \alpha E_{(v,c)|i}(v\tilde{q})] - \phi(i)$$

or, equivalently,

$$\tilde{P} + \alpha\beta\gamma i^2(v_H - c_L) - \tilde{q}\ \{(1 - \alpha)[c_H - \beta i(c_H - c_L)] + \alpha[v_L + \gamma i(v_H - v_L)]\} - \phi(i)$$

This latter expression identifies three effects from an increase in investment i on the seller's payoff:

• The first effect $[\alpha\beta\gamma i^2(v_H - c_L)]$ refers to the fact that the seller captures a share α from the surplus generated by investing. For $\alpha < 1$, this in itself is insufficient to avoid underinvestment.

• The second effect $[\tilde{q}(1 - \alpha)\beta i(c_H - c_L)]$ arises because, by investing, the seller improves his own default payoff. Just as in the earlier cases, this provides additional incentives to invest and the more so the higher the default option $\tilde{q}$.

• The third, countervailing, effect $[-\tilde{q}\alpha\gamma i(v_H - v_L)]$, is due to the fact that, by investing, the seller improves the default option *of the buyer*. This externality results in a *disincentive* to invest. Once again, the effect is stronger the higher the default option $\tilde{q}$.

The last two effects are linear in $\tilde{q}$, which does not appear in the first effect. Raising $\tilde{q}$ thus raises incentives to invest if and only if

$$\alpha\gamma(v_H - v_L) \leq (1 - \alpha)\beta(c_H - c_L)$$

If this condition is not satisfied—which happens if α or γ is large or β is small, for example—then setting $\tilde{q} = 0$ is optimal: The null contract is the optimal initial contract. One case that is very intuitive is $\beta = 0$: When the seller's investment only improves the valuation of the buyer and not the seller's cost, positive default options only improve the buyer's bargaining position when the seller invests more. Consequently, they act as a disincentive to invest and are counterproductive in comparison with the null contract.[2]

Che and Hausch, moreover, have shown that no message-contingent contract can improve on simple contracts of the form ($\tilde{P}$, $\tilde{q}$). This is thus a general lesson from the entire holdup literature we have considered here, whether the optimal contract achieves the first-best outcome (as in ADR or Noldeke-Schmidt) or not (as in Hart-Moore or Che-Hausch): By relying on equilibrium renegotiation, it is possible to derive simple optimal contracts.

12.3.4   Complexity

The contracts we have discussed so far in this chapter assume unverifiability of the state of nature but not of trades, a type of unverifiability stressed in the Grossman-Hart-Moore incomplete-contract paradigm. One reason trades may not be contractable, however, is the excessive *complexity* involved in specifying ex ante the nature of transactions: The exact specifications of ex post transactions may not be known yet—for example, if we are talking of new products and if investment concerns R&D. The mechanism-design question is then, What can contracts achieve when actions are contractable ex post but not ex ante, especially in "complex" environments?

Maskin and Tirole (1999a, 1999b) have identified conditions under which ex ante noncontractability of actions is irrelevant, thereby questioning the incomplete-contract methodology à la Grossman-Hart-Moore. Their key observation is that, while Grossman, Hart, and Moore assume non-contractability of actions ex ante, they assume that the *payoff consequences* of the various actions that could be taken ex post can be *foreseen*. This foresight is indeed necessary in order to be able to make rational investment choices before uncertainty is realized. But, remarkably, it also allows Maskin and Tirole to construct a mechanism (which builds upon subgame-perfect-implementation results) that does not require specifying actions ex ante. Instead, the mechanism specifies transfers and the right to make offers ex post contingent on announcements about the state of nature (and its payoff consequences).

Maskin and Tirole make an important methodological contribution. Their approach, however, is rather abstract, and we shall only discuss it in this

---

2. Bernheim and Whinston (1998b) expand on this point in a more general setting.

chapter in the context of a specific holdup model developed by Segal (1999a). Segal's main goal is in fact to define a notion of complexity of the trading environment and to relate it to the effectiveness of contracting. In his setting, when complexity grows without bounds, contracting loses its power and we are left with the null contract, just as in Che and Hausch (1999). Segal thus provides a foundation for contractual "incompleteness" connected to the difficulty of specifying in advance the realization of uncertainty. In this section, we develop Segal's insight while relying on the formulation, results, and proofs contained in Hart and Moore (1999), who simplify the analysis and illustrate and qualify the results of Maskin and Tirole (1999a).

Assume a contracting problem between two risk-neutral agents, a buyer and a seller. Only the seller can invest to raise the surplus from trade. The problem has three stages: in stage 1 contracting takes place, in stage 2 the seller invests, and in stage 3 the state of nature is observed by both parties and trade takes place. Assume it is always efficient ex post to trade one unit of a good, or "widget," but there is uncertainty ex ante about which "type" of widget should be traded. There are initially N types of widgets. Types are contractible ex post. One type only should be traded. Call it the "special" widget, generating constant valuation v for the buyer and random cost c for the seller. Ex ante, $c \in \{c_L, c_H\}$, with $c_L < c_H < v$ and $\Pr(c_L) = i$, where $\phi(i)$ is, as before, the seller's investment cost. There are thus no direct externalities. The other widgets are called "generic," with production cost for the seller equal to[3]

$$c_n^g = c_L + \frac{n}{N}(c_H - c_L), \quad \text{for } n = 1, \dots, N-1$$

The problem ex post is that of recognizing which is the special widget among the N possible widgets. The parameter N is thus a measure of complexity. As will become clear, the key fact will be that, as N becomes large, c_n^g "fills" the interval $[c_L, c_H]$.

Assume complete symmetry ex ante across widgets, both in terms of the probability of being the special one and in terms of production cost when generic. A state of nature is a cost realization of the special widget and a permutation of the $N - 1$ generic widgets plus the special one. Each state

---

3. The seller's investment has no impact on the cost of generic widgets. This assumption is made only for simplicity.

of nature is thus equally likely. Finally, assume that c and the c_n^g's are observable but unverifiable at stage 3.

The first best involves trading the special widget in all states of nature and setting investment so as to solve

$$\max_i \{i(v - c_L) + (1 - i)(v - c_H) - \phi(i)\}$$

What happens under noncontractibility of i and unverifiability of c and the c_n^g's? Intuitively, the answer to this question may depend on whether the parties can or cannot commit not to renegotiate, and on whether widget types can or cannot be described ex ante.

12.3.4.1   No Renegotiation

Even if the widgets cannot be described at stage 1 (but remember they can be at stage 3), the first best can be achieved provided the parties can commit not to renegotiate: Just set up a mechanism in which the seller can make the buyer a take-it-or-leave-it offer at stage 3. Since he is endowed with full bargaining power, the seller will choose the first-best investment level.

This result is consistent with Maskin and Tirole's claim that ex ante nondescribability may not matter: Clearly, since the first best can be achieved without specifying ex ante any explicit message-contingent outcome,[4] being able to perform such ex ante description adds nothing.

While the no-renegotiation benchmark is exceedingly simple, things become much more involved when the parties cannot commit not to engage in subsequent Pareto-improving renegotiations.

12.3.4.2   Renegotiation

Assume for simplicity that the buyer has full bargaining power in renegotiation. Call P_i the expected price obtained by the seller if his cost is c_i. The seller chooses his investment i to solve

$$\max_i \{i(P_L - c_L) + (1 - i)(P_H - c_H) - \phi(i)\}$$

First-best investment obtains if $P_L = P_H$, but investment decreases when $P_H - P_L$ increases. In particular, in the absence of a prior contract, the buyer

---

4. With one exception: "No trade" has to be contractable ex ante, since the buyer must be allowed to decline the seller offer. Maskin and Tirole derive their results under the assumption that there is at least one level of trade (e.g., no trade) that is contractable ex ante.

offers the seller $P_i = c_i$ ex post, which leads the seller to choose $i = 0$.

The striking result from this model is that, even if the widgets can be described at stage 1, because of the parties' inability to commit not to engage in Pareto-improving renegotiations, the optimal contract implies $i \to 0$ when $N \to \infty$. The gains from contracting thus vanish when com-plexity grows without bounds and the parties might as well not bother to sign any initial contract. Note that this result generalizes to any distribution of bargaining powers in the renegotiation process, as well as to bilateral investments.

Let us now establish this result. The underlying logic is to observe how incentive-compatibility requirements translate into post-renegotiation prices that depend almost one for one on the cost realization of the seller, just as under the null contract.

Specifically, take any mechanism M. Define a state of nature (L, τ) as one where the special widget costs c_L and where the $N - 1$ generic widgets are arranged according to a permutation τ. Without loss of generality, take the special widget to be widget 1, and have widgets $2, 3, \ldots, N$ cost

$$c_L + \frac{1}{N}(c_H - c_L), \quad c_L + \frac{2}{N}(c_H - c_L), \quad \ldots, \quad c_L + \frac{N-1}{N}(c_H - c_L)$$

respectively. Denote the equilibrium strategies of the two parties when playing mechanism M in state of nature (L, τ) as $m_B(L, \tau)$ and $m_S(L, \tau)$ (that is, their announcements, truthful or not, of the state of nature that is mutually revealed to them). Define the price $P(L, \tau)$ as the equilibrium price at which the special widget is traded in state (L, τ), possibly after renegotiation. This yields surpluses $v - P(L, \tau)$ for the buyer and $P(L, \tau) - c_L$ for the seller.

Consider now state of nature (H, τ'), with cost c_H for the special widget and a new permutation of the widgets: The special widget becomes widget N, and widgets $1, 2, 3, \ldots, N - 1$ now cost

$$c_L + \frac{1}{N}(c_H - c_L), \quad c_L + \frac{2}{N}(c_H - c_L), \ldots, \quad c_L + \frac{N-1}{N}(c_H - c_L)$$

Denote the equilibrium strategies of the two parties when playing mechanism M in state of nature (H, τ') as $m_B(H, \tau')$ and $m_S(H, \tau')$, and define the price $P(H, \tau')$ as the equilibrium price at which the special widget is traded in state (H, τ'), possibly after renegotiation.

What does incentive compatibility of truthful reporting of the state of nature imply for prices $P(L, \tau)$ and $P(H, \tau')$? Let us focus on the following two incentive constraints:

1. In state of nature (H, τ'), the seller should not play as if the state of nature were (L, τ).

2. In state of nature (L, τ), the buyer should not play as if the state of nature were (H, τ').

Both unilateral deviations amount to the players choosing a pair of strategies $[m_B(H, \tau'), m_S(L, \tau)]$. Without loss of generality, assume that mechanism M prescribes, upon such a pair of announcements, a starting point of renegotiation where the buyer has to pay the seller an amount $\tilde{P}$ and where widget n is traded with probability x_n, while no trade happens with probability

$$1 - \sum_{n=1}^{N} x_n \geq 0$$

Since we assumed full bargaining power for the buyer in renegotiation, the incentive constraint in state of nature (H, τ') to avoid deviation 1 by the seller is

$$\tilde{P} - \sum_{n=1}^{N} x_n \left[c_L + \frac{n}{N}(c_H - c_L) \right] \leq P(H, \tau') - c_H$$

Similarly, in order to avoid deviation 2 by the buyer in state of nature (L, τ), and keeping in mind that the ex post efficient trade will result anyway, what we need is for the seller not to lose from this deviation, or

$$\tilde{P} - \sum_{n=1}^{N} x_n \left[c_L + \frac{n-1}{N}(c_H - c_L) \right] \geq P(L, \tau) - c_L$$

These two inequalities imply

$$P(H, \tau') - P(L, \tau) \geq c_H - c_L - \sum_{n=1}^{N} \frac{x_n}{N}(c_H - c_L) \geq \frac{N-1}{N}(c_H - c_L)$$

This condition has to be satisfied for any pair (τ, τ'), and therefore, since all permutations are equally likely, the expected price the seller receives when his cost is c_H, minus the expected price he receives when his cost is c_L, is at least

$$\frac{N-1}{N}(c_H - c_L)$$

which tends to $c_H - c_L$ when $N \to \infty$. Consequently, the seller obtains none of the gains from investing, just as without any prior contract. We have thus established the result.

The lessons of this result are twofold. First, as in Maskin and Tirole (1999), we have a case here where ex ante describability of widgets once again does not matter: dropping it cannot hurt, since in the limit there is already no value of contracting even with ex ante describability. Second, what matters here is not whether widgets are describable ex ante but whether the parties can commit not to engage in ex post Pareto-improving renegotiations.

Let us end with an important point concerning the interpretation of this result. The proof has focused on incentive compatibility for states of nature (L, τ) and (H, τ'). These states differ in the cost level of the special widget: widget 1, the special one in state (L, τ), costs c_L, while widget N, the special one in state (H, τ'), costs c_H. More importantly, the two states of nature are "extreme" in the cost differences of the these two widgets when they are not special: widget N is the *most expensive* generic widget in state (L, τ), while widget 1 is the *cheapest* generic widget in state (H, τ'). As a result, it is particularly difficult to prevent the seller from claiming that the state of nature is (L, τ) when it is in fact (H, τ') (so that widget 1 rather than N should be produced) and conversely for the buyer. In this model the cost difference between the most expensive and cheapest generic widgets increases with N, the "complexity" of the environment. Reiche (2003a) makes the point, however, that the value of contracting in this kind of setting can also go to zero if the seller's investment is "ambiguous," that is, has a value that can be negative if the wrong ex post action is taken (because of technological complementarity between the investment and the specific widget to be produced). Ambiguity works, just like complexity, because it generates the same negative correlation between the cost of the ex post efficient widget and the cost of the "associated" ex post inefficient widget as in states (H, τ) and (H, τ').

12.3.4.3   Describability

Although describability did not matter in the preceding analysis, Hart and Moore also provide an example where it does. This is a variation on the previous analysis that has *no* uncertainty. Assume then, without loss of generality, that widget 1 is always the special widget, while widgets 2 to N are the generic ones, costing, respectively,

$$c_L + \frac{1}{N}(c_H - c_L), c_L + \frac{2}{N}(c_H - c_L), \ldots, \quad c_L + \frac{N-1}{N}(c_H - c_L)$$

Here, with describability, it is easy to achieve the first-best outcome: write a specific-performance contract where the parties agree to trade at stage 3 one unit of widget 1 at a fixed price, for example, v.

Instead, without describability at stage 1, we are in the same setup as in the previous subsection, with no benefit of contracting when complexity grows without bound, that is, when N becomes large. Indeed, assume there are N "names" at stage 1, each of which is equally likely to describe the special widget at stage 3, and these are the only ways to describe widgets at stage 1. So, as Hart and Moore (1999, p. 125) write, "Even though the buyer and the seller know at stage 1 which widget is the special one, they have no words to describe it, other than the N names, any one of which may turn out to be appropriate at stage 3." This problem is thus the same as the one considered in the previous subsection where, without commitment against Pareto-improving renegotiation, there is asymptotically no value of contracting when complexity grows.

In contrast to the Maskin-Tirole result, describability matters here because of the combined effect of *renegotiation and risk neutrality:* When renegotiation can be assumed away, first-best implementation can be obtained despite undescribability, as in section 12.3.4.1. When the parties are risk averse, renegotiation-proofness can to some extent be circumvented by "creating risk," and thus ex post inefficiency, following some messages sent by the parties. In such a case, Maskin and Tirole manage to construct mechanisms that still achieve first-best implementation despite undescribability. As the preceding example shows, this result is not possible anymore under risk neutrality.

12.4   Ex Post Unverifiable Actions

The previous section focused first on ex ante and ex post contractable actions, and then, in the last subsection, on ex ante noncontractable but ex post contractable actions. We now focus on ex ante *and* ex post noncontractable actions. This type of actions has in fact already been considered earlier: Think of the *effort choice of moral-hazard models,* a choice that is indeed noncontractible, so that the agent has to be given an incentive scheme in order to exert effort. While in classical moral-hazard models the identity of the agent is exogenously given, one can endogenize *who* has to make the effort decision, that is, who has the *authority* over a given action. Several models of the literature can be reinterpreted as generalizations of the moral-hazard paradigm in order to analyze issues of allocation of authority. The next subsections discuss in turn optimal financial contracting and the distinction between "real" and "formal" authority.

12.4.1   Financial Contracting

12.4.1.1   Financial Constraints and Contingent Control

To illustrate this point we now provide a somewhat different illustration of the Aghion and Bolton (1992) model, which was already discussed in Chapter 11. Namely, we reinterpret it as a "complete-contract" model with ex post unverifiable actions. In this version of the model, at date 0 an entre-preneur/manager needs an amount K from an investor to start a project, which yields a random verifiable profit that can be either 0 ("failure") or 1 ("success") at date 2. The distribution of profit depends on the realization of the state of nature θ and on an action to be taken at date 1. Assume that at date 1 the state of nature θ gets revealed and is verifiable. What is not verifiable, however, is the action that is to be taken at date 1. Think, for example, of actions like business strategies where "the devil is in the details" and where these details cannot be included in a contract, so that the only thing that can be done is to "put somebody in charge of the job." Date-0 contracts can thus specify divisions of the final profit as well as control allo-cations (that is, who can take the action at date 1), contingent on the state of nature θ.

To be specific, assume that two actions can be taken: "Reorganization" (R), which for simplicity yields a probability of success p_R whatever the state of nature, and "continuation" (C), which yields a probability of success p_i in state θ_i, where $i = 1, 2, 3$, where $p_1 < p_2 < p_3$ and all three θ_i's are equiprob-able at date 0. States of nature are thus monotonic in the relative attrac-tiveness of the continuation action. Assume also that the entrepreneur obtains an extra private benefit h under continuation. For example, under reorganization, she loses existing quasi-rents.

Let us concentrate on the case where

$$p_1 + h < p_R < p_2 + h$$

but

$$p_2 < p_R < p_3$$

Recall that the investor cares only about financial returns, while the entrepreneur—who has no financial resources to start with—has a payoff equal to her private benefit plus her financial return. Under the preceding inequalities, the ex post efficient action is C except in state θ_1, while the action that maximizes monetary financial returns is action R except in state θ_3. Finally, assume that the project has positive financial NPV if the ex post efficient action is taken in all states of nature, that is,

$$(p_R + p_2 + p_3)/3 > K$$

The first-best contract is the one where the ex post efficient action is taken at date 1 while satisfying the individual-rationality constraint of the investor (that of the entrepreneur will be automatically satisfied given the assumption that she has no funds of her own). How can one contractually achieve the first best?

One can first note that the first best can be achieved through a *contingent-control contract,* where the investor is given control when $\theta = \theta_1$ while the entrepreneur is given control in state θ_2 (who has control in state θ_3 is irrelevant), and where the entire financial return is given to the investor. Such a contract, which we already discussed in Chapter 11, leads here to efficient decision making in all three states of nature. Moreover, it satisfies the investor's individual-rationality constraint because the project has been assumed to have a positive financial NPV under ex post efficient decisions.

Consider now contracts that have noncontingent control. *Entrepreneur control* requires giving the entrepreneur substantial financial returns if ex post efficient actions have to be chosen without renegotiation. Specifically, inducing the entrepreneur to choose action R in state θ_1 requires

$$wp_R \geq wp_1 + h$$

where w is the entrepreneur's wage in state of nature θ_1 when the project succeeds (it is optimal to give the entrepreneur a zero wage when it fails). Intuitively, the entrepreneur has to be given a big enough share of the return when the project succeeds to compensate for the loss of private benefit when reorganization is chosen. But this requirement conflicts with investor individual rationality if

$$\left[\left(p_R - \frac{h}{p_R - p_1}\right) + p_2 + p_3\right]\Big/3 < K$$

in which case the project cannot start.

However, insisting on a renegotiation-proof contract is excessive, because under entrepreneur control, ex post efficient decisions are *always guaranteed*. Indeed, as discussed in Chapter 11, the investor has the financial resources to *buy back control* to prevent an inefficient ex post action choice by the entrepreneur. Note, however, that this type of contract produces *equilibrium-contingent control*. Moreover, it requires giving the entrepreneur in equilibrium at least an expected monetary reward equal to h in state θ_1. This is the minimum needed to induce her to choose the ex post efficient action R and thereby give up private benefit h associated with action C. This monetary concession conflicts with investor individual rationality if

$$[(p_R - h) + p_2 + p_3]/3 < K$$

While allowing for renegotiation makes it more likely to meet the individual-rationality constraint of the investor, there are thus cases where it will not work.

What about *investor control*? The investor's individual rationality can be satisfied in this case—for example, by giving him the entire financial return of the project. However, as stressed in Chapter 11, the problem is now to avoid inefficient reorganization. To avoid this outcome without renegotiation would require penalizing the investor in state θ_2 if *the project succeeds*! This approach is indeed the only way to induce the investor to choose the continuation action in this state. Consequently, if we assume (following Innes, 1990) that individual financial payoffs have to be monotonic in the total financial return of the project, the contract has to involve equilibrium renegotiation in order to induce ex post efficiency. In turn, this requires giving the entrepreneur some money in state θ_2 to allow her to buy back control and choose the efficient continuation action. Indeed, as stressed by Aghion and Bolton (1992), despite the fact that there is no asymmetry of information between the parties, renegotiation can fail to reach ex post efficiency in the presence of wealth constraints. The only way to achieve efficient decisions in all states of nature is to give the entrepreneur a sum $p_R - p_2$ in state θ_2, in order to allow her to "buy back" control from the investor in this state. Through equilibrium renegotiation, this contract therefore exactly replicates the outcome of the contingent-control contract described earlier.

12.4.1.2   Rationalizing Outside Equity and Debt

The preceding model has focused on ex post actions that were not contractable. Pursuing the parallel with moral hazard models, we now add an earlier stage with an effort choice for the entrepreneur. This allows us to rationalize the existence of two outside investors, rather than one as in the Aghion-Bolton model, as shown by Dewatripont and Tirole (1994a). Consider the following timing:

• At date 0, the entrepreneur obtains funding K, and the financial contract is signed.
• At date $0'$, the entrepreneur chooses effort $a \in \{a_L, a_H\}$.
• At date 1, first-period profit $\pi_1 \in \{0, 1\}$ is realized, with $\Pr(\pi_1 = 1 \mid a_H) = p_H > p_L = \Pr(\pi_1 = 1 \mid a_L)$.
• At date $1'$, action $A \in \{C, R\}$ has to be chosen. As in the previous subsection, action C stands for "continuation," and action R stands for "reorganization."
• At date 2, second-period profit π_2 is realized.

In terms of payoffs, assume for simplicity that the entrepreneur cares only about private benefits and costs, and that (1) effort a_H involves an extra cost $\psi > 0$ relative to effort a_L, and (2) as in the previous subsection, action C gives the manager an extra private benefit h relative to action R. As before, however, investors are risk neutral and care only about financial profits. Investors will thus share among themselves the financial profits $\pi_1 + \pi_2$.

As in the previous subsection, assume that financial profits are verifiable but that the action A and the effort of the entrepreneur are not. Contracts can thus specify divisions of total profits $\pi_1 + \pi_2$ as well as allocations of control over action A, both potentially contingent on first-period profit π_1.

We have here a double moral-hazard problem: The entrepreneur has to be given incentives to exert effort, and the investor in control of action A may have to be given incentives to take the proper action. Assume that it is efficient to implement the high effort a_H. This action choice will be in the interest of the entrepreneur if and only if the probability of continuation depends sufficiently strongly on the effort level, or if and only if

$$h[\Pr(C \mid a_H) - \Pr(C \mid a_L)] \geq \psi \qquad \text{(IC)}$$

What about the choice of action A? Assume that, at date 1, an unverifiable signal s_u is realized, simultaneously with first-period profit. This unverifiable signal determines the density of second-period profit π_2: Call this density $f_A(\pi_2 \mid s_u)$ when action A is chosen, and assume the following:

- $E(\pi_2 \mid C, s_u) - E(\pi_2 \mid R, s_u)$ increases with s_u and takes value 0 for $s_u = \hat{s}_u$.
- Action C is riskier than action R for each s_u in the sense that, controlling for the difference in expectations, action C involves an increase in risk à la Rothschild and Stiglitz (1970) in comparison with action R.

The first assumption is a normalization: It simply means that the unverifiable signals, the s_u's, are ranked according to their differences in expected second-period profits across actions. The second assumption is the crucial one: It says that continuation leads to a higher variability of second-period profits than reorganization. It is a natural assumption whenever reorganization involves selling divisions, reducing the size of operations, and the like—that is, actions that reduce the variance of future returns.

Let us now turn to optimal contracting. Take the point of view of investors, who want to induce high effort while maximizing expected second-period profits. These profits are maximized by choosing action C whenever $s_u \geq \hat{s}_u$. However, if, for the sake of exposition, the unverifiable signal s_u is assumed to be uncorrelated with entrepreneurial effort, second-period-profit maximization then fails to induce high effort from the entrepreneur: She faces the same probability of reorganization whatever her effort choice. Consequently, a trade-off arises between inducing effort and inducing ex post profit maximization. Since first-period profits are assumed to be correlated with effort, high effort can be induced only if the probability of reorganization is positively correlated with first-period profit. As in classical moral-hazard problems, the optimal contract minimizes ex post inefficiency subject to satisfying the incentive constraint (IC). Without computing the result explicitly, we can say that this contract would lead to a second-best contract defined by a pair (s_{u0}^*, s_{u1}^*), where $s_{u0}^* > \hat{s}_u > s_{u1}^*$ and where first-period profit $\pi_1 = 0$ leads to action C being chosen whenever $s_u > s_{u0}^*$ while first-period profit $\pi_1 = 1$ leads to action C being chosen whenever $s_u > s_{u1}^*$.

How can different control structures achieve this second-best outcome when the actions and the signal s_u are unverifiable? First, note that *entrepreneur control* simply cannot, and is in fact very bad. Indeed, the entrepreneur, who only cares about h, then chooses to continue whatever the signal s_u, a choice that is not ex post efficient and moreover fails to induce high effort. Second, while *single-investor control* leads to second-period-profit maximization, it fails to induce high effort from the entrepreneur, as explained earlier (this conclusion remains true whenever s_u is correlated with entrepreneurial effort, but insufficiently so).

A structure that can achieve the second best is *dual, contingent investor control,* that is, giving control to an investor with a "bias" in favor of action C after high first-period profit realization and to an investor with a "bias" in favor of action R after low first-period profit realization.[5] If these biases are strong enough, the entrepreneur chooses high effort, in order to maximize the probability of having high first-period profit.

How does one generate such biases with risk-neutral investors? Since, by assumption, action C is riskier than action R, a bias in favor of action C is induced by giving the investor in control a claim that is *convex* in total profit, that is, an *equity-like claim*; similarly, a bias in favor of action R is induced by giving the investor in control a claim that is *concave* in total profit, that is, a *debtlike claim*. And since the investor in control has to be given incentives to choose the right action, a second investor is needed to act as "budget breaker," that is, to receive the residual profit. The model therefore predicts either *noncontingent control with the investor in control holding a contingent claim* (similar to equity after $\pi_1 = 1$ and similar to debt after $\pi_1 = 0$) or *contingent control* (equity control after $\pi_1 = 1$ and debt control after $\pi_1 = 0$) *with noncontingent debt and equity claims*.

To give an example, consider the following case, where action R yields second-period profit $\pi_2 = r$ with probability γ and $\pi_2 = 0$ with probability $(1 - \gamma)$, while action C yields second-period profit $\pi_2 = 1$ with probability s_u and $\pi_2 = 0$ with probability $(1 - s_u)$. Assume $0 < r < 1, s_u \in [0, \bar{s}_u]$, and $\bar{s}_u > \gamma$. This assumption implies $\hat{s}_u = \gamma r$ for some $\hat{s}_u < \bar{s}_u$, and if there is a single investor, this is the cutoff used to decide whether to continue or not. Instead, with debt and equity, if there is an amount of debt D, an equity holder in control continues if and only if $s_u(1 - D) \geq \gamma(r - D)$, or if and only if

$$s_u \geq \gamma \frac{r - D}{1 - D} \equiv s_u^E(D)$$

Let us thus consider having two investors, an equity holder and a long-term-debt holder with an amount of debt D^*. The variable D^* can be set

---

5. For simplicity, we assume away renegotiation here. See Dewatripont and Tirole (1994a) for an extension with perfect renegotiation.

to ensure second-best implementation after high first-period profit ($\pi_1 = 1$). Specifically, giving control to equity in this case means that reorganization takes place if and only if $s_u \geq s_{u1}^*$ provided that D^* satisfies $s_{u1}^* = s_u^E (D^*)$. How do we then make sure that, after low first-period profit ($\pi_1 = 0$), reorganization takes place if and only if $s_u \geq s_{u0}^*$? If $s_{u0}^* < \gamma$, for any debt level $D \leq r$, the debt holder is excessively tough with the entrepreneur, since he chooses reorganization if and only if $s_u \leq \gamma$. The equity holder, however, would be ready to buy back control from the debt holder if $s_u > s_u^E(D)$, and the more so the higher the unverifiable signal s_u. Specifically, the equity holder is ready to make an early repayment of an amount P_E toward long-term debt D whenever

$$s_u[1-(D-P_E)]-P_E \geq \gamma(r-D)$$

Intuitively, paying early means paying with a higher probability, but it allows the equity holder to take the riskier action C. Consequently, second-best implementation can be achieved after low first-period profit ($\pi_1 = 0$) as follows: The debt holder is given control initially, unless the equity holder pays the debt holder an amount P_E^* toward long-term debt, which is such that

$$s_{u0}^*\left[1-\left(D^*-P_E^*\right)\right] \; P_E^* = \gamma(r-D^*)$$

Under this condition, the equity holder buys back control from the debt holder after low first-period profit if and only if s_u is such that $\gamma \geq s_u \geq s_{u0}^*$, which yields second-best implementation.

Though this is only a simple example where exact implementation of the second-best rule happens in a realistic fashion, the more robust lesson from this subsection is the following: In a world of noncontractable actions (concerning both the entrepreneur/manager and the investors) and contractable profits, one can naturally find a role for the optimal coexistence of two financial securities that combine contingent-control rights and nonlinear income rights in a way that resembles standard debt and equity.

12.4.2   Formal and Real Authority

Aghion and Tirole (1997) also focus on noncontractable actions, which in their setup amounts to choosing a project that the agent has to work on. There are initially $N \geq 3$ potential projects. Project $k \in \{1, 2, \ldots, N\}$ gives the principal a private benefit H_k and the agent a private benefit h_k.

Initially, these various projects are indistinguishable from one another. On the one hand, at least one of them is sufficiently bad that choosing one project at random is worse for both parties than undertaking no project (with associated payoff normalized to zero in this case). On the other hand, the parties know in advance that the best project for the principal gives him $H > 0$ while it gives the agent $\beta h > 0$, and that the best project for the agent gives her $h > 0$ while it gives the principal $\alpha H > 0$. Call α and β the "congruence parameters," and assume that they are positive but smaller than one. The higher these parameters, the more congruent the preferences of the two parties. Note that partial congruence is built into the setup in any case, since one has assumed that (1) the two parties agree that choosing a project at random is worse than undertaking no project; and (2) they each prefer to allow the other party to choose his or her favorite project rather than undertaking no project (since α and β are assumed to be positive).

These assumptions about congruence are crucial given the *information-acquisition* technology: While both parties are initially uninformed about the private benefits associated with individual projects, they can each exert effort to improve their information. Specifically, the principal can at cost $\psi_P(E)$ (increasing and convex in E) become *fully informed* with probability E about project benefits, while he remains *fully uninformed* with probability $1 - E$. Similarly, the agent can at cost $\psi_A(e)$ (increasing and convex in e) become fully informed with probability e about project benefits, while she remains fully uninformed with probability $1 - e$.

The timing of the game is as follows: In stage 1, the parties contract; in stage 2, they exert effort to acquire information about individual project payoffs; finally, in stage 3, a decision can be taken on which project to undertake, if any. Assuming that efforts are privately chosen and that parties only care about their private benefits,[6] the contract only consists in an allocation of authority for stage 3. As Aghion and Tirole stress, what can be contractually allocated is solely "formal" authority, that is, who has the *right* to take the decision. This differs from "real" authority, that is, who *actually* takes the decision. Indeed, given the partial congruence built into the model, a party endowed with formal authority chooses to undertake a project only if he or she is informed about project benefits; otherwise, he or she *transfers* authority to the other party (or equivalently, asks the other party for a

---

6. This assumption is made for the sake of presentation and can be generalized (see Aghion and Tirole, 1997).

recommendation and follows it). In turn, this other party chooses a project or makes a recommendation only if he or she is informed about project benefits. Otherwise, no project is undertaken.

Given this continuation equilibrium in stage 3, if the contract allocates formal authority to the principal, the payoffs for the principal and the agent (U_P and u_A, respectively) upon choosing their effort levels are

$$U_P = EH + (1 - E)e\alpha H - \psi_P(E)$$

$$u_A = E\beta h + (1 - E)eh - \psi_A(e)$$

These conditions reflect the fact that the principal chooses his favorite action whenever he is informed about individual project payoffs, while the agent's information matters only when the principal is uninformed. In stage 2, simultaneous effort choice leads to the following first-order conditions:

$$(1 - \alpha e)H = \psi'_P(E)$$

$$(1 - E)h = \psi'_A(e)$$

As indicated by the second first order condition, higher effort E by the principal crowds out effort e by the agent, who understands that her effort matters with a lower probability. There may therefore be a gain for the principal to commit to exerting lower effort, for example, by choosing an agent who is more congruent with him (that is, an agent "with a higher α").[7] In this case, indeed, the principal exerts less effort, as indicated by the first first-order condition: He is less worried about being uninformed because the project chosen by the agent when she is the only one informed leads to a lower relative loss for the principal.

Another way for the principal to induce the agent to work harder is to *delegate* her formal authority on project choice (this is equivalent, in the Grossman-Hart-Moore approach, to *selling the underlying asset* necessary to get the project going). In this case, given the continuation equilibrium in stage 3, the payoffs for the principal and the agent upon choosing their effort levels are

$$U_P = e\alpha H + (1 - e)EH - \psi_P(E)$$

$$u_A = eh + (1 - e)E\beta h - \psi_A(e)$$

---

7. Aghion and Tirole also look at increases in the "span of control" of the principal as a way for him to commit to spend less effort per agent, since he has more projects to acquire information about.

The agent now chooses her preferred action whenever she is informed, while the principal's information matters only when the agent is uninformed. Simultaneous effort choice now leads to the following first-order conditions:

$$(1-e)H = \psi'_P(E)$$

$$(1-\beta E)h = \psi'_A(e)$$

A comparison of these first-order conditions with the ones where the principal has formal authority indicates that the agent exerts more effort and the principal exerts less effort under delegation. Indeed, the two effort levels are strategic substitutes, reinforcing the fact that the individual endowed with formal authority has more incentives to exert effort, ceteris paribus, since he or she can have the first go at choosing the action.

The Aghion-Tirole paper delivers a rich set of predictions about authority in organizations, all this in a very simple model.[8] From the point of view of contract theory, it is also a good example of the tractability of models with noncontractable actions but contractable control allocations.

12.5   Ex Post Unverifiable Payoffs

In this final section we explore a model by Bolton and Rajan (2001) where, as before, authority rests on an informational advantage, but unlike before is sustained by an ongoing relation built on trust. Authority is modeled not just as a decision right or action but as the act of giving orders that are expected to be executed. The model compares two modes of transacting, the negotiation/contracting mode and the authority mode. In the contracting mode, the services or goods to be provided by a "seller," as well as the terms of trade, are spelled out in detail in a spot contract. In the authority mode, the buyer writes a long-term employment contract with the seller, specifying only the terms of employment, leaving the details of which service to provide in any given period unspecified. In this mode, the buyer directs the seller to perform a specific service in each period. The seller only has the choice of executing the order or quitting. There are no ongoing negotiations about which service to provide or at what terms.

---

8. See also Burkart, Gromb, and Panunzi (1997) for a corporate finance application. where shareholder dispersion acts as a commitment device to "empower" management.

What are the costs of contracting that make it possible for authority to supersede the contracting mode? In the Bolton and Rajan model, the main source of contracting costs is private information and unobservability of payoffs. It is assumed that the buyer (the "boss" in the authority mode) knows more about the costs and benefits of a particular service than the seller. The latter learns his true costs from carrying out a service only after the fact. The spot contract cannot specify terms contingent on realized costs, as costs (in utility terms) are essentially unobservable. The most the seller can hope for then is to obtain compensation for expected costs at the time of signing the contract. But a spot contract where terms of trade reflect only expected costs and not actual costs of a particular service may induce the buyer to sometimes demand excessively costly services. This is the source of inefficiency that an authority mode may be able to overcome.

How can the authority mode overcome this contractual inefficiency? Because the authority mode is based on a long-term contract and an ongoing relationship, the timing of the seller's payments can be made more flexible. The buyer can now compensate the seller with a bonus after the latter has carried out a particularly costly service. The buyer's incentive to pay such bonuses is supported by the seller's threat to dissolve the relationship should the buyer not compensate him adequately. Given that the buyer is induced to always fully cover the seller's costs ex post, the buyer is also induced to choose the action that maximizes net surplus. In other words, the buyer chooses the first-best action in the authority mode, and thus generates an efficiency gain, which would be lost should the seller (employee) decide to quit. It is the prospect of losing this rent that preserves the buyer's incentives to fully cover the seller's costs and induce him to stay.

To be specific, consider a contractual situation between two risk-neutral parties who may interact repeatedly over time. At any given date t, the buyer can write a contract with the seller specifying the nature of the service to be provided, as well as financial terms. For simplicity there are only two types of services (or actions) that the seller can provide; denote them by a_1 and a_2. At any given time the buyer demands at most one of these two services. Provision of the service is observable and verifiable, so that a contract can be written specifying a payment contingent on execution of the action.

The two parties' payoffs are normalized to zero in the event of no trade. If they agree on the provision of a service a_i at some price P_i $(i = 1, 2)$, their payoffs are

$$v(a_i, \theta) - P_i$$

for the buyer and

$$P_i - c(a_i, \theta)$$

for the seller. These payoffs depend on a state of nature θ (which belongs to a finite set θ). Specifically, assume that

$$v(a_i, \theta) \in \{v_L, v_H\} \quad \text{and} \quad c(a_i, \theta) \in \{c_L = 0, c_H\}$$

with

$$0 < c_H < v_L < v_H$$

In addition, assume that at each date t there is an independent draw of a new state θ, with each state being equiprobable. As in Segal (1999a), this assumption captures the idea that the precise nature of a service required by the buyer at any given moment changes over time and in an unpredictable manner.

The set of states comprises all possible configurations of payoffs for the two actions, $\{c(a_1, \theta), c(a_2, \theta), v(a_1, \theta), v(a_2, \theta)\}$, so that there are 16 distinct states of nature. Under these assumptions, provision of some service is efficient in all states of nature. The (first-best) efficient service in any given state is the one maximizing net gains from trade

$$v(a_i, \theta) - c(a_i, \theta)$$

We shall assume, moreover, that

$$v_H - c_H < v_L$$

That is, it is more efficient to produce the low-valuation, low-cost service than the high-valuation, high-cost service.

As explained previously, a central assumption underlying the entire analysis is that the buyer privately observes the realized state of nature at any given date before any contract is drawn. The seller learns his true cost of providing the service only while providing it. In other words, the buyer has superior information about the seller's cost of providing the service. The critical informational assumption to obtain an efficient mode of transaction based on command and authority is that one of the contracting parties (the one ultimately exercising authority) has superior information. If, as is the case in Chapter 7, the buyer had private information about $v(a_i, \theta)$ and the seller about $c(a_i, \theta)$, then authority would not obviously emerge as an efficient mode of transacting.

The two parties are drawn from a pool of anonymous buyers and sellers. Once they are matched, they can choose to engage in a spot transaction or to interact repeatedly over time in an employment relation. There are, thus, two alternative modes of contracting: a market mode and an employment mode. Under the market mode, the buyer and seller are drawn from the pool of buyers and sellers every period. They meet in the marketplace and write a spot contract for the provision of a service at that period. Following provision of the service, the seller is compensated and the contractual relationship dissolves.

Under the employment mode, the buyer and seller write a long-term contract. This is de facto an employment contract where the seller becomes the employee and the buyer the employer. The contract specifies the following:

1. A wage payment in every period.

2. A discretionary bonus to be paid at the end of each period, which varies with the seller's cost of performing the prescribed task.

3. A signing-up fee as well as a severance payment.

The employment contract does not specify what tasks the employee/seller is required to perform. Instead, it is a mutual understanding that he will execute the action prescribed by the employer/buyer at any time in the (foreseeable) future, as long as she sticks to the implicit agreement of compensating him with discretionary bonus payments when costs incurred in executing prescribed actions happen to be high. This contract can be terminated at will by either party, in which case the contractual relationship ends forever.

Whichever mode the parties choose, it is assumed that their presence in the market may end forever at the end of any period t with an exogenously given probability $\gamma > 0$. This probability of termination serves the dual function of discounting the future and measuring the expected frequency of interaction of contracting parties in this market.

12.5.1   The Spot-Contracting Mode

At the beginning of any period, the buyer and seller write a spot contract specifying the service that the seller is to provide, as well as the terms of trade. The buyer knows her own payoff and the seller's cost of providing the service. She makes a take-it-or-leave-it contract offer, which the seller can accept or reject. If the seller rejects, he gets a reservation payoff of $\bar{u}$. Thus a spot contract is a pair $\{a, P(a)\}$, where $P(a)$ denotes the payment to the seller for providing service a. The spot-contracting game can be analyzed as a simple informed-principal problem as in Myerson (1983) or Maskin and Tirole (1990). It could potentially have many different solutions. Bolton and Rajan (2001) argue that a natural solution to this contracting game can be characterized as the solution to a slightly modified ex ante problem, which admits a unique solution.

The modified problem is a contracting problem where the buyer and seller agree on an incentive-compatible state-contingent spot contract before the state of nature is realized and observed by the buyer. Applying the revelation principle, an ex ante efficient spot contract is a pair of state-contingent action and compensation schedules $\{a(\theta), P[a(\theta)]\}$ that maximizes the buyer's expected payoff subject to meeting the following incentive-compatibility and individual-rationality constraints:

$$\max_{a(\theta), P[a(\theta)]} \frac{1}{16} \sum_{\theta} \{v[a(\theta), \theta] - P[a(\theta), \theta]\}$$

subject to

$$\frac{1}{16} \sum_{\theta} \{P[a(\theta), \theta] - c[a(\theta), \theta]\} \geq \bar{u} \qquad \text{(IR)}$$

and, for all $(\theta, \hat{\theta}) \in \Theta \times \Theta$

$$v[a(\theta), \theta] - P[a(\theta), \theta] \geq v[a(\hat{\theta}), \theta] - P[a(\hat{\theta}), \hat{\theta}] \qquad \text{(IC)}$$

Note first that, in order to be incentive compatible, a contract has to specify a constant payment for the same action chosen in two different states of nature, that is,

$$P[a(\theta), \theta] = P[a(\theta)]$$

Incentive-compatible contracts thus take the form $\{a(\theta), P[a(\theta)]\}$.

Second, an optimal contract has to be such that $P[a(\theta)] = P$. To see this point, note that any contract with

$$\Delta P \equiv |P(a_1) - P(a_2)| > v_H - v_L$$

induces the same choice of service by the buyer in all states of nature: She simply picks the cheaper service available, say service a_1 [if $P(a_1) < P(a_2) - (v_H - v_L)$]. The net expected total surplus from such a contract is

$$\frac{1}{4}v_L + \frac{1}{4}v_H + \frac{1}{4}(v_H - c_H) + \frac{1}{4}(v_L - c_H)$$

or

$$\frac{1}{2}v_L + \frac{1}{2}v_H - \frac{1}{2}c_H$$

This contract is dominated by a contract with $\Delta P \le v_H - v_L$. Indeed, under the latter contract, the buyer optimizes in a lexicographic order, first, by selecting the service in each state that maximizes $v(a, \theta)$ and, second, when both services have the same gross return $[v(a_1, \theta) = v(a_2, \theta)]$, by picking the cheaper service (since she is then indifferent). It is easily shown that the total net surplus is then

$$\frac{1}{4}v_L + \frac{3}{4}v_H - \frac{1}{2}c_H$$

Note finally that picking the cheaper service with the lower price (as opposed to the one with the lower cost) is not cost minimizing. The total surplus from trade could be increased in the latter class of contracts by setting $\Delta P = 0$, so that the buyer, when indifferent between the two actions, could choose the less costly service. Straightforward computations indicate that the total net surplus is then

$$\frac{1}{4}v_L + \frac{3}{4}v_H - \frac{3}{8}c_H$$

Consequently, the ex ante second-best contract is such that

$$P(a_1) = P(a_2) = P = \frac{3}{8}c_H + \bar{u}$$

Importantly, note that the contract with $P[a(\theta)] = P$ does not achieve the same surplus as a first-best contract, which implements an action plan to maximize $v(a, \theta) - c(a, \theta)$. As is easily shown, the first-best outcome yields an expected surplus of

$$\frac{3}{8}v_L + \frac{5}{8}v_H - \frac{1}{4}c_H$$

In other words, under the ex ante second-best contract, there is a shortfall in profits of

$$\frac{3}{8}v_L + \frac{5}{8}v_H - \frac{1}{4}c_H - \left[\frac{1}{4}v_L + \frac{3}{4}v_H - \frac{3}{8}c_H\right] = \frac{1}{8}[v_L - (v_H - c_H)] > 0$$

To sum up: the ex ante optimal spot contract takes a very simple form: It is a sales contract specifying a state-independent identical price for each service. The price is set at a level such that the seller is compensated for the costs he is expected to incur. Under such a contract, an inefficiency arises because the buyer's objective is to maximize $(v - P)$ instead of $(v - c)$. We now turn to the employment contract and show that one equilibrium under this contract may yield the first-best payoff.

12.5.2   The Employment Relation and Efficient Authority

Consider now the situation where a buyer and seller have elected to remove themselves from the large pool of anonymous agents that constitute the market and to enter into a long-term employment contract. Such a contract entails an obligation on the part of the seller/employee to carry out the buyer/employer's directions or commands. In exchange the buyer/employer commits to a flow wage payment w, and also promises discretionary bonus payments b to be paid in the event that the employee has to carry out a particularly onerous task. The contract is open ended and at will. In other words, either party is free to quit at any time. In particular, the buyer/employer is free to fire the seller/employee should the latter fail to execute her commands. The contract has an indefinite duration and ends either when one of the parties decides to quit or when an exogenous event occurs that induces separation. Recall that the probability of such an event occurring at any given time is denoted by $\gamma > 0$. In sum, the employment contract described here is a simple form of *relational contract* as analyzed in Chapter 10.

The relation specifies the following sequence of events in every time period t:

1. The buyer learns the state of nature that prevails in period t and directs the seller to provide a given service $a_t \in \{a_1, a_2\}$.

2. The seller responds by either executing the buyer's demand, thereby learning the cost $c(a_t, \theta)$ of doing so, or by quitting, having decided not to execute her order.

3. If the seller executes the buyer's order, the buyer must choose whether to pay a compensatory bonus to the seller.

Let $h_t = \{(c_0, a_0), (c_1, a_1), \ldots, (c_{t-1}, a_{t-1})\}$ denote the history of the employment relation up to period t shared by both parties. It is the sequence of *executed actions* and *realized costs* for the first t periods of time, beginning with time period $t = 0$ (realized benefits could also be part of the history, but these turn out to be redundant information here). Given (h_t, θ_t) where θ_t is the prevailing state at time period t, the buyer's strategy is a pair $\{a_t(\theta_t, h_t), b_t(\theta_t, h_t)\}$ and the seller's strategy is an execute/quit rule $x_t(a_t, h_t) \in \{0, 1\}$, where $x = 1$ when the seller decides to execute the prescribed action and $x = 0$ when he decides to quit.

As we know from Chapter 10, the optimal employment *relational contract* maximizes the expected surplus from the employment relation, subject to satisfying incentive and participation constraints. Obviously, when the employment contract induces first-best equilibrium play, it is efficient. Bolton and Rajan characterize the employment contract for which first-best equilibrium play can be supported for the largest interval of termination probabilities γ. This contract is given by the following:

1. A bonus payment just large enough to induce the employer to always choose a cost-minimizing action. This requires that

$$b \ge v_H - v_L.$$

When this inequality holds, it is not in the employer's interest to order a high cost action in order to gain $(v_H - v_L - b)$.

2. A wage payment just sufficient to ensure participation by the employee. Assuming $\bar{u} = 0$, this means

$$w + \frac{1}{4}(b - c_H) \ge 0$$

3. First-best action choice—$a_t(\theta_t, h_t) = a^{FB}(\theta_t)$—and promised bonus payments—$b_t(\theta_t, h_t) = \min\{c(a_{t-1}, \theta_{t-1}), b\}$—as long as the employee has executed all previous orders; otherwise, $a_t(\theta_t, h_t) = \max_a v(a, \theta_t)$ and $b_t(\theta_t, h_t) = 0$.

4. Execution of employer orders—$x_t(a_t, h_t) = 1$—as long as the seller has made the promised bonus payments—$b_{t-1}(\theta_{t-1}, h_{t-1}) = \min\{c(a_{t-2}, \theta_{t-2}), b\}$—otherwise refusal to carry out the order—$x_t(a_t, h_t) = 0$.

The employer's present expected payoff under the optimal relational contract is then

$$\frac{1}{\gamma}\left(\frac{3}{8}v_L + \frac{5}{8}v_H - \frac{1}{4}c_H\right)$$

This expression compares with the present expected payoff by engaging in a sequence of spot contracts given by

$$\frac{1}{\gamma}\left(\frac{1}{4}v_L + \frac{3}{4}v_H - \frac{3}{8}c_H\right)$$

The equilibrium under the employment relation obtains only if it is in the employer's interest to pay the bonus $b = v_H - v_L$ whenever the employee was ordered to choose an action with cost c_H. If the employer decides to renege on the promised bonus payment, the employment relation dissolves, so that the most she can hope to obtain from such a deviation is

$$b + \frac{1-\gamma}{\gamma}\left(\frac{1}{4}v_L + \frac{3}{4}v_H - \frac{3}{8}c_H\right)$$

If, however, she does not renege, she obtains at least

$$\frac{1-\gamma}{\gamma}\left(\frac{3}{8}v_L + \frac{5}{8}v_H - \frac{1}{4}c_H\right)$$

Consequently, the employer makes the promised bonus payment only if

$$\frac{1-\gamma}{\gamma}\left(\frac{3}{8}v_L + \frac{5}{8}v_H - \frac{1}{4}c_H\right) \geq b + \frac{1-\gamma}{\gamma}\left(\frac{1}{4}v_L + \frac{3}{4}v_H - \frac{3}{8}c_H\right) \tag{12.1}$$

If this condition holds, it is a best response for the employee to execute the prescribed action as long as he continues receiving compensatory bonus payments, and otherwise to quit. Similarly, if this condition holds, it is a best response for the employer to choose $a_t(\theta_t, h_t) = a^{FB}(\theta_t)$ and $b_t(\theta_t, h_t) = \min\{c(a_{t-1}, \theta_{t-1}), b\}$ as long as the seller has executed all previous orders [and otherwise to set $a_t(\theta_t, h_t) = \max_a v(a, \theta_t)$ and $b_t(\theta_t, h_t) = 0$].

If, however, condition (12.1) does not hold, the employment relation is not sustainable. There is thus a cutoff $\hat{\gamma}$ defined as

$$0 < \hat{\gamma} = \frac{[v_L - (v_H - c_H)]}{[8(v_H - v_L) + v_L - (v_H - c_H)]} < 1 \tag{12.2}$$

such that, if the probability of termination γ is smaller than or equal to $\hat{\gamma}$, the internal-transaction mode organized around an authority relation dominates the spot-contracting mode.

This result summarizes in simple terms the main factors that underlie the choice between spot contracting and authority:

• The less durable the relation, that is, the higher the probability of termination γ, the less likely it is for a buyer and seller to engage in an employment relation.

• The larger the scope of "exploitation" of the seller/employee by the buyer/employer (as measured by the size of $v_H - v_L$), the less likely is the emergence of an employment relation.

Remarkably, these factors are closely related to those emphasized by Simon (1951) in his theory of the employment relation (see Chapter 11). Finally, note that, by allowing for general probability distributions over states of nature, this theory would also be able to stress that the employment relation is less likely to emerge when there is less uncertainty as to the nature of the service desired by the buyer.

12.6   Summary and Literature Notes

This chapter has focused on the observable-but-unverifiable-information paradigm, and began with the pioneering contribution by Maskin (1977). He was the first to highlight the power of revelation mechanisms when it is common knowledge that agents share information that is unavailable to the principal, because one can compare their announcements and reward them on the basis of this comparison. Maskin, moreover, constructed mechanisms/contracts that achieve unique Nash implementation after having identified necessary conditions for implementation. This work has inspired a large literature summarized in Moore (1992). Within this literature, the work by Moore and Repullo (1988) shows that the set of implementable functions is significantly larger when one moves from unique Nash implementation to unique subgame-perfect implementation.

This implementation literature has, however, been criticized on two grounds: first and foremost because the mechanisms it has identified do not seem to be used in real-world settings, and second because they typically commit individuals to play inefficient outcomes on some equilibrium paths, and are therefore not renegotiation-proof. Subsequent contributions, however, have shown that the introduction of renegotiation "may kill two birds with one stone":[9] Relying on equilibrium future renegotiation permits implementation of optimal outcomes using simple and realistic initial contracts.[10] This possibility has been shown in this chapter in the specific context of the holdup problem. In this setting, the specifics of the environment (potential availability of default options, potential ability to influence bargaining powers in renegotiation, presence or absence of direct investment externalities) determine whether first-best outcomes can be achieved or not. As we have shown, one often cannot improve upon simple contracts like an option to sell (as in Noldeke and Schmidt, 1995), a default option tied to a penalty for delayed trade (as in Aghion, Dewatripont, and Rey, 1994), or a simple pair of prices for trade/no trade (as in Hart and Moore, 1988).

In some extreme cases, the null contract is even the optimal contract. For example, as shown by Che and Hausch (1999), it may be inefficient to sign an initial contract with a positive default level of trade in a setting where the seller's investment directly increases the buyer's valuation for the good, since the buyer benefits from the seller's investment through her ability to request the default trade.[11] An alternative setting in which the null contract may be approximately optimal is the one considered by Segal (1999a), where the *type of good* to be traded ex post is unverifiable: In this case, when the environment becomes very complex, as measured by the unboundedly large number of possible types of goods that can be traded, the value of contracting goes to zero when commitment not to renegotiate is assumed away.[12]

The preceding results have been derived under the assumption that actions (e.g., the level or nature of trade) are contractable both ex ante and ex post. Even under this assumption, the results of Che-Hausch and Segal can be seen as providing foundations for the Grossman-Hart-Moore

9. Of course, assuming away the parties' ability to commit not to take advantage of future Pareto-improving opportunities clearly reduces the set of implementable outcomes. For a general analysis of implementation with renegotiation, see Maskin and Moore (1999) and Segal and Whinston (2002).

10. Aghion, Dewatripont, and Rey (2002) make the point more generally that contracts can often be seen as partially influencing an underlying game that the contracting parties are bound to play in the future. This "partial contracting" interpretation should be contrasted with "classical" mechanism design à la Maskin (1999) or Moore-Repullo (1988) where the game the agents play is completely endogenous.

11. Bernheim and Whinston (1998b) consider a more general setting where signing a contract with fewer clauses (i.e., with more "ambiguity") improves the parties' incentives to behave efficiently in the relationship.

12. Reiche (2003a) explores a setting where investment is "ambiguous," that is, has a value that can be negative if the wrong ex post action is taken. In this case, the value of contracting also goes to zero in the absence of increasing complexity. And Reiche (2003b) is the first attempt to analyze the issues raised by Segal in an asymmetric information context.

incomplete-contract paradigm, which strictly limits the power of ex ante contracting. The argument invoked to justify such limitations is that actions are contractable ex post but not ex ante. As shown by Hart and Moore (1999), what often matters, however, for the power of ex ante contracting is not whether actions are contractable ex ante but whether parties can commit not to engage in future Pareto-improving renegotiation of the contract. This finding is consistent with the general results of Maskin and Tirole (1999a), who show that first-best outcomes can be achieved under full commitment despite ex ante noncontractability of actions.[13] As shown by Hart and Moore (1999), the irrelevance of ex ante noncontractability of actions is not valid, however, if the contracting parties are both risk neutral and unable to commit not to renegotiate the initial contract.

The preceding debate on the "foundations of incomplete contracting" has proceeded under the assumption that actions are noncontractable ex ante but contractable ex post. An alternative route is to focus on actions that are contractable neither ex ante nor ex post. Such actions are similar to the effort variable in moral-hazard models, which the principal can never contract upon: The agent is by assumption "in charge" of choosing the effort level. Assuming that actions are not even contractable ex post directly leads to a theory of authority, when one is able to choose *who* is in charge of a given action. We have shown in this chapter how the pioneering contribution of Aghion and Bolton (1992) on debt as a contingent-control device can be reinterpreted quite simply in terms of a "complete contract" setting with ex ante and ex post noncontractable actions. Other contributions that have built on ex ante and ex post noncontractable actions to investigate applications in corporate finance or the theory of organizations include Dewatripont and Tirole (1994a), Legros and Newman (2000), Hart and Moore (2000), and Hart and Holmström (2002). Aghion and Tirole (1997) have enriched the paradigm by distinguishing between "formal authority," the *right* to take decisions, and "real authority," the *ability* to take decisions, which often requires appropriate knowledge. Burkart, Gromb, and Panunzi (1997) and Dessein (2002) have used this setup in a corporate finance context, while Dessein (2004) and Aghion, Dewatripont, and Rey (2004) have further explored the connection between information transmission and authority in organizations.

---

13. See also Maskin and Tirole (1999b) and Maskin (2002) for specific illustrations and Tirole (1999) for a general discussion.

We have concluded this chapter by discussing how a repeated game with ex post unverifiable payoffs can provide an alternative theory of authority. We have based our discussion on a model due to Bolton and Rajan (2001). This approach is closely related to more reduced-form models of authority with implicit cooperation in relational contracts by Bull (1987), MacLeod and Malcomson (1989), Wernerfelt (1997), Kreps (1997), Baker, Gibbons, and Murphy (2002), Halonen (2002), and Levin (2003), among others.

Though we have covered quite an extensive set of models in this chapter, let us end by mentioning two additional approaches that try to endogenize contractual incompleteness. First, Anderlini and Felli (1994) have explored the role of bounds on the complexity of contracts, a topic worth pursuing in the future together with other approaches to "bounded rationality." Second, various papers have considered a signaling explanation of contract incompleteness. For example, a football player may forgo an injury insurance clause in his contract in order not to signal that he thinks he is accident-prone (Spier, 1992); a supplier may forgo a penalty for breach of contract by his buyer in order not to signal that he is afraid of potential competitors (Aghion and Bolton, 1987); and, similarly, not signing a long-term labor contract or debt contract may signal that one is not afraid to go back on the labor or capital market (Hermalin, 1988; Diamond, 1993). Finally, Aghion and Hermalin (1990) have argued that legal restrictions on contracts may limit this kind of (wasteful) signaling.

13 Markets and Contracts

This chapter considers a limitation on contracting that is very different from the one discussed in the previous two chapters: instead of considering the impossibility of contracting on some states of nature or actions, this chapter considers limits on the number of parties that can be part of the same contract. Specifically, we shall consider *competition* between multiple principals that each simultaneously offer agents bilateral contracts. In a way, we already considered, in Part III, a form of *intertemporal competition* in the case of a *single principal;* for example, in Chapter 9, a durable-good monopoly's desire to maximize profits in future conflicts with its overall profit-maximization motive as of now. We were, however, able to reinterpret such intertemporal competition in terms of additional constraints on the initial "grand contract." Here instead, with competition between principals, we are closer to an industrial organization setup, where bilateral contracts are the strategic variables of the game.

This chapter provides only selected coverage of the large number of models of market competition with bilateral contracts. It starts by covering by now classical ideas on market breakdown and existence of equilibrium problems under adverse selection, work due in particular to Akerlof and to Rothschild and Stiglitz. This material considers exclusive bilateral contracting. The chapter continues with an exploration of competition with exclusive contracts when contract offers are made sequentially and early contractual agreements can be set up to create a barrier to entry for future competitors. The chapter then proceeds with an analysis of nonexclusive contracting, which has been the subject of more recent work—with the analysis of "common-agency" games in particular. Finally, we close the chapter with an analysis of the link between product market competition and incentives, treating in turn competition between principal-agent pairs and the disciplinary role of product market competition on managers.

13.1 (Static) Adverse Selection: Market Breakdown and Existence Problems

In this section we cover the classic contributions of Akerlof (1970) and of Rothschild and Stiglitz (1976). We offer a unified treatment of their ideas by focusing on a single application: an insurance problem.

Thus, consider the insurance problem with individuals defined by their probability p_i of having an accident (with, say, $p_1 < p_2 < \ldots < p_N$) and type p_i being represented in proportion α_i in the population of individuals. Specifically, an individual has wealth w and utility $u(w)$ without an accident, whereas he suffers an income loss L and has utility $u(w - L)$ following an accident. Utility is increasing and concave, so that individuals are ready to pay an insurance premium for being fully insured at actuarially fair rates. However, if there is perfect competition between risk-neutral insurers and full information, the insurance premium I_i paid by individuals of type i is such that

$$I_i = p_i L$$

In this case, we know that risk-averse individuals strictly benefit from insurance, because they obtain a payoff of

$$u(w - I_i) > p_i u(w - L) + (1 - p_i) u(w)$$

13.1.1   The Case of a Single Contract

Assume now that only individuals know their own types, that is, their own accident probability p_i. Moreover, *assume, as in Akerlof (1970), that only one type of contract, here for simplicity a full-insurance contract, is available.* In this case, only one premium level I will emerge in equilibrium. For an individual to accept the equilibrium contract, we must have $u(w - I) \geq p_i u(w - L) + (1 - p_i) u(w)$. This means that only individuals with a high enough risk of accident will seek insurance. Note also that, just as in the analysis of credit rationing under adverse selection in Chapter 2, raising the price (here, the premium) of insurance worsens the pool of informed parties that accept the contract. With a finite number of types, at worst there can be an equilibrium with insurance solely for the highest-risk type p_N. For another equilibrium to exist with, say, types p_j *to* p_N accepting the contract, we need

$$u(w - I) \geq p_i u(w - L) + (1 - p_i) u(w) \quad \text{for } i = j, j+1, \ldots, N$$

$$u(w - I) < p_i u(w - L) + (1 - p_i) u(w) \quad \text{for } i = 1, 2, \ldots, j-1$$

and

$$\sum_{i=j}^{N} \alpha_i I = \sum_{i=j}^{N} \alpha_i p_i L$$

Intuitively, we need to find a break-even insurance premium I that makes it profitable for all types j to N to accept to pay I. The challenge is that the lower the risk of an accident for an individual, the less valuable is a given insurance contract. Any contract that pools several types has lower-risk individuals subsidizing higher-risk individuals, for the insurer to break even on average. On the one hand, if high-risk individuals are too costly (that is, have very high accident probabilities) or too numerous, then lower-risk individuals will prefer not to be insured at all. On the other hand, if utility is concave enough and the p_i's close enough, all types will pool; in this case, everybody will get insurance just as with full information.

With adverse selection, things can thus differ from full information in that (1) low-risk types may prefer not to be insured; (2) in the extreme case, only the highest-risk individuals will be covered (we have a "degenerate" market); and (3) there can be multiple equilibria; in this case, equilibria are Pareto-ranked: any individual who is insured prefers to be pooled with as many lower-risk individuals as possible, to enjoy more favorable cross-subsidization; moreover, since insurance is voluntary, individuals are better off in equilibria where they choose to be insured.

Note, however, that the equilibrium with maximum coverage is constrained Pareto-efficient: given the constraint of a unique contract, there is no way to satisfy the zero-profit condition for insurers and to make it attractive for lower-risk individuals to join in the pool, because cross-subsidization would be too unfavorable for them. A government without better information on individual types, however, could improve total surplus by subsidizing all insurance contracts, while having equal lump-sum taxation on all individuals: with perfect competition among insurers, the subsidy would be translated into a lower premium, therefore offsetting the taxation for those who choose to be insured; moreover, the subsidy would increase the attractiveness of insurance, making more types ready to join the pool of insurees.[1]

The preceding analysis exactly parallels that in the original Akerlof model, where uninformed buyers are facing sellers of used cars of unknown qualities, but where it is common knowledge that sellers know the quality of their own car and where reservation prices are increasing in quality, since the alternative to selling is to keep using one's car. Consequently, just as here where raising the insurance premium worsens the pool of insurees, in the Akerlof model lowering the price of used cars worsens the pool of sellers. Therefore, it may become impossible to trade any other cars than

---

1. See the recent paper by Bisin, Geanakoplos, Gottardi, Minelli, and Polemarchakis (2004) for a general statement of this result.

the worst ones in a world where, under symmetric information, all cars would be sold in equilibrium.

One final remark: In our insurance setup, we do not have "full market breakdown," that is, the absence of trade in the worst possible equilibrium. This outcome is possible in Akerlof's model but does not arise here because we have assumed that everybody trades under full information. Consequently, it is always profitable to offer an insurance contract acceptable only to the "worst" type. If instead the worst type were not able to trade under full information, the presence of adverse selection can then give rise to complete market breakdown as the only equilibrium.

13.1.2   The Case of Multiple Contracts

Following Rothschild and Stiglitz (1976), let us now allow for multiple contracts and screening. In particular, one can introduce the possibility of deductibles. Two types ($p_1 < p_2$) suffice to illustrate the main insights from their analysis. What Rothschild and Stiglitz have shown is that (1) if insurers are allowed to engage in "cream skimming" by offering better terms to low-risk individuals, pooling equilibria will fail to exist; (2) separating equilibria will also fail to exist if the proportion of high-risk individuals is low enough in the population; and (3) if an equilibrium does exist, it is constrained Pareto-efficient.

The maintained assumption in Rothschild and Stiglitz's analysis is that insurance contracts are *exclusive*: each individual can take on only a single insurance contract. Section 13.3 will look at nonexclusive contracts, while section 13.2 will endogenize the degree of exclusivity, by allowing for contractual penalties for switching contractual partners.

The game considered by Rothschild and Stiglitz is as follows: In stage one, insurers can offer individuals contracts that are pairs (I_i, D_i), where, as before, I_i is the insurance premium while D_i is the deductible. If an individual of type i accepts this contract, she obtains an expected payoff

$$p_i u(w - D_i - I_i) + (1 - p_i)u(w - I_i)$$

In stage two, individuals choose the best possible insurance contract or decide to remain uninsured, in which case they obtain an expected payoff $p_i u(w - L) + (1 - p_i)u(w)$.

Rothschild and Stiglitz assume that insurers are committed to honoring these contracts once they have been offered, even if insurers end up losing money on them. In equilibrium, however, they have to earn zero profits, because insurers compete à la Bertrand: if an insurer is earning positive profits by offering some stage-one insurance contracts [say, pairs (I_i, D_i), for $i = 1, 2$], an inactive insurer could take away these profits by offering exactly the same menu of contracts, but with a slightly lower insurance premium for everybody (that is, ask for $I_i - \varepsilon$, with $\varepsilon > 0$ but arbitrarily small and constant across i's). This insurer would now earn strictly positive profits.

What are the candidate zero-profit equilibria? First, these cannot be *pooling equilibria* because of "cream-skimming" behavior. To be precise, assume an active insurer is earning zero profits by pooling risks, that is, by attracting low-risk and high-risk individuals in proportions β and $(1 - \beta)$ with the contract (I_j, D_j), such that:

$$I_j = [p_1\beta + p_2(1 - \beta)](L - D_j)$$

An inactive insurer could then earn strictly positive profits by entering the market and offering a lower-premium, higher-deductible contract (I_k, D_k) that is attractive only to low-risk individuals. For this to be the case, the new contract has to simultaneously satisfy the constraints:

$$p_1 u(w - D_k - I_k) + (1 - p_1)u(w - I_k) \geq p_1 u(w - D_j - I_j) + (1 - p_1)u(w - I_j)$$

and

$$p_2 u(w - D_k - I_k) + (1 - p_2)u(w - I_k) < p_2 u(w - D_j - I_j) + (1 - p_2)u(w - I_j)$$

These inequalities imply that:

$$(p_2 - p_1)[u(w - D_j - I_j) - u(w - D_k - I_k)] \geq (p_2 - p_1)[u(w - I_j) - u(w - I_k)]$$

Since $p_2 > p_1$, it is possible to find $D_k > D_j$ and $I_k < I_j$ such that these inequalities are satisfied. An entrant can therefore manage to attract only low-risk individuals. Can it also make positive profits? Yes, and this result can be shown as follows: Consider a contract (I_k, D_k) that would leave low-risk types indifferent in comparison with the earlier contract (I_j, D_j). In this case, if the new contract is very close to the old one, that is, if the premium and the deductible are not changed much, the insurer will make almost the same (strictly positive) profit on low-risk types as under the pooling contract, only slightly less because of slightly worse insurance. Moreover, it will not lose money anymore on high-risk types, since this contract does not attract any of those risks. This contract can thus be profitably offered by an entrant, a result which proves that there exist no pooling equilibria.

Can there be *separating equilibria*? As we learned in Chapter 2, these clearly have to involve full insurance for high-risk types: there is no reason to distort their choice of insurance, because low-risk individuals do not have any incentive to "pretend" to be high risk. Due to perfect competition, insurers will earn zero profits on high-risk individuals; simultaneously, low-risk individuals will be offered the best possible partial insurance contract conditional on being unattractive to high-risk individuals. Specifically, equilibrium contracts (I_1, D_1) and (I_2, D_2) will have to be such that

$$D_2 = 0$$

and

$$I_2 = p_2 L$$

while (I_1, D_1) solves

$$\max p_1 u(w - D_1 - I_1) + (1 - p_1)u(w - I_1)$$

such that

$$I_1 \geq p_1(L - D_1)$$

and

$$u(w - I_2) \geq p_2 u(w - D_1 - I_1) + (1 - p_2)u(w - I_1)$$

This pair of contracts is *constrained Pareto-efficient* among the set of separating contracts: indeed, they support a "least-cost separating equilibrium," since insurance is maximized for high risks, and maximized subject to the incentive constraint for low risks.

The problem is that this pair of contracts may also fail to be an equilibrium, in which case we have nonexistence of a competitive equilibrium: by looking at the preceding maximization program, one can note first that the contract offered to low risks does not depend on the proportions α_1 and α_2 of low risks and high risks in the economy; and second that the contract will involve a larger deductible the larger the difference $p_2 - p_1$ between low risks and high risks. As a result, in order to induce separation and to avoid the cross-subsidization between types associated with pooling, low risks may end up facing a lot of risk. If the proportion of high risks is low enough in the economy, low risks would in fact be better off being pooled with high risks, in order to enjoy full insurance. Moreover, since high risks can only benefit from pooling, an inactive insurer could earn positive profits by entering and offering a single full-insurance contract that would Pareto-dominate the preceding separating contracts. This move would, however, eliminate the candidate separating equilibrium. And this outcome would imply nonexistence of equilibrium, because a pooling contract cannot be an equilibrium either, as we have demonstrated.

Recall from Chapter 3 that a similar issue arises in signaling models: the Cho and Kreps (1987) equilibrium is also the least-cost separating equilibrium, and it can also be Pareto-dominated. It survives as a perfect Bayesian equilibrium, however, thanks to the Cho-Kreps out-of-equilibrium beliefs. Here instead, in a screening context, there are no off-equilibrium beliefs to consider: individuals just have to compare two insurance contracts with known payoffs.

However, our ruling out pooling equilibria, together with the consequent nonexistence of equilibrium, does depend on the fact that we allow firms to steal customers from one another in a "targeted" way. This possibility exists in the Rothschild-Stiglitz setup because high risks stick with the initial pooling contract, which could bankrupt the insurer that offers it, once low risks have gone. Several authors have proposed solutions to this nonexistence problem by modifying this latter assumption:

- Wilson (1977) considers the notion of *anticipatory equilibrium;* under this concept, deviations that would become unprofitable if the initial contracts were *withdrawn* are not allowed (the initial contracts could become unprofitable and be withdrawn when they are competing against the deviating offer). With this restriction on allowable deviations, pooling equilibria may survive against deviations with separating contracts if the deviation causes the initial pooling contract to be unprofitable. Indeed, the withdrawal of the initial pooling contract then, in turn, causes the deviating contract to be unprofitable (since following the withdrawal of the initial pooling contract, the deviating contract attracts all types, and is unprofitable as a consequence).

- Riley (1979) instead defines the notion of *reactive equilibrium;* here, one does not allow deviations that would become unprofitable if they led competitors to react by *adding new contracts*. This in fact allows the least-cost separating contract to survive as a reactive equilibrium, because we know that it can be broken only by pooling contracts, which themselves can be broken by a separating contract.

Several authors have tried to provide game-theoretic foundations for these analyses. For example, Hellwig (1987) looks at a game where, in stage 1, firms make offers to individuals, in stage 2 offers can be withdrawn, and in stage 3 individuals choose between the remaining offers. He shows that the Wilson equilibrium is a perfect Bayesian equilibrium of this game, and even the unique "stable" one (in the terminology of Kohlberg and Mertens, 1986, who have built upon the "intuitive criterion" of Cho and Kreps). In contrast, Engers and Fernandez (1987) look at the same game as Hellwig's except that stage 2 is replaced by successive rounds in which firms can add contracts to the set of contracts already on offer. They show that the Riley equilibrium is a perfect Bayesian equilibrium of this game but that there may be other equilibria too, which can be supported by "trigger strategies" similar to those used to support equilibria in repeated games. It remains an open question whether either the Wilson or Riley equilibrium would continue to exist in the larger, more natural, game where in stage 2 offers can be added or withdrawn.

13.2   Contracts as a Barrier to Entry

In many market settings buyers do not get all competing contract offers at the same time. Often buyers may, for example, already have insurance coverage from an existing insurer when a new entrant appears with more attractive terms. More generally, when sellers make contract offers sequentially, then early sellers may attempt to lock customers into long-term contracts by imposing penalties on the buyer in the event of early termination.

It is not obvious a priori that contracts that lock in customers in this way would ever be agreeable to buyers. After all, buyers only stand to lose by limiting competition among sellers. As Aghion and Bolton (1987) have shown, however, there may still be gains from trade for the buyer and initial seller at the expense of future more efficient sellers in signing such "exclusive" contracts. In short, contracts that specify penalties for early termination can be used to extract efficiency rents from future entrants.

To see how this works, consider the following simple example adapted from Ziss (1996). Suppose that there are two transaction periods, $t = 0$ and $t = 1$. In period 0 an incumbent firm can offer a service at cost $c_I > 0$. A (representative) buyer is willing to pay at most $v = 1$ for the service. Suppose that $c_I \leq \frac{1}{2}$ for simplicity. This assumption implies in particular that there are gains from trade between the buyer and seller. In period 1 a new entrant may be able to provide the service at cost c_E.

As there is only one firm in period 0, the price of the service will be $p_0 = 1$. In period 1, however, entry will occur whenever $c_E \leq c_I$, ensuring that competition will take place. Suppose that the incumbent firm has only signed a spot insurance contract with the buyer in period 0; then in period 1 the buyer is "up for grabs" when entry occurs, and Bertrand price competition between the incumbent and the entrant ensures that the equilibrium price will be $p_1 = c_I$. When entry does not occur, then the incumbent continues to charge the "monopoly price" $p_1 = 1$.

Assuming for simplicity that the prior probability distribution of the entrant's future cost c_E is uniformly distributed on the interval $[0, 1]$, the buyer's ex ante expected payoff under spot contracting is given by

$$(1 - c_I)c_I$$

and the incumbent's payoff is

$$1 - c_I + (1 - c_I)^2$$

Suppose now that the incumbent and buyer sign a long-term contract in period 0 specifying a price for the service in both periods p_0 and p_1 as well as a penalty for early termination $d > 0$. Under such a contract the buyer would agree to switch to the entrant in period 1 only if the entrant's offer p_E is so low that

$$1 - p_E \geq 1 - p_1 + d$$

The probability of entry under such a contract is then

$$\Pr(\text{entry}) = \Pr(c_E \leq p_1 - d) = p_1 - d$$

Notice that in a Bertrand equilibrium in period 1 the entrant would only need to offer a price $p_E = p_1 - d$ to attract the buyer, so that the buyer's expected payoff under such a long-term contract is simply $(1 - p_0) + (1 - p_1)$.

The incumbent's ex ante expected payoff, however, is

$$p_0 - c_I + (p_1 - c_I)(1 - p_1 + d) + d(p_1 - d)$$

Given that the buyer always has the option of only accepting a spot contract from the incumbent, the long-term contract (p_0, p_1, d) is acceptable to the buyer only if

$$(1-p_0)+(1-p_1) \geq (1-c_I)c_I$$

Therefore, the incumbent seller's problem is to choose (p_0, p_1, d) to solve the following maximization problem:

$$\max_{(p_0,p_1,d)} \{p_0 - c_I + (p_1 - c_I)(1 - p_1 + d) + d(p_1 - d)\}$$

subject to

$$(1-p_0)+(1-p_1) \geq (1-c_I)c_I$$

Notice that the incumbent seller can set $p_0 = 1$ without loss of generality. Therefore, the incumbent's problem reduces to choosing d to maximize

$$(1 - c_I) + (1 - c_I)^2 [(1 - c_I)c_I + d] + d[1 - (1 - c_I)c_I - d]$$

Solving for the optimal d, one observes that

$$d^* = \frac{1 + (1 - c_I)(1 - 2c_I)}{2} > 0$$

and

$$\text{Pr(entry)} = p_1 - d^* = \frac{c_I}{2}$$

Two important observations emerge from this simple analysis. First, it is always preferable for the incumbent to sign a long-term contract with the buyer, which partially locks the buyer in. Second, this contract tends to reduce competition overall because the probability of entry under the long-term contract is $c_I/2$, as opposed to c_I under spot contracting.

The long-term contract serves as a device to extract part of the efficiency rent of the new entrant. As in the classic contracting problems discussed in Chapter 2, the optimal contract trades off rent extraction and allocative efficiency. The difference here is that it is a buyer-seller coalition that does the rent extraction at the expense of a more efficient future seller. The general implication of this analysis is that "contract markets" may not give rise to the same efficient competitive outcome as competitive markets for goods. By writing exclusionary contracts, buyer and seller coalitions can distort competition and produce inefficient equilibrium outcomes.

These implications go beyond the preceding simple illustrative example. They are also robust to a number of generalizations. As can be readily verified, the long-term contract continues to give rise to the same inefficient exclusion even if it can be renegotiated ex post, as long as the entrant's cost c_E remains private information. When the entrant's cost is public information, then inefficient exclusion can still arise when there are many buyers and when the entrant gains from increasing returns to scale. As can be readily checked, the incumbent seller can then achieve an equilibrium outcome where every buyer accepts a long-term exclusionary contract in a subgame-perfect equilibrium.

13.3   Competition with Bilateral Nonexclusive Contracts in the Presence of Externalities

We now relax the assumption that contracts are exclusive and consider contractual situations where the principal may freely sign multiple bilateral contracts with different agents. The larger the number of agents the principal can contract with, the more complex the multilateral contracting game the parties are involved in. The fine details of such a contracting game in reality—who gets to make the first contractual offer, what happens when multiple offers are made and some are turned down, what is the order of counteroffers, and so on—may be so complex that they may be virtually impossible to keep track of in a formal analysis of optimal contracting.

Accordingly, one strand of the literature has taken a cooperative-game approach to the analysis of these complex contracting games, which suppresses most institutional details of the contracting process and focuses instead on "reasonable" properties any equilibrium outcome must satisfy (see Ray and Vohra, 1997, for a notable contribution in this vein). Another approach has been to generalize the classical Walrasian competitive equilibrium framework to allow for asymmetric information and contracting with nonexclusive contracts. Under this approach, the objective is to characterize equilibrium contractual outcomes and to determine the existence of competitive equilibria and their efficiency. Some of the most notable contributions in this line are by Prescott and Townsend (1984), Gale (1992), Dubey, Geanakoplos, and Shubik (1996), Bisin and Gottardi (1999), and Bisin and Guaitoli (1998).

In keeping with most of the earlier parts of the book, we shall cover only the theoretical analyses that take a noncooperative game-theoretic approach to modeling competition in nonexclusive contracts. We refer the reader interested in the other two approaches to the works we have cited.

The main advantages of the noncooperative approach have been nicely formulated by Gale as follows:

Issues of tractability aside, the (noncooperative) approach remains an ideal towards which economic theory ought to strive. The virtue of the noncooperative approach is that every detail of the environment is made explicit. The extensive form describes all the institutional details of the market, the information that is available to the players and the actions they can take. It determines a unique feasible outcome for every possible profile of player strategies, not just the equilibrium strategies. Finally, it avoids the embarrassment of the invisible hand: everything that happens in equilibrium can be attributed to the actions of the players. (1992, p. 229)

A potential drawback of this approach to keep in mind, however, is that it unfortunately predicts outcomes that tend to be sensitive to fine institutional details, such as who makes the contracting offers, whether public commitments are available, and whether the parties are engaged in a one-shot game or interact repeatedly. It is then always a concern that an inadequate institutional representation of a particular contracting situation may have led to the wrong predictions on the efficiency of particular contractual arrangements.

The problem of nonexclusive contracting arises in many contexts. For example, it is common in insurance markets, as has been stressed in the classic contribution by Pauly (1974). His article is one of the first to argue that an insuree's inability to commit not to contract with multiple insurers can result in "overinsurance" and ultimately undermine the insuree's welfare. It is also a well-recognized problem in credit markets, where the risk of "debt dilution" arises when a borrower can borrow from multiple different sources (see, e.g., Fama and Miller, 1972; White, 1980). Other situations include upstream firms supplying inputs to multiple competitors, a firm selling a product with network externalities, and auctions and bidding with externalities (e.g., the spectrum auctions, takeover bids, etc.).

Rather than analyze one of these particular settings, like insurance contracting or borrowing and lending, we shall attempt to highlight the principles and factors that are common to all these situations by analyzing a general model of contracting between one principal and multiple agents due to Segal (1999b).

In this contracting problem, one principal can engage in a bilateral contractual relation with any of N agents facing him $(i = 1, 2, \ldots, N)$.[2] Let

---

2. In the literature on common agency problems the terminology is often the reverse, with a single agent facing N principals (see Bernheim and Whinston, 1985, 1986a, 1986b).

$x_i \in X_i \subseteq R^+$ denote the trade with agent i and let t_i the payment from agent i to the principal. Then, $\mathbf{x} = (x_1, \dots, x_N)$ denotes the trade profile with all N agents. The principal's payoff under this trade profile is given by

$$\sum_{i=1}^{N} t_i + f(\mathbf{x})$$

while each agent i's payoff is

$u_i(\mathbf{x}) - t_i$

Importantly, we shall allow for an agent j's trade x_j to impose an *externality* on another agent $i \neq j$, in two ways. First, agent j's trade may increase or decrease the principal's payoff of trading with agent i. Second, agent j's trade may increase or decrease agent i's payoff of trading with the principal.

We shall consider two alternative one-shot contracting games:

• The *offer game,* where the principal makes all the contract offers and each agent can only accept or reject her own contract offer. This game, considered in Segal (1999b), is descriptive of the following contracting situations in the literature: (1) a large upstream firm selling inputs to multiple competitors (as in McAfee and Schwartz, 1994, or Hart and Tirole, 1990); (2) a firm selling a product with network externalities (as in Katz and Shapiro, 1986); (3) an auction of an object where possession of the object by one agent imposes externalities on others (as in Jehiel and Moldovanu, 1996, or Jehiel, Moldovanu, and Stacchetti, 1996); (4) a raider attempting a hostile takeover of a target firm by making a *tender offer* to the shareholders of the target company (as in Grossman and Hart, 1980, 1988, and Harris and Raviv, 1988b, 1989); (5) a big risk-averse individual buying insurance from several insurance companies (as in Pauly, 1974, or Kahn and Mookherjee, 1998); and finally (6) a borrower taking a loan from several banks (as in White, 1980, and Bizer and DeMarzo, 1992).

• The *bidding game,* where the individual agents make bilateral offers to the principal. This is the *common agency* game analyzed in Bernheim and Whinston (1986b). This game-form has been used to describe contracting situations involving (1) multiple manufacturers distributing their product through a common retailer (Bernheim and Whinston, 1985), (2) multiple shareholders writing bilateral incentive contracts with a manager

(Bernheim and Whinston, 1985, 1986a), and (3) lobby groups influencing a government agency (Bernheim and Whinston, 1986a; Grossman and Helpman, 1994, 2002; Dixit, Grossman, and Helpman, 1997).

We begin our analysis of bilateral, nonexclusive contracting, with externalities between a principal and multiple agents by considering first the offer game.

13.3.1 The Simultaneous Offer Game

For expositional purposes it is helpful to restrict attention to situations where

1. individual trades are bounded one-dimensional trades: $x_i \in X_i = [0, \bar{x}_i]$.
2. all N agents are identical.
3. the welfare of the contracting parties depends only on the aggregate level of trade:

$$f(\mathbf{x}) + \sum_{i=1}^{N} u_i(\mathbf{x}) \equiv W\left(\sum_{i=1}^{N} x_i \right) \tag{13.1}$$

with $W'(0) > 0$ and $W''(\cdot) < 0$.

We consider in turn two contracting scenarios, one where all the contract offers are publicly observed by all agents, and the other where bilateral contracts between the principal and any agent j are not observed by the other agents $i \neq j$. As we shall highlight, the observability or nonobservability of bilateral contracts can make a critical difference for the efficiency of the overall contracting outcome.

13.3.1.1 Publicly Observable Contracts

The principal begins the contracting game by making a set of bilateral contract offers $\{(x_i, t_i)\}$, $i = 1, \ldots, N$. Each bilateral contract thus involves a level of trade x_i with agent i and a transfer to the principal t_i. Importantly, none of the bilateral contracts is contingent on the level of trade agreed to by other agents $j \neq i$. If we were to consider contracts with some agent i that are contingent on the trades agreed to by the other agents, we would effectively allow for a form of multilateral contract. The purpose of this section, however, is to explore what would happen when the parties do not engage in complete multilateral contracting. For expositional reasons it is helpful to focus on the extreme case where no form of interdependence among agents is controlled directly through some multilateral contractual clauses. We shall, however, briefly discuss an intermediate case when we consider menu auctions.

In practice, most multilateral contracting situations involve a *nexus of bilateral contracts,* which attempt to deal with the interdependence of agents' contracts only in a very limited form. There are many reasons for this contractual incompleteness, which we do not attempt to capture explicitly here. Rather, as in Chapter 11, we limit ourselves here to exploring the consequences of this contractual incompleteness for equilibrium outcomes.

Having received the principal's contract offers, the N agents follow by simultaneously making an *accept/reject* decision. If all agents accept their respective contract offers, they get payoffs $u_i(\mathbf{x}) - t_i$ for $i = 1, 2, \ldots N$. Instead, an agent j who would have unilaterally rejected her offer would get a payoff $u_j(0, \mathbf{x}_{-j})$, where $\mathbf{x}_{-j}$ denotes the vector of trades with all agents other than agent j.

Notice that given a set of bilateral contract offers $\{(x_i, t_i)\}$ there may be multiple equilibria in the continuation accept/reject coordination game. This is the case, for example, if the offers $\{(x_i, t_i)\}$ are such that, for all agents

$$u_i(\mathbf{x}) - t_i \geq u_i(0, \mathbf{x}_{-i})$$

but also

$$u_i(x_i, \mathbf{0}) - t_i < u_i(0, \mathbf{0})$$

where $\mathbf{0}$ denotes the vector $\mathbf{x}_{-i} = (0, \ldots, 0)$.

Whenever the contract offers induce such multiple equilibria in the continuation game, we shall assume that all agents always coordinate on the most efficient equilibrium. Under that assumption there is no loss of generality in restricting attention to contract offers $\{(x_i, t_i)\}$ such that every agent i ends up accepting her contract. For all such contract offers, the optimal set of offers for the principal keeps each agent on her reservation utility and specifies transfers t_i such that, for all i,

$$u_i(\mathbf{x}) - t_i = u_i(0, \mathbf{x}_{-i})$$

Substituting for all the t_i in the principal's objective, the optimal set of trades $\{x_i\}$ is then determined by maximixing the objective

$$f(\mathbf{x}) + \sum_{i=1}^{N} u_i(\mathbf{x}) - \sum_{i=1}^{N} u_i(0, \mathbf{x}_{-i}) \qquad (13.2)$$

Comparing objectives (13.1) and (13.2), one then immediately observes that the optimal set of contracts for the principal implement a socially efficient outcome if and only if $u_i(0, \mathbf{x}_{-i}) \equiv u_i(0, \mathbf{0})$ for all i and $\mathbf{x}_{-i}$. That is, the Coase theorem applies in this multilateral contracting situation with externalities if and only if the *nontraders* remain unaffected by the trades of the other agents with the principal. In other words, whenever bilateral trades impose *externalities on nontraders*—be they positive $[\partial u_i(0, \mathbf{x}_{-i})/\partial x_j > 0]$ or negative $[\partial u_i(0, \mathbf{x}_{-i})/\partial x_j < 0]$—the equilibrium of the bilateral contracting game may depart from social efficiency. An inefficiency arises in this case, as the principal is attempting to extract the *externality rents on nontraders* $u_i(0, \mathbf{x}_{-i})$. However, without such externalities, total welfare of the contracting parties is maximized, as there is no asymmetric information and therefore no information rents to be extracted.

Under our assumption that only the aggregate level of trade matters for total welfare, the principal's problem can be reduced to solving

$$\max_{X = \sum_i x_i} W(X) - R(X)$$

where

$$R(X) = \min_{x} \left[\sum_{i=1}^{N} u_i(0, \mathbf{x}_{-i}) \,\middle|\, \sum_{i=1}^{N} x_i = X \right]$$

When externalities are positive (negative), $R(X)$ is weakly increasing (decreasing) in X. To see this point, consider the case of positive externalities and take any $X' \leq X$. Let $\mathbf{x}$ be the vector associated with X in $R(X)$ and $\mathbf{x}'$ the vector associated with X'. We then have $\sum x_i = X$ and $\sum x_i' = X'$. Define $x_i'' = x_i - (X - X')/N$, and $\mathbf{x}''$ for the corresponding vector. With positive externalities, it must then be the case that

$$R(X') \leq \sum_{i=1}^{N} u_i(0, \mathbf{x}_{-i}'') \leq \sum_{i=1}^{N} u_i(0, \mathbf{x}_{-i}) = R(X)$$

which establishes that $R(X)$ is weakly increasing in X. The reasoning is similar for negative externalities.

Therefore, if we denote by X^* the aggregate level of trade that maximizes total welfare and by $\hat{X}$ the aggregate level of trade that maximizes the principal's payoff, it is easy to see that under positive externalities we have $\hat{X} \leq X^*$, while under negative externalities we have $\hat{X} \geq X^*$.[3] In the case of positive (negative) externalities on nontraders, the principal prefers to underprovide (overprovide) the good or service in order to reduce the rents associated with nonparticipation, and thus get agents to accept contracts with higher transfers.

This general result helps unify a number of disparate insights in the literature on multiagent contracting:

1. In the absence of externalities on nontraders—for example, in the case of insurance provision by multiple insurers or in the case of a new technology with network externalities and no prior substitutes—there is no reason to expect the contracting outcome in a publicly observable contracting process to be inefficient, *since the principal can extract all the rents associated with equilibrium trades without inducing any distortions.*

2. In the case of positive externalities on nontraders, as in a hostile takeover where efficiency is increasing in the proportion of shares tendered to the raider,[4] the principal is likely to commit to trades that are *lower* than would be socially optimal, in order to reduce equilibrium externality rents to nontraders.

3. In the case of negative externalities on nontraders, as in the case of input provision by an upstream firm to competing downstream firms (an application that we will detail later), the principal is likely to contract on trades that are *higher* than is socially optimal, in order to reduce all agents' equilibrium externality rents.

13.3.1.2 Privately Observable Contracts

In some of the applications that we have mentioned it is unlikely that the principal is actually engaging in publicly observable contracting negotiations or is able to commit to observable levels of trade with each of the agents. Accordingly, the contract-theory literature has explored the implications for equilibrium outcomes of *secret* bilateral contracting in

---

3. Things are in fact somewhat more complicated than it appears at first: as pointed out by Segal (1999b), in many applications X^* and $\hat{X}$ will not be single-valued. The result he derives, however, points to equilibrium trades that are lower (higher) than the level of trade that maximizes the total welfare of the contracting parties in case of positive (negative) externalities.

4. See Burkart, Gromb, and Panunzi (1998) for a model of takeovers with this property.

multilateral-contract settings involving externalities. In particular, Hart and Tirole (1990) and McAfee and Schwartz (1994) investigate the case of an input provider contracting with several downstream competitors, and Katz and Shapiro (1986) look at the case of an industry with network externalities. This section covers some of the main lessons from this literature.

We now assume that each agent i observes only her own contract offer (x_i, t_i). When agent i receives an offer from the principal, she now has to *guess* what other offers the principal has made to the other agents to decide whether or not to accept her own offer (x_i, t_i). Furthermore, the principal's offer to agent i may be a signal of the form of the offers to agents $j \neq i$, so that the contracting game with bilateral secret offers is, in effect, a complex signaling game. We know from Chapter 3 that signaling games may have a plethora of perfect Bayesian equilibria when out-of-equilibrium beliefs are not restricted. To be able to make sharper predictions about equilibrium outcomes, several restrictions on out-of-equilibrium beliefs have been considered for contracting games with secret bilateral contracts (see McAfee and Schwartz, 1994, for an extensive discussion of reasonable out-of-equilibrium beliefs for such contracting games). The most common restriction (or "refinement") that has been considered is the notion of *passive beliefs*, first introduced by McAfee and Schwartz (1994), which amounts to saying that, when observing an out-of-equilibrium contract offer (x_i', t_i'), agent i believes that all other offers remain the equilibrium offers.

We follow the literature here and characterize equilibrium outcomes of the contracting game when out-of-equilibrium beliefs are restricted to be passive. Under passive beliefs, when $(\hat{\mathbf{x}}, \hat{\mathbf{t}})$ denotes the equilibrium contract profile, agent i accepts an offer (x_i, t_i) if and only if

$$u_i(x_i, \hat{\mathbf{x}}_{-i}) - t_i \geq u_i(0, \hat{\mathbf{x}}_{-i})$$

Restricting attention, as before, to equilibrium outcomes where all agents accept their contract offers, the principal chooses equilibrium trades x_i to maximize the payoff

$$\sum_{i=1}^{N} t_i + f(\mathbf{x})$$

subject to each agent's participation constraint.

At the optimum again, all the participation constraints are binding. Substituting for all the t_i in the principal's objective, we find that optimal trades in a passive belief equilibrium are given by

$$\hat{x}_i \in \arg\max_{x_i} g(x_i, \hat{\mathbf{x}}_{-i}) \equiv f(\mathbf{x}) + \sum_{i=1}^{N} u_i(x_i, \hat{\mathbf{x}}_{-i}) - \sum_{i=1}^{N} u_i(0, \hat{\mathbf{x}}_{-i})$$

As always, when one imposes a sharp restriction on out-of-equilibrium beliefs, as we have done here, the question arises whether a refined perfect Bayesian equilibrium exists at all. As one might expect, it is possible to show that when $g(x, \hat{\mathbf{x}})$ is a continuous function and is quasi-concave in $\mathbf{x}$, then a passive belief equilibrium does indeed exist.

Note that here the reservation utilities $u_i(0, \hat{\mathbf{x}}_{-i})$ enter as constants and do not affect the equilibrium solution $\{\hat{x}_i\}$. This fact implies, in particular, that for every agent i the equilibrium trade $\hat{x}_i$ satisfies

$$\hat{x}_i \in \arg\max_{x_i} f(x_i, \hat{\mathbf{x}}_{-i}) + u_i(x_i, \hat{\mathbf{x}}_{-i})$$

This condition for optimality is referred to as *pairwise proofness* by McAfee and Schwartz (1994). The optimal trade for an individual agent cannot be directly altered by changing the trades offered to the other agents. This is a critical difference with the previous contracting problem, where contract offers were publicly observable. Now each bilateral contract maximizes the bilateral surplus between agent i and the principal. This result does not mean, however, that the overall multilateral surplus is maximized. Indeed, total surplus is not maximized *in the presence of externalities at equilibrium trade levels,* for then it is not possible to adjust an individual trade level specified in a bilateral contract to changes in other agents' trade levels.

There is one special case where the welfare optimum is attained. If at the welfare-maximizing trade vector $\mathbf{x}^*$ all agents' payoffs are such that $u_i(x_i^*, \mathbf{x}_{-i})$ is independent of $\mathbf{x}_{-i}$, then this trade vector can be supported as a *passive-belief* equilibrium. To see this point, note that, by the definition of a passive-belief equilibrium $\hat{\mathbf{x}}$, we have

$$f(\hat{\mathbf{x}}) + \sum_{i=1}^{N} u_i(\hat{\mathbf{x}}) \geq f(\mathbf{x}^*) + \sum_{i=1}^{N} u_i(x_i^*, \hat{\mathbf{x}}_{-i})$$

The condition that at $\mathbf{x}^*$ all agents' payoffs are such that $u_i(x_i^*, \mathbf{x}_{-i})$ is independent of $\mathbf{x}_{-i}$ then implies that

$$f(\mathbf{x}^*) + \sum_{i=1}^{N} u_i(x_i^*, \hat{\mathbf{x}}_{-i}) = f(\mathbf{x}^*) + \sum_{i=1}^{N} u_i(\mathbf{x}^*)$$

Since $\mathbf{x}^*$ maximizes

$$f(\mathbf{x}) + \sum_{i=1}^{N} u_i(\mathbf{x})$$

$\mathbf{x}^*$ is therefore also a *passive-belief* equilibrium.

In general, the distortion relative to the welfare optimum depends on the sign of the externalities at the efficient trade level. Assuming again that only the aggregate level of trade matters for the total welfare of the contracting parties, Segal (1999b) shows that when externalities are positive (negative), aggregate equilibrium output $\hat{X}$ is below (above) the socially efficient level X^*. We leave it to the reader to verify this simple claim.

Finally, note that when one compares the outcomes under publicly observable and privately observable contracts, the relevant externalities that the principal is attempting to internalize and appropriate are different. In the former contracting problem, the relevant externality to determine the direction of the distortion of equilibrium outcomes relative to efficiency is the one on nontraders, while in the latter contracting problem the relevant externality is the one affecting all traders at the socially efficient trade level. Given that different externalities are involved, it is not too surprising that in general the ranking of the two contracting outcomes in terms of efficiency is ambiguous. That is, in general it is not possible to say whether the nonobservability of bilateral contracts results in greater or less efficiency. An example will make this comparison more concrete.

13.3.1.3   Application: Input Provision to Competing Downstream Firms

This example is adapted from Hart and Tirole (1990) and McAfee and Schwartz (1994). An upstream firm, with a monopoly on an efficient input production technology, produces inputs at unit production costs, which we normalize to zero, and may sell these inputs to potentially two downstream firms (1 and 2), who compete à la Cournot in the final goods market. The inverse demand function in the final goods market is the simple linear downward-sloping function

$$p = 1 - x_1 - x_2$$

where x_i is the output of downstream firm $i = 1, 2$. One unit of output for each downstream firm requires one unit of input. While each downstream firm may purchase the required inputs from this efficient upstream firm, it can also purchase its inputs from an inefficient competitive fringe at unit price $\bar{p} > 0$.

Clearly here it is socially efficient for both downstream firms to procure their inputs from the efficient upstream firm. Moreover, the joint profits of all three firms,

$$\Pi = (1 - x_1 - x_2)(x_1 + x_2)$$

are maximized by setting

$$(x_1 + x_2) = \frac{1}{2}$$

In our previous notation this example is such that $f(\mathbf{x}) = 0$, since costs are zero for the upstream firm, and

$$u_i(x_i, x_j) = (1 - x_i - x_j)x_i$$

What about externalities on nontraders? They may arise here as a result of the downstream firms' option to buy inputs from the inefficient competitive fringe. Specifically, if a downstream firm i rejects the contract from the upstream firm and expects its competitor to produce x_j, it purchases inputs from the competitive fringe to maximize its profits

$$(1 - x_i - x_j - \bar{p})x_i$$

so that its best response as a "nontrader" with the efficient upstream firm is given by

$$x_i = \max\{0, (1 - x_j - \bar{p})/2\}$$

and its payoff as a nontrader is

$$u_i(0, x_j) = [\max\{0, (1 - x_j - \bar{p})/2\}]^2$$

If the competitive-fringe production costs are so high that it is not profitable for the downstream firms to procure any inputs from the fringe, then the nontraders' payoff is always zero and there are no externalities of trading by one downstream firm on the nontrading firm. In that case, contracting with publicly observable bilateral contracts results in an outcome that maximizes the joint profit of all three firms.

Otherwise, the equilibrium under publicly observable contracts is inefficient and is given by the solution to

$$\max_{x_i, x_j} \sum_{i,j=1,2, i \neq j} (1 - x_i - x_j)x_i - (1 - x_j - \bar{p})^2 / 4$$

As can easily be seen, this solution involves setting $(x_1 + x_2)$ above the efficient level of $\frac{1}{2}$. Specifically, equilibrium trades are then given by

$$x_1 = x_2 = x' = \frac{1}{3} - \frac{\bar{p}}{9}$$

Note that this solution requires $\bar{p} \leq \frac{3}{4}$, for when $\bar{p} = \frac{3}{4}$ then $x' = \frac{1}{4}$, so that production using outside inputs ceases to be advantageous for a nontrading downstream firm. The upstream firm can thus sell half of the monopoly quantity at a price of $t_i = \frac{1}{8}$, which leaves each downstream firm with a zero rent if both accept this offer. For lower levels of $\bar{p}$, however, the upstream firm is better off expanding the volume of sales beyond the level that maximizes joint profits, in order to reduce the rents each downstream firm can obtain by exploiting the outside option of procuring inputs from the competitive fringe.

As Hart and Tirole (1990) have highlighted, under privately observable contracts the upstream firm's monopoly position is undermined by its inability to commit not to supply more than the monopoly inputs to the downstream firms. To see this point, observe that under privately observable contracts the upstream firm chooses the level of trade with downstream firm i to maximize total bilateral profits from the trade with firm i, taking as given the expected level of trade with downstream firm j (which we can denote by $\tilde{x}_j$). Thus the upstream firm is setting (x_i, t_i) to solve

$$\max_{x_i, t_i} t_i$$

subject to

$$u_i(x_i, \tilde{x}_j) - t_i \geq u_i(0, \tilde{x}_j)$$

Downstream firm i's participation constraint can be rewritten as

$$(1 - x_i - \tilde{x}_j)x_i - t_i \geq (1 - \tilde{x}_j - \bar{p})^2 / 4$$

Since the expected level of trade $\tilde{x}_j$ is like an exogenous parameter (in a *passive-belief* equilibrium), the solution to the bilateral profit maximization problem is

$$x_i = \frac{1 - \tilde{x}_j}{2}$$

By symmetry, we also have

$$x_j = \frac{1 - \tilde{x}_i}{2}$$

Solving these two equations so that $\hat{x}_i = \tilde{x}_i$ for $i = 1, 2$, we obtain the equilibrium trades $\hat{x}$ under privately observable contracting. This equilibrium outcome is none other than the Cournot competition outcome with $\hat{x}_1 = \hat{x}_2 = \frac{1}{3}$.

Comparing the outcomes under publicly and privately observable contracts, we thus observe that the joint profits of firms are higher under publicly observable contracts, as long as $\bar{p} > 0$. This is not to say, however, that welfare is maximized under publicly observable contracts. Moreover, while firms are better off under publicly observable contracting, consumers are clearly better off under privately observable contracting.

13.3.2   The Sequential Offer Game

In many multilateral contracting situations it is unreasonable to think that the principal will engage in bilateral contracts simultaneously with all agents. It is more likely that the principal first signs up one agent and then turns to a second agent and so on. For example, an insuree may contract first with a primary insurer and in a second step take on secondary insurance.

While several of the insights obtained in the previous section also apply to situations where the principal contracts sequentially with agents, there are also some important differences, which we highlight in this section. In particular, a major difference under sequential contracting, which has important consequences for equilibrium outcomes, is that the first agent(s) to sign a contract will take into account the potential impact of a change in their contract on future contracts. This assumption is in contrast with the assumption of *passive beliefs*, where each bilateral contract is determined as if it had no impact on other trades.

Much of the discussion in this section is based on the simple and elegant treatment of an insurance-contracting problem with moral hazard under nonexclusive contracts by Kahn and Mookherjee (1998). Consider a risk-averse principal facing N perfectly competitive risk-neutral insurance companies (agents). Without insurance, the principal has wealth w in the event of *no accident* and $(w - L)$ in the event of an *accident*. His utility of wealth is a strictly increasing and concave function $u(\cdot)$. The principal can *exercise caution* to reduce the risk of an accident. If he is cautious, the probability of an accident is p_L, while if he is not, it is $p_H > p_L$. The principal incurs a utility cost $\psi > 0$ for being cautious. We assume that being cautious is profitable for the principal in the absence of insurance. That is,

$$p_L u(w - L) + (1 - p_L)u(w) - \psi \geq p_H u(w - L) + (1 - p_H)u(w)$$

We shall also assume that when he is perfectly insured at actuarially fair terms his payoff is higher when he can commit to be cautious:

$$u[p_L(w - L) + (1 - p_L)w] - \psi \geq u[p_H(w - L) + (1 - p_H)w]$$

Thus, under first-best contracting, the principal is perfectly insured and exercises caution. Insurance companies compete to supply insurance and make zero profits in equilibrium. The principal then obtains a payoff of

$$u[p_L(w - L) + (1 - p_L)w] - \psi$$

Under second-best contracting, when the principal's cautiousness is not observable and he cannot commit to be cautious, we know from Chapter 4 that perfect insurance is generally suboptimal. Consider, first, the benchmark situation where the principal can commit to an exclusive insurance contract with a single insurer. Without loss of generality, the insurance contract can be represented as a pair (I, D), where I is the *premium* and $D > 0$ is the *deductible* (which means that in case of an accident the insurance company pays the principal only an amount $L - D$). We shall assume here that being cautious is always efficient even under moral hazard. Therefore, the second-best contracting problem for the principal can be written as

$$\max_{I,D} p_L u(w - I - D) + (1 - p_L)u(w - I) - \psi$$

subject to

$$I \geq p_L(L - D)$$

and

$$p_L u(w-I-D)+(1-p_L)u(w-I)-\psi \geq p_H u(w-I-D)+(1-p_H)u(w-I)$$

The first constraint is a participation constraint for the insurance company. It has to at least break even by providing insurance, under the assumption that the principal takes proper care to avoid accidents. The second constraint is the incentive constraint for the principal, that is, here, by convention, the insuree.

It is convenient to work directly in terms of the principal's wealth in the two states of nature. For this purpose, define the no-accident wealth as $w_N = w - I$ and the accident wealth as $w_A = w - I - D$.

The second-best problem can then be rewritten after some simple manipulations as

$$\max_{w_A, w_N} p_L u(w_A)+(1-p_L)u(w_N)-\psi$$

subject to

$$p_L w_A + (1-p_L)w_N \leq w - p_L L$$

and

$$(p_H - p_L)[u(w_N) - u(w_A)] \geq \psi$$

The first constraint is binding at the optimum, since otherwise w_N can be raised, thereby raising the maximand and relaxing the second constraint. The incentive constraint will also be binding at the optimum, since otherwise we can improve insurance for the principal at an unchanged expected profit for the insurer. Thus the second-best contract requires a strictly positive deductible D (that is, $w_A < w_N$) in order to induce the principal to be cautious. This application is just another illustration of the classical trade-off between risk sharing and incentives, which we have discussed at length in Chapter 4.

Consider now what happens when the principal cannot commit to writing a single exclusive insurance contract. Assume that, no matter what contracts the principal has already signed with insurers, he can always go and offer any insurer a new, *supplementary* insurance contract before choosing his level of care. All bilateral contracts are assumed to be publicly observable. As a result of the principal's inability to commit to a single primary insurer, the second-best outcome we have just described cannot be attained anymore.

More specifically, *once signed,* any contract where the incentive constraint binds can subsequently be improved upon *by the principal.* This result can be seen by the following reasoning: (1) in the second-best contract, the principal's payoff is the same whether he is cautious or not, since the incentive constraint binds; (2) suppose that, contrary to the second-best outcome, the principal decides not to be cautious; (3) he can then increase his payoff by obtaining full insurance by taking on supplementary insurance; (4) the secondary insurer realizes that the principal will face a higher risk of an accident and will take that into account in setting the premium, but the new contract is still profitable for the principal and the secondary insurer. Of course, by taking on secondary insurance, the principal and the secondary insurer impose a negative externality on the primary insurer, who would strictly prefer the principal to be cautious.

If the second-best contract, and more generally any contract where the incentive constraint is binding, cannot be an equilibrium outcome under nonexclusive contracting, what contracts can be equilibrium outcomes? As with renegotiation in Chapter 9, we can, without loss of generality, think of the equilibrium outcome as implemented with a single primary contract, for which the principal has no incentive to take out supplementary insurance.

There are only two possibilities here for a *third-best* contract (with non-exclusive contracting). Either this contract induces the principal to be cautious, or it does not. It is obvious that if the principal is not exercising caution, then the optimal contract is a full-insurance contract with a risk of an accident of p_H. Given the zero-profit condition for insurers, we have in that case

$$w_A = w_N = \tilde{w} = w - p_H L$$

which gives the principal a payoff of $u(w - p_H L)$.

Two cases are then possible: either $u(w - p_H L)$ is lower than the no-contract payoff

$$u_N \equiv p_L u(w - L) + (1 - p_L) u(w) - \psi$$

or it is higher.

Case 1: $u(\tilde{w}) < u_N$ In this case, the third-best equilibrium contract induces the principal to exert caution, and the optimal amount of insurance is given by the solution to

$$\max_{w_A, w_N} p_L u(w_A) + (1 - p_L) u(w_N) - \psi$$

subject to

$$p_L w_A + (1 - p_L) w_N \leq w - p_L L$$

and

$$p_L u(w_A) + (1 - p_L) u(w_N) - \psi \geq u[p_H w_A + (1 - p_H) w_N]$$

Note that the second constraint is now stronger than our familiar incentive constraint. This constraint implies that a contract inducing a high level of caution can be an equilibrium contract only if it cannot be improved upon by a supplementary insurance contract with no caution (and the best such contract involves full insurance). When this *third-best* incentive constraint binds, our familiar incentive constraint is redundant: indeed, the supplementary contract strictly improves upon the contract (w_A, w_N) *if the agent chooses not to exercise caution.*

In equilibrium, this third-best incentive constraint will be binding. Otherwise, it would be possible to improve on the insurance arrangement while maintaining nonnegative profits for the insurer.

Case 2: $u(\tilde{w}) \geq u_N$ In this case, it is possible that there is no way to reach a higher utility level than $u(\tilde{w})$. This is the case, for example, when the initial wealth pair $(w - L, w)$ involves an expected utility for the principal that is not much lower than the second-best level. However, if under the initial wealth pair $(w - L, w)$ the principal has a much lower utility than the second-best level, it is possible that the equilibrium outcome is the same as in Case 1.

To summarize: The principal's inability to commit not to enter into other contracts lowers his equilibrium payoff. However, the extreme outcome of full insurance and no caution is not necessarily the only third-best equilibrium outcome. Instead, another possible outcome is for the principal to limit the amount of insurance he gets from a primary insurer even more than he would under a second-best contract. He has to do this to be able to resist the subsequent temptation to obtain supplementary insurance.

An analysis very similar to the preceding can be performed for the situation where the principal is a borrower who sequentially borrows to invest in a project that also requires effort to raise its continuation value. Bizer and DeMarzo (1992) consider such a contracting problem, where externalities are limited because debt is prioritized but are nonetheless present because higher total debt means lower effort by the principal (Myers', 1977, familiar *debt-overhang* problem mentioned in Chapter 4). Nonexclusivity then results in higher interest rates and indebtedness, and in lower effort by the principal.

13.3.3   The Bidding Game: Common Agency and Menu Auctions

In some multilateral contracting situations it is the agents who initiate contract offers, or bids.[5] This is the case, for example, in procurement contracting, where government agencies typically invite bids rather than make offers to individual contractors. When agents make bids, the dimension of the coordination problem between agents is significantly increased. Where in the offer game the coordination problem among agents arises only in their accept/reject decisions, in the bidding game the coordination problem arises in the contracts they offer and the accept/reject decisions of the principal they induce. Not surprisingly, given the greater potential for coordination failures in the bidding game, much of the early literature on *common agency* and *menu auctions* has focused on this issue. Here, therefore, we concentrate on illustrating how the efficient contractual outcome may not arise in equilibrium because of a coordination failure among agents in a simple example due to Bernheim and Whinston (1986a).

They consider a multiobject auction without externalities, where the principal initially owns M objects and his valuation for each of the objects is normalized to zero. He faces N agents who can, in a first stage, submit nonnegative bids for any of the possible combinations of the objects. In a second stage, the principal chooses the allocation of these objects so as to maximize his total monetary payoff. This game has two noteworthy features: First, we have an auction setting where each object can be allocated only to a single individual. Second, given that all transfers are nonnegative, the principal is always weakly better off accepting all offers, so that we can dispense with all parties' participation constraints.

To be more specific, let us focus here on a principal putting up two items for auction, x_a and x_b. Two agents with preferences for the two items are represented in the following payoff matrix:

---

5. Note that the literature is known as the *common-agency* literature; that is, the names *principal* and *agent* are reversed in comparison with the terminology used in this chapter.

Allocations	Agent 1 Payoff u_1	Agent 2 Payoff u_2
Nothing	0	0
x_a	6	5
x_b	5	6
x_a and x_b	8	7

Given this payoff structure, the efficient allocation is for agent 1 to get x_a and agent 2 to get x_b. Under this outcome the total surplus from trade is 12. There exists, however, an inefficient subgame-perfect-equilibrium outcome of this game where bidder 1 gets both items and a surplus of trade of only 8 is obtained (while the principal gets a payoff of 7). This equilibrium outcome is obtained if the two agents each submit the following equilibrium bids [denoted by $t_i(\cdot)$]:

$$t_i(x_a + x_b) = 7 \quad \text{and} \quad t_i(x_a) = t_i(x_b) = 0$$

To see that these are indeed equilibrium bids, note that if bidder 1 *only* bids for both items, bidder 2 can never gain by bidding for a single item only, and vice versa. There are other equilibria, however. In particular, define a *globally truthful* schedule with utilities u_i^* for $i = 1, 2, \ldots, N$ as a payment schedule where for each individual i and each allocation x, we have

$$u_i[x, t_i(x, u_i^*)] = u_i^*$$

This is a payment schedule where each agent i ends up *truthfully revealing her marginal willingness to pay* for all positive levels of trade, and therefore obtains a constant payoff whatever the (positive) level of trade. In the preceding example, we can rewrite globally truthful schedules as

$$t_1(x_a + x_b) = 8 - u_1^*, \quad t_1(x_a) = 6 - u_1^*, \quad \text{and} \quad t_1(x_b) = 5 - u_1^*$$

for agent 1 and

$$t_2(x_a + x_b) = 7 - u_2^*, \quad t_2(x_a) = 5 - u_2^*, \quad \text{and} \quad t_2(x_b) = 6 - u_2^*$$

for agent 2.

For globally truthful schedules to be equilibria, they have to be mutual best responses, given the optimal choice of the principal. Note that, since the principal cannot make any offer, each agent will give him a zero marginal surplus from trading with her. If the principal trades only with agent i, who moreover offers a globally truthful schedule, he chooses to sell both objects, and he thus obtains as payment $t_i(x_a + x_b)$. Not giving any additional surplus from trading with an additional agent means that the payments $t_i(x_a + x_b)$ for $i = 1, 2$ are equalized across agents and are equal to the revenue the principal obtains from trading with both agents. But trading with both agents under globally truthful schedules makes sense for the principal only if it involves selling x_a to agent 1 and x_b to agent 2. This transaction takes place at a total price of

$$t_1(x_a + x_b) - 2 + t_2(x_a + x_b) - 1 = 2t_i(x_a + x_b) - 3$$

By the preceding reasoning, these conditions imply

$$t_i(x_a + x_b) = 3$$

so that in equilibrium x_a is sold to agent 1 at a price of 1 and x_b is sold to agent 2 at a price of 2. This is an equilibrium for the following reasons:

1. The principal is maximizing his surplus by selling the two objects in this way, given the two schedules put forward by the agents.

2. Agent 1 has a utility level of 5 and could not get more by deviating and trying to get both objects from the principal.

3. Similarly, agent 2 has a utility level of 4 and could not get more by deviating and trying to get both objects from the principal.

One can show that an equilibrium with globally truthful schedules always exists, and that it is efficient in the absence of externalities, that is, when agents' payoffs depend only on their own trades with the principal. This conclusion is intuitive, because under globally truthful schedules, the principal faces constant utility levels for all the agents he is trading with.

The preceding example therefore shows that going from offer games to bidding games has two implications: (1) coordination failures are likely to be endemic, but (2) in the absence of externalities there exists an efficient equilibrium where agents submit globally truthful schedules.

13.4   Principal-Agent Pairs

Introducing contracting questions in industrial organization is very natural: most situations of oligopolistic competition involve "managerial firms" where agency problems typically arise. What is the impact of these agency problems on the equilibrium outcome of oligopoly models? And is there a *strategic value* for principal-agent contracts?

These questions have been studied by a first generation of papers that have assumed contracts to be *publicly observable* and parties to be able to *commit not to renegotiate* them. For example, Fershtman and Judd (1987) focus on a duopoly where firm i is represented by two risk-neutral, symmetrically informed individuals: a shareholder/principal and a manager/agent. The game considered has two stages. In stage 1 each principal-agent pair has to agree on a linear managerial incentive scheme

$$w_i = \alpha_i q_i + \beta_i \pi_i$$

where the managerial compensation w_i depends linearly on the output q_i sold by the firm and its profit level π_i. Once these contracts have been (simultaneously) signed, in stage 2 of the game the α_i's and β_i's become public information and competition takes place, in (static) Cournot or Bertrand[6] fashion.

As is familiar from industrial organization, strategic considerations differ between Cournot and Bertrand competition, because the first corresponds to the case of strategic substitutability (downward-sloping reaction functions) and the second to strategic complementarity (upward-sloping reaction functions):[7] in the Cournot case, it pays to commit to being tougher because doing so induces the competition to become softer, while in the Bertrand case, getting the competition to become softer is achieved by being softer too. Consequently, the outcome of the two-stage game implies positive sales incentives ($\alpha_i > 0$) when stage 2 is modeled as Cournot competition, while negative sales incentives ($\alpha_i < 0$) result under Bertrand competition. By comparison, in the benchmark case without any strategic considerations, only profits would be remunerated ($\alpha_i = 0$).

The preceding result is not without problems. First, one can regret that, as is usual with these strategic models, the prediction depends crucially on the nature of competition between the firms, which is itself often hard to determine. Second, and this is a criticism more specific to this model, how

6. Assume that the two firms' products are differentiated, in order to keep reaction functions continuous.

7. See, for example, Bulow, Geanakoplos, and Klemperer (1985) and Fudenberg and Tirole (1984).

can we justify the assumption that the parties can commit to an incentive scheme that is not renegotiation-proof? Indeed, while it is in the interest of each principal-agent pair to have the other pair *believe* that they will deviate from pure profit maximization, once stage 2 is reached each pair would like to secretly return to profit maximization for each given level of the stage-2 choice variable of the other pair. In fact, if secret renegotiation were allowed after stage 1, under symmetric information within each principal-agent pair they would each revert back to $\alpha_i = 0$, and this move would be anticipated by the other pair, so that contracts would lose all strategic value.[8]

Introducing asymmetric information within each pair is a natural solution to prevent perfect renegotiation. This idea is by now familiar from Chapter 9: ex post Pareto-improving renegotiation is more difficult in the presence of asymmetric information because it typically implies that the uninformed party has to concede rents to (some types of) the informed party. The strategic value of renegotiation-proof contracts in the presence of asymmetric information has first been investigated by Dewatripont (1988) in a setting where contracting takes place between an incumbent firm and a third party (e.g., a labor union) before the potential entry of a competitor. Contracting is designed to commit the firm to high post-entry output. It is assumed to take place before the firm learns its private information (about its own cost, say). However, if the firm has learned its cost by the time the entry decision occurs, renegotiating away the excessively high post-entry output is hard because the union will be afraid (and rightly so) of losing rents in the form of lower wages. Consequently, as long as the ex post allocative inefficiency is not too high, it will be renegotiation-proof. Contracts thus keep some strategic value with asymmetric information, even when ex post Pareto-improving renegotiation is unavoidable.

One can thus rely on asymmetric information to restore the strategic value of contracts in the presence of renegotiation. Note two caveats, however: first, Dewatripont has not addressed the problem of ambiguity of the impact of contracts depending on whether competition is of the Cournot or Bertrand type; second, the reasoning has relied on a model

---

8. A third problem concerns the fact that Fershtman and Judd consider only a specific subset of feasible contracts, namely, contracts linear in sales and profits. Katz (1991) shows that, by allowing more general contractual forms, one can generate many potential equilibria in this game.

where renegotiation happens at the *interim stage* (once the informed party
has learned its type) while initial contracting took place at the initial stage
(before the informed party had learned its type). What about secret renegotiation just after the initial contract has been signed and before any new
information has arrived? This is what would make renegotiation easiest.
Could it eliminate any strategic value of contracting?

These questions are analyzed in depth by Caillaud, Jullien, and Picard
(1995). Let us illustrate their conclusions using one of their examples. It
assumes a Cournot duopoly with market demand defined by $p = 0.5(5 - a - b)$, where a and b are the output levels of the two firms A and B. Let us
focus on asymmetric information at firm A. Assume that the principal has
no private information and has payoff $\pi(a, b, t) = 0.5(5 - a - b)a - t$, while
the agent has private information on her unit cost θ_i and has payoff
$u(a, t, \theta_i) = t - \theta_i a$. The principal thus receives the revenue of the firm
and pays a transfer t to the agent to cover her own cost. As for the private
information, assume that it is common knowledge that the agent can have
two equiprobable cost realizations $\theta_1 = 1 - \delta$ and $\theta_2 = 1 + \delta$, with δ not too
large.[9]

The game consists of three stages:

• The first stage is the initial public contracting stage. In this setup, it will
be enlightening to focus on very simple contracts of the form "The principal accepts paying the agent an unconditional amount R."

• The second stage is the secret renegotiation stage: the principal offers the
agent a new contract of the form $t(a, b)$. If the agent refuses, then the principal pays the agent the initially agreed amount R (and, given the payoff
function of the agent, we shall have zero output from this firm). If the agent
accepts, we move to the third stage and to Cournot competition between
the agents of the two firms. Note that, while the other firm has observed the
initial contract, and thus R, it does not observe the new contract $t(a, b)$ or
whether it is accepted or not.

• In the third stage, the agent learns her type θ_i. She can stay in the market,
in which case there is a simultaneous choice of outputs (call it a_i for the
type-i agent of firm A and b for firm B). The agent is also assumed to be
able to quit at any moment and obtain a zero payoff (while producing zero
output).

---

9. One can verify that $\delta \leq 0.3$ is sufficient for the following discussion.

Both the initial public contracting and the secret renegotiation are thus assumed to happen before the agent has learned her type. This assumption makes renegotiation as easy as possible; therefore, obtaining any strategic value for contracting is hardest.

Let us assume that an initial contract has been signed, with associated payment R from the principal to the agent in stage 3 if stage-2 renegotiation has failed. Assume moreover that the principal can make a take-it-or-leave-it offer to the agent in the secret renegotiation stage. What will be his best offer? It will be convenient to think not in terms of an outcome (t_i, a_i), but in terms of (u_i, a_i), noting that $t_i \equiv u_i + \theta_i a_i$. Given an expected output b from the other firm, the best offer from the point of view of the principal will solve

$$\max_{u_i, a_i} \sum_i 0.5\{0.5(5 - a_i - b - 2\theta_i)a_i - u_i\}$$

subject to

$$2\delta a_1 \geq u_1 - u_2 \geq 2\delta a_2 \tag{IC}$$

$$u_i \geq 0 \quad \text{for } i = 1, 2 \tag{EPIR}$$

$$0.5u_1 + 0.5u_2 \geq R \tag{EAIR}$$

The principal thus maximizes his expected revenue, net of the transfer to the agent, subject to the two incentive constraints [the agent should have an incentive to choose (t_i, a_i) when her type is θ_i] and to the ex post and ex ante participation constraints [constraints (EPIR) and (EAIR), respectively]. While ex post the agent cannot have a negative payoff, from an ex ante point of view, the constraint concerns the initial contract that has given her the possibility of obtaining a transfer R at no cost.

The full-information contract involves dropping the incentive constraints, which implies maximizing $0.5(5 - a_i - b - 2\theta_i)a_i$ for each θ_i. This operation yields the standard Cournot best response, which we can denote by $A_i^*(b) \equiv 0.5(5 - b) - \theta_i$. What if we start instead with asymmetric information and without an initial contract, that is, with $R = 0$? This approach means solving the preceding program without the ex ante constraint (EAIR). From Chapter 2 we know that one type will have the same output as without the incentive constraint but will earn rents, while the other will have no rents but an output distorted downward. Specifically, one can verify that the output levels will be $a_1 = A_1^*(b)$, while $a_2 = A_2(b, 0) \equiv 0.5(3 - b) -$

$3\delta < A_2^*(b)$. The rents for the agent of type θ_1 are equal to what she would get by mimicking type θ_2, that is, $2\delta a_2$ (since $u_2 = 0$ and $u_1 = u_2 + 2\delta a_2$), which we can denote by $2R^0(b)$. From an ex ante perspective, the expected rents of the agent are thus $R^0(b)$.

As long as the initial contract gives the agent a transfer $R \le R^0(b)$, it will be irrelevant, and everybody will expect secret renegotiation to deliver an output response $\{A_1^*(b), A_2(b, 0)\}$. But what if the initial contract specifies a transfer for the agent in excess of $R^0(b)$? Then the trade-off between rent extraction and allocative efficiency is modified, because the initial contract requires that more rents be conceded, in expected terms, to the agent. The efficient way to do so is for the principal to give rents to type θ_1, which at least allows him to reduce the underprovision of output by type θ_2. If the public initial contract implies a transfer R somewhat in excess of $R^0(b)$, secret renegotiation will imply $u_2 = 0$, $u_1 = 2R$, $a_1 = A_1^*(b)$, and $a_2 = R/\delta$ (this last expression is obtained from the relation $u_1 = u_2 + 2\delta a_2$). For higher R's, output a_2 can rise up to its first-best level, in which case higher R's then imply higher utility levels for both types at unchanged output levels.

We thus see that, by modifying the trade-off between rent extraction and allocative efficiency, an initial contract offering rents to the agent has an impact on the output levels that are secretly (re)negotiated between the principal and the agent. Specifically, a more generous initial contract leads to less allocative inefficiency for type θ_2, and thus a higher expected output level by firm A for any given level of output b by firm B. Under Cournot competition, a higher output is attractive as it implies a reduction of equilibrium output b.

Specifically, assuming that firm B has a marginal cost of 2, its reaction function is $b = 1.5 - (a_1 + a_2)/4$. In the absence of an initial contract, one can check that the equilibrium involves $b \equiv b_0 = 1 + 2\delta/3$, $a_1 = A_1^*(b_0)$, and $a_2 = A_2(b_0, 0)$. This contract gives the agent a level of expected rents $R^0(b_0)$. It is then *strictly* in the interest of the principal to give the agent an initial contract with a slightly higher payment than $R^0(b_0)$: it implies only a *second-order loss* for a given output b (given the upward adjustment of a_2), while delivering a *first-order gain* in terms of reduction of the output b of the other firm (from the reaction function, b goes down by 25% of the increase in a_2).

In the Cournot setting, not signing an initial contract is thus not an equilibrium, despite the fact that secret renegotiation is expected right after the initial contract has been signed and thus in the absence of any new information. The equilibrium initial contract offers rents to the agent that limit the need to reduce output below its full-information Cournot level, thereby shifting upward the reaction function of the firm and lowering the equilibrium output of the other firm.

What about a (differentiated) Bertrand setting now? If we keep the same game as before except for having price competition in the last stage instead of quantity competition, we have the same role for initial contracting: by offering rents to the agent initially, one limits the downward distortion of output relative to its full-information level. Here, however, the strategic effect of the initial contract is detrimental: since it makes the firm "tougher," its competitor also becomes tougher. There is no use for an initial contract that grants rents to the agent in order to limit the underproduction that adverse selection creates. Caillaud, Jullien, and Picard show that no stage-zero contract will be signed under Bertrand competition.

Their approach can thus be seen as having "killed two birds with one stone." By allowing for secret renegotiation, it has enhanced realism but also reduced the ambiguity of the role of strategic contracting: since it can only make the firm tougher by reducing the underproduction due to adverse selection, it is only used under quantity competition à la Couruot. Their analysis also leads to an unambiguous policy conclusion: when it is effective, strategic contracting raises output and welfare.

13.5   Competition as an Incentive Scheme

The previous sections have considered a variety of environments where contracting has strategic effects. We end here by asking how in turn contracting and the size of agency costs are influenced by the competitive environment. This question is an old one, encapsulated in the famous saying by Hicks (1935): "The best of all monopoly profits is a quiet life." The presumption that competitive pressures limit agency problems and result in higher efficiency is indeed widespread.[10] Theoretical analyses, however, offer a cautionary perspective on this question: there is often an ambiguous relation between competition and agency costs, because competition simultaneously has two effects: (1) a change in the agent's effort

---

10. See, for example, the influential management work of Porter (1990).

for a *given* incentive scheme; and (2) a change in the incentive scheme chosen by the principal.

This question will be investigated using a model due to Schmidt (1997) where the agent's effort is driven both by financial incentives and by a threat of liquidation (and the associated loss of private benefits). A change in competition then affects both the threat of liquidation and the equilibrium incentive scheme the agent faces. Before analyzing this model, let us stress that it does not exhaust the possible effects of a change in competition. For example, several studies consider the *information effect* of an increase in competition: if a firm faces competitors, relative performance evaluation (as in Chapter 8) becomes possible. Though exploiting this information can, ceteris paribus, increase the payoff of the owner of the firm, the effect on the manager's effort is ambiguous (see Nalebuff and Stiglitz, 1983; Hart, 1983b; Scharfstein, 1988; and Hermalin, 1992). Other effects can also be ambiguous: as shown by Hermalin (1992), this observation is true for the effect of a change in competition on a manager's disutility of effort and attitude toward risk.

Schmidt's model considers a principal-agent problem where effort by the agent serves to decrease the marginal cost of production. Specifically, while initially the cost of the firm is c_H, the agent can decrease this cost to c_L with probability $p \in [0, 1]$ at an effort cost $\psi(p)$. To make the problem well behaved, assume $\psi', \psi'' > 0$, $\psi(0) = \psi'(0) = 0$, and $\lim_{p \to 1} \psi(p) = \infty$. Consider a three-stage problem: first a contracting stage, then a stage where the agent chooses effort, and finally a stage where the principal decides to liquidate the firm or to continue its operations. Under liquidation, we normalize the financial value of the firm, as well as the agent's private benefit, to zero. In the absence of liquidation, the agent obtains a positive private benefit h, and we define the financial value of the firm, in reduced form, as

$$\pi(c, \phi, \varepsilon)$$

where, ceteris paribus, $\pi(c, \phi, \varepsilon)$ decreases in its cost $c \in \{c_H, c_L\}$ and also in the degree of competition ϕ. The value of the firm is also assumed to depend on a noise term ε, which has cumulative distribution $F(\varepsilon)$. To simplify the analysis, assume that liquidation is never attractive for the principal if the cost of the firm is low; that is, $\pi(c_L, \phi, \varepsilon) \geq 0$ for all ϕ and ε.

If the agent receives a wage w, the payoffs of the principal and agent are, respectively,

$$U^P = \max\{0, \pi(c, \phi, \varepsilon)\} - w$$

and

$$u^A = w - \psi(p) + \lambda h$$

where $\lambda = 1$ if the principal does not liquidate the firm and $\lambda = 0$ otherwise. Note that these expressions implicitly assume that the liquidation decision is noncontractable; therefore, the principal will always make the decision that maximizes the ex post financial value of the firm, and moreover the wage the agent will receive cannot depend on this decision. It is, however, assumed that the cost realization is verifiable, so that the principal can offer the agent a wage w_i for cost realization c_i, with $i \in \{H, L\}$. Both parties have been assumed to be risk neutral. In order to make the moral-hazard problem relevant, assume that the agent is wealth constrained, in the sense that $w_i \geq 0$.

Define $l(\phi)$ as the probability of liquidation under cost c_H, and define

$$\Pi_i(\phi) = \int_\varepsilon \max\{0, \pi(c_i, \phi, \varepsilon)\} dF(\varepsilon)$$

The variable $\Pi_i(\phi)$ is thus the expected value of the firm under cost c_i and competition parameter ϕ. For a given degree of competition ϕ, one can then define the principal's first-best problem as

$$\max \, p[\Pi_L(\phi) - w_L] + (1-p)[\Pi_H(\phi) - w_H]$$

subject to

$$p(w_L + h) + (1-p)\{w_H + [1 - l(\phi)]h\} - \psi(p) \geq \bar{u}$$

where $\bar{u}$ is the agent's exogenous ex ante outside payoff. It implies a probability of low cost $p_{FB}(\phi)$ such that

$$\psi'[p_{FB}(\phi)] = \Pi_L(\phi) - \Pi_H(\phi) + l(\phi)h$$

In words, the first best requires that the marginal cost of effort is equated to its marginal benefit, in terms of (1) higher financial value of the firm and (2) lower probability of liquidation and associated loss of private benefit for the agent.

Turning now to the second best, we have to add the following incentive and limited-liability constraints:

$$p \in \arg\max_{\tilde{p}} \, \tilde{p}(w_L + h) + (1 - \tilde{p})\{w_H + [1 - l(\phi)]h\} - \psi(\tilde{p})$$

and

$$w_i \geq 0 \quad \text{for } i = H, L$$

For simplicity, assume that this problem is globally concave (and therefore admits a unique optimum), which is ensured by the following assumption:

$$2\psi''(p) + p\psi'''(p) > 0 \quad \text{for all } p \tag{13.3}$$

Since we consider a problem with only two cost realizations, the incentive constraint can be replaced by the agent's first-order condition if we assume an interior solution for p:

$$w_L - w_H + l(\phi)h - \psi'(p) = 0$$

The optimum can then be derived as follows: First, if the presence of moral hazard prevents the first best from being reached, we have an optimal high-cost wage $w_H(\phi) = 0$. Second, the first-order incentive constraint implies an optimal low-cost wage

$$w_L(\phi) = \psi'(p) - l(\phi)h$$

Third, assuming that $\bar{u}$ is low enough that the agent's participation constraint does not bind given the limited-liability constraints, the whole problem can be rewritten simply as

$$\max p[\Pi_L(\phi) - \psi'(p) + l(\phi)h] + (1 - p)\Pi_H(\phi)$$

which implies that the second-best low-cost probability $p_{SB}(\phi)$ is defined by

$$\Pi_L(\phi) - \psi'[p_{SB}(\phi)] + l(\phi)h - p_{SB}(\phi)\psi''[p_{SB}(\phi)] - \Pi_H(\phi) = 0$$

From this optimality condition, one can now compute the effect of an increase in competition, that is, of an increase in ϕ, on the agent's effort choice:

$$\frac{dp_{SB}(\phi)}{d\phi} = \frac{[\partial\Pi_L(\phi)/\partial\phi - \partial\Pi_H(\phi)/\partial\phi] + hdl(\phi)/d\phi}{2\psi''[p_{SB}(\phi)] + p_{SB}(\phi)\psi'''[p_{SB}(\phi)]}$$

By the concavity assumption (13.3), the denominator of this expression is strictly positive. The numerator is the sum of two parts:

• The second part $hdl(\phi)/d\phi$ is positive. It reflects a "threat-of-liquidation effect": more severe competition means that the agent works harder for a given wage difference $w_L - w_H$, in order to reduce the risk of losing her private benefit.

• The first part of the numerator, $\partial \Pi_L(\phi)/\partial \phi - \partial \Pi_H(\phi)/\partial \phi$, which has a potentially ambiguous sign, reflects a "value-of-cost-reduction effect." A change in competition affects the attractiveness for the principal of inducing the agent to reduce costs. This will affect the wage contract (w_H, w_L) that the principal will offer the agent.

Two comments are in order here. First, the positive sign of the threat-of-liquidation effect relies on the assumption that more competition raises the impact of cost differences on the probability of liquidation (since this probability has been assumed to stay equal to zero for a low-cost firm, whatever ϕ may be). The general point is that more competition will partly alter effort incentives under unchanged wage levels, because of its impact on the threat of liquidation. Second, the value-of-cost-reduction effect can easily be negative and outweigh the other effect. Indeed, the value for the principal of cost reduction by the agent can go down when competition becomes fiercer.

This effect can be illustrated in the case of symmetric Bertrand competition with $N \geq 2$ firms. In this case, profits are always zero, except when there is a single firm that has a low cost c_L, in which case this firm earns strictly positive profits, which we denote by Π. As for private benefits, assume that a firm with cost c is liquidated if and only if there exists at least one firm with strictly lower cost than c in the market (otherwise, it will produce a positive quantity, whether it earns positive profits or not). Under these assumptions, the probability of liquidation of firm i when it has a low cost is zero, while when it has a high cost, it is $l(\phi) = 1 - (1 - p_j)^{N-1}$, assuming that all other firms have an individual probability of low cost p_j. Similarly, when it has a low cost, firm i has a probability $(1 - p_j)^{N-1}$ of earning Π. Consequently, in a symmetric equilibrium, the second-best individual low-cost probability p_N is defined by

$$\psi'(p_N) + p_N \psi''(p_N) = (1 - p_N)^{N-1} \Pi + \left[1 - (1 - p_N)^{N-1}\right]h$$

Indeed, the LHS of the equation is the marginal cost of an increase in effort, including the increase in rent that goes to the manager. The RHS is the marginal benefit of an increase in effort, which has two components: (1) the profit Π when one is alone in having a low cost, times the probability that no other competitor has a low cost, and (2) a private benefit that one obtains with probability one rather than $(1 - p_N)^{N-1}$ (that is, only when no competitor has a low cost). By the concavity assumption (13.3), the LHS is increasing in p_N. The RHS is instead decreasing in p_N provided $\Pi > h$. In this case, a rise in competition, that is, in N, implies a decrease in the probability of low cost p_N. This result follows because, when the number of competitors increases, the value of exerting effort in terms of increased profits goes down: this value is zero when at least one competitor is successful at lowering costs, and this event occurs more frequently—for a given individual effort level—the higher the number of competitors.

Note that this argument assumes that there are at least two firms in the market. Schmidt shows that the comparison between monopoly and duopoly can go either way in this setup, depending in particular on the levels of monopoly profits under c_L and c_H. When a duopoly implies more effort than a monopoly, we have a nonmonotonic relation between productivity and the number of firms in the market, with the highest productivity for two firms.

13.6   Summary and Literature Notes

This chapter has focused on situations where several individuals sign competing contracts, whereas in previous chapters we were always looking at "grand contracts." We first stressed competition in exclusive contracts, with the classical analyses of Akerlof (1970), when offering a menu of contracts is impossible, and Rothschild and Stiglitz (1976), when it is allowed. In the first case, multiple Pareto-ranked outcomes can coexist. The worst one can involve complete market breakdown, while the best one is constrained Pareto-efficient. In the second case, the main issue is failure of existence of equilibrium. This stands in sharp contrast with signaling models, where extreme multiplicity is the norm. We have highlighted, however, that nonexistence can be avoided if one constrains the ability of the parties to steal only the desirable customers from their rivals, as stressed by Wilson (1977) or Riley (1979).

Another effect of adverse selection on competition, which we have not explored in this chapter, is to dampen competitive forces (see Greenwald, 1986, for a particularly elegant analysis of reduced competition in the labor market when current employers have more information about the productivity of their employees than prospective employers).

Some models endogenize the degree of contractual exclusivity. In particular, Aghion and Bolton (1987) show that an incumbent firm and its customers may find it advantageous to sign a contract where customers have to pay a penalty for buying from an entrant rather than the incumbent, because this pushes the entrant to offer more favorable terms to these customers.

A more recent literature has considered competition with nonexclusive contracts. A unifying perspective is put forward by Segal (1999b). Pauly (1974) was the first to point out that an insuree's inability to commit not to contract with multiple insurers can lead to overinsurance and lower insuree welfare. More generally, we made the distinction between the *offer game* (the principal makes all the offers) and the *bidding game* (the competing agents make the offers). These two games lead to the following insights:

• In the offer game, when contracts are publicly observable, inefficiency arises in the presence of *externalities on nontraders,* which prompt the principal to distort trade so as to relax individual participation constraints.

• When contracts are private in the offer game, what matters instead is the presence of *externalities at equilibrium trade levels,* which are not internalized by the principal because they are unobservable to individual agents. Note that private contracting in the offer game requires specifying individual beliefs for each individual offer received from the principal. We focused on *passive beliefs* (see, for example, McAfee and Schwartz, 1994), whereby each individual agent, when observing an out-of-equilibrium contract offered by the principal, believes that the other offers remain unchanged.

• The preceding insights were derived under simultaneous offers. With sequential offers instead, an individual correctly predicts the impact of current contracting on future contracting. In the insurance case, while overinsurance can result from nonexclusive contracting, underinsurance is also possible, as a "commitment device" against eventual overinsurance (see, for example, Kahn and Mookherjee, 1998).

• As for the bidding game, we have focused on the key new issue relative to the offer game, namely the *coordination problem* that can arise from the coexistence of offers made by different parties and its associated potential inefficiency. This inefficiency disappears, however, in the absence of externalities between agents, when one focuses on *globally truthful equilibria* (see, for example, Bernheim and Whinston, 1986a).

Section 13.3 discussed the many applications of this setting. Let us stress that the bidding game, whose analysis has been pioneered by Bernheim and Whinston (1985, 1986a, 1986b), has led to many important applications, for example, to political economy and trade (see in particular the book by Grossman and Helpman, 2002). On the theoretical front, we should mention the work on common agency with adverse selection by Martimort and Stole (2002), as well as the recent work by Segal and Whinston (2003) on "robust common agency."

Section 13.4 focused on the strategic use of contracts in an industrial organization context, that is, on competition between "principal-agent pairs." Early work (e.g., Fershtman and Judd, 1987)[11] pointed out the desirability of using contracts between shareholders and managers as a way to commit to non-profit-maximizing behavior and thereby influence rivals. Katz (1991), however, has shown how this idea could lead to extreme multiplicity of equilibria. Moreover, while it is profitable to have an opponent believe one is not maximizing profit, deviations from profit maximization are not immune to renegotiation (see Dewatripont, 1988). In this section we developed the contribution of Caillaud, Jullien, and Picard (1995), who establish the strategic value of public contracts *even when they can be immediately and secretly renegotiated* (see also Bolton and Scharfstein, 1990). Their usefulness lies in altering the participation constraints of the agent in various states of nature in a way that ends up reducing the well-known allocative inefficiency arising with contracting under adverse selection. When reducing this allocative inefficiency leads to a "favorable" change in the behavior of competitors, the contract has strategic value. In the setting of Caillaud, Jullien, and Picard, for example, an initial contract that reduces underproduction is useful in a Cournot setting but not in a Bertrand setting.

Finally, whereas section 13.4 focused on the role of contracts on product market competition, section 13.5 instead looked at the impact of competition on contracts and agency costs. The literature, pioneered by Hart (1983b), has highlighted the ambiguous effect of competition on managerial effort—for example, with respect to the ability to rely on relative performance evaluation (see Scharfstein, 1988, and also Hermalin, 1992, for a more general analysis). Here, we have not discussed this effect and we have concentrated instead on the relation between the intensity of competition—

---

11. See also Bonnano and Vickers (1988) and Brander and Lewis (1986).

simply parametrized by firm profitability and the threat of bankruptcy—and managerial effort with endogenous managerial incentive schemes. As shown by Schmidt (1997),[12] more competition has two implications: First, the relation between effort and the probability of bankruptcy is affected by a change in competition, which affects managerial effort *for an unchanged incentive scheme;* second, the value of effort for the owner/principal is affected by a change in competition, which leads to a change in the equilibrium incentive scheme. In general, both effects can be ambiguous. In Schmidt's setting, reasonable examples suggest an inverted U-shaped effort level, that is, one with highest effort for intermediate degrees on competition.

12. See also Aghion, Dewatripont, and Rey (1999) and Raith (2003).

APPENDIX

14 Exercises

In this chapter we collect a set of exercises (classified by chapter) that are meant not only to review basic concepts and methods introduced in the previous chapters, but also to explore ideas and applications that we have not had the space to cover in the main body of the book. Some of these questions are based on articles that we have not fully covered in the text. Others are based on teaching material accumulated over the years by ourselves and other instructors of contract theory at the Université Libre de Bruxelles, the Massachusetts Institute of Technology, and Princeton University.

Chapter 2

Question 1

Consider the following monopoly screening problem: A government agency writes a procurement contract with a firm to deliver q units of a good. The firm has constant marginal cost c, so that its profit is $P - cq$, where P denotes the payment for the transaction. The firm's cost is private information and may be either high (c_H) or low (c_L, with $0 < c_L < c_H$). The agency's prior belief about the firm's cost is $\Pr(c = c_L) = \beta$, and it makes a take-it-or-leave-it offer to the firm (whose default profit is zero).

1. If $B(q)$ denotes the (concave) benefit to the agency of obtaining q units, what is the optimal contract for the agency?

2. Compare this second-best solution with the first-best one, obtained if costs are known by the agency. Discuss the results.

3. What would the first-best and second-best solutions be if c, instead of taking two values, were uniformly distributed on $[\underline{c}, \overline{c}]$, with $0 < \underline{c} < \overline{c}$?

Question 2

Consider the monopoly problem analyzed in section 2.1, but assume that the monopolist has one unit of the good for sale, at zero cost, while the buyer can have the following utility:

$$\theta_L - T$$

or

$$\log(\theta_H - T)$$

The buyer's risk aversion thus rises with her valuation. Show that the seller can implement the first-best outcome (that is, sell the good for sure, leave no rents to either type of buyer, and avoid any cost of risk in equilibrium) by using a random scheme.

Question 3

A monopolist can produce a good in different qualities. The cost of producing a unit of quality s is s^2. Consumers buy at most one unit and have utility function

$$u(s|\theta) = \begin{cases} \theta s & \text{if they consume one unit of quality } s \\ 0 & \text{if they do not consume} \end{cases}$$

The monopolist decides on the quality (or qualities) it is going to produce and price. Consumers observe qualities and prices and decide which quality to buy if at all.

1. Characterize the first-best solution.

2. Suppose that the seller cannot observe θ, and suppose that

$$\theta = \begin{cases} \theta_H & \text{with probability } 1 - \beta \\ \theta_L & \text{with probability } \beta \end{cases}$$

with $\theta_H > \theta_L > 0$. Characterize the second-best solution and consumers' informational rents.

3. Suppose now that θ is uniformly distributed on the interval $[0, 1]$. Characterize the second-best optimal quality-pricing schedule.

Question 4

Consider an economy with a continuum of agents who produce output q by supplying input a (for effort) with the individual production function $q = \theta a$, where θ is an idiosyncratic productivity parameter. The productivity density in the population is given by $f(\theta)$ with support $[\underline{\theta}, \bar{\theta}]$ [where $f(\theta) > \varepsilon > 0$]. All agents have the same utility function $u(c) - a$, with $u' > 0$ and $u'' < 0$.

1. What is the distribution of output and consumption in the economy when all agents live and work in autarcy?

2. Suppose that all agents in this economy can write an insurance contract before they know their productivity type. All agents are identical ex ante,

and their future productivity is i.i.d. with density $f(\theta)$. What is the optimal insurance contract when θ and a are observable ex post? What is the optimal insurance contract when only θ is observable? What is the optimal contract when neither θ nor a is observable ex post and $f(\theta)/[1 - F(\theta)]$ is monotonically increasing?

3. Interpret the last solution. Show that the marginal premium is given by

$$P'(\theta) = (\theta u'[c(\theta)] - 1)c'(\theta)$$

and

$$P'(\underline{\theta}) = P'(\overline{\theta}) = 0$$

Discuss this solution.

Question 5

Consider an economy in which firms want to go public. A typical private firm is owned by a risk-averse entrepreneur with personal wealth W_0 and increasing, strictly concave von Neumann–Morgenstern utility function u_F. Firms are worth $\theta + \varepsilon$, where θ and ε are independent real-valued random variables. The quantity ε is realized in the future, and its realization is unknown to everybody at the time of the interaction. It has mean 0. The realization of θ, however, is known to the entrepreneur but to no one else. Assume θ can take two values, $\theta_L < \theta_H$, where θ_L occurs with probability β, and θ_H with probability $1 - \beta$. This is common knowledge, as well as the fact that $\beta\theta_L + (1 - \beta)\theta_H > 1$. There is a monopolistic investment bank that proposes the terms of the initial public offering placed with the market. The offering is a pair $(x, T) \in [0, 1] \times \mathbb{R}^+$, where $1 - x$ is the fraction of the firm sold to the market in exchange for a payment of T to the entrepreneur. The investment bank acts as if it is risk neutral and maximizes total expected market profits from the sale:

$$U_I(x, t, \theta) = (1 - x)\theta - T$$

The safe interest rate is normalized to 0. The strategic interaction considered is the following: first, nature chooses θ, then the bank proposes the terms of the offering, and finally the entrepreneur decides about the acceptance or rejection of the offer.

1. Write down the entrepreneur's expected utility as a function of x, t, and θ.

2. Determine the first-best terms of the offering. Why will the first best not be realized in the present setting?

3. Write down the problem as a screening problem. Explain briefly.

4. Which constraints will bind at the optimum?

5. What allocation will the type-θ_L entrepreneur obtain at the optimum?

6. Solve the screening problem fully.

7. What elements of your solution are typical of screening problems? Is anything surprising?

8. Make a conjecture for the outcome under competition between investment banks.

Chapter 3

Question 6

Consider a firm that can invest an amount I in a project generating high observable cash flow $C > 0$ with probability θ and 0 otherwise: $\theta \in \{\theta_L, \theta_H\}$ with $\theta_H - \theta_L \equiv \Delta > 0$ and $\Pr[\theta = \theta_L] = \beta$. The firm needs to raise I from external investors who do not observe the value of θ. Assume that $\theta_L C - I > 0$. Everybody is risk neutral, and there is no discounting.

1. Suppose that the firms can only promise to repay an amount R chosen by the firm (with $0 \le R \le C$) when cash flow is C and 0 otherwise. Can a good firm signal its type?

2. Suppose now that the firm also has the possibility of pledging some assets as collateral for the loan: Should a "default" occur (the firm being unable to repay R), an asset of value K to the firm is transferred to the creditor whose valuation is xK with $0 < x < 1$. The size of the collateral K is a choice variable. Give a necessary and sufficient condition for the "best" perfect Bayesian equilibrium to be separating. How does it depend on β and x? Explain.

Question 7

Consider the following modification of the Myers-Majluf (1984) model. Suppose that the asset in place can take three ex post values, $A = 0, 1, 2$, and let $\gamma = \text{Prob}(A = 1)$ and $\mu = \text{Prob}(A = 2)$. The new project, however, has a safe value $V_N > I$, where I is the start-up cost of the new project. Suppose that the firm can be of two different types, G and B, where $(\gamma, \mu) \in \{(\gamma_B, \mu_B), (\gamma_G, \mu_G)\}$, with $\gamma_G > \gamma_B$, but

$$E[A_G] \equiv \gamma_G + 2\mu_G = \gamma_B + 2\mu_B \equiv E[A_B]$$

Solve for the set of perfect Bayesian equilibria under, respectively, equity financing and debt financing. Discuss.

Question 8

A firm has a project requiring an investment of 20 at $t = 0$ for a sure return of 30 at $t = 1$. There is no discounting. The investment cost has to be raised from the financial market. Assume that a new equity issue is proposed. Potential new investors are uncertain about the value of the firm's assets in place: $A \in \{50, 100\}$ with $\Pr[A = 100] = 0.1$.

1. Suppose that investors believe that both types of firms invest. What fraction of the firm's equity has to be issued to new investors? What are the payoffs to existing shareholders if they undertake the project? Are these beliefs reasonable?

2. Suppose that investors believe that only bad firms issue new equity. Same questions.

3. Suppose now that shareholders commit at $t = 0$ to a wasteful advertising campaign at $t = 1$ after the project return is realized. The advertising expenditure is an irreversible action on the part of the firm that results in a drop in profits of K. The size of the expenditure is a choice variable. Show that a good firm can signal its type through such expenditures. Discuss.

Question 9

Consider a two-period model with no discounting. An entrepreneur has a project generating a random cash flow $C \in \{\underline{C}, \overline{C}\}$ at $t = 1$ where $\overline{C} - \underline{C} \equiv \Delta > 0$ and $\Pr[C = \overline{C}] \equiv \theta$. The (project) type $\theta \in \{\theta_L, \theta_H\}$, with $\theta_H > \theta_L$, is the entrepreneur's private information, and the (common knowledge) market prior is $\Pr[\theta = \theta_L] \equiv \beta$. The project requires an investment I at $t = 0$ that the entrepreneur needs to raise from the (competitive) market. Assume that $\underline{C} + \theta_L \Delta > I > \underline{C}$. The entrepreneur is assumed to be restricted to issuing debt only or equity only.

1. Show that there exist perfect Bayesian equilibria in which both types issue debt. Which one among these equilibria is preferred by θ_H

entrepreneurs? Show that there may exist perfect Bayesian equilibria in which both types issue equity. Which one among these equilibria is preferred by θ_H entrepreneurs? And do θ_H entrepreneurs prefer this equilibrium to their most preferred debt equilibrium? Explain.

2. In the remainder of the problem, assume that the entrepreneur incurs a nonpecuniary cost of financial distress $K > 0$ whenever she is unable to meet a repayment at $t = 1$. Give conditions on K for a pooling equilibrium with debt to exist. Give conditions on K for a separating equilibrium to exist. Can θ_H entrepreneurs be better off with $K > 0$ than with $K = 0$ (in their preferred equilibrium)?

Chapter 4

Question 10

Take a standard moral-hazard problem where the principal considers offering the agent a lottery rather than a fixed payment w_i if output q_i is observed. Specifically, the agent would receive in this case w_{ij} with probability $p_{ij} \geq 0$, with $j = 1, 2, \ldots, m$ and

$$\sum_{j=1}^{m} p_{ij} = 1$$

Assume the agent's utility function is $u(w) - \psi(a)$. Show that such a randomizing incentive scheme cannot be optimal if the principal is risk neutral and the agent is strictly risk averse.

Question 11

Consider a risk-averse individual [with utility function of money $u(\cdot)$] with initial wealth W_0 who faces the risk of having an accident and losing an amount x of her wealth. She has access to a perfectly competitive market of risk-neutral insurers who can offer schedules $R(x)$ of repayments net of the insurance premium. Assume that the distribution of x, which depends on accident-prevention effort a, has an atom at $x = 0$: $f(0, a) = 1 - p(a)$ and $f(x, a) = p(a)g(x)$ for $x > 0$. Assume $p''(a) > 0 > p'(a)$. The individual's (increasing and convex) cost of effort, separable from her utility of money, is $\psi(a)$. Determine the first-best and second-best insurance contracts. Discuss.

Question 12

Consider a principal-agent problem with three exogenous states of nature, θ_1, θ_2, and θ_3; two effort levels, a_L and a_H; and two output levels, distributed as follows as a function of the state of nature and the effort level:

State of nature	θ_1	θ_2	θ_3
Probability	0.25	0.5	0.25
Output under a_H	18	18	1
Output under a_L	18	1	1

The principal is risk neutral, while the agent has utility function $\sqrt{w}$ when receiving monetary compensation w, minus the cost of effort, which is normalized to 0 for a_L and to 0.1 for a_H. The agent's reservation expected utility is 0.1.

1. Derive the first-best contract.

2. Derive the second-best contract when only output levels are observable.

3. Assume the principal can buy for a price of 0.1 an information system that allows the parties to verify whether state of nature θ_3 happened or not. Will the principal buy this information system? Discuss.

Question 13

Consider the modified linear managerial-incentive-scheme problem, where the manager's effort, a, affects current profits, $q_1 = a + \varepsilon_{q_1}$, and future profits, $q_2 = a + \varepsilon_{q_2}$, where ε_{q_t} are i.i.d. with normal distribution $N(0, \sigma_q^2)$. The manager retires at the end of the first period, and the manager's compensation cannot be based on q_2. However, her compensation can depend on the stock price $P = 2a + \varepsilon_P$, where $\varepsilon_P \sim N(0, \sigma_P^2)$. Derive the optimal compensation contract $t = w + fq_1 + sP$. Discuss how it depends on σ_P^2 and on its relation with σ_q^2. Compare your solution with that in the chapter.

Question 14

Consider the following principal-agent problem. There is a project whose probability of success is a (a is also the effort made by the risk-neutral agent, at cost a^2). In case of success the return is R, and in case of failure the return is 0. The parameter R can take two values, X with probability λ and 1 with probability $1 - \lambda$. To undertake the project, the agent needs to borrow an amount I from the principal. The sequence of events is as follows:

• First, the principal offers the agent a debt contract, with face value D_0. The agent accepts or rejects this contract.

• Second, nature determines the value R that would occur in case of success. This value is observed by both principal and agent. The principal can then choose to lower the debt from D_0 to D_1.

• The agent chooses a level of effort a. This level is not observed by the principal.

• The project succeeds or not. If the project succeeds, the agent pays the minimum of R and the face value of debt D_1.

Answer the following questions:

1. Compute the subgame-perfect equilibrium of this game as a function of I, λ, and X.

2. When do we have $D_1 < D_0$? Discuss.

Question 15

An entrepreneur has two projects available, each requiring an investment outlay of 6 at $t = 0$. The first project generates cash flow $C_1 \in \{5, 45\}$ at $t = 1$. The second project generates cash flow $C_2 \in \{0, 48\}$. The probability of getting a high cash flow is in each case equal to a, where a also denotes the level of effort of the entrepreneur. The entrepreneur has cost of effort of $40a^2$ and can choose between three effort levels: $a \in \{0, \frac{1}{3}, \frac{1}{2}\}$. The firm has no assets in place. Everybody is risk neutral, and there is no discounting. The two projects are mutually exclusive.

1. If the entrepreneur can self-finance, what level of effort will she choose under each project? Which project is worth investing in?

2. Suppose now that the entrepreneur is cash constrained and that the project is entirely financed with debt. What face value D of debt should the entrepreneur choose under each project? Which project does she end up choosing if she can get an unconditional loan, that is, a loan that does not depend on which of the two projects she decides to invest in? Discuss.

3. Can the entrepreneur do better by issuing a fraction s of equity instead of financing the project with debt?

Question 16

Consider a target firm with widely dispersed ownership (atomistic risk-neutral shareholders) facing a takeover bid from a risk-neutral "raider." The monetary value per share under incumbent management is normalized to zero. Once the raider has gained control, she obtains a private benefit $Z \geq 0$ and can also exert effort a at private cost $ka^2/2$, which generates a value per share of aV_R where $V_R > k$.

Gaining control requires acquiring 50% of the shares of the target (the security voting structure is "one share, one vote"). Assume the raider does not own any shares prior to making the offer. There are no costs to the takeover other than the price the raider has to pay. Incumbent management is assumed to remain passive.

The raider makes a public tender offer of a price per share of b. This offer is "unrestricted" and "conditional"; that is, the raider buys all the shares tendered provided at least 50% of the shares of the firm are tendered. Faced with this offer, target shareholders noncooperatively choose whether to tender or not (assume that they think their tendering decision will not affect the outcome of the takeover).

1. Derive the posttakeover value per share, given that the raider has gained control and holds a fraction of shares $s \geq 50\%$.

2. At what bid price b will the raider be able to acquire a fraction of shares $s \geq 50\%$?

3. Derive the raider's optimal offer b^* and optimal posttakeover ownership stake s^*, respectively, when $Z = 0$ and $Z > 0$.

4. Is the raider's optimal bid efficient; that is, does it maximize the sum of shareholder and raider returns?

Chapter 5

Question 17

Consider a seller of a single item facing two potential buyers. The item is either worth v_H or $v_L < v_H$ (the buyers agree on these valuations; that is, it is a "common-value environment", as defined in Chapter 7) and the common prior probability is $\Pr(v = v_H) = 0.5$.

Suppose that the seller privately receives an estimate of the value of the item from an expert (in the form of a signed written letter) prior to the sale. There are n possible estimates e_i, with $i = 1, \ldots, n$. Assume $E[v|e_i] = v_i$ such that

$$v_1 < v_2 < \cdots < v_n$$

The buyers have no information about what the estimate is likely to be. Their beliefs are

$$\Pr(e_i) = \frac{1}{n}$$

1. Show that the unique equilibrium of the game where the seller sells the object through an ascending-price auction (or "English auction"; see Chapter 7) is for the seller to first disclose the content of the expert's estimate to the bidders.

2. What is the equilibrium in the English auction when the seller must pay a cost $K > 0$ to obtain an expert's assessment?

Question 18

Consider the following stylized example of trading by two risk-neutral market makers, each of them small enough so that the *direct* influence of their trade on the stock prices is negligible. It is common knowledge that one of the traders will become informed about the true underlying value of a stock with probability β, while the other always remains uninformed. Assume each market maker can trade up to one unit twice in succession. The question is, should the market makers be required to disclose their first trade before they initiate their second trade? The question is considered at an ex ante stage where both market markers are identical and neither knows who will become informed (if any). So, at stage 0, the market makers must decide whether to introduce mandatory disclosure of trades at stage 1.

Prior to stage 1, the stock is worth either 110 or 90, with equal probabilities, so that the stock price is 100. At the beginning of stage 1, one market maker becomes informed about the value of the stock with probability β, while the other remains uninformed.

For the first trade, assume the uninformed market maker buys with probability 0.5 and sells with probability 0.5. Following the first trade, there may be mandatory or voluntary disclosure. Then a second trade can be initiated by both informed and uninformed market makers.

1. What are the ex post payoffs of the informed and uninformed traders under mandatory disclosure and no mandatory disclosure, respectively?

2. When is mandatory disclosure better from an ex ante perspective than no mandatory disclosure?

3. When there is no mandatory disclosure, when is there voluntary disclosure? Discuss.

Question 19

Consider a two-period model with no discounting. A risk-neutral entrepreneur has a project generating at $t = 1$ a random cash flow $\pi \in \{\pi_L, \pi_H\}$ with $\pi_H > \pi_L$ and $\beta \equiv \Pr[\pi = \pi_L]$. The project requires an investment I at $t = 0$ that is raised from a risk-neutral creditor in a competitive capital market. Suppose that at $t = 1$ the entrepreneur observes π, but the creditor can verify π only by incurring a monitoring cost K (assume that verification costs are small enough for financing to be viable). Let

$$\beta \pi_L + (1 - \beta)\pi_H > I + K$$

and $I > \pi_L > K$, and assume that repayments must be nonnegative.

1. Assume that only deterministic monitoring contracts are feasible. Derive an optimal financial contract. Explain why there is no unique optimal contract within this setting.

2. Show that random verification is optimal. Explain.

3. Focus again on deterministic contracts, and suppose now that the entrepreneur is risk averse while the creditor remains risk neutral. Identify the unique optimal contract. Explain.

Question 20

Consider a financial contracting problem between a wealth-constrained, risk-neutral entrepreneur and a wealthy risk-neutral investor. The cost of investment at date $t = 0$ is I. The project generates a random return on investment at date $t = 1$ of $\pi(\theta, I) = 2 \min \{\theta, I\}$, where θ is the state of nature, uniformly distributed on $[0, 1]$.

1. Characterize the first-best level of investment, I^{FB}.

2. Suppose that the realized return at $t = 1$ is freely observable only to the entrepreneur. A cost $K > 0$ must be paid for the investor to observe $\pi(\theta, I)$. Derive the second-best contract under the assmptions of (a) deterministic verification and (b) zero expected profit for the investor, taking into account that repayments cannot exceed realized returns (net of inspection costs).

3. Show that the second-best optimal investment level is lower than I^{FB}.

Chapter 6

Question 21

A risk-neutral profit-maximizing monopolist producing two goods, good 1 and good 2, faces a consumer with utility function $v_1 q_1 + v_2 q_2 - T$, where T is the payment from the consumer to the monopolist, q_i is the quantity of good $i (i = 1, 2)$ bought by the consumer, and v_i is the consumer's valuation for good i. The monopolist's cost is $c(q_1) + c(q_2)$. Each consumer valuation v_i can take two values, v_i^L and v_i^H. Define $\Delta v_i \equiv v_i^H - v_i^L > 0$. Assume that v_1 and v_2 are independently distributed and $\Pr(v_i = v_i^L) = \beta_i$. The monopolist does not observe the realization of the v_i's, but their distribution is common knowledge.

1. Suppose that the monopolist decides to treat the contract-design problem as two separate problems, one for each good. What is the second-best outcome?

2. Assume that the monopolist now decides to consider a general contract instead of two separate ones. How many (IC) constraints does the monopolist face? How many (IR) constraints? (Do not write them down.)

3. Consider the relaxed problem with only the following constraints: (a) the (IR) constraint for type (v_1^L, v_2^L); and (b) the following four (IC) constraints: for type (v_1^H, v_2^L) versus type (v_1^L, v_2^L), (IC1); for type (v_1^L, v_2^H) versus type (v_1^L, v_2^L), (IC2); for type (v_1^H, v_2^H) versus type (v_1^H, v_2^L), (IC3); and for type (v_1^H, v_2^H) versus type (v_1^L, v_2^H), (IC4). Write down this relaxed problem.

4. Show that for this relaxed problem the (IR) constraint for (v_1^L, v_2^L) is binding. Show that constraints (IC1) and (IC2) are also binding. Use these results to eliminate from the monopolist's problem the payments it gets from types (v_1^L, v_2^L), (v_1^H, v_2^L), and (v_1^L, v_2^H). That is, write the relaxed problem as a maximization problem with respect to quantities and the payment the monopolist gets from type (v_1^H, v_2^H), subject to the two constraints (IC3) and (IC4).

5. Write the Lagrangian of this last problem. Denote by λ_1 and λ_2 the Lagrange multipliers of (IC3) and (IC4), respectively. Show that $\lambda_1 + \lambda_2 = 1/[(1 - \beta_1)(1 - \beta_2)]$. Show that the quantities of good $i(i = 1, 2)$ sold to the types who have a high valuation for that good are as in part 1 of this question. Discuss.

6. Write down the first-order conditions for the quantities of good $i(i = 1, 2)$ sold to the types who have a low valuation for that good. Show that λ_1 and λ_2 are strictly positive. Compare them to the answer of part 1. Discuss.

7. Consider the symmetric case $v_1^L = v_2^L = v^L$, $v_1^H = v_2^H = v^H$, $\beta_1 = \beta_2 = \beta$. Show that the solution to the relaxed problem is also the solution to the initial problem.

Question 22

Consider an agent who works for a risk-neutral principal. The agent can allocate time to $n + 1$ tasks. Call a_i the amount of time spent on task $i(i = 0, 1, 2, \ldots, n)$. The principal cares only about task 0, getting output $q = a_0 + \varepsilon$, where ε is normally distributed with mean 0 and variance σ^2. The agent, however, derives a benefit $v_i(a_i)$ from spending time on tasks $i = 1, 2, \ldots, n$. She has CARA risk preferences, and her utility function is

$$-e^{-\eta[w-\psi(a_0+a_1+\cdots+a_n)+v_1(a_1)+v_2(a_2)+\cdots+v_n(a_n)]}$$

where $\psi(a_0 + a_1 + \ldots + a_n)$ is the cost of time, with ψ' and $\psi'' > 0$ and $\psi(0) = 0$. Assume also that $v_i' > 0$, $v_i'' < 0$, and $v_i(0) = 0$, and that optimization with respect to the a_i's leads to interior solutions. Call w_0 the agent's reservation wage.

1. Derive the first-best outcome. Discuss.

2. Assume that the principal does not observe the a_i's chosen by the agent, but only q and whether the agent can engage at all in any of the tasks 1, 2, ..., n. Assume the principal can offer the agent a linear incentive scheme

$t + sq$ and he can also choose the subset S of tasks the agent is allowed to engage in (that is, for any other task j, the principal can force $a_j = 0$). Determine the optimal subset S as a function of s. What happens when $s = 1$? Compare with the answer in part 1 of this question. What happens when s drops below 1? Discuss.

Question 23

Consider a risk-neutral principal who has to take a decision $d \in \{A, 0, B\}$. The optimal decision depends on a random parameter $\theta = \theta_A + \theta_B$. Ex ante, we have $\Pr(\theta_A = -1) = \beta = \Pr(\theta_B = 1)$ and $\Pr(\theta_A = 0) = 1 - \beta = \Pr(\theta_B = 0)$. Moreover, θ_A and θ_B are independently distributed. Assume that the optimal decision is A if $\theta = -1$, 0 if $\theta = 0$, and B if $\theta = 1$. Let K be the cost to the principal of not taking the optimal decision for any θ.

The principal has access to a population of risk-neutral agents who, by spending one unit of effort looking at θ_i ($i = A, B$), can obtain hard evidence that $|\theta_i| = 1$. Specifically, if $\theta_i = 0$, no evidence is found, while if $|\theta_i| = 1$, hard evidence (that is, evidence that cannot be forged) is found with probability p. Agents' utility functions are $w - n\psi$, where w is their wage, n the number of units of effort expended by the agent ($n = 2$ means that the agent looks at both θ_A and θ_B), and ψ the unit cost of effort.

1. What is the first-best effort level in this case? When is it optimal to have two units of effort expended?

2. Assume that agents privately choose effort but can be paid per piece of evidence provided. Can the first-best effort level be achieved while leaving no rents to the agent(s)? Does it matter whether one or two agents (expending, respectively, two or one units of effort) are hired by the principal? Does the outcome depend on agents' limited-liability constraint $w \geq 0$?

3. Assume now that the hard evidence is automatically transmitted to the principal but that contracts can be contingent only on the *decision* taken by the principal, and not on the amount of information generated by the agent(s). What is the optimal contract for the principal [i.e., the contract that minimizes the expected cost of wrong decisions plus the wage bill to be conceded to the agent(s)] when a single agent is hired by the principal? And when two agents are hired by the principal? Again, does the outcome depend on agents' limited-liability constraints?

4. Assume finally that, whenever the hard evidence is generated, it is first obtained by the agent, who can then decide whether or not to disclose it to the principal. Does this new sequence of moves change the conclusion reached in part 3 of this question?

Question 24

A risk-averse entrepreneur [with strictly increasing utility function $u(\cdot)$] produces random output q, uniformly distributed on $[0, \bar{q}]$, with $\bar{q} > 0$. The entrepreneur wants to diversify risk by writing a risk-sharing contract with a risk-neutral financier (with initial wealth $W \geq \bar{q}$), specifying a transfer to the entrepreneur contingent on realized output.

Output is observable to the entrepreneur. It is also observable to the financier unless the entrepreneur falsifies her accounts. After observing the realization of q, the entrepreneur can produce a falsified output report R at cost

$$\psi(q, R) = \tfrac{1}{4}(q - R) + \tfrac{1}{2}c(q - R)^2$$

where $c > 0$. Suppose that the entrepreneur is protected by limited liability and that her reservation utility $\bar{u}$ is higher than $\bar{q}/2$.

1. Characterize the first-best contract.

2. A contract with no output falsification is such that $R(q) = q$ for all $q \in [0, \bar{q}]$. Show that the first-best contract would lead to falsification. Derive the entrepreneur's equilibrium falsification in response to the first-best contract.

3. What is the optimal no-falsification contract? Show that the optimal contract with no falsification is linear in output q (hint: all incentive constraints are satisfied as long as the contract is locally incentive-compatible at any $q \in [0, \bar{q}]$).

4. Explain why a contract with falsification may dominate the optimal contract with no falsification when $c \to +\infty$.

Chapter 7

Question 25

Consider a public-good problem represented by a decision $d \in [0,1]$. Decision d has an impact on N individuals: Individual $i = 1, 2, \ldots, N$ has (differentiable) utility function $v_i(d, \theta_i) - T_i$, where θ_i is a privately known parameter and T_i is the payment made by the individual to the "planner." The socially efficient decision is

$$d^*(\theta) = \arg\max \sum_i v_i(d, \theta_i)$$

where $\theta \equiv (\theta_1, \ldots, \theta_N)$.

1. Derive the "Groves mechanism," that is, the direct revelation mechanism that implements $d^*(\theta)$ as a *dominant strategy equilibrium*. Show that it is unique. To do so, show that social efficiency implies

$$\theta_i = \arg\max_{\tilde{\theta}_i} \sum_j v_j[d^*(\theta_{-i}, \tilde{\theta}_i), \theta_j]$$

where $\tilde{\theta}_i$ is any announcement that individual i could make. Use this result and the IC constraint for individual i to derive the Groves mechanism as the solution of a differential equation, which is unique up to a constant.

2. Show that budget balance [i.e., $\sum_i T_i(\theta) = 0$ for all θ] in the Groves mechanism can be satisfied if and only if $d^*(\theta)$ is "$(n-1)$-separable." Note that a function $F(m)$, with $m \equiv (m_1, m_2, \ldots, m_n)$, is $(n-1)$-separable if and only if it can be written as

$$\sum_i F_i(m_{-i})$$

3. Rather than insisting on dominant-strategy implementation, focus on *Bayesian implementation*. Assume that the θ_i's are distributed independently. Show that there always exists a budget-balancing mechanism that leads to truth telling as a Bayesian equilibrium. To do so, start with a Groves mechanism and redistribute the surplus/deficit among the agents so as to leave the IC constraints unaffected.

Question 26

Consider a continuum of sellers and a continuum of buyers, each of measure 1. Each seller owns initially one unit of the good. Seller valuations for that good (denoted by v_S) are i.i.d. on $[\underline{v}_S, \bar{v}_S]$ with density $f_S(v_S)$. Each buyer is potentially interested in buying one unit of the good. Buyer valuations (denoted by v_B) are i.i.d. on $[\underline{v}_B, \bar{v}_B]$ with density $f_B(v_B)$. Assume that $\underline{v}_B < \underline{v}_S$.

Call $x_S(v_S)$ the seller's probability of selling given an announced v_S, and $x_B(v_B)$ the buyer's probability of buying given an announced v_B. Call $T_S(v_S)$

the seller's payment (to a "planner") given an announced v_S, and $T_B(v_B)$ the buyer's payment (to a "planner") given an announced v_B. Consider the "Walrasian mechanism," defined by

$$x_S(v_S) = 1 \quad \text{and} \quad T_S(v_S) = P \qquad \text{if } v_S \leq P$$

$$x_S(v_S) = 0 \quad \text{and} \quad T_S(v_S) = 0 \qquad \text{if } v_S > P$$

$$x_B(v_B) = 1 \quad \text{and} \quad T_B(v_B) = -P \qquad \text{if } v_B \geq P$$

$$x_B(v_B) = 0 \quad \text{and} \quad T_B(v_B) = 0 \qquad \text{if } v_B < P$$

1. Show that the IC constraints and IR constraints are satisfied for any price P.

2. Show that there exists a price P such that trade is efficient and balancedness is satisfied.

3. Compare with the Myerson-Satterthwaite (1983) result.

Question 27

A decision where to locate a hazardous-waste dump is taken through an auction between n towns in a given country. Call d_i town i's disutility from taking on the dump. Assume the d_i's are uniformly and independently distributed on $[0, 1]$. Call T_i the transfer the town requests for taking the hazardous-waste dump. The lowest bidder gets the dump and receives its requested transfer, which is paid equally from the other towns. Compute the symmetric equilibrium of this auction. Is this an efficient allocation mechanism? Discuss.

Question 28

Consider a two-person, independent private-value auction with valuations uniformly distributed on $[0, 1]$. Consider the following assumptions on utilities: (a) bidder $i (i = 1, 2)$ has utility $v_i - P$ when she wins the object and has to pay P, while her outside option is normalized to zero; (b) bidder $i (i = 1, 2)$ has utility $\sqrt{v_i} - P$ when she wins the object and has to pay P, while her outside option is normalized to zero.

1. Compare the seller's expected revenue in cases (a) and (b) for the Vickrey auction.

2. Compare the seller's expected revenue in cases (a) and (b) for the (linear) symmetric bidding equilibrium of the first-price, sealed-bid auction.

3. Discuss.

Question 29

Consider an auction setting where a risk-neutral seller of a house faces two potential risk-neutral buyers. Buyer 1 is a real-estate agent who knows the market value of the house perfectly. Buyer 2 does not know the market value of the house, and the same goes for the seller. The seller is determined to sell the house, while each buyer is uninterested in buying at a price higher than the expected value of the house. The value of the house v is either v_H or v_L with $v_H > v_L$, and the seller's and buyer 2's ex ante beliefs are given by $\beta \equiv \Pr(v = v_L)$. Except for the realization of v, all the preceding information is common knowledge.

1. Show that buyer 2 obtains an expected payoff of zero in the first-price sealed-bid auction.

2. Which of the following standard auctions maximizes the seller's expected revenue: the English, Vickrey, or Dutch auction?

3. What is the optimal auction?

4. Assuming now that v is uniformly distributed on the interval $[0, 1]$, characterize the Bayesian equilibrium in the first-price sealed-bid auction. What is the equilibrium payoff of the uninformed buyer?

Chapter 8

Question 30

Consider a risk-neutral principal who employs two agents, $i = 1, 2$, who can produce an amount $q_i = f(a_i, \varepsilon_i)$, where a_i is agent i's effort level and ε_i is a random shock with (atomless) density $g(\varepsilon_i)$. The ε_i's are identically and independently distributed. Each agent has an outside opportunity level of utility normalized to zero. Agents are not wealth constrained.

1. Assume first that each agent i is risk neutral, with utility equal to monetary compensation, w_i, minus a convex cost of effort $\psi(a_i)$. Assuming that a positive level of production is desirable, derive the first-best outcome where each agent has a zero expected payoff. Show how it can be achieved through an incentive scheme where each agent is rewarded according to her output only. Show how it can also be achieved (assuming that a symmetric pure-strategy Nash equilibrium exists) through a simple tournament where the agent who is "behind" in terms of individual output is paid an amount W_l and the one who is "ahead" is paid an amount W_w. Discuss.

2. Assume now that each agent i is risk averse, with utility equal to $u(w_i) - \psi(a_i)$, where $u(\cdot)$ is strictly increasing and concave. Extend the class of possible relative-performance incentive schemes to $W_1(q_1, q_2)$ and $W_2(q_1, q_2)$. Consider any pair (a_1, a_2) that can be sustained as a Nash equilibrium as a result of these incentive schemes and that also gives each agent a nonnegative expected utility level. Show that this pair of effort levels can also be sustained in this way by a pair of incentive schemes $W_1(q_1)$ and $W_2(q_2)$ that lacks relative performance evaluation and that does not have a higher expected cost for the principal. Discuss.

Question 31

Two agents can work for a principal. The output of agent i, $i = 1, 2$, is $q_i = a_i + \varepsilon_i$, where a_i is agent i's effort level and ε_i is a random shock. The ε_i's are independent of each other and normally distributed with mean 0 and variance σ^2.

In addition to choosing a_2, agent 2 can engage in a second activity b_2. This activity does not affect output directly, but rather reduces the effort cost of agent 1. The interpretation is that agent 2 can *help* agent 1 (but not the other way around). The cost functions of the agents are

$$\psi_1(a_1, b_2) = \frac{1}{2}(a_1 - b_2)^2$$

and

$$\psi_2(a_2, b_2) = \frac{1}{2}a_2^2 + b_2^2$$

Agent 1 chooses her effort level a_1 only after she has observed the level of help b_2. Agent i's utility function is exponential and equal to

$$-e^{-\eta[w_i - \psi_i(a_i, b_2)]}$$

where w_i is the agent's income. The agent's reservation utility is -1, which corresponds to a reservation wage of 0. The principal is risk neutral and is restricted to linear incentive schemes. The incentive scheme for agent i is

$$w_i = z_i + v_i q_i + u_i q_j$$

1. Assume that a_1, a_2, and b_2 are observable. Solve the principal's problem by maximizing the total expected surplus with respect to a_1, a_2, and b_2. Explain why $a_1 > a_2$.

2. Assume from now on that a_1, a_2, and b_2 are not observable. Solve again the principal's problem. Explain why $u_1 = 0$.

3. Assume that the principal cannot distinguish whether a unit of output was produced by agent 1 or agent 2. The agents can thus engage in *arbitrage*, claiming that all output was produced by one of them. Assume that they will do so whenever it increases the sum of their wages. Explain why the incentive scheme in part 2 leads to arbitrage. What additional constraint does arbitrage impose on the principal's problem? Solve this problem, and explain why $u_1 > 0$.

Question 32

Two agents work for a principal. The output of agent i, $i = 1, 2$, is $q_i = a_i + \varepsilon_i$, where a_i is agent i's (privately observed) effort level and ε_i is a random shock. The ε_i's are normally distributed with mean 0 and variance-covariance matrix

$$\begin{pmatrix} 1 & \rho \\ \rho & 1 \end{pmatrix}$$

Agent i's utility function is

$$-e^{-\eta[w_i - ca_i^2/2]}$$

where w_i is the agent's income. Each agent's reservation wage is 0. The principal is risk neutral and is restricted to (symmetric) linear incentive schemes. Specifically, the incentive scheme for agent i is

$$w_i = z + vq_i + uq_j$$

Agents can collude by writing a side contract before efforts are chosen. Assume agent 1 can make the following take-it-or-leave-it contract offer to agent 2:

$$s = \phi(q_1 - q_2) + \varphi$$

1. Derive the optimal side contract for an arbitrary incentive scheme (v, u), assuming that effort choices cannot be part of the side contract.

2. Show that the principal can without loss of generality restrict attention to collusion-proof contracts.

3. Derive the optimal collusion-proof contract. Discuss.

4. Would the principal benefit if collusion were made impossible? How would the answer change if agents could write a side contract conditional on effort choices?

Question 33

A (risk-neutral) municipal government considers funding an investment project put forward by an association (also risk-neutral). The cost of the project is known, but the government is unsure about its social value, and its assessment is at odds with that of the association. Specifically, if the project is of "good quality," its social value (net of the cost of the project) as assessed by the government is $\theta_G > 0$, while the association would derive a private benefit $v_G > 0$ from seeing it go through. If instead the project is of "bad quality," its net social value is $\theta_B < 0$, but the association would derive a private benefit v_B, higher than v_G, if it went through. The association knows the quality of the project, while the government's (common-knowledge) belief is $\Pr(v_B) = \beta$.

In the absence of information, the government is ready to fund the project, since we assume $\beta\theta_B + (1 - \beta)\theta_G > 0$. However, since taxation is distortionary, the government has net value $\lambda > 0$ for each unit of revenue raised from the association. However, the government would be unwilling to allow a bad-quality project to go through even if it were able to charge the association for its full private benefit; that is, we assume $\theta_B + \lambda v_B < 0$.

Assume that the government has access to a (risk-neutral) "expert" who, when the project is of bad quality, manages to obtain an (unfalsifiable) proof of this fact with probability p, but observes "nothing" with probability $(1 \quad p)$; "nothing" is also observed with probability 1 when the project is of good quality. The expert starts with no financial resources and can therefore only be rewarded. The association is assumed to observe when the expert obtains a proof of bad quality, while the government has to be "alerted" by the expert.

1. Derive first the optimal scheme for the government when it cannot rely at all on the expert.

2. What is the optimal scheme when the government can rely on the expert and when collusion between the expert and the association is impossible because the expert is "honest"?

3. What is the optimal scheme when the government can rely on the expert but the expert is "self-interested" and the association can promise the expert a side payment for not alerting the government when he obtains a proof of bad quality? Assume the collusion technology is such that, for every unit of money the association pays, the expert only collects an equivalent of $k < 1$ units of money.

4. What is the optimal scheme when the government is unsure about the prospect for collusion, because it believes that with probability γ the expert is "honest" and with probability $1 - \gamma$ he is "self-interested"?

Chapter 9

Question 34

Consider a two-period durable-goods monopoly problem where a seller faces a single buyer with reservation utility for the durable good $v \in \{v_L, v_H\}$ with $v_H > v_L > 0$. The seller's prior belief about the buyer's reservation utility is $\Pr(v = v_H) = 0.5$. The seller's cost of producing the good can also take two equally likely values: $c \in \{c_L, c_H\}$ with $c_H > c_L \geq 0$. Seller costs and buyer reservation values are independently distributed and are private information. Assume

$$v_L - c_L \geq \frac{v_H - c_L}{2}$$

and

$$v_L - c_H < \frac{v_H - c_H}{2}$$

The common discount factor is given by $\delta > 0$.

1. Under what conditions does a pooling equilibrium exist in the first period where

(a) both types of seller set a first-period price

$$p_1 = v_H - \frac{\delta}{2}(v_H - v_L)$$

(b) the type-v_H buyer accepts this price with probability

$$\gamma = \frac{v_H + c_H - 2v_L}{v_H - v_L}$$

and the type-v_L buyer rejects it with probability 1; and (c) following a period-1 rejection, the type-c_L seller sets $p_2^l = v_L$ in the second period and the type-c_H seller sets $p_2^H = v_H$ in the second period?

2. Explain why the seller gains from having private information about costs when his cost is c_L, but not when it is c_H.

Question 35

Consider a two-period regulation model where the "type" of the firm is endogenous. Initially, the regulator offers a revenue function $R_1(q)$ specifying the payment it offers for output level q. Then, the firm sinks a (privately observed) amount I that determines its per-period production cost $c(q, I)$ [with $c(0, I) = c_q(0, I) = 0, c_{qq}(q, I) > \varepsilon > 0$, and $c_I(q, I) < 0$], and chooses to produce quantity q_1, which leads to first-period payoff

$$R_1(q_1) - c(q_1, I) - I$$

If instead the firm quits, it earns $-I$ and the game is over. If the firm has chosen q_1, the regulator's first-period payoff is $q_1 - R_1(q_1)$.

In the second period, after having observed q_1, the regulator offers $R_2(q)$, upon which the firm either quits (leading to a zero payoff for both parties in period 2) or chooses q_2, with associated second-period payoffs $R_2(q_2) - c(q_2, I)$ and $q_2 - R_2(q_2)$ for the two parties.

1. What is the full-commitment strategy of the regulator?

2. In the absence of commitment, show that this game has no pure-strategy perfect Bayesian equilibrium with $I > 0$.

Question 36

Consider the soft-budget-constraint setting discussed in Chapter 9 (section 9.1.3), with the following variation: Assume that each individual investor is infinitesimal, but can, in a first stage of the game, join a "small creditor," with one unit of funds in total, or a "large creditor," with two units of funds. Assume away agency problems between the manager running this undertaking and the small investors. Beyond this initial stage, the setting is as in section 9.1.3.

1. Assuming first a pure adverse selection setting for entrepreneurs (that is, the good entrepreneur can choose only a "quick" project), determine the equilibrium (assuming that creditors plagued by the soft budget constraint can never hope to get a higher probability of good entrepreneurs than the population average β—to get rid of "Rothschild-Stiglitz nonexistence problems" discussed in Chapter 13).

2. Add moral hazard for good entrepreneurs; that is, they can choose between the "quick" project and a "good but slow" project, whose payoffs are as in section 9.1.3.3. When is there is a single equilibrium of the game? When are there two (Pareto-ranked) equilibria?

Question 37

Consider the following investment/insurance problem under private information:

A risk-averse agent invests an amount $p/2$ in a project with random income shocks in two periods $t = 1, 2$, with

$$w_1 = \begin{cases} 1 & \text{with probability } p \\ 0 & \text{with probability } 1-p \end{cases}$$

and $w_2 \in \{0, 1\}$, with

$$\begin{cases} \Pr(w_2 = 1|w_1 = 1) = \gamma \leq p \\ \Pr(w_2 = 1|w_1 = 0) = \mu \geq p \end{cases}$$

where $\gamma > 0.5$ and $p < 1$. The agent's utility function is time separable: $U(c_1; c_2) = u(c_1) + u(c_2)$ with $u(c)$ taking the following piecewise linear form:

$$u(c) = \begin{cases} \dfrac{1}{2} + \dfrac{1}{2}\left(c - \dfrac{1}{2}\right) & \text{for } c \geq \dfrac{1}{2} \\ c & \text{for } c < \dfrac{1}{2} \end{cases}$$

The agent can obtain insurance against the income shocks at actuarially fair rates at the beginning of every period.

1. Characterize the first-best optimal consumption allocation under the assumption that the agent cannot do any private saving.

2. Assuming that income shocks are private information, show that when only spot contracts are feasible, the agent cannot get any insurance.

3. Suppose that the agent can borrow from and lend to a bank at zero interest rate. Characterize the agent's optimal payoff under borrowing and lending.

4. When is insurance in the form of borrowing and lending an optimal contract?

Chapter 10

Question 38

Consider a two-period principal-agent problem, where, in period 1, the agent chooses effort level a, which produces independently and identically distributed profit outcomes in each period, $q_1 \in \{q_L, q_H\}$ and $q_2 \in \{q_L, q_H\}$. The profit outcome q_H occurs with probability $p(a)$—a strictly increasing function of a—and the outcome q_L with probability $[1 - p(a)]$, with $1 > p(a) > 0$ for all $a \in [0, \bar{a}]$, where $\bar{a} < \infty$. The agent's utility function is $u(w) - a$, with $u' > 0$; $u'' < 0$. The agent can neither borrow nor save, so that she is forced to consume what she earns in each period. The principal is risk neutral and can borrow or lend at zero interest rate.

1. Let $\{w_L, w_H, w_{LL}, w_{LH}, w_{HL}, w_{HH}\}$ denote the agent's profit-contingent compensation in periods 1 and 2. Show that the optimal contingent-compensation contract must satisfy the equation

$$\frac{1}{u'(w_i)} = \frac{p(a)}{u'(w_{iH})} + \frac{1 - p(a)}{u'(w_{iL})}, \quad \text{for } i = L, H$$

2. Using Jensen's inequality show that

$$w_i \le p(a)w_{iH} + [1 - p(a)]w_{iL}, \quad \text{for } i = L, H$$

under the optimal contract, when $1/u'$ is concave.

3. Suppose now that under the preceding optimal contract the agent is allowed to save and borrow at date 1 following the realization of q_1. Explain why she would want to save.

Question 39

A firm has assets in place and a new investment opportunity, and lives for three periods. In period $t = 0$, the firm's debt structure is chosen (that is, its level of short-term debt D_1 maturing at $t = 1$, and long-term debt D_2 due at

$t = 2$). At $t = 1$, the assets in place yield a return C_1, and a new investment opportunity appears that requires an investment outlay I. At $t = 2$, the assets in place yield a further return C_2, and the new investment project generates a cash flow C_N, if it has been undertaken at $t = 1$. At $t = 2$, the firm is liquidated and proceeds are distributed to investors. That is, outstanding debt claims are repaid, when feasible, and the residual proceeds are distributed to shareholders. The cash flows C_1 and C_2 are known at $t = 0$, but C_N remains uncertain until $t = 2$. Ex ante it is common knowledge that $C_N \in \{C_L, C_H\}$ with $C_H > I > C_L > 0$ and $\Pr[C_N = C_H] \equiv \gamma$.

The firm is run by a manager who decides whether or not to undertake the project at $t = 1$. The manager is an empire builder. She always chooses to undertake the project if she can. So, if there is sufficient financial slack at $t = 1$, the manager will invest. If this is not the case, the manager will turn to a new lender (bank) for a loan to fund the investment outlays. (Funds borrowed at $t = 1$ can also be used to repay D_1.) Debt raised at $t = 1$ is junior to all existing debt, but senior to equity. The debts D_1 and D_2 cannot be renegotiated. If the firm defaults at $t = 1$, there is a bankruptcy cost $k > 0$ and the firm is liquidated. (There are no bankruptcy costs if the firm defaults at $t = 2$.) Finally, all agents are risk neutral, and the riskless rate of return is zero.

1. Suppose that $C_1 = D_1$. Does this assumption prevent the manager from undertaking projects with a negative net present value (NPV) at $t = 1$? That is, how much additional funding can the manager raise, and what projects will be undertaken?

2. Relax the assumption that $C_1 = D_1$. State the condition (as a function of D_1 and D_2) for the manager to be able to undertake the new project.

3. What are the optimal values of D_1 and D_2? What values of D_1 and D_2 ensure that the investment will be undertaken if and only if its NPV is positive? Explain the role of short-term debt in affecting managerial investment behavior.

4. Now assume that C_1 is a random variable independent of C_N and with the known probability distribution $C_1 \in \{C_1^L, C_1^H\}$ with $C_1^H > C_1^L$ and $\Pr[C_1 = C_1^H] \equiv \eta$. Assume also that all projects have a negative NPV and that $I > C_1^H - C_1^L$. What are the optimal values of D_1 and D_2?

5. Drop the assumption in part 4 that all projects have a negative NPV. Suppose instead that the uncertainty about C_N is resolved at $t = 1$. That is,

at the time the investment is made, the return is known. Assume further that $C_H = 2I = 4C_L$. (C_1 continues to be a random variable). Show that for $I > C_1^H - C_1^L$, it is optimal to set $D_1 = C_1^L$ and $D_2 > C_2$. Explain why risky long-term debt dominates risky short-term debt in this case.

6. Assume now that the opposite condition holds, that is, $I < C_1^H - C_1^L$. Show that risky short-term debt is necessary to avoid overinvestment. What are the costs associated with avoiding overinvestment?

Question 40

Consider a variant of Holmström's (1982a) career-concern model: There are two identical periods. After the second period the manager retires. The output of the manager in period t is

$$q_t = \theta + a_t \varepsilon_t + (1 - a_t) e_t$$

where θ is the manager's unknown ability, $a_t \in [0, 1]$ is the manager's unobserved action, ε_t is an unobserved stochastic return term, and e_t is an observed stochastic return term. One may think of the manager's action as a decision to allocate a dollar between a firm-specific project, which returns ε_t, and a market project, which returns e_t. The allocation is known only to the manager.

The market pays the manager her expected value in each period $w_t = E[q_t|I_t]$, which depends on the market's information I_t and its expectation of the manager's action. Assume that the market's and the manager's first period beliefs about ability are such that θ is normally distributed with mean m_θ and precision (the inverse of the variance) h_θ. Beliefs in the second period are updated based on inferences about a_1, the observed outcome q_1, and the observed market return e_1.

Assume that the returns ε_t and e_t are independent across time as well as from one another. Each is normally distributed with zero mean and with precisions h_ε and h_e, respectively. The manager is strictly risk averse. Her preferences can be described by

$$u(w_1, w_2) = \sum_{t=1}^{2} (E[w_t] - \eta \operatorname{var}[w_t])$$

where w_t is her income in period t, E is the expectation operator, and var is the variance operator. The coefficient of risk aversion η is greater than

0. Note that there is no cost associated with choosing a_t. However, a_t is constrained to lie in the interval [0,1].

1. Write down the equations that characterize a rational-expectations (self-fulfilling) equilibrium for this model.

2. Show that in the rational-expectations equilibrium the manager will necessarily choose the first-period allocation $a_1 = 0$; that is, she will invest all the money in the market project.

3. Would this conclusion be altered if we instead assumed that the firm-specific project had an expected return $E(\varepsilon_t) = 1$? Discuss.

Chapter 11

Question 41

An upstream supplier invests x dollars in period $t = 0$ in acquiring technical skills to produce customized software in period $t = 1$ for a downstream producer. The type of software required and the terms of trade can only be specified in period $t = 1$. The total surplus from trading the software in period $t = 1$ is given by $v(x)$, where $v(\cdot)$ is a strictly increasing, strictly concave function with $v'(0) > 1$, which is bounded above [$v(x) \to M < +\infty$ as $x \to +\infty$]. In period $t = 1$ the upstream and downstream producers are locked in a bilateral bargaining situation, resulting in an efficient trade and in a 50/50 split of the surplus from trade.

1. Explain why ex post spot contracting results in ex ante underinvestment.

2. Suppose now that a new computer to run the software is also available in period $t = 1$. With this new computer, total ex post surplus generated by the software increases from $v(x)$ to $V(x) = f[v(x)] > v(x)$, where $f' \geq 0$ and $f'' \leq 0$. What is the first-best level of investment in skills in period $t = 0$ given that the contracting parties have access to this new computer in period $t = 1$? Is this first-best investment level always higher than the first-best level of investment obtained when access to the new computer is denied?

3. Suppose now that the new computer can be owned either by (a) the upstream producer, (b) the downstream buyer, or (c) a third party owner. Under up- or downstream ownership there will be bilateral ex post bargaining resulting in a 50/50 split of the total surplus. Under third-party ownership of the new computer, there is trilateral ex post bargaining, and the

owner of the computer gets the full marginal contribution of the computer, $V(x) - v(x)$, while the other two parties split the surplus $v(x)$ in half. Show that up- or downstream ownership dominates third-party ownership if $f' > 1$, but third-party ownership dominates when $\frac{1}{2} < f' < 1$.

4. Explain why upstream, downstream, or third-party ownership may dominate when $f' < \frac{1}{2}$.

5. How would your answers to parts 3 and 4 change if the trilateral bargaining solution were given by the Shapley value?

Question 42

Consider the following vertical integration problem: There are two risk-neutral managers, each running an asset a_i where $i = 1, 2$. Both managers make ex ante investments. Only ex post spot contracts regulating trade are feasible. Ex post trade at price P results in the following payoffs: $R(x_1) - P$ for manager 1 and $P - C(x_2)$ for manager 2, where the x_i's denote ex ante investment levels.

If the two managers do not trade with each other, their respective payoffs are

$$r(x_1, A_1) - P_m \qquad \text{and} \qquad P_m - c(x_2, A_2)$$

where A_i denotes the collection of assets owned by manager i. In this problem, $A_i = \emptyset$ under j-integration, $A_i = \{a_1; a_2\}$ under i-integration, and $A_i = \{a_i\}$ under nonintegration.

As in the Grossman-Hart-Moore setting, it is assumed that

$$R(x_1) - C(x_2) > r(x_1, A_1) - c(x_2, A_2)$$

for all $(x_1, x_2) \in [0, \bar{x}]^2$ and all A_i,

$$R'(x_1) > r'(x_1, \{a_1, a_2\}) \geq r'(x_1, \{a_i\}) \geq r'(x_1, \emptyset) \geq 0$$

and

$$-C'(x_2) > -c'(x_2, \{a_1, a_2\}) \geq -c'(x_2, \{a_i\}) \geq -c'(x_2, \emptyset) \geq 0$$

1. Characterize the first-best allocation of assets and investment levels.

2. Assuming that the managers split the ex post gains from trade in half, identify conditions on $r'(x_i, A_i)$ and $c'(x_i, A_i)$ such that nonintegration is optimal.

3. Under the same assumption on ex post bargaining, identify conditions on $r'(x_i, A_i)$ and $c'(x_i, A_i)$ such that integration under the ownership of manager 1 is optimal.

4. Suppose now that

$$r(x_1, A_1) - P_m < \frac{R(x_1) - C(x_2)}{2}$$

for all $x_1 \in [0, \bar{x}]$ and all A_1. Suppose also that

$$P_m - c(x_2, A_2) > \frac{R(x_1) - C(x_2)}{2}$$

for all $x_2 \in [0, \bar{x}]$ and all A_2. Under these assumptions, bargaining under an outside option would give the following outcome:

Equilibrium payoff of manager 1: $R(x_1) - C(x_1) - [P_m - c(x_2, A_2)]$

Equilibrium payoff of manager 2: $[P_m - c(x_2, A_2)]$

In other words, manager 2 gets her outside option. In what way would the analysis and results about optimal ownership allocations and equilibrium investment levels change under this new bargaining solution?

Question 43

Consider a firm seeking outside finance. At date 0, the firm needs to raise I and has no liquid funds. At date 1, it will have (verifiable) assets in place worth A and generate liquid returns C_1 that are assumed to be nonverifiable by outsiders (for example, because they are private information to the firm). We have $C_1 = C_1^H$ with probability β and $C_1 = 0$ with probability $1 - \beta$, where $\beta C_1^H \geq I$. The firm does not know the realization of C_1 at date 0. At date 2 the firm also has long-term returns (future earnings prospects) C_2, which are also unverifiable. The realization of C_2 will be known to the firm already at date 1. We have $C_2 = C_2^H$ with probability γ and $C_2 = C_2^L$ with probability $1 - \gamma$, and $C_2^H > C_2^L > A$.

A contract between the firm and an outside investor is a pair of functions (P, L), where $P = P(\theta)$ and $L = L(\theta)$ depend on the information $\theta = (C_1, C_2)$ available at date 1. $P \leq C_1$ is the firm's payment made out of C_1, and $L \leq A$ is the firm's payment made by liquidating assets. If an amount L of assets is liquidated, long-term earnings to the firm will be $(1 - L/A)C_2$.

The firm and outside investors are risk neutral. At date 0, outside investors have costs of funds equal to one and offer competing investment contracts. The firm then chooses the most preferred one (randomizing if offers are identical), and this contract is executed. Formally, therefore, at date 1 the firm announces its information, and the payments specified in the contract are carried out.

1. Write down the parties' utility functions and the contracting problem at date 0.

2. What is the first-best allocation?

3. Show that in the (second-best) optimal contracting problem the functions P and L must be monotone in C_2. Interpret.

4. Solve the contracting problem and discuss.

5. Now suppose that the parties will renegotiate date-1 inefficiencies whenever possible, that is, whenever the firm has the funds to compensate the investor for not liquidating. Suppose also, to simplify matters, that information is symmetric ex post, that is, that the investor observes θ (but that θ is still nonverifiable). Suppose finally that in these renegotiations the firm has all the bargaining power (that is, makes a take-it-or-leave-it offer to the investor). Determine the optimal renegotiation-proof contract.

6. Compare your results in part 5 to those in part 4.

Question 44

An entrepreneur with no initial wealth has a project that requires an initial investment K and whose output can take two values: $q \in \{0, 1\}$. The market interest rate is normalized to zero. The entrepreneur offers a financial contract to an investor. After the initial investment, both parties observe the realization of the state of the world, $\theta \in \{B, G\}$, which, however, is not observable by a court and thus is not contractable. Instead, a contract can be contingent on the realization of a binary signal, s, which is verifiable in a court. The signal is distributed as follows: If $\theta = G$, then $s = 1$ with probability one. If $\theta = B$, then $s = 1$ with probability γ and $s = 0$ with probability $1 - \gamma$. Assume that γ is sufficiently small but strictly positive.

In each state of the world, an action a has to be taken: $a \in \{S, C\}$, where S is interpreted as "stop" (downsize, liquidate) and C is interpreted as "continue." The probability of high output depends on the realized state of the world and on the action chosen: $\Pr[q = 1|\theta, a] = a_\theta$. (Note that a_θ also expresses the expected monetary return of the project given action a and state θ.) While the investor cares only about monetary returns, the entrepreneur also has a private nonmonetary benefit h from choosing C rather than S. Monetary and nonmonetary returns satisfy the following inequalities:

$$C_G < S_G < C_G + h$$

$$C_B + h < S_B$$

$$S_G - C_G < S_B - C_B$$

Actions cannot be described in an ex ante contract. Instead, a contract specifies control rights, that is, it specifies which party has the right to choose the action. Besides, the contract specifies the entrepreneur's compensation as a function of the realized s and q. If the party in control chooses an action that is not Pareto optimal, the parties can try to renegotiate to an optimal outcome. Assume that the entrepreneur has all the bargaining power in renegotiation.

1. For each of the following control structures, find the values of K for which a contract implementing the first-best action choice is feasible: (a) entrepreneurial control; (b) investor control; (c) contingent control (E has control when $s = 1$, I has control when $s = 0$).

2. Under what conditions does each control structure dominate?

3. Compare your results with Proposition 5 in Aghion and Bolton (1992).

Chapter 12

Question 45

Consider a public good problem. There are $N \geq 3$ agents. The indicator variable y is equal to 1 if the good is supplied and 0 if not, and $t_i \in \mathbb{R}$ is the transfer to agent i. The preferences of agent i are quasi-linear: $\theta_i y + t_i$ with $\theta_i \in \mathbb{R}$. We want to study social choice correspondences, $f(\cdot)$, that we can implement in Nash equilibrium.

1. Show that monotonicity implies that $f(\cdot)$ satisfies the following two conditions:

CONDITION 1   Consider $\theta = (\theta_1, \ldots, \theta_N)$ and $(y, t_1, \ldots, t_N) \in f(\theta)$ such that $y = 1$. Consider also $\phi = (\phi_1, \ldots, \phi_N)$ such that $\phi \geq \theta$ (this means that $\forall i$, $\phi_i \geq \theta_i$). We then have $(y, t_1, \ldots, t_N) \in f(\phi)$.

CONDITION 2   Consider θ and $(y, t_1, \ldots, t_N) \in f(\theta)$ such that $x = 0$. Consider also ϕ such that $\theta \geq \phi$ (this means that $\forall i,\ \theta_i \geq \phi_i$). We then have $(y, t_1, \ldots, t_N) \in f(\phi)$.

2. Consider now $f(\cdot)$ that satisfies conditions 1 and 2. Show that it is monotonic.

3. Show that $f(\cdot)$ satisfies no veto power. Conclude that $f(\cdot)$ is implementable in Nash equilibrium.

4. Show that we can implement an $f(\cdot)$ that satisfies efficient supply [that is, $\forall \theta$ and $\forall (y, t_1, \ldots, t_N) \in f(\theta)$, $y = 1$ if and only if $\sum_{i=1}^{N} \theta_i \geq 0$] that does not involve transfers when $y = 0$ and that is balanced [i.e., $\forall \theta$ and $\forall (y, t_1, \ldots, t_N) \in f(\theta),\ \sum_{i=1}^{N} t_i = 0$].

5. Explain why these results are satisfactory if one cares only about efficiency (efficient supply and not throwing money away) but much less satisfactory if one cares about a "fair" sharing of the cost of the public good.

Question 46

Consider an environment with three individuals (1, 2, and 3) and five outcomes, A, B, C, D, and E. Individual 1 can be of two types, which we call θ_1 and ϕ_1. The same is true for individual 2, who can be of type θ_2 or ϕ_2. Instead, individual 3 has constant preferences. Individual preferences are as follows:

• Individual 1's preferences are summarized by $A > B > C > D > E$ when she is of type θ_1, and by $B > A > E > D > C$ when she is of type ϕ_1.

• Individual 2's preferences are summarized by $A > B > C > D > E$ when she is of type θ_2, and by $B > A > E > D > C$ when she is of type ϕ_2.

• Finally, individual 3's preferences are summarized by $E > D > C > B > A$.

The social-choice function $f(\cdot)$ is defined as follows:

$$f(\theta_1, \theta_2) = A, \quad f(\theta_1, \phi_2) = D = f(\phi_1, \theta_2), \quad \text{and } f(\phi_1, \phi_2) = B$$

1. Show that $f(\cdot)$ is monotonic and satisfies No Veto Power and is therefore implementable in Nash equilibrium.

2. Show that it cannot be implemented in dominant strategies, however.

Question 47

Consider an implementation setup without investment but with risk-sharing. Assume that the parties, a buyer and a seller, have the following utility functions:

$$u_b[v(q, \theta) - P]$$

$$u_s[P - c(q, \theta)]$$

where u_b, v, and u_s are increasing and concave functions, c is an increasing and convex function, and $v(q, 0) = 0$ and $c(q, 0) = 0$ for all θ's. Contracting takes place before θ is known, and trade (P, q) after θ has been observed by both parties.

1. Describe the first best in this setup.

2. Assume that θ is observable but not verifiable, and that the parties cannot commit not to renegotiate but can contractually agree on message-contingent default options and allocations of the entire bargaining power to one party. Construct a revelation game that implements the first best without equilibrium renegotiation.

3. Can a contract without messages but with equilibrium renegotiation implement the first best? Interpret.

Question 48

Consider the contracting problem seen in sections 12.3.1 and 12.3.2, but, rather than assuming

$$c_H > v_H > c_L > v_L$$

assume

$$v_H > c_H > v_L > c_L$$

1. Compute the first-best outcome.

2. What is the optimal option contract under the assumptions made by Noldeke and Schmidt (1995)?

3. What happens if option contracts are not feasible because the buyer can always claim that the seller failed to deliver the good, so that we are in the at-will-contracting world of Hart and Moore (1988)?

4. What would happen if, starting from a Hart-Moore world, "trade" rather than "no trade" were to be the ex post disagreement outcome?

Question 49

Consider a buyer-seller model where the seller can make a costly investment i in quality enhancement. Their respective payoff functions are

$$P - cq - i$$

for the seller, and

$$v(q, i) - P$$

for the buyer, where $v_{qi} > 0$; that is, the effect of a rise in quality enhancement on the buyer valuation $v(\cdot)$ is increasing in the quantity traded q. In addition, P and c stand for price and marginal production cost, as in Chapter 12.

Prices and quantities are assumed to be contractable, while quality is observable but not contractable. The timing of the game is as follows: In stage 0, the parties write an initial contract. In stage 1, the seller chooses i (which then becomes a sunk cost). In stage 2, with probability 0.5, the buyer can make an offer (P, q), while with the remaining probability 0.5 it is the seller who can make an offer (P, q). Finally, in stage 3, the party who did not make the offer in the previous stage can either accept the offer or choose to stick to the initial contract.

1. What are the first-best levels of q and i?

2. What are the equilibrium levels of q and i in the absence of an initial contract [or, equivalently, with an initial contract $(P_0, q_0) = (0, 0)$]?

3. Suppose that the initial contract can only consist in a single pair (P_0, q_0). What will the equilibrium contract be, as well as the associated quality level?

4. Add now to the previous case the following at-will-contracting provision for the buyer. First, when the seller makes the offer in stage 2, the buyer can in stage 3 accept it, accept the initial contract (P_0, q_0), or choose to walk away, that is, choose outcome $(0, 0)$. Second, when the buyer makes the offer in stage 2, the buyer can choose between (P_0, q_0) and $(0, 0)$ if the seller does not accept the buyer's stage-2 offer. What is the impact of this at-will-contracting provision on the equilibrium q and i?

5. If we assume away direct externalities and have payoff functions $v(q) - P$ for the buyer and $P - c(i)q - i$ for the seller [with $c'(i) < 0$], show that choosing a single pair (P_0, q_0) as initial contract is now optimal.

Question 50

Consider a simplified version of the problem in Segal (1999a) and Hart and Moore (1999), with only two widgets, widget 1 and widget 2. Widget 1 costs the seller 0 to produce, while widget 2 costs the seller 1 to produce. Valuations are uncertain, however: in the "good state of nature," widget 1 gives the buyer utility $v > 1$ while widget 2 gives her zero utility; the "bad state of nature" is the opposite case, in that it is widget 2 that gives the buyer utility $v > 1$ while widget 1 gives her zero utility (note that surplus is thus higher in the good state). At investment cost i^2, the seller can induce a probability i that the state of nature is good (and thus $1 - i$ that it is bad).

1. Derive the first best in this environment.

2. Assume that the buyer has full bargaining power in renegotiation. What will be the investment level without the contract if payoffs are mutually observable ex post?

3. Explain how a contract can induce the first best if widgets can be contractually identified by their number ex post and if the parties can commit not to renegotiate the contract.

4. Assume widgets can be contractually identified by their number both ex post and ex ante, but the parties cannot commit not to renegotiate the contract (and the buyer has full bargaining power in the renegotiation). To what extent does contracting reduce the underinvestment of the seller relative to the first best? (Following the lines of the proof detailed in section 12.3.4.2, look at the two following incentive constraints: the one where the buyer considers claiming that the state is bad while it is in fact good, and the one where the seller considers claiming the state is good while it is in fact bad).

5. Discuss this result and compare it with Segal's result.

Question 51

Consider the Aghion-Tirole (1997) model described in Chapter 12. Assume quadratic effort costs:

1. Compute the principal's payoff with and without delegation. Derive the comparative statics of the maximum of these two payoffs with respect to α and β. Discuss.

2. What is the effect of relaxing the assumption that $\alpha > 0$?

3. What is the effect of relaxing the assumption that, if uninformed, the agent would not "choose a project at random"? Specifically, call $\gamma_P < 0$ the principal's payoff from the agent's random choice, and $\gamma_A > 0$ the associated agent's payoff. What is the outcome of the game under these assumptions?

Chapter 13

Question 52

Consider an agent with CARA utility function

$$-e^{-\eta(w-ca^2/2)}$$

where w is monetary compensation and a is effort. Her certainty-equivalent reservation wage is w_0. Output $q = a + \varepsilon$, where ε has a normal distribution $N(0, \sigma^2)$. Two risk-neutral principals (who do not observe a) are interested in q: principal 1 gets a benefit $B_1 q$ and principal 2 gets a benefit $B_2 q$. The agent could be a government agency, and the principals could be political interest groups.

1. Assuming that the principals can join forces and offer the agent a contract $w = t + sq$ to maximize $(B_1 + B_2)q$, what is the optimal contract for them (a) when they can observe and contract on a and (b) when they cannot observe a?

2. Assume that each principal i independently offers a contract $w_i = t_i + s_i q$, that contract offers are simultaneous, and that the agent can only either accept both contracts [in which case she obtains $t_1 + t_2 + (s_1 + s_2)q$] or refuse both. Compute the equilibrium level of $s_1 + s_2$, and compare it with the level of s obtained in part 1. Discuss.

Question 53

Consider an agent who works for two risk-neutral principals ($i = 1, 2$) and produces $q_i = a_i + \varepsilon_i$ for principal i where a_i is effort and the ε_i's are independently and normally distributed with mean 0 and variance σ_i^2. The agent's utility function is

$$-e^{-\eta\left(w-a_1^2/2-a_2^2/2\right)}$$

where w is monetary compensation. Principals are restricted to making simultaneous noncooperative contract offers that are linear in output levels. The agent can accept 0, 1, or both contracts. Her certainty-equivalent reservation wage is 0.

1. Assume each principal can observe only his own output q_i and thus offers a contract $w_i = t_i + s_i q_i$. Compute the Nash equilibrium contracts and effort levels. How do they compare to the optimal contract where the principals can join forces and offer contracts that maximize their joint payoff? Discuss.

2. Assume each principal can observe both output levels and thus offers a contract $w_i = t_i + s_i q_i + f_i q_j$. Compute the equilibrium contracts and effort levels. Compare with the solution in part 1.

Question 54

Consider a public project that a firm can build at cost $\theta \in [\underline{\theta}, \overline{\theta}]$. The firm knows the realization of θ, but regional governments believe it to be distributed according to a density $f(\theta)$ and cumulative distribution function $F(\theta)$ [with $F(\theta)/f(\theta)$ nondecreasing in θ].

There are two regional governments ($i = 1, 2$), with social benefit S_i in region i (positive or negative, depending on employment or environmental considerations, for example). Each government i can set a (negative or positive) transfer T_i that the firm receives if and only if it builds the project.

The firm's payoff is

$$u = d(T_1 + T_2 - \theta)$$

where $d = 1$ if the project is built and 0 otherwise. Government i's payoff is

$$V_i = d[S_i - (1 + \lambda)T_i] + u/2$$

where λ is the shadow cost of public funds.

1. What is the first-best value θ^* such that the project should be built if and only if $\theta \leq \theta^*$?

2. Assuming from now on that θ is private information to the firm, consider first the case where the regional governments join forces and choose $T = T_1 + T_2$ so as to maximize $V_1 + V_2$. Derive the optimal transfer T and the value θ^c such that the firm builds the project if and only if $\theta \leq \theta^c$.

3. Now assume that the regional governments set the T_i's noncooperatively. Derive the equilibrium T_i's and the value θ^{nc} such that the firm builds the project if and only if $\theta \leq \theta^{nc}$.

4. Discuss and compare the answers obtained in parts 1, 2, and 3.

References

Abreu, D., P. Milgrom, and D. Pearce. (1991). "Information and Timing in Repeated Partnerships." *Econometrica*, 59, 1713–33.

Abreu, D., D. Pearce, and E. Stacchetti. (1990). "Toward a Theory of Discounted Repeated Games with Imperfect Monitoring." *Econometrica*, 58, 1041–63.

Adams, W. J., and J. L. Yellen. (1976). "Commodity Bundling and the Burden of Monopoly." *Quarterly Journal of Economics*, 90, 475–98.

Admati, A. R., and P. Pfleiderer. (2000). "Forcing Firms to Talk: Financial Disclosure Regulation and Externalities." *Review of Financial Studies*, 13, 479–519.

Aghion, P., and P. Bolton. (1987). "Contracts as a Barrier to Entry." *American Economic Review*, 77, 388–401.

———. (1992). "An Incomplete Contracts Approach to Financial Contracting." *Review of Economic Studies*, 59, 473–94.

——— (1997). "A Theory of Trickle-Down Growth and Development." *Review of Economic Studies*, 64, 151–72.

———. (2003). "Incomplete Social Contracts." *Journal of the European Economic Association*, 1, 38–67.

Aghion, P., M. Dewatripont, and P. Rey. (1994). "Renegotiation Design with Unverifiable Information." *Econometrica*, 62, 257–82.

———. (1999). "Agency Costs, Firm Behavior, and the Nature of Competition." CEPR Discussion Paper 2130.

———. (2002). "On Partial Contracting." *European Economic Review*, 46, 745–53.

———. (2004). "Transferable Control." *Journal of the European Economic Association*, 2, 115–38.

Aghion, P., and B. Hermalin. (1990). "Legal Restrictions on Private Contracts Can Enhance Efficiency." *Journal of Law, Economics and Organizations*, 6, 381–409.

Aghion, P., and J. Tirole. (1997). "Formal and Real Authority in Organizations." *Journal of Political Economy*, 105, 1–29.

Akerlof, G. (1970). "The Market for Lemons." *Quarterly Journal of Economics*, 84, 488–500.

Alchian, A. A., and H. Demsetz. (1972). "Production, Information Costs, and Economic Organization." *American Economic Review*, 62, 777–95.

Allen, F., and G. Faulhaber. (1989). "Signaling by Underpricing in the IPO Market." *Journal of Financial Economics*, 23, 303–23.

Allen, F., and D. Gale. (2000). *Comparing Financial Systems*. Cambridge, MA: MIT Press.

Anderlini, L., and L. Felli. (1994). "Incomplete Written Contracts: Undescribable States of Nature." *Quarterly Journal of Economics*, 109, 1085–1124.

Anderson, E. (1985). "The Salesperson as Outside Agent or Employee: A Transaction Cost Analysis." *Marketing Science*, 4, 234–54.

Anderson, E., and D. C. Schmittlein. (1984). "Integration of the Sales Force: An Empirical Examination." *RAND Journal of Economics*, 15, 385–95.

Aoki, M. (1986). "Horizontal vs. Vertical Information Structure of the Firm." *American Economic Review*, 76, 971–83.

Armstrong, M. (1996). "Multiproduct Nonlinear Pricing." *Econometrica*, 64, 51–75.

———. (1999). "Price Discrimination by a Many-Product Firm." *Review of Economic Studies*, 66, 151–68.

———. (2000). "Optimal Multiobject Auctions." *Review of Economic Studies*, 67, 455–83.

Armstrong, M., C. Cowan, and J. Vickers. (1994). *Regulatory Reform—Economic Analysis and the UK Experience*. Cambridge, MA: MIT Press.

Armstrong, M., and J. C. Rochet. (1999). "Multidimensional Screening: A User's Guide." *European Economic Review*, 43, 959–79.

Arrow, K. J. (1963). *Social Choice and Individual Values*, 2nd ed. New York: Wiley.

———. (1964). "The Role of Securities in the Optimal Allocation of Risk-Bearing." *Review of Economic Studies*, 31, 91–6.

———. (1970). *Essays in the Theory of Risk Bearing*. Amsterdam: North-Holland.

Asquith, P., and D. W. Mullins, Jr. (1983). "The Impact of Initiating Dividend Payments on Shareholders' Wealth." *Journal of Business*, 56, 77–96.

Atkeson, A., and R. E. Lucas. (1992). "On Efficient Distribution with Private Information." *Review of Economic Studies*, 59, 427–53.

Azariadis, C. (1975). "Implicit Contracts and Underemployment Equilibria." *Journal of Political Economy*, 83, 1183–1202.

———. (1983). "Employment with Asymmetric Information." *Quarterly Journal of Economics*, 98, Supplement, 157–72.

Azariadis, C., and J. E. Stiglitz. (1983). "Implicit Contracts and Fixed Price Equilibria." *Quarterly Journal of Economics*, 98, Supplement, 1–22.

Bagwell, K. (2001). "Introduction". In K. Bagwell (ed.), *The Economics of Advertising*. Cheltenham, UK: Edward Elgar.

Bagwell, K., and M. Riordan. (1991). "High and Declining Prices Signal Product Quality." *American Economic Review*, 81, 224–39.

Baily, M. N. (1974). "Wages and Employment under Uncertain Demand." *Review of Economic Studies*, 41, 37–50.

Bajari, P., and S. Tadelis. (2001). "Incentives versus Transaction Costs: A Theory of Procurement Contracts." *RAND Journal of Economics*, 32, 387–407.

Baker, G. P. (1992). "Incentive Contracts and Performance Measurement." *Journal of Political Economy*, 100, 598–614.

———. (2000). "The Use of Performance Measures in Incentive Contracting." *American Economic Review*, 90, 415–20.

Baker, G. P., R. Gibbons, and K. J. Murphy. (1994). "Subjective Performance Measures in Optimal Incentive Contracts." *Quarterly Journal of Economics*, 109, 1125–56.

———. (2002). "Relational Contracts and the Theory of the Firm." *Quarterly Journal of Economics*, 117, 39–84.

Baliga, S. (1999). "Monitoring and Collusion with 'Soft' Information." *Journal of Law, Economics, and Organization*, 15, 434–40.

Baliga, S., and T. Sjostrom. (1998). "Decentralization and Collusion." *Journal of Economic Theory*, 83, 196–232.

Banerjee, A. (2003). "Contracting Constraints, Credit Markets, and Economic Development." In M. Dewatripont, L. Hansen, and S. Turnovsky (eds.), *Advances in Economics and Econometrics: Theory and Applications, Eighth World Congress of the Econometric Society*, vol. 3, 1–46. Cambridge, UK: Cambridge University Press.

Banerjee, A. V., and A. F. Newman. (1991). "Risk-Bearing and the Theory of Income Distribution." *Review of Economic Studies*, 58, 211–55.

———. (1993). "Occupational Choice and the Process of Development." *Journal of Political Economy*, 101, 274–98.

Baron, D. P., and D. Besanko. (1984). "Regulation, Asymmetric Information, and Auditing." *RAND Journal of Economics*, 15, 447–70.

Baron, D. P., and R. B. Myerson. (1982). "Regulating a Monopolist with Unknown Costs." *Econometrica*, 50, 911–30.

Beaudry, P., and M. Poitevin. (1993). "Signaling and Renegotiation in Contractual Relationships." *Econometrica*, 61, 745–82.

Bebchuk, L., J. Fried, and D. Walker. (2002). "Managerial Power and Rent Extraction in the Design of Executive Compensation." *University of Chicago Law Review*, 69, 751–846.

Becker, G. S. (1968). "Crime and Punishment: An Economic Approach." *Journal of Political Economy*, 76, 169–217.

Beckmann, M. J. (1977). "Management Production Functions and the Theory of the Firm." *Journal of Economic Theory*, 14, 1–18.

Beggs, A. W. (2001). "Queues and Hierarchies." *Review of Economic Studies*, 68, 297–322.

Berglof, E. (1994). "A Control Theory of Venture Capital Finance." *Journal of Law, Economics, and Organization*, 10, 247–67.

Berglof, E., and E. von Thadden. (1994). "Short-Term Versus Long-Term Interests: Capital Structure with Multiple Investors." *Quarterly Journal of Economics*, 109, 1055–84.

Berle, A. A., and G. Means. (1932). *The Modern Corporation and Private Property*. New York: Macmillan.

Bernanke, B., and M. Gertler. (1989). "Agency Costs, Net Worth, and Business Fluctuations." *American Economic Review*, 79, 14–31.

Bernheim, B. D. (1991). "Tax Policy and the Dividend Puzzle." *RAND Journal of Economics*, 22, 455–76.

Bernheim, B. D., and A. Wantz. (1995). "A Tax-Based Test of the Dividend Signaling Hypothesis." *American Economic Review*, 85, 532–51.

Bernheim, B. D., and M. D. Whinston. (1985). "Common Marketing Agency as a Device for Facilitating Collusion." *RAND Journal of Economics*, 16, 269–81.

———. (1986a). "Menu Auctions, Resource Allocation, and Economic Influence." *Quarterly Journal of Economics*, 101, 1–31.

———. (1986b). "Common Agency." *Econometrica*, 54, 923–42.

———. (1998a). "Exclusive Dealing." *Journal of Political Economy*, 106, 64–103.

———. (1998b). "Incomplete Contracts and Strategic Ambiguity." *American Economic Review*, 88, 902–32.

Bester, H. (1985). "Screening versus Rationing in Credit Markets with Imperfect Information." *American Economic Review*, 75, 850–55.

———. (1992). "Credit Screening." In *The New Palgrave Dictionary of Money and Finance*. London and Basingstoke: MacMillan.

Bester, H., and M. Hellwig. (1987). "Moral Hazard and Equilibrium Credit Rationing: An Overview of the Issues." In G. Bamberg and K. Spreman (eds.), *Agency Theory, Information, and Incentives*, 135–67. Berlin: Springer.

Bester, H., and R. Strausz. (2001). "Contracting with Imperfect Commitment and the Revelation Principle: The Single Agent Case." *Econometrica*, 69, 1077–98.

Bhattacharya, S. (1979). "Imperfect Information, Dividend Policy, and 'the Bird in the Hand' Fallacy." *Bell Journal of Economics*, 10, 259–70.

Bhattacharya, S., J. Glazer, and D. Sappington. (1992). "Licensing and the Sharing of Knowledge in Research Joint Ventures." *Journal of Economic Theory*, 56, 43–69.

Bhattacharya, S., and F. Lafontaine. (1995). "Double-Sided Moral Hazard and the Nature of Share Contacts." *RAND Journal of Economics*, 26, 761–81.

Bhattacharya, S., and A. V. Thakor. (1993). "Contemporary Banking Theory." *Journal of Financial Intermediation*, 3, 2–50.

Binmore, K. (1992). *Fun and Games: A Text on Game Theory*. Lexington, MA: Heath.

Binmore, K. G., A. Rubinstein, and A. Wolinsky. (1986). "The Nash Bargaining Solution in Economic Modeling." *RAND Journal of Economics*, 17, 176–88.

Bisin, A., J. Geanakoplos, P. Gottardi, E. Minelli, and H. Polemarchakis. (2004). "Markets and Contracts." *Journal of Mathematical Economics,* forthcoming.

Bisin, A., and P. Gottardi. (1999). "Competitive Equilibria with Asymmetric Information." *Journal of Economic Theory*, 87, 1–48.

Bisin, A., and D. Guaitoli. (1998). "Moral Hazard and Nonexclusive Contracts." C. V. Starr Center for Applied Economics, New York University, Working Paper 98–24.

Bizer, D., and P. DeMarzo. (1992). "Sequential Banking." *Journal of Political Economy*, 110, 41–61.

Bolton, P. (1987). "The Principle of Maximum Deterrence Revisited." UC-Berkeley Working Paper 8749.

Bolton, P., and M. Dewatripont. (1994). "The Firm as a Communication Network." *Quarterly Journal of Economics*, 109, 809–40.

Bolton, P., F. Pivetta, and G. Roland. (1997). "Optimal Sale of Assets: The Role of Noncash Bids." Mimeo, ECARES and Princeton.

Bolton, P., and A. Rajan. (2001). "The Employment Relation and the Theory of the Firm: Arm's Length Contracting versus Authority." Mimeo, Princeton.

Bolton, P., and H. Rosenthal. (2003). "Political Intervention in Debt Contracts." *Journal of Political Economy*, 101, 1103–34.

Bolton, P., and D. S. Scharfstein. (1990). "A Theory of Predation Based on Agency Problems in Financial Contracting." *American Economic Review*, 80, 93–106.

———. (1996). "Optimal Debt Structure and the Number of Creditors." *Journal of Political Economy*, 104, 1–25.

———. (1998). "Corporate Finance, the Theory of the Firm, and Organizations." *Journal of Economic Perspectives*, 12, 95–114.

Bolton, P., J. Scheinkman, and W. Xiong. (2003). "Executive Compensation and Short-termist Behavior in Speculative Markets." NBER Working Paper w9722.

Bolton, P., and M. D. Whinston. (1993). "Incomplete Contracts, Vertical Integration, and Supply Assurance." *Review of Economic Studies*, 60, 121–48.

Bolton, P., and C. Xu. (2001). "Ownership and Managerial Competition: Employee, Customer, or Outside Ownership." London School of Economics, Discussion paper TE/01/412.

Bonnano, G., and J. Vickers. (1988). "Vertical Separation." *Journal of Industrial Economics*, 36, 257–65.

Boot, A. W. A., and A. V. Thakor. (1993). "Self-Interested Bank Regulation." *American Economic Review*, 83, 206–12.

Borch, K. H. (1962). "Equilibrium in a Reinsurance Market." *Econometrica*, 30, 424–44.

Brander, J., and T. Lewis. (1986). "Oligopoly and Financial Structure: The Limited Liability Effect." *American Economic Review*, 76, 956–70.

Brennan, M. J., and A. Kraus. (1987). "Efficient Financing under Asymmetric Information." *Journal of Finance*, 42, 1225–43.

Bull, C. (1987). "The Existence of Self-Enforcing Implicit Contracts." *Quarterly Journal of Economics*, 102, 147–59.

Bull, C., A. Schotter, and K. Weigelt. (1987). "Tournaments and Piece Rates: An Experimental Study." *Journal of Political Economy*, 95, 1–33.

Bulow, J. (1982). "Durable-Goods Monopolists." *Journal of Political Economy*, 90, 314–32.

Bulow, J., J. D. Geanakoplos, and P. D. Klemperer. (1985). "Multimarket Oligopoly: Strategic Substitutes and Complements." *Journal of Political Economy*, 93, 488–511.

Bulow, J., and J. Roberts. (1989). "The Simple Economics of Optimal Auctions." *Journal of Political Economy*, 97, 1060–90.

Bulow, J., and K. Rogoff. (1989). "A Constant Recontracting Model of Sovereign Debt." *Journal of Political Economy*, 97, 155–78.

Burkart, M., D. Gromb, and F. Panunzi. (1997). "Large Shareholders, Monitoring and the Value of the Firm." *Quarterly Journal of Economics*, 112, 693–728.

———. (1998). "Why Higher Takeover Premia Protect Minority Shareholders." *Journal of Political Economy*, 106, 172–204.

Caillaud, B., R. Guesnerie, and P. Rey. (1992). "Noisy Observation in Adverse Selection Models." *Review of Economic Studies*, 59, 595–615.

Caillaud, B., R. Guesnerie, P. Rey, and J. Tirole. (1988). "Government Intervention in Production and Incentives Theory: A Review of Recent Contributions." *RAND Journal of Economics*, 19, 1–26.

Caillaud, B., B. Jullien, and P. Picard. (1995). "Competing Vertical Structures: Precommitment and Renegotiation." *Econometrica*, 63, 621–46.

Calvo, G., and S. Wellisz. (1978). "Supervision, Loss of Control and the Optimal Size of the Firm." *Journal of Political Economy*, 86, 943–52.

———. (1979). "Hierarchy, Ability, and Income Distribution." *Journal of Political Economy*, 87, 991–1010.

Chandler, A. (1962). *Strategy and Structure: Chapters in the History of the Industrial Enterprise.* Cambridge, MA: MIT Press.

———. (1977). *The Visible Hand: The Managerial Revolution in American Business.* Cambridge, MA: Harvard University Press.

———. (1990). *Scale and Scope: The Dynamics of Industrial Capitalism.* Cambridge, MA: Harvard University Press, Belknap Press.

Chang, C. (1990). "The Dynamic Structure of Optimal Debt Contracts." *Journal of Economic Theory*, 52, 68–86.

Chari, V. (1983). "Involuntary Unemployment and Implicit Contracts." *Quarterly Journal of Economics*, 98, Supplement, 107–22.

Chatterjee, K., and W. Samuelson. (1983). "Bargaining under Incomplete Information." *Operations Research*, 31, 835–51.

Che, Y. K., and I. Gale. (1998). "Standard Auctions with Financially Constrained Bidders." *Review of Economic Studies*, 65, 1–21.

Che, Y. K., and D. B. Hausch. (1999). "Cooperative Investments and the Value of Contracting." *American Economic Review*, 89, 125–47.

Chiappori, P., I. Macho, P. Rey, and B. Salanié. (1994). "Repeated Moral Hazard: The Role of Memory Commitment and the Access to Credit Markets." *European Economic Review*, 38, 1527–53.

Cho, I. K., and D. M. Kreps. (1987). "Signaling Games and Stable Equilibria." *Quarterly Journal of Economics*, 102, 179–221.

Chung, T. Y. (1991). "Incomplete Contracts, Specific Investments, and Risk-Sharing." *Review of Economic Studies*, 58, 1031–42.

Clarke, E. H. (1971). "Multipart Pricing of Public Goods." *Public Choice*, 2, 19–33.

Coase, R. H. (1937). "The Nature of the Firm." *Economica*, 4, 386–405.

———. (1960). "The Problem of Social Cost." *Journal of Law and Economics*, 3, 1–44.

———. (1972). "Durability and Monopoly." *Journal of Law and Economics*, 15, 143–9.

Compte, O. (1998). "Communication in Repeated Games with Imperfect Private Monitoring." *Econometrica*, 66, 597–626.

Constantinides, G., and B. D. Grundy. (1989). "Optimal Investment with Stock Repurchase and Financing as Signals." *Review of Financial Studies*, 2, 445–65.

Crémer, J. (1980). "A Partial Theory of the Optimal Organization of Bureaucracy." *Bell Journal of Economics*, 11, 683–93.

———. (1995). "Arm's Length Relationships." *Quarterly Journal of Economics*, 110, 275–95.

Crémer, J., and F. Khalil. (1992). "Gathering Information before Signing a Contract." *American Economic Review*, 82, 566–78.

Crémer, J., and R. P. McLean. (1985). "Optimal Selling Strategies under Uncertainty for a Discriminatory Monopolist when Demands Are Interdependent." *Econometrica*, 53, 345–61.

———. (1988). "Full Extraction of the Surplus in Bayesian and Dominant Strategy Auctions." *Econometrica*, 56, 1247–57.

Dasgupta, P., and E. Maskin. (2000). "Efficient Auctions." *Quarterly Journal of Economics*, 115, 341–88.

Dasgupta, P. S., P. J. Hammond, and E. S. Maskin. (1979). "The Implementation of Social Choice Rules: Some General Results on Incentive Compatibility." *Review of Economic Studies*, 46, 185–216.

d'Aspremont, C., and L. Gérard-Varet. (1979). "Incentives and Incomplete Information." *Journal of Public Economics*, 11, 24–45.

Debreu, G. (1959). *The Theory of Value: An Axiomatic Analysis of Economic Equilibrium*. New York: Wiley.

DeMarzo, P., and M. J. Fishman. (2002). "Optimal Long-Term Financial Contracting with Privately Observed Cash Flows." Mimeo, Kellogg School of Management, Northwestern University, Evanston, IL.

DeMeza, D., and B. Lockwood. (1998). "Does Asset Ownership Always Motivate Managers? Outside Options and the Property Rights Theory of the Firm." *Quarterly Journal of Economics*, 113, 361–86.

DeMeza, D., and D. C. Webb. (1987). "Too Much Investment: A Problem of Asymmetric Information." *Quarterly Journal of Economics*, 102, 281–92.

Demski, J. S., and D. M. Kreps. (1982). "Models in Managerial Accounting." *Journal of Accounting Research*, 20, 117–48.

Demski, J., and D. Sappington. (1984). "Optimal Incentive Contracts with Multiple Agents." *Journal of Economic Theory*, 33, 152–71.

———. (1987). "Hierarchical Regulatory Control." *RAND Journal of Economics*, 18, 369–83.

———. (1991). "Resolving Double Moral Hazard Problems with Buyout Agreements." *Rand Journal of Economics*, 22, 232–40.

Dessein, W. (2002). "Authority and Communication in Organizations." *Review of Economic Studies*, 69, 811–38.

———. (2004). "Information and Control in Alliances and Ventures." *Journal of Finance*, forthcoming.

Dewatripont, M. (1988). "Commitment through Renegotiation-Proof Contracts with Third Parties." *Review of Economic Studies*, 55, 377–89.

———. (1989). "Renegotiation and Information Revelation over Time: The Case of Optimal Labor Contracts." *Quarterly Journal of Economics*, 104, 589–619.

Dewatripont, M., I. Jewitt, and J. Tirole. (1999a). "The Economics of Career Concerns, Part 1: Comparing Information Structures." *Review of Economic Studies*, 66, 183–98.

———. (1999b). "The Economics of Career Concerns, Part 2: Application to Missions and Accountability of Government Agencies." *Review of Economic Studies*, 66, 199–217.

Dewatripont, M., P. Legros, and S. Matthews. (2003). "Moral Hazard and Capital Structure Dynamics." *Journal of the European Economic Association*, 1, 890–930.

Dewatripont, M., and E. Maskin. (1990). "Contract Renegotiation in Models of Asymmetric Information." *European Economic Review*, 34, 311–21.

———. (1995a). "Contractual Contingencies and Renegotiation." *RAND Journal of Economics*, 26, 704–19.

———. (1995b). "Credit and Efficiency in Centralized and Decentralized Economies." *Review of Economic Studies*, 62, 541–55.

Dewatripont, M., F. Maskin, and G. Roland. (1999). "Soft Budget Constraints and Transition." In E. Maskin and A. Simonovits (eds.), *Planning, Shortage and Transformation*, 143–55. Cambridge, MA: MIT Press.

Dewatripont, M., and G. Roland. (1992). "Economic Reform and Dynamic Political Constraints." *Review of Economic Studies*, 59, 703–30.

Dewatripont, M., and J. Tirole. (1994a). "A Theory of Debt and Equity: Diversity of Securities and Manager-Shareholder Congruence." *Quarterly Journal of Economics*, 109, 1027–54.

———. (1994b). *The Prudential Regulation of Banks*. Cambridge, MA: MIT Press.

———. (1999). "Advocates." *Journal of Political Economy*, 107, 1–39.

———. (2003). "Further Notes on Advocacy." Mimeo, ECARES and IDEI, Toulouse.

Diamond, D. W. (1984). "Financial Intermediation and Delegated Monitoring." *Review of Economic Studies*, 51, 393–414.

———. (1991a). "Debt Maturity Structure and Liquidity Risk." *Quarterly Journal of Economics*, 106, 709–37.

———. (1991b). "Monitoring and Reputation: The Choice between Bank Loans and Directly Placed Debt." *Journal of Political Economy*, 99, 689–721.

———. (1993). "Seniority and Maturity of Debt Contracts." *Journal of Financial Economics*, 53, 341–68.

———. (1997). "Liquidity, Banks, and Markets." *Journal of Political Economy*, 105, 928–56.

Diamond, D., and P. Dybvig. (1983). "Bank Runs, Deposit Insurance, and Liquidity." *Journal of Political Economy*, 91, 401–19.

Dionne, G. (ed.). (2000). *Handbook of Insurance*. New York: Kluwer Academic Publishers.

Dixit, A. (1996). *The Making of Economic Policy*. Cambridge, MA: MIT Press.

———. (1997). "Power of Incentives in Private vs. Public Organizations." *American Economic Review*, 87, 378–82.

Dixit, A., G. Grossman, and E. Helpman. (1997). "Common Agency and Coordination: General Theory and Application to Government Policymaking." *Journal of Political Economy*, 105, 752–69.

Dubey, P., J. Geanakoplos, and M. Shubik. (1996). "Default and Efficiency in a General Equilibrium Model with Incomplete Markets." Yale University, Cowles Foundation Discussion Paper 879R. New Haven, CT.

Dutta, P. K., and R. Radner. (1994). "Optimal Principal-Agent Contracts for a Class of Incentive Schemes: A Complete Characterization and the Rate of Approach to Efficiency." *Economic Theory*, 4, 483–503.

Edlin, A. S., and S. Reichelstein. (1996). "Holdups, Standard Breach Remedies, and Optimal Investment." *American Economic Review*, 86, 478–501.

Engers, M., and L. Fernandez. (1987). "Market Equilibrium with Hidden Knowledge and Self-Selection." *Econometrica*, 55, 425–39.

Eswaran, M., and A. Kotwal. (1985). "A Theory of Contractual Structure in Agriculture." *American Economic Review*, 75, 352–67.

Fairburn, J. A., and J. M. Malcomson. (2001). "Performance, Promotion, and the Peter Principle." *Review of Economic Studies*, 68, 45–66.

Fama, E. F., and M. H. Miller. (1972). *The Theory of Finance*. Hinsdale, IL: Dryden Press.

Farrell, J. (1987). "Information and the Coase Theorem." *Journal of Economic Perspectives*, 1, 113–29.

Faure-Grimaud, A. (2000). "Product Market Competition and Optimal Debt Contracts: The Limited Liability Effect Revisited." *European Economic Review*, 44, 1823–40.

Faure-Grimaud, A., J. J. Laffont, and D. Martimort. (2003). "Collusion, Delegation and Supervision with Soft Information." *Review of Economic Studies*, 70, 253–80.

Felli, L. (1996). "Preventing Collusion through Discretion." London School of Economics, Discussion Paper TE/96/303.

Fershtman, C., and K. L. Judd. (1987). "Equilibrium Incentives in Oligopoly." *American Economic Review*, 77, 927–40.

Fishman, M. J., and K. M. Hagerty. (1995). "The Mandatory Disclosure of Trades and Market Liquidity." *Review of Financial Studies*, 8, 637–76.

Freixas, X., R. Guesnerie, and J. Tirole. (1985). "Planning under Incomplete Information and the Ratchet Effect." *Review of Economic Studies*, 52, 173–91.

Freixas, X., and J. Rochet. (1997). *Microeconomics of Banking*, Cambridge, MA: MIT Press.

Fudenberg, D., B. Holmström, and P. Milgrom. (1990). "Short-Term Contracts and Long-Term Agency Relationships." *Journal of Economic Theory*, 51, 1–31.

Fudenberg, D., D. K. Levine, and E. Maskin. (1994). "The Folk Theorem with Imperfect Public Information." *Econometrica*, 62, 997–1039.

Fudenberg, D., and J. Tirole. (1983). "Sequential Bargaining with Incomplete Information." *Review of Economic Studies*, 50, 221–47.

———. (1984). "The Fat-Cat Effect, the Puppy-Dog Ploy, and the Lean and Hungry Look." *American Economic Review*, 74, 361–66.

———. (1990). "Moral Hazard and Renegotiation in Agency Contracts." *Econometrica*, 58, 1279–319.

———. (1991). *Game Theory*. Cambridge, MA: MIT Press.

Gale, D. (1992). "A Walrasian Theory of Markets with Adverse Selection." *Review of Economic Studies*, 59, 229–55.

Gale, D., and M. Hellwig. (1985). "Incentive-Compatible Debt Contracts: The One-Period Problem." *Review of Economic Studies*, 52, 647–63.

———. (1989). "Repudiation and Renegotiation: The Case of Sovereign Debt." *International Economic Review*, 30, 3–31.

Garicano, L. (2000). "Hierarchies and the Organization of Knowledge in Production." *Journal of Political Economy*, 108, 874–904.

Garvey, G., and T. Milbourn. (2003). "Incentive Compensation When Executives Can Hedge the Market: Evidence of Relative Performance Evaluation in the Cross-Section." *Journal of Finance*, 58, 1557–82.

Geanakoplos, J. D., and P. Milgrom. (1991). "A Theory of Hierarchies Based on Limited Managerial Attention." *Journal of Japanese and International Economies*, 5, 205–25.

Gertner, R., D. Scharfstein, and J. Stein. (1994). "Internal Versus External Capital Markets." *Quarterly Journal of Economics*, 109, 1211–30.

Gibbard, A. (1973). "Manipulation of Voting Schemes: A General Result." *Econometrica*, 41, 587–601.

Gibbons, R., and K. J. Murphy. (1992). "Optimal Incentive Contracts in the Presence of Career Concerns: Theory and Evidence." *Journal of Political Economy*, 100, 468–505.

Goldberg, V. P. (1976). "Regulation and Administered Contracts." *Bell Journal of Economics*, 7, 426–48.

Gordon, D. F. (1974). "A Neoclassical Theory of Keynesian Unemployment." *Economic Inquiry*, 12, 431–59.

Goswami, G., T. Noe, and M. Rebello. (1995). Debt Financing under Asymmetric Information." *Journal of Finance*, 50, 633–59.

Grafen, A. (1990). "Biological Signals as Handicaps." *Journal of Theoretical Biology*, 144, 517–46.

Green, E. J. (1987). "Lending and the Smoothing of Uninsurable Income." In E. C. Prescott and N. Wallace (eds.), *Contractual Arrangements for Intertemporal Trade*, 3–25. Minneapolis: University of Minnesota Press.

Green, J. R., and C. Kahn. (1983). "Wage Employment Contracts." *Quarterly Journal of Economics*, 98, Supplement 173–89.

Green, J. R., and J. J. Laffont. (1977). "Characterization of Satisfactory Mechanisms for the Revelation of Preferences for Public Goods." *Econometrica*, 45: 427–38.

———. (1979). *Incentives and Public Decision Making*. Amsterdam: North Holland.

Green, J. R., and S. Scotchmer. (1995). "On the Division of Profit in Sequential Innovation." *RAND Journal of Economics*, 26(1), 20–33.

Green, J. R., and N. Stokey. (1983). "A Comparison of Tournaments and Contracts." *Journal of Political Economy*, 91, 349–64.

Greenwald, B. C. (1986). "Adverse Selection in the Labor Market." *Review of Economic Studies*, 53, 325–48.

Gromb, D. (1994). *Contributions to Financial and Industrial Economics*. Ph.D. thesis. Ecole Polytechnique, Paris.

Grossman, G. M., and E. Helpman. (1994). "Protection for Sale." *American Economic Review*, 84, 833–50.

———. (2002). *Interest Groups and Trade Policy*. Princeton, NJ: Princeton University Press.

Grossman, S. J. (1981). "The Informational Role of Warranties and Private Disclosure about Product Quality." *Journal of Law and Economics*, 24, 461–83

Grossman, S. J., and O. D. Hart. (1980). "Disclosure Laws and Takeover Bids." *Journal of Finance*, 35, 323–34.

———. (1982). "Corporate Financial Structure and Managerial Incentives." In J. McCall (ed.), *Economics of Information and Uncertainty*. Chicago, IL: University of Chicago Press.

———. (1983a). "An Analysis of the Principal-Agent Problem." *Econometrica*, 51, 7–45.

———. (1983b). "Implicit Contracts under Asymmetric Information." *Quarterly Journal of Economics*, 98, Supplement, 123–56.

———. (1986). "The Costs and Benefits of Ownership: A Theory of Vertical and Lateral Integration." *Journal of Political Economy*, 94, 691–719.

———. (1988). "One Share/One Vote and the Market for Corporate Control." *Journal of Financial Economics*, 20, 175–202.

Grossman, S. J., O. D. Hart, and E. S. Maskin. (1983). "Unemployment with Observable Aggregate Shocks." *Journal of Political Economy*, 91, 907–28.

Grout, P. A. (1984). "Investment and Wages in the Absence of Binding Contracts: A Nash Bargaining Approach." *Econometrica*, 52, 449–60.

Groves, T. (1973). "Incentives in Teams." *Econometrica*, 41:617–31.

Groves, T., and J. Ledyard. (1977). "Optimal Allocation of Public Goods: A Solution to the Free-Rider Problem." *Econometrica*, 45, 783–809.

Guesnerie, R. (1992). "The Arrow-Debreu Paradigm Faced with Modern Theories of Contracting." In L. Werin and H. Wijkander (eds.), *Contract Economics*. Oxford: Blackwell.

Guesnerie, R., and J. J. Laffont. (1984). "A Complete Solution to a Class of Principal-Agent Problems with an Application to the Control of a Self-Managed Firm." *Journal of Public Economics*, 25, 329–69.

Gul, F., H. Sonnenschein, and R. Wilson. (1986). "Foundations of Dynamic Monopoly and the Coase Conjecture." *Journal of Economic Theory*, 39, 155–90.

Halonen, M. (1997). "A Theory of Joint Ownership." University of Bristol, Discussion Paper 437.

———. (2002). "Reputation and the Allocation of Ownership." *The Economic Journal*, 112, 539–58.

Hansmann, H. (1996). *The Ownership of Enterprise*. Cambridge, MA: Belknap Harvard.

Harris, M., and B. Holmström. (1982). "A Theory of Wage Dynamics." *Review of Economic Studies*, 49, 315–33.

Harris, M. and A. Raviv. (1979). "Optimal Incentive Contracts with Imperfect Information." *Journal of Economic Theory*, 20, 231–59.

———. (1988a). "Corporate Control Contests and Capital Structure." *Journal of Financial Economics*, 20, 55–86.

———. (1988b): "Corporate Governance: Voting Rights and Majority Rules." *Journal of Financial Economics*, 20, 203–35.

———. (1992). "Financial Contracting Theory." In J. J. Laffont (ed.), *Advances in Economic Theory: Sixth World Congress of the Econometric Society*, vol. 2, 64–150. Cambridge, UK: Cambridge University Press.

Harsanyi, J. C. (1967–68). "Games with Incomplete Information Played by 'Bayesian' Players," parts 1 to 3. *Management Science*, 14, 159–82, 320–34, 486–502.

Hart, O. (1983a). "Optimal Labor Contracts Under Asymmetric Information: An Introduction." *Review of Economic Studies*, 50, 1–35.

———. (1983b). "The Market Mechanism as an Incentive Scheme." *Bell Journal of Economics*, 14, 366–82.

———. (1995). *Firms, Contracts, and Financial Structure*. Oxford: Oxford University Press.

———. (2000). "Financial Contracting." Nancy Schwartz Lecture, Northwestern University, Evanston, IL.

Hart, O., and B. Holmström. (1987). "The Theory of Contracts." In T. F. Bewley (ed.), *Advances in Economic Theory: Fifth World Congress of the Econometric Society*, 71–155. Cambridge, UK: Cambridge University Press.

———. (2002). "Vision and Firm Scope." Harvard University Working Paper.

Hart, O., and J. Moore. (1988). "Incomplete Contracts and Renegotiation." *Econometrica*, 56, 755–85.

———. (1989). "Default and Renegotiation: A Dynamic Model of Debt." MIT Working Paper No. 520, Cambridge, MA.

———. (1990). "Property Rights and the Nature of the Firm." *Journal of Political Economy*, 98, 1119–58.

———. (1994). "A Theory of Debt Based on the Inalienability of Human Capital." *Quarterly Journal of Economics*, 109, 841–79.

———. (1998). "Default and Renegotiation: A Dynamic Model of Debt." *Quarterly Journal of Economics*, 113, 1–41.

———. (1999). "Foundations of Incomplete Contracts." *Review of Economic Studies*, 66, 115–38.

———. (2000). "On the Design of Hierarchies: Coordination Versus Specialization." Harvard University Working Paper.

Hart, O., A. Shleifer, and W. Vishny. (1997). "The Proper Scope of Government: Theory and an Application to Prisons." *Quarterly Journal of Economics*, 112, 1127–61.

Hart, O., and J. Tirole. (1988). "Contract Renegotiation and Coasian Dynamics." *Review of Economic Studies*, 55, 509–40.

———. (1990). "Vertical Integration and Market Foreclosure." *Brookings Papers on Economic Activity*, 1990, 205–86.

Haubrich, J. G., and R. G. King. (1990). "Banking and Insurance." *Journal of Monetary Economics*, 26, 361–86.

Heavner, D. L. (1999). *Economic Essays on the Organization of Firms*. Ph.D. thesis, University of Chicago, Graduate School of Business.

Hellwig, M. (1987). "Some Recent Developments in the Theory of Competition in Markets with Adverse Selection." *European Economic Review*, 31, 319–25.

Hermalin, B. E. (1988). *Three Essays on the Theory of Contracts*. Ph.D. thesis, MIT, Cambridge, MA.

———. (1992). "The Effects of Competition on Executive Behavior." *RAND Journal of Economics*, 23, 350–65.

Hermalin, B. E., and M. L. Katz. (1991). "Moral Hazard and Verifiability: The Effects of Renegotiation in Agency." *Econometrica*, 59, 1735–53.

Hicks, J. R. (1935). "Annual Survey of Economic Theory: The Theory of Monopoly." *Econometrica*, 3, 1–20.

Holmström, B. (1979). "Moral Hazard and Observability." *Bell Journal of Economics*, 10, 74–91.

———. (1982a). "Managerial Incentive Problems—A Dynamic Perspective." In *Essays in Economics and Management in Honor of Lars Wahlbeck*. Helsinki: Swedish School of Economics. (See also *Review of Economic Studies*, 1999.)

———. (1982b). "Moral Hazard in Teams." *Bell Journal of Economics*, 13, 324–40.

———. (1983). "Equilibrium Long-Term Contracts." *Quarterly Journal of Economics*, 98, Supplement, 23–54.

Holmström, B., and P. Milgrom. (1987). "Aggregation and Linearity in the Provision of Intertemporal Incentives." *Econometrica*, 55, 303–28.

———. (1990). "Regulating Trade among Agents." *Journal of Institutional and Theoretical Economics*, 146, 85–105.

———. (1991). "Multitask Principal-Agent Analyses: Incentive Contracts, Asset Ownership, and Job Design." *Journal of Law, Economics and Organization*, 7, 24–52.

———. (1994). "The Firm as an Incentive System." *American Economic Review*, 84, 972–91.

Holmström, B., and J. Roberts. (1998). "The Boundaries of the Firm Revisited." *Journal of Economic Perspectives*, 12, 73–94.

Holmström, B., and J. Tirole. (1989). "The Theory of the Firm." In R. Schmalensee and R. Willig (eds.), *Handbook of Industrial Economics*. Amsterdam: Elsevier.

———. (1993). "Market Liquidity and Performance Monitoring." *Journal of Political Economy*, 101, 678–709.

Inderst, R., and H. Muller. (2003). "Internal vs. External Financing: An Optimal Contracting Approach." *Journal of Finance*, 58, 1033–62.

Innes, R. D. (1990). "Limited Liability and Incentive Contracting with Ex-Ante Action Choices." *Journal of Economic Theory*, 52, 45–67.

Itoh, H. (1991). "Incentives to Help in Multiagent Situations." *Econometrica*, 59, 611–36.

———. (1993). "Coalitions, Incentives, and Risk Sharing." *Journal of Economic Theory*, 60, 410–27.

Jacklin, C. J. (1987). "Demand Deposits, Trading Restrictions, and Risk Sharing." In E. C. Prescott and N. Wallace (eds.), *Contractual Arrangements for Intertemporal Trade*, 26–47. Minneapolis: University of Minnesota Press.

Jaffee, D. M., and F. Modigliani. (1969). "A Theory and Test of Credit Rationing." *American Economic Review*, 59, 850–72.

Jaffee, D. M., and T. Russell. (1976). "Imperfect Information, Uncertainty, and Credit Rationing." *Quarterly Journal of Economics*, 90, 651–66.

Jehiel, P., and B. Moldovanu. (1996). "Strategic Nonparticipation." *RAND Journal of Economics*, 27, 84–98.

Jehiel, P., B. Moldovanu, and E. Stacchetti. (1996). "How (Not) to Sell Nuclear Weapons." *American Economic Review*, 86, 814–29.

Jensen, M. C., and W. H. Meckling. (1976). "Theory of the Firm: Managerial Behavior, Agency Costs and Ownership Structure." *Journal of Financial Economics*, 3, 305–60.

Jewitt, I. (1988). "Justifying the First-Order Approach to Principal-Agent Problems." *Econometrica*, 56, 1177–90.

———. (1997). "Information and Principal-Agent Problems." Mimeo, Oxford and Bristol.

Jin, L. (2002). "CEO Compensation, Diversification, and Incentives." *Journal of Financial Economics*, 66, 29–63.

John, K., and J. Williams. (1985). "Dividends, Dilution and Taxes: A Signaling Equilibrium." *Journal of Finance*, 40, 1053–70.

Jullien, B. (2000). "Participation Constraints in Adverse Selection Models." *Journal of Economic Theory*, 93, 1–47.

Kahn, C. M., and D. Mookherjee. (1998). "Competition and Incentives with Nonexclusive Contracts." *RAND Journal of Economics*, 29, 443–65.

Kahn, C., and J. Scheinkman. (1985). "Optimal Employment Contracts with Bankruptcy Constraints." *Journal of Economic Theory*, 35, 343–65.

Kaldor, N. (1934). "The Equilibrium of the Firm." *Economic Journal*, 44, 60–76.

Kamien, M. I., and N. L. Schwartz. (1991). *Dynamic Optimization: The Calculus of Variations and Optimal Control in Economics and Management*. Amsterdam: North-Holland.

Kanbur, R. (1979). "Impatience, Information and Risk Taking in a General Equilibrium Model of Occupational Choice." *Review of Economic Studies*, 46, 707–18.

Kandori, M., and H. Matsushima. (1998). "Private Observation, Communication and Collusion." *Econometrica*, 66, 627–52.

Kaplan, S., and P. Stromberg. (2003). "Financial Contracting Theory Meets the Real World: An Empirical Analysis of Venture Capital Contracts." *Review of Economic Studies*, 70, 281–315.

Katz, M. L. (1991). "Game-Playing Agents: Unobservable Contracts as Precommitments." *RAND Journal of Economics*, 22, 307–28.

Katz, M., and C. Shapiro. (1986). "Technology Adoption in the Presence of Network Externalities." *Journal of Political Economy*, 94, 822–41.

Keren, M., and D. Levhari. (1979). "The Optimum Span of Control in a Pure Hierarchy." *Management Science*, 25, 1162–72.

———. (1983). "The Internal Organization of the Firm and the Shape of Average Costs." *Bell Journal of Economics*, 14, 474–86.

Kihlstrom, R., and J. Laffont. (1979). "A General Equilibrium Entrepreneurial Theory of Firm Formation Based on Risk Aversion." *Journal of Political Economy*, 87, 719–48.

Kim, S. K. (1995). "Efficiency of an Information System in an Agency Model." *Econometrica*, 63, 89–102.

Kiyotaki, N., and J. Moore. (1997). "Credit Cycles." *Journal of Political Economy*, 105, 211–48.

Klein, B., R. G. Crawford, and A. A. Alchian. (1978). "Vertical Integration, Appropriable Rents, and the Competitive Contracting Process." *Journal of Law and Economics*, 21, 297–326.

Klein, B., and K. B. Leffler. (1981). "The Role of Market Forces in Assuring Contractual Performance." *Journal of Political Economy*, 89, 615–41.

Klemperer, P. (2002). "What Really Matters in Auction Design." *Journal of Economic Perspectives*, 16, 169–89.

———. (2003). "Why Every Economist Should Learn Some Auction Theory." In M. Dewatripont, L. Hansen, and S. Turnovsky (eds.), *Advances in Economics and Econometrics: Theory and Applications,*

Eighth World Congress of the Econometric Society, vol. 1, 25–55. Cambridge, UK: Cambridge University Press.

Knight, F. (1921). *Risk, Uncertainty and Profit*. Boston: Houghton Mifflin.

Kocherlakota, N. (1996). "Implications of Efficient Risk Sharing Without Commitment." *Review of Economic Studies*, 63, 595–610.

Kofman, F., and J. Lawarrée. (1993). "Collusion in Hierarchical Agency." *Econometrica*, 61, 629–56.

Kohlberg, E., and J. F. Mertens. (1986). "On the Strategic Stability of Equilibria." *Econometrica*, 54, 1003–38.

Kornai, J. (1979). "Resource-Constrained versus Demand-Constrained Systems." *Econometrica*, 47, 801–19.

———. (1980). *Economics of Shortage*. Amsterdam: North Holland.

Kornai, J., E. Maskin, and G. Roland. (2003). "Understanding the Soft Budget Constraint." *Journal of Economic Literature*, 41, 1095–136.

Kreps, D. (1990). *A Course in Microeconomic Theory*. Princeton, NJ: Princeton University Press.

Krishna, V. (2002). *Auction Theory*. San Diego, CA: Academic Press.

Laffont, J. J., and D. Martimort. (1997). "Collusion under Asymmetric Information." *Econometrica*, 65, 875–911.

———. (1998). "Collusion and Delegation." *RAND Journal of Economics*, 29, 280–305.

———. (2000). "Mechanism Design with Collusion and Correlation." *Econometrica*, 68, 309 42.

———. (2002). *The Theory of Incentives: The Principal-Agent Model*. Princeton, NJ: Princeton University Press.

Laffont, J. J., and E. Maskin. (1979). "A Differentiable Approach to Expected Utility Maximizing Mechanisms." In J. J. Laffont (ed.), *Aggregation and Revelation of Preferences*. Amsterdam: North-Holland.

Laffont, J. J., and M. Meleu. (1997). "Reciprocal Supervision, Collusion and Organizational Design." *Scandinavian Journal of Economics*, 99, 519–40.

Laffont, J. J., and J. Tirole. (1986). "Using Cost Observation to Regulate Firms." *Journal of Political Economy*, 94, 614–41.

———. (1988a). "The Dynamics of Incentive Contracts." *Econometrica*, 56, 1153–75.

———. (1988b). "Repeated Auctions of Incentive Contracts, Investment and Bidding Parity." *RAND Journal of Economics*, 19, 516–37.

———. (1990). "Adverse Selection and Renegotiation in Procurement." *Review of Economic Studies*, 57, 597–625.

———. (1991) "Provision of Quality and Power of Incentive Schemes in Regulated Industries." In W. Barnett, B. Cornet, C. d'Aspremont, J. J. Gabszewicz, and A. Mas-Colell (eds.), *Equilibrium Theory and Applications: Proceedings of the Sixth International Symposium in Economic Theory and Econometrics*, 161–96. Cambridge, UK: Cambridge University Press.

———. (1993). *A Theory of Incentives in Procurement and Regulation*. Cambridge, MA: MIT Press.

Lal, R. (1990). "Improving Channel Coordination through Franchising." *Marketing Science*, 9, 299–318.

Lazear, E. P. (1995). *Personnel Economics*. Cambridge, MA: MIT Press.

Lazear, E. P., and S. Rosen. (1981). "Rank-Order Tournaments as Optimum Labor Contracts." *Journal of Political Economy*, 89, 841–64.

Legros, P., and H. Matsushima. (1991). "Efficiency in Partnerships." *Journal of Economic Theory*, 55, 296–322.

Legros, P., and S. Matthews. (1993). "Efficient and Nearly Efficient Partnerships." *Review of Economic Studies*, 60, 599–611.

Legros, P., and A. F. Newman. (2000). "Competing for Ownership." CEPR Discussion Paper 2573.

Leland, H. E., and D. H. Pyle. (1977). "Informational Asymmetries, Financial Structure, and Financial Intermediation." *Journal of Finance*, 32, 371–87.

Leppamaki, M. (1998). "Nonmonetary Collusion and Optimal Use of Information." University of Helsinki, Working Paper 437.

Levin, J. (2003). "Relational Incentive Contracts." *American Economic Review*, 93, 835–57.

Lewis, T. R., R. Feenstra, and R. Ware. (1989). "Eliminating Price Supports: A Political Economy Perspective." *Journal of Public Economics*, 40, 159–85.

Lewis, T. R., and D. E. M. Sappington. (1989). "Countervailing Incentives in Agency Problems." *Journal of Economic Theory*, 49, 294–313.

———. (1997). "Information Management in Incentive Problems." *Journal of Political Economy*, 105, 796–821.

———. (2000). "Contracting with Wealth-Constrained Agents." *International Economic Review*, 41, 743–67.

Ligon, E., J. Thomas, and T. Worrall. (2002). "Informal Insurance Arrangements in Village Economies." *Review of Economic Studies*, 69, 209–44.

Lucas, R. (1992). "On Efficiency and Distribution." *Economic Journal*, 102, 233–47.

Ma, C. T. A. (1988). "Unique Implementation of Incentive Contracts with Many Agents." *Review of Economic Studies*, 55, 555–72.

———. (1991). "Adverse Selection in Dynamic Moral Hazard." *Quarterly Journal of Economics*, 106, 255–75.

———. (1994). "Renegotiation and Optimality in Agency Contracts." *Review of Economic Studies*, 61, 109–29.

Ma, C. T. A., and A. Weiss. (1993). "A Signaling Theory of Unemployment." *European Economic Review*, 37, 135–57.

Macho-Stadler, I., and J. D. Perez-Castrillo. (1993). "Moral Hazard with Several Agents: The Gains from Cooperation." *International Journal of Industrial Organization*, 11, 73–100.

———. (1998). "Centralized and Decentralized Contracts in a Moral Hazard Environment." *Journal of Industrial Economics*, 46, 489–510.

MacLeod, W. B. (2003). "Optimal Contracting with Subjective Evaluation." *American Economic Review*, 93, 216–40.

MacLeod, W. B., and J. M. Malcomson. (1988). "Reputation and Hierarchy in Dynamic Models of Employment." *Journal of Political Economy*, 96, 832–54.

———. (1989). "Implicit Contracts, Incentive Compatibility, and Involuntary Unemployment." *Econometrica*, 57, 447–80.

———. (1993). "Investment, Holdup, and the Form of Market Contracts." *American Economic Review*, 83, 811–37.

Malcomson, J. M. (1997). "Contracts, Holdup, and Labor Markets." *Journal of Economic Literature*, 35, 1916–57.

Malcomson, J. M., and F. Spinnewyn. (1988). "The Multiperiod Principal-Agent Problem." *Review of Economic Studies*, 55, 391–407.

Marschak, T., and S. Reichelstein. (1995). "The Communication Requirements for Individual Agents in Networks and Hierarchies." In J. Ledyard (ed.), *The Economics of Informational Decentralization: Complexity, Efficiency and Stability*. Hingham, MA: Kluwer Press.

———. (1998). "Network Mechanisms, Informational Efficiency, and Hierarchies." *Journal of Economic Theory*, 79, 106–41.

Martimort, D. (1996). "Exclusive Dealing, Common Agency, and Multiprincipals Incentive Theory." *RAND Journal of Economics*, 27, 1–31.

———. (1999). "The Life Cycle of Regulatory Agencies: Dynamic Capture and Transaction Costs." *Review of Economic Studies*, 66, 929–48.

Martimort, D., and L. Stole. (2002). "The Revelation and Taxation Principles in Common Agency Games." *Econometrica*, 70, 1659–73.

Mas-Colell, A., M. D. Whinston, and J. Green. (1995). *Microeconomic Theory*. New York, NY: Oxford University Press.

Maskin, E. (1977). "Nash Equilibrium and Welfare Optimality." Mimeo, MIT. (Published in 1999 in the *Review of Economic Studies*, 66, 23–38.)

———. (1997). Private Communication.

———. (2002). "On Indescribable Contingencies and Incomplete Contracts." *European Economic Review*, 46, 725–33.

———. (2003). "Auctions and Efficiency." In M. Dewatripont, L. Hansen, and S. Turnovsky (eds.), *Advances in Economics and Econometrics: Theory and Applications, Eighth World Congress of the Econometric Society*, vol. 1, 1–24. Cambridge, UK: Cambridge University Press.

Maskin, E., and J. Moore. (1999). "Implementation and Renegotiation." *Review of Economic Studies*, 66, 39–56.

Maskin, E., and J. Riley. (1984a). "Monopoly with Incomplete Information." *RAND Journal of Economics*, 15, 171–96.

———. (1984b). "Optimal Auctions with Risk Averse Buyers." *Econometrica*, 52, 1473–1518.

———. (1985). "Input versus Output Incentive Schemes." *Journal of Public Economics*, 28, 1–23.

———. (1989). "Optimal Multiunit Auctions." In F. Hahn (ed.), *The Economics of Missing Markets, Information, and Games*, 312–35. Oxford: Clarendon Press.

———. (2000). "Asymmetric Auctions." *Review of Economic Studies*, 67, 413–38.

Maskin, E., and J. Tirole. (1990). "The Principal-Agent Relationship with an Informed Principal, 1: The Case of Private Values." *Econometrica*, 58, 379–409.

———. (1992). "The Principal-Agent Relationship with an Informed Principal, 2: Common Values." *Econometrica*, 60, 1–42.

———. (1999a). "Unforeseen Contingencies and Incomplete Contracts." *Review of Economic Studies*, 66, 83–114.

———. (1999b). "Two Remarks on the Property-Rights Literature." *Review of Economic Studies*, 66, 139–49.

Mathewson, G., and R. Winter. (1985). "The Economics of Franchise Contracts." *Journal of Law and Economics*, 28, 503–26.

Matthews, S. A. (1983). "Selling to Risk Averse Buyers with Unobservable Tastes." *Journal of Economic Theory*, 30, 370–400.

———. (1995). "Renegotiation of Sales Contracts." *Econometrica*, 63, 567–89.

———. (2001). "Renegotiation of Moral Hazard Contracts under Limited Liability and Monotonicity." *Journal of Economic Theory*, 97, 1–29.

McAfee, R. P. (1993). "Mechanism Design by Competing Sellers." *Econometrica*, 61, 1281–1312.

McAfee, R. P., and J. McMillan. (1987a). "Auctions and Bidding." *Journal of Economic Literature*, 25, 699–738.

———. (1987b). "Competition for agency contracts." *RAND Journal of Economics*, 18, 296–307.

McAfee, R. P., J. McMillan, and M. D. Whinston. (1989). "Multiproduct Monopoly, Commodity Bundling, and Correlation of Values." *Quarterly Journal of Economics*, 104, 371–83.

McAfee, R. P., and M. Schwartz. (1994). "Opportunism in Multilateral Vertical Contracting: Nondiscrimination, Exclusivity, and Uniformity." *American Economic Review*, 84, 210–30.

Melumad, N., D. Mookherjee, and S. Reichelstein. (1995). "Hierarchical Decentralization of Incentive Contracts." *RAND Journal of Economics*, 26, 654–72.

Meyer, M., and J. Vickers. (1997). "Performance Comparisons and Dynamic Incentives." *Journal of Political Economy*, 105, 547–81.

Milgrom, P. R. (1981a). "Good News and Bad News: Representation Theorems and Applications." *Bell Journal of Economics*, 12, 380–91.

———. (1981b). "Rational Expectations, Information Acquisition, and Competitive Bidding." *Econometrica*, 49, 921–43.

———. (2004). *Putting Auction Theory to Work*. Cambridge, MA: Cambridge University Press.

Milgrom, P. R., and J. Roberts. (1982). "Limit Pricing and Entry under Incomplete Information: An Equilibrium Analysis." *Econometrica*, 50, 443–59.

———. (1986a). "Price and Advertising Signals of Product Quality." *Journal of Political Economy*, 94, 796–821.

———. (1986b). "Relying on the Information of Interested Parties." *RAND Journal of Economics*, 17, 18–32.

———. (1992). *Economics, Organization and Management*. Englewood Cliffs, NJ: Prentice Hall.

Milgrom, P. R., and R. J. Weber. (1982). "A Theory of Auctions and Competitive Bidding." *Econometrica*, 50, 1089–1122.

Mirrlees, J. A. (1971). "An Exploration in the Theory of Optimum Income Taxation." *Review of Economic Studies*, 38, 175–208.

———. (1974). "Notes on Welfare Economics, Information and Uncertainty." In M. Balch, D. McFadden, and S. Wu (eds.), *Essays in Equilibrium Behaviour under Uncertainty*. Amsterdam: North-Holland.

———. (1975). "The Theory of Moral Hazard and Unobservable Behaviour, Part 1." Mimeo, Oxford. (Published in 1999 in the *Review of Economic Studies*, 66, 3–21.)

———. (1976). "The Optimal Structure of Incentives and Authority Within an Organization." *Bell Journal of Economics*, 7, 105–31.

———. (1986). "The Theory of Optimal Taxation." In W. Hildenbrand and H. Sonnenschein (eds.), *Handbook of Mathematical Economics*, vol. 3. Amsterdam: North Holland.

Modigliani, F., and M. Miller. (1958). "The Cost of Capital, Corporation Finance, and the Theory of Investment." *American Economic Review*, 48, 261–97.

Mookherjee, D. (1984). "Optimal Incentive Schemes with Many Agents." *Review of Economic Studies*, 51, 433–46.

Mookherjee, D., and I. Png. (1989). "Optimal Auditing, Insurance, and Redistribution." *Quarterly Journal of Economics*, 104, 399–415.

Moore, J. (1992). "Implementation in Environments with Complete Information." In J. J. Laffont (ed.), *Advances in Economic Theory: Sixth World Congress of the Econometric Society*, vol. 1, 182–282. Cambridge, UK: Cambridge University Press.

Moore, J., and R. Repullo. (1988). "Subgame-Perfect Implementation." *Econometrica*, 56, 1191–1220.

Mussa, M., and S. Rosen. (1978). "Monopoly and Product Quality." *Journal of Economic Theory*, 18, 301–17.

Myers, S. C. (1977). "Determinants of Corporate Borrowing." *Journal of Financial Economics*, 5, 147–75.

Myers, S. C., and N. S. Majluf. (1984). "Corporate Financing and Investment Decisions When Firms Have Information That Investors Do Not Have." *Journal of Financial Economics*, 13, 187–221.

Myerson, R. B. (1979). "Incentive Compatibility and the Bargaining Problem." *Econometrica*, 79, 61–73.

———. (1981). "Optimal Auction Design." *Mathematics of Operations Research*, 6, 58–73.

———. (1983). "Mechanism Design by an Informed Principal." *Econometrica*, 51, 1767–97.

———. (1991). *Game Theory: Analysis of Conflict*. Cambridge, MA: Harvard University Press.

Myerson, R. B., and M. A. Satterthwaite. (1983). "Efficient Mechanisms for Bilateral Trading." *Journal of Economic Theory*, 29, 265–81.

Nalebuff, B. J., and J. E. Stiglitz. (1983). "Prizes and Incentives: Towards a General Theory of Compensation and Competition." *Bell Journal of Economics*, 14, 21–43.

Newbery, D. M. G., and J. E. Stiglitz. (1979). "The Theory of Commodity Price Stabilization Rules: Welfare Impacts and Supply Responses." *Economic Journal*, 89, 799–817.

Noldeke, G., and K. M. Schmidt. (1995). "Option Contracts and Renegotiation: A Solution to the Holdup Problem." *RAND Journal of Economics*, 26, 163–79.

Noldeke, G., and E. van Damme. (1990). "Signalling in a Dynamic Labour Market." *Review of Economic Studies*, 57, 1–23.

Okuno-Fujiwara, M., A. Postlewaite, and K. Suzumura. (1990). "Strategic Information Revelation." *Review of Economic Studies*, 57, 25–47.

Palfrey, T. R. (1992). "Implementation in Bayesian Equilibrium: The Multiple Equilibrium Problem in Mechanism Design." In J. J. Laffont (ed.), *Advances in Economic Theory: Sixth World Congress of the Econometric Society*, vol. 1, 283–323. Cambridge, UK: Cambridge University Press.

Pauly, M. V. (1974). "Overinsurance and Public Provision of Insurance: The Roles of Moral Hazard and Adverse Selection." *Quarterly Journal of Economics*, 88, 44–62.

Pearce, D., and E. Stachetti. (1998). "The Interaction of Implicit and Explicit Contracts in Repeated Agency." *Games and Economic Behavior*, 23, 75–96.

Peltzman, S. (1975). "The Effects of Automobile Safety Regulation." *Journal of Political Economy*, 83, 677–725.

Porter, M. (1990). *The Competitive Advantage of Nations*. New York: Free Press.

Povel, P., and M. Raith. (2004). "Optimal Debt with Unobservable Investments." *RAND Journal of Economics*, forthcoming.

Prat, A. (1997). "Hierarchies of Processors with Endogenous Capacity." *Journal of Economic Theory*, 77, 214–22.

Prescott, E. C., and R. M. Townsend. (1984). "Pareto Optima and Competitive Equilibria with Adverse Selection and Moral Hazard." *Econometrica*, 52, 21–45.

Qian, Y. (1994). "Incentives and Loss of Control in an Optimal Hierarchy." *Review of Economic Studies*, 61, 527–44.

Radner, R. (1981). "Monitoring Cooperative Agreements in a Repeated Principal-Agent Relationship." *Econometrica*, 49, 1127–48.

———. (1985). "Repeated Principal-Agent Games with Discounting." *Econometrica*, 53, 1173–98.

———. (1986a). "Repeated Moral Hazard with Low Discount Rates." In W. P. Heller, R. M. Starr, and D. Starrett (eds.), *Uncertainty, Information, and Communication, Essays in Honor of Kenneth J. Arrow*, vol. 3, 25–64. Cambridge, UK: Cambridge University Press.

———. (1986b). "Repeated Partnership Games with Imperfect Monitoring and No Discounting." *Review of Economic Studies*, 53, 43–57.

———. 1992. "Hierarchy: The Economics of Managing." *Journal of Economic Literature*, 30, 1382–1415.

———. 1993. "The Organization of Decentralized Information Processing." *Econometrica*, 61, 1109–46.

Raith, M. (2003). "Competition, Risk and Managerial Incentives." *American Economic Review*, 93, 1425–36.

Rajan, R. G., and L. Zingales. (1998). "Power in a Theory of the Firm." *Quarterly Journal of Economics*, 113, 387–432.

———. (2001). "The Firm as a Dedicated Hierarchy: A Theory of the Origin and Growth of Firms." *Quarterly Journal of Economics*, 116, 805–52.

Ramakrishnan, R. T. S., and A. V. Thakor. (1991). "Cooperation Versus Competition in Agency." *Journal of Law, Economics and Organization*, 7, 248–83.

Ray, D., and R. Vohra. (1997). "Equilibrium Binding Agreements." *Journal of Economic Theory*, 73, 30–78.

Reiche, S. (2003a). "Ambivalent Investment and the Hold-Up Problem." Mimeo, London School of Economics.

———. (2003b). "Incomplete Contracts and Inefficient Renegotiation." Mimeo, London School of Economics.

Rey, P., and B. Salanié. (1990). "Long-Term, Short-Term and Renegotiation: On the Value of Commitment in Contracting." *Econometrica*, 58, 597–619.

———. (1996). "On the Value of Commitment with Asymmetric Information." *Econometrica*, 64, 1395–1414.

Rhodes-Kropf, M., and S. Viswanathan. (2000). "Corporate Reorganizations and Noncash Auctions." *Journal of Finance*, 55, 1807–49.

Riley, J. G. (1979). "Informational Equilibrium." *Econometrica*, 47(2), 331–60.

———. (1985). "Competition with Hidden Knowledge." *Journal of Political Economy*, 93, 958–76.

———. (1989). "Expected Revenue from Open and Sealed Bid Auctions." *Journal of Economic Perspectives*, 3, 41–50.

Riley, J. G., and W. F. Samuelson. (1981). "Optimal Auctions." *American Economic Review*, 71, 381–92.

Riordan, M. H., and D. E. M. Sappington. (1987a). "Awarding Monopoly Franchises." *American Economic Review*, 77, 375–87.

Riordan, M., and D. Sappington. (1987b). "Information, Incentives and Organizational Mode." *Quarterly Journal of Economics*, 102, 243–63.

Roberts, K. (2000). "A Reconsideration of the Optimal Income Tax." In P. Hammond and G. Myles (eds.), *Incentives, Organization, and Public Economics—Papers in Honour of Sir James Mirrlees*. Oxford: Oxford University Press.

Rochet, J. C., and P. Choné. (1998). "Ironing, Sweeping, and Multidimensional Screening." *Econometrica*, 66, 783–826.

Rochet, J. C., and L. Stole. (2002). "Nonlinear Pricing with Random Participation." *Review of Economic Studies*, 69, January, 277–311.

———. (2003). "The Economics of Multidimensional Screening." In M. Dewatripont, L. Hansen, and S. Turnovsky (eds.), *Advances in Economics and Econometrics: Theory and Applications, Eighth World Congress of the Econometric Society*, vol. 1, 150–97. Cambridge, UK: Cambridge University Press.

Rogerson, W. P. (1985a). "The First-Order Approach to Principal-Agent Problems." *Econometrica*, 53, 1357–67.

———. (1985b). "Repeated Moral Hazard." *Econometrica*, 53, 69–76.

Roland, G. (2000). *Transition and Economics: Politics, Markets, and Firms*. Cambridge, MA: MIT Press.

Rosen, S. (1982). "Authority, Control, and the Distribution of Earnings." *Bell Journal of Economics*, 13, 311–23.

———. (1986). "Prizes and Incentives in Elimination Tournaments." *American Economic Review*, 76, 701–15.

Ross, S. (1973). "The Economic Theory of Agency: The Principal's Problem." *American Economic Review*, 63, 134–39.

Rothschild, M., and J. Stiglitz. (1970). "Increasing Risk I. A Definition." *Journal of Economic Theory*, 2, 225–43.

———. (1976). "Equilibrium in Competitive Insurance Markets: An Essay on the Economics of Imperfect Information." *Quarterly Journal of Economics*, 90, 630–49.

Rubinstein, A. (1979). "Equilibrium in Supergames with the Overtaking Criterion." *Journal of Economic Theory*, 21, 1–9.

———. (1982). "Perfect Equilibrium in a Bargaining Model." *Econometrica*, 50, 97–110.

Rubinstein, A., and M. E. Yaari. (1983). "Repeated Insurance Contracts and Moral Hazard." *Journal of Economic Theory*, 30, 74–97.

Saez, E. (2001). "Using Elasticities to Derive Optimal Income Tax Rates." *Review of Economic Studies*, 68, 205–29.

Sah, R. K., and J. E. Stiglitz. (1986). "The Architecture of Economic Systems: Hierarchies and Polyarchies." *American Economic Review*, 76, 716–27.

Salanié, B. (1997). *The Economics of Contracts: A Primer*. Cambridge, MA: MIT Press.

Sappington, D. (1983). "Limited Liability Contracts Between Principal and Agent." *Journal of Economic Theory*, 29, 1–29.

———. (1984). "Incentive Contracting with Asymmetric and Precontractual Knowledge." *Journal of Economic Theory*, 34, 52–70.

Satterthwaite, M. A. (1975). "Strategy-Proofness and Arrow's Conditions: Existence and Correspondence Theorems for Voting Procedures and Social Welfare Functions." *Journal of Economic Theory*, 10, 187–217.

Schaffer, M. E. (1989). "The Credible-Commitment Problem in the Center-Enterprise Relationship." *Journal of Comparative Economics*, 12, 359–82.

Scharfstein, D. (1988). Product Market Competition and Managerial Slack." *RAND Journal of Economics*, 19, 147–55.

Scharfstein, D., and J. Stein. (1990). "Herd Behavior and Investment." *American Economic Review*, 80, 465–79.

Schmidt, K. M. (1997). "Managerial Incentives and Product Market Competition." *Review of Economic Studies*, 64, 191–213.

Segal, I. (1999a). "Complexity and Renegotiation: A Foundation for Incomplete Contracts." *Review of Economic Studies*, 66, 57–82.

———. (1999b). "Contracting with Externalities." *Quarterly Journal of Economics*, 114, 337–88.

Segal, I., and M. Whinston. (2002). "The Mirrlees Approach to Mechanism Design with Renegotiation (with Applications to Hold-Up and Risk Sharing)." *Econometrica*, 70, 1–45.

———. (2003). "Robust Predictions for Bilateral Contracting with Externalities." *Econometrica*, 71, 757–91.

Shapiro, C., and J. E. Stiglitz. (1984). "Equilibrium Unemployment as a Worker Discipline Device." *American Economic Review*, 74, 433–44.

Shavell, S. (1979a). "On Moral Hazard and Insurance." *Quarterly Journal of Economics*, 93, 541–62.

———. (1979b). "Risk-Sharing and Incentives in the Principal and Agent Relationship." *Bell Journal of Economics*, 10, 55–73.

———. (1994). "Acquisition and Disclosure of Information Prior to Sale." *RAND Journal of Economics*, 25, 20–36.

Shin, H. (1998). "Adversarial and Inquisitorial Procedures in Arbitration." *RAND Journal of Economics*, 29, 378–405.

Simon, H. A. (1951). "A Formal Theory of the Employment Relationship." *Econometrica*, 19, 293–305.

Spence, A. M. (1973). "Job Market Signaling." *Quarterly Journal of Economics*, 87, 355–74.

————. (1974). *Market Signaling: Informational Transfer in Hiring and Related Screening Processes.* Cambridge, MA: Harvard University Press.

Spence, A. M., and R. J. Zeckhauser. (1971). "Insurance, Information, and Individual Action." *American Economic Association*, 61, 380–87.

Spier, K. (1992). "Incomplete Contracts and Signaling." *RAND Journal of Economics*, 23, 432–43.

Stein, J. (1989). "Efficient Capital Markets, Inefficient Firms: A Model of Myopic Corporate Behavior." *Quarterly Journal of Economics*, 104, 655–69.

Stiglitz, J. E. (1974). "Incentives and Risk Sharing in Sharecropping." *Review of Economic Studies*, 41, 219–55.

Stiglitz, J. E., and A. Weiss. (1981). "Credit Rationing in Markets with Imperfect Information." *American Economic Review*, 71, 393–410.

Stokey, N. L. (1981). "Rational Expectations and Durable Goods Pricing." *Bell Journal of Economics*, 12, 112–28.

Stole, L., and J. Zwiebel. (1996a). "Intrafirm Bargaining under Nonbinding Contracts." *Review of Economic Studies*, 63, 375–410.

————. (1996b). "Organizational Design and Technology Choice under Intrafirm Bargaining." *American Economic Review*, 86, 195–222.

Strausz, R. (1997). "Delegation of Monitoring in a Principal-Agent Relationship." *Review of Economic Studies*, 64, 337–57.

Sutton, J. (1986). "Noncooperative Bargaining Theory: An Introduction." *Review of Economic Studies*, 53, 709–24.

Thomas, J., and T. Worrall. (1990). "Income Fluctuation and Asymmetric Information: An Example of a Repeated Principal-Agent Problem." *Journal of Economic Theory*, 51, 367–90.

Tirole, J. (1986). "Hierarchies and Bureaucracies: On the Role of Collusion in Organizations." *Journal of Law, Economics and Organization*, 2, 181–214.

————. (1988). *The Theory of Industrial Organization.* Cambridge, MA: MIT Press.

————. (1992). "Collusion and the Theory of Organizations." In J. J. Laffont (ed.), *Advances in Economic Theory: Sixth World Congress of the Econometric Society*, vol. 2, 151–206. Cambridge, UK: Cambridge University Press.

————. (1999). "Incomplete Contracts: Where Do We Stand?" *Econometrica*, 67, 741–81.

Townsend, R. M. (1979). "Optimal Contracts and Competitive Markets with Costly State Verification." *Journal of Economic Theory*, 21, 265–93.

————. (1982). "Optimal Multiperiod Contracts and the Gain from Enduring Relationships under Private Information." *Journal of Political Economy*, 90, 1166–86.

Tuomala, M. (1990). *Optimal Income Tax and Redistribution.* Oxford: Clarendon Press.

van Damme, E. (1983). *Refinements of the Nash Equilibrium Concept.* Berlin: Springer-Verlag.

Van Zandt, T. (1995). "Continuous Approximations in the Study of Hierarchies." *RAND Journal of Economics*, 26, 575–90.

————. (1998). "The Scheduling and Organization of Periodic Associative Computation: Efficient Networks." *Review of Economic Design*, 3, 93–127.

————. (1999). "Real-Time Decentralized Information Processing as a Model of Organizations with Boundedly Rational Agents." *Review of Economic Studies*, 66, 633–58.

Varian, H. R. (1990). "Monitoring Agents with Other Agents." *Journal of Institutional and Theoretical Economics*, 146, 153–74.

Vauhkonen, J. (2002). "An Incomplete Contracts Approach to Financial Contracting: A Comment." *Economics Bulletin*, 7, 1–3.

Vayanos, D. (2003). "The Decentralization of Information Processing in the Presence of Interactions." *Review of Economic Studies*, 70, 667–95.

Vickrey, W. (1961). "Counterspeculation, Auctions, and Competitive Sealed Tenders." *Journal of Finance*, 16, 8–37.

von Neumann, J., and O. Morgenstern. (1944). *Theory of Games and Economic Behaviour*. Princeton, NJ: Princeton University Press.

von Thadden, E. L. (1995). "Long-Term Contracts, Short-Term Investment and Monitoring." *Review of Economic Studies*, 62, 557–75.

Walsh, C. (1995). "Optimal Contracts for Central Bankers." *American Economic Review*, 85, 150–67.

Webb, D. C. (1992). "Two-Period Financial Contracts with Private Information and Costly State Verification." *Quarterly Journal of Economics*, 107, 1113–23.

Weiss, A. (1980). "Job Queues and Layoffs in Labor Markets with Flexible Wages." *Journal of Political Economy*, 88, 526–38.

———. (1983). "A Sorting-cum-Learning Model of Education." *Journal of Political Economy*, 91, 420–42.

Weitzman, M. (1976). "The New Soviet Incentive Model." *Bell Journal of Economics*, 7, 251–7.

Welch, I. (1989). "Seasoned Offerings, Imitation Costs, and the Underpricing of Initial Public Offerings." *Journal of Finance*, 44, 421–49.

Wernerfelt, B. (1997). "On the Nature and Scope of the Firm: An Adjustment Cost Theory." *Journal of Business*, 70, 489–514.

Whinston, M. D. (1990). "Tying, Foreclosure, and Exclusion." *American Economic Review*, 80, 1–26.

White, M. (1980). "Public Policy toward Bankruptcy: Me-First and Other Priority Rules." *Bell Journal of Economics*, 11, 550–64.

Williamson, O. E. (1967). "Hierarchical Control and Optimum Firm Size." *Journal of Political Economy*, 75, 123–38.

———. (1971). "The Vertical Integration of Production: Market Failure Considerations." *American Economic Review*, 61, 112–23.

———. (1975). *Markets and Hierarchies*. New York: Free Press.

———. (1979). "Transaction-Cost Economics: The Governance of Contractual Relations." *Journal of Law and Economics*, 22, 233–61.

———. (1985). *The Economic Institutions of Capitalism*. New York: Free Press.

Wilson, C. (1977). "A Model of Insurance Markets with Incomplete Information." *Journal of Economic Theory*, 16, 167–207.

Wilson, J. Q. (1989). *Bureaucracy: What Government Agencies Do and Why They Do It*. New York: Basic Books.

Wilson, R. B. (1968). "The Theory of Syndicates." *Econometrica*, 36, 119–32.

———. (1993). *Nonlinear Pricing*. New York: Oxford University Press.

Winton, A. (1995). "Costly State Verification and Multiple Investors: The Role of Seniority." *Review of Financial Studies*, 8, 91–123.

Zahavi, A. (1975). "Mate Selection—A Selection for a Handicap." *Journal of Theoretical Biology*, 53, 205–14.

Ziss, S. (1996). "Contracts as a Barrier to Entry: Comment." *American Economic Review*, 86, 672–74.

Author Index

Subject Index